Baptist Reconsideration
of Baptism and Ecclesiology

European University Studies

Europäische Hochschulschriften
Publications Universitaires Européennes

Series XXIII
Theology

Reihe XXIII Série XXIII
Theologie
Théologie

Vol./Bd. 716

PETER LANG

Frankfurt am Main · Berlin · Bern · Bruxelles · New York · Oxford · Wien

Lennart Johnsson

Baptist Reconsideration of Baptism and Ecclesiology

A Presentation of the Baptist Union of Sweden and a Study of its Official Response to *BEM* in Relation to the Public Discussions primarily amongst its Pastors and Theologians

PETER LANG
Europäischer Verlag der Wissenschaften

Die Deutsche Bibliothek - CIP-Einheitsaufnahme

Johnsson, Lennart:

Baptist reconsideration of baptism and ecclesiology : a
presentation of the baptist union of Sweden and a study of its
official response to BEM in relation to the public discussions
primarily amongst its pastors and theologians / Lennart
Johnsson. - Frankfurt am Main ; Berlin ; Bern ; Bruxelles ; New
York ; Oxford ; Wien : Lang, 2000
   (European university studies ; Ser. 23, Theology ;
   Vol. 716)
   Zugl.: Uppsala, Univ., Diss., 1999
   ISBN 3-631-37721-5

ISSN 0721-3409
ISBN 3-631-37721-5
US-ISBN 0-8204-5380-3

© Peter Lang GmbH
Europäischer Verlag der Wissenschaften
Frankfurt am Main 2000
All rights reserved.

Printed in Germany 1 2   4 5 6 7

www.peterlang.de

Doctoral dissertation presented at the Theological Faculty, Uppsala University 1999

Abstract

Johnsson, Lennart, 1999: Baptist Reconsideration of Baptism and Ecclesiology. A Presentation of the Baptist Union of Sweden and a Study of its Official Response to *BEM* in Relation to the Public Discussions primarily amongst its Pastors and Theologians.

This dissertation presents in Part I the Baptist Union of Sweden in an historical and ecumenical context from the 1840's onwards, dealing with both divisions, for example the Pentecostal Movement (1913), the Örebro (Baptist) Mission (1936/37), and ecumenical strivings concretized in amongst other things ecumenical congregations.

Its official response to *BEM* (Part II) gives a more traditional, closed Baptist opinion on baptism. Baptism cannot be the basis of church unity wanted by *BEM*.

In the analysis in Parts II and III, the study shows, however, that fundamental Baptist principles, introduced in Part I and which recur throughout the dissertation, i.e. believers' baptism, congregationalism, the authority of the Bible, are reconsidered due mainly to the principle of freedom. This is evident especially in Part III, dealing with the public discussions within the Baptist Union of Sweden at the congregational level from 1970's onwards. There are compromises and diversity: there are at least two different baptismal theologies and practices within the Union; for example recognition of (and even Baptist pastors administering) infant baptism, questioning of "re-baptism" and of believers' baptism as proper biblical *baptism of metanoia*, indiscriminate believers' baptism. The Baptist ecumenical commitment and involvement in concrete examples of unification have influenced and contributed to a reconsideration of baptism.

All this has implications for Baptist identity, opening up possibilities of church unity on the basis of both types of baptisms, and also membership on the basis of faith alone. There is a reconsideration of Baptist identity.

The reality is more complex and ambiguous than is apparent in official documents. This may be a memento to the World Council of Churches and Faith and Order, as well as to ecumenical work in general at all levels in all churches.

Keywords: Baptism, *Baptism of metanoia*, Indiscriminate baptism, Infant baptism, "Re-baptism", Reconsideration of baptism, "Baptism, Eucharist and Ministry" *(BEM)*, Baptist identity, Baptist movement, Baptist Union of Sweden, Blessing of children, Churches respond to *BEM*, Ecclesiology, Ecumenical congregations, Ecumenism, Faith and Order, Integration, Reception, Sacrament, Unity, World Council of Churches.

Lennart Johnsson, Department of Theology, Uppsala University, Box 1604, S-751 46 Uppsala, Sweden

To Eva

1 Cor. 13

Contents

Part II

The Official Response of the Baptist Union of Sweden to BEM

Part III

Public Discussions within the Baptist Union of Sweden

Acknowledgements

This book originated as a doctoral thesis. Before this publication for a wider readership it has been slightly revised.

This thesis has a long history. It has been written concurrently with full-time work as a university chaplain (Church of Sweden) in Uppsala, teacher at the University of Uppsala and Johannelunds teologiska högskola (The Johannelund School of Theology) in Uppsala, in the last few years as vicar of Wederslöfs Parish in the diocese of Växjö in the southern part of Sweden, and for the last few terms as teacher and head of Religious Studies at Växjö University.

I want above all to thank my supervisor Professor Sven-Erik Brodd. If I have at times almost given up this project, he has encouraged, inspired and given me support. During the years he has untiringly and with great interest followed my work, read my thesis in different versions and discussed them with me. More than anything else this has helped me to complete the task.

I also want to thank Associate Professor Torsten Bergsten. He has encouraged me, given me much good advice in constructive and dynamic discussions, as well as critical remarks on my thesis. I am also grateful to Johnny Jonsson, a teacher at Teologiska Högskolan Stockholm (The Stockholm School of Theology). He has read my thesis, contributed with important remarks and helped me in many ways. I want to thank the dialogue group between the Church of Sweden and the Baptist Union of Sweden. For constructive theological and practical discussions, and friendship I want to thank especially the Baptist delegates, the present General Secretary Sven Lindström, Gunilla Arlinger, Ingvar Gustafsson, and once again Johnny Jonsson,

Sven-Gunnar Lidén and Karin Wiborn, but also the delegates from the Church of Sweden, the Bishop Biörn Fjärstedt, Lena Bohman, Stina Eliasson, Birgitta Larsson and Kjell Petersson.

I am grateful to my friends and colleagues in Växjö University and its Department of Humanities. Thank you for all your support and encouragement!

Special thanks to my good friend, Revd. Dr. Christopher Meakin, who has helped me with the task of checking the English and correcting my "Swinglish" and given me much advice.

Finally I want to thank my wonderful wife Eva and children Andreas, Samuel and Christoffer. Without their support and encouragement, this study would not have been finished. What you all have done for me, and sorry to say also suffered, no one will ever understand. Eva, you have had to carry too heavy a burden. Thanks for all your understanding, encouragement, support and love – usually unknown to others. I dedicate this book to you.

Introduction

Aim and Method

After years of studying at both the faculty of theology and at the faculties of arts and sciences at the University of Uppsala, I began to work on a dissertation in Studies in Faiths and Ideologies. The title of the dissertation was *Beasley-Murray's dopuppfattning* (Beasley-Murray's View on Baptism).[1]

Following on from this dissertation and due to interest in ecumenism in general, and in the work within Faith and Order in particular, it was a matter of course for me, to continue my research within ecumenism and ecclesiology and to begin to analyse the Baptist responses to the document *Baptism, Eucharist and Ministry*, also called *the Lima Document*.[2] The task was, however, too far-reaching and very soon the importance of restriction became obvious.[3] I decided therefore to work with the

---

[1]   Johnsson, Lennart, *Beasley-Murray's dopuppfattning*, 1987. See more below at the end of the *Introduction*, where I briefly discuss this dissertation. From my study, finished in 1987, I am in one way not surprised at the continuing development of his theology in regard to baptism. It is expressed especially in 1994, when he suggests that Baptist congregations might recognize infant baptism in as much as those baptized by infant baptism should not be "re-baptized". See Beasley-Murray, George, Raymond, "The Problem of Infant Baptism. An Exercise in Possibilities." *Festschrift Günther Wagner*, 1994, pp. 1-14.

[2]   *Baptism, Eucharist and Ministry*, 1982. In the following abbreviated *BEM*.

[3]   The set of problems which is dealt with in the thesis is probably not unique to the Baptist Union of Sweden, but to make comparisons

official response on baptism by the Baptist Union of Sweden to *BEM* (see Part II). This official response of the Baptist Union of Sweden is in the following abbreviated *BUS*.[4] The task also involves a presentation of the Baptist Union of Sweden, its history and the Baptist Union in an ecumenical context (see Part I). Further I study what I call *public discussions* about baptism in this denomination, but primarily from the 1970's until the beginning of the 1990's (see Part III), to ascertain if there is a reconsideration of baptism and thus ecclesiology within the Baptist Union, when comparing *BUS* and these *public discussions.*

Through this study I am trying to understand the response of the Baptist Union of Sweden to *BEM*. The question is, however, if this response necessarily tells the whole truth about the opinion of the Baptist Union. This is why I think it valuable also to include in this study the public discussions. In these we may find opinions similar to those in *BUS*, but possibly also others. I also want to put the thesis in a context, in order to understand better Part II and III, by looking at the history of the Baptist Union of Sweden, both its problems with divisions, and also its strivings towards church unity. Relevant information about the organization of the Union and its statistics, and also about Swedish society at the time of the development of the Baptist movement in the 19th century is provided. In this way we ought to get a more comprehensive picture of the Baptist Union.

The thesis is written for an international readership. It is a case-study which may hopefully be of some general international interest as it investigates more closely how one local response to *BEM* has come into existence, how the work advanced, and also follows the discussions within that denomination during that time. To compare an official response of a denomination with public discussions within that denomination is a method which hopefully also can be used in other contexts and research, fully conscious of the difficulties involved in such a procedure.

The Baptist Union of Sweden stands apart in comparison with the Church of Sweden, the Catholic Church etc. (especially concerning for example baptism), and certainly it constitutes a minority together with some other churches on the Swedish religious-sociological scene. Even a Christian or religious minority

---

between the Baptist Union of Sweden and other churches in their responses to *BEM* etc., falls outside the scope of this investigation.

4   See appendix.

demands particular attention and is an important task for research, not least from an ecumenical standpoint. Without doubt the Baptist Union of Sweden both directly and indirectly has played an ecumenical role. It has been a partner in the ecumenical (especially Free Church) dialogue in Sweden.

We must not either forget that the Baptist Union of Sweden belongs to an international Baptist context. It is a member of the Baptist World Alliance (BWA). BWA was established in 1905, and it has grown from 6 million at its start to about 38 million baptized members in about 150 nations in the beginning of the 1990's.[5] The major thing that all these members seem to agree about completely is believers' baptism - mostly and preferably by immersion.[6]

The general opinion on what characterizes Baptists is that they teach, preach and practise only believers' baptism. We may call attention to the fact that the Baptists appeared on the scene as a protest and corrective to other churches, which sometimes have been accused of practising so-called indiscriminate baptism (as BEM more or less explicitly also does) or non-baptisms, i.e. infant baptism is rejected as a baptism. Believers' baptism and believers' congregation have been two well-known principles and they have in many respects given the Baptist Union of Sweden its identity.

One of the tasks in this thesis is to examine the hypothesis that the Baptist Union of Sweden still says a categorical "no" to infant baptism as a genuine or proper baptism - which among other things implies a "yes" to "re-baptism".[7] Further, I will try to ascertain whether the Baptist Union still persists in saying that a Baptist congregation is equivalent to the members who have been

---

5   *Svenska Baptistsamfundets Årsbok* 1992-93, p. 8. The number of Baptists is in fact higher than these figures indicate, since more people who are not (yet) baptized by believers' baptism live in Baptist congregations. See more about this problem, and also about the term *those ministered to (betjänade)*, below, chapter 4.

6   See for example "Tomma ord - eller?", [editorial], VP, No. 30, 1985, p. 2. Another significant point where the Baptists are in agreement is about freedom of religion, but this is not unique to Baptists.

7   See for example David Lagergren, former General Secretary in the Baptist Union of Sweden, who states in 1978 that there are no signs, as far as he knows, of a change of the view of baptism within the Baptist Union of Sweden. ("... i dagens läge finns inga tecken som jag känner till vare sig inom Missionsförbundet eller Baptistsamfundet till en förändring av dopsynen."), "Så ser ledare för andra samfund på SMF", [David Lagergren], *Liv och frihet*, 1978, p. 293.

baptized by believers' baptism (by immersion) or whether there are any tendencies towards a change concerning baptism and ecclesiology, in theory and practice. After all, baptism has ecclesiological and ecumenical implications,[8] and it is closely related to, and often regarded as an expression of, the unity of the church. Therefore also ecclesiology, ultimately the Baptist Union of Sweden *in oikumene,* will be dealt with.[9]

Baptism has during the centuries been of fundamental importance to the churches - because of above all the commandment of Jesus Christ to baptize. Baptism has been both unifying and divisive. The view of baptism has often been a controversial issue, resulting in different teachings, understandings and practices of baptism - in relation to other topics such as ecclesiology, ecumenism, faith etc. - contributing to divisions within the church. The doctrine has not only concerned theory (baptismal teaching) but also practice, i.e. how baptism ought to be administered, and the "correct" time for baptism etc. There have been generally speaking two main streams: one advocating infant baptism and an ecclesiology built on it; the other, however, built exclusively on believers' baptism and a concomitant ecclesiology. The latter has also denied infant baptism as a baptism, implying so-called "re-baptism".

Different processes during the centuries have caused revisions and changes in regard to both baptismal teaching and baptismal practice. During recent decades there has been a steady growth in ecumenical matters, including baptism and ecclesiology, where the World Council of Churches, *WCC,* has played an essential role. The emphasis on baptism in *BEM* is well known. We know also about the relevance of baptism to the churches working towards church unity. The Baptists seem, however, in relation to most of the other denominations and churches, on account of their emphasis on believers' baptism to be farthest from that kind of church unity which is built on *one baptism,* which also includes infant baptism.

---

8   "Different baptismal practices are always a problem, but the problem becomes urgent when baptism is put in relation to incorporation into the congregation." Lagergren, David, *Enhetsförslaget och dopfrågan,* 1969, p. 5.

9   To make the Baptist reconsideration of baptism and ecclesiology and thus also Baptist identity clear, presentation of the context is restricted mainly to such things as are of importance in order to solve the task of this thesis.

Due amongst other things to the difficulties with baptism, not least in the work for church unity, where baptism many times has been a stumbling-block, it is understandable that the Faith and Order Commission has invited churches to prepare official responses to BEM "at the highest appropriate level of authority",[10] also discussing the issue of baptism. It can then be assumed that these responses are representative - so for example BUS. Besides BEM, many other international, bilateral and multilateral dialogues (before and especially after the Second Vatican Council) have become an urgent appeal to many churches and denominations.[11]

The principal task of this thesis is to study and reflect on baptism, both its doctrine and practice, in the Baptist Union of Sweden. What kind of baptismal theology and baptismal practice do we find in this Baptist Union? One of many problems in a study like this is that there is neither an official authorized Confession, nor any binding teaching authority, as in for example the Roman-Catholic or Lutheran Churches - except the Bible alone. The Baptist movement is a popular movement in the positive sense, arising and growing from below. This is also expressed ecclesiologically by the principle of congregationalism. Therefore, it is also difficult to find formulated, authorized Swedish Baptist theology.

In this doctoral thesis it is natural to start with the internationally and ecumenically well known document BEM.[12]

---

[10] BEM p. x.

[11] "The decade of the 1970's which lies behind us was a time when the churches reached a number of new and pioneering theological agreements. The wealth of documents collected in this volume speaks for itself. One might say these past years have been a decade of steady growth in ecumenical consensus." Growth in Agreement, 1984, p. 2. It is also said that "the time has now come to bring together in one volume the many documents published in different places around the world in journals, symposia and church publications or press services in order to give a first general survey and much needed global view of what has been achieved so far." Ibid.

[12] The results after years of thorough preparation and four years' work of the theological steering committee under Max Thurian constituted the basis of the concluding discussion at the Lima Commission in 1982. Among the experts who were involved in the work of the steering committee we may mention the Baptist theologian Günther Wagner. William H Lazareth states: "Under the guidance of the Holy Spirit, the answer to all this work and prayer was unprecedented in the modern

There is something new in *BEM*, but there were also ideas circulating before *BEM* which are reinforced by it. *BEM* is, as Max Thurian writes,

> the fruit of a long history of study and dialogue. Four world conferences (Lausanne 1927, Edinburgh 1937, Lund 1952, Montreal 1963) and ten plenary meetings of the Faith and Order Commission (from Chicester 1949 to Lima 1982, taking in on the way the meetings in Bristol 1967 and Accra 1974 which were important stages in the evolution of the Lima document) signpost the course of this history.[13]

That *BEM* has played a decisive role in the ecumenical process can be seen among other things in all the responses to *BEM* and the in many ways unprecedented discussions at many levels all over the world.[14] The main issues concern baptism, eucharist and ministry in the work towards the visible unity of Christ's body. In the preface to *BEM*, it is said concerning the Faith and Order Commission: "During the last fifty years, most of its conferences have had one or another of these subjects at the centre of the discussion."[15]

---

ecumenical movement. Basic convergence was achieved on many essential parts of the apostolic faith that had formerly divided the churches and prevented them from sharing in eucharistic and conciliar fellowship together. While such theological agreements will not guarantee Church unity, they certainly can help to overcome many of the mistaken or outdated reasons frequently given to justify our disunity." *Growing Together in Baptism, Eucharist and Ministry*, 1982, p. 5.

[13] *Churches respond to BEM*, Vol. I, 1986, pp. 2f. See also pp. 1-12. For the history and the roots of *BEM*, see *A Documentary History of the Faith and Order Movement 1927-1963*, 1963, and *A Documentary History of Faith and Order 1963-1993*, 1993. Concerning the world conference in Montreal 1963, it could be described as the first really ecumenical world conference, since even the Roman Catholic Church participated. Concerning the origin and development of the World Council of Churches, see Visser't Hooft, W.A., *The Genesis and Formation of the World Council of Churches*, 1982.

[14] *Churches respond to BEM*, Vols. I-VI, 1986-1988. We can also note that the Roman Catholic Church, not a member of *WCC*, officially responded for the first time to an ecumenical document. Günther Gassmann writes: "The convergence document on 'Baptism, Eu-charist and Ministry' (BEM) has received extraordinarily wide attention from the member churches of the World Council of Churches and *beyond*." *Churches respond to BEM*, Vol. I, 1986, p. v. Italics mine.

[15] *BEM*, preface, p. viii.

BEM does not present itself as a consensus document but a "reception-text", a convergence document. The explicit aim of the Commission is

> to proclaim the oneness of the Church of Jesus Christ and to call the churches to the goal of visible unity in one faith and one eucharistic fellowship, expressed in worship and common life in Christ, in order that the world might believe.[16]

And *BEM* stresses concerning the issue of baptism that

> Mutual recognition of baptism is acknowledged as an important sign and means of expressing the baptismal unity given in Christ.[17]

Because of the impulses coming from among other things the WCC and Faith and Order in Geneva, it became necessary to discuss baptism within the different churches and denominations, including also Baptist ones. The *BEM*-process is thus not concluded but still continuing, and my thesis may be regarded as a small expression of the process that is taking place on a much larger scale at both congregational and denominational, as well as national and international levels.

Discussing these issues we come to another difficult and closely related topic, that of reception. *BEM* calls for one kind of reception, *a formal one.* There is, however, as far as I can see, a danger with the kind of reception which *BEM* initiates and of which *BUS* is an example, in that the responses to *BEM* may be polite, discrete and cautious, mostly on a theoretical level.

From the study in Part II, I try to discover *BUS'* position on different questions and identify a theological profile in *BUS'* understanding of baptismal theology and baptismal practice in an ecclesiological context. These two documents, *BEM* and *BUS*, are different both in their origin and their character. Despite this I have not chosen to analyse them separately. If I had first analyzed *BEM* and then *BUS*, the comparison would have involved problems, since *BUS* is dependent on *BEM* and cannot be read in the same way. The latter is a document understandable on its own, whilst *BUS* is not. They belong together and the analysis ought to be done in this connected way.

There is on the other hand *an informal reception* which is reflected in the public discussions, and which may indicate better

---

[16] By-Laws, quoted in *BEM*, the preface p. viii.

[17] *B 15.*

the ideas on the grass-roots level.[18] The process of reception is one involving not only the highest appropriate level of authority but also the local, congregational level, i.e. as a matter of fact all believers. It may be of interest to see what *BUS* says and compare this with the study of the public discussions.

From this study of baptism and ecclesiology in *BUS* and the public discussions we will also probably gain more knowledge partly of the situation and identity of Swedish Baptists, and partly of Baptist identity in the *oikumene,* i.e. the relation and interaction between the Baptist Union of Sweden and other churches and denominations. The ecumenical process, taking place at different levels, is thus partially dealt with. The Baptist Union of Sweden, especially at the local, congregational level, is affected by and involved in ecumenical congregations. There is a great number of Baptists who are members of this kind of congregation.[19] There is therefore reason to suppose that this phenomenon directly or indirectly, together with other aspects such as the secularization, urbanisation and pluralism of society, would contribute to a Baptist reconsideration of baptism and ecclesiology. A change of view on baptism, both regarding teaching and practice, is possibly taking place within the Baptist Union of Sweden with implications for its ecclesiology and identity. A challenging question is how open (in theory and in practice) the Baptist Union of Sweden can be without losing its identity.

---

[18] Concerning the problem of reception, see for example *Theologischer Konsens und Kirchenspaltung,* 1981, and see also in Swedish Thunberg, Lars, "Om receptionen av ekumeniska texter", *Ekumeniken och forskningen,* 1992, pp. 201-215.

[19] Palm, Irving, "Frikyrkofolket och ekumeniken", *Tro & Tanke* 1993:5, pp. 77, 85. See also more below.

Material

How do we conduct such an inquiry into Baptist reconsideration of baptism and ecclesiology? In this question one restriction is implied concerning the material which forms the basis of the task. For Part II it is (as, of course, has been understood) primarily *BEM* and *BUS*. The latter is a homogeneous material, which is a result of another homogeneous document, *BEM*.

In Part III, I have used a material of a different character, as we do not find *one* articulated Swedish Baptist theology. This has meant that my work has been more difficult to carry out but also more fascinating. The material for the study in Part III is to a great extent to be found in *Veckoposten,* the official weekly magazine of the Baptist Union of Sweden until 1992, when it was merged with *Sändaren.* It could be fruitful to refer to some of this, in order to illustrate other approaches within the Baptist Union of Sweden which are rarely or never referred to in the so-called major works.[20]

Veckoposten must be regarded as central to the Baptist Union and its members. It has been the major instrument in giving expression to the identity of the Baptist Union. It has been the official organ of the Baptist Union and the voice of the leadership internally vis à vis the Baptist community and externally vis à vis other denominations, churches and society. It also constituted a unifying element in the Baptist Union, for the individual Baptist

---

[20] "What is true of all learning processes is also true of the ecumenical learning process: *it begins at home with ourselves.* How we achieve 'unity in diversity' in our own ecclesial family, if we achieve it at all, will influence directly the way in which this 'unity in diversity' is envisaged and achieved in the wider ecumenical field, and thus influence how the present crisis in respect of this concept is overcome." Meyer, Harding, "'Unity in diversity' - A Concept in Crisis", *Ekumeniken och forskningen,* 1991, p. 53. Italics mine. See for example what the then chairman of *BWA,* Knud Wümpelmann, states: "The most important thing is always the contribution of the local congregation", Swedberg, Bo, "Knud Wümpelmann, ledare för 35 miljoner baptister: -Det viktigaste är alltid lokalförsamlingens insats", *VP,* No. 21/22, 1991, p. 20.

as well as for Baptist congregations and the denomination, perhaps the only one apart from the General Conference, Central Board, and General Secretary. In addition to those in *Veckoposten*, some other articles, mainly by Baptists in other publications, are used.

I have intentionally chosen not to work with opinion polls but with already available printed material. Using opinion polls in this case would possibly involve the risk that through my questions I would start a new discussion within the Baptist Union. The investigation would then have been determined by *my* questions and problems. I am now analysing an already existing discussion.

Since baptism is a delicate issue and it is therefore especially important to give as nuanced a picture as possible, I have often allowed people to speak for themselves by giving quotations, as well as references, in order to indicate the breadth and depth within the Baptist Union of Sweden, and to point to theologians and pastors (and also some laymen) of different kinds who have had significance in different ways.

The multiplicity implies that a few Baptists in this study may be regarded as untypical, even among the Swedish Baptists. It seems, however, evident to me that personal and individual contributions are something which characterizes the Baptist Union. This appears among other things in personal testimony, in believers' baptism, in the fight for freedom (of religion (faith), conscience, speech) etc. That there are in principle, as already stated, no Confessions/Creeds or other official documents on Baptist doctrine, as in many other churches and denominations, creates problems. As a solution to this dilemma I found it natural to let individual Baptists speak for themselves in my thesis.[21] Quotations and references may sometimes seem to be too abundant. This can, of course, also be questioned, but I have found it helpful in order to do the material the greatest possible justice.

---

[21] Most quotations from Swedish sources in the notes have been translated into English. Some, especially in Part II and III, have not been, because those particular quotations are to show nuances in the Swedish language for those interested. It is evident from the references which quotations are translations from Swedish to English. For any overall evaluation the texts left in Swedish do not, however, play any greater part. Irrespective of italics or underlining in an original text, only italics are used in the thesis both in my own text and also in the quotations.

I have collected a comprehensive sample of an extensive material, at the centre of which we find *Veckoposten*. After putting it together I create the arena, the public discussions, with a built-in comparative method, which also constitutes a basis for a comparison with *BUS* and *BEM*.[22] I am conscious of the dilemma that these individual Baptists are not always representative of the Baptist Union of Sweden but are only speaking for themselves – with some exceptions as for instance when the General Secretaries make utterances on behalf of the Union. However, through working with a fairly comprehensive material with many different opinions, I can nevertheless try to structure the opinions of these individual theologians and pastors, and relate them to each other. In this way I hopefully give a more complete picture of the baptismal theology and baptismal practice within the Baptist Union of Sweden, by describing these opinions, rather than by only studying an official document.

BUS is an example of teamwork "at the highest appropriate level of authority", while in the public discussions we find individuals who without doubt can be more outspoken in articles, statements etc. than an official document normally can be.

On the question of how representative *BUS* is, there is no simple answer, since we do not know how many Baptists agree or disagree with *BUS*. We do, however, know quantitatively how many worked on *BUS*, and qualitatively that they were leaders taking up certain positions. Further, it can be noted that differing opinions, presumably of varying representative character, can be found in *Veckoposten*.[23] We do not get a complete answer either to

---

[22] A similar approach could be used in the study of other churches on various theological questions, and perhaps also in the study of for example party politics on official policy statements in relation to debates in the media.

[23] It would indisputably also have been useful to make a closer study of *Veckoposten* itself and its significance for the development within the Baptist Union, as well as a study of a wider context, i.e. its ecumenical significance. It could be asked whether there has been any more or less conscious censuring in *Veckoposten*, which has been hinted at by the General Secretary David Lagergren, see below Part I, chapter 9.5.2. and by the Baptist pastor Ruben Mild, see Part III, chapter 8.1. and 8.2.1. Have for example some people not written articles at all since they have assumed these would not have been published etc.? There are undoubtedly some people who write more frequently than others. Of course, *BEM* and *BUS*, as well as articles in the denominational press, in for instance *Veckoposten*, *Svensk Veckotidning* (the organ of Mission Covenant Church of Sweden) and *Missionsbaneret* (the organ of Örebro

the question of how representative the public discussions are. In the public discussions we may suppose that there are leading pastors who take different positions but also ordinary laymen.

Is it feasible to compare a coherent document such as *BEM* or *BUS* with an often heterogeneous material such as *Veckoposten?* In one sense they are not comparable entities. Nevertheless, this comparison might eventually point to some trends which are not to be found at the official level, but are realities within the denomination at both congregational and denominational levels, and thus of great value in this research.

There are two obvious levels in the Baptist Union of Sweden, that is the *denominational level*, where we find the General Secretaries, the Central Board etc., and the *congregational level*, where we find pastors,[24] laymen etc. To give a concise picture of the Baptist Union of Sweden, which at the same time is as representative as possible, is a difficult task. But both the denominational level and the congregational level must be included, qualitatively and quantitatively. *Veckoposten* partly reflects the denominational level, partly the congregational level, a forum for ordinary Baptist members and also for non-Baptists who want to give their opinions on different issues.

There is one name which I ought especially to mention already in this context, that of one of the leading Swedish Baptist theologians, Torsten Bergsten. He is a layman, Doctor of Divinity and associate professor. One may perhaps be surprised at how often his name appears in this thesis, but he is one of the most influential Baptist theologians in Sweden. He is also known internationally, among other things through his doctoral thesis in 1961, *Balthasar Hubmaier. Seine Stellung zu Reformation und Täufertum: 1521-1528*. He must be regarded as a pioneer in the Swedish theological and ecumenical discussions. He has been influenced by the international theological debate on baptism after the Second World War as well as himself contributing to it,

---

(Baptist) Mission), reports etc., all have given rise to discussions and reactions on the issues of baptism and church unity. We can also observe that a more or less explicit dialogue was carried on between the denominational newspapers. What is written by one newspaper could be an important incitement to another. This is another interesting task which ought to be dealt with more than is the case in this thesis; it may be another research-project in the future.

[24] The term preacher *(predikant)* is also used, although less frequently than earlier in Baptist history.

through among other things his article about baptism and the church in 1957, translated into English in 1959.[25] And Lars Eckerdal, a former professor of theology at the university of Lund, currently the bishop of the diocese of Gothenburg, especially mentions Torsten Bergsten as one of the persons who has brought new ideas to the Baptist Union of Sweden on the issue of baptism.[26] Bergsten has through his ecumenical contacts on the national as well as the international level continually presented studies in theology, maintaining what we may call an "open" or "radical" Baptist ecumenical attitude. He is one of the most prolific Baptist debaters in Sweden with a large production of articles. We can suppose that he gives voice to at least some Baptists who for different reasons cannot be so outspoken as he himself is. Therefore, he has a central place in our study as an authority and a representative of a less traditional section of the Baptists, particularly dealt with in Part III. We can also note that he was not involved in the work on BUS.

I have had to make difficult choices in my work with this thesis. In addition to the material, another delimitation is that of chronology, which may lead to discussion and even dispute. These two problems are interrelated. That there is a continuing discussion within the Baptist Union does not make it easier. I have, however, decided to deal mainly with the 1970's and 1980's, apart from the presentation of the Baptist Union of Sweden and its history, since BEM appeared in 1982 and BUS in 1985. This gives the opportunity partly to make an analysis of the response of the Baptist Union of Sweden to BEM, partly to study the public discussions contemporaneous with BEM and the response of the Baptist Union to BEM, and also to look at what was going on in the Baptist Union of Sweden just before, during and after BEM.

One possibility, which I considered especially when working with Part III, was to divide that study into two parts, one dealing

---

25 Bergsten, Torsten, "Baptism and the Church. Baptist Faith and Practice in a Biblical and Ecumenical Light", *The Baptist Quarterly*, Vol. 18, No. 3, 1959, pp. 125-131, and No. 4, 1959, pp. 159-171, [Orig: "Dopet och församlingen. Baptistisk tro och praxis i biblisk och ekumenisk belysning", *Dopet Dåben Dåpen.* Tre nordiska teologiska uppsatser, Stockholm 1957, pp. 5-23.].

26 Eckerdal, Lars, *Vägen in i kyrkan*, 1981, p. 373. Eckerdal mentions the work of Bergsten, "Dopet och församlingen. Baptistisk tro och praxis i biblisk och ekumenisk belysning", *Dopet Dåben Dåpen*, 1957.

with the period before *BEM* and the other after. Since, however, there is no such distinct and obvious turning-point to be found in the Baptist Union of Sweden in connection with *BEM*, I have decided not to divide the study in that way.

The main presentation in my thesis deals thus with the years 1975-1992, but there will be a number of digressions both backwards and forwards in time in order to enlarge the context and understanding of the debate. As a starting point I have chosen 1975, as we can follow the discussion which then had been going on for some time within the Baptist Union of Sweden as a result of events within it in 1969, when two congregations (one from the Baptist Union of Sweden, the other from the Mission Covenant Church of Sweden) were united. Further, open membership was discussed and partly recognized within the Baptist Union that year. This resulted in a change of statutes a couple of years later in 1972. The last Free Church Conference also took place in 1969. And added to this the so-called *Tresamfundssamtalen* (Trilateral Denominational Consultations) between the Baptist Union of Sweden, the United Methodist Church in Sweden and the Mission Covenant Church of Sweden started in the same year. In other words a new expansive ecumenical period had started with rethinking and creative discussions, changes etc., not least through the development of the ecumenical congregations especially in the 1970's and onwards - the 1970's has been designated as the decade of congregational amalgamation.[27] And 1992 has been chosen as the upper limit since I can in this way follow *Veckoposten* until its last number in that year.

The criteria for choosing the period from the 1970's and onwards are thus simply pragmatic and, of course, they can be criticized in many ways. However, I can satisfy the requirement of some kind of continuity and of contextualisation in the discussion that follows. Not least the development of the ecumenical congregations made this period an intensive time for the Baptist Union of Sweden, a process which still continues even if less intensively, with consequences and implications in different areas.

How much of the historical context ought to be dealt with in order to understand *BUS* and the public discussions? Some issues which are referred to in the thesis, primarily in Part I,

---

[27] Bergsten, Torsten, "Kyrkotillhörighet - medlemskap - bekännelse", *Tro och Liv*, No. 1, 1980, p. 33. See more below.

concerning for example Baptist history, have already been studied by the Baptists Nils Johan Nordström (1880-1943), Gunnar Westin (1890-1967), David Lagergren (b. 1919) and Torsten Bergsten (b. 1921), but for a Swedish-speaking public, whilst this thesis is written for an international forum. I decided, however, that it is necessary for such an international forum to give an account of the Baptist Union of Sweden, so that they will better understand the problems dealt with in Parts II and III, from an historical, ecumenical perspective.

This thesis does not claim to give a complete picture. There is much more which could have been further developed, to get a more comprehensive, contextualised picture of the Baptist Union of Sweden and a better understanding of the difficult issues concerning baptism: for example about baptism, water-baptism and Spirit-baptism, its relation to other issues such as pneumatology or theology in the strict sense, i.e. the view of God. The questions of authority, the relation between Scripture, Tradition and traditions (written and unwritten),[28] could, of course, have been dealt with in a thesis like this. At the very best some of the different topics are touched on cursorily. Other subjects must be completely passed over. I do not pretend to cover the whole debate. Certainly much remains to be done within this field and much can thus be added to this thesis, but I want only to point to some theological and ecumenical problems regarding baptism, looking for significant aspects and tendencies, in the light of the process in which the Baptist Union is involved, both in itself and in relation to other churches/denominations in Sweden with consequences in ecclesiology and ecumenism.

---

[28] See the definition given in *Baptism, Eucharist & Ministry 1982-1990*, Faith and Order paper No. 149, 1990. Tradition refers to the comprehensive process of the transmission of the Gospel in the power of the Holy Spirit, from which the scriptures and also ecclesial traditions arise, while traditions refer to these various ecclesial traditions which developed in the course of the centuries. *Baptism, Eucharist & Ministry 1982-1990*, 1990, pp. 131f. We may note that while other churches, for example the Roman Catholic, refer to tradition, Baptists often refer to Baptist heritage - certainly with different understandings and meanings.

Previous Research

Scholars have shown little interest in Baptist theology, at least in Sweden. The Baptist Union of Sweden, its history and theology, has been dealt with in Swedish theological research mostly from an historical perspective and mainly by Baptists.[29] This circumstance can be regarded as one incitement for our study. Understandably it is impossible to give a complete picture of the history of the Baptist movement in Sweden, including the divisions and the ecumenical work of the Baptist Union of Sweden etc., in a few pages. I will thus only give a selection of aspects, which can hopefully bring into relief some dimensions of this phenomenon, and in this way also lead to a better understanding of, and provide a context for, Part II, *BUS/BEM*, and Part III, the public discussions. For recent decades I have to a great extent used original sources, but for earlier Swedish Baptist history the presentation is mainly based on the research and litterature which is available.

---

[29] See as regards older research for example Nils Johan Nordström, Gunnar Westin; then the two books by David Lagergren (1989, 1994); and it is also dealt with in other contexts, above all by Torsten Bergsten.

I also want to mention a couple of other works by non-Baptists, for example Samuelsson, Owe, *Sydsvenska baptister inför myndigheter*, 1998. He deals with Baptists in a special geographic area, the southern part of Sweden, during the years 1857-1862. Lars Eckerdal is another non-Baptist who has studied the Baptist Union of Sweden and its history especially concerning liturgical development. Eckerdal, Lars, *Vägen in i kyrkan*, 1981, pp. 370-380.

There are other works - mostly written from an historical perspective - dealing with the origin and development of different revivalist movements in Sweden, and in that context also with for instance the origin and development of the Baptist movement (in a special area, i.e. in a diocese or county) or of one or more Baptist congregations. See for instance references in Samuelsson, Owe, *Sydsvenska baptister inför myndigheter*, 1998 pp. 11-15.

Disposition

The thesis is in three parts. In Part I a presentation and an outline of the history of the Baptist Union of Sweden is given especially in an ecumenical context, in order to understand Parts II and III better. Part II is a study and analysis of *BUS*, a response to *BEM* "at the highest appropriate level of authority", i.e. of the discussion and dialogue on the official level. In Part III, I look at *the public discussions*, which have a different character than *BUS*. The questions and problems are, however, on the whole the same. The thesis ends with a conclusion with some remarks about the Baptist reconsideration of baptism and ecclesiology and the Baptist Union of Sweden in ambiguity and in a process of integration.

Part I is a comprehensive introduction to or presentation of the Baptist Union of Sweden, intended for above all an international public. To get a better understanding of *BUS* and also the public discussions, it is of importance to describe the context of the Baptist Union of Sweden from its very beginning until the present time, including its relations (or not) to other denominations and churches on practical as well as theoretical levels.

That believers' baptism has been central during the whole history of the Baptist Union of Sweden is well known, even if it is not always explicit in all contexts in Part I. Believers' baptism has been one of the most fundamental principles of the Baptist Union and it has also been a cause of controversies and conflicts from the beginning (with the then monolithic State Church) and onwards. The question of baptism has been involved also in other questions concerning for instance ecclesiology and ecumenism.

In Part I, I present some fundamental principles of the Baptist movement. Thereafter something in general terms is said about the organization of the Baptist Union and some statistics of the Baptist Union are given. We will look at the origin, history and development of the Baptist movement and the Baptist Union of Sweden. Something is also said about Swedish society and the State Church (which after 1862 became more independent from the State and was called the Church of Sweden), at the time when the Baptist Union of Sweden developed in the middle of the 19th century. We will study a process within the Baptist Union coterminous with the existence of the Baptist movement in

Sweden until this day, resulting partly in divisions partly in ecumenical strivings.

Baptist openness may be regarded as one keyword. This openess can be seen also in its ecumenical commitment (discussions about and also realizations of co-operation in different ways), possibly first more implicit in its history, later on, however, more and more explicit, which may be seen as also influencing baptismal theology and practice (Baptist identity). The ecumenical strivings have become concrete in many ways not least in later decades – during the period I am especially studying, in Parts II and III, i.e. in the 1970's and onwards - in conferences, meetings, studies, consultations and especially in the so-called ecumenical congregations.[30] It may also be said in this context that Part I has more of a descriptive character than the other parts which are more analytic.

In Part II, I conduct a more detailed analysis of the response of the Baptist Union of Sweden on baptism to *BEM*, in order to discover the official Baptist attitude. We can assume that the Baptist Union in its response to *BEM* was forced to proceed with great care on account of its history, where it has been caught between two poles which both encourage and inhibit it. We will also among other things see if there is convergence or divergence between this response of the Baptist Union of Sweden and *BEM* itself.

In the light of the concept "one baptism" in *BEM* I will discuss whether it is possible to talk about "one baptism" when we, as a matter of fact, are confronted with different opinions, views and practices, such as infant baptism, believers' baptism and "re-baptism". Other topics which will be dealt with are for example the blessing of children, the faith-context, the expressive/symbolic - instrumental/sacramental view of baptism, as well as the celebration of baptism. The questions of ecclesiology, baptism and membership/belonging and a discussion about the recognition of baptism and church unity will also be included.

Part III is a study of *the public discussions* in the light of the same or similar questions as are treated in Part II, to see if there

---

[30] It may be objected that through this presentation of ecumenical congregations in this part, I anticipate Parts II and III. This may be true in one way. I believe, however, that it is of advantage to the reader in order to get a better understanding on the whole of the Baptist Union of Sweden when proceeding to Part II and especially Part III.

are different emphases or alternative opinions within the Baptist denomination. In other words, is the result of the analysis of the Baptist response to *BEM* concerning baptism congruous with or divergent from the public discussions within the Baptist Union? Do we from the study in Parts II and III find two or more different teachings and practices of "the one baptism"? One might be representative of *BEM*, which in brief implies recognition of infant baptism as valid, and rejects "re-baptism". The other might be representative of *BUS*, which implies rejection of infant baptism as valid, and advocates "re-baptism"? I will further ask whether we find from this study any change in the Baptist Union, that is a changed or new identity among the Swedish Baptists (within Baptist congregations and the denomination) in comparison with traditional Baptism. Further, what kind of implications does an eventual Baptist reconsideration of baptism have for the identity of the Baptist Union of Sweden, the Baptist congregations and the ecumenical work towards the unity of the church.

Part III deals mostly with local congregations and those Baptists who have participated in theological and ecumenical discussions. This means for the most part leading theologians and pastors, but also some ordinary, mainly Baptist, participants.

In the conclusion the question of Baptist reconsideration of baptism and ecclesiology is discussed in the light of the results in the thesis.

It is very crucial in the reading of this thesis to keep in mind that the Baptist Union of Sweden has been and still is in a period of development, with all the problems and questions such a period implies for a study like this.

Questions of Terminology

There are, of course, difficulties with the qualification of terms. More than one objection can probably be raised against such definitions. A reservation must also be mentioned: there are some terms which are used in a relatively open way. I mention below some of the terms which are used in the thesis.

A term which is problematic is *Free Church.* A Free Church is a church or denomination which is "free" in relation to the State. In

Sweden this applies legally for instance to the Baptist Union of Sweden as well as the Catholic Church. However, in the thesis this term will refer neither to the Catholic Church, nor the Orthodox, but to denominations originating in the 19th century and later, such as the Baptist Union of Sweden, the Mission Covenant Church of Sweden, the Örebro (Baptist) Mission etc.

Congregational level. By this term I mean a local congregation, i.e. a congregation or the members of a particular congregation, (referring to a pastoral unit), i.e. the grass roots. In Baptist tradition the term *congregation* is usually used, while the term *church* is usually used in other traditions.

Denominational level applies to the overall system, the Central Board *(missionsstyrelse)*, the General Secretary, the national level.

Infant baptism (barndop): the baptizand is "passive" not giving a personal "conscious response". In polemic writings the terms *pouring (begjutning)* or *sprinkling (bestänkning)* may be used, inferring that this act is not a baptism.

Believers' baptism (troendedop) means baptizing a person in water and in the name of the Trinity, where the baptizand is "active", i.e. gives a personal "conscious response" to the Gospel and to God. I will not use the term *adult baptism (vuxendop)*, since this can be misleading – people who are not yet regarded as adults can also give a "conscious response", making a personal confession or testimony of faith.

The term *"re-baptism" (omdop)* means baptizing in water and in the name of the Trinity a person who has formerly been baptized as an infant. I am aware that this term is not used in a Baptist context but by those who regard such a baptism as a second baptism. It is in spite of this used in this thesis for lack of a better alternative, but with brackets to indicate that it is not a generally accepted term.

I use the term *proper baptism* (or *genuine*), which is a baptism which is recognized as valid. And *improper baptism* is a baptism which has been "wrongly performed" but it can yet be recognized as valid. *Invalid baptism* is thus not recognized as a baptism at all. In using these distinctions *proper/improper* and *valid/invalid*, I am not committing myself to their meaning and use in for example Catholic sacramental theology. They are intended as formal analytical distinctions, which will become apparent in my use of them later in the thesis.

Closed membership (slutet medlemskap) means that believers' baptism is regarded as a necessary condition of being a member of a Baptist congregation.[31]

Associate membership (associativt medlemskap) means that a person who is a member of (or belongs to) one denomination (for example Baptist) at the same time for some reason joins a congregation belonging to another denomination (for instance Methodist) without leaving his original denominational affiliation. In other words, an individual can keep his membership in the congregation in the place where the person in question earlier lived and at the same time be associate member in another congregation belonging to another denomination in the place to which the person moves. The term *associate membership* was introduced into the Swedish Free Church movement at the Free Church Conference in 1953.[32]

Open membership (öppet medlemskap) means that a Baptist congregation welcomes on the basis of a personal profession of faith people who are baptized by infant baptism or are not necessarily baptized at all - neither by believers' baptism nor by infant baptism. The Baptist congregation, which earlier had

---

[31] Concerning the term *membership (medlemskap)*, I also want to mention *belonging (tillhörighet)*. I have understood that it is difficult to make a distinction in the international debate, nevertheless it is made in Sweden. See more below.

[32] Bergsten, Torsten, *Frikyrkor i samverkan*, 1995, pp. 146f. See also Bergsten, Torsten, "Associativt och öppet medlemskap", *Baptistpredikanternas studieblad*, No. 2, 1964, pp. 9-12. Bergsten writes among other things that associate membership is intended for a limited time and has the nature of a temporary arrangement. Ibid. p. 10. In 1965 the Central Board *(Missionsstyrelsen)* of the Baptist Union of Sweden said in its recommendation concerning associate membership, that a condition for this must still be that those who associate with the congregation fully identify themselves with Baptist preaching and practice, even if they themselves cannot share the Baptist position on everything. See for example Lagergren, David, "Svar:", *VP*, No. 27, 1978, p. 10. As far as Lagergren knows the associative members have been allowed to have positions of trust in a Baptist context. Ibid.

There has been an ambiguity concerning associate membership within the Baptist Union. One cause which has been given is that this kind of membership decreases the demand for clear Baptist preaching. See for example *Svenska Baptistsamfundets Allmänna konferenser Stockholm 1963 Linköping 1964. Svenska Baptistsamfundets Ungdomsförbunds (SBUF) årskonferenser Västerås 1963 Sjövik 1964*, 1964, p. 111.

demanded believers' baptism for membership, in spite of this fact gives them full membership.[33] Open membership has been common for a long time, for instance in England, but began within Swedish Baptism first in the 1960's, which caused dramatic debates.[34]

The year 1969 may be regarded as a turning point for the Baptist Union of Sweden. As stated previously, open membership was recognized by the General Conference that year, with a change of statutes in 1972. Today open membership is quite common within the Baptist Union of Sweden.

Transferred membership (överfört medlemskap) is a kind of open membership. Transferred membership means for example that a Baptist congregation welcomes people from *other* congregations as full members, believers who for example have been *baptized* by infant baptism, and gives them full membership without baptizing them by believers' baptism, *or* believers who have not been baptized at all. People who regard their infant baptism as a valid baptism can thus be transferred from a congregation practising infant baptism to a Baptist congregation.[35]

Closed communion (slutet nattvardsbord) means that only members of the congregation or only believers and baptized are

---

33 See Bergsten, Torsten, "Baptismen, trosfriheten och ekumeniken", *Liv och tjänst*, 1988, p. 198. See also Bergsten, Torsten, "Förändring genom konfrontation och dialog. Svenskt perspektiv", *Samfund i förändring*, 1997, pp. 42ff., Bergsten, Torsten, "Enheten i Kristus", *Tro, Frihet, Gemenskap*, 1998, pp. 229f., where he discusses associate and open membership.

34 A discussion about this can be found in *Baptistpredikanternas studieblad*. See for example Bergsten, Torsten, "Associativt och öppet medlemskap", *Baptistpredikanternas studieblad*, No. 2, 1964, pp. 9-12. He writes on both associate and open membership that they are a deviation from traditional Swedish Baptist practice. Ibid. p. 10. Concerning open membership, he writes that within Swedish Baptism this has hardly been tried [i.e. in the 60's, remark mine]. Ibid. p. 11; see also Bergsten, Torsten, "På väg mot fördjupad gemenskap", *Dokument från Örebro*, 1969, pp. 61-78.

35 See for example Bergsten, Torsten, "Baptismen, trosfriheten och ekumeniken", *Liv och tjänst*, 1988, p. 198; Bergsten, Torsten, "Förändring genom konfrontation och dialog. Svenskt perspektiv", *Samfund i förändring*, 1997, p. 43.

welcome to participate at the Lord's table. This practice began, however, to cease in the middle of the 20th century.[36]

Open communion (öppet nattvardsbord) means that everyone who believes in Jesus Christ is welcome to take part in the Lord's Supper.[37]

I use the above mentioned terms *closed* and *open* in Swedish Baptism, also in another sense. Using them I interpret the process and development within the Baptist Union, where *closed* means a traditional, conservative Baptist attitude, while *open* means a more pluralistic, liberal Baptist one.

I also use the terms *subjective* and *objective* but not as evaluative expressions but as neutral terms. By *subjective* I mean a conscious act of faith, the emphasis is on the role of the person; while by *objective* the role of the person is subordinated.

We will meet the terms *ecumenism, ecumenical* etc.,[38] and also *ecumenical congregation.*[39] As a matter of fact this designation is improper as long as it does not concern *all* Christians in a place. By *ecumenical congregation* I mean a congregation which has been formed by the union of two or more different congregations, belonging/affiliated to more than one denomination and where we find people who are members of, or affiliated to, different denominations and not just to one church or denomination. Furthermore, the newly established congregations which have been ecumenical from the beginning are also included. We find thus different kinds of ecumenical congregation.

---

36 Bergsten, Torsten, *Frikyrkor i samverkan*, 1995, p. 177.

37 Bergsten, Torsten, "Enheten i Kristus", *Tro, Frihet, Gemenskap*, 1998, pp. 228f.

38 Professor Per Erik Persson makes the remark about ecumenism, that it may not only concern unity, the process towards utopia, but also conflict solving and the causes of division. Persson, Per Erik, "Forskning om ekumenik - en inledning", *Ekumeniken och forskningen*, 1992, pp. 11f. See also Brodd, Sven-Erik, *Ekumeniska perspektiv*, 1990, pp. 9f.; Brodd, Sven-Erik, "Ekumenik. Skärningspunkt mellan idé och verklighet", *Kyrkans liv*, 2nd ed., 1993, pp. 284-304.

39 Other terms in Swedish are: *unionsförsamling (union congregation), ekumenisk frikyrkoförsamling (ecumenical free church congregation), gemensam församling (common congregation), förenad församling (united congregation), samverkande församling (co-operative congregation).* The accepted term in Swedish since 1990 is *gemensam församling (common congregation).*

Some Short Remarks about my Dissertation: "Beasley-Murray's dopuppfattning"

I want to summarize the results of my study of George Raymond Beasley-Murray's view on baptism. He belongs to those Baptist theologians who have had (and still have) great importance in the process of reconsideration which parts of the Baptist fellowship, particularly in Europe, have experienced in later decades. Beasley-Murray has been an important source of inspiration in this work and thus also for Swedish Baptism.

He is one of the first European Baptist theologians who seriously deals with the problem of baptism after the many debates and discussions which took place all over Europe especially from the 1940's and onwards, much on account of Karl Barth's and Emil Brunner's writings,[40] and ecumenical work (Faith and Order, WCC etc.). Without doubt Beasley-Murray has in more than one way through his work in books, articles, debates etc., contributed to reflection on and reconsideration of the issue of baptism. He has had an impact not least on the Baptist movement itself with respect to the issue of baptism. He has therefore paved the way for a process from what we may call a more traditional Baptist symbolic view of baptism towards a more open and complementary view. He has also contributed to dialogues with other churches, denominations and traditions, making dialogue possible between different positions at different levels.

In the dissertation I ask a number of fundamental questions, and analyse some features of Beasley-Murray's view of baptism. I examine in particular the relationship between baptism and faith.

---

[40] See for example Barth, Karl, "Die kirchliche Lehre von der Taufe", *Theologische Studien* 14, 1947, (orig. 1943), questioning infant baptism. See also his book a couple of decades later, *Die kirchliche Dogmatik*, Band 4: Die Lehre von der Versöhnung. Teil 4: Das christliche Leben: (Fragment): die Taufe als Begründung des christlichen Lebens, 1967. The questioning of infant baptism was brought to the forefront in the 1930's and 1940's also by Emil Brunner. Brunner started proposing a view which questioned infant baptism on theological grounds in connection with a visit to Uppsala in 1937. See Brunner, Emil, *Wahrheit als Begegnung*, 1938, pp. 136-140.

The concepts of symbol and sacrament are discussed in relation to the traditional symbolic view of baptism (represented by Zwingli, Calvin, Barth and the Baptist movement) and the sacramental view of baptism (represented by Augustine, Thomas ab Aquino and Luther). There are, of course, different accents, interpretations, and even divergent and different views within each respective tradition, as concerns the action of God and/or man, faith and grace etc. This discussion constitutes the setting of the discussion about baptism as symbol or sacrament by Beasley-Murray. He is of the opinion that Baptists have not shown sufficient appreciation of the sacramental meaning of baptism, that too often baptism has been understood by Baptists as having no more than symbolic value. Beasley-Murray has taken an intermediary position between those maintaining a traditional symbolic view of baptism and those maintaining a traditional sacramental view. He writes:

> In the light of the foregoing exposition of the New Testament representations of baptism, the idea that baptism is a purely symbolic rite must be pronounced not alone unsatisfactory but out of harmony with the New Testament itself.[41]

The concepts of faith ("fides qua", "fides quae" and "fiducia") are discussed in the dissertation and the use of these terms and concepts by Beasley-Murray. I look at such aspects as for example faith *before, in* and *after* baptism; as well as the different aspects of faith, (faith as knowledge, conversion, *metanoia*, response, trust, obedience) and faith as a gift etc. Beasley-Murray distinguishes between faith in the external and in the internal sense - faith as response in the former sense, i.e. confession of faith; and prayer in the latter sense. The response ought to be made *in* baptism, and the right biblical baptism is according to Beasley-Murray believers' baptism. This baptism is partly an action of God and partly an act of man (his response, faith). Sacrament means thus in this context a commitment by oath between two partners, God and man. In spite of his more sacramental view of baptism, his opinion excludes, as I understand it, the teaching and practice of infant baptism. He means that it is the response of man to God which releases the

---

[41] Beasley-Murray, George Raymond, *Baptism in the New Testament*, 1976, p. 263. First published in 1962. See also Beasley-Murray, George Raymond, *Baptism Today and Tomorrow*, 1966, especially the chapter *Baptism, A Symbol or Sacrament?* pp. 13-41.

power of the resurrection of Jesus Christ. He does not say that infant baptism is not baptism, but that it is a different baptism. There are thus two sorts of baptism, one for children who cannot profess their faith and one for those that can.

I study further the relation between baptism (i.e. believers' baptism) and faith. Beasley-Murray is of the opinion that baptism and faith should not be separated; that baptism and faith could be seen, without pressing the point, as the interior and exterior aspects of the same thing. To distinguish baptism and faith as Baptist tradition has done, with the order "faith then baptism", is thus according to Beasley-Murray a misinterpretation of the New Testament, just as much as the order prevalent in other denominations, "baptism then faith". Baptism should as the crucial element be integrated with faith into *one act*, believers' baptism. In the New Testament, according to Beasley-Murray, exactly the same spiritual gifts are associated with baptism and faith, and God's gift through baptism and through faith is identical, salvation in Christ. The operation of baptism and faith is the same, i.e. the believer's death and resurrection with Christ and eternal life. If faith, that is the commitment, is lacking, baptism is only an external rite and therefore meaningless. It must be a question of *in baptism by faith*, where faith is the means of reception.

One conclusion of the analysis is that there is a tendency in the argumentation of Beasley-Murray to imply that faith without baptism is sufficient for man to be saved and thus to be associated with the death and resurrection of Jesus Christ. God gives everything to faith (brings the person from death to life), but nothing to baptism if faith is absent. It is faith, the commitment *(sacramentum)*, which is essential. So the identification of baptism with faith is valid only on certain presuppositions.

Part I

The Baptist Union of Sweden

A Presentation

1. Introduction

In this section, I will describe the history of the Baptist Union of Sweden from its early beginnings in the 1840's until the 1990's, and say something about the Baptist Union of Sweden in a 19th century historical context. The pioneerperiod of the Baptist movement is discussed when the State Church is in a process of change, on account of different movements in society and also of revivalist movements, which contributed to "the end" of the State Church system.

The Baptist Union of Sweden has from the beginning of its history been a movement which has had to deal with divisions. Something must thus be said about the Baptist Union and some of the divisions, for instance the Pentecostal Movement, and the Örebro (Baptist) Mission.[1] The development of the Baptist Union has also included ecumenical strivings, on both an international and national level, which will be discussed in this part as well as in Part III.

The Baptist Union of Sweden has taken part in different ecumenical contexts. I therefore discuss a number of different ecumenical strivings (for example some conferences, consultations and studies), and the ecumenical congregations and different reactions towards this phenomenon. Other expressions of ecumenism such as for example common service manuals, common hymn book etc. are also dealt with.

All this is of importance as a context for Part II, and not least Part III. Such a survey cannot be complete. Much has already been written. There are above all some major Swedish works by the Baptists Gunnar Westin, Nils Johan Nordström, David Lagergren and Torsten Bergsten. Hopefully this section could, however, function as a brief history lesson on the Baptist Union for readers of

---

[1] *Örebro (Baptist) Mission* is the English term which I use. In Swedish, however, it has been called *Örebro Missionsförening* (Örebro Mission Society) - also *Örebro in- och utländska missionsförening* - and from 1964 it was called *Örebro Missionen/Örebromissionen* (Örebro Mission) or only *ÖM*.

this thesis and as an "apéritif" to further in-depth studies by other researchers.

First, however, I want to describe the principles of the Baptist movement in general and then a general view of the organization of the Baptist Union of Sweden, giving some statistics etc.

2. Some Fundamental Principles of the Baptist Movement

It is not easy to characterize briefly what makes a Baptist "a Baptist" or what gives a "Baptist" identity. In short: *who* is a Baptist? There are, however, some principles which have been more or less associated with the Baptists.

Ever since the ancient church and up to the 16th century it is the consistent Catholic and Orthodox tradition of infant baptism which has been predominant. There have, however, during the centuries been movements of protest against this teaching and practice. Since the 16th century Anabaptist and Baptist movements have preached, taught and practised their characteristic *believers' baptism.*[2] This implies that the validity of infant baptism is denied and that "re-baptism" is practised, when necessary. Baptists have had great difficulties, with tensions and conflicts with the "established" churches, and even persecutions of different kinds have occurred. Baptists have been controversial on account of their opinion concerning baptism and have through their attitude, in relation to churches and denominations practising infant baptism, contributed to questions about baptism and ecclesiology being of interest, but they have also been a stumbling-block in the work towards church unity.

Believers' baptism is according to traditional Baptist teaching a symbolic act of obedience and confession of faith.[3] It is, together with Holy Communion or the Lord's Supper, recognized as a New Testament ordinance. Baptism symbolizes the death, burial and

---

[2] Concerning Baptist writings on baptism, see for example *A Bibliography of Baptist writings on baptism 1900-1968,* 1969.

[3] Faith usually means in this Baptist context a personal, conscious response of the believer, i.e. baptizand, which has as its presupposition the hearing of a message. The message is heard through the Word of Christ and results in a (sudden and radical) *metanoia.* Man answers (directly) in faith and gives his conscious response to the call of God and is baptized by believers' baptism.

resurrection of the baptizand or believer with Christ. While Baptists cannot recognize infant baptism as a valid baptism, this logically implies that the Baptists represent an alternative to the unanimity of many other churches and denominations teaching, preaching and practising infant baptism. These regard baptism (infant baptism as well as believers' baptism - if this is not a so-called "re-baptism") as the basis for ecclesial unity. The latter opinion is the principal line today in the declarations of many of the churches/denominations in the world, which is also confirmed in *BEM*. The latter writes about "Our common baptism" and "our one baptism".[4]

Another principle is *the authority of the Bible*, and especially of the New Testament,[5] which has led to serious study of the Bible.[6] The Baptists hold the principle of biblical authority as the sole authority for the theology and practice of baptism. For Baptists the Bible is the sole rule of faith and practice *(sola Scriptura)*, the Holy Spirit the guide and interpreter, and Jesus is regarded as the ultimate authority in belief and practice. Jesus is the only Lord, the norm by which the Scriptures have to be interpreted and understood. Of course we are conscious that the authority of the Bible may mean different things to all the different churches and denominations, and sometimes even within one and the same church.[7]

A theological opinion or position has, however, seldom if ever, been held only biblical grounds, but it is developed in a context where other causes are involved such as cultural, sociological elements. The Bible is to be read through different "spectacles". There is thus also within the Baptist Union of Sweden "tradition". It is a question of a doctrinal tradition which is very flexible.

---

[4] *B 6.*

[5] See for instance Franzén, Bert, "Tro och liv i förändring", *Tro, Frihet, Gemenskap*, 1998, p. 193; Nordström, Nils Johan, *De frikyrkliga och statskyrkoproblemet*, 1922, pp. 84ff.

[6] Baptists have in general had a critical attitude towards historical-critical study of Bible-texts. Even if there has been such an opposition to historical-critical study, a certain openness is to be found within the Baptist Union of Sweden from the 1920's, which also caused tensions within the Union. Lagergren, David, *Framgångstid med dubbla förtecken*, 1989. p. 101.

[7] The authority of the Bible is a topic which ought to be dealt with much more than is possible in this thesis.

We find amongst the Baptists another typical mark, *the principle of congregationalism*. Baptists assert that a congregation is in principle free from every other authority. The congregation is regarded, especially by the traditional or strict Baptists, as a community of believers. The membership is then limited to those who have been baptized by believers' baptism by immersion, who by their own free will respond to the offer of the Gospel in faith, life and ministry, i.e. closed membership.[8] A genuine, personal conversion and the competence of each individual in matters of faith are thus presupposed in order to be a member, and baptism is for believers and believers only. Repentance and saving faith or trust in Christ are two sides of the one coin, called conversion. Through this baptism the believer makes a public statement of his faith, that Christ is the Lord - whom he wants to follow. There is an emphasis on congregational polity, i.e. the visible church manifested as the local gathered community of believers. The congregation is competent under Jesus Christ to interpret and administer his laws. The church ultimately being seen to consist of *congregatio sanctorum loci*, i.e. a congregation of believers in one place, characterizes Congregationalism.[9] The Baptists have, however, "wider contexts", for instance national conventions, unions, associations, the Baptist World Alliance etc., and are not at all isolationist.

In mentioning congregationalism, we can note that there is an ambiguity in theology and organization within the Baptist denominations concerning for example the attitude towards

---

[8] It is stated in a Swedish Baptist report: "Through personally receiving the message of Christ as Lord and Messiah, as Saviour, that is through faith and also baptism in the name of Jesus Christ people become members of the congregation - the church." ("Genom personligt mottagande av ordet om Kristus som Herre och Messias, som Frälsare, d.v.s. genom tro och därtill dop i Jesu Kristi namn blir människor medlemmar i församlingen - kyrkan.") "Svenska Baptistsamfundet och Kyrkornas Världsråd. En studierapport", 1965, p. 3, [unpublished paper]; and it is said in the annual report of the Central Board *(Missionsstyrelsens årsberättelse)* in 1963, that the congregation is a believers' congregation and baptism believers' baptism. *Svenska Baptistsamfundets Allmänna konferenser Stockholm 1963 Linköping 1964. Svenska Baptistsamfundets Ungdomsförbund (SBUF) årskonferenser Västerås 1963 Sjövik 1964*, 1964, p. 7. See, however, below about the open membership practised within the Baptist Union of Sweden since 1970's.

[9] The claim of the complete independence of a congregation is problematic. I will discuss this more below.

congregationalism and episcopalism. We can for example read about how the former General Secretary Birgit Karlsson (b. 1935), Sweden, meets the *Baptist bishop* Janis Tervits in Latvia[10]

Congregationalism also implies among other things that the Baptists do not in principle have official authorities or binding Confessions, except the Bible. Nevertheless there have been Creeds or Confessions to express the Baptist faith, also within the Baptist Union of Sweden.[11] The Central Board *(Missionsstyrelsen)* writes in 1990/91:

> Baptists sometimes describe themselves as a movement without Confessions of Faith, and thereby wish to emphasize the right and responsibility of the individual to seek for himself in Scriptures after support for his conviction. It would be oversimplified to ignore the occasions when Baptists have found it both right and urgent to formulate their faith.[12]

There are thus Creeds or what are preferably called by many Baptists themselves Confessions of Faith. Baptists do not give their Confessions the same formal status as for instance the Lutheran

---

[10] Lantz, Ragni, "Birgit Karlsson: -Det ljusnar för kristna i öst", *VP*, No. 43, 1989, p. 2. See also "Baptist-biskop besökte Sverige", *VP*, No. 2, 1988, p. 3, it concerns bishop Kabwe-ka-Uza, Zaire. Compare, for example, the episcopal Baptist Union in Zaire/Congo with the Southern Baptists.

[11] Hans Sundberg and Berit Åqvist (Baptist pastors – see, however, more below) write that in spite of the opposition of Baptists to Confessions of Faith there are examples of these. They refer to Lumpkin, *Baptist Confessions of Faith*, where for example also the Confession of the first Baptist congregation in Stockholm, from 1856, is included (this Confession of Faith had been formulated by the Baptists in U.S.A., brought to Sweden by F.O. Nilsson and was accepted by this congregation in 1856). Sundberg, Hans, Åqvist, Berit, "Bekännelse och bärande idéer", *Liv och tjänst*, 1988, p. 100. See also Lumpkin, W.L., *Baptist Confessions of Faith*, (rev. ed.), 1969; Parker, G. Keith, *Baptists in Europe. History and Confessions of Faith*, 1982; Fahlgren, Sune, "Baptismen och baptisternas gudstjänstliv", *I enhetens tecken*, 1994, pp. 259ff., referring among other things to the significance of the Confession of Faith for Baptists as evidenced by F. O. Nilsson's letter of farewell before the banishment. Concerning Nilsson, se more below. Fahlgren also mentions the Swedish Baptist Confession of Faith (approved in 1848) for the first Swedish Baptist congregation, called *Den svenska baptistförsamlingen*, in Borekulla, Landa parish, which was a translation of the German Confession of Faith from 1847. Ibid. p. 259. Note the international contacts and influences.

[12] *Svenska Baptistsamfundets Årsbok* 1990/91, p. 38. See also "Unikt: baptister utarbetar trosbekännelse", *VP*, No. 9, 1977, p. 1.

Confessional documents have for Lutherans.[13] Statutes are likewise written in the local congregations and they are revised at regular intervals. Furthermore, worship must not necessarily follow any strict order or manual - some follow one, but not "slavishly". If there is a manual, it is regarded as guidance.

The *principle of freedom*, or the spirit of freedom, has already been spoken of. Through the centuries Baptists have fought for freedom of thought, freedom of speech and freedom of religion, and have had a passion for liberty.[14] Freedom includes also a responsibility - ultimately to be faithful to God. This principle of freedom implies a certain freedom for each Baptist congregation - for instance vis à vis other Baptist congregations and the Central Board - which has also led to the possibility of a certain freedom as regards doctrines and the interpretations of different doctrines.[15]

This principle includes religious liberty and freedom of conscience. A person must have the freedom to follow his conscience and his conviction about faith, which also includes respect for the convictions of others. This implies that, for instance, membership of a congregation is a question of a voluntary and individual standpoint. In other words, it is up to the individual person himself to choose and decide. For Baptists a person is not born into a congregation or a church. Therefore it is from a general point of view inconceivable for Baptists to practise a baptism which

---

[13] Sundberg and Åqvist write that a Swedish Baptist Confession of Faith was approved in 1861 and has never formally ceased to be valid, even if it has hardly had "any decisive meaning as an authoritative Confession of Faith." Sundberg, Hans, Åqvist, Berit, "Bekännelse och bärande idéer", *Liv och tjänst*, 1988 p. 102. Cf. for instance *Svenska Baptistsamfundets Årsbok* 1981, p. 81, where the Union expresses hesitation towards written Confessions of Faith.

[14] See an interesting discussion by Bergsten about there being a risk with this ideal of individual and collective freedom, in that there is a tendency to dissolution of the collective fellowship of faith. Bergsten, Torsten, "Döparrörelsen 450 år", *VP*, No. 33/34, 1975, p. 3. See also Janarv, Ruben, "Baptisterna och friheten", [del 4], *VP*, No. 17, 1978, p. 10.

[15] "On the arrival of the Baptist movement in Sweden it was natural to adopt this ecclesiology [congregational, remark mine]. Each congregation was independent which also led to a certain freedom of interpretation of doctrine. The great, common doctrinal question was, however, believers' baptism, that is adult baptism by immersion after a personal confession of faith. This was as G. Westin says 'of constitutive importance for the type of ecclesiology Baptists represent.'" Struble, Rhode, *Den samfundsfria församlingen och de karismatiska gåvorna och tjänsterna*, 1982, p. 21.

excludes this act of the will, i.e. infant baptism.[16] Faith is a personal voluntary commitment to God. It is the individual relationship to God which is emphasized, and this is regarded as a covenant with God.

We find another distinctive feature among the Baptists in *Pietism*. It is a matter of the importance and priority of *each single individual's personal and immediate encounter with God.*[17] This does not in any way exclude the idea, or realization, of fellowship, the *communio sanctorum*, but the condition of this fellowship is that the individual person has had a "special" encounter with the living God. These individuals meet, however, together in fellowship, *communio*, in the congregation for worship etc.[18] We find thus a close connection between these two, individual pietism and fellowship; they are dependent on each other.[19]

Even if baptism involves a voluntary personal commitment on the part of the individual believer, it is also the responsibility of the congregation and leads to membership in that community. Therefore, the Baptist understanding of baptism cannot be described in a simplistic way as individualistic.

In the Baptist tradition we also find another characteristic, "puritanism". There is a longing for, and attempt to realize, the "pure" congregation. Believers are in the world but not of the world. The practice of congregational (or church) discipline has been one instrument in trying to maintain "pure" congregations.[20]

---

[16] See for example Janarv, Ruben, "Baptisternas grundsatser och dopet", [del 5], *VP*, No. 27, 1978, p. 8.

[17] The Baptist pastor Harry Månsus is of the opinion that there is in fact only one focus for the Baptists, from which their views of baptism and congregation are derived, the individual's encounter with the living God. Månsus, Harry, "Baptistsamfundet och 80-talets folkväckelse", *VP*, No. 27, 1979, p. 4.

[18] Concerning Baptist spirituality in regard to worship, see Fahlgren, Sune, "Baptismens spiritualitet - speglad i gudstjänstlivet. Svenskt perspektiv", *Samfund i förändring*, 1997, pp. 104-114.

[19] See for example Bert Franzén. He holds that each single person has to decide about baptism and membership, and also describes the role of fellowship for Baptists. Franzén, Bert, "Tro och liv i förändring", *Tro, Frihet, Gemenskap*, 1998, pp. 206-212.

[20] See the discussion about this in for example Nordström, Nils Johan, *De frikyrkliga och statskyrkosystemet*, 1922, especially pp. 87-91. Congregational discipline, practised especially in the beginning of the Baptist history but also

As a consequence of the principle of freedom one of the most important tenets of the Baptist movement has been advocacy of the separation of church and State.[21] During the Enlightenment, freedom of religion increased in Sweden, but not until 1951 was it fully guaranteed for everyone by law, in the Freedom of Religion Act of 1951.[22] Today everyone has the right to choose whether to be a member of or belong to a church or religious body, Christian or non-Christian, or not.

It may therefore be proposed that in general three characteristics or principles determine the identity of Baptists. All these three are, of course, derived from the fundamental principle, the principle of biblical authority, which is presupposed. This statement of principles is important. It plays a certain part in the discussion which follows later on in the thesis.

---

until the 1960's, concerns things like clothing, hair (especially for women), dance, cinema etc. See Kennerberg, Owe, *Innanför eller utanför*, 1996. He studies not only Baptist congregations, but also congregations of the Pentecostal Movement and of the Mission Covenant Church of Sweden. See also Lagergren, David, *Framgångstid med dubbla förtecken*, 1989, p. 21; Lidén, Sven Gunnar, Tema: "Svensk baptistungdom och dess verksamhet", *Tro, Frihet, Gemenskap*, 1998, p. 83.

[21] This question has also been debated several times among the Swedish Baptists from its origin and onwards, see for example Nordström, Nils Johan, *De frikyrkliga och statskyrkoproblemet*, 1922, especially pp. 94-160, but also pp. 161-195.

[22] "The work of The 'Dissenter Act' committee led as could be expected to a completely new law, the Freedom of Religion Act of 1951". Lagergren, David, *Förändringstid*, 1994, p. 216. First in 1951 a Swedish citizen was allowed not to belong to any religious institution.

3. Organization

This chapter is a presentation of the organization of the Baptist Union of Sweden. The latter consists of congregations. It is in other words the congregations and their members which are connected to the Union. According to its statutes the Baptist Union of Sweden is a Christian denomination, a union of congregations.[23] It can be mentioned that the Baptist congregations also according to the statutes are organized in districts.[24] Already in 1861, we find a decision about division into districts, the district regulations.

The emphasis is on the word "denomination" and not "church".[25] The former General Secretary David Lagergren gives a definition of denomination:

A Christian denomination is a fellowship of congregations. The Baptist denominations are congregationalist, i.e. the congregations themselves joined together voluntarily in this fellowship and can influence it through sending representatives to the conferences of the denomination and in other ways.[26]

And Lagergren mentions that the denomination has four functions: to be a spiritual community; to be a community of faith; to be a working-community; to be the basis of ecumenism.[27] He

---

[23] See for example *Svenska Baptistsamfundets Årsbok* 1979, p. 117.

[24] Ibid, see also for example *Svenska Baptistsamfundets Årsbok* 1989, p. 202. In 1992 there were about 250 congregations in 17 districts. Bexell, Oloph, "Kyrkor i Sverige", *Kyrkans liv*, 2nd ed., 1993, p. 82.

[25] In for instance 1971 it was even explicitly said that the Baptist Union of Sweden is not a church. *Svenska Baptistsamfundet*, 1971-1972, p. 139, [årsbok].

[26] Letter from David Lagergren 20.12 1988 to Bergsten, quoted in Bergsten, Torsten, "Samfundsmedvetande och kongregationalism i svensk frikyrklighet", *Kyrkohistorisk årsskrift* 93, 1993, p. 144. It originates from Bergsten, Torsten, "Kyrka, samfund och den radikala kongregationalismen. Tro och Liv-symposium 26-27 jan 1989", 1989, [unpublished paper].

[27] Letter from David Lagergren 20.12 1988 to Bergsten, quoted in Bergsten, Torsten, "Samfundsmedvetande och kongregationalism i svensk frikyrklighet",

does not unfortunately expand on what these functions involve.

Another former General Secretary, Birgit Karlsson, says:

> The Baptists have always asserted on the basis of the New Testament... that the congregation consists of those who by their own free will have answered in the affirmative the call of the Gospel to faith, life and ministry.[28]

Her statement refers partly to the principle of biblical authority and partly also, as did Lagergren's, to the principle of freedom. Karlsson writes: "The voluntary character is only possible for those who have their own free will."[29] This voluntariness excludes the baptism of infants. This will, of course, be discussed more below.

The Baptist Union of Sweden advocates as already mentioned the principle of congregationalism, which implies that the Baptist Union does not *in principle* have any central authority. It claims thus to defend what it considers to be the congregational structure of the New Testament, avoiding superstructures and headquarters. Each local congregation is sovereign both in relation to other congregations and in relation to the Union - and also to the State. I intentionally write "in principle". For there is reason to question this, as becomes evident for example in the establishment of the Baptist Union of Sweden and the appointment of a General Secretary etc., i.e. the congregationalist principle, strictly interpreted, did not work in practice.[30] So in spite of the principle of congregationalism, there

---

Kyrkohistorisk årsskrift 93, 1993, p. 144. It can be observed that Lagergren does not use the term *church (kyrka)* but *denomination (samfund)*.

[28] Karlsson, Birgit, "Dopet - en central fråga när församlingar går samman. Missionsföreståndaren kommenterar", *VP*, No. 40, 1987, p. 10.

[29] Ibid.

[30] See for example the annual report of the Baptist Central Board *(Missionsstyrelsens årsberättelse)*; note, however, the term *but (men)* in the quotation. It states that the individual congregation according to Baptist understanding of the nature of the congregation works independently *"but* in responsibility for the fellowship, which the denomination is and in different ways gives expression to. It is our conviction that the independence of the congregation and loyalty towards the denomination are compatible, both practically and spiritually." *Svenska Baptistsamfundets Allmänna konferenser Stockholm 1963 Linköping 1964. Svenska Baptistsamfundets Ungdomsförbunds (SBUF) årskonferenser Västerås 1963 Sjövik 1964*, 1964, p. 8. Italics mine.

Bergsten also confirms that the principle of congregationalism is problematic. Bergsten, Torsten, "Samfundsmedvetande och kongregationalism i svensk frikyrklighet", *Kyrkohistorisk årsskrift* 93, 1993, p. 133. He mentions the resolution on a common denominational organization and that the

is within the Baptist Union of Sweden a well-developed organization. The appointment of a General Secretary is thus an event which points to something which is more than the local congregation and the principle of congregationalism, interpreted in a more absolute way. In spite of proposals already in the 19ᵗʰ century to appoint a General Secretary, the first General Secretary *(missionsföreståndare)* was chosen in 1932.[31] The General Secretary is the person who together with the Central Board leads the work at the national level. The title "General Secretary" is, according to the response of the Baptist Union of Sweden to *BEM*, secular, "but the person who holds it is in function equal to a bishop in episcopalian churches."[32] To write about a General Secretary, and also to equate

administration of Foreign Missions *(Yttre Missionen)* contributed to the establishment of the Swedish Baptist Mission Society *(Sällskapet Svenska Baptistmissionen).* Ibid p. 133 and pp. 136f. And Eckerdal writes that there was a Baptist co-ordinating organization from the beginning. He mentions for example annual meetings, an administration committee (1857), the division into districts (1861), and the adopting of a Swedish Baptist Confession in 1861. Eckerdal, Lars, *Vägen in i kyrkan,* 1981, p. 370. At the General Conference in 1889 a common denominational organization *(samfundsorganisation)* was established, which was called *Sällskapet Svenska Baptistmissionen,* (The Swedish Baptist Mission Society). Nordström, Nils Johan, *Svenska Baptistsamfundets historia.* Andra delen, 1928. See also Westin, G., *Svenska Baptistsamfundets historia 1887-1914,* 1965, where Westin also discusses the difficulties of congregationalism in the Baptist Union of Sweden.

That this principle of congregationalism was not consistently maintained by the Baptist Union, but the latter organized itself as a denomination and has district structures etc., was one of the reasons for division within the Baptist Union and the development of the Pentecostal Movement - concerning this division see more below. Concerning congregationalism in the Baptist Union of Sweden, see also for instance Westin, Gunnar, *Den kristna friförsamlingen genom tiderna,* 3ʳᵈ ed., 1955, especially pp. 371-377; Struble, Rhode, *Den samfundsfria församlingen och de karismatiska gåvorna och tjänsterna,* 1982, pp. 21-24.

[31] Bergsten, Torsten, "Samfundsmedvetande och kongregationalism i svensk frikyrklighet", *Kyrkohistorisk årsskrift* 93, 1993, p. 133. Fear of the episcopate is given as one cause of the delay. Ibid. p. 144. Hjalmar Danielson (1881-1955) was the first General Secretary of the Baptist Union of Sweden. Jakob Byström (1857-1947) had, however, for decades been the leader of the denomination until 1932. Lagergren, David, *Framgångstid med dubbla förtecken.* 1989, p. 184.

[32] *Churches respond to BEM,* Vol. IV, 1987, p. 209. It is stated: "Recently a

this to a bishop, is in the light of the beginning of Baptist history in Sweden significant.[33]

A theologically interesting observation, which may be mentioned in discussing congregationalism and episcopalism, is that the Baptist pastor Edvin Hallberg (b. 1901) as early as 1938 warned against an exclusive sovereignty of the local congregation. He writes:

> We must not overemphasize the sovereignty of the local congregation so that we ignore the comprehensive view which was important for Christ and his apostles.[34]

And

> St. Paul does not talk about the many bodies but about *one* body. He cannot then have in mind only one individual congregation but all... The body is not only a foot or a hand but the whole organism.[35]

Later on in this article he continues:

> Someone may object: at the time of the Apostles there was no Central Board? On the contrary the apostles were a Central Board, appointed by Jesus himself.[36]

And Hallberg states:

> The apostles personified the fellowship of the denomination... Certainly the apostles did not act as a unified board, but the leadership of the Christian mission was in their hands, a leadership which no local congregation ignored.[37]

Torsten Bergsten makes a comment on Hallberg's work:

---

woman pastor was unanimously elected as the general secretary of the Union." Ibid. This refers to Birgit Karlsson, a person whom we will subsequently meet several times in this study. It is also said: "The primary and close attachment of the threefold ministry, including the ministry of *episkopé*, to the local church is a reason for us as a non-episcopalian church not to choose the title of bishop for those who serve several churches in their regional or nationwide functions." Ibid. p. 210.

[33] See also Bergsten, Torsten, "Samfundsmedvetande och kongregationalism i svensk frikyrklighet", *Kyrkohistorisk årsskrift* 93, 1993, pp. 131-150.

[34] Hallberg, Edvin, *Samfundstanken i Apostlagärningarna*, 2nd ed., 1939, p. 17.

[35] Ibid. p. 16. [Concerning Eph. 1.]

[36] Ibid. p. 25.

[37] Ibid. p. 26.

A view of the denomination is indicated in which, more powerfully than by Ongman and also in an episcopal way, the apostolate is emphasized as the uniting force, an *episkopé* appointed by Christ himself. According to this view the Baptist Union is not a Mission Society, as it was called in 1889, but in a deeper sense a Christian denomination.[38]

Through elected members the congregations meet at the General Conference *(allmänna konferensen)* for consultations, in order to elect representatives to the Central Board *(missionsstyrelse)* and other officials, and ordain pastors and missionaries.[39] The "bishop", the General Secretary, is appointed by the General Conference. It may give recommendations but not directives concerning common issues such as for example foreign missions and home missions, ecumenical work etc. The General Conference is the highest decision-making organ of the Baptist Union.[40] The General Secretary is an ex officio member, the others are elected by the General Conference for a limited period.[41] The Central Board is an executive body for foreign and home missions, with the task of guiding the work of the Baptist Union, preparing commissions for the General Conference, carrying out the resolutions, appointing and dismissing officials, administering property of the denomination etc.

I also want to mention two important instruments of the Baptist Union of Sweden: *Veckoposten*[42] and *Betelseminariet.*[43] *Veckoposten*

---

[38] Bergsten, Torsten, "Samfundsmedvetande och kongregationalism i svensk frikyrklighet", *Kyrkohistorisk årsskrift* 93, 1993, pp. 143f. I will return to John Ongman later on. It can be briefly mentioned that Ongman, 1844-1931, was a Baptist pastor and later on became the leader of the Örebro (Baptist) Mission, which before the separation in 1936/37 worked within the Baptist Union of Sweden.

[39] It may be noted that in the middle of the 1980's fifty five percent of the Baptist congregations had a pastor as leader *(föreståndare)*, whilst the others were led by laymen. *Svenska Baptistsamfundets Årsbok* 1986, p. 61.

[40] Bergsten, Torsten, "Svenska Baptistsamfundet", *Svenska Trossamfund*, 8th ed., 1990, p. 68.

[41] See *Svenska Baptistsamfundets Årsbok* 1988, pp. 72-77, especially p. 72, § 5, p. 73, § 5, p.76, § 11 and p. 77, § 11, *Svenska Baptistsamfundets Årsbok* 1989, pp. 202-204; *Svenska Baptistsamfundets Årsbok* 1990/91, pp. 190-192. See also for example "Beslutskonferens", [editorial], *VP*, No. 16, 1991, p. 2.

[42] The first number of *Veckoposten* was published in 1868. It is stated that number 0! was published on the 3rd December 1868. See Jonsson, Gunnar, O, *Ett hundra år med baptistförsamlingen Ebeneser Stockholm*, 1983, p. 7.

no longer exists. *Veckoposten* and *Svensk Veckotidning*, the organ of the Mission Covenant Church of Sweden, amalgamated as a new weekly in 1992, called *Sändaren*. This is now common to both the Baptist Union of Sweden and the Mission Covenant Church of Sweden. The two theological colleges, *Betelseminariet* of the Baptist Union and *Teologiska Seminariet på Lidingö* of the Mission Covenant Church of Sweden were closed in 1993 when *Teologiska Högskolan Stockholm, THS,* (Stockholm School of Theology) was founded as an interdenominational school of theology, to train pastors and missionaries. It also runs other courses and programs such as The Human Rights Programme.[44]

---

[43] The Bethel Seminary *(Bethelseminariet,* later spelled *Betelseminariet),* was founded in 1866 in Stockholm as a school for preachers. It has been of great importance for the expansion of the work in Sweden, and also for the work in the foreign missions, training pastors and missionaries. See *Betelseminariet 100 år,* 1966. The Bethel Seminary has been called the heart of the Baptist Union of Sweden, *(Baptistsamfundets hjärta).*

The Baptist Theological Seminary in Rüschlikon, Switzerland, must also be mentioned in this context. A large number of Swedish Baptist pastors and theologians have been there for further studies. It was opened in 1949 and it has been owned and run until 1989 by the Southern Baptists. Ohm, Sven, "Rüschlikon-seminariet vårt!", *VP,* No. 25, 1989, pp. 2f. The work at Rüschlikon was ended in 1995 and the school, The International Baptist Theological Seminary, was moved to Prague. See Lindvall, Magnus, Åqvist, Berit, *Tema:* "Utbildning och det tryckta ordet", *Tro, Frihet, Gemenskap,* 1998, p. 179.

[44] "Utbildning för tjänst", sektion 2, *Sändaren,* No. 38, 1993, pp. 1-20. See also Swedberg, Bo, "-Fri teologihögskola bra för ekumeniken", *VP,* No. 40, 1992, p. 6; Åqvist, Berit, "Berit Åqvist om samverkan med Lidingö: -Inte ekumenik i uppgivenhetens tecken", *VP,* No. 40, 1992, pp. 8f.; Ahlefelt, Annika, "'Nya Teologiska högskolan ska motverka kyrkosplittring'", *Svenska Kyrkans Tidning,* No. 40, 1993, p. 19, [Church of Sweden]; Pastorsutbildning med nya perspektiv, [editorial], *VP,* No. 13/14, 1991, p. 2; Lindvall, Magnus, Åqvist, Berit, *Tema:* "Utbildning och det tryckta ordet", *Tro, Frihet, Gemenskap,* 1998, pp. 176-178; There have earlier been discussions about increased co-operation between the denominations and the theological colleges, see for example "Utökat samarbete mellan Betelseminariet och Örebro Missionsskola leder till alternativ akademisk examen", *VP,* No. 2, 1977, p. 16.

4. Some Statistics on the Baptist Union of Sweden 1856-1995

Statistics are a complicated matter, but I will nevertheless give some statistics on members of the Baptist Union of Sweden, which may be looked upon as elementary but hopefully be of some help in understanding its history and development.

Many Baptist congregations are small today, less than 15 or 25 members, and even less than 10 members.[45] The cost of running such congregations becomes greater per person in such cases. To this must be added that the average age of the members in many of these congregations is high.[46] We can further notice that in the last few years many Baptist congregations have decreased especially in the countryside. On the whole recruitment is not very high. "Det finns en väg", 1982, (There Is a Way), gives some figures illustrating the problem of recruitment within the Baptist Union of Sweden. It says that in 1982 it had 5146 children in 287 Sunday schools and 216 teenagers in 42 youth classes (kristendomsskolor). Sunday

---

[45] Skog writes that in 1990 about 90 Baptist congregations have between 1 and 10 members, 45 Baptist congregations between 11 and 20 members. The largest at the time, Norrmalms in Stockholm, had 520 members and Ebeneser also in Stockholm 440 members, in Gothenburg 470 members and Örebro 440 members. Skog, Margareta, "Frikyrkoras medlemstal i landets kommuner 1990", Tro & Tanke 1992:4, p. 108.

[46] "Det finns en väg", 1982, p. 50, [unpublished paper].

"Det finns en väg" is a report by a working party appointed by the Baptist Central Board (missionsstyrelse), to work with problems to do with the future of the Baptist Union of Sweden. The working party consisted of the following persons: Börje Hammarroth, Nils Kahlroth, Gunnar Kjellander, David Lagergren, Ingvar Paulsson, Lars Georg Sahlin, Bo Swedberg and Berit Åqvist. This report is one example of the Baptist Union's attempt to adjust to the new situation arising from the ecumenical congregations; see more below. "Det finns en väg" is among other things influenced by the British Baptists' Signs of hope (Hoppfulla tecken) from the end of the 1970's. See Lagergren, David, "Frikyrkans framtidsväg", VP, No. 43, 1991, p. 4.

school has decreased since 1950 by 1000 - 1500 children a year, from 40,000 30 years ago to 5000 at the present.[47] It states: "Many congregations have given up!"[48] From 1975 to the middle of the 1990's the Baptist Union of Sweden has lost 18% of its members.[49]

The reasons for decline are not easy to identify, but one of the natural recruitment sources is certainly enormously weakened by the decrease of children in the Sunday schools. The difficulty in recruiting children and youngsters has caused worry among Baptists. In 1987 Birgit Karlsson states that the most serious observation in the Baptist annual report is the "catastrophic decline in the work of the congregations among children and youth."[50] Two of many other causes, related to the decrease both of children, young people and adults, may be secularization and urbanization, and the general changes in society. In short: negative trends.

Something else, which I want to mention already in this context, is the ecumenical congregations. The development of the ecumenical congregations from the 1970's and onwards has influenced the statistics in the last decades.[51] Looking at the statistics below, for the years 1980- and onwards, it seems evident that the decline in members has suddenly ceased. It is claimed that the deceleration of the downward trend in the last years is to a great extent due to the fact that also members in ecumenical congregations, who are members for instance of the Mission Covenant Church of Sweden, are counted among the members of the Baptist Union of Sweden. The Mission Covenant Church of Sweden and other denominations acted similarly.[52] In other words

---

[47] "Det finns en väg", 1982, pp. 37f., [unpublished paper]. See also Svärd, Stig, "Den halvfärdiga bron – och hammaren som väntar på oss", VP, No. 17, 1982, p. 3.

[48] "Många församlingar har gett upp!" "Det finns en väg", 1982, p. 38, [unpublished paper].

[49] Skog, Margareta, "Antal medlemmar i valda samfund 1975-1996", Tro & Tanke 1996:6, p. 47. See, however, also the discussion below in this chapter about the new concept "ministered to".

[50] Karlsson, Birgit, "Från min horisont", VP, No. 21, 1987, p. 4. See also Lundkvist, Sven, "Medlemsrekrytering och motiv för medlemskap", Frikyrkosverige, 1979, p. 34.

[51] See also below chapter 9.5.1.

[52] "Medlemstal", [editorial], VP, No. 44, 1986, p. 2.

there are many members who have been counted twice.[53]

We have to notice that children (who are not baptized by believers' baptism) are not included in the statistics of the Baptist Union of Sweden. The figures for the period 1856-1995 are as follows:[54]

1856	886	1940	46,705
1860	4311	1950	37,633
1870	8617	1960	31,881
1880	18,928	1965	29,360
1890	33,479	1970	26,110
1900	40,759	1975	23,391
1910	51,259	1980	21,187
1920	60,913	1985	21,095
1930	63,399	1990	20,512
1934	68,151[55]	1995	19,442[56]

---

[53] Criticism has been raised against this procedure. See for example the editorials, "Siffror till eftertanke", [editorial], VP, No. 18, 1987, p. 4; "Att räkna medlemmar", [editorial], VP, No. 5, 1990, p. 2. Skog writes also about this problem, Skog, Margareta, "Frikyrkornas medlemstal i landets kommuner 1990", Tro & Tanke 1992:4, p. 106, and Palm, Irving, "Frikyrkofolket och ekumeniken", Tro & Tanke 1993:5, p. 51.

[54] All statistical information until 1970 (except 1934) in Gustafsson, Berndt, Svensk Kyrkogeografi, 1971, p. 58. See also pp. 56-64. Note, however, Nordström, who gives the following figures, 1860 4930; 1870 8617, 1880 19,279; 1889 33,479. Nordström, Nils Johan, Svenska Baptistsamfundets historia. Andra delen, 1928, p. 339. Concerning 1975 to 1990, see Skog, Margareta, "Antalet medlemmar i valda samfund 1975-1992", Tro & tanke 1992:11, p. 60. See also pp. 45-61.

[55] 68,151 is given in Hallqvist, Anders, Westblom, Per, Tema: "Viktiga händelser i Baptistsamfundets historia", Tro, Frihet, Gemenskap, 1998, p. 248. Before the Örebro (Baptist) Mission broke away from the Baptist Union, the latter had thus in 1934 more than 68,000 members. The total decrease in the Baptist Union of Sweden between 1935 and 1942 was 25,000. Lagergren, David, Framgångstid med dubbla förtecken, 1989, p. 203, footnote 23.

[56] Skog, Margareta, "Antal medlemmar i valda samfund 1975-1996", Tro & Tanke 1996:6, p. 53. Some statistics of other churches in Sweden may be mentioned. There are four groups or Church-families in Sweden: the Catholic, the Orthodox, the Free Church and the Lutheran, the last including the Church of

It can be noted that a new term was introduced at the end of the 1980's, *number ministered to (antal betjänade)*. This is an attempt to get a better picture of the number who are "active" in the denomination. This implies that not only the "members" are counted but also those are registered who in one way or another participate actively in the life/services etc., of the denomination.[57] Concerning the number of "those ministered to" there are the following statistics for the Baptist Union, 31,554 (1990), 35,773 (1995).[58]

Sweden and the Swedish Evangelical Mission *(Evangeliska Fosterlandsstiftelsen, EFS)*. Note that the number of members in all the churches and denominations including the Baptist Union of Sweden, except the Catholic and the Orthodox Eastern Churches where the membership is connected with (infant-) baptism, presupposes some kind of an act of confession of faith. In addition to the Church of Sweden, the largest Christian denominations represented in Sweden are the following in 1990, in parentheses statistics for 1975. The Roman Catholic Church 140,177 (70,206), the Orthodox and Eastern Churches 97,148 (50,500), [the increase of these churches depends to a large extent on immigration, my remark]; the Pentecostal Movement 97,282 (93,566), the Mission Covenant Church of Sweden 77,058 (83,892), the Swedish Evangelical Mission 22,982 (26,456), the Örebro (Baptist) Mission 22,384 (19,966), the Salvation Army 26,656 (36,565), the Swedish Alliance Mission 13,411 (13,844), the United Methodist Church in Sweden 5344 (8059), the Scandinavian Independent Baptist Union 1034 (1149), the Swedish Holiness Mission/Holiness Union Mission 5021 (4882). [Observe that the Swedish Holiness Movement changed its English, not Swedish, name in the middle of the 1980's to the Holiness Union Mission.] Skog, Margareta, "Antalet medlemmar i valda samfund 1975-1992", *Tro & Tanke* 1992:11, p. 60. See also the investigation presented in *Frikyrkosverige*, 1979; especially Lundkvist, Sven, "Medlemsrekrytering och motiv för medlemskap", *Frikyrkosverige*, 1979, pp. 21-34; Källstad, Thorvald, "Frikyrkofolkets ekumeniska vilja", *Frikyrkosverige*, 1979, pp. 55-71; Lundkvist, Sven, "Demografiska och socio-ekonomiska data", *Frikyrkosverige*, 1979, pp. 73-88, plus the appendices with tables.

[57] Concerning the discussion about "those ministered to", see Skog, Margareta, "Antalet medlemmar i valda samfund 1975-1989", *Religion och Samhälle* 1989:9, especially pp. 14-17, pp. 21-23; Skog, Margareta, "Antal medlemmar i valda samfund 1975-1996", *Tro & Tanke* 1996:6, pp. 45-55.

[58] Skog, Margareta, "Antalet medlemmar i valda samfund 1975-1989", *Religion och Samhälle* 1989:9, p. 55.

I also want in this context to give the numbers of those baptized within the Baptist Union of Sweden from 1970-1995:

1970	316	1985	267
1975	292	1990	163
1980	251	1995	104[59]

[59] Letter to Lennart Johnsson: Skog, Margareta, 17/1/97. In parenthesis it can be mentioned that there has been a lively debate in Swedish mass media especially in the 1990's, and particularly within the Church of Sweden. It concerns a number of ministers in the Church of Sweden who have been "re-baptized" in a Baptist context (the Baptist Union of Sweden, the Pentecostal Movement). The question has been whether they should be allowed because of this to continue their work as priests within the Church of Sweden. Whether some of them are counted in these statistics will not be dealt with here.

5. Swedish Society in a 19th Century and Early 20th Century Historical Perspective

In order to get a better understanding of the origin and development of the Swedish Baptist movement in the 19th century, some general, introductory remarks may be made about Swedish society and also about the State Church or "National Church".[60]

The State Church system may be looked upon as a result of a process ever since the Swedish Reformation of making Swedish church-life uniform, upheld by the teaching and preaching of the Lutheran doctrines and through Royal Ordinances.[61] The Ecclesiastical Law 1686 and its baptismal obligation, the so-called forced baptisms (tvångsdop) should be mentioned - the terms compulsory, coercive or enforced baptisms are also used. Until the middle of the 19th century it was compulsory for every Swedish citizen to be baptized according to the order of the State Church. Infant baptism was thus a compulsory civil act, irrespective of whether the parents were believing Christians or not. Neglect of this duty had serious consequences regarding a person's civil rights.[62] This coercion was regarded by the Baptists among others as an improper custom, and they among others protested against what

---

[60] Membership in that Church and citizenship in the nation have been closely linked.

[61] Concerning the history of the Reformation in Scandinavia, see for instance the great work of Garstein, Oskar, Rome and the Counter-Reformation in Scandinavia, Vol. I (1539-1583), 1963; Rome and the Counter-Reformation in Scandinavia, Vol. II (1583-1622), 1980; Rome and the Counter-Reformation in Scandinavia, 46, 1992; Rome and the Counter-Reformation in Scandinavia, 47, 1992. Concerning especially the Swedish context (Swedish Church history during the years 830-1989), see for example Petrén, Erik, Kyrka och makt, 1990.

[62] Bert Franzén writes about the forced baptisms in Sweden in the 19th century at the beginning of the Baptist movement, Franzén, Bert, "Barnen och församlingen. Guds försprång kan behållas", VP, No. 24/25, 1986, p. 5. See also Samuelsson, Owe, Sydsvenska baptister inför myndigheter, 1998, especially pp. 16-32, pp. 201-208.

they considered as "sacramental Christianity" (sakramentskristendom).[63] The Baptists began to baptize people in Sweden by believers' baptism, which in fact was illegal. Prohibited "re-baptisms" were thus taking place. The forced baptisms continued within the State Church/Church of Sweden until the end of the 19th century.[64]

Attempts to preserve the local parishes of the State Church intact are continued until about 1850. Swedish society in the 19th century was, however, in a process of change and the time of the uniform monolithic church was at an end. There were political and economic changes in the country. Revivalist movements were criticizing the national State Church. It may, however, be of importance to note that there were also revivalist movements within the State Church during the first decades of the 19th century.[65] Voluntary unions and associations were established, based upon individual commitment, and secessions from the State Church occurred. The former collective view of the unity and life of the church was thus challenged. Meeting-houses and "village prayer meetings" (byaböner) are started and new local congregational structures can

---

[63] The concept "sacramental christening" (sakramentskristning) was used later on among Baptists, so for example by Gunnar Westin in a talk 1944, which caused reactions from the Church of Sweden (for example Bishop Yngve Brilioth who later became the archbishop of Uppsala and also Ruben Josefson who also was later to become archbishop). See Bergsten, Torsten, Frikyrkor i samverkan, 1995, p. 169.

[64] Brodd, Sven-Erik, Dop och kyrkotillhörighet enligt Svenska kyrkans ordning, 1978, p. 58. In this book Brodd also argues that baptism shall determine whether one belongs to the church. Bring, Ragnar, Dop och medlemskap i kyrkan, 1979, may be regarded as a reaction to Brodd's work. As regards the question of compulsory baptism and the relation between baptism and belonging for the Church of Sweden, see Brodd, Sven-Erik, "Dop och kyrkotillhörighet i Svenska kyrkan", Ekumenisk samsyn om dop och kyrkotillhörighet, 1978, pp. 25-32. See also Hermansson, Werner, Enhetskyrka, folkväckelse, församlingsgemenskap, 1968.

[65] See for example Petrén, Erik, Kyrka och makt, 1990, especially pp. 269-271. As concerns the independent revivalist movements, especially during the last part of the 19th century, see Walan, Bror, "De utomkyrkliga väckelserörelserna under senare hälften av 1800-talet", Väckelse och kyrka i nordiskt perspektiv, 1969, pp. 184-214, for the Baptists especially pp. 189-195. Concerning revivalist movements within the Church of Sweden, see Martling, Carl Henrik, "De inomkyrkliga väckelserörelserna under förra hälften av 1800-talet", Väckelse och kyrka i nordiskt perspektiv, 1969, pp. 155-183, including also the bibliographical overview, pp. 182-183.

be noticed, where people were gathering because of a common faith, to work together and try to unite all believers irrespective of church-affiliation in different kinds of alliances. This may be regarded as one kind of unity-model.[66]

With reference to the revivals during the 19th century something may be said about the Evangelical Alliance *(Evangeliska Alliansen)*, established in Sweden in 1847. The idea came to Sweden some years earlier through mission and temperance societies and the activity of among others the Methodist minister George Scott (1804-1874) from England, who was in Sweden, particularly in Stockholm, between 1830 and 1842.[67] Just as the movement inspired by Anglo-Saxon trends was fluid, so the boundaries between Baptists and Non-Baptists were also fluid.[68]

The influences from Anglo-American piety developed with hitherto unknown strength and were of decisive significance for the Swedish popular revival. All this gave the impetus to the Free Church movement *(frikyrkorörelsen)*. New ideas and impulses were coming to Sweden from abroad: Evangelicalism and Methodism from England, Presbyterianism from Scotland. The Swedish Baptist movement emanates from the 19th century neo-evangelical popular revival and Anglo-American influences.[69] It originates partly in the Swedish Lutheran Pietistic movement *(svensk-lutherskt läseri)* and partly in American and German Baptism.

---

[66] Examples of this unity-model are Y.M.C.A., established in Sweden in 1887, and Y.W.C.A., established in 1889.

[67] Westin, Gunnar, *George Scott och hans verksamhet i Sverige* I, 1929.

[68] Whilst students in Uppsala Anders Wiberg - one of the Baptist pioneers, see more below - and Carl Olof Rosenius (1816-1868) – the latter regarded as one of the spiritual fathers of the Swedish Evangelical Mission - were both for some time associates of the Methodist preacher George Scott, in Stockholm.

[69] Concerning the development of the neo-evangelical movement and the Evangelical Alliance, see Walan, Bror, *Församlingstanken i Svenska Missionsförbundet*, 1964; Hermansson, Werner, *Enhetskyrka, folkväckelse, församlingsgemenskap*, 1968; Brodd, Sven-Erik, "Ekumeniska perspektiv. Om kristna enhetssträvanden i Sverige", *Svenska Trossamfund*, 8th ed., 1990, pp. 185f.; Samuelsson, Owe, *Sydsvenska baptister inför myndigheter*, 1998, pp. 33ff. Westin writes also about this Anglo-American influence, see Westin, Gunnar, *George Scott och hans verksamhet i Sverige* I, Stockholm 1929. Concerning the American influences, see also Samuelsson, Owe, *Sydsvenska baptister inför myndigheter*, 1998, pp. 3f. And Nordström also discusses the impetus and appearance of the Swedish Free Church movement, Nordström, Nils Johan, *De frikyrkliga och statskyrkoproblemet*, 1922, pp. 15-73.

Some other Free Churches, such as the Mission Covenant Church of Sweden and the Swedish Alliance Mission (first called Scandinavian Alliance Mission (Skandinaviska Alliansmissionen)), are offshoots of 19th century Swedish revivalist movements. Others, such as the United Methodist Church in Sweden, trace their roots to various English and American revival influences. In spite of some attempts in the 19th century to unite the revivalist movements, these failed among other things on account of the Baptist view of baptism and congregation.[70]

Of course the new means of communication - understood in a broad sense - were of importance for the changes and the circulation of new influences in Sweden. Through the Elementary School Law (folkskolestadgan) in 1842 literacy was increasing. That papers, periodicals, tracts, etc. were accessible to more people was of great importance, giving possibilities of propagating different opinions. The mobility of people was at this time considerably increased. Some other things which also have contributed to changes may be mentioned. In 1855 compulsory church attendance was abolished.[71] We may also mention the Conventicle Act of 1858.[72] This replaced that of 1726,[73] with the consequence that anybody who wished was in principle permitted to preach the Word of God and that it was permitted for people to gather for unofficial prayer meetings or acts of worship and to read Scripture outside the State Church. In practice there were, however, restrictions on Baptists and others. Sandewall writes:

> The alteration of the law which took place in 1858 has usually been looked upon as one of the folk revival's great victories. The sources, however, give another impression. On the contrary, the number of lawsuits increased sharply... [it] implied during the first years after the revision, deterioration for the revival, compared with the situation during the time of the old

---

[70] See for instance Bergsten, Torsten, "Enheten i Kristus", Tro, Frihet, Gemenskap, 1998, pp. 217f.

[71] Note that in spite of this forced baptisms continued. Brodd, Sven-Erik, Dop och kyrkotillhörighet enligt Svenska kyrkans ordning, 1978, p. 59.

[72] Conventicle is an act of worship led by laymen.

[73] The Conventicle Act of 1726 was complemented with regulations and a decree of 1762, which "limited and hampered the application of the old Conventicle Act." Sandewall, Allan, Konventikel- och sakramentsbestämmelsernas tillämpning i Sverige 1809-1900, 1961, pp. 200f. See also Karlsson, Birgit, "150 händelserika år", Tro, Frihet, Gemenskap, 1998, pp. 15-18.

Conventicle Act. [---] Later in the 1860's, however, the number of lawsuits diminished considerably, and it was soon only a matter of the odd prosecution here and there.[74]

Yet another act in 1868 replaced the 1858 Act.[75]

In 1860 the first religious freedom act, also called the Dissenter Law, entitled a Swedish citizen to convert to another denomination recognized by the State.[76] As a matter of fact Swedish Baptists could not leave the Swedish Church until 1951 (The Freedom of Religion Act),[77] since the Baptist Union refused to apply to the Crown for recognition as an approved denomination in accordance with the Religious Freedom Act of 1860/1873. Baptists among others remained thus for the most part within the State Church, and were legally its members.[78] But, of course, "the freedom" had a price for some, i.e. to follow personal religious conviction concretized in for example believers' baptism, which was regarded by the State Church as "re-baptism", or to refrain baptizing infants. It could result in loosing employment, home etc., or fines and even prison. Some emigrated and others were exiled.[79]

---

[74] Sandewall, Allan, *Konventikel- och sakramentsbestämmelsernas tillämpning i Sverige 1809-1900*, 1961, pp. 201f.; see also pp. 93ff.

[75] See Sandewall, Allan, *Konventikel- och sakramentsbestämmelsernas tillämpning i Sverige 1809-1900*, 1961, discussing the Conventicle and also the Sacramental Acts and their application in Sweden. See especially pp. 67ff., (concerning 1858), and pp. 96ff., (concerning 1868). The Conventicle Act of 1868 remained until 1952. It had, however, not been used for several decades. Ibid. p. 163. See also ibid. pp. 167ff., about lay administration of the sacraments, baptism and Holy Communion, the so-called Sacramental law (1855) etc. See also Sandewall, Allan, "Konventikelplakatets upphävande - ett gränsår i svensk religionsfrihetslagstiftning?", *Kyrkohistorisk Årsskrift* 57, 1957, pp. 136-152; *På stugmötenas tid*, 1958; Jonsson, Gunnar, O, *Ett hundra år med baptistförsamlingen Ebeneser Stockholm*, 1983 p. 6; Samuelsson, Owe, *Sydsvenska baptister inför myndigheter*, 1998, pp. 16-32.

[76] Westin, Gunnar, *Den kristna friförsamlingen i Norden*, 1956, pp. 11-21. Samuelsson, Owe, *Sydsvenska baptister inför myndigheter*, 1998, pp. 19-21, p. 29. There was also a Dissenter Law in 1873; it was in principle the same as that of 1860, but it was slightly more lenient.

[77] This year Baptist pastors were also given the licence to solemnize marriages.

[78] Sandewall, Allan, *Konventikel- och sakramentsbestämmelsernas tillämpning i Sverige 1809-1900*, 1961, p. 204.

[79] Åqvist, Berit, "Förord", *Tro, Frihet, Gemenskap*, 1998, p. 7; Karlsson, Birgit, "150 händelserika år", *Tro, Frihet, Gemenskap*, 1998, pp. 11-14, pp. 21-23;

Neither the beginning of industrialization,[80] nor the emigration of more than 1 million people from Sweden to the U.S.A. between 1850 and 1914 (and also to Germany, Denmark and other countries), should be forgotten. Some emigrated on account of their religious faith, as for instance some Baptists.

Something should be said in this context about the relationship of the Baptist Union, and also the other Free Churches, to the State Church, especially concerning the practice of baptism within the latter.

A stumbling block for the Free Churches, and especially for the Baptist Union of Sweden, has been the State Church system. This concerns many questions - ideological, economic, and practical etc. - for example the question of membership.[81] Many Free Church members have, however, asked for baptism from the State Church, especially in the first decades of the 20th century. The Free Church Conference *(Frikyrkomötet)* in 1919, with about 500 elected representatives of the Baptist Union of Sweden, the Mission Covenant Church of Sweden and the United Methodist Church in Sweden, found this situation threatening. An appeal was issued to Free Church people to respect the demands of denominational loyalty by not going to the State Church ministers, but by turning to their congregations' own superintendents and preachers for

---

Westblom, Anne, *Porträtt:* "Pedagog i Dalabygd", *Tro, Frihet, Gemenskap,* 1998, pp. 164f. Franzén writes about "The struggle for freedom" *(Kampen för frihet),* Franzén, Bert, "Tro och liv i förändring", *Tro, Frihet, Gemenskap,* 1998, pp. 200-205. Samuelsson writes that during the 1850's and 1860's the Swedish Baptists were regarded as apostates (since they regarded infant baptism as completely meaningless) and therefore they were considered to be "non-Christians". Because of this the Baptists were for example refused banns and marriage. Samuelsson, Owe, *Sydsvenska baptister inför myndigheter,* 1998, p. 237, see also pp. 165-177, pp. 201-208; Dahlbäck, Eva, "Trosprov vara baptist – miste lärartjänst", *VP,* No. 1/2, 1975, p. 11.

[80] In addition to this the trade union movement must be mentioned.

[81] Most babies until 1996 became automatically, by birth, members of the Church of Sweden (without any baptism at all), if the mother was a member of that church. Changes in this arrangement were, however, taking place and today membership or belonging, *(tillhörighet),* (of newborn children) is related to baptism. "Automatic membership by birth" has ceased in the Church of Sweden. Concerning the change, see *Svensk författningssamling,* (SFS), 1995:1211. Lag om ändring i kyrkolagen (1992:300). Tredje avdelningen. Kyrkotillhörighet i Svenska kyrkan. 3 kap. Om kyrkotillhörighet. §§ 1-15, 1996.

baptism and other church acts.[82] For, in spite of the changes in Sweden in the 19th century and in the early 20th century, many members of the Free Churches did often ask for baptism and other ceremonies from the State Church/Church of Sweden (as a matter of fact right up to the middle of the 20th century). It was important for the individual's social status at a time when a person - until the beginning of the 20th century - had to be baptized in the State Church for example in order to enter into marriage and have access to higher education.

Against the background of the above mentioned aspects and historical perspective, pointing to changes taking place in Swedish society and in the State Church (later the Church of Sweden), we may look more closely at the Baptist Union of Sweden.

---

[82] See Andersson, Axel, *Svenska Missionsförbundet*, del I, 1928, especially pp. 305f. Concerning the Free Church Conference, see more below, chapter 9.1.

6. The First Years of the Baptist Union of Sweden - A Discussion Primarily about Baptism and Holy Communion

The Baptist movement has been regarded as the first major distinctively Free Church movement in Sweden. During the 1850's the Baptists consolidated into congregations.[83] The general opinion is that Swedish Baptism was "born" in 1848 when what were probably the "first" believers' baptisms were administered in Sweden by the Danish Baptist preacher A P Förster[84] - of course with the exception of the "missionary baptisms" earlier (in the Middle Ages and onwards) – and the first congregation was founded.[85] In a Confession of Faith *(trosbekännelse)*, approved in

---

[83] To get a fuller picture of the history of the Baptist Union of Sweden see Nordström, Nils Johan, *Svenska Baptistsamfundets historia.* Första delen 1923, Andra delen 1928; Nordström, Nils Johan, *En kulturbild från 1800-talets religiösa brytningstid,* 1926; *Svensk baptism genom 100 år,* 1948; Westin, Gunnar, *Kyrkor, sekter och kristen gemenskap,* 1941; Westin, Gunnar, *Den kristna friförsamlingen i Norden,* 1956; Westin, Gunnar, *I den svenska frikyrklighetens genombrottstid,* 1963; Westin, Gunnar, *Svenska Baptistsamfundet 1887-1914,* 1965; *Stockholms Första Baptistförsamling 1854-1954,* 1954; Lagergren, David, *Framgångstid med dubbla förtecken,* 1989; Lagergren, David, *Förändringstid,* 1994; Bergsten, Torsten, *Frikyrkor i samverkan,* 1995; Lindvall, Magnus, "Baptismen – en rörelse i tiden", *Samfund i förändring,* 1997, pp. 9-27. Lindvall deals most with the Baptist Union of Sweden, (but shortly also with Denmark, Norway and Finland, especially pp. 12-14); *Tro, Frihet, Gemenskap,* 1998.

[84] Hallqvist, Anders, Westblom, Per, *Tema:* "Viktiga händelser i Baptistsamfundets historia", *Tro, Frihet, Gemenskap,* 1998, p. 241.

[85] Nordström, Nils Johan, *En kulturbild från 1800-talets religiösa brytningstid,* 1926; Drake, Adolf, Borgström, J.A., *Svenska baptisternas historia under de första 50 åren 1848-1898,* 1898, pp. 63-83 and pp. 131-185. Cf. Lagergren, David, "När föddes baptismen i Sverige?", *VP,* No. 42, 1980, p. 2, where Lagergren against Nordström mentions that a believers' baptism had already occurred in 1847. See also Lagergren, David, "Vallfartsort och väckelsehärd", *VP,* No. 34/35, 1980, p. 2.

These baptisms taking place outside the State Church during the following

1848, of the first Baptist congregation in Sweden,[86] it is stated in Article 10:

> Through baptism we are received into Christ's congregation on earth, and the Lord has ordained this to be a means of grace for us.[87]

In Article 8 we read:

> We believe that holy baptism, which is authorized by Christ and which according to the clear statement of the New Testament shall remain in the church until his return, consists in the person who is to be baptized being immersed by an ordained minister of the Lord in water in the name of the Father, the Son and the Holy Spirit and thereafter being raised up. Only in this way is the divine command fulfilled, and the deep original meaning of this command of Christ preserved.[88]

I want also to draw attention to the question of membership, and give an example which illustrates the complexity of the questions concerning incorporation into a church, i.e. the local congregation, and also the relation between baptism and membership. In Article 10 it is said about admission that,

> an admission of a new member can occur only *by a vote* after prior acquaintance with his spiritual state and after personal confession of faith. At such a vote it is most desirable that unanimity among the voters is

---

years caused trouble in different ways. A term which is used in this context is *lekmannadopstriden (laybaptism conflict)*. See Holte, Ragnar, "Svenska kyrkan och lekmannadopet. En studie till det utgående 1800-talets kyrkohistoria", *Kyrkohistorisk Årsskrift* 50, 1950, pp. 165-215; Henningsson, Karl-Åke, *Striden om lekmannadopet*, 1956; Brodd, Sven-Erik, *Dop och kyrkotillhörighet enligt Svenska kyrkans ordning*, 1978, pp. 67ff.

[86] i.e. *Den svenska baptistförsamlingen*, in Borekulla, Landa parish.

[87] "Genom döpelsen blifwa wi upptagna uti Christi Församling på jorden, och Herren har förordnat den till ett Nådemedel för oss." In Nordström, Nils Johan, *En kulturbild från 1800-talets religiösa brytningstid*, 1926, p. 63. See also Fahlgren, Sune, "Baptismen och baptisternas gudstjänstliv", *I enhetens tecken*, 1994, pp. 259ff.

[88] "Wi tro, att den Heliga Döpelsen... skall stå fast i kyrkan till hans återkomst, deruti består, att den som döpes skall af en dertill förordnad Herrans tjenare i Fadrens, Sonens och den Heliga Andas namn neddoppas under vattnet och åter ur detsamma upplyftas. Endast på detta sätt blifwer den Gudommeliga befallningen uppfylld, och den djupa ursprungliga betydelsen av denna Christi ordning bibehållen." In Nordström, Nils Johan, *En kulturbild från 1800-talets religiösa brytningstid*, 1926, pp. 61f.

reached.[89]

The Baptist Union of Sweden *(Svenska Baptistsamfundet)* was in one way established in 1857 when the first General Conference was held.[90] But as a matter of fact it was first at the conference in 1866 that the idea of a national Baptist Missionary Association was proposed.[91] And at the conference of Baptist congregations 1889 a common denominational organization was formed called the Society for Swedish Baptist Mission, *(Sällskapet Svenska Baptistmissionen).*[92] The name indicates the great importance of mission for the Swedish Baptists, which is still the case.

A name associated with the first years of the Baptist movement in Sweden is Fredrik Olai (or Olaus) Nilsson (1809-1881) - originally after his conversion a Methodist.[93] He is commonly designated as the pioneer of Swedish Baptism and the first Baptist preacher in Sweden.[94] Nilsson was baptized by believers' baptism in Hamburg in 1847. He was expelled from Sweden in 1851 for propagating "heresy", and went abroad to among other places the U.S.A., but returned from the U.S.A. to Sweden in 1860. He went back, however, to the U.S.A. in 1868 and died there in 1881.

---

[89] "En ny medlems intagande kan endast efter föregående bekantskap om hans själstillstånd och efter personlig aflagd bekännelse *genom röstning ske.* Wid en sådan omröstning är det på det högsta önskanswärdt, att enhällighet af rösterna finner rum." In ibid. p. 66. Italics mine.

[90] Westin, Gunnar, *Svenska Baptistsamfundet 1887-1914,* 1965, p. 393. Nineteen delegates from eight different districts of Sweden were assembled. The next year, 1858, a second conference was held with about one hundred delegates. That was before any law of Religious Freedom was promulgated in Sweden. According to Westin, the Baptist Union of Sweden existed in a very loose form from the united Baptist congregations of the 1850's. Ibid. See also Samuelsson, Owe, *Sydsvenska baptister inför myndigheter,* 1998, pp. 45ff.

[91] Nordström, Nils Johan, *Svenska Baptistsamfundets historia.* Andra delen, 1928, p. 125.

[92] Ibid. pp. 131-135.

[93] Nordström, Nils Johan, *En kulturbild från 1800-talets religiösa brytningstid,* 1926, pp. 24ff.; Lindberg, Alf, *Väckelse, frikyrklighet, pingströrelse,* 1985, pp. 15ff.

[94] In the beginning of Swedish Baptist history the terms *preacher (predikant)* or *teacher (lärare)* were preferred instead of *pastor,* a term which was too reminiscent of the church tradition they had rejected. Franzén, Bert, "Tro och liv i förändring", *Tro, Frihet, Gemenskap,* 1998, p. 209.

Another pioneer of the Baptist movement is Anders Wiberg (1816-1887).[95] Wiberg was in America for some years. The exiled F.O. Nilsson baptized him in Copenhagen in 1852. Anders Wiberg is one of the leading personalities during the first 40 years of Swedish Baptism and has been characterized as the best-informed and most theologically educated leader of Swedish Baptism. He had from childhood had connections with the neo-evangelical movement but worked for nine years as a minister in the State Church, until 1851, before he became a Baptist.

In a book by Wiberg published in 1852, the Baptist teaching about baptism and congregation is given its first explicit exposition in Sweden. The name of the book was *Hvilken bör döpas? och Hvaruti består dopet? Undersökning grundad uppå den heliga Skrifts vittnesbörd och den christna kyrkans historia*, (Who Should be Baptized? And What Does Baptism Consist of? An Investigation Based on the Witness of Holy Scripture and the History of the Christian Church).[96] And through this book Baptist doctrine was spread in Sweden.

Another important means of promoting Baptist ideas was the periodical *Evangelisten*, (The Evangelist), started by Wiberg in 1856. Further, the periodical already mentioned *Wecko-Posten*,[97] which started in 1868, must be included in this context.

Wiberg and Swedish Baptism advocated a different view of children than the predominant Lutheran view at that time in Sweden. The Swedish Lutherans taught the importance of baptizing children due to the doctrine of original sin since baptism snatches the infants out of the Devil's mouth and makes them the possession

---

95 Bergsten, Torsten, "Anders Wiberg - väckelseman, samfundsledare och teolog", *Kyrkohistorisk årsskrift* 81, 1981, pp. 84-93; Lindberg, Alf, *Väckelse, frikyrklighet, pingströrelse*, 1985, pp. 19ff.; Bergsten, Torsten, "Enheten i Kristus", *Tro, Frihet, Gemenskap*, 1998, pp. 217f.

96 This work is to a large extent according to Westin a revision of English Baptist books, Westin, Gunnar, *I den svenska frikyrklighetens genombrottstid*, 1963, p. 135.

97 Since 1930 spelled *Vecko-Posten* (later on *Veckoposten*), which started as *Nyhetsbladet*. *Nyhetsbladet* was from the beginning a complement to *Evangelisten*. Franzén, Bert, "Adolf Drake - han skapade Veckoposten", *VP*, No. 38, 1992, pp. 8f.; Lagergren, David, "Borgström och Byström - ett radarpar!", *VP*, No. 39, 1992, pp. 8f.; Lindvall, Magnus, Åqvist, Berit, *Tema:* "Utbildning och det tryckta ordet", *Tro, Frihet, Gemenskap*, 1998, pp. 182-185.

of God.[98] Anders Wiberg repudiated, however, the argumentation from the Bible for infant baptism. Wiberg interpreted Mark. 10:13-16 in the following way: small children are, generally speaking, predetermined for the Kingdom of God. Why should children be excluded when those who are similar to them (i.e. after the conversion) are admitted to the Kingdom of God?[99] We can also observe that original sin is a reality for Wiberg; small children are not without original sin or pure. All have sinned in Adam. Children are in spite of this not under judgment. They have been purified through the blood of the Saviour.[100]

The young Swedish Baptist movement did, in consequence of this interpretation of the Bible, officially dissociate itself from the Lutheran teaching and practice of infant baptism. And in 1862 Anders Wiberg and Lars Wilhelm Henschen, a member of the municipal court in Uppsala, wrote a critical petition to the Government on account of the Dissenter Act in 1860. The petition was delivered, signed by many Baptists (about 4000 persons, i.e. a majority of the Baptists in Sweden at that time). In this very detailed document it is said:

> We believe that infants will be blessed without any external means on account of the words of Christ that the Kingdom belongs to such as these... for those, to whom the Kingdom belongs without being baptized, will certainly, although they die in such a state, be blessed.[101]

---

[98] See for example Brodd, Sven-Erik, *Dop och kyrkotillhörighet enligt Svenska kyrkans ordning*, 1978, pp. 23-25, and pp. 35ff.

[99] Wiberg, Anders *Hvilken bör döpas? och Hvaruti bestâr dopet?*, 1852, p. 194.

[100] Ibid. p. 195. "Wiberg here confirms that he is a General Baptist, that is a supporter of the idea of a general choice by grace." Bergsten, Torsten, "Barnet i frikyrkan. En historisk-teologisk studie", *Tro och Liv*, No. 3, 1985, p. 6.

[101] In Nordström, Nils Johan, *Svenska Baptistsamfundets historia*. Andra delen, 1928, p. 26. Wiberg states also: "Att späde barn blifva salige utan alla utvärtes medel, tro vi på grund af Christi blotta ord, att 'sâdana hörer himmelriket till' (Matth. 19:14); hvilket sistnämnde ställe icke med ringaste skäl kan påstås hafva någon hänsyftning på dopet. Tvärtom kan man deraf draga den slutsats, att dopet icke är nödvändigt till barnens salighet; ty den, till hvilken himmelriket hörer, utan att han är döpt, blir, om han dör under sådant tillstånd, visserligen salig. Att antaga det odöpte barn, som dö förr, än deras medvetande utvecklats, skulle blifva hvarken salige eller osalige, medgifver ej 'den rena evangeliska läran' (jfr Rom. 14:10. 2 Kor. 5:10. Matth. 25:32)." Ibid, see also pp. 19-45; Westin, Gunnar, *Den kristna friförsamlingen i Norden*, 1956, pp. 52-54. Bergsten writes in 1985 that Wiberg's interpretation is probably representative of the Swedish Free Church also today. Bergsten,

Wiberg like Broady[102] held according to Bergsten a *symbolic view of baptism*, but it is not an absolutely strict symbolic view. There is a hint that he did regard baptism as a means of grace, or something close to this view.[103]

In addition to infant baptism, another question was that of Holy Communion and membership, i.e. the demand for "pure" congregations, that the congregations should consist only of believers who have experienced salvation and made a public confession of their faith and been baptized by believers' baptism.

The question of Holy Communion (or the Lords' table) was discussed already in the 1850's. At the second General Conference in 1858, the most important theme for discussion was closed or open Holy Communion. In the discussion two Baptist representatives from Great Britain (Edward Steane and John Howard Hinton) and two from Germany (Johann Gerhard Oncken and Julius Köbner) participated. The Germans pleaded for closed Holy Communion - which also at that time was the predominant practice among the American Baptists - which implied that only Christians baptized by believers' baptism ought to be admitted to the Holy Communion. The two from the English Baptist Union, however, pleaded for open Holy Communion. Swedish Baptists decided on closed Holy Communion,[104] and from that time and

---

Torsten, "Barnet i frikyrkan. En historisk-teologisk studie", *Tro och Liv*, No. 3, 1985, p. 6.

[102] Concerning Broady see more below.

[103] Bergsten writes that Wiberg represents a Reformed, symbolic view of baptism. Bergsten, Torsten, "Anders Wiberg, dopet och de kristnas enhet", Tro och Liv, No. 4, 1988, p. 18. Bergsten continues that Wiberg did, however, come very close to regarding baptism as a means of grace, *(nådemedel)*. Ibid. p. 19, see also p. 25. Bergsten states that he adopted a golden mean between the American Baptist theology, which onesidedly emphasized that baptism is a symbolic act, and the Lutheran, which regarded baptism as a means of grace, where God acts with the human being, with the infant as well. Bergsten, Torsten, "Anders Wiberg - väckelseman, samfundsledare och teolog", Kyrkohistorisk årsskrift 81, 1981, p. 90. As a matter of fact Wiberg writes in a statement in 1850 (observe before he became a Baptist) about baptism as a sacrament. "Om det kristliga dopet tror och håller jag, hvad Herren Jesus själf stadgat uti instiftelseorden till detta sakrament..." in Nordström, Nils Johan, *Svenska Baptistsamfundets historia.* Första delen, 1923, p. 76. See also Bergsten, Torsten, "Förändring genom konfrontation och dialog. Svenskt perspektiv", *Samfund i förändring*, 1997, pp. 30ff.

[104] We find, however, an apology for closed Holy Communion already in Wiberg

about 100 years on it was closed Holy Communion which was the rule in the Baptist Union of Sweden.[105] There was a minority which wanted open Holy Communion. These people were, however, not expelled from the Baptist fellowship of faith. Freedom of faith was respected.

We may also note that the General Preachers' Conference *(allmänna predikantmötet)* in 1897 proposed that Holy Communion ought not to be open to those who did not belong to the Baptist congregation. This was changed in 1919: "the extremely restrictive attitude that the denomination had held for a long time was abandoned in 1919."[106] Closed Holy Communion was, however, predominant until the 1940's.

The leader of the Baptist Union after Wiberg was Knut Oscar Broady (1832-1922). He was called to be head of the Baptist preachers' school, i.e. the Bethel Seminary *(Betelseminariet)*. For forty years he was its leader.[107] Through Broady, influenced by American Baptism, the Reformed view was strengthened within the Swedish Baptist movement, for example concerning the doctrine of baptism.[108] The Reformed, symbolic interpretation of baptism

---

1854. Wiberg, Anders, *Det Christliga Dopet,* 1854.

[105] Lagergren, David, "Nattvarden i Svenska Baptistsamfundet 1848-1910", *När vi bryter det bröd...,* 1981, pp. 89-100. See also Carlsson, Else-Marie, "Nattvarden i Svenska Baptistsamfundet 1910-1970", ibid. pp. 101-119; Persson, Larsåke W., "Nattvarden i Svenska Baptistsamfundet på 1970-talet", ibid. pp. 120-154; Bergsten, Torsten, "Förändring genom konfrontation och dialog. Svenskt perspektiv", *Samfund i förändring,* 1997, pp. 36-39.

[106] "...den hyperrestriktiva hållning som samfundet länge intagit, bröts upp 1919." Lagergren, David, *Framgångstid med dubbla förtecken,* 1989, p. 60.

[107] The forty years of work at the *Betelseminariet* by Adolf Drake (1833-1906) should not be forgotten either, and his work with *Veckoposten.* Franzén, Bert, "Adolf Drake - han skapade Veckoposten", *VP,* No. 38, 1992, pp. 8f. See also Åqvist, Berit, *Porträtt: "Baptistisk hövding", Tro, Frihet, Gemenskap,* 1998, pp. 237-239. Other key persons in the *Betelseminariet* who are of importance for this thesis are - besides Broady's successor, Principal Carl Eric Benander (1861-1956), then Principal Nils Johan Nordström (1880-1943), after him Fredrik Hedvall (b. 1892) - David Lagergren (b. 1919), Bert Franzén (b. 1926) and thereafter Berit Åqvist. They have all in different ways made an impact on the development of the Baptist Union.

[108] Westin, Gunnar, *Den kristna friförsamlingen genom tiderna,* 3rd ed., 1955, p. 56; Walan, Bror, "De utomkyrkliga väckelserörelserna under senare hälften av 1800-talet", *Väckelse och kyrka i nordiskt perspektiv,* 1969, p. 192. See also

79

became predominant in the Baptist Union of Sweden for more than 100 years - until the present time.[109]

The relation to the Northern Baptist Convention and the support of its American Baptist Foreign Mission Society (ABFMS) for the Baptist Union of Sweden was, of course, of importance. Lagergren writes that the Baptist Union of Sweden from the very beginning was noticed abroad and that the Northern Baptist Convention rightly regarded itself as mother denomination of Swedish Baptism. ABFMS considered the Baptist work in Sweden as one of its most important results and it gave it financial support from the beginning in 1850 and until 1930.[110] Leading Swedish Baptist pastors had studied and worked in the U.S.A. They had a critical attitude towards British Baptist leaders, for instance towards both C.H. Spurgeon and J.H. Shakespeare.[111]

Franzén, Bert, "Tro och liv i förändring", *Tro, Frihet, Gemenskap*, 1998, pp. 189-190. Fahlgren writes: "Inte minst Broady... kom att bli en förkämpe för en antisakramental syn." Fahlgren, Sune, "Baptismen och baptisternas gudstjänstliv", *I enhetens tecken*, 1994, p. 263.

[109] Bergsten, Torsten, "Dopet igår och idag", *Tro och Liv*, No. 2, 1979, p. 5. It can also be noted that Broady's view of Holy Communion is discussed in the literature. Lagergren, David, *Framgångstid med dubbla förtecken*, 1989, pp. 156f.

[110] Ibid. pp. 189ff.; Westin, Gunnar, *Den kristna friförsamlingen i Norden*, 1956, p. 66; Nordström, Nils Johan, *Svenska Baptistsamfundets historia*. Andra delen, 1928, pp. 141-155. We can also mention that Wiberg's book *Det Christliga Dopet*, 1854, was printed in the U.S.A.

The *ABFMS* continued to support the Baptist Union of Sweden, and contributed for example to the building up of the Bethel Seminary. See for example *Svenska Baptistsamfundet*, 1969-1970, p. 177, [årsbok]; *Svenska Baptistsamfundet*, 1970-1971, p. 171, [årsbok], etc. A significant question for future research is how much dependence on and influences from America have affected the Baptist Union of Sweden during the years? How has the financial dependence controlled the Baptist Union? One can wonder if certain conditions for receipt of financial support were (at least implicitly) stipulated.

[111] Lagergren, David, *Framgångstid med dubbla förtecken*, 1989, p. 191.

7. Some Divisions within the Baptist Movement

Ever since the Baptists were consolidated in the Baptist Union of Sweden, the questions of baptism, ecclesiology and Baptist identity have been in a process of development and divergent views concerning both doctrinal and practical issues have arisen. Sometimes they have given rise to various divisions.

7.1. Some Baptist Movements and Divisions

Already in about 1860 a separation from the Baptist Union of Sweden occurred. Hundreds of members left the Union. The main cause was the so-called doctrine of sinlessness, associated with a man named August Sjödin.[112]

The American and British revivals strongly influenced Swedish spiritual life and in the beginning of the 1870's a more extensive division occurred. The reasons for this split depended mainly on differences in doctrine. In opposition to the Baptist Union of Sweden a divergent opinion was put forward concerning among other things reconciliation, sanctification, eschatology and the doctrine of sinlessness, asserting that complete sinlessness was already possible during life on earth. The division depended also on practical issues, such as the organization and the employment of trained pastors. The leader was Helge Åkeson (1831-1904). He dissociated himself from among other things the doctrine of so-called objective atonement.[113] In 1872 he was expelled from the Baptist Union. Concerning the question of sanctification, Baptist congregations were divided, and it resulted also in some congregations being expelled from the Baptist Union of Sweden. The

---

[112] Nordström, Nils Johan, *Svenska Baptistsamfundets historia.* Andra delen, 1928, pp. 57-90 (about the doctrine of sinlessness); Westin, Gunnar, *Den kristna friförsamlingen genom tiderna*, 3rd ed., 1955, p. 364; Bergsten, Torsten, "Samfundsmedvetande och kongregationalism i svensk frikyrklighet", *Kyrkohistorisk årsskrift* 93, 1993, p. 135.

[113] Åkeson had a similar view of the atonement to that of Paul Peter Waldenström. Waldenström is regarded, together with Erik Jakob Ekman, as the founder of the Mission Covenant Church of Sweden, established in 1878. Concerning this denomination see chapter 9.4.2. below.

establishment of the Scandinavian Independent Baptist Union *(Fribaptistsamfundet)*, was thus a fact in 1872.[114]

The Swedish Holiness Mission *(Helgelseförbundet)* may also be mentioned in this context, established in 1887, originating from an evangelical prayer-fellowhip. Edvard Hedin (1856-1921) is regarded as the founder. First in the 1920's the Swedish Holiness Mission developed into a separate denomination with a Baptist baptismal theology.[115]

The Pentecostal Movement, as well as the Örebro (Baptist) Mission, also ought to be mentioned here. These last two will be dealt with in more depth in the following sections.

7.2. The Baptist Union of Sweden and Two Major Divisions

In the beginning of the 20th century, new movements that emphasized spiritual experience were appearing. There was a new type of preaching within Swedish Free Church Christianity about baptism in the Holy Spirit, about the gifts of the Spirit and the life of the Holy Spirit.[116] These movements had a tendency to establish new "special" groups and congregations for their followers. They influenced the Free Churches and, of course, also the Baptist congregations. The attitude to the New Movement *(Nya rörelsen)* or "the second blessing", later called the Pentecostal Revival and after

---

[114] Westin, Gunnar, *Den kristna friförsamlingen i Norden*, 1956, pp. 61f.; Westin, Gunnar, *Den kristna friförsamlingen genom tiderna*, 3rd ed., 1955, p. 364; Nordström, Nils Johan, *Svenska Baptistsamfundets historia*. Andra delen, 1928, pp. 57-90 and pp. 205-217. See also Struble, Rhode, *Den samfundsfria församlingen och de karismatiska gåvorna och tjänsterna*, 1982, pp. 10f.; Lindberg, Alf, *Väckelse, frikyrklighet, pingströrelse*, 1985, pp. 57ff.; Lagergren, David, "Från Wiberg till Pethrus", *VP*, No. 45, 1985, p. 6.

[115] Concerning these Baptist movements, see Bexell, Oloph, "Kyrkor i Sverige", *Kyrkans liv*, 2nd ed., 1993, pp. 81-84. See also, concerning the Scandinavian Independent Baptist Union, Isacsson, Seth, "Fribaptistsamfundet", *Svenska Trossamfund*, 8th ed., 1990, pp. 73-78, and concerning the Swedish Holiness Mission/Holiness Union Mission, Davidson, Birger, "Helgelseförbundet", ibid. pp. 79-84.

[116] Lagergren, David, *Framgångstid med dubbla förtecken*, 1989, p. 100. Lagergren writes that baptism in the Holy Spirit was a special experience, largely unknown to the Swedish Baptists before 1905-1907. Preaching about this met resistance. Ibid.

a time the Pentecostal Movement *(Pingströrelsen)*, resulted in a split within Swedish Baptism.[117]

There have been many crisis, difficulties, problems and divisions between individual Christians, among congregations etc., ever since that time. And tensions between leading persons within the Baptist Union of Sweden occurred which amongst other things resulted in two different branches. One is the Pentecostal Movement, which does not count itself as a church or denomination, with its leader Lewi Pethrus (1884-1974). The other is the Örebro (Baptist) Mission *(Örebro Missionsförening)*, with its leader John Ongman (1844-1931).[118]

7.2.1. The Baptist Union of Sweden and the Pentecostal Movement

Apparently it took some years before the Pentecostal Movement achieved a substantial breakthrough and seriously influenced the development of the Baptist Union.[119] It is particularly one *Baptist* congregation which has been associated with the development of the Pentecostal Revival/Movement, Stockholms sjunde baptistförsamling (the Seventh Baptist Congregation of Stockholm), which was given the name Filadelfiaförsamlingen, founded in 1910. It was at that time the fastest growing Baptist congregation in Sweden. In 1913 this congregation was expelled from the Baptist Union of Sweden, together with its pastor and charismatic leader

---

[117] Concerning the Swedish Pentecostal Revival, see Asp, Samuel, "Den svenska pingstväckelsen", *Svenska Trossamfund*, 8th ed., 1990, pp. 91-100.

[118] Concerning the Örebro (Baptist) Mission, see Sundberg, Kerstin, "Örebromissionen", *Svenska Trossamfund*, 8th ed., 1990, pp. 85-90; Westin, Gunnar, *Svenska Baptistsamfundet 1887-1914*, 1965, dealing with, besides the Baptist Union of Sweden, *den nya rörelsen*, (the New Movement) later named *Pingströrelsen* (the Pentecostal Movement), and the Örebro (Baptist) Mission. See also "Svenska Baptistsamfundet och Kyrkornas Världsråd. En studierapport", 1965, pp. 69f., [unpublished paper]; Bergsten, Torsten, *Frikyrkor i samverkan*, 1995, pp. 85-90, and pp. 184-195; Karlsson, Birgit, "150 händelsrika år", *Tro, Frihet, Gemenskap*, 1998, pp. 28-31.

[119] Struble is of the opinion that neither the Scandinavian Independent Baptist Union nor what would become Örebro (Baptist) Mission gave rise to anything new. They wanted rather to *renew* old forms. The Pentecostal Revival, however, implied a radically new way of thinking and action. Struble, Rhode, *Den samfundsfria församlingen och de karismatiska gåvorna och tjänsterna*, 1982, p. 11. See also Lagergren, David, "Från Wiberg till Pethrus", *VP*, No. 45, 1985, p. 6.

Lewi Pethrus. The Pentecostal Revival grew under the leadership of that congregation to become the Pentecostal Movement.[120] In the subsequent decades thousands of Baptists went over to the Pentecostal Movement. Many families and congregations were split. This started a painful process in the Baptist community.[121] In 1921 the membership losses from the Baptist Union to the Pentecostal Movement were so great that it was necessary to have a special statistical column for those who left. However, in spite of this division and the obvious difficulties with losses, the Baptist Union was able to grow between 1914-1934.[122]

The formal reason for the expulsion of Filadelfiaförsamlingen from the Baptist Union was the matter of the Lord's table. Lewi Pethrus allowed believing and baptized (of course through believers' baptism) persons without being members in a local Baptist congregation to participate in Holy Communion (first later on designated with the term open Holy Communion). He broke then consciously with Baptist orthodoxy concerning Holy Communion.[123] The main reason for the division which was mentioned was the "New Movement" with its teaching about baptism in the Holy Spirit.[124] And *Veckoposten* argued against speaking in tongues.[125]

---

[120] Carlsson, Bertil, *Organisationer och beslutsprocesser inom Pingströrelsen*, 1974, pp. 20-27; Lagergren, David, *Framgångstid med dubbla förtecken*, 1989, pp. 46-50; Lindberg, Alf, *Väckelse, frikyrklighet, pingströrelse*, 1985, especially pp. 143-260.

[121] Lagergren, David, *Framgångstid med dubbla förtecken*, 1989, pp. 63-68; Struble, Rhode, *Den samfundsfria församlingen och de karismatiska gåvorna och tjänsterna*, 1982, pp. 17-21, pp. 28ff.; Kvist, Edvin, "Mot nya tider", *Mot nya tider*, 1938, p. 51.

[122] Lagergren, David, *Framgångstid med dubbla förtecken*, 1989, pp. 21f.

[123] See Struble, Rhode, *Den samfundsfria församlingen och de karismatiska gåvorna och tjänsterna*, 1982, pp. 248f.; Lagergren, David, *Framgångstid med dubbla förtecken*, 1989, pp. 46ff. See also Lagergren, David, "Är en gemensam dopsyn en förutsättning för gemensamt nattvardsfirande?", 1976, pp. 1-2, [conference documentation].

[124] This question, about baptism in the Holy Spirit with speaking in tongues, caused according to Struble the first and greatest division. Struble, Rhode, *Den samfundsfria församlingen och de karismatiska gåvorna och tjänsterna*, 1982, p. 18. And Lewi Pethrus himself gives this explanation of the expulsion of Filadelfiaförsamlingen from the Baptist Union. There was the "official reason" of the Lord's table, but he mentions also another reason which the leaders of the Baptist Union have not officially recognized, but nonetheless admitted, i.e. that Filadelfiaförsamlingen unreservedly took sides with the New

Another reason for the division that also must be mentioned in this context was the developing radical congregationalism of Lewi Pethrus. His opinion was that denominations and district organizations were unacceptable and erroneous.[126] He states: "The very root of division among God's people is the issue of denominationalism."[127] This implied that no organization involved in Christian activity should exist besides the independent local congregation.[128]

Bergsten states in this context: "It is evident that LP [i.e. Lewi Pethrus, remark mine], personally maintained the central *episkopé*-function within the Pentecostal Movement."[129] We can note this in

Movement, i.e. the Pentecostal Movement. Pethrus, Lewi, "Vår ställning till andra kristna", *Pethrus, Lewi, Samlade skrifter*, Band 6, 1958-1959, p. 167, [published orig. in 1931, my remark]. See also Westin, Gunnar, *Svenska Baptistsamfundet 1887-1914*, 1965, pp. 217ff.; "Baptisterna och Anden", [editorial], VP, No. 6, 1979, p. 2; Franzén, Bert, "Anden och det kristna livet, I, Döpta i en och samma ande", VP, No. 34, 1987, p. 7, writing that a distinction was made between water baptism and baptism in the Holy Spirit.

[125] Struble, Rhode, *Den samfundsfria församlingen och de karismatiska gåvorna och tjänsterna*, 1982, p. 18.

[126] Pethrus, Lewi, "De kristnas enhet. Kan detta mål nås genom de moderna samfundsorganisationerna?", *Pethrus, Lewi, Samlade skrifter*, Band 4, 1958, p. 142, [published orig. in 1919, my remark.]

[127] "Själva roten till splittringen bland Guds folk är samfundstanken." Ibid. p. 144. Westin says concerning Pethrus' writing, that he himself is ready to prove quite the opposite, i.e. that division is the cause of the denominations. Westin, Gunnar, *Samfund och enhet*, 3rd ed., 1920, p. 32. Recent research, see for example Struble and Lagergren, has shown that nothing indicates that Baptist pastor Lewi Pethrus was in principle an opponent of denominational organizations before his expulsion from the Baptist Union of Sweden. But in connection with the crisis of 1913 Pethrus has stated himself that he had a spiritual experience that made him conscious of the error of the Baptists. Struble, Rhode, *Den samfundsfria församlingen och de karismatiska gåvorna och tjänsterna*, 1982, pp. 28ff.; Lagergren, David, *Framgångstid med dubbla förtecken*, 1989, pp. 46ff.; Bergsten, Torsten, "Samfundsmedvetande och kongregationalism i svensk frikyrklighet", *Kyrkohistorisk årsskrift* 93, 1993, p. 135.

[128] See Pethrus, Lewi, "Vår ställning till andra kristna", *Pethrus, Lewi, Samlade skrifter*, Band 6, 1958-1959, pp. 166-183, where Pethrus writes about the reasons for the breach.

[129] Bergsten, Torsten, "Samfundsmedvetande och kongregationalism i svensk frikyrklighet", *Kyrkohistorisk årsskrift* 93, 1993, p. 140.

spite of the independent tendencies within the Pentecostal Movement.[130] The Pentecostal Movement has also, not least due to its leader Lewi Pethrus, had a reserved, not to say negative, attitude towards ecumenism.[131] The division between the Baptist Union of Sweden and the Pentecostal Movement resulted in a schism, which later on would prove to be impossible to repair.[132]

Both the expulsion of 1872 and that of 1913 had, according to Lagergren, "their formal cause in the district regulations of 1861 and their material justification in what the Baptists then thought was right doctrine."[133] Whatever the causes may have been, and there are as we understand more than one, these divisions have limited the Baptist Union of Sweden in more than one sense.

---

[130] Bertil Carlsson points out that there is among other things centralization within the Pentecostal Movement, despite its advocacy of the independence of the local congregations. Carlsson, Bertil, *Organisationer och beslutsprocesser inom Pingströrelsen*, 1974. And Struble writes that it is difficult to state exactly when the Pentecostal Revival became a uniform movement of Pentecostal congregations. A crucial step in that direction was the expulsion of Filadelfiaförsamlingen in 1913. Struble, Rhode, *Den samfundsfria församlingen och de karismatiska gåvorna och tjänsterna*, 1982, p. 225. See also Westin, Gunnar, *Samfund och enhet*, 3rd ed., 1920; Bergsten, Torsten, "Samfundsmedvetande och kongregationalism i svensk frikyrklighet", *Kyrkohistorisk årsskrift* 93, 1993, pp. 135ff.

[131] Pethrus was for example negative towards the establishment of the Free Church Committee for Co-operation, *(Frikyrkliga Samarbetskommittén)*, in 1918. See Pethrus, Lewi, "Ett brännande spörsmål", *Evangelii Härold*, 7 Nov. 1918, p. 177. In the same article he writes about denominations as an unbiblical institution. Some years later, 1927, he criticized also the idea of an alliance *(allianstanken)*, the world ecumenism appearing in Stockholm in 1925 and the participation of the Free Churches in that meeting. Pethrus, Lewi, "De frikyrkligas allianssträvanden och pingstväckelsen", *Evangelii Härold*, 15 Dec. 1927, pp. 641-643. Concerning the attitude of the Pentecostal Movement to ecumenism until 1947, see Struble, Rhode, *Den samfundsfria församlingen och de karismatiska gåvorna och tjänsterna*, 1982, pp. 145-154; see also Bergsten, Torsten, *Frikyrkor i samverkan*, 1995, p. 67; Bergsten, Torsten, "Enheten i Kristus", *Tro, Frihet, Gemenskap*, 1998, p. 220.

[132] Lagergren, David, *Framgångstid med dubbla förtecken*, 1989, p. 82.

[133] Lagergren, David, "Från Wiberg till Pethrus", *VP*, No. 45, 1985, p. 6.

7.2.2. The Baptist Union of Sweden and the Örebro (Baptist) Mission

Another regrettable and more considerable division in the Baptist Union of Sweden is the development of the Örebro (Baptist) Mission. Even in this case the question of baptism in the Holy Spirit played its part.

In the beginning of the 1890's the Baptist pastor John Ongman (1844-1931) returned after a long stay in the U.S.A. to Sweden and Örebro. He was the originator of lively activity and established his own organization, *Örebro Missionsförening*, in 1891. In 1897 the Baptist congregation Filadelfia was established in Örebro with Ongman as its leader. No division occurred at that time, but the seed of a division was, however, sown.[134]

From the beginning the Örebro (Baptist) Mission worked within the Baptist Union of Sweden. But Örebro was developing as a second centre in the Union. The founding of Örebro (Baptist) Mission School *(Örebro Missionsskola)* in 1908 played a great part in the coming division between the Baptist Union and Örebro (Baptist) Mission as well as the latter's Foreign Missions.[135] Further there were two of almost everything - two mission centres, two Central Boards, two preachers' schools, two evangelist-missions, two publishing houses, two weeklies etc.,[136] and all this within the same Baptist Union. Örebro (Baptist) Mission developed more and more towards becoming a "denomination" within the Baptist Union. In 1936-37 the division became unavoidable.

The explanation of the departure from the Baptist Union was that views, such as ecumenism which were foreign to the original Baptist movement had been accepted and practised by persons within the Baptist Union. Of course the statutes approved in 1936 must also be mentioned.[137] Through these statutes there was "a

---

[134] Westin, Gunnar, *Svenska Baptistsamfundet 1887-1914*, 1965, pp. 53-68; Struble, Rhode, *Den samfundsfria församlingen och de karismatiska gåvorna och tjänsterna*, 1982, p. 11.

[135] Lagergren, David, *Framgångstid med dubbla förtecken*, 1989, p. 101, see also pp. 69ff.; Westin, Gunnar, *Svenska Baptistsamfundet 1887-1914*, 1965 pp. 255-261.

[136] In 1921 Örebro (Baptist) Mission began to publish its own weekly *Missions-Baneret.*

[137] Lagergren, David, *Förändringstid*, 1994, pp. 80f.

tendency towards a change-over from a ministering mission society towards a kind of denomination."[138] In 1937 and 1938, whole congregations announced their departure from the Baptist Union. In 1937, 7856 Baptist members resigned their membership of the Baptist congregations, but in 1938 the number was less, 4161.[139] Some congregations chose, however, to stay affiliated to the Baptist Union of Sweden and at the same time to be affiliated to the Örebro (Baptist) Mission, in so-called doubly affiliated congregations *(dubbelsamverkande församlingar)*.[140] The division was, however, a reality. It was a process above all at the local, congregational level.[141]

---

[138] "... en tendens till övergång från 'tjänande missionssällskap till ett slags kyrkosamfund'." Ibid. p. 81. Something else which, according to Lagergren, embittered the division of the Union more than anything else was the conflict over the chapels. If a congregation left the Baptist Union all its property remained in the hands of the Union. Ibid. p. 45. See also pp. 45-49; *Enade och åtskilda*, 1989, pp. 156-162.

[139] Lagergren, David, *Förändringstid*, 1994, pp. 82f.

[140] That congregations have had a connection with or been affiliated to more than one denomination is thus not something new which has developed during the 1970's and later; see more below. We may note a difference on the question of membership between the Baptist Union of Sweden and Örebro (Baptist) Mission. In the Baptist Union an individual is a member of a congregation and that congregation is affiliated to *(ansluten)* the Baptist denomination. Within the Örebro (Baptist) Mission there was a so-called individual membership; it was a Mission Society with individuals as members. It was the person himself, the individual - not the congregation - who was a member of that "denomination" or rather society *(förening)*.

Örebro (Baptist) Mission continued until 1996/97, when Interact *(NYBYGGET - kristen samverkan)* started, where there are also affiliated congregations. (The Baptist Union of Sweden has decided not to be involved but to take a reserved attitude.) This implies that Örebro (Baptist) Mission is now involved in a new context or a new denomination, Interact, together with the Holiness Union Mission and the Scandinavian Independent Baptist Union. See for example Skog, Margareta, "Frikyrkosamfundens medlemstal i landets kommuner 1995", *Tro & Tanke* 1997:3, p. 69.

[141] Lagergren states: "As far as the written material allows one to judge the development of the events, the leading men in Örebro were less active in urging departure than leaders of the denomination thought. The initiative seems rather to come from the local level." Lagergren, David, *Förändringstid*, 1994, p. 83. "It appears as if neither the leaders in Stockholm nor in Örebro had any real influence on the development when the ball had started rolling." Ibid. p. 79. See also *Mot nya tider*, 1938, on the whole question and especially

One of the most apparent differences between the Baptist Union and the Örebro (Baptist) Mission concerned the doctrine of baptism in the Holy Spirit. The Örebro (Baptist) Mission made a distinction between *baptism in water* and *baptism in the Holy Spirit*, the latter being a particular experience in the life of the Christian.[142] There were, of course, other differences, for instance apocalyptic, eschatology and the view of the Bible.[143] As already indicated, the question of denominational structure was another difficult and divisive issue. Lagergren does also mention an at first glance odd reason for disunity, the question of sport. There was according to some people a connection between sport *and* dance and alcohol; sport maybe also drawing youth away from Christ.[144] Another controversial issue was the question of whether women could also be trained and sent out as evangelists. Ongman advocated this,[145] but not the Baptist Union of Sweden at that time.[146] An additional

---

Fridén, George, ".Jag tror på vår framtid", *Mot nya tider*, 1938, pp. 30f.

[142] Lagergren, David, *Förändringstid*, 1994, pp. 29-33 and p. 81.

[143] While Broady had a more optimistic view of the future, Ongman held the opinion that it would end in a catastrophe. Lagergren, David, *Framgångstid med dubbla förtecken*, 1989, p. 100. And in the end of the 1920's there were, according to Lagergren, two new causes of tension, historical-critical research and the already-mentioned ecumenical movement. Ibid. p. 91, see also p. 101; Sollerman, Erik, "Rent religiöst har ÖM och BM förts närmare varandra", *VP*, No. 28/29, p. 7.

[144] Lagergren, David, *Förändringstid*, 1994, pp. 42-44.

[145] See for example Lindberg, Erik, "John Ongman - en förkämpe för kvinnans rätt", *VP*, No. 31/32, 1992, pp. 8f.

[146] The Bible school in Örebro was established in 1891. It aimed also to send women evangelists, "which at that time was an abomination to the brothers in Stockholm." ("… vilket vid den tiden var en styggelse för bröderna i Stockholm.") "Svenska Baptistsamfundet och Kyrkornas Världsråd. En studierapport", 1965, pp. 69f., [unpublished paper]. First in 1958 it became possible for a woman to be a pastor within the Baptist Union of Sweden. Nowadays there are no problems with women as (Baptist) pastors within the Baptist Union, and a woman, Birgit Karlsson, was for several years also General Secretary of the Baptist Union of Sweden. She became a pastor in 1959. See Lantz, Ragni, "Kvinnor träder fram", *Tro, Frihet, Gemenskap*, 1998, pp. 117-135. It can be noted that in 1993 Birgit Karlsson was appointed as chairman in European Baptist Federation (EBF), which was questioned by one of the member denominations - the Rumanian. They could not accept her as the chairman *since she was a pastor*. The following year the Rumanians, however, made amends to her and asked her forgiveness. Ibid. p. 121.

cause of the division was the Baptist ecumenical commitment to among other things the Swedish Ecumenical Council, *(Svenska Ekumeniska Nämnden)*, founded in 1932, and the Swedish Ecumenical Association *(Svenska Ekumeniska Föreningen)*.[147] It can be mentioned that the principal of the Bethel Seminary, Nils Johan Nordström, acknowledged in 1933 the aims of the ecumenical movement in a speech at the constitutive meeting of the Ecumenical Association, and in an article which had previously appeared in *Veckoposten*. This was, however, criticized by other Baptists.[148]

The relation between these denominations, the Baptist Union and the Örebro (Baptist) Mission, has been characterized by an ambiguity.[149] The former has on some occasions, for instance at the General Conferences in 1948, 1956 and 1965, given expression to a desire for a radical reconsideration of the relations with the Örebro (Baptist) Mission. Örebro (Baptist) Mission maintained, however, a more reserved or restricted attitude.[150]

Parenthetically it can be mentioned that the question of whether women deacons are biblical and consistent with Baptist tradition was discussed in for example 1952. Jonsson, Gunnar, O, *Ett hundra år med baptistförsamlingen Ebeneser, Stockholm*, 1983, p. 53.

[147] The Ecumenical Committee originated in strivings for peace and was reorganized in 1932 to form the Swedish Ecumenical Council with the Swedish Ecumenical Association becoming a subsidiary organization. Lagergren, David, *Förändringstid*, 1994, p. 34, see also pp. 34-42. In 1971 the latter was integrated into the Swedish Ecumenical Council.

[148] Lagergren writes about Nordström's openness towards ecumenism: "This was without doubt a new note within the Baptist movement which had continually talked about the New Testament *congregation* consisting of those who have been *baptized by believers' baptism*, and still restricted the Lord's table to them. Reactions came also. The editor of Veckoposten wrote some critical articles... Most of the opposition came from the ÖM-influenced [Örebro (Baptist) Mission, remark mine] part of the denomination." Lagergren, David, *Förändringstid*, 1994, p. 34. Italics mine. See also Bergsten, Torsten, "Enheten i Kristus", *Tro, Frihet, Gemenskap*, 1998, pp. 215-216, where Bergsten writes about Nordström as a prominent figure in ecumenism, and refers in connection with this to among other things Nordström's work *De frikyrkliga och statskyrkoproblemet*, 1922.

[149] We will have reason to discuss the relations between these denominations more below, see especially chapter 9.4.1.

[150] "Svenska Baptistsamfundet och Kyrkornas Världsråd. En studierapport", 1965, pp. 69f., [unpublished paper].

As far as we can see, during the years there has been a complicated process, where we find different within the Baptist Union currents and seeds of dissension which, as time went on, resulted in or contributed to among other things the divisions which are mentioned above. The divisions have, of course, influenced the Baptist Union of Sweden in more than one way, as regards theology, ideology, psychology, number of members, economy etc. Whatever the causes may be, it will probably be evident that among other things the views on baptism, Holy Communion and congregation have been contributory causes to the Baptist Union *sometimes* being characterized as anti-ecumenical. If all these divisions had not occurred, the Baptist Union would with great probability have been a larger denomination. There was therefore hesitation towards ecumenism within the Baptist Union of Sweden.

At the same time there have been through the decades leaders and congregations which have worked for co-operation with other denominations, above all at the Free Church level. There is thus also to be found a process within the Baptist Union going from, in general terms, a negative attitude to ecumenism towards a more open and favourable attitude. This implied involvement in and commitment to ecumenical contexts, which also became as we have seen one of the reasons for the disruptions and divisions within the Baptist Union. Both the Pentecostal Movement and the Örebro (Baptist) Mission were negative to among other things the developing ecumenism and critical of what they found within the Baptist Union, namely a "churchism" and an ecumenical commitment.

8. Ecumenical Strivings - from an International Viewpoint

Baptists have generally speaking become more and more involved in ecumenical work worldwide. They have been participants in dialogues (bi- and multilateral), both national and international, with other Baptist groups and Free Churches and with the major churches. In recent years the Baptist World Alliance *(BWA)* has participated in international, bilateral dialogues.[151] The Baptist Union of Sweden is a member of the Baptist World Alliance. It must also be mentioned that it was first in the years 1984-1988 that an international dialogue took place between the Baptists and the Catholics.[152]

Of course many subjects have been dealt with in these contexts, but some issues have been more frequent at the international, ecumenical level, not least within the WCC. They are the issues of baptism and church unity. In *Baptism, Eucharist & Ministry 1982-1990* it is stated:

Particularly from the 1961 New Delhi assembly onwards Faith and Order has contributed to the reflection on the nature and goal of the unity of the

---

[151] See for example *Baptists and Lutherans in Conversation. A Message to our Churches,* 1990; Rothermundt, Gottfried, "Ein Dialog beginnt. Die baptistisch-lutherischen Gespräche seit 1979", *Ökumenische Rundschau,* No. 36, 1987, pp. 321-331.

[152] See for example "'Summons to Witness to Christ in Today's World': A report on the Baptist-RC International Conversations, 1984-88", *One in Christ,* No. 3, 1990, pp. 238-255; and also concerning international Baptist-Catholic dialogues *Dokumente wachsender Übereinstimmung,* Band II, 1982-1990, 1992, pp. 374-391; concerning Baptist-Lutheran dialogues, ibid. pp. 189-216; concerning Baptist-Reformed dialogues, *Dokumente wachsender Übereinstimmung,* Band I, 1931 bis 1982, 1991 (2nd ed.), pp. 102-122. Concerning the problem of consensus and reception, see for example *Theologischer Konsens und Kirchenspaltung,* 1981, especially interesting contributions by Harding Meyer, who writes about "Wer ist sich mit wem worüber einig? Überblick über die Konsenstexte der letzten Jahre", pp. 15-30, and also by Peter Lengsfeld, about "Ökumenische Spiritualität als Voraussetzung von Rezeption", pp. 126-134.

church (Uppsala assembly 1968, section I, Commission meetings at Louvain 1971, Accra 1974 and Bangalore 1978, consultation at Salamanca 1973 and Nairobi assembly 1975).[153]

Baptists around the world have, however, as has also been stated previously, originally and generally been hesitant about ecumenical strivings and the ecumenical movement, even if there from time to time have been exceptions.[154] As regards Faith and Order and the WCC, certain Baptist Unions did, however, after some hesitation, participate in Faith and Order in 1942 and in the WCC in 1948, in Amsterdam.

The Baptist Union of Sweden has during the decades had an ambivalent attitude to the WCC and ecumenism. The words of the former General Secretary David Lagergren are striking when he characterizes the attitude of the Baptist Union of Sweden to ecumenism as "a sign of contradiction".[155] They apply to both international, national central/denominational and local/congregational levels.

---

[153] *Baptism, Eucharist & Ministry 1982-1990,* 1990, p. 6. As regards the questions of baptism and unity see among others *One Lord, One Baptism,* 1960; *The New Delhi Report* 1961, 1962; *Louvain 1971,* 1971, see especially *On the Way to Communion in the Sacraments,* pp. 35-53, and *Unity of the Church - Unity of Mankind* pp. 169-211. We note that Roman Catholic theologians took part in the work of the Faith and Order movement as full members for the first time in Louvain. Ibid. p. 5. See also *Ecumenical Perspectives on Baptism, Eucharist and Ministry,* 1983; *One Baptism, One Eucharist and a mutually recognized Ministry,* 1975; *Uniting in Hope,* 1975; *Nairobi 1975,* 1976; *Bangalore 1978,* 1979, where the abbreviation *"BEM"* (Baptism, Eucharist and Ministry) is used for the first time.

[154] One early example of an exception is from the beginning of the 19th century: the Baptist William Carey. In a letter he writes to Andrew Fuller: "... would it not be possible to arrange a conference at the Cape of Good Hope for all Christian denominations from all over the world once every ·tenth year? I sincerely recommend such a plan." Quoted in "Svenska Baptistsamfundet och Kyrkornas Världsråd. En studierapport", 1965, p. 70, [unpublished paper]. On this statement it has been said: "In Carey's ecumenical vision, we encounter one of the earliest initiatives to a succession of Mission Conferences arranged in the second half of the 19th century which would culminate in the World Mission Conference in Edinburgh 1910, which resulted in the establishment of the International Missionary Council 1921." Ibid. See also my dissertation, Johnsson, Lennart, *Beasley-Murray's dopuppfattning,* 1987, pp. 36ff.

[155] "Ekumeniken var sålunda - och skulle länge förbli - ett motsägelsens tecken inom Svenska Baptistsamfundet." Lagergren, David, *Framgångstid med dubbla förtecken,* 1989, p. 164.

During the crisis that resulted in the painful division between the Baptist Union and the Örebro (Baptist) Mission in the 1930's, ecumenism, as noted above, was *one* of the difficult questions which caused the schism. And the ecumenical movement was widely looked on as "a threat to true biblical faith and to the freedom and independence of the churches and the congregations."[156] A reserved attitude towards ecumenism could also be observed for instance at the Free Church Conference in 1924, concerning the preparations for the ecumenical meeting in Stockholm in 1925 under the supervision of Archbishop Nathan Söderblom. Hesitations were expressed about the fact that the Roman Catholic Church was also included.[157] This Meeting in 1925, where also the two Swedish Baptist leaders N.J. Nordström and J. Byström did participate,[158] is usually regarded as the first World Conference, where the isolation between churches and denominations was overcome. It paved the way for the decisions which were later made, i.e. the constituting of the *WCC* in Amsterdam in 1948 etc.

Torsten Bergsten also gives an account of the Baptist Union of Sweden and its attitude towards the *WCC* and ecumenism:

> When the World Council of Churches appeared, it was regarded by many [Baptists, my remark] as a mouthpiece of liberal theology, aiming at a dictatorial super-church. In some eyes the WCC was an ominous sign that the last day was at hand. These apprehensions were exaggerated and misleading, producing an anti-ecumenical atmosphere which prevented the Baptist Union of Sweden from joining the WCC.[159]

A couple of decades later, it is said in the final report in 1965 from the committee, "Svenska Baptistsamfundet och Kyrkornas Världsråd. En studierapport", in an evaluation of a possible Baptist Union of Sweden membership in the *WCC*, presented to the Central

---

[156] Bergsten, Torsten, "Baptismen, trosfriheten och ekumeniken", *Liv och tjänst,* 1988, p. 192; Lagergren, David, *Framgångstid med dubbla förtecken,* 1989, pp. 91ff.

[157] Ibid. p. 160. *Veckoposten* already in 1914 expressed criticism of Söderblom, at his appointment as the Archbishop that year, primarily on account of the reputation that Söderblom had as a liberal theologian. Ibid.

[158] Sundström, Erland, "Babylonisk sköka – konungens brud", *VP,* No. 23, 1975, pp. 8f.

[159] Bergsten, Torsten, "Baptismen, trosfriheten och ekumeniken", *Liv och tjänst,* 1988, p. 192.

Board of that denomination:

> The committee is of the opinion that it is evident, partly that the statement that the World Council of Churches in its present state is identical with the Babylonian harlot in Revelation 17-18 is groundless, partly that the idea of Christian unity is firmly established in the New Testament.[160]

Further it is said:

> In this complex situation, the committee is of the opinion, that every step which in complete faithfulness to the Word of God can be taken towards a gradual overcoming of Christian division also ought to be taken. The committee considers that the entrance of the Baptist Union of Sweden into the World Council of Churches is such a step. The development of the World Council of Churches so far is in general such that our denomination can and ought to support it.[161]

The Baptist Union of Sweden did not, however, become a member of the WCC at that time, in the 1960's, nor is it so today. It has, however, since 1961 been indirectly involved in the work of the WCC. In 1961 the International Missionary Council was integrated into the organization of the WCC, and the Baptist Union of Sweden has been a member of the International Missionary Council's

---

[160] "Studiekommittén anser, att det tydligt framgår, dels att påståendet att Kyrkornas Världsråd i sin nuvarande form skulle vara identisk med den babyloniska skökan i Uppenbarelseboken 17-18 saknar grund, dels att den kristna enhetstanken är fast förankrad i Nya Testamentet.", "Svenska Baptistsamfundet och Kyrkornas Världsråd. En studierapport", 1965, pp. 95f., [unpublished paper]. The Baptist members of this committee were the editor Bert Franzén, pastor Ruben Jansson (surname later changed to Janarv) and pastor Edvin Österberg, but also pastor Fredrik Almstad, Göte Aourell, Dagny Berg, Fritz Eldebo, Inger Eskilsson, Efraim Fraim, Gunnar Langerud, Hans Oddestad, Gunnel Sjöberg, Eric Strutz, Nils Sundholm, Arvid Svärd, pastor Joel Sörenson, Simon Öberg, Gerd Öman.

[161] "I denna komplexa situation anser studiekommittén, att varje steg, som i full trohet till Guds ord kan tagas till ett successivt övervinnande av den kristna splittringen, också bör tagas. Studiekommittén anser, att Svenska Baptistsamfundets anslutning till Kyrkornas Världsråd är ett sådant steg. Kyrkornas Världsråds hittillsvarande utveckling är i stort sett sådan, att vårt samfund både kan och bör ge det sitt stöd." Ibid. p. 96. In another part of this report, it is stated: "It is particularly regrettable bearing in mind its size that the Southern Baptists have not yet joined the WCC..." ("Det är särskilt beklagligt med hänsyn till dess storlek att inte Sydstatsbaptistsamfundet ännu gått in i Kyrkornas Världsråd.") Ibid. p. 83. See also *Svenska Baptistsamfundets Allmänna konferenser Stockholm 1963 Linköping 1964. Svenska Baptistsamfundets Ungdomsförbunds (SBUF) årskonferenser Västerås 1963 Sjövik 1964*, 1964, p. 70.

Swedish partner, the Swedish Missionary Council, since 1922.[162]

The criticisms and caution concerning the WCC depend on among other things misunderstandings and prejudices about the nature of the WCC. There has in recent years been an increasingly more favourable evaluation of the work of the WCC within the Baptist Union of Sweden. In a Baptist editorial in 1986 it is stated: "The opposition which has often been imagined to exist between the revivalist movements and ecumenism does not apply any longer."[163] Of course BEM has also played a crucial role in this ecumenical process. The Baptist Berndt Sehlstedt writes:

> Internationally in the light of 'Baptism, Eucharist and Ministry', the different views of baptism in the various church traditions are adjusting to each other (as for baptismal practice there is strong recognition of the Baptist tradition).[164]

And Torsten Bergsten writes in an unofficial commentary to the translation of BEM into Swedish:

---

[162] As regards the Baptist Union of Sweden and its relation to the ecumenical movement see "Svenska Baptistsamfundet och Kyrkornas Världsråd. En studierapport", 1965, [unpublished paper], where we explicitly find a description of the ambiguity and ambivalence within the Swedish Baptist Union towards the WCC. See also the discussions in some of the annual books of the Baptist Union of Sweden, for example Svenska Baptistsamfundets Årsbok 1961-1962, pp. 19f.; Svenska Baptistsamfundets Årsbok 1962-1963, pp. 22f.; Svenska Baptistsamfundets Årsbok 1963-1964, p. 26; Svenska Baptistsamfundets Årsbok 1986, pp. 70ff. Further Franzén, Bert, "Den enhet vi söker", [editorial], VP, No. 38, 1975, p. 2; "Uppbyggelse och nytta", [editorial], VP, No. 21, 1986, p. 2; Bergsten, Torsten, "Baptismen, trosfriheten och ekumeniken", Liv och tjänst, 1988, pp. 192f.; Bergsten, Torsten, "Enheten i Kristus", Tro, Frihet, Gemenskap, 1998, pp. 221f. Torsten Bergsten was a member of the Faith and Order Commission 1968-1974, and an observer at the meeting in Uppsala 1968. Bergsten, Torsten, Frikyrkor i samverkan, 1995, p. 207.

[163] "Motioner", [editorial], VP, No. 12, 1986, p. 2. And in another editorial in 1987, it is said: "There is more reason than some will admit, to be thankful for the many impulses to renewed reflection about questions of Christian unity which during the years have emanated from the WCC. Without these impulses we would probably with great probability have an even longer distance to go than is the case now, before Christian unity will be discernible among us." "Samtala!", [editorial], VP, No. 14, 1987, p. 4. See also Svenska Baptistsamfundets Årsbok 1986, pp. 70-74.

[164] Sehlstedt, Berndt, "Dopfrågan", VP, No. 25/26, 1983, p. 10. See also "Årskonferensens förhandlingar: Evangelisationens vägar den mest samlande frågan", VP, No. 21, 1986, p. 3.

As many times before the far-reaching ecumenical consensus on the views of baptism, Holy Communion and ministry, which has been growing within Christianity owing to the long and persevering efforts of Faith and Order, can be noted with joy.[165]

We do, however, find varying attitudes towards ecumenism within the Baptist Union of Sweden. In short, it is a sensitive question,[166] and one of the difficult issues is believers' baptism.

---

[165] Bergsten, Torsten, "Kontroversiella rekommendationer", *Dop, Nattvard, Ämbete,* 2nd ed., 1983, p. 134. It is interesting to note that Bergsten does not write convergence but consensus.

[166] See "Motioner", [editorial] *VP,* No. 12, 1986, p. 2; "Frikyrklig samordning och Kyrkornas världsråd tas upp i massmotioner", *VP,* No. 12, 1986, p. 3; Naess, Kurt, "Vad hände med motioner om Kyrkornas världsråd?", *VP,* No. 50, 1990, p. 7; "Birgit Karlsson svarar:", *VP,* No. 50, 1990, p. 7.

9. Ecumenical Strivings - from a National Viewpoint

The ecumenical strivings on a national and denominational level are, of course, related to the international discussions and in one way or another also related to the discussion about baptism and ecclesiology. In spite of the exclusiveness of the Baptist Union of Sweden - not least in the light of its beginning as a Baptist movement in relation to the State Church - regarding for example the questions of baptism, the Lord's table, ecclesiology, we find increasing tendencies to movements towards church unity in the Baptist Union of Sweden. The ecumenical strivings, more or less strongly expressed, are often inspired by a vision of and a prayer for the realization of the unity of all Christians, which first and foremost for most of the Baptists implies the realization of one united Free Church. The Baptist denomination has throughout the years made an active contribution not least to Free Church co-operation.

In this chapter,[167] I want to present what I call *Ecumenical Strivings - from a National Viewpoint* or Free Church Ecumenism. This includes the Free Church Conferences, the founding of the Free Church Committee for Co-operation, as well as the idea of a Free Church Federation, and other different attempts to unite with other denominations. Some consultations, theological documents and ecumenical studies are briefly presented as well as some other conferences and meetings which in one way or another relate primarily to baptism and ecumenical work. As far as concerns recent decades the so-called *Tresamfundssamtalen* (Trilateral Denominational Consultations), between the Baptist Union, the

---

[167] For a more detailed account of the subject studied in this chapter, see above all Bergsten, Torsten, *Frikyrkor i samverkan*, 1995, where he well describes the ecumenical development of the Swedish Free Churches, from the first Joint Conference between the Baptist Union of Sweden, the Mission Covenant Church of Sweden and the United Methodist Church in Sweden in 1905, up to 1993; and also Lagergren, David, *Framgångstid med dubbla förtecken*, 1989; Lagergren, David, *Förändringstid*, 1994.

Mission Covenant Church of Sweden and the United Methodist Church in Sweden, are considered, as well as other attempts at reunion. The documents *Gemensam grund* (Common Foundation), *Gemensam väg* (Common Path) as well as the ecumenical conferences, *Graninge I, II* and *III*, are discussed.

To provide a better background understanding of the section about the ecumenical congregations, I also want to discuss especially the relations between the Baptist Union of Sweden and the Pentecostal Movement, the Örebro (Baptist) Mission and Mission Covenant Church of Sweden. The two last denominations have a special place in the context of the ecumenical congregations. Thereafter the ecumenical congregations from about the 1970's and onwards are dealt with. The reactions towards this phenomenon, a local ecumenical development which resulted in changed structures with different constellations of congregations having a mixture of for instance different theologies of baptism, are also mentioned. I want to present some statistics to illuminate the development of the ecumenical congregations. The participation of the Baptist Union in other ecumenical contexts is mentioned, such as *Sampsalm* (an ecumenical hymn book) and the common books of worship.

9.1. **Free Church Ecumenism: Free Church Conferences, The Free Church Committee for Co-operation,The Free Church Federation**

The common Free Church theology of conversion and believers' congregations has in practice been sufficient for many Baptists to enable them to have closer relationships with other Free Churches.[168] But there have been and still are theologically controversial questions and inbuilt differences of opinion between these denominations, which understandably from time to time have come to the fore during work towards unity.

In 1905 three Free Churches, the Baptist Union of Sweden, the United Methodist Church in Sweden (we can note that the Methodist Church has an episcopal view of the church) and the Mission Covenant Church of Sweden, gathered for a first Free Church Conference in Stockholm.[169] In 1910 the second Free

---

[168] Lagergren, David, *Framgångstid med dubbla förtecken*, 1989, p. 151.

[169] This type of co-operation was in practice for many years restricted to these three denominations, especially at the central, denominational level. Bergsten,

Church Conference took place, and in 1918 these three denominations established *Frikyrkliga Samarbetskommittén* (the Free Church Committee for Co-operation). This Committee and the Free Church Conferences have for decades played a significant role in the Swedish ecumenical process.[170] The background to the Free Church Committee for Co-operation is to be found in among other things *predikantförbunden* (the Preachers' Associations).[171] We must not forget the role and the initiative of *Fria Kristliga Studentföreningen (FKS)* (the Free Christian Student Association) in this organization (i.e. the Free Church Committee for Co-operation).[172] Between 1919 and 1969 Free Church Committee for

---

Torsten, *Frikyrkor i samverkan*, 1995, pp. 13-116. Besides the establishment of the BWA the same year, in 1905, *Svenska Baptisternas Ungdomsförbund, SBUF*, (the Swedish Baptist Youth Association) was also established. Lidén, Sven Gunnar, Tema: "Svensk baptistungdom och dess verksamhet", *Tro, Frihet, Gemenskap*, 1998, pp. 78f.

[170] Concerning Free Church co-operation and the development of the Free Church Committee for Co-operation etc., see Bergsten, Torsten, *Frikyrkor i samverkan*, 1995. See also for example some of the articles in *Tro & Liv*, No. 4, 1943: Julén, J., "Frikyrkligt samarbete", *Tro och Liv*, No. 4, 1943, pp. 150-165; Modén, K.A., "Tillbakablickar och framtidssyner, Minnen och intryck I", *Tro och Liv*, No. 4, 1943, pp. 173-175; Norman, Aug. V., "Tillbakablickar och framtidssyner, Minnen och intryck II", *Tro och Liv*, No. 4, 1943, pp. 175-176; Nyrén, J., "Tillbakablickar och framtidssyner, Minnen och intryck III", *Tro och Liv*, No. 4, 1943, pp. 177-178; Lundahl, J.E., "Tillbakablickar och framtidssyner, Minnen och intryck IV", *Tro och Liv*, No. 4, 1943, pp. 178-181; Benander, C.E., "Tillbakablickar och framtidssyner, Minnen och intryck V", *Tro och Liv*, No. 4, 1943, pp. 181-183; Danielson, Hj., "Tillbakablickar och framtidssyner, Minnen och intryck VI", *Tro och Liv*, No. 4, 1943, pp. 183-184; Larsson, Rich, "Tillbakablickar och framtidssyner, Framtidsuppgifter", *Tro och Liv*, No. 4, 1943, pp. 184-187.

In 1963 the name *Frikyrkliga Samarbetskommittén* (the Free Church Committee for Co-operation) was changed to *Sveriges Frikyrkoråd* - abbreviated "SFR" - (Swedish Free Church Council). Since 1993 it is reorganized as *Sveriges Frikyrkosamråd* – abbreviated "FSR" - (the Swedish Free Church Consultative Council).

[171] "Membership in the Preachers' Associations was from the beginning restricted to preachers of the Mission Covenant Church of Sweden, the Baptist Union of Sweden, the United Methodist Church in Sweden and the Swedish Evangelical Mission, and the priests of the State Church." Bergström, Erik, "Stockholms Evangeliska Predikantförbunds tillkomst och utveckling", *I endräktens tecken*, 1922, p. 12, see also pp. 5-13.

[172] Bergsten, Torsten, *Frikyrkor i samverkan*, 1995, pp. 22ff. *Fria Kristliga*

Co-operation arranged Free Church Conferences,[173] and it was a co-ordinating and consultative body for work between the Free Churches.

At the Free Church Conferences in 1919 and 1924 the difficult issues of the Baptist doctrine and practice of baptism, Holy Communion etc., were avoided. At the Free Church Conference in 1929, the problem was, however, brought to light, among other things the question of shared communion (*gemensam nattvard*). At this Free Church Conference the Baptists rejected a proposal from the Free Church students in Uppsala for shared communion.[174] In spite of this a small opening is to be discerned, and we may notice the emphasis put by some of the youth on work towards church unity. The Baptist Union maintained, however, closed Holy Communion and drew a boundary line between those baptized by believers' baptism and other Christians.

In the 1930's, 1940's and onwards Free Church ecumenism became of greater interest. Ecumenical strivings and the idea of a federal Free Church developed in the 1930's,[175] and from 1940 onwards there were attempts to establish a Free Church Federation. There was a desire to widen the number of denominations to include more than the three mentioned but measures were postponed. Attempts were, however, made. Lagergren comments on the fact that the Baptist Jacob Byström spoke at the Free Church Conference in 1934 of the need for greater unity with movements like the Swedish Holiness Mission and the Pentecostal Movement. Nothing happened at that time. At the Free Church Conference in 1939 *Veckoposten* suggested that this meeting should be changed into a *national assembly of*

Studentföreningen was established in 1912. Ibid. p. 22.

[173] Bergsten mentions the eleven Free Church Conferences (1905, 1910, 1919, 1924, 1929, 1934, 1939, 1953, 1958, 1964, 1969), and the establishment of the Free Church Committee for Co-operation. Bergsten, Torsten, *Frikyrkor i samverkan*, 1995.

[174] Lagergren, David, *Framgångstid med dubbla förtecken*, 1989, pp. 154ff.

[175] "The idea of a federal Free Church was proposed in the 1930's... The Free Christian Student Association spread the idea in letters to the governing Boards of the Baptist Union of Sweden, the United Methodist Church in Sweden and the Mission Covenant Church of Sweden." *På väg mot frikyrklig enhet*, 1953, p. 209; see also Nicklasson, Gösta, *Missionsförbundet och ekumeniken*, 1971; Bergsten, Torsten, *Frikyrkor i samverkan*, 1995, pp. 112ff.

revivalists (väckelsefolkets riksting). Veckoposten published some figures which showed that the three denominations in the Free Church Committee for Co-operation had about 174,000 members, while the "revivalist denominations" outside the Free Church Committee for Co-operation, including the Swedish Evangelical Mission *(EFS)*, had 246,000 members.[176]

After *Fria Kristna Riksmötet* (the Free Christian National Assembly) in 1944,[177] the possibility was investigated of widening the circles so that all denominations and movements which built on the grace of God received in personal faith should also be included. The invitation was accepted by the Scandinavian Independent Baptist Union, the Salvation Army, the Swedish Holiness Mission, the Swedish Salvation Army and the Örebro (Baptist) Mission. The Swedish Evangelical Mission and the Pentecostal Movement declined. The Meeting in 1944 was a success; the rapprochement between the three denominations in the Free Church Committee for Co-operation and the other denominations was essentially encouraged.[178]

At the Free Christian National Assembly in 1947 the number of denominations in the Free Church Committee for Co-operation was increased. In the autumn of 1947 the latter could announce that the Scandinavian Independent Baptist Union, the Swedish Holiness Mission, the Swedish Salvation Army and the Örebro (Baptist) Mission had joined it. Later on in 1952 the Swedish Alliance Mission joined. The Pentecostal Movement did, however, stay outside the Free Church Committee for Co-operation.[179] At the Free Christian National Assembly in 1950, the question of unity was discussed, and the idea of establishing a federative Swedish Free Church was proposed.[180] In 1953 *Det allmänna frikyrkliga mötet* or

---

[176] Lagergren, David, *Förändringstid*, 1994, p. 228.

[177] It can be noted that in the same year, 1944, a conference of *Baptist* movements also took place - see below.

[178] Lagergren, David, *Förändringstid*, 1994, p. 228. The reason for starting these Free Christian National Assemblies was the changes taking place especially in the 1930's within the Swedish Free Church movement (the growth of the Pentecostal Movement, the division between the Baptist Union and Örebro (Baptist) Mission etc.). Bergsten, Torsten, *Frikyrkor i samverkan*, 1995, p. 119.

[179] Lagergren, David, *Förändringstid*, 1994, p. 229. See also Bergsten, Torsten, *Frikyrkor i samverkan*, 1995, pp. 119ff.

[180] Ibid. pp. 137f. This idea of a federal Free Church and union churches arose

frikyrkomötet (the General Free Church Conference) recommended that a Free Church Federation should be established. The basis of this federation would be a common view of the local Christian community and the challenge of evangelisation.[181] The General Conferences of the Mission Covenant Church of Sweden and the United Methodist Church in Sweden approved the proposal, as did the Baptist Union of Sweden in principle.[182] The other five denominations shelved the question. The proposal for a *frikyrkoförbund* (Free Church Association) in 1953 came, however, to nothing and in 1955 the Free Church Committee for Co-operation noted that the proposal had been dropped.[183] In 1969 the last Free Church Conference took place.[184]

Proposals to establish a Free Church Federation or some kind of church unity had been raised already in the 19th century,[185] and

---

out of the experiences among other things in Great Britain, where union churches consisting of Baptist and Congregationalist congregations were established according to an agreement made in 1910. Rudén discusses this. He also mentions America and the attempt to establish a reunion between the Northern Baptist Convention and the Disciples; and *Bund der Freikirchlichen Gemeinden* in Germany, which is a union between three Free Churches. Rudén, Erik, "Samarbete mellan de frikyrkliga", *Tro och Liv*, No. 7/8, 1948, pp. 310f.

[181] See Cedersjö, Björn, "På väg till enhet i tron!? Ef. 4:13. En kartläggning och analys av ett antal lärosamtal (åren 1963-1988) där frikyrkorna i Sverige deltagit", 1989, p. 4, [unpublished paper]. See also *På väg mot frikyrklig enhet,* 1953.

[182] Bergsten, Torsten, *Frikyrkor i samverkan,* 1995, p. 192.

[183] Swedberg, Bo, *Frikyrka på väg,* 1961, pp.7-8; Bergsten, Torsten, *Frikyrkor i samverkan,* 1995, pp. 139-143.

[184] Bergsten, Torsten, *Frikyrkor i samverkan,* 1995, p. 160. It is stated that the 11th Free Church Conference in 1969 will with all certainty be the last meeting of that kind. Bergsten, Torsten, "Ekumenik, vision och verklighet", *Tro och Liv,* No. 1, 1986, p. 9, see also pp. 5f. See, however, *G* 72 etc. below.

[185] P.P. Waldenström expresses the idea of a unification of Baptists *(baptister)* and Independent/Free Lutherans *(fria lutheraner)* already in 1870. This did not, however, take place. What happened was that still another denomination was created the Mission Covenant Church of Sweden, which was established in 1878. Bergsten, Torsten, "Anders Wiberg, dopet och de kristnas enhet", *Tro och Liv,* No. 4, 1988, p. 12. See also Swedberg, Bo, *Frikyrka på väg,* 1961, pp. 7-29, pp. 53-63; "Det finns en väg", 1982, especially pp. 17-19, p. 53, [unpublished paper]; *Tecken om enhet,* 1991; Swedberg, Bo, "Baptistledarna: - Nu krävs vidgade perspektiv i vårt arbete för kristen enhet", *VP,* No. 13/14,

also as noted in this study, on different occasions in the 20th century.

There have been, as we have seen, difficulties in realizing this idea of a Free Church Association or Federation. The idea of some kind of church unity still exists within the Baptist Union of Sweden, and we will have an opportunity to come back to this issue in the following sections, and also in Part III.

It is obvious that all the breakdowns have been considered as failures among Christians and have also disillusioned many Christians about their vision of church unity, especially as a union of the denominations. Others were, however, of the opinion that the longing for unity was so great within the Swedish Free Churches that in spite of the failures to establish a Free Church Federation or union, the ecumenical strivings and progress would continue. So they did, with ecumenical and theological studies, consultations, meetings etc., at different levels, not least at the local level, i.e. among the congregations. In the following sections I will give some examples of this.

9.2. Ecumenical Consultations

Other attempts at ecumenism were made. For example the so-called Trilateral Denominational Consultations starting at the end of the 1960's. These consultations, in which among others the Baptist Union of Sweden participated, were a discussion about a common Free Church. Several Free Churches gathered on the initiative of the United Methodist Church in Sweden and the Mission Covenant Church of Sweden for deliberations about establishing a new Free Church in Sweden.

Besides the Baptist Union of Sweden, there were the following denominations: the United Methodist Church in Sweden, the Mission Covenant Church of Sweden and the Swedish Salvation Army. More denominations were later involved in these deliberations. These were the Örebro (Baptist) Mission, the Scandinavian Independent Baptist Union, the Swedish Holiness Mission and the Swedish Alliance Mission. Many of these

---

1991, p. 5; "Vägen till målet", [editorial], *VP*, No. 39, 1991, p. 2; Bergsten, Torsten, "Att respektera varandras dop", *VP*, No. 9, 1992, p. 12. See also below where I discuss attempts at reunion.

denominations eventually left, however, the negotiations about a new church federation. There were only three denominations left which were ready to carry on with the talks. They were the Baptist Union of Sweden, the Mission Covenant Church of Sweden and the United Methodist Church in Sweden.[186] They discussed a federal Free Church and continued the work for the goal of achieving church unity. This project went on during the period 1969-1971.[187]

Of course the General Assembly of the WCC in Uppsala in 1968 was a stimulus to Swedish ecumenical work, also to these talks.[188] By April 1971 a total breakdown was, however, a fact, or rather the Trilateral Denominational Consultations were suspended.[189]

---

[186] See for example Bergsten, Torsten, "Ekumenik, vision och verklighet", Tro och Liv, No. 1, 1986, p. 6. We can note that the three denominations are the same as those involved in the Free Church Conference in 1905 and which also paved the way for Frikyrkliga Samarbetskommittéen (the Free Church Committee for Co-operation) in 1918, later, from 1963, Sveriges Frikyrkoråd (the Swedish Free Church Council).

[187] The Trilateral Denominational Consultations can be seen as a fruit of conversations on a joint Free Church in January 1969. See Lagergren, David, Enhetsförslaget och dopfrågan, 1969. In this context the Free Church Conference, 17-19 March 1969, in Örebro can be mentioned. There were more than 1000 representatives from almost 500 congregations within the 8 denominations belonging to Frikyrkorådet (the Swedish Free Church Council). See Dokument från Örebro, 1969. In this document Torsten Bergsten gives some reflections worth considering in the work towards church unity, Bergsten, Torsten, "På väg mot fördjupad gemenskap", Dokument från Örebro, 1969, pp. 61-78.

[188] Bergsten writes about this meeting in Uppsala as "a milestone in the international ecumenical development." Bergsten, Torsten, "Ekumenik, vision och verklighet", Tro och Liv, No. 1, 1986, p. 4.

[189] The causes of this have been discussed. Sometimes the United Methodist Church in Sweden has been singled out, and especially the newly appointed Methodist bishop in Sweden, Ole Borgen. Källstad comments on the words of the bishop, "Let us stop!", i.e. stop the plans for unification and federation of these denominations, that the new Methodist bishop's statement, in a press release the 3rd October 1970, came as a cold shower. Källstad states that the Methodist Annual Conference in 1971 was for many Methodists "a traumatic experience." Källstad, Thorvald, "Metodistkyrkan och tresamfundssamtalen", Tro och Liv, No. 5, 1979, p. 40, see also pp. 38-42. The failure of these consultations depends of course more or less on all three denominations. The issue of believers' baptism was one stumbling block. It is said that it was clear to the Baptist Union that it could not compromise on the Baptist view of baptism and congregation. Svenska Baptistsamfundet, 1971-1972, p. 177, [årsbok], and also pp. 178-181; see also Svenska Baptistsamfundet, 1970-

Thereafter the initiative in Free Church ecumenism was in the hands of the Swedish Free Church Council.[190]

A further ecumenical consultation was proposed, the Quadrilateral Denominational Consultations. The Methodist Thorvald Källstad was one of its initiators in 1979. Once again the intention of this project was to achieve church unity at the denominational level. The denominations which were involved in the discussions this time were the United Methodist Church in Sweden, the Swedish Evangelical Mission, the Mission Covenant Church of Sweden and the Church of Sweden. The Baptist Union of Sweden was not involved but reactions came from it. David Lagergren gives his reaction to these talks:

> For many years more believers' baptisms have been conducted in the Mission Covenant Church of Sweden than in the Baptist Union of Sweden. It would therefore have serious consequences for the position of believers' baptism in Sweden, if the Mission Covenant Church of Sweden should be absorbed into such an ecumenical church where the pressure to practise infant baptism would be very strong.[191]

The existence of ecumenical congregations - belonging to both the Baptist Union of Sweden and the Mission Covenant Church of Sweden - makes the situation, according to Lagergren, even more problematic, "if the Mission Covenant Church of Sweden should go in one direction and the Baptist Union of Sweden in another."[192]

Of course baptism, infant baptism and/or believers' baptism, was a problem in this ecumenical context. Only too soon these preparations broke down and the Quadrilateral Denominational Consultations remained nothing more than an idea.

The Church of Sweden and the Mission Covenant Church of

1971, pp. 172f., [årsbok]; *Svenska Baptistsamfundet,* 1972-1973, p. 171, [årsbok]; Nicklasson, Gösta, *Missionsförbundet och ekumeniken,* 1971, pp. 29-101; "Ekumenik på 80-talet", [editorial], *VP,* No. 44, 1978, p. 2; Freij, Torbjörn, "Uppbrott, kollaps och sedan...? Så växte det frikyrkliga samarbetet fram – del II", *VP,* No. 45, 1978, p. 10.

[190] Bergsten, Torsten, *Frikyrkor i samverkan,* 1995, p. 281. Parenthetically I want to mention a document of 1995, which once again is another expression of ecumenical strivings of the three "old" denominations, see *Gemensam tro,* 1995.

[191] Lagergren, David, "Fyrsamfundsamtal?", *VP,* No. 11, 1979, p. 2.

[192] Ibid.

Sweden had, however, carried on another dialogue, started in 1964, i.e. even some years before the Trilateral Denominational Consultations had started and the proposal for the talks between four denominations was first mentioned.[193]

The already mentioned Free Christian Student Association, which ought to be studied more closely, must be briefly discussed here.[194] This organization started in 1912, and it published 1917-1922 the periodical *Frikyrklig Tidskrift* (the Free Church Journal),[195] followed by *Frikyrklig Ungdom* (Free Church Youth), 1923-1971. The name changed in 1954 to *Kristet Forum* (Christian Forum).[196] The editorial

---

[193] Ulla Bardh writes that the Mission Covenant Church of Sweden and the Church of Sweden have been conducting a dialogue with each other since 1964. Already during the period of the Trilateral Denominational Consultations "the double dialogue" of the Mission Covenant Church of Sweden was questioned in Free Church circles. Bardh, Ulla, "Preliminär skrivning av idépapper om SMF och ekumeniken med anledning av det s.k. folkrörelseprojektet 'Ju mer vi är tillsammans...', där SMF representerar väckelserörelserna", [s.a.], p. 16, [unpublished paper]. And in 1966 the direction of the Mission Covenant Church of Sweden was the subject of discussion in among other things *Svensk Veckotidning;* See also *Liv och frihet,* 1978, pp. 174f.; Nicklasson, Gösta, *Missionsförbundet och ekumeniken,* 1971, pp. 102-136. Concerning the talks between the Church of Sweden and the Mission Covenant Church of Sweden (1964-1970), see *Samtal om samverkan,* 1971. And as far as concerns the Church of Sweden and its dialogues, see for example also Fagerberg, Holsten, *Svenska kyrkan i ekumeniska samtal,* 1987:1.

[194] In 1966 it changed its name to *Frikyrkliga Studentrörelsen* (the Free Church Student Movement). Bergsten writes that the Free Christian Student Movement sometimes has been a disturbing source of new ideas (*obekväm idégivare*) for the Swedish Free Church movement during its almost 70 years. In 1971 the Free Church Student Movement ceased to exist as a Free Church organization and founded, together with *kyrkliga studentrörelsen* (the youth movement of the Church of Sweden), *Kristna Studentrörelsen i Sverige* (KRISS), (the Student Christian Movement in Sweden). Bergsten, Torsten, *Frikyrkor i samverkan,* 1995, p. 161. See also ibid. pp. 22-32; Bergsten, Torsten, "Ekumenik, vision och verklighet", *Tro och Liv,* No. 1, 1986, p. 9. *Fria Kristliga Gymnasiströrelsen (FKG),* (the Free Christian Secondary School Movement), started in 1915 may also be mentioned. Bergsten, Torsten, *Frikyrkor i samverkan,* 1995, p. 24.

[195] Lagergren, David, *Framgångstid med dubbla förtecken,* 1989, pp. 151f. Bergsten gives, however, the years 1918-1922, Bergsten, Torsten, *Frikyrkor i samverkan,* 1995, p. 24.

[196] Ibid.

staff of this periodical were N.J. Nordström (Baptist Union of Sweden), S. Wisborg (Mission Covenant Church of Sweden) and A. Strömstedt (United Methodist Church in Sweden). It was in the spring of 1918 that these men proposed that a Free Church Co-operation Committee should be appointed, which also happened.[197]

It is obvious that the questions of baptism and church unity were discussed in all this. In the following sections I will give some examples of this.

9.3. Free Church Identity Studies and Ecumenical Studies/ Consultations on Baptism

The questions of baptism, infant baptism, believers' baptism and "re-baptism", as well as the position of children in the congregation, were in the course of the 1930's and above all during the 1940's and 1950's discussed in Europe. All this resulted in studies, discussions, consultations, dialogues, publications etc., on baptism. All this also made an impact on the Baptist movements, with implications and consequences in the 1960's and later. The discussions about baptism were to a great extent caused by the questioning of infant baptism on biblical and theological grounds by Karl Barth and Emil Brunner. The Baptist Union of Sweden has, as has earlier been remarked, also been involved in and influenced directly and indirectly by national and international debates, dialogues and works on theological and ecumenical issues.[198]

The question of identity and the new ecumenical situation, not least because of the ecumenical congregations,[199] resulted in important studies within *Sveriges Frikyrkoråd* (the Swedish Free Church Council). Working parties produced two documents,

---

[197] Lagergren, David, *Framgångstid med dubbla förtecken*, 1989, pp. 151f.

[198] We can note that Karl Barth's book, *Die kirchliche Lehre von der Taufe*, 1947, was published in Swedish by the Baptists' publishing company *Westerbergs* in Stockholm, with the title *Det kristna dopet*, 1949. See also Johannes Schneider, one of the Baptists who together with George Raymond Beasley-Murray has given baptism a sacramental interpretation. Kurt Aland, Oscar Cullmann, Joachim Jeremias among others have in different ways also made contributions to the discussion about baptism in general and to the debate for and against infant baptism in particular.

[199] See chapter 9.5. below.

Gemensam grund (Common Foundation), 1963, and *Gemensam väg* (Common Path), 1968. They were of great consequence for subsequent developments and partly indicated how much the Swedish Free Churches had in common theologically, partly that there were also dividing lines.

In *Gemensam grund*,[200] in which the former General Secretary David Lagergren among others participated,[201] a theological foundation for an enlarged co-operation between the Free Churches, including the Baptist Union is presented.[202] On the whole there is a far-reaching unity on theological matters, even if there are different accents. In *Gemensam grund* both the agreements and the differences of opinion in the denominations are shown. Concerning the struggle for Christian unity, four phases are outlined: 1) an invisible unity in Christ, 2) an initial visible unity between individuals and between denominations, 3) a deepened visible unity, 4) the final unity in Jesus Christ.[203] The question of baptism is discussed and it is a theological issue which is regarded as a serious problem in a Free Church co-operation, aiming at a real unity.[204] The mode of baptism is discussed, as well as the question of baptism and congregation, and the connection of baptism with the Holy Spirit. *Gemensam grund* gives support to both believers' baptism and infant baptism.[205] As for the meaning of

---

200 *Gemensam grund* was published on the initiative of the Swedish Free Church Council. Concerning the background to this study, see Nicklasson, Gösta, *Missionsförbundet och ekumeniken*, 1971; Cedersjö, Björn, "På väg till enhet i tron!? Ef. 4:13. En kartläggning och analys av ett antal lärosamtal (åren 1963-1988) där frikyrkorna i Sverige deltagit", 1989, pp. 4, 11, [unpublished paper]; Bergsten, Torsten, *Frikyrkor i samverkan*, 1995, p. 171.

201 The working party consisted of Thorvald Källstad (United Methodist Church in Sweden), David Lagergren (Baptist Union of Sweden), Lars Lindberg (Mission Covenant Church of Sweden), Hårold Norburg (Swedish Holiness Mission), Folke Thorell (Örebro (Baptist) Mission), Stig Wikström (Swedish Alliance Mission).

202 In the preface it is said that it is hoped that the book will lead to discussions and studies within the Swedish Free Churches and perhaps even in the Church of Sweden about the Christian faith and Christian unity. *Gemensam grund*, 1963, p. 6.

203 Ibid. pp. 43ff.

204 Ibid. p. 35.

205 Ibid. pp. 29-36.

baptism *Gemensam grund* discerns three main interpretations: 1) Baptism is regarded as a gift of God, an action of God. The emphasis is on what God does and gives. Baptism is regarded as a means of grace, and this view of baptism is described as sacramental. 2) Baptism is regarded as a confession of faith and obedience, a confirmation of conversion. The emphasis is on man, what man does. God is, however, not understood as passive. He gives a particular blessing to those who confess and obey. This view is called symbolic. Baptism is not a means of salvation. 3) Baptism is regarded as an act of blessing. Baptism is neither a means of salvation nor a confession of faith. The emphasis is on conversion and personal faith.[206] It is stated that baptism for the Free Churches is necessary for membership of a congregation, but "that *membership* in exceptional cases can be acquired *without baptism.* "[207] It is mentioned that many congregations have introduced open Holy Communion,[208] for the same motives as those given by Erik Rudén (1906-1987) 15 years earlier.[209]

As concerns children and the question of infant baptism, the report says:

> The Free Church view on children is largely uniform and that according to this view children are like the rest of humanity under the rule of sin and death. They have, however, not yet committed any personal sins. The Kingdom of God belongs to children, and therefore they do not need to be baptized, to be delivered from original sin. On this basic view among other things infant baptism as well as believers' baptism are justified in the Free Churches. The argument for practising infant baptism is that the Kingdom of God belongs to them.[210]

---

[206] Ibid. pp. 31f.

[207] "... men att *medlemskap* undantagsvis kan vinnas *utan dop*". Ibid. p. 34. Italics mine.

[208] Ibid. p. 38, see also pp. 37-39.

[209] See Lagergren, David, *Förändringstid*, 1994, p. 230. The utterance by Rudén in 1948 - see Rudén, Erik, "Samarbete mellan de frikyrkliga", *Tro och Liv*, No. 7/8, 1948, pp. 305-312, discussed more below - is one example of the significance a leader's words can have. It indicates what the role and function of a leader as authority can imply - positively or negatively. (Of course "timing" sometimes also plays a certain role, i.e. the leader says something which is right in time.)

[210] *Gemensam grund*, 1963, p. 31.

We here meet the questions of anthropology and ecclesiology, which will be discussed more below.

We find for example the following significant observations in this report: every view of believers' baptism cannot be looked upon as symbolic; further every view of infant baptism cannot be looked upon as sacramental.[211] It is also indicated in the report that dividing lines and different opinions, concerning for example baptism, are to be found not only between the denominations but also within one and the same denomination.[212] From this the conclusion is drawn that practical co-operation can take place in several areas in spite of differences of opinion and that the question of baptism in the long run calls for renewed common Bible study. This is necessary in order to create a solid basis for the unity of the Free Churches.[213] It is also said:

> In the first place we are of the opinion that if real unity shall be achieved in the Swedish Free Churches, it is necessary that the doctrinal questions are treated with greater seriousness and care... Secondly, we are of the opinion that it is desirable that the denominations continue with official and/or unofficial discussions with each other on the question of unity.[214]

In short, a serious desire for unity is expressed.

What happened after this? Perhaps the period immediately afterwards could be called a period of consideration and reflexion before another study started which resulted in the document *Gemensam väg* in 1968.[215]

In *Gemensam väg*,[216] reflection on baptism was deepened. One

---

[211] Ibid. p. 32.

[212] Ibid.pp. 35f.

[213] Ibid. p. 36.

[214] Ibid. pp. 45.f.

[215] Eckerdal writes, however: "The immediate result of the report was silence, but the Free Church Council decided, however, to continue the study through a considerably enlarged theological working party with members nominated by the member denominations. The main issue was how to overcome the conflicts among others on the question of baptism. When the report was to be published in 1968, it was called *Gemensam väg*." Eckerdal, Lars, *Vägen in i kyrkan,* 1981, p. 395.

[216] *Gemensam väg* is like *Gemensam grund* published on the initiative of the Swedish Free Church Council. The theological working party behind the former consisted of 18 persons. From the Baptist Union of Sweden, Torsten

part of the article called *Dopet* (Baptism) is about baptism in the New Testament, the other about baptism in Swedish Free Churches, where different views on the question of baptism are brought together.[217] It is stated in the report, that there are still conflicts of opinion concerning the question of baptism between the denominations, but in spite of different views of baptism and varying practice the different denominations co-operate.[218] Some proposals for achieving Free Church unity are also presented in the book. One of the proposed ways towards this church unity is both infant baptism and believers baptism taking place within the same congregation.[219] The question of open Holy Communion is once again discussed. It is also recommended.[220]

A book which also ought to be briefly mentioned in this context is *En bok om dopet i ekumenisk belysning* (A Book on Baptism from the Ecumenical Point of View), 1965.[221] In the preface to this book

---

Bergsten, Ruben Janarv, David Lagergren; Örebro (Baptist) Mission, Linné Eriksson, Gösta Tunehag; the Mission Covenant Church of Sweden, Gösta Hedberg, Sven Hemrin, Lars Lindberg; Swedish Alliance Mission, Knut Svensson, Stig Wikström; Swedish Salvation Army, Folke Holmlund; Scandinavian Independent Baptist Union, August Peterson, Halvard Åberg; Swedish Holiness Mission, Stig Abrahamsson, Härold Norburg; the United Methodist Church in Sweden, Thorvald Källstad, chairman, Gunnar Larsson, Torsten Wedar. On this study see also Cedersjö, Björn, "På väg till enhet i tron!? Ef. 4:13. En kartläggning och analys av ett antal lärosamtal (åren 1963-1988) där frikyrkorna i Sverige deltagit", 1989, pp. 4, 11 [unpublished paper]; Bergsten, Torsten, *Frikyrkor i samverkan*, 1995, p. 171.

[217] *Gemensam väg*, 1968, pp. 27-34.

[218] Ibid. pp. 33f. See the preface by Thorvald Källstad, ibid. p. 9; Eckerdal, Lars, *Vägen in i kyrkan*, 1981, p. 395.

[219] *Gemensam väg*, 1968, pp. 62f. Besides the proposal already mentioned (2. about various baptismal practices within one and the same congregation), there are: 1. Associative membership. 3. Open membership without infant baptism. 4. Two congregations in one church building. 5. One congregation affiliated to two or more denominations. 6. Congregations with different baptismal practices within one and the same denomination. 7. An autonomous ecumenical congregation. Ibid. pp. 61-67.

[220] Ibid. p. 39.

[221] In this book there are contributions and commentaries by the following: from the Baptist Union of Sweden, Torsten Bergsten, Bert Franzén; the Mission Covenant Church of Sweden, Sven Hemrin; the United Methodist Church in Sweden, Thorvald Källstad; the Pentecostal Movement, Willis Säwe; the

the hope is expressed by Torsten Bergsten that the book will create a salutary ecumenical unease within Swedish Christianity. It is said that every denomination basing itself on the New Testament professes *one* baptism. In spite of this the sacrament of unity has, however, been one of the stumbling blocks in the way of the work towards Christian unity.[222]

The issue of baptism also turns up in three famous consultations at Graninge outside Stockholm. These conferences, *Graninge I* (1974), *II* (1976) and *III* (1979), were arranged by *Svenska Ekumeniska Nämnden* (the Swedish Ecumenical Council). The impetus for them came from the charismatic movement and *riksmötet* (the National Christian Conference) in Gothenburg 1972, called *G 72*, which may be called another milestone in the ecumenical process in Sweden.[223] At the National Christian Conference in Gothenburg, it was recommended that the question

---

Church of Sweden, Anders Nygren, Kjell Byström, Ludvig Jönsson and Edvin Larsson. The first part of this book about the meaning of baptism is a translation of the last part, *The Meaning of Baptism* in the Faith and Order report *One Lord, One Baptism*, 1960. There is also an introduction by Bishop Anders Nygren, the Church of Sweden. The second part has the title *Svensk dopdebatt* (Swedish Debates on Baptism). Representatives of five different churches/denominations write concerning the view and practice of baptism in their own church in the light of the document *The Meaning of Baptism*. The third part is a translation of *Ye Are Baptized*, 1961. This is a survey by Lukas Vischer of the practice and view of baptism and confirmation in most of the different church traditions in the world.

222 *En bok om dopet i ekumenisk belysning*, 1965, p. 8. Bert Franzén also makes a contribution to this book and writes an article called *Dopet som kallelse och gåva* (Baptism as Call and Gift). He writes concerning the report *The Meaning of Baptism*: "There is reason to ask whether the consensus reached in the work of the commission is not ultimately from an ecumenical viewpoint an illusion, in the sense that the different denominations draw very different practical conclusions from the common foundation... The problems one wanted to avoid are still left, the work of the commission helps us to tackle them from a new angle." Franzén, Bert, "Dopet som kallelse och gåva", *En bok om dopet i ekumenisk belysning*, 1965, p. 63.

223 See Bergsten, Torsten, *Frikyrkor i samverkan*, 1995, pp. 124f. *Svenska Baptistsamfundet*, 1973-1974, pp. 169-170, pp. 187-188, [årsbok]; The National Christian Conferences were: "G 72" in Göteborg 1972, "V 77" in Västerås 1977, "J 83" in Jönköping 1983 and "Ö 89" in Örebro 1989. These National Christian Conferences can be seen as a sort of continuation of the report of the Free Church Conferences ended in 1969. See also Bergsten, Torsten, "Ekumenik, vision och verklighet", *Tro och Liv*, No. 1, 1986, p. 9.

of baptism ought to be brought up in discussions between the Swedish churches and denominations.[224] The Swedish Ecumenical Council invited representatives to a conference about this in 1974 at Graninge.

In Gothenburg the initial idea was to hold that baptism is the foundation of unity in Christ. The question which first and foremost according to *G 72* was to be answered at the recommended conference was "if unity in the question of baptism was a precondition for intercommunion."[225]

Graninge I 1974, had the theme *Dopet i kyrkornas gemenskap* (Baptism in the Fellowship of Churches). This was in fact the first Swedish ecumenical conference with baptism as its theme. The purpose of this conference was: 1) to bring ecumenical work on the question of baptism, which in Sweden had resulted in the book *En bok om dopet i ekumenisk belysning*, 1965, to the fore once more. 2) to actualise, starting from the New Testament, different interpretations of baptism and at the same time to test critically the different opinions in the light of the word of Scriptures and the testimony of the Spirit. 3) to try to find formulations which express both common and divergent positions.[226]

---

[224] See "Konferens kring temat 'Dopet i kyrkornas gemenskap'", 1974, p. 1, [conference documentation]. See also "Utkast till rapport till V-77. Dopet och de kristnas enhet", 1976, p. 1, [conference documentation].

[225] "... om enighet i dopfrågan är en förutsättning för gemensamt nattvardsfirande." "Konferens kring temat 'Dopet i kyrkornas gemenskap'", 1974, p. 1, [conference documentation]. See also Karlsson, Birgit, "G 72 -en manifestation av enhet", *Året*, 1972, pp. 17-23. A committee report may be mentioned, *Gemensamt nattvardsfirande*, 1975, which after "G 72" dealt with the issue of whether a common view of baptism is a condition for shared Holy Communion, where particularly the practice of "re-baptism" is pointed out as an ecumenical problem. It states that in principle baptism is understood as a condition for admission to Holy Communion. *Gemensamt nattvardsfirande*, 1975, p. 231. Further writings about baptism in Sweden in the 1970's, *Dopet - en Guds gåva*, 2nd ed., 1975; (see a comment by Lagergren on this book, Lagergren, David, "Tro och dop", *VP*, No. 3, 1975, p. 2); *Kyrkan och dopet*, 1974; Ruuth, Anders, *Dopets rikedom enligt Bibeln och bekännelseskrifterna*, 1975; Petersson, Kjell, *Kyrkan, folket och dopet*, 1977; Brodd, Sven-Erik, *Dop och kyrkotillhörighet enligt Svenska kyrkans ordning*, 1978, pp. 16-19; Brodd, Sven-Erik, *Dop - Kyrka - Struktur*, 1980, pp. 9-15; *Ekumenisk samsyn om dop och kyrkotillhörighet*, 1978, which is a dialogue between the Church of Sweden and the Roman Catholic Diocese of Stockholm.

[226] "Konferens kring temat 'dopet i kyrkornas gemenskap'", 1974, p. 1, [conference documentation].

At this conference about 60 people participated, representing different denominations. The representatives from the Baptist Union were the principal of the *Betelseminariet* Bert Franzén (b. 1926) and senior lecturer Torsten Bergsten. Bert Franzén contributed with an introductory talk about *Dopet som ekumeniskt problem* (Baptism as an Ecumenical Problem).[227] And Torsten Bergsten gave a lecture about *Dopet i internationell belysning* (Baptism in an International Perspective).[228]

In the conference statement it is said that the talks have been held in an open atmosphere and have pointed to convergence on the central meaning of baptism. Conscious that there nevertheless are various opinions on important questions, they want to continue with talks in the hope of attaining the unity in understanding and practice that the Bible presupposes and has in view.[229]

Bert Franzén gave afterwards a presentation and analysis of the conference in the article *Dopet som gemenskapsfaktor* (Baptism as a Community Creating Factor).[230] He is of the opinion that the conference only partially realised its aim. He wants to characterize the conference more as a beginning than a terminal point.[231]

In 1976 it was time for *Graninge II*. The Swedish Ecumenical Council also arranged this. Its purpose can be seen as a continuation of *Graninge I*. The theme was *Tron och dopet* (Faith and Baptism). Also at this conference about 60 people participated, representing different denominations. The representatives from the Baptist Union of Sweden were the General Secretary David Lagergren, the principal Bert Franzén, pastor Ruben Janarv (b.

---

227 Franzén discusses baptism and church membership and the problem of "re-baptism". Franzén, Bert, "Inledningsanförande till grupparbete: Dopet som ekumeniskt problem", 1974, p. 23, [conference documentation].

228 Bergsten, Torsten, "Dopet i internationell belysning", 1974, pp. 33f., [conference documentation].

229 "Uttalande från konferensen (1974-12-13)", 1974, p. 57, [conference documentation].

230 Franzén, Bert, "Dopet som gemenskapsfaktor", *Tro och Liv*, No. 5, 1975, pp. 194-197.

231 Ibid. 195; see also Franzén, Bert, "Dopet i kyrkornas gemenskap", [editorial], *VP*, No. 1/2, 1975, pp. 2, 14; Arvidson, Thorvald, "Dopet – gemenskap eller söndring", *VP*, No. 1/2, 1975, p. 3.

1926) and New Testament Scholar, David Hellholm (b. 1941).[232] David Lagergren spoke on the subject *Är en gemensam dopsyn en förutsättning för gemensamt nattvardsfirande?* (Is a Common View of Baptism a Condition for Open Holy Communion?)[233] David Hellholm delivered a lecture on the subject *Pistis - baptisma. Ett försök att analysera trons förhållande till dopet utifrån Rom 6* (Pistis - Baptisma. An Attempt to Analyse the Relation of Faith to Baptism from Rom. 6).

Hellholm abandons a traditional Baptist theological outlook and is an example of a more pluralistic, open-minded attitude. He says that in the same way as we today are clear that there is not *one* christology, nor *one* ecclesiology, nor *one* understanding of faith in the New Testament, the realisation that we do not either have *one* theology of baptism in the New Testament is beginning to make itself felt. That *one* theology of baptism does not exist does not, of course, make the situation easier.[234]

As a result of *Graninge II* a preliminary report was sent to the National Christian Conference in Västerås 1977 (called *V 77*). It is said in this report:

> Formerly people met in controversial talks where each side tried to prove that the other side was wrong. Nowadays we are in the process of trying to understand and learn from each other. This atmosphere of mutual confidence has characterized these Graninge-conferences.[235]

---

[232] At this conference Torsten Bergsten did not participate. We can also observe that there is no woman representing the Baptist Union of Sweden.

[233] Lagergren, David, "Är en gemensam dopsyn en förutsättning för gemensamt nattvardsfirande?", 1976, pp. 1-2, [conference documentation]. This question was originally the reason for the Graninge conference about baptism. The talk by Lagergren was an introduction to the work of a particular committee. He writes: "Open Holy Communion amongst Baptists is a clear negative answer to the question of whether a common view of baptism is a presupposition for intercommunion... The division in baptismal practice is painful, not least, for Baptists". ("Den 'öppna kommunionen' bland baptisterna utgör alltså ett klart nej-svar på frågan om gemensam dopsyn är en förutsättning för gemensamt nattvardsfirande... Dock upplevs klyftan i doppraxis smärtsam, inte minst för baptister, och vi ser fram mot den dag, hur nära eller avlägsen den än må vara, då dopet återställts till sin ursprungliga enhet.") Ibid. p. 2.

[234] Hellholm, David, "Pistis - baptisma. Ett försök att analysera trons förhållande till dopet utifrån Rom 6", 1976, p. 1, [conference documentation].

[235] "Förr möttes man i stridssamtal där vardera parten bara försökte bevisa att den andre hade fel. Nu håller vi på att förstå och lära av varandra. Denna

It is further said in the report that the Baptists declared openly, during the two above-mentioned conferences *Graninge I* and *II*, the difficulties they themselves have in putting their view of baptism into practice. The Baptists said that the new insights they have about both the semi- and unconscious levels of the psyche and about man's dependence upon the environment he lives in have made it more difficult to decide when a personal faith exists.

And what is to be said to a person, who in the light of new faith-experiences doubts that the faith in which he/she once as a youth was baptized, actually was worthy of the name Christian faith?[236]

We do find some openings, which are of interest from ecumenical and theological perspectives.

I want to say something briefly about the last Graninge-conference in 1979. *Graninge III* had the theme *Att tillhöra Guds folk - om tro och kyrkotillhörighet* (Belonging to the People of God - Faith and Church-Membership).[237] About 70 people participated, from leading and responsible positions in the Swedish churches and denominations.[238] Once again almost all the Christian churches and denominations were represented. From the Baptist Union of Sweden we find Torsten Bergsten, who delivered an introductory lecture on the theme *Kyrkotillhörighet - medlemskap - bekännelse*

---

atmosfär av ömsesidigt förtroende satte sin prägel på Graninge-konferenserna." "Utkast till rapport till V-77. Dopet och de kristnas enhet", 1976, p. 3, [conference documentation].

[236] "Och vad säger man till en människa som i ljuset av nya troserfarenheter råkar i tvivel om att den tro, som hon en gång i ungdomen blev döpt på, verkligen var värd att kallas en kristen tro?" Ibid. pp. 3f. See also Lagergren who writes on *Graninge II*, that the representatives of the Baptist denominations declared in a statement, that there is a largely common view of baptismal doctrine but this cannot be applied to infant baptism, that infant baptism is not a biblical baptism. Lagergren, David, "Dopsamtal", *VP*, No. 3, 1977, p. 2.

[237] See *Tro och Liv*, No. 1, 1980, which contains all the lectures and section-reports from *Graninge III*.

[238] Among others the then General Mission Secretary within the Mission Covenant Church of Sweden, Lars Lindberg participated. He gave an introductory lecture about *Folkkyrka – folkrörelse* (National Church - Popular Movement), Lindberg, Lars, "Folkkyrka - folkrörelse", *Tro och Liv*, No. 1, 1980, pp. 20-26, and professor Per Erik Persson gave a lecture *Att tillhöra Guds folk* (To Belong to God's People), Persson, Per Erik, "Att tillhöra Guds folk", *Tro och Liv*, No. 1, 1980, pp. 4-11.

(Church belonging - Membership - Confession).[239] He discusses the subject from two viewpoints: partly in a concrete, practical-theological material from the Swedish Free Church world at this time, partly as a theological reflection on the ecumenical development which the material reflects. These reflections result partially according to Bergsten in a modest contribution to a Catholic-Baptist dialogue.[240] Once again the issue of baptism was treated.

In the two last mentioned conferences, *Graninge II* and *Graninge III*, it was said that baptism was not an isolated event but a process.[241]

Still another report from the Örebro (Baptist) Mission can be added. It is a study about baptism, *Vattnet som förenar och skiljer* (Water Which Unites and Divides).[242] Questions are arising, it is said, on the local ecumenical level, where Christians from different baptismal traditions and different views of congregation are meeting. In this report there is a discussion about this, the interpretation of baptism and about baptismal practice in an ecumenical perspective. It is also stated that the document may also be seen in an international perspective, that baptism during recent decades has been an issue dealt with in the churches worldwide. "One expression of this is the current report 'Baptism, Eucharist and Ministry'".[243] This report has, of course, been of interest to the Baptist Union of Sweden and other denominations.[244]

---

[239] Bergsten, Torsten, "Kyrkotillhörighet - medlemskap - bekännelse", *Tro och Liv*, No. 1, 1980, pp. 33ff.

[240] Ibid. p. 33. We will have an opportunity to come back to this lecture. See Part III, chapter 8.2.2.

[241] See also for example Svensson, Nils-Eije, "'Att tillhöra Guds folk' - Graninge III handlade om tro och kyrkotillhörighet", *Tro och Liv*, No. 1, 1980, pp. 2f.

[242] *Vattnet som förenar och skiljer*, 2nd ed., 1986. This report is also in *Enade och åtskilda*, 1989, pp. 13-72. The working party consisted of Lennart Thörn (chairman), David Allén, Sune Fahlgren, Hans Lundin, Joel Sahlberg, Tord Ström and Bo Wettéus.

[243] *Vattnet som förenar och skiljer*, 2nd ed., 1986, p. 48.

[244] See for example Bergsten, Torsten, "Öppet nattvardsbord, överfört medlemskap och en öppen baptism", *VP*, No. 3, 1986, p. 6; "Öppning om dopet", *VP*, No. 24/25, 1986, p. 2; Juhlin, Lars, "Behövs dopet?", *VP*, No. 40, 1989, p. 7; Selinder, Per-Magnus, "Öppning i dopfrågan", *Svensk Veckotidning*,

In order to understand the ecumenical strivings and especially the development of the ecumenical congregations better, there is reason to concentrate particularly on the relations of the Baptist Union of Sweden to two denominations. They are the Örebro (Baptist) Mission and the Mission Covenant Church of Sweden, which will be dealt with in the next section, together with the relation to the Pentecostal Movement.

9.4. Relations between the Baptist Union of Sweden and Some Other Denominations

9.4.1. Relations between the Baptist Union of Sweden and the Pentecostal Movement and the Örebro (Baptist) Mission – Attempts at Reunion

After the sections about divisions in the Baptist movement, we should look at some attempts at reunification within the Baptist movement.

In the years 1916-1919 the Baptist Union of Sweden tried to reunite with the Pentecostal Movement, partly through the efforts of Pastor John Ongman who in 1916 tried to get the Pentecostal congregations back into the Baptist Union, and partly through the Annual Conference of the Baptist Union in 1919. These efforts failed. The failure was due among other things to the Pentecostal view of the independent local church (samfundsfria församlingen).[245] In the year 1919 Lewi Pethrus discussed Christian unity in his book De kristnas enhet (Christian Unity). Unity of the Spirit is according to Pethrus the only foundation of Christian unity.[246]

No. 22, 1986, p. 2.

[245] Concerning the attempt of the Baptist Union to reunite with the Pentecostal Movement 1916-1919, and the answer of Lewi Pethrus, see Struble, Rhode, Den samfundsfria församlingen och de karismatiska gåvorna och tjänsterna, 1982, pp. 36-53.

[246] Pethrus, Lewi, "De kristnas enhet. Kan detta mål nås genom de moderna samfundsorganisationerna?", Pethrus, Lewi, Samlade skrifter, Band 4, 1958, pp. 129-179. See also Struble, Rhode, Den samfundsfria församlingen och de karismatiska gåvorna och tjänsterna, 1982, pp. 145f.; Bergsten, Torsten, "Samfundsmedvetande och kongregationalism i svensk frikyrklighet", Kyrkohistorisk årsskrift 93, 1993, pp. 136f.

During the 1930's, when the division between the Örebro (Baptist) Mission and the Baptist Union occurred, there were ecumenical strivings to unite the congregations which left the Baptist Union with the Pentecostal Movement. Lewi Pethrus and the Pentecostal Movement thus tried, after a time of isolation and an ecumenically negative view, to unite the Örebro (Baptist) Mission and the Pentecostal Movement in 1937/1938, but without any success.[247] After this failure with the Örebro (Baptist) Mission, new attempts were made. The Pentecostal Movement and the Baptist Union approached each other. Lewi Pethrus made once again an initial contact. As one reason for this unity Pethrus mentioned the common method and view of baptism. The term *döparenhet (Baptist unity)* was used.[248] In 1944 a conference of Baptist movements took place. There were participants from the Baptist Union of Sweden, the Scandinavian Independent Baptist Union, the Swedish Holiness Mission, the Örebro (Baptist) Mission and the Pentecostal Movement at this conference in Filadelfiakyrkan in Stockholm.[249] Other conferences also between Baptist congregations *(döparförsamlingar)* took place that year,[250] and in the following years. For example representatives of Pentecostal congregations and the congregations co-operating with the Örebro (Baptist) Mission met in Örebro in 1946 at a conference on mutual understanding. But it did not result in the denominations being united.[251] And the

---

[247] Lagergren writes that the question about Baptist unity was remarkably enough first put by Pethrus already in 1937. Lagergren, David, "Svenska baptistsamfundet och Örebromissionen - En tillbakablick", VP, No. 7, 1985, p. 12; Struble, Rhode, *Den samfundsfria församlingen och de karismatiska gåvorna och tjänsterna*, 1982, pp. 154-160.

[248] See Alf Lindberg who describes the Baptist attempts at unity during the 1930's and 1940's, Lindberg, Alf, *Väckelse, frikyrklighet, pingströrelse*, 1985, pp. 220-223; Struble, Rhode, *Den samfundsfria församlingen och de karismatiska gåvorna och tjänsterna*, 1982, pp. 166ff.; Lagergren, David, *Förändringstid*, 1994, p. 220, p. 231; Lagergren, David, "Från Wiberg till Pethrus", VP, No. 45, 1985, p. 6.

[249] Bergsten, Torsten, *Frikyrkor i samverkan*, 1995, pp. 186ff.

[250] Lagergren mentions for example conferences in Ludvika and Örnsköldsvik in 1944. Lagergren, David, *Förändringstid*, 1994, p. 231, see also pp. 231ff.; Struble, Rhode, *Den samfundsfria församlingen och de karismatiska gåvorna och tjänsterna*, 1982, pp. 166ff. We may call to mind the Free Christian National Conference, which also took place the same year, in 1944.

[251] *Enhetskonferensen i Örebro*, 1946; Struble, Rhode, *Den samfundsfria*

attempt at uniting the Baptist Union and the Örebro (Baptist) Mission had also to wait.[252]

It might be said that during a long period the situation in one way has been the same, i.e. that the Baptist Union of Sweden has not been able to integrate with other denominations on the denominational level. There was, however, a tendency towards change within the Baptist Union. It concerned among other things the relation to the Örebro (Baptist) Mission.

Before the Trilateral Denominational Consultations took place between 1969-1971, another round of talks took place between the Baptist Union and the Örebro (Baptist) Mission. In 1965 the Board of the Baptist Union of Sweden took the initiative for a dialogue with the Örebro (Baptist) Mission. We can note that the bilateral talks between the Baptist Union and the Örebro (Baptist) Mission went on 1965-1969. In 1969 the talks about a common Free Church were, however, interrupted, and this, some argue, on account of the participation of the Baptist Union in the Trilateral Denominational Consultations.[253] In 1976, some years after the Trilateral Denominational Consultations were "ended", the conversations between the Baptist Union and the Örebro (Baptist) Mission, interrupted in 1969, were resumed.

In 1983 the Baptist Union of Sweden and the Örebro (Baptist) Mission had a partially common Annual Conference, the first since the division into two mission societies in 1937.[254] And the first

församlingen och de karismatiska gåvorna och tjänsterna, 1982, pp. 174ff. This conference was according to Struble an internal agreement between the Pentecostal Movement and the Örebro (Baptist) Mission. But the question about organization, on both sides, was the great obstacle to a fusion between these two. Ibid. p. 177 and p. 179. See also Lagergren, David, *Förändringstid*, 1994, pp. 231-235; Bergsten, Torsten, *Frikyrkor i samverkan*, 1995, pp. 186f.

252 Lindberg, Alf, *Väckelse, frikyrklighet, pingströrelse*, 1985, pp. 220-223; Lagergren, David, *Förändringstid*, 1994, pp. 236ff.; Lagergren, David, "Svenska baptistsamfundet och Örebromissionen - En tillbakablick", *VP*, No. 7, 1985, p. 12.

253 *Tecken om enhet*, 1991, p. 5; Bergsten, Torsten, "På väg mot fördjupad gemenskap", *Dokument från Örebro*, 1969, pp. 61-78; Bergsten, Torsten, *Frikyrkor i samverkan*, 1995, pp. 163f.

254 "En historisk konferens?" [editorial], *VP*, No. 19/20, 1983, p. 2; See also "De har funnit varandra! Men hur går det för SB och ÖM?", *VP*, No. 21, 1983, p. 1; Wiktell, Sven, E., "Öppenhjärtig intervju. Hur ser missionsföreståndarna på de många arbetsuppgifterna?", Ibid. pp. 10-11; Wiktell, Sven, E., "Försoningens

common Conference of the Baptist Union of Sweden and the Örebro (Baptist) Mission was held in 1990.[255]

In 1986 the two Central Boards (missionsstyrelserna) of the Baptist Union and the Örebro (Baptist) Mission met for the first time to talk about mutual relations and tasks. From both denominations the idea was expressed that the aim of the work must be a fusion, a reunion, even if some hesitation also can be discerned.[256] It is interesting for instance to note the difference in the reports from *Veckoposten* and *Missionsbaneret* (the latter the organ of Örebro (Baptist) Mission). There are evidently different attitudes and the headlines speak their silent language. *Veckoposten* writes: "Co-operation strengthens links - A good omen for the future",[257] and in *Missionsbaneret* it is: "Örebro (Baptist) Mission and the Baptist Union in joint board meeting: What can

---

gemenskap vid Herrens bord", Ibid. pp. 3, 13.

See also Lagergren, David, "Svenska baptistsamfundet och Örebromissionen - En tillbakablick", VP, No. 7, 1985, p. 12, and also for instance Erik Sollerman who writes: "If the Baptist Union has changed its attitude towards the charismatic message, then the Örebro (Baptist) Mission has changed its attitude towards ecumenical co-operation and appears today as a very co-operative ecumenical fellowship." Further he states: "The conclusion of this attempt at an analysis is, however, that the Baptist Union and the Örebro (Baptist) Mission have been brought closer to each other and that which was a great problem in the 1930's is no longer relevant or separating." Sollerman, Erik, "Rent religiöst har ÖM och BM förts närmare varandra", VP, No. 28/29, 1979, p. 7; Sahlberg, Joel, "Svensk baptism i framtiden", VP, No. 1, 1979, p. 12; Freij, Torbjörn, "Tre baptistprofiler kommenterar 'baptistfederationen'", VP, No. 4, 1979, p. 10. Concerning the relation between the Baptist Union of Sweden and the Örebro (Baptist) Mission, and a historical background to both these denominations, see also Cedersjö, Björn, Fahlgren, Sune, "Från separation till växande gemenskap. Relationen Svenska Baptistsamfundet – Örebromissionen som den speglas i protokollen från samtalsdelegationen 1965-1986", 1987, [unpublished paper]; Enade och Åtskilda, 1989.

[255] "Två samfund", [editorial], VP, No. 23, 1990, p. 2; " -Så mycket gemensamt!", VP, No. 23, 1990, p. 1.

[256] Swedberg, Bo, "En historisk händelse - och sedan?" VP, No. 5, 1986, p. 2; Swedberg, Bo, "Det var missionsstyrelserna ense om: Praktisk samverkan förenar", VP, No. 5, 1986, p. 6; "Detta lovar en god fortsättning", VP, No. 5, 1986, p. 6; Lindström, Sven, "Jesusglöd i levande församlingar", VP, No. 5, 1986, p. 7. See also the discussion some years earlier, Lagergren, David, "ÖM och SB", VP, No. 4, 1981, p. 2.

[257] "Samverkan stärker banden - Bådar gott för framtiden", VP, No. 5, 1986, p. 1.

they both do together?"[258]

The conversations resumed in 1976 went on until the beginning of 1991.[259] Co-operation between the Baptist Union and the Örebro (Baptist) Mission was brought to the fore and a new kind of Baptist federation was proposed.[260] The talks continued thus until the beginning of 1991, when the leaders of the two denominations said that the bilateral talks should cease.[261] A fusion between the denominations did not seem at that time to be imminent. The development of an increasing number of ecumenical congregations was expected to lead to a possible broader solution,[262] a union consisting of the Baptist Union, the Mission Covenant Church of Sweden and the Örebro (Baptist) Mission. Voices critical of the fact, that the talks between the two involved denominations had ceased, are also to be discerned (see for instance in *Veckoposten*). Of course the questions of baptism and ecclesiology are involved, as well as the view of the Bible, in this discussion about church unity. Some are of the opinion that it is better to unite (first) with another Baptist denomination, i.e. with Örebro (Baptist) Mission, than with for instance the Mission Covenant Church of Sweden.[263]

---

[258] Ringsvåg, Ingemar, "ÖM och Baptistsamfundet i gemensamt styrelsemöte: Vad kan de båda göra tillsammans?", *Missionsbaneret*, No. 4, 1986, p. 3.

[259] *Tecken om enhet*, 1991, p. 5.

[260] See for example Cedersjö, Björn, Fahlgren, Sune, "Från separation till växande gemenskap. Relationen Svenska Baptistsamfundet – Örebromissionen som den speglas i protokollen från samtalsdelegationen 1965-1986", 1987, p. 20, [unpublished paper].

[261] A declaration was then made by the leaders (Sigvard Karlehagen, Gustav Sundström, Ingvar Paulsson, Birgit Karlsson), "Nu är tiden inne för nya perspektiv i enhetssamtalen", [Sigvard Karlehagen, Gustav Sundström, Ingvar Paulsson, Birgit Karlsson], *VP*, No. 12, 1991, p. 3.

[262] Ibid. See also "Mot nya horisonter?", [editorial], *VP*, No. 12, 1991, p. 2; Naess, Kurt, "Glädjande klarsyn", *VP*, No. 24, 1991, p. 8; Stenström, Tomas, "Till rätt adressat?", *VP*, No. 14, 1992, p. 4.

[263] See for example Mild, Ruben, "Var det nödvändigt?", *VP*, No. 18, 1991, p. 4; "Det uppgivna målet om enhet. Förenade församlingar beklagar deklaration", [Kent Malmqvist], *VP*, No. 21/22, 1991, p. 16; "Att missa målet", [Wilhelm Salomonson, Jan Lundahl, Ingrid Samuelsson], *VP*, No. 21/22, 1991, p. 16; Nordin, Nils, G., "Öppet brev om samverkan mellan samfunden", *VP*, No. 24, 1991, p. 8; Swedberg, Bo, "Kristianstad: Här fungerar en gemensam församling", *VP*, No. 11, 1992, pp. 8f.; Jansson, Martin, "Hur skall det bli med Baptistsamfundet?", *VP*, No. 15, 1992, p. 12; Roman, Bertil, "Tre bilder", *VP*,

The isolationist tendencies that guided the Örebro (Baptist) Mission in the 1930's have, however, evidently changed during later decades and the Örebro (Baptist) Mission has drawn nearer other denominations.

Another rapprochement between the Baptist Union of Sweden and the Örebro (Baptist) Mission may be pointed out, namely that the Baptist publishing house *Westerbergs Förlag*, which existed until 1985, merged with the publishing house of the Örebro (Baptist) Mission, *Libris*. The Örebro (Baptist) Mission (Interact) and the Baptist Union of Sweden have, however, not yet been united on the central "denominational" level.

9.4.2. Relations between the Baptist Union of Sweden and the Mission Covenant Church of Sweden

In this context we should say something more about the Mission Covenant Church of Sweden,[264] because this denomination, as well as the Örebro (Baptist) Mission, is dealt with especially in connection with ecumenical congregations later on in my study. The Mission Covenant Church of Sweden is not a Baptist but a Reformed-Lutheran denomination and is a member of the WCC.

There have been discussions between the Baptist Union of Sweden and the Mission Covenant Church of Sweden during recent decades. There has also been and there still is co-operation between these two denominations, particularly in the establishing of ecumenical congregations, in spite of (partially) different views of for instance baptism. We can note that some local congregations of the Mission Covenant Church of Sweden co-operate today also with the Church of Sweden,[265] and that the Mission Covenant Church of

---

No. 9, 1992, p. 12.

[264] Concerning the Mission Covenant Church of Sweden, see for example Eldebo, Runar, "Svenska Missionsförbundet", *Svenska Trossamfund*, 8th ed., 1990, pp. 57-63; *Liv och frihet*, 1978; Bredberg, William, *P.P. Waldenströms verksamhet till 1878*, 1948; Bredberg, William, *Sällskap - samfund - kyrka?*, 1962; Hermansson, Werner, *Enhetskyrka, folkväckelse, församlingsgemenskap*, 1968; Walan, Bror, *Församlingstanken i Svenska Missionsförbundet*, 1964; Walan, Bror, *Året 1878*, 1978; Walan, Bror, *Fernholm och frikyrkan*, 1962.

[265] Bergsten writes that the Mission Covenant Church of Sweden at the time of Örebro 1969 was involved in ecumenical talks with a number of Free Churches and also, since 1964, with the Church of Sweden. Bergsten, Torsten, *Frikyrkor i samverkan*, 1995, pp. 163f. See also Bardh, Ulla, "Preliminär skrivning av idépapper om SMF och ekumeniken med anledning av det s.k. folkrörelseprojektet 'Ju mer vi är tillsammans... ', där SMF representerar

Sweden has conducted official talks with the Catholic diocese of Stockholm.[266]

The Mission Covenant Church of Sweden was established in 1878 as a mission society, a breakaway from the Swedish Evangelical Mission.[267] It was as a matter of fact from the beginning something more than a mere mission society within the Church of Sweden and became gradually a congregationalist denomination. Two of the then leaders had been priests in the State Church, Paul Peter Waldenström (1838-1917) and Erik Jakob Ekman (1842-1915). In opposition to the Swedish Evangelical Mission one of these leaders of the Mission Covenant Church of Sweden, P.P. Waldenström, taught the doctrine of subjective atonement. These two prominent figures within the Mission Covenant Church of Sweden held, general speaking, two different views of baptism, and the Mission Covenant Church of Sweden has thus since its beginnings had a Baptist vein. This depends above all on E.J. Ekman and A. Fernholm who argued for believers' baptism.[268] P.P. Waldenström pleaded, however, for infant baptism.[269] Waldenström held the opinion that in order to be allowed access to Holy Communion it was enough to be a believer - to be baptized was thus not necessary. After many debates and meetings he proposed the following with regard to the view of membership in the congregation: "The congregation receives as members those who

---

väckelserörelserna", [s.a.], p. 16, [unpublished paper]. See also the previous discussion.

[266] It can also be mentioned that the Swedish Salvation Army united with the Mission Covenant Church of Sweden in 1988. It forms today a non-territorial district within the Mission Covenant Church of Sweden.

[267] The Swedish Evangelical Mission was established 1856 as an independent organization within the State Church. Different opinions in the teaching about the atonement and about who was allowed to participate in Holy Communion resulted in it later splitting and the Mission Covenant Church of Sweden was established.

[268] Walan, Bror, *Församlingstanken i Svenska Missionsförbundet*, 1964, pp. 283-289. Andreas Fernholm first worked as a priest within the State Church, thereafter as a Baptist preacher and later on he worked within the Mission Covenant Church of Sweden.

[269] We can note that in the hymnal of the Mission Covenant Church of Sweden in 1893 there were four hymns for baptism, two for infant baptism and two for believers' baptism.

believe in Christ."[270]

At present both infant baptism and believers' baptism are practised (both by sprinkling and immersion) within the Mission Covenant Church of Sweden.[271] This would not be remarkable *per se* - this is the case for instance in the Church of Sweden - if it were not for the fact that it is possible for a person to be "re-baptized", i.e. that one and the same person within the Mission Covenant Church of Sweden may be baptized twice (i.e. both by infant baptism and by believers' baptism, in this case "re-baptism"), even within the same congregation. And at least as a theoretical possibility by the same pastor. The churches or chapels usually have a baptismal pool and a baptismal font.[272]

In addition to this we can note that it is, according to Lars Lindberg, possible in special circumstances of a pastoral nature to be a member of a congregation of the Mission Covenant Church of Sweden even without any baptism.[273] At the same time baptized children are not formally allowed to be members of the congregation.[274] Furthermore it may be mentioned that both open membership and open Holy Communion are practised.

---

[270] See Eldebo, Runar, "Svenska Missionsförbundet", *Svenska Trossamfund*, 8th ed., 1990, p. 58. Italics mine.

[271] Ibid. p. 60.

[272] "Också dopgrav och dopfunt brukar finnas väl synliga." Ibid. p. 61.

[273] See Lars Lindberg: "Inom SMF säger vi *ja till dopet*, det är en gåva från Gud, det är ett sakrament. Dopet framställs inte i Svenska Missionsförbundet som ett krav utan som en gåva och en möjlighet. Av själavårdsmässiga skäl kan man t o m få bli medlem i en församling, om man har blivit blockerad inför dopet. Men det är slarvigt att säga, att man i Svenska Missionsförbundet 'inte behöver döpas'." Lindberg, Lars, "Dop och omdop", *Svensk Veckotidning*, No. 22/23, 1987, p. 2.

[274] Erik Lindberg writes: "The position of the Mission Covenant Church of Sweden is more difficult to understand. They baptize children, *but for what purpose?* They are not allowed to belong to the church... Rigid dogmatism still prevents the smallest children from having their names put in the membership register of the congregation. Few of them become members as adults." Lindberg, Erik, "Erik Lindberg om frikyrkans framtid 'Börja förnya eller dö ut'", *Broderskap*, No. 50/52, 1993, p. 6. Italics mine. See Eldebo, who also states that children formally are outside membership, ("barnen står alltså formellt utanför medlemskap."). Eldebo, Runar, "Svenska Missionsförbundet", *Svenska Trossamfund*, 8th ed., 1990, pp. 59f.

We find at least two traditions going hand in hand within the Mission Covenant Church of Sweden, and this results sometimes in problems and also tensions within the denomination itself and in the congregations. There is also an ambiguity both among pastors and the members as regards the teaching and practice of baptism. This ambiguity is not, as pointed out above, a new feature of the Mission Covenant Church of Sweden arising in the 1970's and 1980's. It has been more or less an ingredient from the very beginning of the history of this denomination.

After the "crash" in 1971, when the Trilateral Denominational Consultations were suspended, it was immediately afterwards difficult to start with this kind of issue at the central denominational level. The talks had, however, as far as we can see, theological after-effects and the questions of baptism and church unity became as time went on increasingly accentuated, not least at the local congregational level among the believers in the different congregations. And the development of the ecumenical congregations from the 1970's and onwards must once again been mentioned. Rapprochements had been made between the Baptist Union of Sweden and the Mission Covenant Church of Sweden. In 1983, after 105 years of working side by side, the two governing Bodies of the Baptist Union of Sweden and Mission Covenant Church of Sweden met.[275]

From the talks between these two denominations since the beginning of the 1970's, not least due to the ecumenical congregations, we may briefly mention the documents which the Baptist Union and the Mission Covenant Church have produced. They are *På väg mot kristen enhet*, 1984, (On the Way Towards Christian Unity) and *På väg mot kristen enhet för församlingar som planerar att förenas*, 1988 (On the Way Towards Christian Unity for Congregations Planning to Unite). Some advice is given in these reports to congregations planning to establish an ecumenical congregation.[276] Other expressions of rapprochement and co-operation are for example the shared weekly *Sändaren* already

---

[275] See Lagergren, David, "Efter etthundrafem år", *VP*, No. 50, 1983, p. 2; "När samfundsstyrelserna möttes: -Vi är på väg mot enheten", *VP*, No. 50, 1983, p. 7. In 1983, as already stated, the Baptist Union of Sweden and the Örebro (Baptist) Mission had also a partially common Annual Conference.

[276] See Fahlgren refering to the first document (1984), Fahlgren, Sune, "Sju samfund - tre handböcker - en gemensam nattvardsliturgi", *Svenskt gudstjänstliv* 62, 1987, p. 37.

mentioned.[277]

There are a significant number of ecumenical strivings and some of these mature in a very practical and concrete way especially in the ecumenical congregations, which will be dealt with next.

9.5. Ecumenical Congregations

9.5.1. Some Statistics

In discussing ecumenical congregations, their origin and development etc., I want to start with the statistics. They will put the ecumenical congregations and their position in a larger context, and possibly point to some tendencies.

From the 1970's onwards a significant ecumenical process has been taking place, especially at the congregational level.[278] There

---

[277] Concerning the background to and start of Sändaren, see for instance Svenska Baptistsamfundets Årsbok 1990/91, pp. 92ff. See also "Tidigare redaktörer. Det räcker med en bra tidning", VP, No. 9, 1989, p. 5; "Gemensam tidning - nu!", [editorial], VP, No. 8, 1991, p. 2; "Förenade församlingar: Gemensam tidning för samfunden -nu!", VP, No. 8, 1991, p. 3; "En tidning", [editorial], VP, No. 21/22, 1991, p. 2; "Gemensam tidning", [editorial], VP, No. 15, 1992, p. 2; "Nya tidningen kommer i höst", VP, No. 27/28, 1992, p. 1; "Ny tidning", VP, No. 27/28, 1992, p. 2; Swedberg, Bo, "Nu är det klart: Den gemensamma tidningen börjar utkomma den 1 november", VP, No. 27/28, 1992, p. 5. There has also been critical voices, see for instance Mild, Ruben, "Åter aktuell dopdebatt", VP, No. 43, 1991, p. 12.

From the beginning the United Methodist Church in Sweden was also interested in participating in this newspaper but later on withdrew. Another weekly common to five denominations ought to be mentioned. It is Petrus which was established in 1993, in which the following denominations were involved: the Holiness Union Mission and the Scandinavian Independent Baptist Union (these became one denomination at New Year 1994, named HF/FB (HF/FB Mission), the Pentecostal Movement, the Swedish Alliance Mission and the Örebro (Baptist) Mission. On account of the establishment of Interact 1996/97 the number of denominations has changed.

[278] The 1970's has been designated by Bergsten as "the decade of congregational amalgamation", (ett församlingssamgåendets årtionde). Bergsten, Torsten, "Kyrkotillhörighet - medlemskap - bekännelse", Tro och Liv, No. 1, 1980, p. 33. He writes concerning the ecumenical congregations: "These congregations represent in my opinion the most interesting and fruitful form of ecumenism in the 1970's and 1980's." Bergsten, Torsten, "Ekumenik, vision och verklighet", Tro och Liv, No. 1, 1986, p. 12. The ecumenical congregations caused the

are a number of different kinds of co-operation and unification between congregations,[279] increasingly influencing individuals, congregations and the central, denominational level. Some statistics can help us to grasp the influence of the development of ecumenical congregations on the Baptist Union of Sweden, on other denominations etc.

In 1985, about 27% of Baptist members were also members of another denomination. In 1990 it had increased to 37%, in 1992 40%, in 1995 44%.[280] We find that the Baptist Union had 342 congregations in December 1989, including the ecumenical congregations, 73 congregations or 21% of these being of the latter type.[281] Some years earlier, in 1985, 63 of the 377 Baptist

---

Baptist Union in 1972 to make the addition to its statutes that, when special reasons exist, membership in the denomination may be accorded to a congregation which has been established through co-operation between on the one hand a Baptist congregation or a group of Baptists and on the other hand a congregation or a group belonging to another denomination. Bergsten, Torsten, "Enheten i Kristus", *Tro, Frihet, Gemenskap*, 1998, pp. 230f. See also below.

[279] This is also to be noted in *Svenska Baptistsamfundets Årsböcker* (the Annuals of the Baptist Union of Sweden) where it is said that a specified number of Baptist congregations have united with congregations of for example the Mission Covenant Church of Sweden and established ecumenical congregations. See for instance *Svenska Baptistsamfundets Årsbok* 1983, p. 81; *Svenska Baptistsamfundets Årsbok* 1984, p. 73; *Svenska Baptistsamfundets Årsbok* 1985, p. 59; *Svenska Baptistsamfundets Årsbok* 1989 p. 62.

[280] Skog, Margareta, "Antalet medlemmar i valda samfund 1975-1992", *Tro & Tanke*, 1992:11, p. 52; Skog, Margareta, "Frikyrkornas medlemstal i landets kommuner 1990", *Tro & Tanke* 1992:4, pp. 106f; Skog, Margareta, "Frikyrkosamfundens medlemsantal i landets kommuner 1995", *Tro & Tanke* 1997:3, p. 74. See also "Mission i Sverige", [editorial], *VP*, No. 11, 1991, p. 2.

[281] In 1989 (31. Dec. 1989), the number of ecumenical congregations, in which the Baptist Union of Sweden was involved was 73. These are divided into the following constellations:

Baptist Union and Mission Covenant Church of Sweden 30 congregations,

Baptist Union and Örebro (Baptist) Mission 28,

Baptist Union, Mission Covenant Church of Sweden and Örebro (Baptist) Mission 6,

Baptist Union, Mission Covenant Church of Sweden and United Methodist Church in Sweden 4,

congregations were united not only with the Baptist Union of Sweden but with other denominations,[282] in 1990, 76 of the about 250 (Margareta Skog corrects her own figure of 250 to 330 in a letter to me) Baptist congregations and in 1995, 81 of 298 or 304 (the last mentioned figures are added to the statistics in the mentioned letter to me) Baptist congregations.[283] Some of the Baptist congregations are, as has already been stated above, small.[284]

Some figures from 1990 give the following information about the number of Baptist members involved with other denominations.

Baptist Union and United Methodist Church in Sweden 1,

Baptist Union, Mission Covenant Church of Sweden and Scandinavian Independent Baptist Union 1,

Baptist Union, Holiness Union Mission, Örebro (Baptist) Mission and Swedish Alliance Mission 1,

Baptist Union, Mission Covenant Church of Sweden, Holiness Union Mission and Swedish Alliance Mission 1,

Baptist Union, Mission Covenant Church of Sweden, Örebro (Baptist) Mission and Scandinavian Independent Baptist Union 1. Palm, Irving, "Gemensamma församlingar - en ny fas i den ekumeniska utvecklingen", Tro & Tanke 1992:4, p. 40. See also Karlsson, Birgit, "Budskapet, gemenskapen och de vita fälten", VP, No. 19/20, 1991, p. 5.

[282] Skog, Margareta, "Frikyrkornas medlemstal i landets kommuner 1985", Religion och Samhälle 1986:13, p. 10. See also "Siffror till eftertanke", [editorial], VP, No. 18, 1987, p. 4.

[283] Skog, Margareta, "Frikyrkosamfundens medlemsantal i landets kommuner 1995", Tro & Tanke 1997:3, p. 74. We can observe that the Baptist Union of Sweden in 1995 had 35 congregations together with the Mission Covenant Church of Sweden, i.e. ecumenical congregations, together 4041 members, and 28 congregations together with Holiness Union Mission/Scandinavian Independent Baptist Union and Örebro (Baptist) Mission, (later on 1996/97 these last mentioned united in Interact, in 1994 the two first mentioned were united), with totally 2484 members. Ibid. See also ibid. pp. 72 ff. Concerning the number of congregations (1990, 250), see Skog, Margareta, "Frikyrkornas medlemstal i landets kommuner 1990", Tro & Tanke 1992:4, p. 106, see also letter to Lennart Johnsson: Skog, Margareta, 24/9/99.

[284] See also Skog, Margareta, "Frikyrkosamfundens medlemsantal i landets kommuner 1995", Tro & Tanke 1997:3, pp. 78f; Karlsson, Birgit, "Från min horisont", VP, No. 21, 1987, pp. 4, 12, where Karlsson discusses the ecumenical congregations, some statistics, and "negative trends" especially concerning children and youth-work in the Baptist congregations.

Baptist Union and Mission Covenant Church of Sweden 3719, Baptist Union of Sweden and Örebro (Baptist) Mission 2405, Baptist Union of Sweden, Mission Covenant Church of Sweden and Örebro (Baptist) Mission 754, Baptist Union of Sweden, Mission Covenant Church of Sweden and United Methodist Church in Sweden 457, Baptist Union of Sweden and United Methodist Church in Sweden 101; Baptist Union of Sweden and other Churches 296.[285]

Without doubt this development has implications on many levels, including theological matters - baptism, ecclesiology, ecumenism etc.

9.5.2. The Origin and Development of Ecumenical Congregations

The background to the development of the ecumenical congregations is complex. It must not be forgotten that the ecumenical congregations are to be understood not least in the context of ecumenical strivings at the beginning of this century and onwards. Among other things the first Free Church Conference in Stockholm 1905, with the Baptist Union of Sweden, the United Methodist Church in Sweden and the Mission Covenant Church of Sweden, and the Free Church Committee for Co-operation, 1918, must be mentioned. The other Free Church Conferences (1905-1969), the youth and student associations and their work, different studies and consultations etc., have all played a role in this process, as well as open Holy Communion, and associative and open membership. Especially since the 1970's the number of ecumenical congregations has been growing, with implications not only on the local, congregational level but also on the denominational level. There has been an interaction, sometimes with tensions, at different levels within the Baptist Union of Sweden and also vis á vis other denominations and churches. I want to mention some causes of the establishment of ecumenical congregations, for there are different reasons for two or more congregations uniting into one. Some have already been indicated above.

A delicate question may be asked: according to the Baptists is the church unity found in the ecumenical congregations to be regarded by those involved as the work of the Spirit, i.e. that there are spiritual causes? Or are these congregations sometimes more or

---

[285] Skog, Margareta, "Antalet medlemmar i valda samfund 1975-1992", Tro & Tanke 1992:11, p. 52.

less forced to unite with each other for social, economic and pragmatic reasons? Probably it is a question of a combination of both. There are thus theological reasons arising from Jesus' prayer for unity, as well as non-theological. Congregations have not always been satisfied with co-existing in division. Sometimes the establishing of ecumenical congregations may be ascribed to practical reasons: different congregations seem to unite with each other in order to compensate for their individual weaknesses - decreasing members, the expense of maintaining buildings etc. The common development in society, urbanization and secularization, have certainly also played a role in this process.[286]

As a starting point for such a development towards establishing an ecumenical congregation, there could be a joint youth group for two different congregations,[287] or the use of the same church building.[288] The question of evangelism or evangelization may be another cause.[289] The charismatic movement, the "Jesus-movement" and the "tent meetings" in the 1960's and onwards, crossing various barriers, sometimes causing problems but mostly reconciliation between denominations, congregations and individuals, may not be forgotten either. There is a whole spectrum of reasons and interactions, and the ecumenical process has taken place both in a defensive spirit (too few members etc.,) but also in an offensive spirit with vigorous and powerful congregations.

---

[286] Irving Palm mentions three main causes of why two or more congregations have established a new congregation: 1) the change in society through urbanization and the development of the welfare state, 2) the decrease of members in the Free Churches, 3) improved ecumenical climate. In Lindberg, Erik, "Gemenskapsgrupper - frikyrkans framtid?", VP, No. 42, 1991, pp. 5f. See also Tecken om enhet, 1991, especially pp. 19-20.

[287] Bergsten already in 1964 writes of a very practical and from my point of view ecumenically interesting aspect which is too often neglected. It concerns Free Church "mixed marriages" (frikyrkliga 'blandäktenskap') which according to him are increasing when young people are meeting across the denominational barriers. Bergsten, Torsten, "Associativt och öppet medlemskap", Baptistpredikanternas studieblad, No. 2, 1964, p. 10.

[288] For an example of this see Lantz, Ragni, "Övervägande positiva reaktioner till samverkan", VP, No. 6, 1986, p. 7.

[289] Lagergren writes: "In several places the establishing of ecumenical congregations has been justified practically by the fact that each congregation on its own has been too weak to manage the task of evangelizing a place." Lagergren, David, "Varför gör inte samfunden mer...", VP, No. 9, 1984, p. 12.

In discussing this, it is of importance to know that there are different kinds of ecumenical congregations. An ecumenical congregation can be:[290]

a) a doubly affiliated congregation *(dubbelansluten församling)* which in most cases implies an older congregation which is affiliated to or co-operates with *(ansluten till/samarbetar med)* two denominations, for instance the Baptist Union of Sweden and the Mission Covenant Church of Sweden.[291]

b) a united congregation *(förenad församling)* is a congregation which has been established due to the fact that two or more congregations have been united and these have established a new congregation with a relation to two or more denominations.

c) a completely new congregation.

In this connection something must also be said about some statements made by the General Secretary of the Baptist Union of Sweden, Erik Rudén, in 1948,[292] statements which have been of importance for the Baptist Union and the development of the ecumenical congregations. They were concerned with "union churches" or ecumenical congregations,[293] and as already mentioned, closed and open Holy Communion,[294] an issue which was brought to the fore within the Baptist Union once again during the 1940's and onwards. This question took in comparison with the earlier position of the Swedish Baptists (closed Holy Communion) a new direction, which has been of importance in different ways, among other things for ecumenism. In 1948, the same year as the

---

[290] Concerning a-c, see *Tecken om enhet,* 1991, pp. 13f.

[291] As for *ansluten till* (affiliated to) applying to the Baptist Union of Sweden and the Mission Covenant Church of Sweden and *samarbetar med* (co-operates with) applying to Örebro (Baptist) Mission, these two concepts mean on the whole the same thing.

[292] Erik Rudén, 1906-1987, was also the General Secretary of the Baptist Union of Sweden in 1965-1971. The years 1955-1959 he was secretary for missions, and 1959-1965 European Secretary in *BWA*.

[293] Rudén, Erik, "Samarbete mellan de frikyrkliga", *Tro och Liv,* No. 7/8, 1948, pp. 305-312. See also Rudén, Erik, "'Union Churches'", *VP,* No. 6, 1965, p. 14; Bergsten, Torsten, *Frikyrkor i samverkan,* 1995, pp. 147-148.

[294] See Rudén, Erik, "Samarbete mellan de frikyrkliga", *Tro och Liv,* No. 7/8, 1948, pp. 305-312.

Baptist Union of Sweden celebrated its hundredth anniversary,[295] Erik Rudén writes that even if he respects those holding to closed Holy Communion, the time has come when Baptists cannot refuse Holy Communion to those who through their faith in Jesus Christ have become His possession. He says:

> To uphold this opinion is almost coercion of conscience in my view... *To practise open Holy Communion when the congregation celebrates the Lord's Supper is on the basis of Baptist belief possible.*[296]

Even if similar ideas had been discussed as early as in the 1850's, Erik Rudén's standpoint indicates something important. He was in conflict with the Swedish Baptist majority, which on the question of Holy Communion had prevailed for a hundred years.[297] Lagergren comments:

> Rudén departed from the main Baptist position on Holy Communion for a hundred years, which entailed admission to Holy Communion being tied to believers' baptism - before 1919 even to membership in an established Baptist congregation.[298]

And on Rudén's words,

> According to my conviction the time has come when we Baptists ought to say this clearly and not bar those from Holy Communion who through their faith

---

[295] Concerning this anniversary see *Svensk baptism genom 100 år,* 1948; Svärd, Arvid, Wange, Per, *Det hundrade året,* 1948; Lagergren, David, *Förändringstid,* 1994, pp. 240-249.

[296] "Att hävda denna mening har för mig fått något av samvetstvång över sig... *Att tillämpa öppen kommunion i församlingens firande av Herrens nattvard är utifrån baptistisk trosuppfattning möjligt."* Rudén, Erik, "Samarbete mellan de frikyrkliga", *Tro och Liv,* No. 7/8, 1948, p. 308.

[297] "Svenska Baptistsamfundet och Kyrkornas Världsråd. En studierapport", 1965, p. 63, [unpublished paper]. See also the discussion above concerning for example the Pentecostal Movement.

[298] Lagergren, David, *Förändringstid,* 1994, p. 229. Another leading Baptist, Gunnar Westin, was one of those representing another attitude. He maintained closed Holy Communion. He was critical of and also hesitant to associative and open membership. See also for example Wiberg, Anders, writing a chapter in *Det Christliga Dopet,* 1854, "Det Christliga Dopet såsom ett Willkor för Ledamotskap i Christi Församling och Delaktighet i Herrans Nattward" (Christian Baptism as a Condition for Membership in the Congregation of Christ and for Participation in Holy Communion), pp. 275-288.

in Jesus Christ have become his possession.[299]

Lagergren makes the comment:

This statement by Rudén was very much welcomed by many within the Baptist Union, but it also offended many more. *Vecko-Posten* referred to the meeting but did not mention the statement.[300]

It was obviously too sensitive. From the beginning of the 1950's open Holy Communion was introduced, and it began then slowly to be practised in most Baptist congregations.

In the 1950's, and above all in the 1960's and 1970's, we can observe a tendency to abandon traditional positions in Swedish Christianity, including the Baptist Union of Sweden. Various local ecumenical councils were established.[301] It can also be mentioned that the Ecumenical Development Week started in 1972 as a consequence of *G 72*, i.e. the National Christian Conference in Gothenburg the same year.[302] In the 1980's and 1990's open Holy Communion has been increasingly regarded as an almost uncontroversial practice within the Baptist Union of Sweden.[303] Erik Rudén's words have had significance for the direction of the Baptist Union from a closed attitude and traditionalism towards

---

[299] Rudén, Erik, "Samarbete mellan de frikyrkliga", *Tro och Liv*, No. 7/8, 1948, p. 308. Rudén's lecture was held at the preachers' meeting in Malmö in the autumn 1948, later printed in *Tro och Liv*, No. 7/8, 1948.

[300] Lagergren, David, *Förändringstid*, 1994, p. 230.

[301] See for instance Brodd, Sven-Erik, "Skärningspunkt mellan idé och verklighet", *Kyrkans liv*, 2nd ed., 1993, p. 302, where Brodd writes about conciliar ecumenism *(rådsekumeniken)* as characterizing the 1960's and 1970's. Bergsten designates the whole period 1905-1993 within the Swedish Free Church movement with this term, i.e. co-operation between congregations and denominations. As examples he mentions *Sveriges Frikyrkoråd* and *Sveriges Kristna Råd*. Bergsten, Torsten, *Frikyrkor i samverkan*, 1995, p. 16.

[302] The Ecumenical Development Week, since 1985 called the Development Forum of the Swedish Churches, deals with the issues of peace and justice.

In talking about the issue of peace, I want to mention the *Life and Peace Institute*, which was founded in 1985 in Uppsala. This may be seen as one consequence of the ecumenical Life and Peace Conference in Uppsala 1983 with about 160 participants representing Orthodox, Catholic, Anglican and Protestant Churches from all parts of the world.

[303] See for example Bergsten, Torsten, "Öppet nattvardsbord, överfört medlemskap och en öppen baptism", *VP*, No. 3, 1986, p. 6.

openness and pluralism, and have played a certain role in the development of ecumenical congregations. For he is open towards ecumenism,[304] even if, of course, the question of baptism is a difficult issue, also for Rudén.[305]

We find, however, a telling observation by Lagergren more than 30 years after the statement by Rudén in 1948. According to him the invitation to other Christians to communicate at Baptist Holy Communions, irrespective of whether baptized or not, is "an ecumenical exception" *(ett ekumeniskt betingat undantag)* which is necessitated by the confused baptismal situation in Christianity.[306] There is, from a theological point of view, therefore still a slight tension over whether baptism *or* faith alone is to be the condition for participation in Holy Communion.

When congregations were united into one, Christians from different congregations, affiliated to different denominations, were brought closer together (among other things through local associative membership, open membership etc.). This process became more concrete above all in the 1970's and onwards, with increasing unity at the local congregational level, not least, of course, in the ecumenical congregations. Furthermore the continuing development of and work within local ecumenical councils and also the charismatic movement, a movement growing above all from below, has had a certain impact. We must not either forget the work of the Baptist Youth Association together with other Youth Associations.[307] This co-operation on different levels plays an

---

[304] Rudén, Erik, "Samarbete mellan de frikyrkliga", *Tro och Liv*, No. 7/8, 1948, pp. 305-312.

[305] "A union of two congregations such as a Baptist and a Methodist or a congregation belonging to the Mission Covenant Church is not possible, unless they have found a common position in questions which divide us. For me baptism is just such a question." Rudén, Erik, "Samarbete mellan de frikyrkliga", *Tro och Liv*, No. 7/8, 1948, pp. 310f.

[306] Lagergren, David, "Barnen och nattvarden", *VP*, No. 49, 1981, p. 2. See "Särskilt yttrande: Barnen och nattvarden" [David Lagergren], *När vi bryter det bröd...*, 1981, pp. 235ff., mentioning both open Holy Communion and open membership as ecumenical exceptions.

[307] See for example Rydlander, Håkan, "SBUF och ÖMU: Återförena baptismen!", *VP*, No. 50, 1983, p. 10. And the youth associations of the three "old" denominations (the Baptist, Mission Covenant Church and Methodist) have in 1991 expressed their intention to co-operate more closely with each other. Suggestions of a fusion between these three youth associations have also been

important role and will probably in the long run be one contributory reason for changes not only on the congregational levels but also on the denominational levels.

Different congregations have, however, in various ways, also before the 1960's, chosen to co-operate with each other on common issues. One example from 1954 may be given, when two different Baptist congregations in Lindesberg, one from the Baptist Union and one from the Örebro (Baptist) Mission, decided to unite.[308] And some *Baptist* congregations have ever since the division in the 1930's co-operated with both the Baptist Union of Sweden and the Örebro (Baptist) Mission.[309]

Something new happened, as has been mentioned several times above, when the two congregations in Höör (in the south of Sweden) were united into an ecumenical congregation in 1969.[310] This congregation was affiliated to *(anslutit sig till)* two Free Church denominations, both the Mission Covenant Church of Sweden and the Baptist Union of Sweden. These two denominations had parted with each other over the view of baptism and conditions of membership. Here we have *two different Church traditions* (an infant-Baptist respectively a believers' Baptist), which are *united into one* ecumenical congregation affiliated not to one but to *two* denominations. It is stated in *Tecken om enhet* that, "This event became the embryo of a new phase in the Free Church ecumenical movement in Sweden."[311] We may suspect that this new phase also

---

discussed. Palm, Irving, "Frikyrkofolket och ekumeniken", *Tro & Tanke* 1993:5, p. 71. See also Part III, for example chapter 9.

[308] Lagergren, David, "Svenska baptistsamfundet och Örebromissionen - En tillbakablick", *VP*, No. 7, 1985, p. 12.

[309] See Bergsten, Torsten, "Baptismen, trosfriheten och ekumeniken", *Liv och tjänst*, 1988, p. 197. See also *Tecken om enhet*, 1991, pp. 16f., making a distinction between older *(äldre)* and younger *(yngre)* ecumenical congregations *(gemensamma församlingar)*. For example some congregations have had relations through almost their entire history with for example both the Swedish Alliance Mission and the Mission Covenant Church of Sweden, (i.e. since the beginning of the 20th century). Ibid. p. 16. The "younger" ecumenical congregations are those established from about the 1970's and onwards.

[310] See for example *Svenska Baptistsamfundet*, 1971-1972, pp. 187-188, and also pp. 197-198, [årsbok]; *Svenska Baptistsamfundet*, 1972-1973, pp. 181-182, [årsbok].

[311] "Denna händelse kom att bli embryot till en ny fas i den frikyrkoekumeniska

had implications thereafter on among other things the issue of baptism.

In spite of the existence and the growth of the ecumenical congregations, the Annual Conference of the Baptist Union decided in 1969 *not to recommend o p e n membership.* It decided namely,

after an intensive discussion and great hesitation, 'not to recommend open membership but neither to reject those congregations which already had decided on this issue or felt compelled to decide positively'. As at the conference in 1858 tolerance prevailed. After this decision more Baptist congregations introduced open membership.[312]

This decision must be regarded as a crucial turning-point for the Baptist Union of Sweden with implications in different areas and subjects - theologically and practically - both within the Union itself but also in relation to other denominations. This event and its importance in the following decades, i.e. 1970's - 1990's, for the Baptist Union can probably not be emphasized too much. The Baptist Union of Sweden was at a crossroads.

What must be noted in this context is the importance of the principle of freedom. For the decision at the Annual Conference in 1969 was made among other things on the condition that each congregation is *free to decide in its own way* in relation to other congregations and also in relation to the Baptist denomination.[313] Its constitution had, however, to be changed in order to fit reality. This meant that congregations which did not correspond to the definition of a Baptist congregation might in spite of this be affiliated to the Baptist Union. A change was therefore made in 1972. This made admission to the Baptist Union possible for a

---

rörelsen i Sverige." *Tecken om enhet,* 1991, p. 2. See also Bergsten, Torsten, *Frikyrkor i samverkan,* 1995, p. 124, and p. 281; Bergsten, Torsten, "Gemensamma församlingar", *Nordisk Ekumenisk Orientering,* No. 2, 1994, pp. 3-5.

[312] Bergsten, Torsten, "Förändring genom konfrontation och dialog. Svenskt perspektiv", *Samfund i förändring,* 1997, p. 43. See also Bergsten, Torsten, "Baptismen, trosfriheten och ekumeniken", *Liv och tjänst,* 1988, p. 197; Bergsten, Torsten, "Enheten i Kristus", *Tro, Frihet, Gemenskap,* 1998, pp. 230f.; *Svenska Baptistsamfundet,* 1969-1970, pp. 146-149, [årsbok], with the heading "Utredning om öppet medlemskap". It states that associate membership may in practice be regarded as open membership. Ibid. p. 148; Lagergren, David, "Svar:", *VP,* No. 27, 1978, p. 10.

[313] See Bergsten, Torsten, "Baptismen, trosfriheten och ekumeniken", *Liv och tjänst,* 1988, p. 197.

congregation which was established through fusion of on the one hand a Baptist congregation or a group of Baptists and on the other hand a congregation or a group belonging to *another* denomination.[314]

Besides Höör, another "famous" ecumenical congregation in Sweden is Valsätrakyrkan in Uppsala - originating in Uppsala Baptist congregation.[315] Gunnar Fridborg writes that Valsätrakyrkan is a new establishment on a broad ecumenical basis - not an amalgamation of already existing congregations. The fellowship had been built up from scratch.[316] In 1975 a group consisting of about 40 people gathered for various activities whilst the church was being built. In 1976 the Uppsala Baptist congregation employed two pastors, each working half time. In April 1976 the church was opened. The group and its activities increased and about 75 people attended services each Sunday. More people were, however, on its list of contacts. Members from different denominations and churches were involved in this new fellowship, which economically and legally was linked to Uppsala Baptist congregation. First in April 1978 the constitution which marked the formation of a new congregation was passed. It did not, however, affect the legal side. About 70 persons became members. Most of them were, however, already members of other denominations. In February 1982 the congregation acquired legal status and became a "juridical subject". Congregational constitution and statutes were approved. At that time it thus became possible for the congregation

---

[314] *Svenska Baptistsamfundet,* 1973-1974, p. 215, [årsbok]. See also *Svenska Baptistsamfundet,* 1971-1972, pp. 197-198 ("motion om ändring av § 1 i Stadgar för Svenska Baptistsamfundet"), [årsbok], and *Svenska Baptistsamfundet,* 1972-1973, pp. 181-182 ("Beträffande stadgeändring"), [årsbok]. See also *Svenska Baptistsamfundet,* 1969-1970, pp. 146-149, ("Utredning om öppet medlemskap"), [årsbok]; Lagergren, David, "Lokalekumeniken och dopet", *VP,* No. 37, 1978, p. 2.

[315] As concerns the background and development of this ecumenical congregation, see Fridborg, Gunnar, "Valsätrakyrkan i Uppsala. En ny typ av ekumenisk församling", *Årsbok,* 1981-1982, pp. 12-17. See also Mattson, Valter, "Behov och problem som den ekumeniska församlingen brottas med. Praktiska, samhälleliga, psykologiska och teologiska aspekter på framväxten av Församlingen i Valsätrakyrkan", 1981, [unpublished paper]; Bergsten, Torsten, "Den gemensamma församlingen - ett tecken om enhet", *Levande,* 1996, pp. 37-53.

[316] Fridborg, Gunnar, "Valsätrakyrkan i Uppsala. En ny typ av ekumenisk församling", *Årsbok,* 1981-1982, p. 16.

to be associated with a denomination. The question was to which denomination would it be affiliated? Valsätrakyrkan had developed out of a Baptist group and with Baptist support, but more and more members had been coming to it from other churches and denominations, some even without any Christian background. Gunnar Fridborg writes that at various times seven Swedish and a couple of foreign denominations were represented in this congregation.[317] It was decided in the congregation in 1982 to try to co-operate with the churches and denominations which were represented in the Swedish Free Church Council. This was, however, experienced by some as provocative and resulted in a report with the theme: *Kan man tillhöra fem samfund?* (Is It Possible to Belong to Five Denominations?)[318] The same year, in 1982, the Baptist Central Board decided to accept Valsätrakyrkan as a full member-congregation within the Baptist Union of Sweden.[319]

---

[317] "... en ganska brokig skara med tidvis sju svenska samfund och ett par utländska representerade." Fridborg, Gunnar, "Ekumenik: Så här fungerar det i Valsätra", *VP*, No. 40, 1982, p. 8. See also Lindberg, Erik, "1+1=mer än 2 vid samgående", *VP*, No. 40, 1991, p. 4.

[318] See Bardh, Ulla, "Dop och medlemskap. En jämförelse mellan två ekumeniska församlingar; Storvreta frikyrkoförsamling och Valsätrakyrkan, baserad på eller speglad i 155 medlemmars svar på en enkät, hösten 1989.", 1990, [unpublished paper], and Bardh, Ulla, "Preliminär skrivning av idépapper om SMF och ekumeniken med anledning av det s.k. folkrörelseprojektet 'Ju mer vi är tillsammans...', där SMF representerar väckelserörelserna", [s.a.], [unpublished paper]. In this last she says that in Valsätrakyrkan there were members from among others the following denominations: the Baptist Union of Sweden, the Mission Covenant Church of Sweden, the Swedish Alliance Mission, the Scandinavian Independent Baptist Union and the Swedish Holiness Mission. She writes: "Valsätrakyrkan fattade det ovanliga beslutet att begära anslutning till samtliga trossamfund, från vilka man hade medlemmar, nämligen BS, SAM, FBS, HF och SMF. Detta upplevdes av de flesta samfundsteologer som ekumeniskt omedvetet och provocerande. Ja, det ledde t.o.m. till en dokumenterad överläggning i Älvsjö, under temat: 'Kan man tillhöra fem samfund?'" Ibid. p. 12. See also Bergsten, Torsten, "Den gemensamma församlingen - ett tecken om enhet", *Levande*, 1996, pp. 43ff.

[319] In *VP*, No. 40, 1982, p. 8, there is a picture of the then General Secretary of the Baptist Union of Sweden David Lagergren and Agneta Magnusson a member of Valsätrakyrkan. It says in the caption that the Central Board (*Missionsstyrelsen*) has decided to welcome Valsätrakyrkans församling as a full member of the Baptist Union of Sweden. ("*Missionsstyrelsen har beslutat välkomna Valsätrakyrkans församling som fullvärdig medlem i Svenska Baptistsamfundet. Detta tog sig ett konkret uttryck i ett handslag mellan David Lagergren och Agneta Magnusson, medlem i Valsätrakyrkan.*") Fridborg,

Still another ecumenical congregation is Sannerudskyrkan. The development towards an ecumenical congregation started with co-operation between a Mission Covenant Church congregation and a Baptist congregation in 1970, when the two congregations, Stora Kils missionsförsamling and Stora Kils baptistförsamling, did youth-work together. The pastor of the Mission Covenant Church congregation, Harry Öberg, was also the pastor of Stora Kils Baptist congregation. In 1979 these two congregations moved to a joint church building, Sannerudskyrkan, where there is both a baptismal font and an open baptismal pool.[320] David Lagergren, General Secretary of the Baptist Union, and Egon Onerup, education secretary of the Mission Covenant Church of Sweden, participated. Lagergren held the inaugural speech.[321]

As we understand it, these two congregations were a church union several years before any congregational constitution was accepted, and before the common statutes had been worked out and been accepted. As an ecumenical congregation, Sannerudskyrkan, was established first in January in 1984, at that time belonging to both the Baptist Union of Sweden and the Mission Covenant Church of Sweden.[322]

Other examples of ecumenical congregations affiliated with both the Baptist Union of Sweden and the Mission Covenant Church of

---

Gunnar, "Ekumenik: Så här fungerar det i Valsätra", VP, No. 40, 1982, p. 8.

[320] One of the former church-buildings was demolished on account of road construction, the other was sold to the Pentecostal congregation. "Stor utmaning att få arbeta för samgående", VP, No. 7, 1984, p. 8.

[321] Wingård, Bengt-Gunnar, "Sannerudskyrkan - gemensam kyrka för missions- och baptistförsamlingarna i Kil invigd", VP, No. 45, 1979, p. 3.

[322] "Stor utmaning att få arbeta för samgående", VP, No. 7, 1984, p. 8. See also Bergsten, Torsten, "Kyrkotillhörighet - medlemskap - bekännelse", Tro och Liv, No. 1, 1980, p. 33; Lantz, Ragni, "Ebbe Sundström: -Teologin får vika om helheten gagnas", VP, No. 50, 1989, p. 2; Lantz, Ragni, "Sannerudskyrkan i Kil. Högt i tak och trångt i bänkarna", VP, No. 50, 1989, pp. 8f., 11.

Another example is the ecumenical congregation in Knivsta - a suburb of Uppsala - called Knivsta Free Church Congregation. In this congregation Baptist members and members of the Mission Covenant Church of Sweden work together. The chairman, Thord-Ove Thordson, says: "we do not want to work only for the members of the Mission Covenant Church and the Baptists but for all the people who live in this area." "I Kil, Knivsta och Järnboås: Allt vanligare att två blir ett", VP, No. 7, 1984, pp. 8f.

Sweden are for example Johannes-kyrkans församling in Boden, and Sköllersta frikyrkoförsamling.[323] Hjortensbergskyrkans församling in Nyköping is another example, with relations to the three "old" denominations – the Baptist Union of Sweden, the Mission Covenant Church of Sweden and United Methodist Church in Sweden;[324] Vretstorps frikyrkoförsamling and Östansjö frikyrkoförsamling, both affiliated with the Baptist Union of Sweden, Mission Covenant Church of Sweden and Örebro (Baptist) Mission.[325]

We will have the opportunity to study this in greater depth below in Part III.

9.5.3. Different Reactions to the Establishment and Existence of Ecumenical Congregations

These constellations in the ecumenical congregations result in there being different theological positions in one and the same congregation. This has, of course, implications for dealing with for instance the issues of baptism and ecclesiology, since different doctrines and practices are brought together under the same roof. The faith and life of the individual Baptist is in this kind of church unity practised and tested together with the experiences of others with other backgrounds, and more or less conscious theologies.

BEM writes: "On the way towards their goal of visible unity, however, the churches will have to pass through various stages."[326] This is true! Some of the stages towards church unity, which can concern theological and/or practical problems, are easy to overcome. Others are, however, difficult and almost impossible to overcome. It can be stated that the ecumenical congregations are on the one hand something positive, a partial realization of church unity. They involve, however, on the other hand challenges. The issue of baptism constitutes a stumbling block in the work of unification. Evidently, the ecumenical congregations have their price. The medal has a reverse side, which should not be neglected.

---

[323] See Bergsten, Torsten, "Kyrkotillhörighet - medlemskap - bekännelse", *Tro och Liv*, No. 1, 1980, pp. 34f.

[324] "Hjortensbergskyrkan, Nyköping: Tre församlingar växte under tio år samman till en enda", *VP*, No. 49, 1983, pp. 8f.

[325] "Efter 126 års parallelldrift. Två förenade församlingar har bildats i södra Närke", *VP*, No. 8, 1988, p. 3.

[326] *BEM* p. ix.

In the Annual of the Baptist Union of Sweden for 1988, it is said that the strains

which a congregation encounters in its life and ministry, are encountered also by ecumenical and co-operating congregations. It is becoming more obvious, that these phases put the theological basis and spiritual tradition to a serious test.[327]

The unifying process has been regarded by some as a threat to the Baptist Union of Sweden and its identity, while some of the former boundary lines between congregations and denominations are more or less changed, or even abolished. The Baptist pastor Ruben Janarv gives open expression to how the difficult process, which has resulted in living side by side with various traditions, can be. He states:

Nobody should think that the result has been reached without agony. Perhaps one has to be a Baptist in order to understand how such a decision can be reached and how difficult it sometimes can be to do this. It is at home one has to learn and practice what ecumenism demands from a practical point of view.[328]

Another Baptist pastor, Edvin Österberg (b. 1905), states that it is wasted labour for the Baptist Union to work for church unity with both the Örebro (Baptist) Mission and the Mission Covenant Church of Sweden.[329] He maintains that in view of the great differences concerning congregation, baptism, eucharist and ministry, church unity must appear as a utopia.[330] The principle of biblical authority also comes to the fore, as well as the principles of believers' baptism and congregationalism. The Baptist Einar Axelson writes about difficult times for those (Baptists) who want to be faithful to the Word.[331] Unifications of congregations result according to him in confusion and possibly divisions.[332]

There are hesitant and critical voices towards this work towards

---

[327] *Svenska Baptistsamfundets Årsbok* 1988, p. 57, [Missionsstyrelsens årsberättelse].

[328] Janarv, Ruben, "Gemensam väg?", *VP*, No. 17, 1983, p. 11.

[329] Österberg, Edvin, "Enhet och samverkan", *VP*, No. 25/26, 1982 p. 10.

[330] Ibid.

[331] Axelson, Einar, "Viktigare än ekumeniken", *VP*, No. 18, 1988, p. 11.

[332] Ibid.

unity, but looking at the opinions on ecumenical congregations among members within the ecumenical congregations themselves there are some obvious tendencies. They are positive towards this work and this in spite of the ambiguities and difficulties indicated above, and also the differences in teachings and practices concerning the issues of baptism and ecclesiology. In an inquiry conducted by *Veckoposten* the members of 40 ecumenical congregations, affiliated with both the Baptist Union of Sweden and the Mission Covenant Church of Sweden, were asked about the situation before and after the unifications.[333] The most common answers from the 30 congregations which answered the inquiry were that after the unification there had been "a considerable improvement" *(avsevärd förbättring)*, or "an improvement" *(enbart förbättring)*.[334] The comparison between before and after a unification consistently shows an improvement in the present situation within ecumenical congregations. It should not be forgotten, however, that there are 10 ecumenical congregations from which we do not get any information in this inquiry about attitudes towards the unifications.[335]

The favourable reactions to the establishment and existence of ecumenical congregations are confirmed in another survey conducted by Irving Palm. Palm points out that Baptists during the period 1978 to 1992 have become even more positive towards unification than before.[336] He states:

> The support for a fusion at the local and the national level is greater within the Baptist Union than within many other denominations. One contributing reason to this is that the denomination includes many ecumenical congregations. Also amongst the members who do not belong to this category

---

[333] Swedberg, Bo, "Enkät ger klart besked: 'Bättre' eller 'mycket bättre' i de förenade församlingarna", *VP*, No. 51/52, 1987, p. 3.

[334] Ibid.

[335] It looks like a conscious strategy on Bo Swedberg's part to plead for ecumenical congregations, and using an important instrument, *Veckoposten*. I am, however, not quite sure that his opinion is representative of the Baptist members at large, but that he in many different ways tries to convince them of the advantages in ecumenical congregations. This is in my opinion discernible. This is another interesting task for research, i.e. to study and analyse what the role of such a creator of public opinion as *Veckoposten* can be.

[336] Palm, Irving, "Frikyrkofolket och ekumeniken", *Tro & Tanke* 1993:5, 1993, p. 70.

of congregation, there are still great sympathies for fusions of congregations as well as of denominations.[337]

He continues:

It is above all the members of the Baptist Union of Sweden and the members of the Mission Covenant Church of Sweden who are in favour of the strivings to unite denominations and local congregations.[338]

In 1988 some ecumenical congregations (in Bålsta, Knivsta, Storvreta, and Valsätrakyrkan in Uppsala) proposed a motion to the Annual Conferences of the three denominations of the Baptist Union of Sweden, the Mission Covenant Church of Sweden and the Örebro (Baptist) Mission, in which it was urged that these conferences should take the initiative to establish a common council.[339] The reason for this was that more and more congregations are affiliated with two or more denominations. The Board of the Mission Covenant Church of Sweden dissociated itself, however, from the proposal, and the Board of the Baptist Union was neither for nor against, whilst the Örebro (Baptist) Mission was hesitant. The three Annual Conferences did in spite of this approve in principle the proposal of the motion and urged *Sveriges Frikyrkoråd* (the Swedish Free Church Council) to set up a working party with the task of working on the questions of a practical, theological and strategical character.[340] In 1989 the Swedish Free Church Council invited all ecumenical congregations and the

---

[337] Ibid. p. 77.

[338] Ibid. p. 85. Concerning other (mainly) positive reactions to the ecumenical congregations, see for example Swedberg, Bo, "Baptister och missionsförbundare om förenad församling i Mölndal: -Det bästa som hänt oss", *VP*, No. 10, 1985, pp. 6f.; Swedberg, Bo, " -Det här är en enhet som vi längtat efter", *VP*, No. 7, 1986, pp. 6f.; Wiktell, Sven, E., "Åseda. Grunden för arbetet är bönegrupperna", *VP*, No. 3, 1989, p. 2; Elmquist, Karl-Axel, "Viktig arbetsgrupp tillsatt: Sex samfund börjar nu samråda om de förenade församlingarna", *VP*, No. 16, 1989, p. 2; "Traditioner och reaktioner", [editorial], *VP*, No. 16, 1990, p. 2; "'Folk uppskattar vår enhet'", *VP*, No. 37, 1990, p. 1; Swedberg, Bo, " -Vi vill ha en öppen kyrka i Fjugesta", *VP*, No. 37, 1990, pp. 8f.; Swedberg, Bo, "600 personer deltog i invigningshögtiden", *VP*, No. 37, 1990, p. 9; "Ingen i Höör ångrar samgående", *VP*, No. 8, 1992, p. 1; Swedberg, Bo, "I Höör längtar man inte tillbaka till det som var", *VP*, No. 8, 1992, p. 7.

[339] "Motionen om ett gemensamt samrådsorgan inom SFR för samfund med gemensamma församlingar", quoted in *Tecken om enhet*, 1991, p. 10.

[340] *Tecken om enhet*, 1991, pp. 9ff.

146

denominations within the Free Christian Association Council (*De Fria Kristna Samfundens Råd*, abbreviated *SAMRÅD*), to send representatives to an introductory conference in order to appoint among other things a working party. The Baptist Union of Sweden was involved and did nominate the Baptist pastors Ulla Bardh (b. 1936) and Valter Mattsson (b. 1931) to this working party, which was called *Arbetsgruppen för gemensamma församlingar* (abbreviated *AGF)* (the Working Party on Ecumenical Congregations). Its work resulted in the report *Tecken om enhet.*[341]

There are, as we have found, different reactions to ecumenical congregations and church unity. Some are openly favourable, just as others are openly negative. We have formed an idea of some of the difficulties and compromises which have to be dealt with for individuals, congregations and denominations. I will continue to discuss the ecumenical congregations and Baptist identity, especially in Part III. I want, however, to conclude this part by giving some more examples of expressions of ecumenism.

---

[341] In this report, *Tecken om enhet*, 1991, also different bi-lateral talks and questions about ecumenical congregations are discussed. See also Palm, Irving, "Gemensamma församlingar - en ny fas i den ekumeniska utvecklingen", *Tro & Tanke* 1992:4, 1992, p. 33; "Vägen till målet", [editorial], *VP*, No. 39, 1991, p. 2; Bergsten, Torsten, "Baptismens dubbla dilemma", *VP*, No. 47, 1991, p. 4; Lantz, Ragni, "Ulla Bardh: -Vi har mycket att lära av de gemensamma församlingarna", *VP*, No. 33/34, 1992, p. 16.

This project, which resulted in *Tecken om enhet*, had as one of its aims to describe, analyze and explain the occurrence of the social phenomenon "ecumenical congregations". It was carried out at the Department of Sociology, Uppsala university, in co-operation with the Swedish Free Church Council and its working party, i.e. *AGF*.

9.6. Other Expressions of Ecumenical Commitment:

9.6.1. Some Organizations

Baptists are also involved in ecumenical work, through such organizations as the Baptist youth, *SBUF*,[342] and *Svenska Baptisternas Kvinnoförbund* (the Swedish Baptist Women's Association). The latter are responsible for Foreign Missions and special gatherings for mission work. Bible studies and the spiritual life will also be mentioned in this context. There is *Frikyrkliga Studieförbundet* (the Free Church Study Association) established in 1947, and *Frikyrkliga Ungdomsrådet* (the Free Church Youth Council). Other organizations in which the Baptist Union has been or still is involved are for example *Diakonia*,[343] *Svenska Missionsrådet* (the Swedish Missionary Council), probably the oldest of the ecumenical bodies; further, *Svenska Ekumeniska Nämnden* (the Swedish Ecumenical Council) founded in 1932, which was until 1992 an ecumenical forum for the Free Church co-operation organizations and the Church of Sweden; *Sveriges Frikyrkoråd* (the Swedish Free Church Council) founded in 1918, and *De fria kristna samfundens råd* (abbreviated *FRISAM)* (the Free Christian Denominational Council), later named *SAMRÅD*, established in 1975.

The Swedish Free Church Council and *SAMRÅD* had among other things the task of encouraging co-operation between different denominations, for example the co-ordination of the Free Church hospital chaplaincies and the work of the Free Church chaplaincies at the universities and colleges. Furthermore, these organizations were bodies to which measures proposed by State commissions were remitted for consideration. They were also the forum where Free Church ecumenical matters were discussed. In 1993 the

---

[342] See for example Lindvall, Karin, *Porträtt:* "Jag älskar söndagsskolan...", *Tro, Frihet, Gemenskap,* 1998, pp. 73f., Lidén, Sven-Gunnar, *Tema:* "Svensk baptistungdom och dess verksamhet", *Tro, Frihet, Gemenskap,* 1998, pp. 75-94. We can among other things mention for example the Free Christian Student Association and its role in the founding of the Free Church Committeee for Co-operation discussed earlier in this thesis etc.

[343] *Diakonia* is the aid organization of seven Free Church denominations, working in about 40 countries. *Svenska Baptistsamfundets Årsbok* 1990/91, p. 57.

Swedish Free Church Council and *SAMRÅD* decided to dissolve themselves and form another new organization, *Sveriges Frikyrkosamråd* (the Swedish Free Church Co-operation Council).[344] Another ecumenical institution is *Sveriges Kristna Råd (SKR)* (the Christian Council of Sweden), that was constituted in 1992 with 56 participants from 20 churches and denominations.[345] Its task is to co-ordinate as much as possible co-operation on the ecumenical level.[346] It is said in an editorial in *Veckoposten:*

> The plans to form the Christian Council of Sweden are in their original intentions possibly one of the most far-reaching ecumenical projects which have ever been launched in our country.[347]

In discussing Free Church ecumenism and general ecumenical strivings, one should not forget the co-operation in broadcasting on radio and eventually television between the different denominations and churches, and its explicit and implicit consequences for ecumenical work in Sweden, both for those who were broadcasting the services - pastors and lay-people - and those who were listening. There was co-operation with the Broadcasting Authority in the 1920's, 1930's and 1940's and onwards, concerning for instance morning prayers and services.[348] All this has significance for ecumenical work.

---

[344] The Swedish Free Church Co-operation Council consisted, in 1993, of the original eight members (three of them are today in Interact) of the Swedish Free Church Council and in addition the Adventists, the Salvation Army and the Pentecostal Movement.

[345] Once again under debate in 1998.

[346] See for example *Svenska Baptistsamfundets Årsbok* 1992-93, pp. 52-54.

In Dec. 1992, after years of discussions and preparation, 20 different Christian churches and denominations were united in *Sveriges Kristna Råd* (the Christian Council of Sweden). Fourteen other denominations were asked but refused, such as the Pentecostal Movement and the Salvation Army. In the steering committee we find at that time the General Secretary of the Baptist Union of Sweden, Birgit Karlsson, the Catholic Bishop Hubertus Brandenburg, the Archbishop of the Church of Sweden, Bertil Werkström, among others. Bergsten, Torsten, *Frikyrkor i samverkan,* 1995, pp. 246f., pp. 267-280; Palm, Irving, "Frikyrkofolket och ekumeniken", *Tro & Tanke* 1993:5, 1993, pp. 37ff.

[347] "Möte med konsekvenser", [editorial], *VP*, No. 38, 1992, p. 2.

[348] Hellström, Jan Arvid, *Samfund och radio,* 1979; Larsson, Rune, *Religion i radio och TV under sextio år,* 1988.

9.6.2. Hymn Books

The ecumenical congregations are evidently indications of the realization of the ecumenical strivings taking place in Sweden, with Baptist members and congregations as one of their main actors. We do, however, find further expressions of ecumenical commitment in the Baptist Union of Sweden.

In the case of the Baptist Union of Sweden and the Örebro (Baptist) Mission we find among other things a common hymn book *Psalm och Sång* (Hymns and Songs), 1966;[349] further a joint publishing house, joint training course for missionaries, joint continuing theological education for pastors, and some pastors' meetings etc.

Sampsalm, published in 1987,[350] is a common hymnal for fifteen denominations, among others the Baptist Union of Sweden.[351] There are 325 hymns which are common to all these churches, i.e. hymns with exactly the same text, melody and even number in all the denominational hymn books. There is a second part of the hymn book which consists of a varying number of hymns specific to each denomination. Since 1987 nine denominations, including the Baptist Union of Sweden, have had this second part in common as well. It is called *Psalmer och Sånger* (Hymns and Songs).[352]

---

[349] In 1919 it was suggested that a hymnal for alliance-meetings be published. Lagergren, David, *Framgångstid med dubbla förtecken*, 1989, p. 153, see also Fridborg, Gunnar, "Nu kommer ditt festtåg, o Gud", *Tro, Frihet, Gemenskap*, 1998, pp. 144f. The first Baptist congregations used besides common revivalist songbooks *Pilgrims-Sånger* (1859), *Andeliga sånger* (1850-77, published in small booklets), also the hymn book of the State Church. Fahlgren, Sune, "Baptismen och baptisternas gudstjänstliv", *I enhetens tecken*, 1994, p. 264, see also ibid. pp. 263-271.

[350] See for example *VP*, No. 42, 1987; *Svenska Baptistsamfundets Årsbok* 1988, pp. 7-8, p. 56.

[351] The fifteen denominations are: the Baptist Union of Sweden, the Adventists, The Scandinavian Independent Baptist Union, the Salvation Army, the Holiness Union Mission, the Catholic Church in Sweden, the Liberal Catholic Church, the United Methodist Church in Sweden, the Pentecostal Movement, the Swedish Alliance Mission, the Swedish Salvation Army, the Church of Sweden, the Mission Covenant Church of Sweden, the Örebro (Baptist) Mission and the Swedish Evangelical Mission. (Observe that a change occurred in 1996/97 with Interact, three denominations have merged into one denomintion. On account of this there are after this event less denominations.)

[352] The nine denominations were the Baptist Union of Sweden, the Adventists, the Scandinavian Independent Baptist Union, the Holiness Union Mission, the

This important step has been regarded as a contributory reason to the Baptist Union of Sweden producing the manual of 1987, to be discussed in the next section, together with other denominations. Another reason which might be mentioned is the new translation of the New Testament into Swedish in 1981.[353]

9.6.3. The Baptist Manuals

The Baptist manuals of 1924, 1940, 1955, 1974 and 1987 also point to significant theological and ecumenical aspects.

At the very beginning of the Baptists' history in Sweden there were no manuals at all. At that time there seemed to be no need for any manuals.[354] Eventually a Swedish Baptist manual came, however, into existence in 1924.[355] There was, at the origin of this first Swedish manual, a desire for uniformity in practice among Baptist congregations. This manual consisted of 34 pages, to be compared with the manual of 1987, which has about 245 pages.

United Methodist Church in Sweden, the Swedish Alliance Mission, the Mission Covenant Church of Sweden, the Örebro (Baptist) Mission.

In *Svenska Baptistsamfundets Årsbok* 1988, it is stated by the Central Board: "Fifteen churches and denominations share the common part and nine Free Churches have joined in *Hymns and Songs*. This is an unique ecumenical work which is now available and makes 1987 a memorable year." Ibid. p. 8, see also p. 56. Zettergren discusses also the new Swedish hymn book, *Sampsalm*, and *Psalmer och Sånger*, Zettergren, Sten-Sture, "En ny psalmbok blir till", *Tro & Liv* No. 1, 1987, pp. 5-9; see also Fahlgren, Sune, "Sju samfund - tre handböcker - en gemensam nattvardsliturgi", *Svenskt gudstjänstliv* 62, 1987, pp. 35-55; Swedberg, Bo, "'Psalmer och Sånger' bidrar till en rikare gudstjänst", *VP*, No. 8, 1989, pp. 2f.; Swedberg, Bo, " -Den lär oss förstå bibelns anknytning till vår vardagsvärld", *VP*, No. 8, 1989, pp. 3, 12; Fridborg, Gunnar, "Nu kommer ditt festtåg, o Gud", *Tro, Frihet, Gemenskap*, 1998, p. 145.

In the hymn book *Hymns and Songs* there is also an order of service where we find something new in an ecumenical order for the Lord's table.

[353] See the preface to *Till församlingens tjänst*, 1987.

[354] Eckerdal, Lars, *Vägen in i kyrkan*, 1981, p. 370.

[355] The title was *Formulär för vigsel, begravning, dop och nattvard*. The task of drawing up a formula for religious ceremonies was assigned by the Preachers' conference to some of its members in 1922. These were C.E. Benander, Hj. Danielson, N.J. Nordström, Th. Wennström and Gunnar Westin.

Besides baptism (three pages),[356] there are in this manual of 1924 orders for weddings, funerals and the Lord's table (Holy Communion).

The next manual was published in 1940.[357] This manual included like the manual of 1924 baptism, wedding, funeral and Holy Communion, and it is a slight revision, as a matter of fact almost identical with the manual of 1924.[358]

In the 1950's, there was, as already has been pointed out, an ecumenical breakthrough also among Baptists which had after-effects in the 1960's and onwards. The influences from abroad, in the study of exegesis and liturgy, the international discussions, ecumenical work etc., reached the Baptist Union of Sweden in different ways. There are thus indications of a complementing of the traditional Baptist view of baptism through impulses coming from abroad. David Lagergren states that a renewal of the Baptist theology of baptism occurred in the 1950's and 1960's. The question is, however, as Lagergren says, "how far the renewal of Baptist baptismal theology has affected members in general."[359]

The Religious Freedom Act 1951 played, however, a certain role in a revision of the Baptist manual. In the manual of 1955, called *Handbok för Svenska Baptistsamfundet* (Manual of the Baptist Union of Sweden),[360] there are in comparison with the two former,

---

[356] As for baptism, it is said in the manual of 1924 that the minister (*dopförrättaren*) reads some appropriate Scriptures at the baptismal pool. The following are suggested: Matt. 28:18-20, Matt. 3:13-15, Acts 2:37-41 and at the end of the service Gal. 3:27.

[357] The title was *Handbok för dop, nattvard, vigsel och begravning inom Svenska Baptistsamfundet.* Hj. Danielson and N.J. Nordström produced this work.

[358] As for the celebration of baptism some Scriptures were read, for instance Matt. 3:13-15, Matt. 28:19f., Acts 2:37-41, Rom. 6:3-4 and after the ceremony for example Gal. 3:27. *Handbok för dop, nattvard, vigsel och begravning inom Svenska Baptistsamfundet*, 1940, p. 7. There are also some introductory notes: the person who is going to be baptized ought to have made an oral confession of faith in Christ, either by telling the story of his conversion or by answering questions on the faith put by the leader of the congregation. This is absent in the manual of 1924.

[359] Lagergren, David, "Tradition och förnyelse II", *VP*, No. 26, 1984, p. 6.

[360] The committee working with this manual consisted of Ernhard Gehlin, Fredrik Hedvall, Manne Lundgren (secretary), Erik Rudén and Ruben Swedberg.

besides baptism, wedding, funeral and Holy Communion, also other religious ceremonies such as a blessing of infants,[361] induction of pastors, commission of deacons and reception of members. In this manual the order of baptism is almost the same as in the manual of 1940.[362]

Lars Eckerdal, writing about the publication of the manual of 1955, states that even if Baptists still at that time asserted that baptism is an act of confession of faith and obedience, there were some tendencies among Swedish Baptists, impressed with the growing ecumenical biblical-theological work, also to take into account the issue of baptism.[363] Concerning the insertion of Acts 8:36-38, Eckerdal says: "Baptism may not only be understood as an act of obedience in faith but also as *God's action.*"[364]

In the middle of the 1960's there is another example of the realization of ecumenical strivings. As already mentioned, the two denominations, the Baptist Union of Sweden and the Örebro (Baptist) Mission, decided to publish a common hymn book in 1966, but some years later in 1974 they also published a common manual, *Handbok för församlingens gudstjänstliv* (A Manual of Congregational Worship).[365] These two liturgical books were, of course, great ecumenical events.[366]

This manual of 1974 is, in comparison with the manual of 1955, expanded with still more religious ceremonies and instructions for pastors (i.e. visiting the sick, legal texts with commentaries, a

---

[361] "The blessing of infants was presumably in practice a relatively new phenomenon, which among other things could constitute an actual alternative to infant baptism." Eckerdal, Lars, *Vägen in i kyrkan*, 1981, p. 374. Concerning the blessing of infants see also *BUS* and the discussion about this in Part II.

[362] There are, however, a couple of additional Bible references as Acts 8:36-38 and Col. 2:12.

[363] Eckerdal, Lars, *Vägen in i kyrkan*, 1981, p. 373.

[364] Ibid. pp. 373f. Italics mine.

[365] *Handbok för församlingens gudstjänstliv*, 1974. The committee working with this manual consisted of the Baptists Erik Rudén, Nils Kahlrot, David Lagergren, from Örebro (Baptist) Mission Joel Boström, Linné Eriksson, Mauritz Gagnerud. See also Fahlgren, Sune, "Baptismen och baptisternas gudstjänstliv", *I enhetens tecken*, 1994, pp. 271-273.

[366] See for example Eckerdal, Lars, *Vägen in i kyrkan*, 1981, p. 376.

memorandum for those who officiate at weddings). There are also more alternatives for example in the orders of baptism and marriage.[367] Something new in this manual is *Gudstjänsten* (The Service) which comes directly after the preface.[368] Thereafter we find baptism, Holy Communion etc.

The next manual, the latest, is from 1987. It is called *Till församlingens tjänst. Handbok för Fribaptistsamfundet, Helgelseförbundet, Svenska Baptistsamfundet, Örebromissionen, Finlands Svenska Baptistsamfund*, (For the Ministry of the Congregation. Manual of the Scandinavian Independent Baptist Union, the Holiness Union Mission, the Baptist Union of Sweden, the Örebro (Baptist) Mission, the Baptist Union of Finland).[369] This manual can also be regarded as a sign of the work towards church unity, for it is not the manual of one denomination, or of two as the manual of 1974. It is as a matter of fact the manual of five denominations, which are Baptist. The fact that five different denominations are involved in publishing a manual must be regarded as an historic event and an important step in ecumenical work.

These later manuals, and especially the manual of 1987,[370] are

---

[367] In the manual of 1955 only marriage has an alternative.

[368] *Handbok för församlingens gudstjänstliv*, 1974, pp. 11ff.

[369] The manual of 1987 has been worked out by a committee which consisted of Lennart Andersson, Bernt Axelsson, Bertil Davidsson, Ruben Janarv, Birgit Karlsson, Larsåke W Persson (secretary), Tord Ström, Gustav Sundström. Ulla Bardh took part in the work of the committee for the first year and was after that replaced by Birgit Karlsson. The work with this manual started in 1983. From the beginning in 1983 a committee was appointed by the Boards of the Baptist Union of Sweden and Örebro (Baptist) Mission. Some time afterwards the Swedish Holiness Mission/Holiness Union Mission joined this committee. In the final stage the Scandinavian Independent Baptist Union and the Baptist Union of Finland have decided to support the work of the committee and recommend their congregations and pastors to use it. See also *Svenska Baptistsamfundets Årsbok* 1988, pp. 56f.

[370] Torsten Bergsten writes that this manual of 1987 gives a solemn official confirmation that the widened and deepened understanding of baptism has now attained general recognition even within the Baptist part of Swedish Christianity. Bergsten, Torsten, "Anders Wiberg, dopet och de kristnas enhet", *Tro och Liv*, No. 4, 1988, p. 25. See also Gustafsson, Ingvar, "Till församlingens tjänst", *VP*, No. 34, 1987, p. 6; Fahlgren, Sune, "Baptismen och baptisternas gudstjänstliv", *I enhetens tecken*, 1994, pp. 273-275.

proof of a growing rapprochement between the Baptist Union of Sweden and other denominations. It has for instance some orders of service and formulations from *Handbok till den kristna församlingens tjänst* (A Manual for the Ministry of the Christian Congregation) published in 1983 by the Mission Covenant Church of Sweden and the Swedish Alliance Mission, which are verbatim or in slightly revised form in this manual. Furthermore, other orders of service, for instance wedding and funeral, follow in general the formulations of the Church of Sweden.

A question arises. Why does it make use of other, even non-Baptist, manuals? As a matter of fact it is explained in the manual itself by the committee which worked it out that it is important that people from different denominations can feel themselves at home with the words and the order on such occasions.[371]

After this presentation at the end of Part I of some expressions of ecumenical commitment, which underline still more the ecumenical strivings within the Baptist Union of Sweden, I will in Part II deal with the ecumenical "convergence" document, *DEM*, and the official response to it of the Baptist Union of Sweden, *BUS*, concerning the issue of baptism. Hopefully, the general survey of the Baptist Union of Sweden – in an ecumenical context – in this part will give the following two Parts II and III a better basis, and also give the international reader of this thesis the possibility of a better understanding of the subject.

---

[371] *Till församlingens tjänst*, 1987, p. 9.

Part II

*The Official Response
of the Baptist Union
of Sweden
to BEM*

1. Introduction

In Part I, I have tried to point out some aspects as a background and context of Parts II and III. The Baptist Union of Sweden has an interesting history and background. It has been involved in different ecumenical contexts. Different ecumenical strivings as well as disruptions and divisions, at both an international and a Swedish central denominational and local congregational level, have therefore been discussed. There are changes and reconsiderations at different levels within the Baptist Union of Sweden and in "ecclesiastical geography" in general. There have, besides divisions within the Baptist Union of Sweden, been tendencies both towards mere co-operation with other denominations and congregations, and also towards federation and fusion.

One expression of all this, taking place in the Baptist Union of Sweden at different levels, is as a matter of fact the response of the Baptist Union of Sweden to *BEM*. Bearing in mind the divergent attitude to baptism in the Baptist movement in comparison with other denominations, it is of interest to note that some Baptist Unions have given a response to *BEM* and in that way taken part in the "reception process". This must be regarded possibly also as a step in the ecumenical process and dialogue.[1] The Baptists have from an international point of view tended to maintain a reserved position and sometimes taken up a critical attitude towards ecumenism, and even rejected ecumenical ambitions. This tendency has meant that Baptists have tended to end up on the margins of the ecumenical movement. Nevertheless, Baptists with their characteristic features have on the other hand had and still have an impetus on the ecumenical movement and also take part in ecumenical matters. This is also confirmed for instance by the

---

[1] The Southern Baptists did not give any answer to *BEM*. That this denomination with its millions of members has shown little interest in ecumenical topics and does not participate more actively in the ecumenical dialogue can of course be regarded as a disadvantage.

responses of the Baptist Unions to *BEM*,[2] and among them we find that of the Baptist Union of Sweden.[3] These responses are ecumenical signs showing a readiness to discuss and work with theological matters together with others, and also to work for church unity. Signs of this kind have actually, as regards the Baptist Union of Sweden, been discerned ever since 1905, when the Baptist Union of Sweden and the Mission Covenant Church of Sweden together with the United Methodist Church in Sweden arranged the first Free Church Conference, in spite of differences concerning the issue of baptism. The participation of the Baptist Union of Sweden has also been seen in different consultations, studies, in ecumenical congregations, in common hymn books, manuals etc.

In the following Parts II and III, I am primarily going to study the Baptist Union of Sweden and its reconsideration of baptism in *BUS*, its official response to *BEM*, *and* the public discussions taking place in that denomination. This also implies that the questions of ecclesiology and ecumenism will be, more or less explicitly, involved in the continuing study. That the Swedish Baptists have given an official response is a special ecumenical event. Günther Gassmann writes that the official responses to *BEM* are

> an indication of where the churches stand with regard to ecumenical convergence on the still dividing issues of baptism, eucharist and ministry. They are also an indication of the ways in which the churches are moving forward in renewal, mutual enrichment and ecumenical commitment in common obedience to God's call and mission for the sake of God's world.[4]

There is, however, a danger with such an attitude. For there is in fact a possibility that the official responses at the national, central level, "at the highest appropriate level of authority"[5] (for instance the response to *BEM* of the Baptist Union of Sweden), are not congruent with what happens at the local, congregational and central, denominational levels, which may appear by studying *the*

---

[2] Concerning the responses of the Baptist Unions to *BEM* see, besides the volumes of *Churches respond to BEM*, Vols. I-VI, 1986-1988, Wagner, Günter, *A Survey of Baptist Responses to "Baptism, Eucharist and Ministry"*, 1986.

[3] See appendix.

[4] *Churches respond to BEM*, Vol. IV, 1987, p. vii. Gassman was then Director, WCC, Faith and Order Secretariat.

[5] *BEM*, preface, p. x.

public discussions within a denomination. These are dealt with in Part III. Possibly we may find some signs of a process within the Baptist Union of Sweden at the local, congregational level, indicating something remarkable which does not appear in *BUS*. Through this study of the public discussions, we can see if there are complementary or alternative opinions within a denomination in relation to the official response, which possibly may point to a polarization or even tension between various levels and groups, with regard for example to the teaching and practice of baptism. There is a possibility that the official response to *BEM* reflects only *one* opinion in a denomination, and that there are other opinions and aspects, which are not to be found in such an official response.

Gassmann is, of course, conscious of such dilemmas, and he writes:

> Even though the official responses are *only one expression* of a much broader process of discussion in the churches, they are of special importance.[6]

And *BEM* itself says:

> Perhaps even more influential than the official studies are the changes which are taking place within the life of the churches themselves.[7]

With these statements in mind it could be valuable to look more closely at the central, denominational and local, congregational levels.

The Third World Conference on Faith and Order in Lund said already in 1952 in the final report: "The Ecumenical Movement is not alive unless it is local."[8] Each church, each congregation, each place, is as a matter of fact of importance in ecumenical work. The New Delhi assembly of the *WCC* in 1961 writes:

> We believe that the unity which is both God's will and his gift to his Church is being made visible as all in each place who are baptized into Jesus Christ and confess him as Lord and Saviour are brought by the Holy Spirit into one fully committed fellowship, holding the one apostolic faith, preaching the one Gospel, breaking the one bread, joining in common prayer, and having a corporate life reaching out in witness and service to all and who at the same

---

6   *Churches respond to BEM*, Vol. IV, 1987, p. vii. Italics mine.

7   *BEM*, preface p. viii.

8   See *A Documentary History of the Faith and Order Movement 1927-1963*, 1963, p. 105.

time are united with the whole Christian fellowship in all places and all ages in such wise that ministry and members are accepted by all, and that all can act and speak together as occasion requires for the tasks to which God calls his people.[9]

In this part the official response of the Baptist Union of Sweden to *BEM* will be studied and analysed.[10] I am primarily going to deal with the basic and complex issue of baptism in *BUS*, the response of the Baptist Union of Sweden to *BEM* 1982, and also some other main issues related to baptism, among other things ecclesiology and church unity. A question to bear in mind during this study is, whether baptism is a basic bond of unity or even *the* basic bond? And is it at all possible to write as *BEM* does about "our one baptism" and "our common baptism"? Or is there possibly more than one baptism in the church, and if so, does this depend on different baptismal practices or on different baptismal understandings?

This study involves, however, a weakness, namely that a certain reiteration is inevitable. The reason for this dilemma is, of course, that different aspects, questions and topics are interwoven with each other.

In chapter 1, something is said about the preparatory process, leading up to *BUS*. Thereafter, in chapter 2, I will study the issue of whether there is a common understanding of baptism. On the basic concept "one baptism" in *BEM*, it can be asked if it is possible to use this concept in view of the actual situation: infant baptism and believers' baptism. This depends, of course, on whether infant baptism and believers' baptism are to be regarded as acceptable forms of one and the same baptism; whether they both are recognized as valid and proper. Concepts which are also treated in chapter 3, and are of importance in a discussion about infant baptism and believers' baptism, are "ecclesiology" and "anthropology". This can be

---

9   *The New Delhi Report*, 1962, p. 116; see *BEM*, preface, p. viii, "It is important to acknowledge that the search for local church union and the search for universal consensus are intimately linked."

10   See *Churches respond to BEM*, Vol. IV, 1987, pp. 200-213. This official response of the Baptist Union of Sweden to *BEM* is abbreviated *BUS* in the thesis. Before this English translation appeared there is the response of the working party on *BEM* (the Swedish version) called "Dop Nattvard Ämbete. Svenska Baptistsamfundets svar på Faith and Order Paper No. 111", 1985, [unpublished paper], abbreviated *Dop* in the thesis. I also note that the translation of *BEM* or the Lima-document into Swedish is called *Dop, Nattvard, Ämbete*.

put concretely in the question of whether a person is a child of God (within the Kingdom, New Covenant) or not by birth.[11] In chapter 4, the blessing of children and the faith-context, i.e. the corporate faith, its relevance and importance, are discussed and this also in relation to ecclesiology and the view of man. The question of the blessing of children and faith-context is concluded in the following chapter 5, in a study of the relation between the blessing of children and infant baptism. What kind of difference, if any, is there between a child who has been blessed and one who has been baptized? In chapter 6, the problematic issue of "re-baptism" is discussed. A fundamental question is whether a baptism can be a "re-baptism". How do BEM and BUS handle this question and the practice of what as a matter of fact is regarded by most churches as "re-baptizing" a person baptized as an infant? In chapter 7, the question of the action of man and/or God in baptism is dealt with, that is if baptism is to be looked upon as an expressive, symbolic or an instrumental and sacramental act. Chapter 8 is a study of the celebration of baptism in BEM and BUS. Among other things I discuss what is necessary in the rite of baptism for it to be recognized as proper and valid. The order of baptism, immersion etc., is also discussed. In chapter 9, an important and delicate subject is studied, i.e. ecclesiology. This concerns among other things the questions of baptism and membership, and the relation between these, for example the significance of baptism (or not) for membership in the ecclesia, the church. In the last chapter 10 in this part, about the recognition of baptism and church unity, it is asked whether there is recognition of one another's baptism and therefore there is a common baptism. Or, if this is not the case, if it will ever be possible, amongst the different denominations with various understandings and practices of baptism and ecclesiology, to attain church unity on the basis of baptism, or if there are other possibilities.

Some questions which we shall keep in mind during our study are thus the following. Do we, with reference to BEM's statement about "our one baptism", find that BUS is on its way towards mutual recognition of baptism? And do we find what we may call a common understanding of baptism in BUS and BEM, regarding its institution and meaning and also regarding the relation between baptism and faith? Or do we in fact have more than one baptism in the church? And if so, is this because of different baptismal understandings or

---

[11] These issues of ecclesiology and anthropology are also dealt with in the other chapters.

different baptismal practices? Where is church unity to be found and manifested according to *BEM* and *BUS*?

2. An Introduction to the Response of the Baptist Union of Sweden to *BEM* and to the Preparatory Process

Each work has its own history and context, so also the responses to *BEM*. They are, of course, products of their own time and context, just as *BEM* itself.

> The Lima document exists as the harvest of a long and patient process of reflection recognized by over a hundred theologians representing all the Christian confessions in Lima in January 1982 as ripe enough for presentation to all the churches.[12]

BEM is, of course, influenced by those who have been involved in its process and who finally wrote the document, by their explicit and implicit aims, their thoughts about the recipients etc.

There is a continual interchange on many levels in different ways. This applies also to *BUS*. Two persons, David Lagergren and Torsten Bergsten, have played an important part in starting the process that resulted in *BUS*. According to Lagergren, Bergsten has called attention to the fact, that in *BEM* the predominance of the major Churches is noticeable, while views characteristic of the Free Churches are more infrequent. Consequently, this ought to be one reason for the Swedish Free Church movement to react to *BEM*. Lagergren hopes that such a process will begin in all the churches and denominations in Sweden, irrespective of whether the denomination belongs to the World Council of Churches or not, for this concerns us all.[13]

A committee or working party, called *BEM-gruppen* (the BEM-group) in the Minutes, was appointed by the Central Board of the

---

[12] Thurian, Max, "Introduction: The Lima document on 'Baptism, Eucharist and Ministry' the event and its consequences", *Churches respond to BEM*, Vol. I, 1986, p. 2.

[13] Lagergren, David, "Nattvard och syndabekännelse", *VP*, No. 8, 1983, p. 2.

Baptist Union of Sweden to give a response to this document.[14] The committee consisted of the following five persons: Bert Franzén (b. 1926), principal at Bethel Seminary, Ruben Janarv (b. 1926), chairman of the Personnel Association - *personalförbundet,* Johnny Jonsson (b. 1946), teacher at Bethel Seminary, David Lagergren (b. 1919), General Secretary of the Baptist Union of Sweden and Stig Sköld (1935-1999), education secretary in the Baptist Union. All these are Baptist pastors. David Lagergren was the chairman and Stig Sköld the secretary at the meetings. They met for more than a year and had 10 meetings.[15] A certain degree of international contact and interaction can be found in the work with *BUS*.[16] We notice that neither women nor laity were represented.

---

[14] We can compare how differently the words "The Faith and Order Commission now respectfully invites all churches to prepare an official response to this text at the highest appropriate level of authority, whether it be a council, synod, conference, assembly or other body" *(BEM* p. x), have been interpreted by different churches and denominations. See for example *BUS* and compare this with other responses to *BEM,* where "... all congregations were offered the opportunity to study and respond as well." (Lutheran Church in America), *Churches respond to BEM,* Vol. I, 1986, pp. 28f.; see also ibid. pp. 111f., (Christian Church (Disciples of Christ)); *Churches respond to BEM,* Vol. II, 1986, pp. 63f., (Church of the Province of New Zealand); ibid. pp. 165f., (Presbyterian Church of Wales) etc.

[15] There are Minutes and Supplements from the meetings, which lay behind the definitive response of *BUS* but which are not to be found in it. By quoting them in the text or in the footnotes, we can follow the discussion of the working party and also get a better understanding of the process which preceded *BUS,* and also of *BUS* itself.

The following meetings were held: 1. 5/10/83, §§ 1-6; 2. 2/11/83, §§ 7-10; 3. 17/1/84, §§ 11-16; 4. 23/2/84, §§ 17-24; 5. 20/3/84, §§ 25-30; 6. 11/5/84, §§ 31-36; 7. 23/8/84, §§ 37-47; 8. 20/9/84, §§ 48-55; 9. 18/10/84, §§ 55-65 [§ 55 occurs twice, partly in the meeting of 20/9/84 and partly in the meeting of 18/10/84. This has, however, no significance for us]; 10. 20/11/84, §§ 66-72.

[16] The working party refers for example to a letter from the Baptist World Alliance. See Minutes 17/1/84, § 12, "Brev från BWA innefattande rapport från utvärderingsgrupp utsedd av BWA och WARC, de reformerta kyrkornas världsallians, att granska resultaten av samtalen mellan de reformerta och baptister 1973-77 (rapporten från 1982) *samt* utdrag ur rapport från WARC Executive Committee, Kappel, 1983, *och* ett brev från BWA och WARC till alla baptister och reformerta." [WARC, i.e. World Alliance of Reformed Churches, remark mine].

During the first meeting it was decided that Ruben Janarv should take the main responsibility for studying the part about Baptism in *BEM* and give his viewpoints. David Lagergren should deal with the Eucharist, Stig Sköld with the Ministry part 1-3, Bert Franzén with the Ministry part 4-6; and Johnny Jonsson should study the commentaries.[17] At the meeting on 18/10/84, it is decided that the chairman David Lagergren should write an introduction to the report of the committee.[18]

At the second meeting, 2/11/83, Ruben Janarv gave his viewpoints and commentaries regarding Baptism in *BEM*.[19] The group was of the opinion that the following main points concerning baptism ought to be mentioned in a response to *BEM:*

1. The question of the mutual recognition of baptism.

2. The justification and limitations of open membership.

3. The meaning of the blessing of children.[20]

It was decided that Ruben Janarv was to work on points 1 and 2, Bert Franzén on point 3.[21]

Concerning other international contacts, see Minutes 23/8/84, § 39, We read: "David Lagergren rapporterar från EBF:s Commission on Doctrine. David delgav vid kommissionens sammanträde sitt eget bidrag till yttrande om Limatextens avsnitt om nattvarden. Andra bidrag vid kommissionen som delges BEM-gruppen är

* London Baptist Association response to 'Baptism, Eucharist and Ministry'

* Thorwald Lorenzen: 'Baptism and Church Membership: Some Baptist positions and their ecumenical implications'

* Noel Dose [Vose, my remark]: 'The Lima Statement on Baptism: A Baptist's Response to the Faith and Order Paper No. 111.'"

See also Minutes 20/9/84, § 51, We read: "Anmäls brev från Geneve (CEC), där stor aktivitet i pågående konsultationer rapporteras. Ingen inbjudan att delta föreligger."

17 Minutes 5/10/83, § 4.

18 Minutes 18/10/84, § 61.

19 See Supplement to Minutes 2/11/83.

20 "Gruppen anser att följande tre huvudpunkter bör belysas i ett kommande yttrande: 1. Frågan om ömsesidigt doperkännande (punkt 15). 2. Det öppna medlemskapets motiveringar och begränsningar. 3. Barnvälsignelsens innebörd." Minutes 2/11/83, § 9.

21 Ibid.

At the next meeting, 17/1/84, Bert Franzén delivered a paper about the blessing of infants, and at the meeting 23/2/84 it was stated that Bert Franzén is to complete his earlier paper about the blessing of infants.[22] The committee also discussed whether a supplement on the blessing of children should be added to B com 12. This contribution could also be used in the question about the mutual recognition of baptism, and even churches practising infant baptism could be recommended to consider the meaning and justification of the blessing of children.[23]

At the last meeting on 20/11/84, it was decided to present the response of the working party on BEM (the Swedish version[24]) to the Central Board of the Baptist Union of Sweden.[25] The Central Board had a meeting 8/3/85 at Kungsholms Baptistkyrka, Stockholm, and decided to approve the response.[26] Among them we find Birgit Karlsson, later the General Secretary after David Lagergren.[27]

---

[22] It can be mentioned that Franzén at this time worked on the issue of the spiritual position of children and the blessing of children, which resulted in the book Guds försprång. 1991, (God's Advantage. On Children and the Kingdom of God).

[23] "I samtalet framförs att en bilaga om barnvälsignelsen kan fogas till kommentaren till punkt IV A 12 [i.e. B com 12, my remark] i Limadokumentets avsnitt om dopet. Inlägget kunde också komma i frågan om ömsesidigt doperkännande och även barndöpande kyrkor kunde rekommenderas av ["att", my remark] överväga barnvälsignelsens motivering och innebörd." Minutes 23/2/84, § 20.

[24] i.e. "Dop Nattvard Ämbete. Svenska Baptistsamfundets svar på Faith and Order Paper No. 111", [1985], [unpublished paper].

[25] Minutes 20/11/84, § 68.

[26] "Svenska Baptistsamfundets svar på Faith and order paper nr 111 om dop, nattvard och ämbete har utsänts till missionsstyrelsens ledamöter.
Missionsstyrelsen beslutar att godkänna yttrandet." Minutes 8/3/85, § 13. See also Svenska Baptistsamfundets Årsbok 1986, p. 53.

[27] The following persons participated in this meeting of the Central Board on 8/3/85: Börje Hammarroth, chairman; Lars Ericson, vice chairman; Ingvar Paulsson, vice chairman; Valter Mattsson, secretary at this meeting. Besides these Sören Andersson, Paul G Dahlberg, Bernt Ekinge, Brita Erlandsson, Lazar Grujic, Ingvar Gustafsson, Elisabeth Hurtig, Birgit Karlsson, Gunnar Kjellander, Anita Larsson, Agneta Magnusson, Margaretha Möller, Ruth Osmund, Ingrid Rudberg, Stig Svärd, Gunnar Sönnerhed, Lennart Åkerblom, Lennart Gustafsson, Sven Ohm, Lilian Åkerblom, Bert

In *BUS* it is stated in the foreword that,

The Baptist Union of Sweden, although not a member of the World Council of Churches, has always followed with great interest the work of the Faith and Order Commission of the WCC. When the Lima document on 'Baptism, Eucharist and Ministry' appeared, it seemed therefore natural that the Baptist Union of Sweden should formulate a response to this document. This response has been worked out by a committee of five persons and has been approved by the executive board of the Union.[28]

Franzén (during the later part of the meeting), Eivor Lönnback, Margaretha Wiktell, Bengt Jansson, Olof Lindström, Bo Swedberg and Ruben Janarv. See Minutes [8/3/85] of the Central Board of the Baptist Union of Sweden.

[28] *BUS* p. 200.

3. Reactions to *BEM's* Understanding of "the one Baptism" in the Church

I am now in this chapter mainly going to study the question of "the one baptism" or "our one baptism" in *BEM* and *BUS*.

It can be noted that *BUS* does not give any explicit answers to the four questions posed by *BEM*, about

-*the extent to which your church can recognize in this text the faith of the Church through the ages; -the consequences your church can draw from this text for its relations and dialogues with other churches, particularly with those churches which also recognize the text as an expression of the apostolic faith; - the guidance your church can take from this text for its worship, educational, ethical, and spiritual life and witness; -the suggestions your church can make for the ongoing work of Faith and Order as it relates the material of this text on Baptism, Eucharist and Ministry to its long-range research project 'Towards the Common Expression of the Apostolic Faith Today'.*[29]

BUS starts immediately with introductory notes on the issue of baptism. I will discuss the paragraphs in *BEM* and the responses of the Baptist Union of Sweden to these, beginning with *B 1*.

What *BEM* writes in section I, paragraph *B 1*, about the institution of baptism, does not result in any explicit comment at all. From this point of view it looks as if *BUS* is in agreement with *BEM*.

In section II, paragraphs *B 2-7* about the meaning of baptism, *BEM* has the following outline:

A. Participation in Christ's Death and Resurrection *(B 3)*.

B. Conversion, Pardoning and Cleansing *(B 4)*.

C. The Gift of the Spirit *(B 5)*.

D. Incorporation into the Body of Christ *(B 6)*.

E. The Sign of the Kingdom *(B 7)*.

---

[29] *BEM*, preface, p. x.

BUS does not *explicitly* comment on or question paragraphs *B 2, B 3, B 4*,[30] but only *B 5*, the gift of the Spirit,[31] and *B 6*, the incorporation into the Body of Christ, where it makes a reservation. Concerning *B 1-7, BUS* writes:

> In accordance with the above [referring to 'Introductory notes' in *BUS*, remark mine] we can agree with what is said here. Yet the indicated difficulty emerges in the last sentence in § 6... Can we in earnest talk about 'our one baptism' as long as baptismal practice in a decisive way divides us?[32]

The problem becomes accentuated by baptismal practice. The committee also mentions this. Janarv writes a commentary in a Supplement to the Minutes:

> Almost everyone agrees on the institution and meaning of baptism, and they have done so for some time now... Note section II D6 [i.e. *B 6*, my remark]. What does for example the Mission Covenant Church of Sweden say about incorporation into the body of Christ? Note that the commentary concerns to a large extent practice, and it is here 'differences' appear.[33]

The reason for the emphasis on baptismal *practice* can be derived from *BEM* itself. In *B com 6* it is stated:

> *The inability of the churches mutually to recognize their various practices of baptism as sharing in the one baptism...*[34]

---

30 Janarv makes a note, in a Supplement to the Minutes, on the Swedish translation of *B 4*, "The baptism... implies confession of sin and conversion of heart." In *Dop, Nattvard, Ämbete* this is translated in the following way, "Det dop... är förbundet med syndabekännelse och hjärtats omvändelse." *Dop, Nattvard, Ämbete*, 2nd ed., 1983, p. 16. Janarv criticizes the Swedish translation and makes the following comment: "Dopet 'innebär' (implies) syndabekännelse och omvändelse, inte enbart 'är förbundet med'." Supplement to Minutes 2/11/83.

31 Concerning the discussion on *B 5*, see below.

32 *BUS* p. 200f.

33 "Dopets (I) instiftelse och (II) innebörd är nästan alla överens om och har varit det ett bra tag... Obs II D 6 [i.e. *B 6*, my remark] - Vad säger t ex SMF om införlivandet i Kristi kropp? Obs att kommentaren i hög grad gäller *praxis*, där framträder 'skillnader'." Supplement to Minutes 2/11/83.

34 In *Dop, Nattvard, Ämbete*, 2nd ed., 1983, it is said: "Kyrkornas oförmåga att erkänna, att deras olika praxis i fråga om dopet ändå representerar delaktighet i ett och samma dop..." (p. 17). Janarv makes the following note on the Swedish translation: "Kommentar: Kyrkornas oförmåga 'inbördes' ((mutually) saknas) att erkänna (att) deras olika praxis ifråga om dopet *som*

Further, it is said in B com 6:

The need to recover baptismal unity is at the heart of the ecumenical task as it is central for the realization of genuine partnership within the Christian communities.[35]

BEM writes in B 6:

Through baptism, Christians are brought into union with Christ, with each other and with the Church of every time and place. Our common baptism, which unites us to Christ in faith, is thus a basic bond of unity... Therefore, our one baptism into Christ constitutes a call to the churches to overcome their divisions and visibly manifest their fellowship.[36]

The question is what BEM's statement about "our one baptism" means, and where the unity is to be achieved according to it? The answer seems to be that the unity is achieved in Christ. The focus for the discussion about baptism is thus put on Christ. Baptism is founded on God's saving action in Christ. There is in other words a christological basis of baptism. He commands baptism, and is the centre where unity is realized. If Christ unites the next question will be: in what way or by what means? The answer is explicit. Christ unites people through baptism, and baptism is thus an instrument. Consequently it urges the churches and denominations to recover this baptismal unity.[37]

(inte: ändå representerar) delaktighet i ett och samma dop. Här är i sv. översättningen en uppmjukning av engelska texten." Supplement to Minutes 2/11/83.

[35] And in Dop, Nattvard, Ämbete, 2nd ed., 1983, this is translated: "Behovet att återupptäcka och återvinna enheten i dopet är en central ekumenisk angelägenhet med tanke på förverkligandet av ett sannskyldigt partnerskap de kristna samfunden emellan." (p. 17). Janarv writes: "'Recover' är översatt: återupptäcka och återvinna 'partnerskap' - ovanligt i svenskan". Supplement to Minutes 2/11/83.

[36] B 6. Italics mine. Max Thurian writes among other things concerning the purpose of the invitation to the churches to receive BEM: "It is a question of discovering whether, in all the diversity of our legitimate and enriching confessional traditions, yet confessing the same fundamental faith of our common creed, we are able and willing to work together for the renewal and unity of the churches. The basis of this work is our one baptism." Thurian, Max, "Introduction: The Lima document on 'Baptism, Eucharist and Ministry' the event and its consequences", Churches respond to BEM, Vol. I, 1986, p. 9. Italics mine.

[37] B com 6.

It seems as if *BEM* relates baptism to what we may call a vertical dimension, emphasizing the importance of the relation to and unity with Christ, and due to this idea it can write about "our one baptism". Unity is achieved in Christ, but the churches are not united since they have not yet seen this. The task is therefore *"to recover baptismal unity"*.[38]

I put, however, a question mark to this: is this possible if there are for example different baptismal practices? *BUS* asks, as we already have noted, if we can talk about "our one baptism" while there are different baptismal practices?[39] What kind of difficulties do we find with this kind of statement in *BUS* when *BEM* mentions "our one baptism"? The question put in *BUS* is challenging. It points implicitly to the possible interpretation that we do not have one baptism but at least two baptisms.

It looks as if the emphasis in *BUS* is put more on the act of baptism, i.e. on baptismal practice. Since there are different baptismal practices, infant baptism and believers' baptism, there seems to be reason not to write about "our one baptism". *BUS* relates baptism to a more horizontal level, i.e. looking at how the various and different baptisms relate to one another. It seems as if it in one sense has misunderstood the text and the intention of *BEM* and therefore cannot agree with it on "our one baptism" since it starts from baptismal practice. *BEM* and *BUS* refer to different things when they discuss "our one baptism". The latter cannot accept that all the so-called baptisms are to be recognized as baptisms. We will discuss this more subsequently.

In section III, paragraphs *B 8-10*, *BEM* deals with the issues of baptism and faith, and also with the lifelong growth into Christ. Of these paragraphs *BUS* deals mainly with *B 8*, about baptism as both God's gift and our human response to that gift.[40] It seems that it does not question *BEM's* statement about this. We can rather find agreement on this point; there seems to be *a common understanding*

---

[38] Ibid.

[39] *BUS* p. 201.

[40] In *B 8* it is stated: "Personal commitment is necessary for responsible membership in the body of Christ." In *Dop, Nattvard, Ämbete*, 2nd ed., 1983, p. 18 this is translated: "Personlig hängivenhet är nödvändig..." Janarv has a note on *B 8*, where he writes: "'Commitment' är översatt 'hängivenhet', 'överlåtelse' är bättre." Supplement to Minutes 2/11/83.

of baptism.[41] *BUS* writes, however, on the fact that there are various baptismal practices: "But various practices indicate different consequences of this common understanding."[42]

Based on the fact that we have various baptismal practices, can we be sure, as *BUS* asserts, that we as a matter of fact have a common understanding of baptism? The answer depends, of course, on *BUS'* interpretation of the concept "common understanding". It would, however, seem possible that the various practices which it refers to are deduced not from a common understanding of baptism, but rather from different understandings of baptism, i.e. that there are implicitly different doctrines of baptism. This may indicate the possibility that it is more than just baptismal practice(s) that divides the denominations with reference to the issue of baptism. Our further investigation will hopefully find an answer to this dilemma.

BEM emphasizes in *B 9* and *B 10*, that baptism is a "life-long growth into Christ" with ethical implications. *BUS* does not explicitly mention or comment on these paragraphs.

So far it can be established that, according to *BUS*, we are not confronted with different baptismal understandings. There is a common understanding of baptism, but there are different baptismal practices. The question must be asked whether it is possible to talk of a common baptism when there are in fact different baptismal practices? Does it not indicate that there are different underlying baptismal understandings and thus at least

---

[41]   *BUS* p. 201. In a Supplement Janarv writes: "Praxis visar emellertid på olika konsekvenser av *denna gemensamma förståelse.*" Supplement to Minutes 23/2/84. Italics mine. And in another Supplement Janarv writes about the disunity in practice: the necessity of baptism is *recognized by all churches*, but it is also here practice which disunites, "Dopets nödvändighet *erkännes av alla kyrkor* - men även här är det praxis som skiljer." Supplement to Minutes 2/11/83. Italics mine.

   Concerning the recognition of baptism by all churches or denominations, compare, however, with the Society of Friends and the Salvation Army. See also *BUS* p. 201 writing: "The Society of Friends and the Salvation Army, for example, do not practise any baptism."

[42]   *BUS* p. 201. In *Dop* we do not find the last quoted sentence from *BUS*, but the following, which is missed in *BUS*: "We appreciate the emphasis on the significance of baptism for Christian hope and a responsible life in the world." ("Vi uppskattar betoningen av dopets betydelse för det kristna hoppet och för ansvarigt liv i världen.") *Dop* p. 2.

two baptisms? This is one of the topics which I want to penetrate in the next chapter.

4. Infant Baptism and Believers' Baptism

In discussing baptism we cannot avoid the two concepts "infant baptism" and "believers' baptism" – although it is a distinction which is often proposed in an oversimplified way as one between unconditional opposites. This is, however, not always the truth. Nevertheless they create associations in many directions - not least concerning the questions of unity and division in the church, a subject which we will also discuss later on in the thesis.[43] In this chapter, I am going to treat the issues of infant baptism and believers' baptism as they are traditionally understood, and also with reference to the question of anthropology and ecclesiology, especially the place of children in the church.

BEM has the following outline in section IV, paragraphs B 11-16, about baptismal practice:

A. Baptism of believers and infants (B 11-13).

(We may note that it has the question of infant baptism and believers' baptism under the heading Baptismal Practice.)

B. Baptism - chrismation - confirmation (B 14).

C. Towards mutual recognition of baptism (B 15-16).

In regard to the issues mentioned above, I am in this chapter mainly going to deal with A, B 11-13.

The question of anthropology is and has been a difficult theological problem, which ought to be discussed more fully than is done in this thesis. Both anthropology and ecclesiology are related in one way or another to baptism. For the view of man has consequences for baptism and ecclesiology, and vice versa, and this subject touches the complex issue of evil, original sin etc. We touch on one sensitive ecclesiological problem, namely the place of children in the church. It is a problem which in its turn depends on anthropology. In order to get a better understanding of the view of man in BUS and BEM, there is a fundamental question to ask: what kind of relation do children have to God by birth?

---

[43] See also Part I, especially chapter 9.

BUS is explicit on this question. Children by birth live "under the atonement of Christ",[44] and this is evidently a common Baptist conviction.[45] For this reason "no special performance is required" according to *BUS*.[46] The "special performance" which is mentioned must allude to infant baptism. According to its view of man, which seems to presuppose that infants are not in bondage, nor under the judgment of sin, no such special performance is needed. Children are by birth free. They are obviously within the Kingdom (Covenant) without any baptism.

Consequently, it seems that it is presupposed that something occurs in a person's spiritual life before believers' baptism can take place - which on a traditional Baptist view should be a *baptism of metanoia* - an "event" of some kind sometime between birth and the baptism proper. This "event" implies that man is no longer within the Kingdom/Covenant. If and when a man becomes conscious about this state and wants to return, i.e. to convert and repent, the right time for the performance of baptism is at hand. The person is then again in the Covenant.

Nevertheless, *BUS* looks for some kind of act for infants and children. Instead of practising baptism, it advocates the blessing of children. While the "event" has not yet happened, baptism seems to be excluded for small infants and children. What does this blessing mean? It is "an expression and a reminder of this situation of life", i.e. that the children live "under the atonement of Christ and also in the protection of the faith of their parents and the church fellowship."[47] The document has a positive view of man. Man is not outside the New Covenant, the Kingdom, by birth.

In *BEM*, however, there seems to be another view of man: man is in bondage by birth. It is more pessimistic. Christian baptism (which includes infant baptism) is "a washing away of sin... [It is]

---

44 *BUS* p. 204.

45 "The blessing of infants in the congregation expresses the general Baptist conviction that the child, though unaware of it, without either faith or baptism, participates in the atonement of Christ and thereby God's grace." Bergsten, Torsten, "Kontroversiella rekommendationer", *Dop, Nattvard, Ämbete*, 2nd ed., 1983, p. 135.

46 *BUS* p. 204.

47 Ibid.

an exodus from bondage".[48] "Thus those baptized are no longer slaves to sin, but free."[49] It is explicitly said in the heading of *B 6*, that baptism is "Incorporation into the Body of Christ". Baptism is "entry into the New Covenant between God and God's people."[50] Further, baptism "unites the one baptized with Christ and with his people."[51] In other words, it mediates salvation, eternal life. The question is, however, if baptism - and all that is said about it, its meaning etc. in *BEM* - is complete when connected "only" to the rite itself or if it has to be completed (with chrism, and the eucharist as in the Orthodox Churches or with some kind of confirmation as in some other churches) for salvation and the *total* initiation. In these paragraphs, *BEM* shows that man is outside the Body of Christ, the church, by birth. Since man belongs like the whole of creation in one way to God, but is fallen, a special act is needed, i.e. baptism.

In *BUS*, however, children belong to the New Covenant by birth. There is an evident difference (with implications). It is stated:

> The Baptists do not adhere to the teaching of inherited sin in the sense that the children already from birth should live under the judgment of sin.[52]

A question arises from this statement: Do human beings live under the atonement of Christ forever, or is it possible to be outside the New Covenant? The answer of the quotation above seems to be that it is possible for man to live under the judgment of sin and thus outside the Covenant. Because of this *BUS* can also talk about conversion as a reality. It is of the opinion that conversion is a fundamental condition for baptism proper, believers' baptism, *a baptism of metanoia.*

We must consequently ask whether baptism according to *BUS* is therefore regarded as a "second entry" into the New Covenant or incorporation into Christ? For it did not, as we have pointed out above, make any explicit comments on *B 1-4*, but seemed to agree with *BEM*, that baptism is "incorporation into Christ... it is entry into the New Covenant between God and God's people."[53] etc. *BUS*

---

[48] *B 2.*

[49] *B 3.*

[50] *B 1.*

[51] *B 2.*

[52] *BUS* p. 204. See also Part III, e.g. chapter 2.2.

[53] *B 1.*

writes concerning *B 1-7*, with the exception of the paragraphs I have mentioned above, *B 5* and *B 6*, concerning especially the issue of "our one baptism": "In accordance with the above we can agree with what is said here."[54]

We find on the one hand that children belong to God and are within the Covenant by birth, and on the other that baptism is an entry into the New Covenant, (since *BUS* does not oppose *BEM* in *B 1-4)*. Self-evidently it is impossible to enter somewhere you already are. There must thus be a presupposition to this second entry into the Covenant. It looks as if there must be the "event" mentioned above - at least in most cases (for it is not explicitly said in *BUS* that a fall is necessary to be baptized). In other words, some kind of a "fall" is normally to be reckoned with in order for baptism to take place. Man lives now under the judgment of sin. He is outside the Body of Christ, the Covenant, and needs to repent and be baptized.[55] The question of whether baptism in this case is a second entry into the Covenant may thus be answered in the affirmative.

A fundamental question, which is not easy to answer, follows from this. Of what does the "fall", which must imply that a person no longer belongs to the New Covenant or does not, in the words of *BUS*, live "under the atonement of Christ", consist?

This view of conversion must presuppose that there is some kind of a change, a "fall", in regard to a person's spiritual position. It is a "fall" from one position to another, from "a", which is the New Covenant, the Body of Christ, to "b", which is something else, that which is contrary to the New Covenant. This "transfer", from one position "a" to another "b", is the presupposition for proper baptism, believers' baptism with a personal conversion and the acceptance of faith, i.e. when the person in question "returns" from "b" to the position of "a".

Furthermore, what is the significance of believers' baptism, if a person does not "transfer" from "a" to "b", but grows up in a Christian environment? In such a case baptism can neither be an entry into the Covenant, nor a baptism of repentance *(metanoia)*. What kind of baptism is it, when the person in question just

---

[54] *BUS* p. 200.

[55] We may just remind ourselves about one central thesis in Baptist teaching, which is to be found in Acts 2:38: "Repent and be baptized, everyone of you, in the name of Jesus Christ for the forgiveness of your sins. And you will receive the gift of the Holy Spirit."

confesses his belonging to God in an act of baptism? I would rather call it a baptism of manifestation (or possibly of obedience), instead of a *baptism of metanoia*. It is nevertheless administered, possibly on the basis of the institution in Matt. 28:18-20.

It seems that this kind of baptism partly undermines the value and meaning of baptism, which *BEM* describes in *B 1-7*, referring to the New Testament, as incorporation into the Body of Christ, a new birth, an exodus from bondage, a liberation into a new humanity, which obviously cannot be applied to a person who already is in the Covenant.[56]

Is it possible in such a case to call this a genuine baptism, a *baptism of metanoia*, since we do not find the presuppositions upon which believers' baptism rests, i.e. personal conversion, returning from position "b" to "a", but (only) confession of faith. Unfortunately we do not get any explicit answers in *BUS* to these questions.

The doctrine of original sin has played an important role during the centuries, often as an argument for the practice of infant baptism. *BEM* seems to hold that doctrine - which could have been discussed more, in particular the connection between baptism and original sin - and thus to be of a different opinion than *BUS* concerning the view of man, which, of course, results in other conclusions.[57] The child is not "only" born into a broken world, it also shares in its brokenness.[58] All this points to the position that children, before being baptized, do not belong to the Covenant, the Body of Christ.

There seems to be, reflected in the view of the newborn, different anthropologies in *BEM* and *BUS*. For the latter children belong to God by birth, they are subject to the love and care of the heavenly Father. Therefore, baptism is not needed at an early age. We can

---

[56] I want to note that the idea of Covenant is to be found in *BEM*, but it could with advantage have been further explicitly developed and also with references to the Old Testament.

[57] *BEM* quotes 1 Cor. 6:11 (Baptism is a washing away of sin), 1 Cor. 10:1-2 (Baptism as an exodus from bondage); Gal. 3:27-28 and 1 Cor. 12:13 (Baptism as a liberation into a new humanity). See *B 2*.

[58] "*The infant is born into a broken world and shares in its brokennes.*" *B com 12*. *BEM* writes also: "By baptism, Christians are immersed in the liberating death of Christ where their sins are buried, where the 'old Adam' is crucified with Christ, and where the power of sin is broken." *B 3*. And in *B com 18* it says: "*those who are baptized into the body of Christ are made partakers of a renewed existence.*"

understand that it dissociates itself from the doctrine of original sin in the sense that children from birth live under sway of sin. According to *BEM*, children do not belong to God (the new Covenant) by birth, and therefore baptism is strongly vindicated. Is there not a risk, however, that *BEM* implicitly contributes to something which it explicitly wants to counteract, i.e. that sometimes – because of this strong emphasis on baptism – so-called indiscriminate baptisms are practised?

These different understandings of man have, of course, implications for whether infant baptism or believers' baptism alone is to be practised. *BUS* pleads one-sidedly for believers' baptism, while *BEM* pleads for both infant baptism and believers' baptism. There are thus two different baptismal practices resulting from different conditions for the validity of baptism, depending on among other things anthropology.

There may nevertheless be a *common understanding* of baptism, but it is not obvious that one can write as *BEM* does about "our one baptism" or "our common baptism". *BEM* itself states clearly that believers' baptism "is the most clearly attested pattern in the New Testament documents."[59] but it does not discuss in detail its reasons for advocating infant baptism, possibly because the existence of infant baptism is implicit or even non-existent in the New Testament. There are hermeneutical problems here, if it is possible to regard these *baptisms* as equivalent, (i.e. if believers' baptism as a matter of fact is compatible with infant baptism). We will have reason to discuss this more below.

---

[59] *B 11.*

5. Faith-Context - with Special Reference to the Blessing of Children

The subject of faith-context, or corporate faith, and the blessing of children will be discussed in this chapter.[60] Since *BUS* does not discuss the topic of children and the faith-context in relation to the more traditional approach – see for example BEM, i.e. where faith-context is related to infant baptism in the discussion - but, for reasons which will become apparent below, in relation to the blessing of children, this chapter has a different character than could possibly be expected. The topic of this chapter may also be of value for the next chapter, where the blessing of children also will be discussed, but then in relation to infant baptism.

It can be noted that the blessing of children has been practised within the Baptist Union of Sweden ever since the middle of the 1930's. The blessing of infants is found for the first time in a Swedish Baptist manual in 1955.[61] Some took place, however, as early as the 1860's.[62]

From the previous discussion we have found that *BUS* has a different argumentation than *BEM* concerning baptism and the place of children in the church. To practise infant baptism is absolutely out of the question for the former. It holds that no special rite or act is needed, i.e. no baptism for infants, since they already are within the Covenant or, as Baptists would prefer to say, the Kingdom of God.

A child is, however, not able to become a member of a Baptist congregation, because of Baptist anthropology and ecclesiology. For according to this it is faith, the conscious response of man, together

---

[60] Sometimes another term is used instead of *blessing of children*, namely *dedication*, but not *BUS*.

[61] *Handbok för Svenska Baptistsamfundet*, 3rd ed., 1955, pp. 83f.

[62] *BUS* p. 204. See also Franzén, Bert, *Guds försprång*, 1991, pp. 88-90.

with believers' baptism, which results in membership in the Baptist congregation. These presuppositions exclude infants from membership. *BUS* is conscious of this dilemma.

A possible solution to the problems with infant baptism and the place of children seems to be found in the blessing of children. *BUS* gives expression to a desire for closer studies on the subject of the place of children. It writes:

> The place and theological foundation of the blessing of children has probably not been given enough attention in this connection but should be the subject of a close study, which hopefully could give a new basis of the question of mutual acceptance of baptismal practices.[63]

A wish for mutual acceptance of baptismal *practices* is thus expressed. It may be of interest to compare *BUS* and *Dop*. In the latter the question of mutual recognition of *baptism* is discussed.[64] However, in the English version, *BUS*, there is more emphasis on baptismal *practices* than in the Swedish text, *Dop*.

The concept "faith" should be analysed here. There is a wide spectrum of difficulties with the concept "faith". Does faith mean the faith found in for example the New Testament or in other documents, in the historic Creeds, in doctrine alone or in doctrine plus practice?[65] There are different interpretations and understandings of faith - faith as trust and confidence, faith as an intellectual assent to doctrines/propositions etc. The classic terms are *fides qua, fides quae* and *fiducia*. Similar problems arise, of course, when discussing the issue of faith-context or corporate faith.

Is there any difference according to *BUS* between children growing up in a faith-context, which possibly may be interpreted as living in Christian (Baptist) families, and children growing up in non-Christian families, i.e. without any (closer) faith-context? In *BUS* the children growing up in Christian (Baptist) homes obviously

---

63 *BUS* p. 202.

64 *Dop* writes: "... frågan om det ömsesidiga doperkännandet." See *Dop* p. 4.

65 Concerning the difficulties with the concept "faith", see for example Ratschow, Carl Heinz, *Die eine christliche Taufe*, 1972, p. 107: "Es ist deutlich, dass dabei der Glaube keineswegs einhellig bestimmbar ist. Dieser Glaube ist bei Thomas die fides catholica als Bekenntnis also der 'Glaube der Kirche'... Bei Luther ist es die fides als poenitentia und fiducia. Bei Calvin ist dieser Glaube die cognitio, die sich auf den Erwählungsratschluss bezieht."

have an advantage. And this is on account of an act that goes back to Jesus' example, that is to say the blessing of children. This act may be regarded as "the possibility as well as the obligation to express 'that children are placed under the protection of God's grace'".[66]

It writes that children live "also in the protection of the faith of their parents" and not "only" this, but also under protection of "the church fellowship".[67] What this protection of the faith of Christian parents and of the Christian fellowship adds to or effects in the children, in comparison with a child who is "only" under the general protection of Christ, we do not get any explicit answer to. But as the child by birth is a child of God, it seems as if this spiritual status in one way or another is looked upon as a threatened state, which Christian parents unlike non-Christian parents are conscious about, and thus these parents try among other things through the blessing of children to help the child to preserve its status as a child of God.

The working party makes several comments on this topic. It considers the question of whether the blessing of children should be given only to those who later on will receive a Christian education.[68] It seems to be implied by Franzén that this act, the blessing of children, should not be carried out where it is known that it will not be followed up by a Christian education, while the blessing of children taking place within a congregation presupposes promises both from parents and from the congregation.[69] What these promises consist of is, however, not specified.

---

[66] *BUS* p. 202, quoting *B 16*: "there is the possibility as well as the obligation to express 'that children are placed under the protection of God's grace' (§ 16) in an act that goes back to Jesus' action." *BUS* quotes *B 16*: "The first may seek to express more visibly the fact that children are placed under the protection of God's grace."

[67] *BUS* p. 204.

[68] Janarv writes: "Man måste dock överväga om barnvälsignelsen skall 'ges' enbart åt den som sedan får en kristen fostran." Supplement to Minutes 2/11/83.

[69] The working party, referring to Bert Franzén, writes in a commentary: "... that when it [the blessing of children, my remark] takes place in the context of the congregation it presupposes promises from both parents and congregation and should have a clear reference to conversion and baptism in the future." ("På frågan om vi kan ge barnvälsignelse i sammanhang där vi *vet* att den inte kommer att följas upp av kristen fostran, menade Bert att när

In spite of the obvious statement, that the blessing of children is an official act involving responsibilities of Christian education, it is stated in the next sentence, that it is, however, possible to take part individually in what is called an "unofficial" blessing of children.[70] Then the presuppositions and responsibilities are evidently changed. There is no explicit discussion of the differences between an official and an unofficial blessing of children.

That it is possible to have the blessing of children in an unofficial way, but not in an official way, i.e. in the congregation, if it is known with certainty that there will not be any Christian education seems strange, not least bearing in mind what is stated in the Supplement to the Minutes about the "official" blessing of children:

> that when it takes place in the context of the congregation it presupposes promises from both parents and congregation and *should have a clear reference to conversion and baptism in the future.*[71]

In *BUS* the reference of the blessing of children to the future is also made explicit. The act

> points towards the day when the young man/woman presumably accepts the Christian faith and the fellowship of the church where he/she has grown up.[72]

But when the blessing of children takes place in another context, in an unofficial way, there are evidently other presuppositions.

On the one hand, it looks as if *BUS* says that no special act is required for children. On the other hand, however, it writes about an obligation to express the fact that children are under the protection of God's grace. The authors "want to comply with the request [by *BEM*, my remark] 'to express more visibly that fact'."[73] But is it possible to express this without any kind of special rite or

---

den sker i församlingens sammanhang förutsätter den löften från såväl föräldrar som församling och bör ha en klar anknytning till omvändelse och dop i framtiden.") Ibid.

70 "Om man individuellt medverkar i en 'icke-officiell' barnvälsignelse är en annan sak." Ibid.

71 "att när den sker i församlingens sammanhang förutsätter den löften från såväl föräldrar som församling och *bör ha en klar anknytning till omvändelse och dop i framtiden."* Ibid. Italics mine.

72 *BUS* p. 204.

73 *BUS* p. 202. *BUS* quotes *B 16*.

act? The answer depends on the meaning of the terms *act* and *performance (rite)*. Is not the blessing of children a kind of act or performance? Of course it is, and indeed it is interesting to see that *BUS* itself uses the term *act*. Mentioning with emphasis the blessing of children, it states: "*The act* as a whole is a marking of the place of the child in the church family".[74]

This seems an ambivalent position, for even if no special act or rite is required to express the fact that children benefit from the atonement of Christ, there is surprisingly enough an obligation to express that fact in order to maintain amongst other things God's priority. The discussion above underlines all the more a possible ambiguity in *BUS* itself, and also in the working party which prepared it.

Concerning corporate faith, many questions can also be put to the material in *BEM*. In what way is this kind of corporate faith at work in the baptizand? Is this kind of faith effective just for a limited period of time or indefinitely? We do not get any answers in *BEM*. The same can also be said about *BUS*. The latter just mentions corporate faith as one point where it sees a possibility of understanding infant baptism and the blessing of children as "related expressions for several momentous parts of the Christian understanding of the children."[75] And it asserts: "Even the blessing of children 'stresses the corporate faith'... and the participation of the child in the fruits of the parents' faith."[76]

If there had been a brief discussion of the concept of "corporate faith", and how this faith is related to the personal belief, it might have helped us to a better understanding of these topics, and of the subject of baptism as a whole. What, according to both *BUS* and *BEM*, is faith (a gift or a human act – both?), and what is "sufficient" faith (in order to make it possible to be baptized by infant baptism according to *BEM*, so that it will not be a question of "indiscriminate baptism"; and according to *BUS* so that it is a question of being ready for believers' baptism)? These are topics which could merit discussion by others.

This discussion about the issues of anthropology, the faith-context, the blessing of children, and the place of children in the

---

[74] *BUS* p. 204. Italics mine.

[75] *BUS* p. 205.

[76] Ibid. Note, however, and compare with the "unofficial" blessing.

church, provokes a fundamental question: when does a child cease to be a child of God? Moreover, when is a person "ready" to be a member of the church, i.e. of a Baptist congregation? We will return later to the discussion of these issues, but first the issue of the blessing of children and infant baptism will be discussed.

6. Infant Baptism as a Blessing of Children

After the discussion in the previous chapter, I want to continue to study the question of the relation between infant baptism and the blessing of children.

As has already been seen, the blessing of children is important for BUS, but what is the content of the blessing of children? The document mentions the following: 1) a thanksgiving to the Lord of Life for the newborn child. 2) an act of prayer for parents and child. 3) and eventually an opportunity for the church to accept its responsibility for the newborn child.[77] It is also pointed out by Franzén in the working party, but not in BUS, that name-giving is possible in the Baptist view in connection with the blessing of children.[78]

---

[77] BUS p. 204.

[78] Minutes 17/1/84, § 14, "Bert Franzén gave a talk about the blessing of children (appendix). Bert points out that from the Baptist point of view it is possible to have a name-giving ceremony in connection with the blessing of children. He suggests further a recommendation to those churches that practise infant baptism, especially those in which there is hesitation about infant baptism, that they seriously discuss the meaning of the blessing of children. The historical and New Testament background should be indicated." ("Bert Franzén föredrar en skrivning om barnvälsignelsen (bilaga). Bert påpekar att namngivning i samband med barnvälsignelse ur baptistisk synpunkt är en möjlighet. Han föreslår vidare en rekommendation till de barndöpande kyrkorna, särskilt sådana där det råder tveksamhet om barndopet, att på allvar ta upp frågan om barnvälsignelsens innebörd. Den historiska och nytestamentliga bakgrunden bör påvisas.")
Bert Franzén is one of those within the Baptist Union of Sweden who has dealt seriously with the subject of the blessing of children and the place of children in the congregation. See for example four articles in Veckoposten, Franzén, Bert, "Barnen och församlingen. Guds försprång kan behållas", VP, No. 24/25, 1986, p. 5; Franzén, Bert, "Barnen och församlingen, II. Texterna om Jesus och barnen", VP, No. 26, 1986, p. 6; Franzén, Bert, "Barnen och församlingen, III. Barn med andlig hemortsrätt", VP, No. 27/28, 1986, p. 7; Franzén, Bert, "Barnen och församlingen, IV. En modell för mognad", VP, No. 29/30, 1986, p. 7. See Franzén, Bert, Guds försprång, 1991, and also the

In spite of the position of *BUS* that it cannot itself recognize or plead for the practice of infant baptism within the Baptist church, an interesting question in this context is whether there is any tendency in this document to recognize at least some infant baptisms in other churches and denominations as valid baptisms? Or does it possibly equate the blessing of children with infant baptism?

> Can such a kind of baptism - as long as this personal response is not given - be said to have another meaning than the blessing of children has in churches where baptism of believers is practised?[79]

In this question there seems to be an implicit answer indicating that *BUS* would possibly tend to consider infant baptism as equal to the blessing of children. As a matter of fact, it states explicitly:

> For Baptists it is possible to look at infant baptism as a form of blessing of children... infant baptism can be looked upon as an alternative to the blessing of children.[80]

The answer to the question asked above is quite clear. In spite of the use of water and of the name of the Trinity in infant baptism, it is not, regardless of the statement about a common understanding of baptism, recognized as a baptism, but it is regarded as a blessing of children, "a form of blessing".[81]

This conclusion seems partly to be justified by the working party's previous discussion of *BEM's* "invitation" (in *B com 12)* to recognize infant baptism and confession of faith on the one hand and the blessing of children and believers' baptism on the other as "equivalent alternatives".[82] Such a recognition may compel the

---

discussions and references in Bergsten, Torsten, "Barnet i frikyrkan. En historisk-teologisk studie", *Tro och Liv,* No. 3, 1985, especially chapter 6. *Barnen och församlingen* (Children and The Congregation), chapter 7. *Två slags medlemskap* (Two Kinds of Membership), and also chapter 8. *Familjekyrka och församlingsbarn* (Family Church and Children of the Congregation).

79   *BUS* p. 202.

80   *BUS* p. 205.

81   Ibid. *BUS* states also: "Many important biblical thoughts and sayings which often are related to the baptism of children can very well be used also for the blessing of children." Ibid.

82   *BEM* writes: *"In some churches which unite both infant-baptist and believer-baptist traditions, it has been possible to regard as equivalent alternatives for entry into the Church both a pattern whereby baptism in infancy is followed by*

Baptists to regard infant baptism as a blessing of children.[83] A possible conclusion may be that baptism will not be necessary for membership.[84] Or another challenging conclusion which might be drawn from such a discussion could be to regard believers' baptism as similar to or even equivalent to an act of confirmation, rather than to baptism. This could be controversial.

According to *BEM*, baptism seems to be the "starting-point" of a process in a Christian's life, where God is the subject. God acts in a special way with the baptizand in and through baptism and begins a life-long "process". "Baptism is related not only to momentary experience, but to life-long growth into Christ."[85] And it writes about baptism in general and places infant baptism and believers' baptism side by side.[86]

BUS cannot agree completely with the view of *BEM* on baptism. Unfortunately it does not comment on the question of baptism and growth. Believers' baptism seems in one way to be regarded *not* as the beginning of a process and growth, but rather the climax of a process, where hearing and receiving the Word results in repentance and conversion - thereafter believers' baptism can take place. Believers' baptism is thus in one way complete:

> We cannot see that baptism has to be completed by another act of sacramental character in order to receive the Holy Spirit or share in the

---

later profession of faith and a pattern whereby believers' baptism follows upon a presentation and blessing in infancy. This example invites other churches to decide whether they, too, could not recognize equivalent alternatives in their reciprocal relationships and in church union negotiations." B com 12.

[83] Supplement to Minutes 2/11/83.

[84] Ibid. Italics mine. Janarv: "Om den troendedöpande kyrkan skall erkänna barndop - trosbekännelse likvärdigt med barnvälsignelse - trosdop, har den då inte tvingats till två slutsatser: 1. barndop är att betrakta som en barnvälsignelse, 2. dop är inte oundgängligen nödvändigt för medlemskap." Concerning the "equivalent alternatives" the Mission Covenant Church of Sweden is mentioned. It is stated: "Obs. vad som säges om likvärdiga alternativ. Det gäller 'vissa kyrkor' av t ex SMF-typ." Ibid.

[85] *B 9.*

[86] "In both cases, the baptized person will have to grow in the understanding of faith." *B 12.* "It [i.e. baptism, my remark] looks towards a growth into the measure of the stature of the fullness of Christ (Eph. 4:13)." *B 8.*

eucharist. That would imply to diminish the meaning of baptism and not take its consequences seriously.[87]

It seems, however, to regard the blessing of children (which also ought to imply infant baptism) under the category of a growth: "So performed and understood the blessing of children is an expression of the Baptist understanding of the children growing up in the church."[88]

It is the blessing of children (also infant baptism if the analysis is correct), not believers' baptism, which according to *BUS* "underlines the being of man as a continuation of a divine act of creation."[89] Due among other things to this, we can understand the hesitation and even disagreement of *BUS* with *BEM's* statement *"that both forms of baptism embody God's own initiative in Christ and express a response of faith made within the believing community."*[90] and that the former cannot agree with the latter's statement for instance that *"Both forms of baptism require a similar and responsible attitude towards Christian nurture."*[91] *BUS* makes the following remark on this last quotation:

> When it is said in the commentary to § 12 [i.e. *B 12*, my remark] that 'both forms of baptism require a similar and responsible attitude towards Christian nurture', it should be pointed out that anyone who has been blessed as a child and consequently is not baptized, is to be regarded as a catechumen, in the proper sense of the word, whose instruction is a preparation for baptism and life as baptized.[92]

Significantly when *BUS* writes about the blessing of children, it quotes *BEM's* statement about *both* forms of baptism, *infant baptism* and believers' baptism:

---

[87] *BUS* p. 202.

[88] *BUS* pp. 202, 204.

[89] *BUS* p. 205. Cf., however, *Dop:* "Barnvälsignelsen understryker *liksom dopet* tillblivelsen av en människa som en fortsättning av den gudomliga skapelseakten." *Dop* p. 8, Italics mine. These two words *liksom dopet* (like baptism) are missing in *BUS*. I hold that one cannot apply the same reasoning to infant baptism as to the blessing of children, see more below.

[90] *B com 12*.

[91] Ibid.

[92] *BUS* p. 202.

The practice of infant baptism emphasizes the corporate faith and the faith which the child shares with its parents... Through baptism, the promise and claim of the Gospel are laid upon the child.[93]

And it comments: "We hesitate to put someone in the situation to have a claim 'laid upon' him as long as there is no possibility of response."[94] The expression "laid upon" ought not to be applied to a child in infant baptism as *BEM* states. It seems, however, to be applicable to believers' baptism according to *BUS*, where evidently a claim may be laid upon a young person or an adult, as there is, in contrast to a child in infant baptism, the possibility of a response.[95]

There are without doubt interesting ideas in *BUS* about the place of children in the church. The blessing of children is one example, and in comparing *BEM* and *BUS* we have discovered so far that there are differentiations. There are obvious difficulties in regarding infant baptism and the blessing of children as alternatives as the latter does. The differences between infant baptism and the blessing of children are among other things the following: the use of water, the intention, the rite or act *(dopformen)*.

As a consequence of *BUS'* view of infant baptism, it seems a logical consequence that it, despite the recommendation of *BEM* (see for example *B 13* and *B com 13*), will continue to practise "re-baptism", i.e. to baptize people who have been "blessed" by infant baptism.

Without doubt the Baptists need (of course together with other denominations) to continue the process which has been started. To consider more seriously the place of the child in the church, to study further the faith of children, the relation between the blessing of children and infant baptism, the relation between corporate faith/faith-context and personal belief, growth in faith after baptism etc.

One conclusion which can be drawn from *BUS* is that both the child who has been blessed in a Baptist congregation and the child who has been baptized by infant baptism, but in its view has not been baptized but "only" blessed, are thus to be regarded as catechumens, "whose instruction is a preparation for baptism and

---

[93]   *B com 12.*

[94]   *BUS* p. 202. See also Supplement to Minutes 2/11/83.

[95]   *BUS* p. 202.

life as baptized."[96] These catechumens are preparing for proper or genuine baptism with a personal conversion and the acceptance of faith - expressed in a personal, conscious response - and a life as baptized.[97]

This view of infant baptism stands in contradiction to BEM, where we find that both baptisms, infant baptism (even if practised in an indiscriminate way) as well as believers' baptism (if "re-baptism" is not practised; see for instance B 16), are regarded as baptisms. There are obviously theological difficulties involved in maintaining that there is *one baptism* in two different forms.

The questioning of infant baptism in BUS gives rise to our next topic: the difficult question of "re-baptism".

---

[96] Ibid. It is said in a Supplement: "Ett tredje 'alternativ' nämns: barnvälsignelse. Med den som bakgrund borde man kunna ge katekumenatet dess rätta plats – 'catechetical instruction'." Supplement to Minutes 2/11/83.

[97] BUS p. 202. In Dop, Nattvard, Ämbete it is stated: "Alla kyrkor döper troende, som kommer från andra religioner... och som accepterar den kristna tron och deltar i kristen undervisning." Dop, Nattvard, Ämbete, 2nd ed., 1983, p. 19. We can observe a comment from Janarv, where he says that the specific meaning of "catechetical instruction", [see B 11, my remark], is lost in the Swedish translation "kristen undervisning". He does not, however, comment or say anything more about this. Supplement to Minutes 2/11/83.

7. The Question of "Re-Baptism"

The previous topics imply a discussion about "re-baptism", a subject which has already been touched on quite a few times. This "practice" has during the centuries given rise to more than one theological discussion, numbers of accusations and different kinds of punishments – including the death penalty. And both *BEM* and *BUS* deal with it.

BEM states simply:

> Baptism is an unrepeatable act. Any practice which might be interpreted as 're-baptism' must be avoided.[98]

In a commentary it underlines this and also the importance of what it calls *"the sacramental integrity of other churches"*.[99] It asks those churches which do not practise infant baptism but only believers' baptism to refrain from "re-baptizing" people.[100]

How does *BUS* interpret this appeal? In what way does it comment on this in all likelihood provocative suggestion to refrain from "re-baptism"? Initially it agrees with it,[101] but makes a very important addition, that the question of whether "re-baptism" is practised or not, depends on *who* interprets the act.[102]

In the preparatory work for *BUS*, it is once again the *practice* of baptism which causes the problem and is thus discussed. It is said in a commentary concerning "re-baptism", that the working party agrees with *BEM's* thesis, but concerning practice which could be

---

[98]   *B 13.*

[99]   *B com 13.*

[100] Ibid.

[101] *BUS* p. 202.

[102] Ibid.

considered "re-baptism", it must be asked who it is that determines that it is in fact so?[103]

An expression in the commentary in *BEM* which resulted in a reaction in *BUS* is "sacramental integrity".[104] The latter does not feel that this applies when baptizing members of a church, where membership is also possible without either baptism or personal response. It mentions explicitly the Church of Sweden in this context.[105] In such circumstances it is difficult to take seriously the accusation that Baptists deny sacramental integrity.[106]

This refusal to accept such an accusation may be questioned, in the light of the fact that Baptists do in fact baptize members of other churches in which neither baptism nor personal response are conditions of membership. The issue of people who are baptized by infant baptism and baptized once again by believers' baptism, which in the opinion of *BEM* must be regarded as a "re-baptism", is a dilemma and relates also to the problem of proselytism.

BUS obviously denies that "re-baptism" is practised. But do any of the priests and pastors who practice infant baptism, and who according to *BUS* look upon infant baptism in the same way, i.e. as a blessing of children, also deny that "re-baptism" is practised? It thinks so.[107]

---

[103] Supplement to Minutes 2/11/83.

[104] *B com 13.*

[105] *BUS* p. 201. Compare, however, open membership in Baptist congregations, where baptism is not either a condition of membership of a Baptist congregation.

[106] *BUS* p. 201. *Dop* writes: "Det blir svårt att under sådana förhållanden ta på allvar den ibland uttalade anklagelsen att vi baptister utför sakramental handling med en annan kyrkas medlem när vi döper den som har sitt medlemskap i *en folkkyrka.*" *Dop* p. 3. Italics mine. And Janarv writes: "Det blir svårt att under sådana förhållanden ta på allvar den ibland uttalade anklagelsen att vi baptister utför en sakramental handling med en annan kyrkas medlem när vi döper den som har sitt medlemskap i *Svenska kyrkan* utan att vara döpt." Supplement to Minutes 23/2/84. Italics mine. And in the Minutes 23/8/84, § 40, it is written: "I fjärde stycket [in the Supplement 23/2/84, my remark] byts 'Svenska kyrkan' mot 'en folkkyrka'."

[107] "For Baptists it is possible to look at infant baptism as a form of blessing of children and *there are examples that priests and pastors who practise infant baptism look upon it in the same way.*" *BUS* p. 205. Italics mine.

It believes it possible to write about a common understanding of baptism, especially regarding its meaning and importance.[108] But if there is a common understanding of baptism, why can it not recognize infant baptism as baptism? An answer is possibly to be discerned in the following quotation:

> Can we in earnest talk about 'our one baptism' as long as *baptismal practice* in a decisive way divides us?[109]

The difficult point is to find out what the expression "baptismal practice" means in the document. Certainly infant baptism would not be recognized as valid, even if this baptism was practised for example by immersion and in the name of Jesus Christ or in the name of the Trinity. We may suppose that something more is included than baptismal practice in order to recognize a baptism; otherwise *BUS* ought to refrain from condoning the baptism of people who have been baptized by infant baptism in a correct way, i.e. in water, possibly even by immersion, and in the name of the Trinity or in the name of Jesus Christ.

In one way it is true that baptismal practice divides the churches. This is not, however, the whole truth. For infant baptism is not recognized by *BUS* and this obviously not only because of the practice, but because of something more: "For Baptists the baptism belongs together with a personal conversion".[110] The personal faith of the baptizand is not only important but absolutely necessary in order to recognize a baptism as valid. Conversion and personal response, a profession of faith, are crucial components in order to recognize baptism as valid - Baptists find support for this in the Bible. And *BEM* is, as previously quoted, of the same opinion that believers' baptism is the most clearly attested pattern in the Bible.[111] In other words, the baptizand ought to have an active role in the rite of baptism.[112] Bergsten is of the opinion that *BEM* in

---

[108] *BUS* p. 200.

[109] *BUS* p. 201. Italics mine.

[110] *BUS* p. 204.

[111] *B 11.*

[112] Note the baptismal formula of the ancient church which had the form of a dialogue between the minister and the baptizand, i.e. the baptizand was active, professing his conscious faith, at the time of his baptism. See Seiler, Herman, "Dop och kyrkotillhörighet i den katolska kyrkan. Dopet som sakramentalt inlemmande i kyrkan", *Ekumenisk samsyn om dop och*

these words is formulating a conviction which inspires every right-minded Baptist.[113]

There is here a delicate issue, relating to "re-baptism": how does faith relate to baptism? Does the validity of baptism depend on the faith of the individual and/or on that of the collective, the corporate faith (i.e. *fides ecclesiae, fides vicaria*)?

In spite of its recognition of the New Testament pattern mentioned above, *BEM* has, however, in contrast to the Baptists, no problems in recognizing infant baptism as valid, and advocating it, although the personal confession of faith does not take place at the time of baptism. *BUS* does not defend "re-baptism" to diminish baptism, but in fact quite the opposite, to exalt it.

For both *BEM* and *BUS* the confession of faith, related to baptism, is important. There is, however, evidently a major difference between them. In the latter this confession of faith must be made in close connection with believers' baptism, which excludes infants. The condition for baptism is thus evident, and this is missing in infant baptism. Is this faith a guarantee that the baptizand will remain a believer in Christ? If not, will another "re-baptism" be necessary (on account of a "re-conversion")? These topics are not discused either in either document.

Personal profession of faith as a condition, advocated by *BUS* and by Baptists in general, does not, however, necessarily concern only the form, the practice, but also the content, the doctrine and teaching. This is not only a question of baptismal practice but also baptismal theology.

The following assumption can be made from the discussion in this chapter. Believers' baptism is recognized as a proper, genuine baptism. This statement presupposes implicitly a possibility of having so-called improper baptisms. The question is whether infant baptism can be regarded by *BUS* as at least an improper baptism. This means that it can be recognized as a baptism. The baptism is thus, in spite of the fact that it is improper, valid and no "re-

---

kyrkotillhörighet, 1978, pp. 39ff., refering to among others Ratzinger, J., "Taufe, Glaube und Zugehörigkeit zur Kirche", *Internationale Katholische Zeitschrift*, 1976, pp. 218ff., and Stenzel, Alois, *Die Taufe. Eine genetische Erklärung der Taufliturgie*, Innsbruck 1958. I will return to the article by Seiler later on in the thesis.

[113] "Så formulerar BEM den övertygelse som besjälar varje rättsinnig baptist." Bergsten, Torsten, "Kontroversiella rekommendationer", *Dop, Nattvard, Ämbete*, 2nd ed., 1983, p. 134.

baptism" is consequently required. We can still use the term *baptism*. Alternatively, we are confronted with the opinion that this kind of baptism, i.e. infant baptism, cannot be recognized as a baptism at all. It is not even improper, it is invalid, which means it is *not* a baptism and therefore, since we cannot use the term *baptism* in this case, believers' baptism is not a "re-baptism" either.

The question of whether "re-baptism" exists or not depends, of course, on how and by whom the concept is interpreted. In an analysis of *BUS* it is, however, evident that the Baptist Union of Sweden will continue to baptize people with believers' baptism, even if they have been baptized (according to *BUS* "blessed") in a not only improper but also from its standpoint invalid infant baptism. So in spite of writing about *"various baptismal practices"*,[114] one "practice", infant baptism, is not recognized as a baptism. For "various baptismal practices" must as a matter of fact refer also to the practice of infant baptism.

> We recommend churches that *baptize children*, and especially those in which uncertainty about infant baptism has arisen, to seriously consider the question of blessing of children.[115]

The question of "re-baptism" is a problem for church unity. So how does *BUS* deal with this sensitive aspect? For this is still a great problem for many churches in the work towards the one church, despite the fact that *BUS* is of the opinion that unity in Christ can be manifested in spite of differences in baptismal practice.[116] Nevertheless, if necessary, it may be possible within Christianity to achieve some kind of unity without baptism as a common basis,[117] questionable as this may be from a theological point of view. For such a position creates problems in a number of ways, for instance with regard to the commandment of Christ to baptize (Matt. 28:18-20).

BUS claims concerning the problem of baptism ("re-baptism") and church unity that the non-recognition of ordained ministries among other churches could in an equivalent way be taken as a

---

[114] *BUS* p. 201. Italics mine.

[115] *BUS* p. 205. Italics mine.

[116] *BUS* p. 202.

[117] See for instance the discussion about alliance ecumenism etc. in for example Part I.

justification for Baptists to continue to maintain their opinion regarding baptism. Baptists do not have any greater difficulties in recognizing (the ordained) ministries of other churches.[118] Baptists do also recognize churches and their members as parts of the Body of Christ,[119] which has resulted in open communion and sometimes also open membership.[120]

It looks as if this "openness" is thought to justify Baptists in continuing to maintain their different opinions and practices concerning baptism, for instance that of "re-baptism".[121] Of course such an argument can be questioned. It is to be noted that *BUS*, in spite of its view on infant baptism, underlines the importance in the light of the discussion in *BEM* about "mutual recognition of baptism",[122] of using a terminology that is not depreciating or insulting. This is, however, an example of using a term such as *infant baptism* but giving it another content than that which is usually implied in the concept.

> However, we want to emphasize that a terminology should be used that is not depreciating or insulting. This would to a great extent contribute to an increasing mutual understanding of our convictions. We Baptists must admit that we have often used the expression 'sprinkling'.[123]

The term *infant baptism* should be used out of respect for those who see it as a valid act when such a baptism is referred to. The description of infant baptism as "sprinkling" should thus cease, since it expresses "repudiation of churches baptizing infants."[124] The significance of the commentary in *BUS* on *B 16* is that it writes about "infant baptism" but gives it a meaning which evidently implies that infant baptism is not a baptism. The question is what advantage is gained if it uses the "right" words, but as a matter of fact means something else (possibly even the exact opposite). For

---

[118] *BUS* p. 202.

[119] Cf., however, the discussion below about some members of the Church of Sweden.

[120] *BUS* p. 202.

[121] Ibid.

[122] *B 15-16*.

[123] *BUS* p. 203.

[124] Ibid.

this kind of argument will surely be apprehended as offensive by some of the churches practising infant baptism, and in particular be more confusing for everyone than using a terminology which is consistent with the content which *BUS* ascribes to it. For to what extent will the right words benefit mutual respect and hopefully also understanding and recognition of each other's baptism in the future,[125] as long as the content of the concept (and the practice of) "infant baptism", in relation to believers' baptism, is regarded not as a baptism but as an act of blessing?

The aspects which we have found in discussing the subject of "re-baptism" cannot be set aside. Such an opinion on "re-baptism" as the one expressed in *BUS* must be interpreted as meaning that one will continue to practise it, in view of the fact that a person who has been baptized by infant baptism is regarded by *BEM* not as "blessed" but as baptized. It is not possible to use the words "our common baptism" and "our one baptism" as the latter does, since it unfortunately must be pointed out that there are different baptismal practices due to different baptismal doctrines. These two, doctrine and practice, do correspond to each other, which has many implications.

There is infant baptism and believers' baptism and thus a differentiation of baptism, with the former not recognized as baptism by some people but equated with the blessing of children, and the latter consequently sometimes seen by others as "re-baptism". Between these two polarized opinions we find a whole spectrum of attempts at compromise to solve this intricate equation.

The discussion about differentiations of baptism may be made clearer in the following way: *BEM* and *BUS* may to a great extent be in agreement in regard to the contents of baptism; there are, however, different conditions for baptism. If the conditions (which I think must also include baptismal theology and not "only" baptismal practice), however, for one or another reason, are not considered to be met, various conclusions can be drawn. It is then sometimes not a baptism but something else, a blessing of children. Or even if not all conditions are present (as for instance the conscious personal response) or if the churches baptizing infants are regarded as really acting wrongly, a baptism may be recognized

---

[125] "The matter in concern - to handle the question of how to look upon one another's baptism - will benefit from a mutual respect which also manifests itself in our choice of words." Ibid.

as improper but nevertheless valid on the basis that it is God who acts and baptizes. Based on this position it is not only possible to speak of a common understanding of baptism but also of a common baptism, which should result in refraining from "re-baptizing".

This discussion of "re-baptism" gives rise to another issue, which will be treated next: the question of an expressive, symbolic "contra" an instrumental, sacramental view of baptism. Still another issue related to this discussion is the relation of faith to baptism, to be discussed more in the chapter *Ecclesiology - Baptism and Membership*.

8. Baptism as an Expressive or an Instrumental Act

In this chapter the relation between expressive/symbolic and instrumental/sacramental views of baptism will be studied. These concepts can have different meanings.[126] We can note that the two concepts "expressive" and "instrumental" do not necessarily contradict each other, i.e. that baptism can be regarded as both an instrumental and an expressive act.

What is characteristic of an expressive view of baptism? I want to qualify the concept "expressive" in the following way: that baptism in this case is exclusively a confirmation of a conscious response in faith to something which has already happened in the believer. The believer, the baptizand himself, expresses this at the time of his baptism. In this view God is not seen as acting in a special, sovereign way in and through baptism, regardless of the state of the baptizand. It is thus the conversion (metanoia), and the conscious personal response, which is the sine qua non which has to take place as closely as possible to the time of baptism. This baptism, a baptism of metanoia, is the climax of a process.[127] The baptizand is

---

[126] The sacraments can be seen either as no more than "symbols", or as "efficacious signs" which impart the grace which they signify. Also in BEM there seems to be an ambiguity, with baptism sometimes seen as a symbol, and other times as an effective sign.

See George Raymond Beasley-Murray who humourously says about the difficulty with the concept "sacrament", that it is like a nylon stocking: it can fit limbs of many shapes! Beasley-Murray, George Raymond, Baptism Today and Tomorrow, 1966, p. 13.

[127] Some Baptists hold, however, that the confession, the conscious response to Christ in faith, has an objective basis in that the work of God is active in the person before his baptism. Nevertheless, what has been given to a person (the faith) is as it were presented to God as a response. In other words, that Baptists have an expressive or subjective understanding of faith and baptism would probably not be accepted by all Baptists. They maintain that the act of faith has an objective foundation in God's action in the person before

thus the active subject (through testimony, response etc.) in the act of baptism. The baptism is further regarded as a symbol of the person's participation in the death and resurrection of Jesus Christ. The immersion symbolizes this especially in a dramatic way, expressing the fact that the person has been converted and has left the "world".

An expressive view may be briefly characterized in the following way. The emphasis in baptism is laid more on the action of the baptizand than on God, who, however, has acted before baptism, at the time when God called the person, and the person in question then repented and responded to the call of God.[128] This conversion is later on, yet as soon as possible, professed in believers' baptism. Baptism is thus also an act of confession and obedience, symbolizing the conversion. This expressive view of baptism has been the predominant one among Swedish Baptists.[129]

There is, however, on the other hand to be found a more sacramental and instrumental view of baptism also among some Baptists.[130] The meaning of the concept "instrumental"/ "sacramental" is that baptism is an instrument of God's own action. God is the real subject in baptism and acts in a special way on the baptizand in and through baptism. Baptism has an effect *per se*,[131]

---

baptism; God's work of salvation in Jesus Christ precedes every human achievement or deed.

[128] The *metanoia* is thus regarded as ultimately caused by God.

[129] "På grund av det reformerta arvet har majoriteten baptister ensidigt framställt dopet som en *bekännelse- och bekräftelsehandling*." Bergsten, Torsten, "Kyrkotillhörighet - medlemskap - bekännelse", *Tro och Liv*, No. 1, 1980, p. 40. Italics mine.

[130] Günter Wagner, who is one of the more internationally famous Baptist theologians, has worked a lot in ecumenical contexts. He writes: "Of course, Beasley-Murray exposed himself to ecumenical dialogue at an early time (if I am not mistaken, as a consultant in the group which produced the document *'One Lord One Baptism'*). We need to remember, though, that 'sacramental' thinking was not unknown among Baptists prior to that. Johannes Schneider's *'Die Taufe im Neuen Testament'* could not be printed by the German Baptist publishing house because of internal censorship. However, strands of sacramental thinking go back to the beginnings of Baptist history." Letter to Lennart Johnsson: Wagner, Günter, 19/2/88. See also Part III, chapter 6.

[131] This view has been criticized by some for seeing the rite itself as the crucial factor, i.e. the baptism itself (not God) has a regenerative power. A slight

i.e. without necessarily any personal response of the baptizand, but, of course, in a faith-context - in the form of the so-called *fides ecclesiae* and *fides vicaria.* The emphasis is, in comparison with the symbolic, expressive view, laid on God's action in baptism.

As we understand it, infant baptism might be justified according to this view. It is God who effects something in baptism. God cleanses, sanctifies and makes man righteous. He washes away sin, and the baptizand dies and is raised to a new life. God is the subject in the rite of baptism, and He acts supremely on the baptizand - which implies that the baptizand can be unaware. (The importance of the faith-context, with the parents, godparents etc., should, of course, not be forgotten.)

The term *sacrament* refers to God's salvific action mediated through particular visible, ecclesial things and actions, which constitutes a special relationship between the person who is baptized and Christ. Some churches put emphasis on the Word, that the Word of God takes precedence over the sacraments. This does not seem to be at the very centre in *BEM.* A classic definition of a sacrament is that it is an outward and visible sign of an inward and spiritual grace. *BEM* states, in the section about the Eucharist:

> Since the earliest days, baptism has been understood as the sacrament by which believers are incorporated into the body of Christ and are endowed with the Holy Spirit.[132]

In baptism, in an instrumental or sacramental view, a person gives nothing to God, but God accepts in spite of this the baptizand. Infant baptism shows that God accepts us unconditionally and that baptism in that case is valid by virtue of God's promise. This is an expression of God's priority and *gratia praeveniens* (prevenient grace). And a child cannot give, but it can receive. In infant baptism a child is also seen as a symbol of the receptive relationship to God.

To be baptized in a Baptist congregation, some kind of a personal presupposition is required in order that the baptism be recognized and regarded as a genuine, valid baptism - even if this takes place by the power of grace, which enables man to "present" something to God, giving an answer, a pledge to God.

---

tendency in this direction may be found in *BEM* as well: baptism is... through baptism... etc. The question has been raised of whether baptism is God's action or human action. The *"ex opere operato"* doctrine is well known; an outward rite effects what it signifies irrespective of faith.

[132] *E com 19.*

A basic question asked by *BUS* is whether baptism does have any effect without a personal response? This question has already been discussed and has been given a negative answer. In a question to *BEM*, *BUS* uses the term *effect*, but it does not itself give any definition of this term. We may assume that the term used by it is to be related to *BEM* in B 2-7.[133] It draws the reasonable conclusion that baptism according to *BEM* must have an effect even if a personal response is not given, since the latter stresses the fact that no baptism can be repeated or made undone.[134] It is not denied by *BUS* that God as a matter of fact acts and even effects "something" in baptism, but, and this is important to note, that he does not in infant baptism but only in believers' baptism. Even if there is the use of water, the name of the Trinity, the reading of Scriptures, the invocation of the Holy Spirit, a faith-context, in brief all the requirements for baptism according to most traditions and churches for it to be duly performed, the validity of baptism depends for *BUS* also on something more. There is a superior criterion: that the person (himself) must act.

It is easy to get the impression from *BUS* that baptism is not and cannot be the sovereign action of almighty God in a human being, as long as at least one condition is lacking. The condition which is required is that the baptizand himself must be a subject and act in a special manner, i.e. in giving a conscious response in faith – as a result of what God previously has done through his Son Jesus Christ, and also what God has done for the person in question, resulting in conversion and baptism. Then the baptizand enters into the New Covenant etc. From that point in time, he is also a member of the (Baptist) congregation. This conscious response can, of course, also be given in the act of baptism according to *BEM*, but it is not absolutely necessary. This implies that not only believers' baptism but also infant baptism is recognized as proper and valid.

BEM advocates an instrumental view of baptism. It is looked upon as a sacrament, i.e. as an instrumental act through which God in a

---

[133] It can be noted that *BEM* itself does not use the term *effect*. Max Thurian writes: "As used in the Lima document, the term 'sign' should be understood in the emphatic sense of 'effective sign'. This is equivalent to the term 'sacrament'." Thurian, Max, "Introduction. The Lima document on 'Baptism, Eucharist and Ministry' the event and its consequences", *Churches respond to BEM*, Vol. I, 1986, p. 10.

[134] "The very stress of the fact that no baptism can be repeated or made undone possibly implies an answer in the affirmative." *BUS* p. 202.

very decisive and special way acts upon the baptizand,[135] even if the latter in infant baptism is not able to give a personal response at the time. Baptism is a participation in Christ's death and resurrection. It is an exodus from bondage and a liberation into a new humanity; it gives a new life in the power of the resurrection of Jesus Christ, and brings the baptizand into union with Christ, with other Christians and with the Church of every time and place.

There is in other words an emphasis on *God's action* in baptism, taking place in a faith-context, for it should not be forgotten that faith is of importance in the rite of baptism also for *BEM.*[136] That it is conscious of the great importance of faith can be discerned in the way in which it admonishes churches practising infant baptism. It writes that especially these churches

> must guard themselves against the practice of apparently indiscriminate baptism and take more seriously their responsibility for the nurture of baptized children to mature commitment to Christ.[137]

And it writes of baptism as both God's gift and *our human response* to that gift.[138] It thus stresses the necessity of a response of faith and the importance of a human response by the baptizand himself at the time of baptism or, if this is not possible on account of age, later on. The response does not have to be, in contrast to *BUS,* a personal conscious response to God by the baptizand himself at the time of his baptism.

The importance of the faith-context is emphasized as concerns infant baptism. *"The practice of infant baptism emphasizes the*

---

[135] Max Thurian writes: "For the Lima document, baptism is quite evidently a sacrament; in other words an effective liturgical sign, a sign which really effects what it signifies in image or symbol... The document does not contain any explicit definition of the sacrament, but the context clearly implies some such definition as the one just given: the sacrament is a liturgical sign which effectively produces in reality that which it signifies in image or symbol." Thurian, Max, "Introduction. The Lima document on 'Baptism, Eucharist and Ministry' the event and its consequences", *Churches respond to BEM,* Vol. I, 1986, p. 10.

[136] The emphasis on the Word is perhaps not as strongly expressed in *BEM* as might be desired. The Word, the sacrament and faith all belong together.

[137] *B 16.*

[138] *B 8.* Italics mine.

corporate faith".[139] (A delicate question to ask *BEM,* as it advocates infant baptism, is whether a faith-context can guarantee a person's Christian upbringing?)

We find at least two possible answers concerning what faith, the response of man, can mean. 1) It can mean that a person answers for himself. This is always the case in believers' baptism. 2) It can mean that the church (in this case meaning parents, guardians, godparents and congregation) takes the responsibility for a person and answers: a) either together with the person who is going to be baptized, b) or in the case of infant baptism, that the church in celebrating baptism answers for this person *(fides ecclesiae)* or that a person answers *(fides vicaria)* instead of the baptizand not yet capable of answering for himself on that occasion. What matters in the latter (2) is that baptism may take place in a faith-context (without a person's conscious response) and that the personal response will hopefully sooner or later occur.[140]

What kind of baptism does *BUS* have in mind when it asks: "Does baptism have any effect without this response?"[141] The answer is, of course, infant baptism. We discover from *BUS'* question to *B 12* in *BEM,* that it has difficulties with its view, that baptism *per se* (an instrumental view) - in a faith-context - could effect something. The personal conscious response is the *sine qua non* in (almost) all Baptist views of baptism.[142]

BUS keeps to a mainly expressive view of baptism according to our definition, but it tends nevertheless to have some instrumental/sacramental aspects. These obviously cannot be applied to infant baptism but only to believers' baptism. There are at the same time clear indications of a critical attitude towards an instrumental/sacramental view of baptism. There is thus a significant difference between the view of baptism in *BUS* and an explicitly instrumental one. Caution is to be found among the Baptists concerning sacramental or instrumental ideas, fearing too heavy a stress on the very act of baptism, a kind of impersonal, magical act and effect on an unaware person at the expense of free

---

[139] *B com 12.*

[140] See *B 15.*

[141] *BUS* p. 202.

[142] "For Baptists the baptism belongs together with a personal conversion and the acceptance of faith which occur later in life." *BUS* p. 204.

will (the principle of freedom), accountability, and ethical responsibility, for which the Baptists call.

It can be noted that *BUS* writes in the section about the Eucharist:

> There is, it seems to us, a tendency towards sacramentalism in this document [i.e. in *BEM*, my remark]. Eager to clarify the meaning of the eucharist, the document gives to this sacrament such a comprehensive function and such a unique position that other elements of Christian worship and Christian experience are eclipsed, such as prayer, Bible study, praise, service and fellowship. All these elements are, to be sure, present in the eucharist but only in part. They can and must function also outside the eucharist.[143]

This statement seems to be applicable not only to the part about the Eucharist, but to *BEM* as a whole, and also to our discussion about the expressive and instrumental views of baptism.

Torsten Bergsten also deals with this "high-church" tendency and writes as a commentary to *BEM*, that there is an imbalance in the Faith and Order dialogues, where the Orthodox and Catholic Churches have a much stronger position than the Reformed and the "Free Churches".[144] He writes that the high-church tendency is more obvious in the section on Ministry than in that on the Eucharist.[145]

To conclude the discussion about expressive and instrumental views of baptism, it can be stated that if we have an instrumental view of baptism, implying the sovereign action of almighty God on a person (even an infant), God "effects" something through baptism (without necessarily any personal response of the baptizand but baptism takes place in a faith-context), and if this person is baptized a "second time", it ought to be regarded as a "re-baptism". Consequently, in the light of the discussion in the last chapter, this

---

[143] *BUS* p. 206.

[144] "Det är uppenbart att den ortodoxt-katolska parten i Faith and Order-samtalen har en långt starkare ställning än den reformert-frikyrkliga. Det är angeläget att denna obalans inte får slå igenom lika starkt i vår hemmaekumeniska situation. Varken ekumenik på Roms eller på Calvins villkor leder fram till det efterlängtade målet, den kristna kyrkans synliga enhet." Bergsten, Torsten, "Kontroversiella rekommendationer", *Dop, Nattvard, Ämbete*, 2nd ed., 1983, p. 139.

[145] "I kapitlet *Ministry* blir den 'högkyrkliga' tendensen i BEM ännu påtagligare än i nattvardsavsnittet." Ibid. p. 136. See also p. 138.

is a denial of "sacramental integrity". However, although *BUS* does not consider the first baptism of people baptized as infants as genuine or proper, it does not accept the accusation of *BEM* that "re-baptism" is a denial of sacramental integrity. Therefore, Baptists feel justified in continuing with this practice.

A consequence of this is in my opinion that it questions whether God can effect something in and through baptism *per se.* In spite of discerning an instrumental aspect in *BUS,* we find that what ultimately is of importance for the validity of baptism is faith, i.e. the personal conscious response, the confession of faith. The emphasis on an expressive view will result in a continued practice of "re-baptism". To look at baptism as an instrumental act implies evidently recognition of infant baptism as a valid baptism. There is also a rejection of "re-baptism". This is the view which *BEM* advocates. What matters according to *BEM* is baptism *per se,* of course in a faith-context.

Obviously both baptisms have their advantages and disadvantages. Believers' baptism on the one hand risks becoming something "subjective", a private affair between God and the believer - depending on the person's intellectual, spiritual abilities to understand and profess the faith, emphasizing personal confession and conversion; infant baptism on the other hand risks becoming something "objective", a mechanical rite effected by the minister, emphasizing baptism as a gift of God, forgetting what should follow, discipleship. Many different questions are involved: anthropology, God's action vis á vis the human act, the meaning and role of the Word, the ministry etc.

9. The Celebration of Baptism

In the light of the previous paragraphs I will in this chapter deal with the section about the celebration of baptism (B 17-23), in particular immersion and the order of baptism.

"Baptism is administered with water in the name of the Father, the Son and the Holy Spirit." (B 17); BEM states earlier: "baptism is in water and the Holy Spirit." (B 14) The conditions are evident in BEM, with or in water and in the name of the Trinity.

Are BEM and BUS in agreement as to how baptism shall be administered? Evidently they seem to be in agreement, for the above statement (i.e. B 17) describes according to BUS "what is necessary about the celebration of baptism."[146]

In the quotations above two prepositions can be observed, "with" and "in", which give us cause to discuss something characteristic of Baptists, namely immersion.[147] BEM has in the quotation above the

---

[146] BUS p. 203. "We agree that 'Christian baptism is in water and the Holy Spirit'". BUS p. 202.

[147] In passing it can be mentioned that infant baptism (as well as believers' baptism) by immersion is practised in some churches, for example sometimes in the Church of Sweden and also in the Orthodox Church.

The following discussion concerning the question of "immersion" is of interest from both an ecumenical point of view and also for the discussion of "re-baptism". Professor Thomas Hopko writes about triple immersion, since some Orthodox question the validity of baptisms not enacted by triple immersion. "While traditional Orthodox practice - scripturally prescribed, liturgically ordered and canonically legislated - is surely that of triple immersion in water in the name of the Father and the Son and the Holy Spirit, it is also the case that baptisms performed in other ways, particularly by pouring or sprinkling water, have been accepted by the Orthodox not only when done outside the canonical boundaries of the Orthodox Church, but even within them... I myself was baptized by *poured water* [italics mine] in a church canonically within the Ecumenical Patriarchate, together with thousands, if not millions of people who were baptized this way within Orthodoxy in recent centuries in Eastern Europe and America. How is this to be taken? Are we now to be *'really baptized'* [italics mine] as some have suggested, and that after years of

phrase "with water", but also states explicitly: "Christian baptism is *in* water and the Holy Spirit".[148] It recommends immersion since it is also an expression of the fact that "the Christian participates in the death, burial and resurrection of Christ."[149]

BUS writes deliberately "baptize in water". The reason for this is, of course, the practice of immersion, which is the common, in fact the only correct method within the Baptist Union of Sweden. An argument for immersion is that "Naturally enough the rich contents of baptism benefits from a form that fully does justice to it".[150]

In the preparatory work we find nevertheless the possibility of an exception to immersion. It is said that "in water" is a more natural way of expressing the form, which we almost without exception use, immersion.[151] The words *så gott som* (almost) point to the possibility of practising baptism without immersion.

---

baptizing ourselves, and offering and receiving the holy eucharist in the Orthodox Church? Such questions must be answered for the sake of peace and unanimity within the Church, for consistency and integrity in our pastoral practices, and for justice and truth in our ecumenical relations and missionary activities.

Surely the criteria for discernment in this matter include the *faith* of the people involved, as well as the *forms* of the ritual which they use. It also involves their actual possibilities, their knowledge, their freedom and their intentions in performing the sacramental rite. It also has to do with the nature of the God in whose name the baptismal act is performed. Can we really believe, for example, that God would require the *'rebaptism'* [italics mine] of those whose intentions were pure, but whose faith and/or ritual forms were defective at the time of their original baptism? The traditional reaction of the Orthodox Church to this question, in my opinion, has clearly been negative." Hopko, Thomas, "Tasks Facing the Orthodox in the 'Reception' Process of BEM", *Orthodox Perspectives on Baptism, Eucharist and Ministry*, 1985, p. 137.

[148] *B 14.* Italics mine.

[149] *B 18.*

[150] *BUS* p. 203. It comments: "For a person who practises immersion it is natural to say 'baptize in water'". Ibid.

[151] "ett naturligare uttryckssätt för den form som vi *så gott som* undantagslöst använder: nedsänkning." *Dop* p. 6. Italics mine. In the preparatory work to *BUS* we find the working party discussing the prepositions "in" and "with". *Dop* writes: "Med beskrivningen i § 17 är det nödvändiga sagt om hur dop skall firas. För den som döps genom nedsänkning är det naturligast att säga 'döpa i vatten', så mycket mer som det är vad som framhålles redan i § 14:

In a comment on *B 18*,[152] *BUS* writes:

We find that immersion does not only express participation in Christ's death, burial and resurrection *but also other factors* as e.g. when the purification that baptism aims at is described by 'washing', Acts 22:16, 'a body washed in pure water', Hebrews 10:22, or as 'the washing of regeneration and renewal in the Holy Spirit', Titus 3:5, or when it is said: 'Baptized into union with him you all put on Christ as a garment', Galatians 3:27.[153]

This looks like an addition to the statement of *BEM*. It is therefore easy from this statement to get the impression that these *other factors* are missing in *BEM*. This is, however, not the case. Even if it does not explicitly mention these "other factors" in *B 18*, it is conscious of them and it also quotes the same Bible references. We find, however, these references in other paragraphs than in *B 18*. In *B 2* we find Titus 3:5 and Galatians 3:27-28; in *B 4* Acts 22:16 and Hebrews 10:22. This indicates possibly that *BEM* and *BUS* use and interpret these references in different ways, that they may be proof of different things for each of them.

Concerning the order of baptism, there are different opinions within the churches and denominations. *BEM* gives a list of elements which should at least find a place within any

---

'Det kristna dopet sker i vatten och Helig Ande.' *Dessutom är det ett naturligare uttryckssätt för den form vi så gott som undantagslöst använder: nedsänkning."* Dop p. 6, italics mine. *Dop* makes an addition regarding "immersion", which does not occur in *BUS*, see the italics.

In Minutes 20/9/84, § 49 it is said: "Angående punkterna 17 och 18 förs en stunds samtal. Särskilt gäller det prepositionerna 'i' (in) och 'med' (with) i samband med ordet 'döpa'. Jämförelser med New English Bible och New International Bible rekommenderas. Punkterna 17 och 18 skall dock stå kvar med tillägget att för den som dopet skett genom nedsänkning är det naturligast att säga 'döpa *i* vatten'." And Janarv writes in Supplement to Minutes 23/2/84: "Med denna beskrivning är det nödvändiga sagt om hur dop skall firas. Vi vill dock hellre säga att dopet sker *i* vatten än *med* vatten, så mycket mer som det är vad som sägs redan i punkt 14: 'Det kristna dopet sker i vatten och Helig Ande.' Dessutom är det ett naturligare uttryckssätt för den form vi så gott som undantagslöst använder: neddoppning."

[152] "In the celebration of baptism the symbolic dimension of water should be taken seriously and not minimalized. The act of immersion can vividly express the reality that in baptism the Christian participates in the death, burial and resurrection of Christ." *B 18*.

[153] *BUS* p. 203. Italics mine.

comprehensive order of baptism. The list consists of: 1) The proclamation of scriptures referring to baptism. 2) An invocation of the Holy Spirit. 3) A renunciation of evil. 4) A profession of faith in Christ and the Holy Trinity. 5) The use of water. 6) A declaration that the persons baptized have acquired a new identity as sons and daughters of God, and as members of the Church, called as witnesses of the Gospel.[154] *BUS* acknowledges the list of elements and mentions explicitly the proclamation of scriptures referring to baptism, the creed and the epiklesis.[155]

There is, however, hesitation regarding what it calls "over-explicit explanations". What does it intend with the following sentence:

> Moreover, we believe that over-explicit explanations can 'rationalize away' the inherent symbolic force of the rite. But we do recognize elements here enumerated which should be included, e.g. the proclamation of the scriptures referring to baptism, the creed and the *epiklesis.156?*

It does not comment on or explain what it means by "over-explicit explanations". But by going to the working party we possibly find an indication of the answer in a commentary to *B 20*, which points out that there was hesitation concerning the renunciation of evil in point 3 above. It says: "There is hesitation and uncertainty about 'renunciation of evil'."[157] This is, however, not explicitly mentioned in *BUS*.

Commenting on *B 20*, it refers to its earlier discussion about *B 18* and writes: "Several elements of the baptismal ritual here enumerated are, in accordance with what was said in item 18 above, included in the very baptismal rite."[158] And it refers to the

---

[154] *B 20.* It makes the following addition: "Some churches consider that Christian initiation is not complete without the sealing of the baptized with the gift of the Holy Spirit and participation in holy communion." Ibid.

One question which ought to have been discussed and developed more especially in *BEM* is, whether baptism is valid in itself, i.e. baptism having for example a saving power in itself, or must it be confirmed by chrism and/or by personal faith of the baptized to be valid?

[155] *BUS* p. 204.

[156] Ibid

[157] "Tveksamhet eller oklarhet rådde om 'avsägelse av det onda'." Supplement to Minutes 2/11/83.

[158] *BUS* p. 204.

discussion about *B 14*, where it explains that baptism does not need to be completed by another act of a sacramental character, i.e. to receive the Holy Spirit or to share in the eucharist.[159] Whether baptism (infant baptism and/or believers' baptism) is complete in itself or whether it has to be completed in some way or another, is, as has already been indicated, a delicate issue.

A further point which may be noted in this discussion about the celebration of baptism concerns *where* the sign of the Spirit is to be found. *BEM* discusses different understandings and mentions three actions where the Spirit may be operative: 1) the water rite itself, 2) the anointing with the chrism and/or 3) the imposition of hands.[160] It adds that some people are of the opinion that the Spirit is operative throughout the rite in all three.[161] It relates the gift of the Spirit in baptism to the liturgy, and gives expression to a desire for more of "such vivid things" in the liturgy, such as the laying on of hands, anointing and the sign of the cross.[162]

Does *BUS* talk at all about the laying on of hands, and if so, what does it mean? It does not, as far as we have found, see the imposition of hands in the baptismal rite as the point when the Holy Spirit is given. It writes:

> the imposition of hands, in the baptismal rite itself or in a special ceremony afterwards, is not associated with the giving of the Holy Spirit but an act of blessing with intercession for the baptized person, a consecration to membership and personal commitment in the Christian church.[163]

It does not explicitly mention where or in what way the Spirit is given. The working party questions whether the topic of the sign of

---

159 *BUS* p. 202.

160 *B 14*.

161 Ibid.

162 *B 19*.

163 *BUS* p. 203. And *Dop* writes: "Vid handpåläggning, i själva dopakten eller i en särskild akt efteråt är det för oss inte särskilt fråga om Andens meddelelse utan en välsignelsehandling med förbön för den som döpts, en 'avskiljning' som medlem i den kristna församlingen till tjänst bland människor." *Dop* p. 5.

the gift of the Spirit is exhaustively treated in *BEM*. And it is asked what the Pentecostals say?[164]

As we have understood, the teaching on the Spirit and on the gifts of the Spirit has been a very delicate issue and still is for the Baptist Union of Sweden. That there is a careful and almost reluctant attitude in *BUS* towards this topic is thus explicable in view of its history.[165]

On *B 21* and *B 22*, *BUS* does not make any comments of importance but agrees evidently with *BEM* on these paragraphs: "Paragraph 21 accords with what has been said about the proclamation of the scriptures referring to baptism in the preceding paragraph."[166]

We can, however, observe that it does not explicitly comment on *BEM's B com 21* as concerns especially the discussion about "indiscriminate baptism",[167] which in one way is surprising considering its view on infant baptism. *BEM* writes:

> *In many large European and North American majority churches infant baptism is often practised in an apparently indiscriminate way. This contributes to the*

---

[164] Janarv: "Är tecknet på den heliga andens gåva så som det uppfattas i olika traditioner uttömmande beskrivet här? Vad säger t ex pingstvännerna?" Supplement to Minutes 2/11/83. The working party wonders what is meant by the claim of some churches, as mentioned in *BEM, B 20*, that Christian initiation is not complete if the baptized person is not sealed with the gift of the Holy Spirit. Ibid. Janarv adds the following note to *B com 14*: "*Within some traditions it is explained that as baptism conforms us to Christ crucified, buried and risen, so through chrismation Christians receive the gift of the pentecostal Spirit from the anointed Son.*", that by "some traditions", the Orthodox and Catholics are described, ("Här beskrivs med 'vissa traditioner' närmast ortodoxer och katoliker.") Ibid.

[165] See Part I, chapter 7.2.1. The relation - on account of for example the charismatic movement - between "baptism in water" and "baptism in the Holy Sprit" (see for example Mark. 1:8) is a topic which ought to be dealt with more profoundly than now is the case in *BEM*. When is the Spirit given and how? Once or many times? What about the freedom of the Spirit to act without visible means? There is diversity in Acts as to whether baptism (in water) is prior to reception of the Spirit, or the Spirit prior to baptism, and the Spirit without baptism etc. There are many questions which need to be dealt with.

[166] *BUS* p. 204.

[167] *BUS* advocates the blessing of children and this as an alternative to infant baptism. *BUS* p. 205, see also Supplement on blessing of children, *BUS* pp. 204f.

reluctance of churches which practise believers' baptism to acknowledge the validity of infant baptism;[168]

The working party, however, dissociates itself from *BEM* and does not accept its argumentation concerning indiscriminate baptism. It states:

> The crucial point on the question of infant baptism is not after all the fact that it is practised indiscriminately.[169]

This is a characteristic comment on *BEM's* attempt to solve the problem of infant baptism and "re-baptism", between churches exclusively practising believers' baptism and churches practising both infant baptism and believers' baptism.

The silence of *BUS* regarding indiscriminate baptism and this statement by the working party indicates on the whole the problem in achieving church unity on the basis of "our common baptism".

On the statement in *B 22,* that baptism is normally administered by an ordained minister, *BUS* writes: "What is said in § 22 applies to us as well."[170] And on *B 23* it wants to underline *BEM's* view that baptism is "intimately connected with the corporate life and worship of the Church".[171]

The agreement between *BUS* and *BEM* which we found at the beginning of this chapter concerning the celebration of baptism may be questioned and discussed. The fact is that something absolutely necessary must be integrated into these aspects, if baptism is to be regarded as a proper, valid baptism by *BUS* and not as a blessing.

We can note so far that *BEM's* description of the celebration of baptism and the agreement of *BUS* with *BEM* (on for instance *B 17),* does not imply a "yes" by the former to every baptism which is administered with or in water and in the name of the Trinity.

---

168 *B com 21b.*

169 "Kommentaren till punkt 21 b) om dem som 'tvekar' att erkänna barndopets giltighet. Den springande punkten i fråga om barndopet är trots allt inte att det praktiseras urskillningslöst." Supplement to Minutes 2/11/83.

170 *BUS* p. 204. It is not my purpose to discuss the meaning of "ordained ministry" for considering baptism as valid, but we can take it for granted that this is not a problem for *BUS.* Concerning the discussion about ministry see also *BUS* pp. 207-213. As I wrote in Part I, many Baptist congregations are not led by any pastor at all, and Baptists have traditionally been hesitant to use the term *pastor/priest,* preferring *preacher.*

171 *BUS* p. 204.

Concerning the celebration of baptism we find thus both agreements and disagreements between the two documents. The non-recognition of infant baptism by *BUS* is without doubt a stumbling block, and the problems with "re-baptism" and indiscriminate baptism, from *BEM's* point of view, still exist.

Practice in infant baptism and believers' baptism (water, the name of the Trinity etc.) is similar. There is possibly a common understanding of baptism. But, in the opinion of *BUS*, some baptismal rites differ so much from each other that one baptismal rite (i.e. infant baptism) cannot be recognized as such but only as an act of blessing. The difference is that in some baptisms (infant baptisms), an absolutely necessary presupposition is missing - the personal conscious response, in others (believers' baptism), however, this is to be found. This presupposition concerns, however, not only baptismal practice but also as a matter of fact the underlying baptismal theology in this baptismal practice. This indicates that there is an underlying interaction between theology and practice. This is not only a question of differences in baptismal practice, as *BUS* seems to regard the problem, there is also a baptismal theology underlying the baptismal practice which decides whether the precondition of baptism is, or is not, present.

In spite of these problems, it seems that it is possible to achieve church unity according to *BUS*.[172] It shows openness towards differences between various baptismal rites, and it states as a comment on *B 20:*

> One baptismal rite may differ from the other by being more or less comprehensive, § 20. Such differences should not impede Christian unity.[173]

The question remains, however, of what the basis of the church and of church unity is in such a case, if baptism cannot be the basis? This brings us to questions of ecclesiology, membership of and belonging to a church, and the relation and function of baptism to church, and to membership, which will be dealt with in the next chapter.

---

[172] "We mean that unity in Christ can be manifested in spite of different baptismal practices." *BUS* p. 202.

[173] *BUS* p. 203.

10. Ecclesiology - Baptism and Membership

One of the most fundamental issues in theology in general, and in the theology of baptism in particular, is ecclesiology. Different kinds of question are involved in this subject. For instance what is the relation between baptism and membership? Is the church equivalent to the baptized or not? What really is the church, and who is "in" and who is "outside" the church? Is the local congregation the same as the church?

One view of the church is that it is a community in the Holy Spirit through baptism, where Christ is the Head. A community becomes a church, the Body of Christ, by God's saving grace through Word and sacrament, and through baptism a person is incorporated into this community of the church. In other words, baptism is *one* mark of the church (but as stated before not of every church or denomination). There are, of course, other marks, such as eucharist, prayer, worship etc. *BEM* writes:

> Through baptism, Christians are brought into union with Christ, with each other and with the Church of every time and place...[174]

The church is the Body of Christ, where every member has a special relation to the Lord, who is the Head, and also a relation to each other. It is universal, but concretized as a local church, usually designated as a local congregation by the Baptists.

BEM makes a distinction between those churches which baptize people at any age, and those which only baptize those who are able to make a confession of faith for themselves.[175] This distinction could be regarded as describing in general terms two different categories of churches. Both are, however, in one way or another baptizing people. This distinction in the description of the churches using these two categories has, however, a weak point which can be questioned; which *BUS* does in fact do:

---

[174] *B 6.*

[175] *B 11, B com 12.*

The list that is presented here is not complete, at any rate not for Swedish conditions. There are churches in which the individual is at liberty to decide not only the form of baptism but also if he should be baptized at all.[176]

And it asks:

... should a church be looked upon as a church if not all or even any of its members are baptized or if the sacraments are neither taken into account nor administered?[177]

This is a challenging question for *BEM*.

As examples of this type of community the Society of Friends and the Salvation Army are mentioned.[178] Neither of these two churches belongs to either of the two categories of churches which *BEM* mentions. From the discussion above it has been established that it proposes that both infant baptism and believers' baptism are to be recognized, but not "re-baptism". For *BUS*, however, it is only believers' baptism which is recognized as valid. This can imply that churches baptizing infants ought in one way to be regarded as equivalent to Quakers and the Salvation Army. In other words, the members of both kinds of churches, for example the Salvation Army (where no baptism is practised) and members of the Church of Sweden (baptized by infant baptism), could be regarded as not baptized. To the question of whether a church where there is no baptismal practice at all could be regarded as a church, we get the answer, which is to be expected, that "churches which are reluctant to recognize infant baptism have been prepared to answer this question in the affirmative."[179] In other words, a church may also include non-baptized members. Without such an opinion *BUS* would get into trouble in many ways, seeming to hold that all churches practising infant baptism (Orthodox, Catholic, Anglican

---

[176] *BUS* p. 201.

[177] Ibid. Concerning the claim in *BEM* that all churches baptize believers, the working party writes: "I gruppen nämndes med anledning av satsen 'Alla kyrkor döper troende...' att det finns undantag. Det finns även de som tar in de som inte är döpta." Supplement to Minutes 2/11/83. See also the discussion in Part I, especially on the Mission Covenant Church of Sweden, where there are different possibilities for membership with or without baptism, with both infant baptism *and* believers' baptism even of one and the same person, i.e. "re-baptism", chapter 9.4.2. See also Part III, chapter 8.2.1.

[178] *BUS* p. 201.

[179] Ibid.

and Lutheran etc.) or which do not practise baptism at all (as the Society of Friends and the Salvation Army) are non-churches.

The opinion of *BUS* that a person can be a member of a church without any baptism must, however, be regarded as a deviation from *BEM's* position:

> Through baptism, Christians are brought into union with Christ, with each other and with the Church of every time and place.[180]

This is also noted by *BUS*.[181] *BEM* regards baptism as incorporation into the Body of Christ, which is the church.[182] The church consists thus of baptized people and baptism is the way into the church, an entry into the New Covenant between God and his people.[183] For *BUS* baptism, although desirable, is not necessarily the way into the church (into Christ) but one way among others.[184]

Concerning the concepts "belonging" *(tillhörighet)*, and "membership" *(medlemskap)*, etc., there are different approaches within the denominations. Many terms circulate and confusion might easily become complete. I will deal briefly with the concepts "belonging" and "membership" in relation to baptism and the congregation/church.

The Swedish researcher Irving Palm mentions that there are three traditional ways of becoming a member of a local congregation within the Free Churches. From the 1960's and onwards there is within some churches a fourth way. The four ways to membership are 1) through repentance and baptism,[185] 2) through the confession of faith,[186] 3) through a certificate of a change of address

---

[180] *B 6.*

[181] *BUS* p. 201.

[182] *B 6.*

[183] *B 1.*

[184] See the discussion above where we have for instance pointed out the tension in *BUS* about whether baptism is to be regarded as "the first" or "the second" entry into the Kingdom, the Covenant.

[185] This is the traditional Baptist way to membership in a congregation. Palm, Irving, "Gemensamma församlingar - en ny fas i den ekumeniska utvecklingen", *Tro & Tanke* 1992:4, p. 57.

[186] For the congregations of the Mission Covenant Church of Sweden this is enough. People are welcomed as members regardless of whether they are baptized by infant baptism, by believers' baptism or not baptized at all. Ibid.

from another congregation,[187] 4) through associative membership.[188] Palm also mentions a fifth type of membership, that of open membership.[189] He does not discuss how these types are related to one another.

BUS writes about a "line of difference between 'belonging' and 'membership'".[190] To make a distinction between belonging and membership can be helpful, but it can also be problematic and confusing. What differences do we find in BUS concerning the two concepts "membership" and "belonging"? Unfortunately, it does not go into any deeper discussion of these concepts, and does not give any clear definition of what "member"/"membership" and "belonging" mean. But from its discussion as a whole, we can find the outline of an answer - of course bearing in mind the risks with such a generalization.

The following differences between "membership" and "belonging" can possibly be identified in Baptist congregations:

1) Member through repentance/conversion, confession i.e. personal conscious response and believers' baptism.

2) Member through repentance/conversion, confession i.e. personal conscious response without believers' baptism or without any baptism at all.

1) Belonging i.e. without any personal conscious response but infant baptism.

2) Belonging i.e. without any personal conscious response but blessing of children.

To exemplify the ambiguity and difficulties with terms and concepts, we find the following reflections in BUS. Even if it accepts that another church may consist of *members* who are *not baptized,* it is hesitant and shows a deep concern about the "increasing number of unchristened members" of the Church of Sweden: "This naturally creates difficulties in ecumenical relations and

---

187 Sometimes described as transferred membership (överfört medlemskap). Ibid.

188 Ibid.

189 Ibid. pp. 57f. See also Introduction, Questions of Terminology.

190 BUS p. 205. See also Franzén, Bert, Guds försprång, 1991, and "Guds försprång i barnens liv", [SEW.], VP, No. 20, 1989, p. 11.

discussions when the church and the importance of sacraments for the church are to be defined."[191]

These unchristened members can hardly include all members who have not been baptized by believers' baptism, but must refer to members who have not been baptized at all, neither by infant baptism nor by believers' baptism. One possible interpretation is that we have the curious state of affairs that *BUS* seems to give some sanction to the practice of infant baptism and regards the decrease of infant baptisms as a problem. It does not seem to have any greater difficulties in writing about children baptized by infant baptism as baptized and members of a church:

> We recommend churches that *baptize children,* and especially those in which uncertainty about *infant baptism* has arisen, to seriously consider the question of blessing of children.[192]

Obviously it does not refer to infants who have given a personal conscious response at the rite of baptism in this recommendation.

We cannot expect that it would support the teaching and practice of infant baptism. So it means something else by this "baptism" than by believers' baptism. The reason for these statements is probably to be found in the desire to use a terminology that is not depreciating or insulting, which has already been discussed in the thesis.[193]

A problem which *BUS* observes among churches practising infant baptism is that some churches on the one hand stress the necessity of baptism but on the other hand accept and justify membership without baptism in their midst. It exemplifies this dilemma by mentioning the Church of Sweden, where there is "an inconsistency between doctrine and practice".[194] At first sight it seems strange that it criticizes the Church of Sweden while it does not for instance criticize the Salvation Army. For unlike the Salvation Army, the Church of Sweden does in fact practise baptism - both infant baptism and believers' baptism. We can, however, understand, after the discussions above, why it draws attention to and criticizes the Church of Sweden. The real problem, with reference to churches

---

[191] *BUS* p. 201.

[192] *BUS* p. 205. Italics mine.

[193] See also *BUS* p. 203.

[194] *BUS* p. 201.

like the Church of Sweden, is that in these churches neither at baptism nor later on a personal response is necessary for membership.[195] This implies at least a theoretical possibility of having a church where members are neither baptized by any baptism, nor have given any personal response.

We do as a matter of fact find that the statement in BUS, about the recognition of other churches' members as members of the Body of Christ,[196] is not wholly applicable, since some members of the Church of Sweden (who are neither baptized nor have given any personal response) are obviously questioned as members of the Body of Christ. The kind of churches which are accepted by BUS are those in which all have given what it would call a personal conscious response to God - but all are not necessarily baptized.

It is understandable that it recognizes churches with unchristened members, since even within the Baptist Union of Sweden itself there are "unchristened members". This is due to the possibility that a person has been baptized by infant baptism and therefore accordingly is not regarded as baptized, but still has in spite of this the possibility of becoming a member of a Baptist congregation. Or secondly it is due to the possibility of being a member of a Baptist congregation without any baptism at all. What matters is the personal conscious response. These must, however, be looked upon as exceptions from a Baptist point of view. It can

---

[195] "We are, however, obliged to observe that there is an inconsistency between doctrine and practice when the necessity of baptism is strongly stressed at the same time as membership without baptism is accepted and justified. Nor is a personal response later on necessary for membership. This is best exemplified in our country by the Church of Sweden with its state church idea and increasing number of unchristened members." BUS p. 201. See also Supplement to Minutes 23/2/84; Minutes 23/8/84, § 40; Dop p. 3. See also Bergsten who finds in Vägen till kyrkan, 1988, two different opinions within the Church of Sweden, one encouraging indiscriminate baptism, the other, however, in agreement with BEM and warning against it. Bergsten, Torsten, "Dop och kyrkotillhörighet", Nordiska röster om dop och kyrkotillhörighet, 1988:4, especially pp. 90f.

[196] "... it is the recognition of other churches and their members as members of the body of Christ that is the reason why open communion and sometimes even open membership are practised in our churches." BUS p. 202. See also the discussion above.

occur on account of the development of open membership and not least because of ecumenical congregations.[197]

The idea that it is not baptism but faith alone that matters can also be applied to the question of participation in the Lord's Supper,[198] i.e. open communion:

> This is, no doubt, the New Testament order: first the breakthrough of the new life in baptism, then the food for this life in the eucharist. But if less importance is attached to the sacraments and *more to faith*, it may be possible to support the practice in most Baptist churches in Sweden to invite all believers to the Lord's table, whether they are baptized or not.[199]

In *BEM*, however, we find that baptism and eucharist are kept together. The condition for participating in Holy Communion is that the participants are baptized.[200]

We can note that *BUS* does not mention anything about *BEM's* statement about children sharing in the eucharist. This is symptomatic. The issue of Holy Communion and children has been a difficulty for Baptists.[201]

---

[197] See Part I, chapter 9.5, where I discuss the ecumenical congregations, and also Part III, for example chapter 7. and chapter 9.

[198] *BUS* p. 206.

[199] Ibid. Italics mine.

[200] *BEM*, (part Eucharist), *E 2, E com 19*.

[201] Ulla Bardh also pays attention to this dilemma. She writes in *Exkurs om barnvälsignelse* (An Excursus on the Blessing of Children): "Personally I would note that BS [the Baptist Union of Sweden, i.e. meaning *BUS* here, my remark] refrains from commenting on one of its own internal problems concerning the relationship of children to baptism, the eucharist and the congregation, namely the question of children's Holy Communion. When BS [the Baptist Union of Sweden, which is not the same as *BUS* here, my remark] carried out its thorough examination of the question of the eucharist, after three years work presented to the denomination in 1981, the question of children's Holy Communion was the only point on which agreement could not be reached. The General Secretary David Lagergren made a reservation to the recommendation of the report that children be admitted to the eucharist with the approval of their parents. His reservation is a clearer Baptist interpretation than the current BS text [i.e. *BUS*, my remark] in order to understand the argumentation of those practising believers' baptism about these difficult questions." ("Personligen noterar jag att BS avstår från att kommentera ett av sina interna problem vad gäller barnets förhållande till dop, nattvard och församling, nämligen frågan om barnkommunion. Då BS

From this chapter about ecclesiology, baptism and membership, we find that one of the most fundamental doctrines for Baptists, believers' baptism, in spite of the Baptist tradition and its principles, and the emphasis on baptism in the New Testament and its commandment to baptize,[202] is not a necessary presupposition for becoming a member of a Baptist congregation. Even if believers' baptism is, of course, desirable, and also is preached and taught, the emphasis on believers' baptism seems to be replaced by faith alone, the personal conscious response which is strongly emphasized by *BUS*. The latter expresses opinions and practices similar to those of the Mission Covenant Church of Sweden.[203]

We may conclude this discussion by noting a tendency in the Baptist Union of Sweden towards a possible shift from what I would call a *"Baptism*-communion movement" to a *"Faith*-communion movement", due especially to the new ecumenical situation caused especially by the ecumenical congregations. It may be stated that the Baptist movement no longer succeeds, in comparison with its earlier history in Sweden, in seeing repentance, confession and baptism as one baptismal act.[204]

The definition of the church and the local congregation has still not been clarified, i.e. whether it is equivalent to the community of the baptized *or* to the fellowship of believers or both. This has, of course, consequences for church unity, if it is understood to be baptismal unity etc. *BEM's* emphasis on baptism, as the incorporation into the Christ, i.e. the church, etc. with implications

---

företog en grundlig bearbetning i nattvardsfrågan, efter tre års arbete presenterad i samfundet 1981, var frågan om barnkommunion den enda punkt där enighet inte kunde uppnås. Missionsföreståndare David Lagergren reserverade sig mot utredningens rekommendation av barns tillträde till nattvarden med föräldrars samtycke. Hans reservation är en klarare baptistisk utläggning än den nu aktuella BS texten för att förstå troendedöpares argumentation kring dessa svåra frågeställningar. (När vi bryter det bröd... sid 235 f.)"), Bardh, Ulla, "Limadokumentet och Sv. Baptistsamfundet. En redogörelse för och kommentar kring Sv. Baptistsamfundets remissvar", 1986, [unpublished paper]. Bardh refers to *När vi bryter det bröd...*, 1981, (where we also find the reservation of Lagergren, ibid. pp. 235f.).

202 See also *B 1*.

203 See Part I, chapter 9.4.2.

204 See Part I.

for the relationship with all who are *baptized* in whatever church or denomination, is thus one model but not the only one in reality.

11. Towards Mutual Recognition of Baptism and Church Unity - A Challenge

In this part, about the official response of the Baptist Union of Sweden to *BEM* concerning the issue of baptism, the Swedish Baptist standpoint primarily regarding baptism and also some other ecclesiological topics related to baptism has been analysed. Following from the previous chapters I want to conclude this part by considering the issue of the recognition of baptism and church unity.

BEM says:

> The union with Christ which we share through baptism has important implications for Christian unity.[205]

It takes it more or less for granted that members of different denominations/churches and local congregations in the world are united with Christ through baptism, and this has implications for Christian unity and ultimately church unity. This statement presupposes that there is an agreement among the churches first of all that baptism constitutes the basis of ecclesiology. Furthermore, that a recognition of baptism exists; and also that there is a mutual recognition of one another's baptism. If, however, there are different baptismal practices and also different baptismal theologies, or no baptism at all (as with for instance the Quakers), obviously other implications ought to be drawn, indicating rather the reverse, i.e. disunity and consequently not church unity on the basis of baptism.

It has been noticed that *BUS* has an ambivalent attitude towards *BEM*. On the one hand, it agrees on one point with *BEM*, for example that the work of Faith and Order

> has led to a common understanding of baptism in *many respects*, especially regarding the meaning and importance of baptism.[206]

---

[205] *B 6*.

[206] *BUS* p. 200. Italics mine. *BUS* writes also: "After all, different churches with various traditions can say the same things about baptism." Ibid.

On the other hand, however, there is a critical attitude. Different presuppositions and diverging opinions can be observed in relation to *BEM*, concerning baptism, ecclesiology and church unity. *BUS* questions for instance its view about "our one baptism" and asks: "Can we in earnest talk about 'our one baptism'...?"[207] For in its opinion, all those baptized by infant baptism do not share in that union through baptism which *BEM* writes about. People who have gone through infant baptism or the blessing of children are regarded as equal by *BUS*. Both these categories ought thus to be considered as catechumens, whose instruction is a preparation for baptism and life as baptized.[208] Such a standpoint has also implications for church unity.

The stance of *BEM* recognizing both baptisms - infant baptism and believers' baptism - and thus having a pattern of unity based upon baptism seems according to *BUS* to end up in a blind alley.[209] The latter says:

> With the present varied practices in different churches it is hardly possible to come to a united standpoint.[210]

We can note that *BEM* does not give any alternatives. Its statement that "Churches are increasingly recognizing one another's baptism as the one baptism into Christ"[211] can thus hardly be applied in the case of the Swedish Baptist document.[212] In the eyes of *BEM*, and of churches practising infant baptism, a continued practice of "re-baptism" will be taking place among Baptists. Church unity on the basis of recognizing one another's baptism, which must include recognition of baptismal practice as well as baptismal theology, seems far away.

BUS' view about different baptismal practices cannot in my opinion exclude but must include different baptismal doctrines. It is

---

[207] *BUS* p. 201.

[208] *BUS* p. 202.

[209] *BUS* p. 200.

[210] Ibid.

[211] *B 15.* See also *B 10:* "Christians discover the full significance of *the one baptism* as the gift of God to all God's people." Italics mine.

[212] To *B 15* Janarv asks: "Är denna beskrivning adekvat?" Supplement to Minutes 2/11/83.

true that it notes: "The difficulties have been evident when it comes to the point of putting the common view into practice."[213] The question which, however, must be asked is why it regards infant baptism as a blessing, if there is a common view on baptism and differences only in baptismal practice? And what does its attitude to infant baptism lead to in relation to the worldwide Church where the need

to recover baptismal unity is at the heart of the ecumenical task as it is central for the realization of genuine partnership within the Christian communities[214]?

For in one sense the baptismal practices of both infant baptism and believers' baptism are in many ways the same possibly due to a common understanding of baptism. Both are, as already has been stated above, conducted in water and in the name of the Trinity, in a faith-context etc.

There are still different theological interpretations with various practical consequences, which sometimes result in non-recognition of baptism. One implication of this is that one church "re-baptizes" a person, while he or she in the opinion of that church is not baptized at all. Another church practising infant baptism estimates, however, this "biblical, proper baptism" as a second one, a "re-baptism", with continuing divisions among and within the churches and a weakened witness to the One Church.

BUS' opinion on baptism has, as we have seen, implications for ecclesiology and church unity. There are different implications in *BUS* and in *BEM*, implications such as the non-recognition of infant baptism, "re-baptism", which in *BEM's* perspective gives rise to problems concerning Christian unity and church unity. Aware of the problematic situation, since baptism (infant baptism, indiscriminate baptism, "re-baptism") is a stumbling block, *BUS* gives a serious suggestion of a solution to the basic and complex issues of infant baptism, believers' baptism and "re-baptism", namely that the blessing of children could possibly be a starting-point towards church unity. It writes:

Churches where infant baptism, and especially those where hesitation about the rise of infant baptism is at stake, should consider the possibility of offering parents blessing of children as an alternative to infant baptism.[215]

---

[213] *BUS* p. 200.

[214] *B com 6.*

A legitimate question follows from this: can church unity be established and manifested without any baptism at all? For what kind of unity does *BUS* refer to in its statement, "that unity in Christ can be manifested in spite of different baptismal practices."[216]? What finally seems to matter is not baptism but faith alone, the personal conscious response to the risen Lord. Baptism is thus no longer regarded as absolutely necessary, not even to be a member of a congregation of the Baptist Union of Sweden.

We are generally speaking confronted with at least two different kinds of models of church unity. One works towards mutual recognition of baptism and puts its emphasis on the latter. This applies to *BEM.* Baptism is something central, and the one baptism *(our one baptism)* is more or less taken for granted. Baptism is the foundation of the church and of the work for church unity. Therefore it is important to recognize one another's baptism. It is baptism,

> our one baptism into Christ [which, my remark] constitutes a call to the churches to overcome their divisions and visibly manifest their fellowship.[217]

In *BUS*, however, the model of church unity cannot for understandable reasons be based upon baptism, since the only baptism which is recognized as proper and valid is believers' baptism - in spite of for example an instrumental, sacramental view of baptism. This standpoint cannot in the perspective of *BEM* be looked upon as a positive contribution to the ecumenical work for mutual recognition of baptism, but rather quite the reverse.

The fact is that ecumenically we are still confronted by a stumbling block with the inability of the churches mutually to recognize themselves as sharing in the one baptism.[218] The starting-

---

215 *BUS* p. 205. Janarv in the working party makes a comment on *B 16:* "Här kan barnvälsignelsen bli ett viktigt inslag." Supplement to Minutes 2/11/83.

216 *BUS* p. 202. In *Dop* it is said: "Vi menar att enheten i Kristus kan komma till uttryck trots olikheter i doppraxis." *Dop* p. 4.

217 *B 6.* See also in *BEM:* "Jesus' life of service, his death and resurrection, are the foundation of a new community which is built up continually by the good news of the Gospel and the gifts of the sacraments. The Holy Spirit unites in a single body those who follow Jesus Christ and sends them as witnesses into the world." *M 1.*

218 *"The inability of the churches mutually to recognize their various practices of baptism as sharing in the one baptism, and their actual dividedness in spite of*

point for the work for church unity is thus not baptism in *BUS*, but partly the blessing of children, partly faith, i.e. the personal conscious response. It is of interest to note this against the background of the origin and development of the Baptist Union of Sweden.[219] A reconsideration of baptism (which includes ecclesiology and ecumenism) is in progress.

Both *BEM* and *BUS* defend believers' baptism on the basis of the New Testament. *BEM* is of the opinion that believers' baptism is "the most clearly attested pattern in the New Testament documents", and according to *BUS* it is the only valid baptism. In spite of these arguments they draw, however, in the discussions about ecumenism and church unity, another consequence than to plead for believers' baptism. For *BEM* recognizes infant baptism as valid, and *BUS* not least significantly is open to bracketing baptism (i.e. believers' baptism) - pleading for faith alone - and working for church unity based on the blessing of infants. New challenges are waiting in the continued work with these important topics: baptism, faith, ecclesiology, ecumenism etc.

In Part III, there will be a discussion about almost the same issues as in this part, but now in the public discussions within the Baptist Union of Sweden. This in order to see if *BUS* reflects the actual situation of the Baptist Union of Sweden or if there are possibly alternative viewpoints or tendencies which are not expressed.

---

mutual baptismal recognition, have given dramatic visibility to the broken witness of the Church." B com 6.

[219] Compare with the Baptist principles and the early Swedish Baptist movement and its earlier fight – out of the biblical commandment to baptize - for believers' baptism, and its costs, where baptism was the *sine qua non*, of course together with conversion, a personal confession etc. See Part I, chapter 2. and chapter 6.

Part III

Public Discussions within the Baptist Union of Sweden

1. Introduction

In Part II, analysing more closely the official response of the Baptist Union of Sweden to *BEM*, at least two baptismal theologies and practices, each of them with different presuppositions, were found. One, represented by *BEM*, recognizes both infant baptism and believers' baptism. *BEM* rejects, however, "re-baptism". *BUS* recognizes only believers' baptism, and is of the opinion that infant baptism is not a baptism at all, which implies an affirmation or at least an acceptance of what other churches and denominations regard as "re-baptism". In our analysis in Part II, infant baptism is for *BUS* more or less equivalent to a blessing. All this implies that we can neither talk about "our one baptism", nor about a mutual recognition of baptism. This has, of course, implications for the issues of ecclesiology, for example incorporation into the Body of Christ, the church and the local congregation, and church unity on the basis of baptism. In brief, baptism as the basis of the call to church unity can be questioned.

In this part, I will try to examine the material that I call the *public discussions*. The same topics will in principle be dealt with as have been dealt with in Part II. This is done by looking at statements and discussions from articles in journals, mainly in *Veckoposten*, but also in some other publications principally by Swedish Baptist pastors and theologians. They concern the questions of baptism, ecclesiology and church unity during the period which mainly precedes and directly follows the publications of *BEM* and *BUS* – the 1970's and onwards. I want to see if the same positions are to be found in the public discussions as in *BUS*, or if there are any complementary, alternative or even divergent positions in relation to it. The public discussions may not necessarily be representative of the Baptist Union in the same way as *BUS*. It can nevertheless be of considerable importance in our study of the Baptist Union of Sweden, widening still more the perspective and putting the Baptist teaching and practice of baptism in context.

2. Infant Baptism and Believers' Baptism: Differentiations and Divergences

2.1. Tendencies to Recognize Infant Baptism as Baptism?

Infant baptism and the Baptist movement is a difficult subject. That infant baptism has been and still is criticized as unbiblical by Baptists in general is obvious. *BUS* does not either recognize infant baptism as baptism, I pointed out this fact in the discussion in Part II. At the same time we have to remind ourselves that infant baptism and the blessing of children were more or less regarded as equivalent. This opinion is, however, according to Lagergren, to be regarded as more favourable than the traditional Baptist rejection of this type of baptism.[1] I want first make some additional comments about the blessing of children in this context before continuing with the issue of infant baptism.

The blessing of children is a late phenomenon in the history of the Baptist Union of Sweden,[2] even if a few took place early in its history.[3] In the manual of 1987 it is said that there is no direct exhortation in the Bible to repeat the act which is found in Mark 10:13ff., but "...congregations and Christian parents have found it natural to express the significance of the example of the Gospel in a simple act in a service."[4] In this manual there are two alternatives

---

[1] Lagergren, David, "Ekumenisk barnteologi", *VP*, No. 17, 1991, p. 6. See also *BUS*.

[2] Franzén, Bert, "Barnen i församlingen. Frågan om tillhörighet och medlemskap", *Tro och Liv*, No. 3, 1985, p. 32. See also Franzén, Bert, *Guds försprång*, 1991, especially pp. 86-95; Franzén, Bert, "Barnen och församlingen, II. Texterna om Jesus och barnen", *VP*, No. 26, 1986, p. 6.

[3] See Part II, chapter 5.

[4] *Till församlingens tjänst*, 1987, p. 98.

for the blessing of children. One of these may be seen as a name-giving ceremony.[5]

The earlier lack of such a rite depended to a great extent on the Baptist opinion that the children of Christian parents are already included in God's act of redemption through Christ without any religious rite.[6] There seems thus in my opinion to be a difference between the children of Christian parents and those of non-Christian parents.

Let us then proceed to the issue of infant baptism. To plead for the traditional Baptist view that no infant baptism is a baptism can be interpreted to imply that all the churches and denominations practising infant baptism lack Christian baptism. In the light of this assertion, the question is if there are any tendencies to recognize infant baptism as baptism, implicitly or explicitly, within the Baptist Union of Sweden, for example in Baptist manuals or in statements and writings by Swedish Baptists.

In the most recent above-mentioned Baptist manual of 1987, there is an interesting detail. An instruction states that in ecumenical services there may be a Renewal of the Baptismal Covenant (Förnyelse av dopförbundet).[7] This may be "a possibility for Christians from different baptismal traditions to confess and preach together the meaning of baptism."[8] In the words of welcome to the service it is stated:

> On different occasions, in different ages and in different connections we have answered and said our 'yes' to the call of God to union with Christ and His congregation. Today we confess that we are Christians, members in His Body... Today we remind ourselves of our conversion, our baptism and our dedication to Christ. In thankfulness we want to renew our covenant with Him, once more give ourselves to Him and to each other.[9]

---

5   Ibid. pp. 98ff.

6   Franzén, Bert, "Barnen i församlingen. Frågan om tillhörighet och medlemskap", Tro och Liv, No. 3, 1985, p. 32.

7   Till församlingens tjänst, 1987, p. 36.

8   Ibid. See also Fahlgren, Sune, "Baptismen och baptisternas gudstjänstliv", I enhetens tecken, 1994, p. 282.

9   "... I dag erinrar vi oss vår omvändelse, vårt dop och vår överlåtelse till Kristus. I tacksamhet vill vi förnya vårt förbund med honom, på nytt överlåta oss åt honom och åt varandra." Till församlingens tjänst, 1987, p. 36.

Note, however, the order: conversion, baptism and dedication to Christ. There is here, even if not a recognition of infant baptism, an opening towards mutual recognition of baptism, as well as an open attitude towards other baptismal traditions.

After this example, statements by two prominent Baptists, David Lagergren and Bert Franzén can be examined. Both have been involved in the work of *BUS*, Lagergren as chairman of the commission. Do any of their statements indicate any kind of recognition of infant baptism, in spite of their response in *BUS* with its evident non-recognition?

Lagergren writes concerning people baptized by infant baptism that "a genuine respect ought to be shown for their faith in their baptism", even if "no objective acknowledgement of the baptism of fellow-Christians is given".[10] This cannot be interpreted as recognition of infant baptism, without pressing the words too much. But it is, however, a minor opening. It expresses respect for other people's faith in their own baptism. There is no unconditional wish to baptize them by believers' baptism, which could have been expected from a traditional Baptist point of view. Respect is the keyword.

According to Bert Franzén a self-critical examination concerning their practice of baptism is desirable for all denominations, to clear away obstacles to achieving a deeper Christian fellowship.[11] Franzén seems to be open to infant baptism. In his book *Guds försprång*, 1991, he even gives recognition to the churches baptizing infants, for guarding certain values. They have "persistently maintained the importance of 'prevenient grace'."[12] Another statement by Franzén must be quoted. In view of the problem of the baptism of very young children, especially among Pentecostals and

---

10 "Där ett objektivt godkännande av medkristnas dop inte föreligger, bör en genuin respekt för deras tro på sitt dop visas." Lagergren, David, *Enhetsförslaget och dopfrågan*, 1969, p. 13.

11 Franzén, Bert, "Dopet som gemenskapsfaktor", *Tro och Liv*, No. 5, 1975, p. 197. See also Franzén, Bert, "Dopet i kyrkornas gemenskap", *VP*, No. 1/2 1975, p. 2; Franzén, Bert, "Inledningsanförande till grupparbete: Dopet som ekumeniskt problem", 1974, p. 23, [conference documentation].

12 "Det finns anledning att erkänna att barndöpande samfund utövat en god vakttjänst just omkring de värden som här uppmärksammas. Man har envist hållit fast vid 'den förekommande nådens' betydelse." Franzén, Bert, *Guds försprång*, 1991, p. 47.

Southern Baptists, he states: "We shall try completely to avoid the baptism of children, not only baptism of infants, in our churches."[13] This is not a recognition of infant baptism, but not an absolute demand to cease with infant baptisms either, only an appeal to avoid them.

Let us consider an article which deals with the opinions of three Baptist pastors concerning baptism and implicitly "re-baptism":[14] *Baptist pastor about baptismal document: Baptists ought to recognize infant baptism.*[15] This looks like proof that people who have earlier been baptized as infants do not necessarily have to be "re-baptized" within the Baptist Union of Sweden. The reader may first get the impression that the title is a statement by Birgit Karlsson. This is, however, not true.[16] There is also a picture of the former General Secretary Birgit Karlsson, which may further contribute to the misunderstanding, and the caption runs: "The time of baptism is not crucial, says the Baptist leader Birgit Karlsson."[17]

The statement in the title is instead from another Baptist pastor (now a famous novelist), Vibeke Olsson. She expresses the opinion that Baptists ought to recognize infant baptism as a baptism for ecumenical reasons, that it would be wrong to be superior and not recognize infant baptisms.[18] This ought consequently to imply

---

13 "Överhuvud taget ska vi försöka undvika barndop, inte bara småbarnsdop, i våra kyrkor." Franzén, Bert, "Barnen och församlingen, IV. En modell för mognad", *VP,* No. 29/30, 1986, p. 7. Bert Franzén suggests in another article that Baptist denominations ought to make a common study on the problem of age. It is especially urgent to involve the Pentecostal Movement, according to Franzén, since the age of the baptizand in Pentecostal congregations is frequently very low. Franzén, Bert, "Dopet i kyrkornas gemenskap", *VP,* No. 1/2, 1975, p. 2. See also Franzén, Bert, *Guds försprång,* 1991; "Guds försprång i barnens liv", [SEW.], *VP,* No. 20, 1989, p. 11.

14 "Re-baptism" will be dealt with more below in chapter 5; see also Part II, chapter 7.

15 "Baptistpastor om dopdokument: -Baptister bör erkänna barndopet", *Svenska Journalen,* No. 1, 1985, p. 12.

16 See also Svenson, Sven, "Missvisande rubrik", *VP,* No. 5, 1985, p. 3.

17 "-Tidpunkten för dopet är inte det allena saliggörande, säger baptistledaren Birgit Karlsson." "Baptistpastor om dopdokument: -Baptister bör erkänna barndopet", *Svenska Journalen,* No. 1, 1985, p. 12.

18 Ibid.

rejection of at least some "re-baptisms". And in the same article, a traditional, closed Baptist position is also put forward by pastor Ruben Janarv. He maintains that the Baptist Union of Sweden cannot recognize infant baptism as a baptism, *"then we would no longer be Baptist congregations."[19]* His statement implies a continued practice of "re-baptism".

Amongst these three opinions (Birgit Karlsson b. 1935, Vibeke Olsson b. 1958, and Ruben Janarv b. 1926), we can distinguish at least two, possibly three, different interpretations. 1) There is recognition of infant baptism and possibly as a result rejection of "re-baptism". 2) Infant baptism is not recognized as valid and consequently there is an acceptance of "re-baptism", which in this interpretation is not regarded as a "re-baptism". 3) Birgit Karlsson seems to propose some kind of "a golden mean" between these two, which indicates an opening. She disregards in one way the difficult question about the validity of baptism *per se*, and does not speak about the act of baptism but about the importance of *baptismal life*. She emphasizes this.[20]

Birgit Karlsson makes another interesting statement in an article about "the baptized infant": *"Of course these should not been baptized once more."[21]* She underlines this statement by saying: "I do not want to baptize such a person again."[22]

These statements by a General Secretary ought to imply that she regards infant baptism as baptism, probably improper but nevertheless valid. Infant baptism is thus not, as in *BUS*, regarded

---

19 *"... då skulle vi nämligen inte längre vara baptistförsamlingar."* Ibid. Italics mine.

20 "För mig är det avgjort viktigaste om en människa – oavsett tidpunkt för dopet – lever i sitt dop och tar det på allvar." "Baptistpastor om dopdokument: -Baptister bör erkänna barndopet", *Svenska Journalen*, No. 1, 1985, p. 12.

21 *"Naturligtvis skall inte dessa döpas en gång till."* Karlsson, Birgit, "Dopet - en central fråga när församlingar går samman. Missionsföreståndaren kommenterar", *VP*, No. 40 1987, p. 11. Italics mine. See also "'En federativ gemenskap'", *VP*, No. 50, 1989, p. 3, where Karlsson, in an interview discussing a fellowship of federative character, is open to the practice of infant baptism.

22 "Jag vill inte heller döpa en sådan person igen". Karlsson, Birgit, "Dopet - en central fråga när församlingar går samman. Missionsföreståndaren kommenterar", *VP*, No. 40 1987, p. 11.

as a "non-baptism" or a blessing but as a valid baptism. We may observe that Birgit Karlsson, in spite of this attitude, approved *BUS* a couple of years earlier.[23]

An at least implicit recognition of infant baptism seems also to be given by the Baptist pastor Harry Månsus (b. 1941).[24] It is also proposed by another Baptist pastor and member of the Board of the Baptist Union of Sweden, that infant baptism should be regarded as a biblical baptism, if a person baptized by such baptism later on becomes a believer. Bearing in mind the history of the Baptist movement and the Baptist principles of baptism and congregation, it is not surprising that the Baptist pastor, Edvin Österberg (b. 1905), designates this development "remarkable".[25]

Torsten Bergsten does also *de facto* give recognition to infant baptism.[26] He maintains that there are *many Baptists* who hold such a view,[27] and that

---

23 See Minutes 8/3/85, § 13.

24 Månsus, Harry, "Bibliskt dop eller surrogatdop?", *Tro och Liv*, No. 5, 1975, p. 218. See also the next section *A Discussion of Believers' Baptism and Baptism of Metanoia*, about the problem, according to Månsus, in baptizing committed Christians (also those baptized by infant baptism!), i.e. those who already are in the church, in Christ.

25 It is Österberg who refers to this unnamed Baptist pastor. See Österberg, Edvin, "Dop och församling", *VP*, No. 42, 1984, p. 4. Österberg writes: "I en av våra större baptistförsamlingar, vars pastor är med i Missionsstyrelsen, fick de församlade del av sin pastors uppfattning i dopfrågan... Han sade, att om en person, som är barndöpt, senare kommer till tro, så skall dennes dop gälla såsom ett bibliskt dop. En märklig utveckling!" Ibid. See also Öman, Torsten, "Frälsningens mottagande", *VP*, No. 25, 1976, p. 4.

26 In opposition to *BUS*' statements about infant baptism, he talks about infant baptism not as a blessing of children but as a valid, even if improper, *(oklart)*, baptism. "Dopet som förenar. En dialog mellan Torsten Bergsten, Svenska baptistsamfundet, och Björn Svärd, Svenska kyrkan", *Till hembygden*, 1988, p. 78.

27 "För egen del har jag och *många baptister* med mig pläderat för uppfattningen att ett barndop bör accepteras och respekteras när den som döpts i späd ålder bekänner sig som döpt kristen och troende församlingsmedlem." Bergsten, Torsten, "Dop och nattvard i de gemensamma församlingarna", *Tro och Liv*, No. 6, 1990, p. 4. Italics mine. This article originated in a talk, Bergsten, Torsten, "Dopsyn och församlingstillhörighet i gemensamma församlingar", 1989, [unpublished paper]. See also Bergsten, Torsten, "Kyrkotillhörighet - medlemskap - bekännelse", *Tro och Liv*, No. 1, 1980,

Within the Swedish Baptist church a more relaxed view of infant baptism is slowly gaining ground.[28]

Interestingly Bergsten argued already in 1957 in favour of recognizing infant baptism as valid.[29] Bergsten's explanation of this changed attitude towards infant baptism among Baptists is significant. To maintain the opinion that infant baptism is a "non-baptism" results, according to him, in totally absurd historical consequences. It is to say

---

especially pp. 42f.; Bergsten, Torsten, "Öppet nattvardsbord, överfört medlemskap och en öppen baptism", VP, No. 3, 1986, p. 6.

[28] "Inom den svenska baptismen vinner långsamt en mera avspänd syn på barndopet terräng." Bergsten, Torsten, "Dop och kyrkotillhörighet", Nordiska röster om dop och kyrkotillhörighet, 1988, p. 91. See also Bergsten, Torsten, "På väg mot ett ömsesidigt doperkännande?", 1989, p. 3, [unpublished paper]; Bergsten, Torsten, "Baptismens dubbla dilemma", 1991, [unpublished paper], later in Bergsten, Torsten, "Baptismens dubbla dilemma", VP, No. 47, 1991, p. 4, where Bergsten comments on the report Tecken om enhet, 1991, and writes about indirect recognition of the practice of infant baptism, (ett åtminstone indirekt erkännande av barndopsseden), in ecumenical congregations, where amongst others the Baptist Union of Sweden is involved; Bergsten, Torsten, "Ekumenisk barnteologi", VP, No. 13/14, 1991, p. 12; Bergsten, Torsten, "Tro och tvivel på barndopet", VP, No. 19/20, 1991, p. 7; Bergsten, Torsten, "Att respektera varandras dop", VP, No. 9, 1992, p. 12.

[29] Bergsten, Torsten, "Dopet och församlingen. Baptistisk tro och praxis i biblisk och ekumenisk belysning", Dopet Dåben Dåpen, 1957, pp. 18-23. See also a translation of this, (already mentioned in Part I), Bergsten, Torsten, "Baptism and the Church. Baptist Faith and Practice in a Biblical and Ecumenical Light", The Baptist Quarterly, Vol. 18, No. 4, 1959, pp. 166-171, with the title "Yes" and "No" to Infant Baptism. Ecumenical Intercommunion.

Another name which once again ought to be mentioned also in this context is Karl Barth. Barth had a critical attitude to infant baptism. He questioned infant baptism for biblical and theological reasons, which caused countless discussions, debates and publications. See for example Barth's work Die kirchliche Lehre von der Taufe, 1947 (orig. 1943), which was published in Swedish in 1949, Det kristna dopet, by the Baptist publishing house Westerbergs in Stockholm. Nevertheless, recognition of infant baptism has, according to Bergsten, sometimes been given by Baptists with reference to above all Karl Barth and his idea about infant baptism as a baptism even if improper. Bergsten, Torsten, "Kyrkotillhörighet - medlemskap - bekännelse", Tro och Liv, No. 1, 1980, p. 42. Whether some Baptists do regard infant baptism as an improper baptism as a result of the view of Karl Barth is, however, a difficult problem. It will not be discussed in this context.

that the majority of Christians through the centuries have never been baptized, in spite of the fact that many have regarded themselves as baptized as infants and, as for instance Luther, have found consolation in the thought of their baptism in times of tribulation.[30]

One reason for Baptists recognizing infant baptism as a valid baptism is thus that they ought not to regard the majority of Christians through the centuries as unbaptized.

Recognition of infant baptism as a baptism has thus been given not only implicitly but also explicitly as a complete and genuine baptism by some of these distinguished Baptists, as well as by others, some would even say "many".[31]

These statements must be considered an indication of BEM's assertion that many churches are on their way "towards mutual recognition of baptism",[32] including the Baptists. This points to a tendency towards a revised or even changed attitude among Baptists. And it is, of course, significant to find a Baptist General Secretary who also publicly recognizes infant baptism as valid. We will return to this, but it can already be mentioned that these pronouncements by Birgit Karlsson have been appreciated by some Baptists, but they have for obvious reasons also caused disturbance among others.[33]

There are, however, not only statements by Baptists giving expression to a more or less open attitude towards infant baptism and even recognition. There are also some Baptist pastors who administer infant baptism.

In a weekly magazine one can read about Baptist pastors who administer infant baptisms and how these pastors during the rite "have felt a blessed direct connection with heaven." It is further

---

30 Bergsten, Torsten, "Svenska kyrkan i den aktuella debatten. Tre perspektiv", *Kyrkohistorisk årsskrift* 84, 1984, p. 35; see also Bergsten, Torsten, "Kyrkotillhörighet - medlemskap - bekännelse", *Tro och Liv*, No. 1, 1980, p. 42.

31 "Många baptister erkänner i dag också barndopet som fullvärdigt dop." Svärd, Björn, "Dopet i fokus", *Dopet i fokus*, 1992, p. 6. See also Aourell, Göte, "Dopet och frikyrklig enhet", *VP*, No. 42, 1992, p. 12; Bergsten, Torsten, "Dop och nattvard i de gemensamma församlingarna", *Tro och Liv*, No. 6, 1990, p. 4.

32 B 15-16 with the title *Towards Mutual Recognition of Baptism*.

33 See chapter 8.2.1. below, where the statements by Birgit Karlsson and others will be discussed and further put in context.

said: "there were many examples of breached walls and demolished boundaries."[34] This may be understandable not least from a traditional Baptist viewpoint.[35] And the examples given above must be looked upon as exceptions and in the context of traditional Baptist history, and of Baptist teaching and practice of baptism, as almost incomprehensible.[36] I also want to recall something I already mentioned in Part I, that baptismal fonts are to be found in a Baptist context in the ecumenical congregations, and thus infant baptisms administered there.[37]

There is obviously an opening towards mutual recognition of baptism. These examples and statements are interesting findings - but we do not know how representative of Swedish Baptists in general they are. This opinion I call an open and pluralist Baptist attitude. It seems partially to come close to *BEM*. Therefore these examples are of great value in regard to the theological discussion and particularly to the ecumenical movement in Sweden, but also in a larger context in the work towards mutual recognition of baptism, towards "our one baptism", and towards church unity. The thesis of *BEM*, that "Churches are increasingly recognizing one another's baptism as the one baptism into Christ..."[38], seems to be realized in a preliminary and partial way. And as a matter of fact not only that, but even Baptist pastors are *practising infant baptism!* The strict "non-recognition" of infant baptism is softened among

---

34 Andersson, Krister, "Levande samtal om förenade församlingar", *Svensk Veckotidning*, No. 42, 1990, p. 2. See also Bergsten, Torsten, "Den gemensamma församlingen - ett tecken om enhet", *Levande*, 1996, p. 50.

35 I will give another example which illustrates some other problems and speaks for itself. In Helsingborgs Baptistförsamling a former minister of the Church of Sweden worked (and is still working) as a pastor. He (Robert Södertun) had not himself been baptized by believers' baptism. "Landet runt", *Trons Värld*, No. 20, 1989, p. 3.

36 See for example in Part I, chapter 2. and chapter 6. (with F.O. Nilsson, Anders Wiberg and his book *Hvilken bör döpas? och Hvaruti består dopet?* etc.).

37 See for example Sannerudskyrkan and Valsätrakyrkan etc. These baptismal fonts may, however, not be fixed, so for example in Valsätrakyrkan. Skog, Margareta, "Antalet medlemmar i valda samfund 1975-1989", *Religion och Samhälle* 1989:9, p. 20. This is also a further example of a changed attitude towards infant baptism within a Baptist (-ecumenical) context.

38 *B 15.*

Swedish Baptists, and one of the most characteristic principles in the history of the Baptists, a fundamental Baptist doctrine, seems to be altered - some may perhaps prefer to say "complemented".

This development is not discussed nor even mentioned in BUS. It is rather a contradiction of the opinion that is advocated in BUS, which we call a traditional, closed Baptist attitude. This may, however, possibly point to an increasing development within the Baptist Union of Sweden after BUS. The dates in the footnotes, when compared with the year of the decision of the Central Board of the Baptist Union of Sweden 1985 to approve the response, i.e. BUS, reveal that most of the references arguing for recognition of infant baptism are after 1985.[39]

2.2. A Discussion of Believers' Baptism and Baptism of Metanoia

It can be questioned whether there is also a reconsideration of believers' baptism of a more profound character amongst Swedish Baptists, especially because of what we have found in the previous section.

In the development of what would become the Baptist Union of Sweden, people came to the conclusion, by reading and studying the Bible, that believers' baptism was the proper biblical baptism and infant baptism was unbiblical, invalid and erroneous. The Baptist biblical principle emphasizes the Bible as the only authority. Ruben Janarv is one of many contemporary Swedish Baptist pastors who himself gives expression to this classic Baptist opinion.[40] He refers to Anders Wiberg's book *Hvilken bör döpas? och*

---

[39] See, however, Bergsten, Torsten, "Dopet och församlingen. Baptistisk tro och praxis i biblisk och ekumenisk belysning", *Dopet Dåben Dåpen*, 1957; Lagergren, David, *Enhetsförslaget och dopfrågan*, 1969. Bergsten later writes in reaction to the contribution by Lagergren: "This makes it clear that there are two different stances on infant baptism amongst Baptists." ("Här åskådliggörs att det inom baptismen förekommer två olika ställningstaganden till barndopet.") Bergsten, Torsten, "Kyrkotillhörighet - medlemskap - bekännelse", *Tro och Liv*, No. 1, 1980, p. 42.

[40] Janarv writes that the first and determining principle for Baptists is the Bible. He maintains, however, that Baptists do not have one single view of the Bible. Janarv, Ruben, "Vem är baptist?" [del 2], *VP*, No. 14, 1978, p. 11. See also Part I, chapter 2.

Hvaruti består dopet?, 1852, (Who Ought to be Baptized? and What Is Baptism?).

Wiberg's initial purpose had been to defend infant baptism, but then he could not against his own conscience "distort the Scripture". Wiberg had, according to Janarv, expressed what baptism primarily is about: the authority of the Bible.[41] It is a *baptism of metanoia* or conversion, when the person in question confesses his faith and as a consequence of this asks for baptism. And Baptists argue, based on the New Testament, that baptism and faith are expressions of the same reality.[42] The New Testament ascribes, according to Harry Månsus, faith and baptism to the same spiritual event - the forgiveness of sins and incorporation into Christ. To be a believer and to be baptized was in early Christian times one and the same experience of salvation. *They coincided in time.*[43] Romans 10:17 and Acts 2:37f. have been determining texts for Baptist teaching about faith and baptism.[44]

The emphasis is laid on two active subjects, God and man; neither God alone, nor baptism *per se*. There is a meeting between God and man. Man coming from sin and the world, of which he, according to traditional Baptist teaching, must repent, and then

---

[41] Janarv, Ruben, "Baptisternas grundsatser och dopet", [del 5], *VP*, No. 27, 1978, p. 8.

[42] Bert Franzén writes: "The baptismal texts [Mark. 1:9-11, Acts 19:1-7, my remark] show that in the ancient church the event of salvation was strictly held together: conversion, faith and baptism in the name of the Father, the Son and the Holy Spirit is what man is called to undergo. In and through this process God, by grace, gives the forgiveness of sins and the gift of the Holy Spirit as an expression of salvation to eternal life." Franzén, Bert, "Dopet i vatten och ande", *VP*, No. 1/2, 1987, p. 5. See also Franzén, Bert, "Dopet och frälsningen. Kommentar till en artikel", *VP*, No. 42, 1989, p. 10; Engberg, Sigurd, "Det kristna dopet", *VP*, No. 8, 1976, p. 4; Bergsten, Torsten, "Dopet i ekumeniskt perspektiv", *VP*, No. 7, 1988, p. 7, Bergsten, Torsten "Dopet i ekumeniskt perspektiv", *VP*, No. 8, 1988 p. 7, and Bergsten, Torsten "Dopet i ekumeniskt perspektiv", *VP*, No. 9, 1988 p. 7, the last three held first as discourses at Örebro Missionsskola, Bergsten, Torsten, "Dopet i ett ekumeniskt perspektiv", 1988, [unpublished paper]; Lagergren, David, "Tro och dop", *VP*, No. 3, 1975, p. 2.

[43] Månsus, Harry, "Bibliskt dop eller surrogatdop?", *Tro och Liv*, No. 5, 1975, p. 214.

[44] Bergsten, Torsten, "Kontroversiella rekommendationer", *Dop, Nattvard, Ämbete*, 2nd ed., 1983, p. 135.

reaching a state of grace. This is *metanoia*, a conversion from darkness to light, from a life in sin to a life in the forgiveness of Christ, from Satan to Christ. And baptism has its right and proper place as close in time as possible to *metanoia*.[45] After the "fall", before conversion, the person is regarded as a sinner and outside the Body of Christ, the Covenant. After conversion he enters (returns to) the Body, and is regarded as a righteous man, a believer. [46]

An issue which should not be forgotten in this context is thus the question of anthropology, the view of man, and original sin.[47] Infants are according to the doctrine of original sin not only influenced by the social environment, but also marked by original sin from birth. This doctrine has involved problems, i.e. whether a child, dying before being baptized, comes to "heaven" or not. The churches upholding the doctrine of original sin maintain a negative view of man.[48] A person must be transformed through baptism in

---

[45] There has been a tendency among Baptists, especially in the early period, to depict in black and white terms the time before and after *metanoia*. This stark contrast can also be found in some old Baptist hymns. See for example in "Psalmer och sånger", 608:5 (Emil Gustafsson 1887): "Sin and world, farewell for ever, you will never have me again..." ("Synd och värld, farväl för evigt, aldrig får du mig igen...") Quoted by Bergsten in "Dopet som förenar. En dialog mellan Torsten Bergsten, Svenska baptistsamfundet, och Björn Svärd, Svenska kyrkan", *Till hembygden*, 1988, p. 86.

[46] There have been slight tendencies in Baptist history to see this approach as implying the idea of sinlessness. In other words, the believer, i.e. the person after his *metanoia*, is regarded as almost completely free from temptation and sin, a completely "new man". Such a view is called by Bergsten a "tendency towards an unrealistic teaching of sinlessness" *(dragning till en orealistisk syndfrihetslära)*. He is of the opinion that such a view is balanced in a salutary way by the pessimism in the Lutheran view of man. This is, according to Bergsten, an example of how Lutheranism and the Free Churches can complete and correct each other in theology and piety, that together they can preach and embody the Gospel in a more enriched way than separated from one another. "Dopet som förenar. En dialog mellan Torsten Bergsten, Svenska baptistsamfundet, och Björn Svärd, Svenska kyrkan", *Till hembygden*, 1988, p. 86. On this problem from an historical perspective see Part I, chapter 7.1. - about August Sjödin for example.

[47] The subject of original sin, already discussed in Part I, will be discussed more also further on in chapter 7. See also Part II, chapter 4.

[48] *BEM* seems also to reckon with original sin, see the discussion in Part II, chapter 4.

250

order to be a child of God and a member of the church. Obviously one important distinction between different churches and denominations is anthropology, seen in whether original sin is accepted as a reality or not.[49]

Baptists do not usually hold the doctrine of original sin.[50] Children are by birth God's children and therefore no special act is necessary from a Baptist point of view in order to transform a newly born baby from one ontological level to another.[51] *BUS* also

---

[49] Franzén writes that the doctrine of original sin is one of the basics where Lutherans and Baptists are divided, implying concrete consequences above all in baptismal practice. Franzén, Bert, "Barnen i församlingen. Frågan om tillhörighet och medlemskap", *Tro och Liv*, No. 3, 1985, p. 36. See also Franzén, Bert, *Guds försprång*, 1991, p. 169.

[50] Bergsten writes: "The Baptist movement of today does not hold the doctrine of original sin." ("Baptismen omfattar i modern tid inte arvsyndsläran.") Bergsten, Torsten, "Dopet i ett ekumeniskt perspektiv", 1988, p. 4, [unpublished paper].

The doctrine of original sin has, however, been held also within the Baptist movement. Anders Wiberg was of the opinion that infants are not by nature innocent children of God. All have sinned in Adam and all are born of sinful seed and by nature children of wrath. See Bergsten, Torsten, "Barnet i frikyrkan. En historisk-teologisk studie", *Tro och Liv*, No. 3, 1985, p. 6f. In spite of this doctrine, children do not, however, according to Wiberg need external means of grace, that is the Word, Baptism, the Eucharist, to be saved. For small children are saved through the general atonement of Christ. Small children are completely free from the debt of original sin. Ibid. p. 7. Bergsten also mentions Balthasar Hubmaier (dead 1528), who calls children, children of wrath. Ibid. p. 4.

The doctrine of original sin has, however, been taught among Baptists even at the present day which must be regarded as an exception. For Bergsten himself seems in some way to reckon with original sin, and this in spite of his statement above that Baptists of today do not hold the doctrine of original sin. He writes on one occasion: "... because of original sin and environment 'the effects' can disappear." ("Alla barn är Guds barn oberoende av dop och tro, detta inte pga skapelseplanet utan pga frälsningsplanet. Församlingen och de kristna föräldrarna kan bevara denna 'effekt', dvs barnets barnaskap hos Gud. Ty pga arvsynd och miljö kan 'effekten' försvinna.") Bergsten, Torsten, "Dop och kyrkotillhörighet", *Nordiska röster om dop och kyrkotillhörighet*, 1988, p. 31.

[51] "Ever since the early days of the Baptist movement the dominant approach has been that the children of Christian parents - if we confine us to these - are included in the divine work of redemption through Christ, without a special ceremony or religious act being necessary in this context." Franzén, Bert, "Barnen i församlingen. Frågan om tillhörighet och medlemskap", *Tro och Liv*, No. 3, 1985, p. 32, (we may note the qualification "Christian

251

explicitly states that infants are regarded as children of God by birth on account of the atonement of Christ.[52]

Bert Franzén expresses the Baptist opinion of original sin in the following way: "after the completed redemptive work of Christ no children are born under the sign of original sin, but under that of love and reconciliation."[53] In other words, the work of Christ is complete and has totally changed the condition of humanity. Infants have from birth a right relation to God; they are the children of God, by birth belonging to and living within his Kingdom, ("under the atonement of Christ" according to *BUS*). And Franzén writes:

> The texts on children do not presuppose faith on their part in order for them to receive the advantages that Jesus says they have. It is the disciples that have to repent not the children. Their minds and hearts are already turned in the right direction. And God has an advantage in their lives.[54]

This results in the complicated fact, which will be dealt with more below,[55] that a person from a Baptist point of view may be a member of the Kingdom of God but not of a local (Baptist) church, of which he becomes a member later on, by believers' baptism.

There are sometimes difficulties in upholding proper believers' baptism, but some Baptist pastors try to. For example, a Baptist pastor, Paul Lilienberg (b. 1923), only practises what he calls a *baptism of metanoia* (*omvändelsedop*),[56] i.e. proper or genuine believers' baptism. Baptists ought, according to him, increasingly to preach and practise the *baptism of metanoia* and not reduce

---

parents"). See also ibid. p. 39; "Frikyrkorna ense: Barnen tillhör Guds rike", [BF.], *VP*, No. 17, 1985, pp. 3, 12; Bergsten in "Dopet som förenar. En dialog mellan Torsten Bergsten, Svenska baptistsamfundet, och Björn Svärd, Svenska kyrkan", *Till hembygden*, 1988, p. 78; *Till församlingens tjänst*, 1987, p. 100. Note, however, the act of blessing of children within the Baptist Union.

52 *BUS* p. 204.

53 "... efter Kristi fullbordade försoningsgärning föds inga barn i arvsyndens tecken utan i kärlekens och försoningens." Franzén, Bert, *Guds försprång*, 1991, p. 169.

54 Ibid. p. 38.

55 See chapter 7.

56 See Freij, Torbjörn, "TV-kyrkan i söndags: 'Det andliga spirandet fortsätter'", *VP*, No. 20/21, 1977, p. 3.

baptism to an act of reception of membership.[57] He means by this that he does not practise "re-baptism" of people who already are Christians.[58]

A concrete example is given in the article, which further illustrates what is meant by a *baptism of metanoia*. Some young people had gone astray, but later on come to faith. At the time of baptism, they descended into the baptismal pool, dressed in their old jeans and an ordinary shirt. After baptism, they changed into white robes, "In this way baptism becomes a visible proof of what this is all about: to be a new creature in Christ."[59] This is an example of a more traditional Baptist view of a genuine or proper believers' baptism, where *metanoia* is interpreted as a radical conversion and baptism takes place close to this event.[60]

Some problems have already been indicated in regard to what I call proper believers' baptism, for example the "time-problem", and the relation between church and the local congregation etc. There are more problems, in my opinion, as for example: when does a child change its "ontological status" (from having a right relation to God) and become a young person, an adult, "disciple", who needs to repent and be baptized? And what does *metanoia* mean and how can baptism and faith coincide as closely as possible in time? Do Baptists themselves succeed in maintaining this so-called proper baptism?

I want to give a couple of examples which illustrate the difficulties indicated above about "the fall" - as one presupposition of *baptism of metanoia* - and in maintaining proper believers' baptism (i.e. keeping faith and baptism close to each other in time). The personal history of one individual is described as follows.

A woman, Ann-Christine Lindholm, was baptized by infant baptism. She grew up in a Christian home within the Salvation Army and became a Salvationist. She was confirmed within the Salvation Army, which implies that she made a personal commitment. Later on she came to the conclusion that believers'

---

57 Ibid.

58 "Vi tillämpar bara omvändelsedop, inte omdop av redan kristna." Ibid. What Lilienberg means by Christian is not clear from this article.

59 Ibid.

60 See also Franzén, Bert, "Dopet och frälsningen. Kommentar till en artikel", *VP*, No. 42, 1989, p. 10, where Franzén points out that baptism was administered close in time to conversion in the New Testament.

baptism was the biblical baptism and was baptized in 1984 in a Baptist congregation. She was in spite of this decision still active within the Salvation Army. Only a year after her believers' baptism she became a member of a Baptist congregation. She began to study theology at the University of Uppsala, but took a sabbatical year and went to the Bible School of Livets Ord (the Word of Life) – affiliated with the so-called Faith Movement - in Uppsala for a year, before she graduated and gained a BD. In 1988 she was ordained as a Baptist pastor.[61]

Another example may be given. A certain youth called Marcus was baptized by believers' baptism at the age of 11. He says, however, that he has believed in Jesus his whole life, "as long as I can remember anyhow."[62] And still another, Birgitta Brynfors, baptized by believers' baptism says: "I have always had a faith, as long as I can remember".[63]

The three individuals referred to above have all according to traditional Baptist teaching, from the very beginning of their lives, i.e. by birth, been within the Kingdom, although not members of any local Baptist congregation. What is to be done with people like the three just mentioned with reference to believers' baptism and incorporation into the church? I will return to this problem below, for such individuals ought to be a challenge to Baptists, where a "fall" and a *metanoia* seems to be a presupposition of baptism,

---

61 Lantz, Ragni, "Ann-Christine Lindholm: Från frälsningssoldat till baptistpastor", *VP*, No. 8, 1988, p. 16. Concerning *Livets Ord*, see more below, chapter 9.

62 "Så länge jag kommer ihåg i alla fall." Sjölén, Berit, "Marcus 11 år 'kan' konferens", *VP*, No. 22, 1985, p. 9.

63 "Jag har alltid haft en tro, så länge jag kan minnas". Swedberg, Bo, " -Att döpas var som att komma hem", *VP*, No. 45, 1989, p. 10. See also Franzén, Bert, *Guds försprång*, 1991, especially pp. 105-113. An interesting discussion is also found in Franzén concerning Baptists' (especially earlier) conscious attempts to bring children and young people to conversion. Franzén, Bert, "Barnen och församlingen. Guds försprång kan behållas", *VP*, No. 24/25, 1986, p. 5; According to Franzén this was done in spite of the fact that Jesus never mentions the necessity of conversion concerning children. ("Jesus talar aldrig om behovet av omvändelse för barn. De har redan vad omvändelsen skulle kunna ge dem... Utan tro och utan omvändelse och dop är riket deras".) Franzén, Bert, "Barnen och församlingen, II. Texterna om Jesus och barnen", *VP*, No. 26, 1986, p. 6. See also Franzén, Bert, "Barnen och församlingen, III. Barn med andlig hemortsrätt", *VP*, No. 27/28, 1986, p. 7.

involving repentance, a conversion from darkness to light. Believers' baptisms are thus sometimes administered within the Baptist Union of Sweden to people who already for a long time have been believers.

Another problem must be that baptism may on the other hand be administered too early in relation to the personal conscious faith, in order to be a proper, biblical *baptism of metanoia.* It is to be expected that erroneous grounds (from a Baptist point of view) sometimes may be the reason for believers' baptism, for example expectations from family or friends.[64]

There is, of course, a special problem for Baptists if baptism is not something done of one's own free will (which is one of the fundamental Baptist principles), but is more or less compulsory. The Baptist pastor Werner Fristedt talks about "children as pressurized believers".[65] It seems as if the confession of faith, and consequently baptism, may be more or less forced on a young person, sometimes in an authoritarian and unhealthy way. He explains:

> Some Christian parents can in a psychologically dominant way determine the faith of their children in such a way that the 'ready-made' faith of the parents is taken over by the children as a faith in authority. The child believes in the faith of its parents. That such a child wants to be baptized and take part in Holy Communion is easy to understand. But it is NOT an action and reception of faith on the basis of the child's own experience of salvation.[66]

This implies that the personal conscious faith of the baptizand at the time of baptism seems not always to be present either within the Baptist Union of Sweden. We may compare with the practice of infant baptism and we find that there are similarities.

---

64 Birgit Karlsson touches on this problem in the article Karlsson, Birgit, "Tillbaka till dopet", *VP*, No. 46, 1987, p. 6. See also Gustafsson, Ingvar, "En väg till salighet", *VP*, No. 25, 1984, p. 4.

65 *"'påtryckstroende' barn".* Fristedt, Werner, "Barn - Dop - Nattvard", *VP*, No. 6, 1976, p. 12.

66 "Men vissa kristna föräldrar kan så dominanspsykologiskt trosprägla sina barn, att föräldrarnas 'färdiga' tro intages av barnet som barnets auktoritetstro. Barnet tror på fars och mors tro. Och att ett sådant barn liksom tyckes vilja vara med i dop och nattvard är ju lätt att förstå. Men det blir ICKE ett trons handlingsfungerande och mottagande utifrån barnets egen frälsningserfarenhet." Ibid.

The question must be raised of whether there is a danger that some believers' baptisms become cultural religious *rites de passage* instead of biblical *baptism of metanoia?* As a matter of fact Bergsten speaks about a fatal ritualisation of baptism also within the Baptist Union(s), that believers' baptism becomes a more or less incomprehensible external act for the baptizand. The teaching takes place at best first *after* baptism.[67] And

> Baptists have just as the great National Churches ended up with a post-baptismal catechumenate. As a result one of the most important features in Baptist baptismal preaching has lost its point.[68]

He argues for the importance of teaching *before* baptism (and thus a time of maturing before baptism takes place).

Then there is once again the danger that baptism may occur too late – from a traditional Baptist point of view - and in another way be "indiscriminate". The suggestion by Bergsten may result in the proper biblical believers' baptism being softened, first faith and then considerably later – after the teaching - baptism.

This raises (once again) the question of the age of baptism and of the dilemma of the ontological status. At what age is a person mature and ready for believers' baptism? When is a baptism actually an infant baptism and when is it believers' baptism? For the age of the baptizands is sometimes so low that it might be difficult to draw a line between infant baptism and believers' baptism. In other words, at what age is a human being capable, in the case of believers' baptism from a Baptist standpoint, of making a serious conscious personal response, taking responsibility for himself and deciding to be baptized or not?[69] This is a hard question to answer. All these problems about age, ontological status, faith, *metanoia,* etc., may contribute to a reconsideration of believers' baptism.

---

[67] Bergsten, Torsten, "Kyrkotillhörighet - medlemskap - bekännelse", *Tro och Liv,* No. 1, 1980, p. 44.

[68] Ibid.

[69] See the discussion above by Franzén, about the problem of baptizing young children, and for example the following references, Franzén, Bert, "Dopet i kyrkornas gemenskap", *VP,* No. 1/2, 1975, p. 2; Franzén, Bert, "Barnen och församlingen, IV. En modell för mognad", *VP,* No. 29/30, 1986, p. 7; Franzén, Bert, *Guds försprång,* 1991; "Guds försprång i barnens liv", [SEW.], *VP,* No. 20, 1989, p. 11.

The Baptist pastor Larsåke W Persson (b. 1945) belongs to those who have observed the "time-problem".

Between faith and baptism there is in the New Testament no room for a period during which to mature. This is, however, often the case for people nowadays, and that is in any case not a result of New Testament teaching. Into what indeed is a man to mature? The dignity to be baptized?? No, whoever believes and is baptized will be saved. (Mark 16:16)... What a tragedy that baptism is understood as an internal religious affair, which Christians squabble about, when it as a matter of fact is an answer to man's longing.[70]

We find that believers' baptism tends sometimes to be more like a rite to become a member of a "society", an association, or sometimes a transitional rite to another denomination - an act of recruitment (*medlemsintagningsakt*) - than the act of becoming a believer.[71]

There are examples pointing to the fact that there have been (and are) difficulties in many ways in maintaining proper biblical believers' baptism, and we find instead temporal disjunctions between faith, *metanoia* and baptism, within the Baptist Union of Sweden. This is manifest for example also in the Baptist manual of 1974, where questions concerning a genuine biblical believers' baptism appear. There is a desire that faith, *metanoia* (conversion) and baptism ought to be kept together and not separated. Therefore because of different wishes, there are not one but two alternative orders for the rite of believers' baptism. This is motivated with the

---

[70] "Mellan tro och dop ryms inte i Nya Testamentet någon mognadsperiod. Det ser vi emellertid ofta hos människor i vår tid och det är i varje fall inte resultat av nytestamentlig undervisning. Vad skulle man förresten kunna mogna till? Värdighet att döpas?? Nej, den som tror och blir döpt han skall bli frälst. (Mark. 16:16)... Vilken tragik att dopet har kommit att uppfattas som någon religiös föreningsangelägenhet som de kristna bråkar om när det i själva verket är svar på människans längtan." Persson, Larsåke W., "Vad betyder det att vara döpt?", *VP*, No. 1, 1978, p. 4.

[71] See Lilienberg above (*"not reduce baptism* to an act of reception of membership!"), in Freij, Torbjörn, "TV-kyrkan i söndags: 'Det andliga spirandet fortsätter'", *VP*, No. 20/21, 1977, p. 3. Italics mine. Already in the 1960's Franzén discusses the problem that membership is understood by many individualistically and in terms of belonging to an association, and that a thorough investigation of the idea of membership in the Free Churches is needed. Franzén, Bert, "Individ och familj i den kristna församlingen", *Familj och församling*, 1960, p. 20.

statement that one of them does not have any New Testament basis.[72]

From the discussion so far, we have understood that personal faith, through conversion, and baptism often have become two different experiences. They are not held strictly together in time, as those advocating proper biblical *baptisms of metanoia* want. There is too great a discrepancy in time. The Baptist pastor, Gunnar Kjellander (b. 1932), also confirms this dilemma:

> ... our position has been the following: to be baptized one must be of a certain type and one must have gone part of the way on the journey together with Christ.[73]

There must obviously be on the basis of the New Testament problems for some Baptists when "the biblical closeness of time", between faith, *metanoia* and baptism, is not maintained. The concept *"metanoia"* is thus in general given only one interpretation, i.e. of a sudden radical conversion, and baptism must be, or ought to be, administered as close as possible to this event in order to be a proper biblical baptism. All believers' baptisms cannot therefore be regarded as *baptisms of metanoia* in a qualified sense.

Some believers' baptisms may in one way, strictly interpreted, be regarded as unbiblical from a traditional, closed Baptist perspective of *baptism of metanoia*, on account of the fact that the two parts - conversion and baptism - have been separated. Some Baptists agree that believers' baptisms are sometimes not *baptisms of metanoia*. In the case of a child growing up in a congregation who later is baptized by believers' baptism, Franzén states that *it is not a baptism of metanoia,* but "a baptism of faith. The child has never turned away, but makes a decision and through baptism assents to

---

72 It is stated in the manual: "Traditionally in Baptist congregations, baptism has been preceded by a confession of faith in the presence of the congregation in a private gathering. This practice has, however, been questioned in recent years, among other things owing to the fact that it does not have any New Testament basis. Therefore it has been thought suitable to introduce two alternative orders in the manual, through which it has also been possible to meet different wishes concerning the shaping of the baptismal rite." *Handbok för församlingens gudstjänstliv,* 1974, p. 22.

73 "...vår inställning [har] varit sådan - för att få döpas måste man vara si och så och man måste ha kommit en bit på vägen i vandringen tillsammans med Kristus." Wiktell, Sven, "Gunnar Kjellander: -Det är dramatik i dopet", *VP,* No.10, 1979, p. 5.

Christ."[74] To baptize a person who already is a believer, a member of a congregation and also previously baptized by infant baptism is according to Bergsten completely wrong. He even calls it "a meaningless act". If a person

already is a living member in the Body of Christ, it is a meaningless act to incorporate him again through baptism... It [the baptism] would be reduced to an act of confession or obedience, deprived of its most profound New Testament contents.[75]

And he writes already in 1960's about this dilemma and has hesitations about baptizing by believers' baptism for example a member of the Mission Covenant Church of Sweden or a Methodist who has been an active member for decades. He is of the opinion that the problem becomes even more complicated if baptism is connected as in the New Testament with the forgiveness of sins and regeneration.

---

[74] "När ett barn som vuxit upp i församlingen döps, är det inte fråga om ett omvändelsedop utan ett trosdop. Barnet har aldrig vänt sig bort, men det gör ett ställningstagande och bejakar Kristus i och med dopet." Franzén in Doyle, Kerstin, "Samling kring barnen och församlingen: Bort med åldersgränser, fram för tant Maja och Erik Fläckman!", VP, No. 21, 1986, p. 10.

[75] "Om vederbörande redan är en personlig kristen, församlingsmedlem och därtill döpt som barn, vore det helt felaktigt att döpa honom eller henne... Om hon redan är en levande lem i denna kropp, är det en meningslös handling att genom ett dop inlemma henne på nytt. Ett sådant dop skulle i annan mening än den tidigare diskuterade bli ett 'oklart' dop. Det skulle reduceras till en bekännelse- och lydnadsakt, berövat sitt djupaste nytestamentliga innehåll." Bergsten, Torsten, "Kyrkotillhörighet - medlemskap - bekännelse", Tro och Liv, No. 1, 1980, p. 43. See also Report of theological conversations. Sponsored by the World Alliance of Reformed Churches and the Baptist World Alliance 1973-1977, referred to and quoted by Bergsten. It states: "We are thankful to God for this mutual recognition of each other's good standing as Christians and for the fact that many Baptist and Reformed churches practise mutual admission to the communion of the Lord's Supper..., we note statements by some Baptist theologians, arguing that baptism is not an appropriate way of receiving into membership of a Baptist church those Christians who have already made a public confession of faith in Christ and have entered into the privileges and responsibilites of membership in some other Christian community." In Bergsten, Torsten, "Kyrkotillhörighet - medlemskap - bekännelse", Tro och Liv, No. 1, 1980, p. 43.

How can a man who already for decades has confessed himself to be a believer in Christ and also belongs to a Christian congregation be regenerated in baptism?[76]

The Baptist pastor Harry Månsus states clearly:

The Baptist churches have not succeeded in keeping to the New Testament baptismal view but have permitted conversion and baptism to be two different decisions, two different experiences, two stations on the way towards the goal.[77]

He states that

one should not continue to baptize committed Christians, i.e. believers or those who already are 'in Christ', independent of whether they are baptized by infant baptism or come from another denomination without any baptism at all.[78]

He is conscious of the fact that this is radical: "This is, of course, a very radical change in the traditional Baptist baptismal practice." But he wants to plead for what in his opinion is biblical baptism.[79]

In other words, faith, *metanoia* and baptism in the Baptist Union of Sweden are not necessarily indissolubly related to one another in time. One of the clearest proofs that believers' baptism is no longer

---

[76] Bergsten, Torsten, "Associativt och öppet medlemskap", *Baptistpredikanternas studieblad*, No. 2, 1964, pp. 11f.

[77] "De troendedöpande kyrkorna har inte förmått hålla fast vid den nytestamentliga dopsynen utan har låtit omvändelse och dop bli två olika beslut, två olika upplevelser, två stationer på vägen mot målet." Månsus, Harry, "Bibliskt dop eller surrogatdop?", *Tro och Liv*, No. 5, 1975, p. 215. See also George Raymond Beasley-Murray in *Introduction: Some Shorts Remarks about my Dissertation: "Beasley-Murray's dopuppfattning"*. He is of the opinion that it is wrong to distinguish baptism and faith as Baptist tradition has done.

[78] "Som en konsekvens av denna bibliska insikt bör man inte längre fortsätta att döpa avgjorda kristna, dvs. sådana som redan är 'i Kristus', oberoende av om dessa är döpta som spädbarn eller om de kommer från ett samfund utan dop överhuvudtaget." Månsus, Harry, "Bibliskt dop eller surrogatdop?", *Tro och Liv*, No. 5, 1975, p. 218.

[79] Ibid. Observe the title, *Biblical Baptism or Surrogate Baptism?* There is a hint in this title that Månsus regards believers' baptism of those who already for some time have been believers as surrogate baptism and not as a biblical baptism.

a *baptism of metanoia* is, according to Månsus, that baptism has almost completely been removed from the public revival meetings.[80]

Birgit Karlsson is, of course, aware of all the difficulties and problems in upholding biblical baptism. She also writes about the dilemma of there being two stages at different times, which implies that the character of believers' baptism as a *baptism of metanoia (omvändelsedop)* has become unclear.[81] She shows, however, openness to the possibility that baptism must not absolutely take place at the time of a person's conversion.[82]

The finding that some believers' baptisms are regarded by Baptists themselves as not in complete agreement with biblical teaching, or even as meaningless acts, is significant. This is what I want to designate *improper believers' baptism.* Some Baptists look as if they are ready almost to call it an act of recruitment. All this also has implications for the issue of ecclesiology. Baptism in the local Baptist congregation cannot always be looked upon by Baptists themselves as incorporation into Christ and his Body, i.e. the universal church and the local congregation, since the person in question from a Baptist point of view is through personal conscious faith in Christ already a believer and in Christ and his Body. Due to these difficulties in maintaining a traditional Baptist *baptism of metanoia,* a very provocative and radical discussion has been started by Harry Månsus. He asks simply: *"Is it not best to abandon baptism altogether?"*[83]

The question must be regarded as remarkable, especially from a Baptist point of view where believers' baptism has been the characteristic mark, although it is in one sense understandable - since baptism, even according to some Baptists, has increasingly tended to be not a proper biblical *baptism of metanoia,* but something else. The dilemma of the Baptists, according to Månsus, can be indicated with slight overstatement by the process of incorporation into a Baptist congregation. It is not sufficient to be a believer or Christian in order to be received as a member in a local

---

[80] Ibid. p. 215.

[81] Karlsson, Birgit, "Baptistisk tro är inte till salu - men vi vill ge den vidare", *VP,* No. 43, 1991, p. 5.

[82] Karlsson, Birgit, "Tillbaka till dopet", *VP,* No. 46, 1987, p. 6.

[83] *"Är det inte bäst att överge dopet helt och hållet?"* Månsus, Harry, "Bibliskt dop eller surrogatdop?" *Tro och Liv,* No. 5, 1975, p. 216.

Christian fellowship. For in addition to this, to qualify the person is obliged to make an act of obedience and confession of faith, i.e. to be baptized through believers' baptism.[84] He mentions among other things the discrepancy which has arisen between the universal church, the Body of Christ, and the local congregation,[85] and that the changed position of baptism has involved a dangerous displacement of theological emphases.[86] Therefore, he seriously discusses abandoning baptism.

According to him, to give up baptism in modern times does not at all imply a depreciation of the rich content of baptism in the ancient church. It is rather an honest acknowledgement of the tragic consequences that the spiritual blindness and unrepentance of men have had. He says that the unfortunate displacement of baptism which has occurred within the Baptist movement is not a gratuitous development but is to a very great degree historically conditioned - on account of continual confrontation with a different practice of baptism – and this has resulted in extremely dangerous consequences. This confrontation has made the question of baptism sensitive and infected so that baptism, instead of being a natural way to God, has become an obstacle for people in search of God. It is above all on account of this that baptism has disappeared from Baptist preaching.[87]

It can be seriously questioned if it is at all possible for baptism to regain its original meaning as an unambiguous and meaningful way to give concrete expression to man's devotion to God and the encounter of God with man. He is of the opinion that today we must ask ourselves if God does not give the forgiveness of sins, rebirth, regeneration, the Holy Spirit and its gifts without any consideration of the different views on baptism. Is it not time to leave this Jewish custom behind us, just as footwashing was abandoned a long time

---

84 See ibid. pp. 215f. See also below, chapter 7. and in Part I, chapter 6. about for example the *vote* in addition to believers' baptism in order to be a Baptist member etc. It is not sufficient either to be baptized by infant baptism and later confess a personal faith - in some kind of confirmation. Cf., however, open membership, and the discussion of ecumenical congregations etc. below.

85 "Dessutom har en mycket ödesdiger diskrepans uppkommit mellan den universella församlingen, Kristi kropp, och lokalförsamlingen." Ibid. p. 215.

86 "Dopets förändrade plats har medfört en farlig förskjutning av de teologiska accenterna." Ibid.

87 Ibid. p. 216.

ago without any greater hesitation? This has already happened for example in the Salvation Army.[88] However, he concludes:

> Even if the abandonment of the practice of baptism is a strong theoretical alternative, it is bound, however, to remain an abstract theological theory, especially bearing in mind that both the Lutheran and the Baptist traditions strongly emphasize baptism as a divine command.[89]

There is thus, according to some Baptists, a change in believers' baptism, so that it not longer is a *baptism of metanoia,* a baptism to Christ. There are, however, also attempts by some Swedish Baptist pastors to maintain and practise what I call the proper biblical *baptism of metanoia,* i.e. a baptism performed at the time of conversion/repentance, which I also have referred to and exemplified. So far it has been indicated that it can be difficult in traditional Baptist doctrine and practice to maintain a biblical *baptism of metanoia.* Either baptism takes place too early or too late in relation to conversion.

The concept *"metanoia"* is difficult. Within the Baptist Union of Sweden there are those who plead for *baptisms of metanoia* in the sense of a sudden conversion followed in as close connection as possible by believers' baptism - where teaching "at the best" follows baptism. There are also those Baptists who maintain that the person to be baptized must have progressed some way in the Christian faith before baptism can be administered. There is a time for maturing in faith. Faith may also have been present since childhood. Since the concepts "metanoia" and "faith" are ambiguous,[90] there are consequently different interpretations and explanations of what *"the baptism of metanoia"* implies.

---

88 Ibid.

89 "Trots att övergivandet av dopet är ett starkt teoretiskt alternativ är det dock dömt att förbli en teologisk skrivbordsprodukt, speciellt med tanke på att både den lutherska och den baptistiska traditionen så starkt betonar dopet som en gudomlig *befallning."* Ibid. pp. 216f. "Även om alla kyrkor idag genom ett enhälligt ekumeniskt beslut övergav dopet, så skulle det dock inte dröja länge till dess en ny dopväckelse bröt fram. Dopet kommer alltid att förbli aktuellt". Ibid. p. 217.

90 An interesting interpretation of what *metanoia* means is given by Torsten Bergsten. He writes that "most human beings succumb to evil and therefore they need, whether baptized as infants or not, to make a change of heart and be reborn. It means consciously becoming what one once unconsciously was a child of God. This is the meaning of conversion." "Dopet som förenar. En dialog mellan Torsten Bergsten, Svenska baptistsamfundet, och Björn Svärd, Svenska kyrkan", *Till hembygden,* 1988, p. 78. We note also, besides this

In Baptist circles there has been a tendency, not least at its very beginning, to overlook the various meanings of conversion. Too often *metanoia* has been considered equivalent to a sudden, radical conversion from one status to another i.e. the idea that conversion is tantamount to a startling and dramatic experience. The most important thing has been to point to a date and time of conversion. This has, as I have tried to point out above, resulted in complications in handling believers' baptism. One can also easily get the impression that the emphasis among Baptists on conversion and *baptism of metanoia* has, if not replaced, at least reduced the importance of continuing personal spiritual growth. *Metanoia* can, however, also mean a life-long process and describe in my opinion a conversion in a continuing process, and denote the complete process of repentance. In other words, the confession of Christ has grown in clarity through a considerable period of time.[91]

In brief, spiritual experience is manifold and it is impossible to determine this experience from a human point of view. There are, of course, many more ways of coming to a living faith and thus coming to baptism than those referred to above.[92]

---

interpretation of *metanoia*, some other topics which are indicated: infant baptism and the absence of original sin.

[91] David Lagergren gives expression to the idea that even if the New Testament emphasizes conversion and baptism as beginnings, what matters is the continuation *(att allt hänger på fortsättningen.)*, Lagergren, David, "Kontinuitet", *VP*, No. 41, 1976, p. 2. Bergsten discusses the subject of conversion on the basis of a survey he has done amongst theological students at three theological seminaries, in Bromma, Lidingö and Örebro. He writes: "In the 55 answers a wide scale of experience and development is detectable, from continuous fellowship with God to a dramatic experience of conversion." Bergsten refers also to an *ÖMU-brochure, (ÖMU-häftet,* [Barn, ungdom och omvändelse: En avgörande fråga! Ett utbildningshäfte för ledare i det kristna barn- och ungdomsarbetet. ÖMU, 1982]), where three different paths to conscious faith are mentioned; they are maturity, commitment and conversion ("mognad, avgörelse och omvändelse"). Radical change is there reserved for the concept of conversion. Bergsten, Torsten, "Barnet i frikyrkan. En historisk-teologisk studie", *Tro och Liv*, No. 3, 1985, pp. 14f.

[92] I will give an example, indicating that the importance of the eschatological perspective, Jesus' second coming, should not either be forgotten in discussing *metanoia*, i.e. a readiness for the final judgement. The example which may speak for itself, from the early Swedish Baptist history, is the story about a woman, Josefina, who was born in 1853 and was baptized in 1878 by immersion in an ice hole, since the small congregation had no baptismal pool. Josefina did not want to wait until the summer when she

It can be deduced so far that the opinion of *BUS*, on infant baptism and believers' baptism, is not the only one within the Baptist Union. I have pointed to reconsideration within the Baptist Union of Sweden, not only in the form of openings towards infant baptism and even recognition of infant baptism - see former section - but also in this section of the view and practice of believers' baptism. There are complementary as well as alternative opinions that undeniably point both to interesting dynamic processes within the Baptist Union itself and to promising openings not least from an ecumenical viewpoint - sometimes moving towards the standpoint of *BEM*.[93] We find that also within the Baptist Union of Sweden reality differs at times from that which is regarded as the prototype of the New Testament. If infant baptism and believers' baptism are not regarded as equivalent, according to some Baptists, we do see a similar phenomenon in regard to believers' baptism. There are concerning believers' baptism differences in baptismal understanding and practice that are not always regarded as equivalent by Baptists themselves. All this has, of course, implications on other issues, as for instance ecclesiology, which already has been indicated and also will be dealt with more later on.

A question may be asked as a result of this section. If Baptists themselves do not always succeed in assuring genuine or proper biblical believers' baptism, but nevertheless recognize such baptisms as valid - some taking place "too late", others "too early" without a living personal faith (and even under pressure, according to some Baptists) - is there not a new basis and a possible opening for Baptists also to regard infant baptism as improper but still valid? I will discuss this among other things in the next section.

---

now had received salvation, for Jesus could come back before that time. Cronsioe, Håkan, "Tack, Veckoposten!", *VP*, No. 43, 1992, p. 15. Sometimes this eschatological aspect seems to be pushed too much into the background in favour of questions of baptismal method, time etc.

[93] Of course, it is in a way easier for the Swedish Baptists of today, at the end of 20th century, to reconsider baptism (both infant baptism and believers' baptism) than it was in the middle of the 19th century with the monolithic church system (with its power, "forced baptisms" etc.), which caused reactions and protests. See Part I, chapter 5. and chapter 6.

3. Faith-Context – with Special Reference to Infant Baptism

For *BEM*, baptism is valid (both infant baptism and believers' baptism) if it has been administered in water and in the name of the Trinity – in other words what many churches regard as "re-baptism" will not be administered. Baptism is valid even if the personal conscious response of the baptizand, the confession of faith, is not present at the time of baptism. In *BUS*, however, the personal, conscious response of the baptizand is the *sine qua non*;[94] otherwise baptism is equivalent to the blessing of children and what many churches regard as "re-baptism" may later on be administered. This opinion is, however, as we have noted, not the only one to be found within the Baptist Union of Sweden.

In this chapter I am going primarily to examine the importance and meaning of the faith-context for the recognition of infant baptism as valid, and this in order to find out if there is an unconditional recognition of all infant baptisms by those Baptists who recognize infant baptism as valid. If not all infant baptisms are recognized but only some of them, I will try to find out what kind of conditions will be used as criteria for an infant baptism to be a valid baptism.

Birgit Karlsson belongs, as we have seen above, to those Baptists who recognize infant baptism as valid. As she understands infant baptism, the intention is that the faith will be passed on to the baptized infant by the family and the congregation, what I call a close faith-context. The faith-context is of importance, in order that this faith will be a consciously accepted faith which later on will be expressed, often in the act of confirmation.[95] The infants are thus taken care of and brought up in the fellowship of the congregation, where they eventually will live and serve. This kind of infant baptism is thus recognized as valid. These persons should not,

---

[94] See also Part I, chapter 2.

[95] Concerning confirmation see more below in this chapter.

according to Karlsson, be baptized again.[96] The most important question for Birgit Karlsson is if a person lives in his baptism and takes it seriously, irrespective of the time or the procedure of baptism. She makes a reservation: "But of course as Baptists we only preach believers' baptism."[97] It is also of interest to note that Karlsson obviously sees some kind of response to God even in infants. She talks for instance about the unreflecting trust as a response of the infant.[98]

A particular problem arises, however, with what is called by Karlsson the National Church tradition, i.e. the Church of Sweden. She says that in this tradition it belongs to "the birth phase" *(födelsefasen)* also to be baptized. The (infant) baptism may thus take place totally independent of the awareness and ability of the family to form and bring up the infants in the baptismal faith of the church.[99] These baptisms are for Karlsson not valid, but a blessing of children. Karlsson writes that "this act of blessing" does not become an initiation into a Christian life in the congregation.[100]

Some infant baptisms are valid, others not, but are regarded as blessing of infants. In *BUS* we found, however, that *all* infant baptisms are considered to be such.

In spite of the use of water, the reading of the Word and that the formula (in the name of the Trinity) has been pronounced over the baptizand etc., infant baptism is sometimes for some Baptists a "non-baptism", when the faith-context, interpreted particularly as the faith of the family, is not present. If faith-context, however, is present, it may be recognized as valid.

Torsten Bergsten, who writes about infant baptism as valid, states also: "It is infant baptism of this kind which is recognized as

---

96 Karlsson, Birgit, "Dopet - en central fråga när församlingar går samman. Missionsföreståndaren kommenterar", *VP*, No. 40, 1987, pp. 10f.

97 "Baptistpastor om dopdokument: -Baptister bör erkänna barndopet", *Svenska Journalen*, No. 1, 1985, p. 12.

98 "Det späda barnet... dess gensvar är den oreflekterade tilliten." Karlsson, Birgit, "Dopet - en central fråga när församlingar går samman. Missionsföreståndaren kommenterar", *VP*, No. 40, 1987, p. 10.

99 Ibid. p. 11. We may recall *BEM's* discussion of indiscriminate baptisms.

100 "Men någon begynnelse till ett kristenliv i församlingen blev inte denna välsignelseakt." Karlsson, Birgit, "Dopet - en central fråga när församlingar går samman. Missionsföreståndaren kommenterar", *VP*, No. 40, 1987, p. 11.

'improper' but yet valid."[101] It is thus explicitly said that only some infant baptisms are recognized as valid. Bergsten is conscious of the dilemma. He thinks that the double approach to infant baptism leads to complications, both practical and theological, but sees the development within the Baptist movement as a seriously intended step towards the "mutual recognition of baptism" to which the authors of *BEM* look forward.[102]

Of course, such a selective recognition also results in problems. And with reference to Bergsten's writings, David Lagergren discusses the risk of subjectivity. He writes about a fatal subjectivity (*en ödesdiger subjektivering*) in recognizing some but not all infant baptisms.[103] His opinion concerning infant baptism is clear-cut.

Already in 1957 (in Swedish) Bergsten encourages the Baptist churches to say a hesitant but necessary "yes" to infant baptism, *if* it is administered in the presence of believing parents and godparents, who solemnly promise to bring up the baptized child in the Christian faith, and remind it of its baptism.[104] There is obviously a condition for Bergsten to recognize every infant baptism as a valid baptism, for from his statements we can infer that other infant baptisms must be recognized as invalid. And he writes also about two types of infant baptism.

---

[101] "Det är barndop av detta slag som ett växande antal baptister i vårt land är beredda att erkänna som 'oklara' men ändå giltiga dop." "Dopet som förenar. En dialog mellan Torsten Bergsten, Svenska baptistsamfundet, och Björn Svärd, Svenska kyrkan", *Till hembygden*, 1988, p. 78.

[102] Bergsten, Torsten, "På väg mot ett ömsesidigt doperkännande?", 1989, p. 3, [unpublished paper].

[103] Lagergren, David, "Ekumenisk barnteologi", *VP*, No. 17, 1991, p. 6. There are two articles by Bergsten, which give rise to this article by Lagergren. Bergsten pleads once again for his flexible attitude to infant baptism. Some infant baptisms are recognized and no "re-baptism" is demanded, on other occasions "re-baptism" may, however, be defended. See Bergsten, Torsten, "Ekumenisk barnteologi", *VP*, No. 13/14, 1991, p. 12; Bergsten, Torsten, "Ekumenisk barnteologi", *VP*, No. 15, 1991. p. 4. I will discuss this dilemma further below.

[104] Bergsten, Torsten, "Baptism and the Church. Baptist Faith and Practice in a Biblical and Ecumenical Light", *The Baptist Quarterly*, Vol. 18, No. 4, 1959, pp. 166-171.

One type of infant baptism is administered in the presence of believing parents and god-parents, who promise solemnly to bring up the baptized child in Christian faith and remind it of its baptism. This promise is fulfilled, and the baptized child is brought up to receive its baptism in faith... Infant baptism acts here quite obviously as a church-building factor.[105]

There is, however, also another type of infant baptism:

But there is a different type of infant baptism as well, to which a 'no' must be said quite frankly from the Baptist side. The Church conception must be rejected that emanates from an indiscriminate infant baptism quite independent of the fact whether the person being baptized receives faith and accepts grace or not.[106]

From these discussions we find therefore that the faith-context plays a determining part in the discussion about the validity of infant baptism. The role of the faith-context is also emphasized by *BEM* in the recognition of infant baptism.[107] Churches practising infant baptism also talk about the necessity of the faith-context.[108]

Then we are faced with another question: what does the concept "faith-context" mean, for are not all baptisms administered in a faith-context? The answer must obviously, in the light of my study, be a "no" – from a general Baptist point of view. I therefore make the distinction between the concepts "faith-context" and "close faith-context" (i.e. the family and/or the congregation). The latter seems to be necessary for those Baptists who are ready to recognize not all but some infant baptisms as valid. One faith-context, which has been mentioned previously and which is closest to the child – the close faith-context - is formed by the parents.[109] If infants of Christian parents are to be baptized, it is more or less presupposed that the parents try to take responsibility for their Christian upbringing. There is then an organic continuity from childhood and

---

[105] Bergsten, Torsten, "Baptism and the Church. Baptist Faith and Practice in a Biblical and Ecumenical Light", *The Baptist Quarterly*, Vol. 18, No. 4, 1959, p. 168.

[106] Ibid. p. 169.

[107] See for instance *B com 12*.

[108] See for instance the Church of Sweden, and the discussion in the next chapter 4. about indiscriminate baptism.

[109] An interesting discussion about *fides vicaria* is found in Franzén, Bert, "Barnen och församlingen, III. Barn med andlig hemortsrätt", *VP*, No. 27/28, 1986, p. 7.

onwards, leading (hopefully) towards conscious faith and confirmation at the age of about 14-15. In such cases we are, according to some Baptists, confronted by valid or "'functioning' infant baptisms",[110] although improper. There are thus infant baptisms *sub conditione*, the confession of faith is expected to take place later in the baptizand's life, for example presumably at the time of confirmation.

In the Baptist Union of Sweden, we do not usually find the concept "confirmation" used. Nor is there any act performed within the Baptist Union called confirmation.[111] Instead there is the concluding ceremony of "faith courses" *(kristendomsskolans avslutning)* – with intercession and a presentation of Christian knowledge (no laying on of hands). In "faith courses" *(kristendomsskola)* and "training for discipleship" *(lärjungaskapsträning)*, the Christian faith is given form and content. Opportunities for spiritual training are also given. In such a context a profession of faith could preferably take place.

Berit Åqvist (b. 1939) discusses, however, Baptist confirmation. The latter can be regarded, according to her, not as a requirement but as a possibility, an open offer for the young person to confirm the faith which already exists or is growing during this period of preparation.[112]

---

[110] "'fungerande' barndop." Bergsten, Torsten, "Dopet i ekumeniskt perspektiv", *VP*, No. 8, 1988, p. 7. See also Svärd, Björn, "Dopet i fokus", *Dopet i fokus*, 1992, p. 6.

[111] There are generally different understandings of confirmation and also its relation to baptism. It can either be a distinctive sacramental rite in the total process of initiation (baptism, chrismation, confirmation, admission to the eucharist), or a kind of reaffirmation of baptismal vows, for instance an occasion for blessing. In *Baptism, Eucharist & Ministry 1982-1990* it is said: "Confirmation is still seen to be serving two different purposes. Some churches see the confirmation as the special sign of the gift of the Spirit in the total process of initiation, others take confirmation above all as the occasion for a personal profession of faith by those baptized at an earlier age." *Baptism, Eucharist & Ministry 1982-1990*, 1990, p. 112. And the Church of Sweden writes: "The order for confirmation has been changed so that the most important part is the renewal of the gift of the baptism in the Holy Spirit." *Churches respond to BEM*, Vol. II, 1986, p. 130. Other aspects which have been important for the Church of Sweden in its confirmation work during this century are confirmation as catechizing the baptized, especially in the manual of 1942; first Holy Communion, and later on evangelization (1978), an act of prayer and blessing (1986/1994).

[112] Åqvist, Berit, "Baptistisk konfirmation", *VP*, No. 33, 1985, p. 2.

There is an interpretation of believers' baptism within the Baptist tradition that de facto sees it as similar to confirmation, for in some cases believers' baptism can be seen as similar to Lutheran confirmation, if a person has lived in, preserved and developed a relation to God since birth.[113] And a Baptist pastor tells of a person baptized by believers' baptism who de facto experienced this act as a confirmation of his faith, a consecration and a definite commitment to Christ.[114]

There are thus for some Baptists "similarities" between different practices, 1) infant baptism *and* the blessing of children, and 2) now believers' baptism *and* confirmation. However, I question whether these similarities are significant.

The faith-context is a keyword, not least for Baptists in order to recognize some infant baptisms, and several aspects are associated with it, for example parents. When the term *Christian parents* is used by Baptists, it seems to mean believers. The mere fact that a person is baptized and formally a member of a church or congregation is, however, not enough to be defined as a Christian or a believer. There has to be some kind of inner, conscious conviction, a personal faith in Jesus Christ. Among Baptists it is presupposed that the child grows up in a conscious faith-context at home and in the congregation,[115] as *BEM* also says: *"The practice of infant baptism emphasizes the corporate faith and the faith which the child shares with its parents."[116]*

---

[113] Bergsten: "Uppfattat på detta sätt liknar dopet i den baptistiska traditionen den lutherska konfirmationen.", "Dopet som förenar. En dialog mellan Torsten Bergsten, Svenska baptistsamfundet, och Björn Svärd, Svenska kyrkan", *Till hembygden*, 1988, p. 79.

[114] Wiktell, Sven, "Gunnar Kjellander: -Det är dramatik i dopet", *VP*, No. 10, 1979, p. 5.

[115] Bergsten, Torsten, "Dop och kyrkotillhörighet", *Nordiska röster om dop och kyrkotillhörighet*, 1988, p. 87. Bergsten mentions that one of the differences between the Church of Sweden and the Baptist Union of Sweden is that in the Church of Sweden it is sufficient for a child's membership of the Church if the parents are formally members of the Church, whereas the Baptist Union of Sweden presupposes that an infant grows up in a conscious faith-context at home, i.e. with Christian parents or at least one Christian parent, and in the congregation. Ibid. (Note, however, the change from 1996 in the Church of Sweden concerning membership/belonging to that church.)

[116] *B com 12.*

It is up to parents and the congregation to guide the baptized child, so that he later on will confess his faith in God and in that way confirm his baptism. Bergsten writes:

In a time when even many Christian families are subject to crisis and divorces, it is important to emphasize that the child needs, in order to develop spiritually, not only believing parents but also access to a living congregation.[117]

The opinion seems to be that if infant baptism is not strictly confined to children of consciously believing Christian parents in the fellowship of a congregation, this type of baptism is emptied of its true Christian meaning and is open to all kinds of interpretation. This would be "a corruption of baptism".[118] If the parents for some reason are not "spiritually alive", there might, however, be possibilities of compensating their shortcomings with godparents and the congregation.

In general terms there are, as mentioned earlier, two different opinions within the Baptist Union of Sweden concerning the validity of infant baptism. Some Baptists, probably the majority, state that infant baptism cannot at all be recognized as valid. The faith-context does not matter. Others, however, who seem according to some to be a growing number, maintain that some infant baptisms under some presuppositions are to be recognized as valid. These different approaches have, of course, different implications also for the view of believers' baptism and the practice of "re-baptism".

A question which is relevant to the discussion about faith-context and the validity of baptism is that of who it is that is to decide about the validity of baptism? Certainly it is held among Baptists that it is not up to them to draw a line between baptism and non-baptism, between Christians and non-Christians, but this is up to God alone.[119] Is it, however, possible to leave the question to God alone? Do we not find that also Baptists themselves, from what we have seen so far, set limits for the validity of baptism - just as

---

[117] Bergsten, Torsten, "Dop och kyrkotillhörighet", *Nordiska röster om dop och kyrkotillhörighet,* 1988, p. 87.

[118] "... förvanskning av dopet", Bergsten, Torsten, "Dop och kyrkotillhörighet", *Nordiska röster om dop och kyrkotillhörighet,* 1988, p. 90. Bergsten refers to the Danish Lutheran theologian Peder Højen, who warns against such a corruption of baptism.

[119] See for example Bergsten, Torsten, "Svenska kyrkan i den aktuella debatten. Tre perspektiv", *Kyrkohistorisk årsskrift* 84, 1984, p. 36.

representatives of other churches and denominations do as well? On the one hand, it is said within the Baptist Union of Sweden that infant baptism is *not* baptism (in for example *BUS)* and, on the other hand, that *some* infant baptisms are recognized as valid baptisms. To set bounds and decide if a baptism is valid or not, "That's up to God."[120] But on the other hand, it is implicitly also maintained that it may be up to the individual (possibly together with his pastor) to decide if the infant baptism in question is to be recognized as valid or not.[121] Bergsten writes that only if a person baptized by infant baptism does not recognize this rite as a Christian baptism, ought he to be "re-baptized" as a believer.[122]

The "re-baptism" may also be administered on account of repentance in a Baptist context, when a person has been baptized by infant baptism but has grown up in a secularized environment and asks for *(believers')* baptism. It is absurd, according to Bergsten, to expect that the Baptist congregation should teach about the meaning of infant baptism, that the converted person should be reminded of his infant baptism and so refrain from believers' baptism.[123] This opinion is proposed on the principle of

---

[120] "Det är Guds ensak." Ibid.

[121] "Var går gränsen? Det kan bara den människa själv avgöra som på uppriktiga grunder önskar medlemskap i en baptistförsamling.", Bergsten, Torsten, "Associativt och öppet medlemskap", *Baptistpredikanternas studieblad,* No. 2, 1964, p. 12. Bergsten states that it is up to the individual to decide also when the baptism should take place. Bergsten, Torsten, "Dop och nattvard i de gemensamma församlingarna", *Tro och Liv,* No. 6, 1990, pp. 6f. See also how Bergsten defines a "true" Christian baptism: "... This is the *objective* side of baptism, which is an instrument for God's dealing with man. But if baptism should be a true Christian baptism, there must be a *subjective* side as well. Just as a promise must be believed in to become effectual and full of blessing *to me,* baptism must be received in faith. In baptism the objective, God's dealing, and the subjective man's reception coalesce into an indissoluble unit, by which man is made a member of the Church, the body of Christ." Bergsten, Torsten, "Baptism and the Church. Baptist Faith and Practice in a Biblical and Ecumenical Light", *The Baptist Quarterly,* Vol. 18, No. 4, 1959, p. 167.

[122] "Endast när en människa, döpt som barn, inte i tro kan bejaka denna handling som ett kristet dop, bör hon kunna döpas om som troende." Bergsten, Torsten, "Kyrkotillhörighet - medlemskap - bekännelse", *Tro och Liv,* No. 1, 1980, p. 42.

[123] "Dopet som förenar. En dialog mellan Torsten Bergsten, Svenska baptistsamfundet, och Björn Svärd, Svenska kyrkan", *Till hembygden,* 1988,

freedom, i.e. that it is up to the individual person himself to estimate the value of "his" baptism and decide if "his" baptism is a baptism or not. Birgit Karlsson also writes that it is up to the individual to decide if his infant baptism is to be recognized as valid or not. She discusses refraining from baptizing a person who recognizes his infant baptism as a baptism.[124]

An interesting finding from the discussion in this chapter concerning faith-context and its importance for the validity of infant baptism, seems to be that faith-context does not necessarily play any role that in the last resort, on the principle of freedom and out of respect for the individual, it is very much in the hands of the baptized individual to decide if his or her infant baptism is valid or not. For even if his baptism is duly administered, with water and in the name of the Trinity, and in addition to that in a faith-context – also in a close faith-context - it is possible that this baptism is not recognized as a valid baptism. Possibly it can be regarded as a blessing, if the individual does not believe in his baptism. This implies in all likelihood the continuing practice of "re-baptism". Or that a person baptized by infant baptism, growing up in a non-Christian context - i.e. without any close faith-context - and living without any personal faith, yet has the possibility of getting his infant baptism recognized as valid, if he later comes to faith in Christ and he himself regards his baptism as valid, for personal and pastoral reasons.

This chapter shows that there are no simple answers to all the questions about faith-context and its meaning for the validity of baptism. What, however, is of importance to note is that some Baptists maintain that some infant baptisms are to be recognized as valid baptisms because of a faith-context. This kind of recognition must nevertheless be regarded as an important step, not only towards mutual recognition of baptism, but also towards the "one baptism" and towards church unity, the *una ecclesia*. It may be considered to be in line with the intention of *BEM:* "When

---

p. 84. See also Bergsten, Torsten, "Ekumenisk barnteologi", *VP*, No. 13/14, 1991, p. 12.

In ecumenical congregations there will sometimes be other premises, since both infant baptism and believers' baptism (also as "re-baptism") are practised.

[124] Karlsson, Birgit, "Tillbaka till dopet", *VP*, No. 46, 1987, p. 6. See also Björn Svärd, "Dopet i fokus", *Dopet i fokus,* 1992, p. 6.

an infant is baptized, the personal response will be offered at a later moment in life... the baptized person will have to grow in the understanding of faith."[125] And it is not difficult to agree with the statement that the Baptist recognition of "functioning" infant baptisms can be regarded as an important step towards the one baptism.[126]

---

[125] *B 12.*

[126] "Det baptistiska erkännandet av de 'fungerande' barndopen kan betraktas som ett viktigt steg hän mot det ena dopet." Bergsten, Torsten, "Dopet i ekumeniskt perspektiv", *VP*, No. 8, 1988, p. 7.

4. Indiscriminate Baptism

In this chapter the question of indiscriminate baptism will be discussed. It is an issue that is problematic for most churches, including the Baptist Union of Sweden.

Infant baptism is not recognized as baptism by *BUS* but may be regarded as equivalent with the blessing of children. There is, however, another possibility in discussing infant baptism that it may be regarded not "only" as a blessing, but may be regarded as an improper baptism, which may be indiscriminate.

The practice of indiscriminate baptism is without doubt one of the contributing reasons, perhaps one of the most important ones, which has forced even Baptists with an open attitude, i.e. recognizing some infant baptisms, to have ambivalent attitudes and make choices which sometimes imply a non-recognition of infant baptism. If infant baptism is to be recognized by Baptists, one presupposition is, as stated in the previous section, that it is administered in a faith-context, otherwise the practice of "re-baptism" must be defended.[127] *BEM* writes that the indiscriminate infant baptisms contribute to

> the reluctance of churches which practise believers' baptism to acknowledge the validity of infant baptism.[128]

---

[127] Bergsten states: "May I be allowed to present an ecumenical Baptist, Free Church dream! In a disestablished Swedish-Lutheran National Church with baptism as the normal criterion of membership both infant baptism and increasingly baptism at a responsible age will be practised. To the extent that the infant baptisms are followed by a personal milieu of faith and conviction they should naturally be respected even by Christians with a Baptist view. *But as long as infant baptism is in addition practised in an indiscriminate way, the same respect cannot be expected from Baptist denominations.*" Bergsten, Torsten, "Dop och kyrkotillhörighet", *Nordiska röster om dop och kyrkotillhörighet*, 1988, p. 92, italics mine. See also the discussion above, chapter 2.1.

[128] *B com 21b.*

From the previous analysis, we see that this is completely correct. And we recall *BEM's* words:

> In order to overcome their differences, believer baptists and those who practise infant baptism should reconsider certain aspects of their practices. The first may seek to express more visibly the fact that children are placed under the protection of God's grace. The latter must guard themselves against the practice of apparently indiscriminate baptism and take more seriously their responsibility for the nurture of baptized children to mature commitment to Christ.[129]

There is a relatively high rate of infant baptism in Sweden, especially administered in the Church of Sweden. This ought to be a challenge to the Baptist Union of Sweden, not least with some Baptists' openness to recognize infant baptism. Therefore, it is surprising that *BUS* does not make any comments on this. The working party, however, mentions indiscriminate baptism.[130] As the Church of Sweden for obvious reasons turns up in this discussion, let us look more closely at the attitude of the Church of Sweden to the question of indiscriminate baptisms.

There are some indications that the Church of Sweden itself officially acknowledges that some of the infant baptisms carried out within it are indiscriminate and that they constitute a problem. This is found in the response of the Church of Sweden to *BEM*. It is said:

> BEM takes up what it calls an 'apparently indiscriminate' way of baptizing in some majority churches (16) [i.e. B 16, my remark]. This is an obstacle for churches which practise 'believers' baptism' as they consider the recognition of infant baptism. The Church of Sweden has reason to consider more closely in which way the significance of baptism shall be made clear for parents of children to be baptized, without making this into an 'examination of faith.'[131]

---

[129] *B 16.* A distinction which may be mentioned: Baptists baptize on the basis of the confession of the baptizand's faith, Lutherans, however, with a view to the faith of the baptizand. For both it is important that baptism takes place *in* faith.

[130] Supplement to Minutes 2/11/83.

[131] *Churches respond to BEM*, Vol. II, 1986, p. 129. In an excerpt from the response of the General Synod in 1985 to *BEM* it says amongst other things: "Recommendations to churches baptizing infants not to do this indiscriminately (no. 16) are taken seriously by the Church of Sweden." Quoted in *Vägen till kyrkan*, 1988, p. 271. See also as concerns the Church of Sweden and the issue of baptism, *Dopet - teologiskt, kyrkorättsligt, pastoralt*, 1984; Ekblad, Lars, *Och hindra dem inte*, 1992.

There is a dilemma on both sides, for infant baptism churches as well as for those exclusively practising believers' baptism.[132]

The rate of infant baptism in the Church of Sweden is still high,[133] in spite of the opinion that Sweden is secularized.[134] In *Vägen till kyrkan*, 1988, (The Way into the Church),[135] there is information which possibly indicates that the Church of Sweden as a matter of fact encourages continuing practice of indiscriminate baptism. For the task of the open National Church *(folkkyrka)* must imply, according to this working party, with reference to Jesus' command to baptize, a constant striving to let all people partake of the grace offered in baptism.[136] It is *de facto* explicitly said that the open

---

[132] See for example Lindberg, Erik, "Lutheraner och baptister: Vi är ense i allt utom dopet", *VP*, No. 4, 1992, p. 5.

[133] The frequency of infant baptism in the Church of Sweden. The number of infant baptisms per year in the Church of Sweden as a percentage of the total annual birth figures.

1970..... 80,7%;	1985 .... 73,5%;
1975..... 82,7%;	1990 .... 71,7%;
1980..... 76,2%;	1995 .... 79,1%.

For 1970 and 1975, Dahlgren, Curt, "Gudstjänstbesök och livsriter under 1970-talet", *Smärre meddelanden* 1980:7, p. 3. For 1980 and 1985, Dahlgren, Curt, "Gudstjänstbesök och livsriter i Svenska kyrkan under 1980-talet", *Tro & Tanke* 1991:10, p. 54. For 1990 and 1995, Straarup, Jørgen, "Den kyrkliga aktivitetens utveckling under 1990-talet" *Tro & Tanke* 1996:6, p. 16.

[134] A study about Swedish secularization and religious attitudes related to the ritual of infant baptism in the Church of Sweden, see Reimers, Eva, *Dopet som kult och kultur*, 1995.

[135] As a result of a decision during the synod of the Church of Sweden of 1983 a working party was appointed to examine the question of baptism and church belonging. This group produced a preliminary report for discussion, *Dop och kyrkotillhörighet*, (SKU) 1985:1, (Baptism and Church Belonging). Later a second report called *Vägen till kyrkan*. (The Way into the Church. On Baptism and Church Belonging). The group worked out on the basis of comments on the previous report a proposal for strengthening the place of baptism in the Church of Sweden and gave two alternative proposals for how church – belonging could be defined in the future.

[136] "Den öppna folkkyrkans uppdrag att, i enlighet med dopbefallningens: 'gör alla folk till lärjungar: döp dem i Faderns och Sonens och den heliga Andens namn', måste innebära en ständig strävan att låta alla människor få del av den i dopet erbjudna nåden." *Vägen till kyrkan*, 1988, pp. 125f.

National Church strives to baptize everybody.[137] These words may, of course, be interpreted in different ways, but it is easy to get the impression that the Church of Sweden will prevent other churches and denominations from baptizing people.

Bergsten also makes a comment on this. He writes that this statement is remarkable and he asks:

> Does the Church of Sweden really want to baptize infants of Free Church, Catholic or Orthodox parents? In that case the Church of Sweden is making proselytes. Does the Church of Sweden want to baptize the infants of explicit atheists or of religiously indifferent parents? In that case it is 'indiscriminate baptism'.[138]

These reactions are understandable, not least from a Baptist point of view. And, of course, when the Church of Sweden explicitly states that it strives to baptize everyone, and de facto has a high rate of infant baptisms, this ought to include some indiscriminate baptisms. As long as infant baptism is practised in an indiscriminate way, the Baptists will surely feel that their mission is not finished and the problems on the question of "re-baptism" will remain.[139]

In conclusion. Many churches and denominations either practising infant baptism or exclusively believers' baptism seem, however, to be in agreement that indiscriminate baptisms are not desirable, although there are different views on what "indiscriminate baptism" is, and also on what the faith-context means for the validity of baptism. As a result of the different views,

---

[137] "När en öppen folkkyrka döper barn - och strävar efter att döpa alla -..." Ibid. p. 126.

[138] Bergsten, Torsten, "Dop och kyrkotillhörighet", Nordiska röster om dop och kyrkotillhörighet, 1988, p. 90.

The statement by the Church of Sweden about striving to baptize everyone, may be interpreted in various ways, either as Bergsten does, or that the Baptismal Commission in Matt. 28:18 does not necessarily mean baptizing all and everyone, i.e. also from other church traditions. One of the members of the working party of the Church of Sweden, Olof Ignérus, is of the opinion that Bergsten has misunderstood this point. He states: "There is no question of the Church of Sweden striving to baptize the children of Baptists." Ignérus, Olof, in Nordiska röster om dop och kyrkotillhörighet, 1988, p. 31.

[139] See also Bergsten, Torsten, "Tro och tvivel på barndopet", VP, No. 19/20, 1991, p. 7, where he writes about "... misuse of Christian baptism." ("... missbruk av det kristna dopet.")

one church accuses the other of practising "re-baptism". Another consequence is that indiscriminate infant baptisms are not recognized as valid by some Baptists who, however, recognize other infant baptisms. We can also note that in a traditional, closed Baptist attitude no infant baptisms are recognized as baptisms. This raises the question of "re-baptism" which will be studied more in the next chapter, also in the light of the reconsideration of believers' baptism.

5. The Question of "Re-Baptism"

We can ask if there are any differences between infant baptism and believers' baptism, besides differences in the ages of the baptizands? They are both baptisms in water and in the name of the Trinity (also in a faith-context in one or other form). Sometimes there is a discontinuity between baptism and faith, not only in infant baptism but also, as I have pointed out above, in believers' baptism. This discontinuity in the case of infant baptism may result in the infant baptism not being recognized as valid, and sometimes "re-baptism" is administered. What happens in the cases of those baptized by believers' baptism, where there is a similar discontinuity? Are these baptisms then regarded as "non-baptisms", resulting in "re-baptisms"? In this chapter the issue of "re-baptism" will be discussed mainly from two different perspectives.

One is from a more traditional point of view. It concerns "re-baptizing" a person who has been baptized by infant baptism. The second one concerns "re-baptizing" a person who has been baptized by believers' baptism. For it is an intriguing finding of this study that due to traditional Baptist teaching and the principle of biblical authority, some "indiscriminate" believers' baptisms occur within the Baptist Union of Sweden itself,[140] because of the "time-problem".

Many Baptists do not recognize infant baptisms as valid, even if there is some kind of a continuity, i.e. that also a close faith-context is present from the very beginning of a person's life (with believing parents, a living congregation), until the time when he himself later on in his life can give his conscious personal witness (in some kind of confirmation).

---

[140] See also Harry Månsus. He writes that, if believers' baptism becomes a part of the preaching of the other churches, then there is no need for administering "indiscriminate" believers' baptism amongst Baptists. They can instead return to the Apostolic baptismal practice, i.e. baptizing people "into Christ". Månsus, Harry, "Bibliskt dop eller surrogatdop?", *Tro och Liv*, No. 5, 1975, p. 218.

To "re-baptize" a person baptized by infant baptism results in problems and difficulties in more than one way, in christology, ecclesiology and church unity.[141] It has been declared in the ecumenical document *Tecken om enhet*, (not exclusively from the Baptist Union of Sweden but from *Sveriges Frikyrkoråd):*

> Certainly there are nowadays a number of examples of Baptists - theologians and laymen - who have started to talk about re-baptism as a problem and sought formulations which might give room for a recognition of the custom of infant baptism. These are, however, not in a majority.[142]

And Torsten Bergsten writes that in the denominations practising believers' baptism a new view of the problem baptism - "re-baptism" is beginning to manifest itself.[143]

Birgit Karlsson expresses on the one hand certain hesitations about believers' baptism as "re-baptism", but she is, however, of the opinion, that it is not possible to prevent a person being baptized by believers' baptism, who during his Christian life realizes that he ought to be baptized in obedience to his conviction, even if this discovery is made a long time after the time of conversion. She talks about such a baptism as improper (*ett oklart dop),* since it is separated in time from the beginning of *metanoia (omvändelsetrons början).* Nevertheless, it must be carried out, since every step taken

---

[141] We may recall another kind of problem for the Baptists in the beginning of the Baptist movement in Sweden when these "re-baptisms" were forbidden and if administered resulted (sometimes) in various penalties (imprisonment, exile etc.). See Part I, chapter 5. and chapter 6.

[142] *Tecken om enhet,* 1991, p. 92.

[143] "Dopet som förenar. En dialog mellan Torsten Bergsten, Svenska baptistsamfundet, och Björn Svärd, Svenska kyrkan", *Till hembygden,* 1988, p. 75. Bergsten held already in the 1960's that many times open membership is more defensible on biblical grounds than a "renewed baptism". Bergsten, Torsten, "Associativt och öppet medlemskap", *Baptistpredikanternas studieblad,* No. 2, 1964, p. 12. See also Bergsten, writing about the constitution of Valsätrakyrkan from 1995 that "another major regulation means that Valsätrakyrkan practises *one* baptism and avoids re-baptism." Bergsten, Torsten, "Den gemensamma församlingen - ett tecken om enhet", *Levande,* 1996, p. 52. Concerning a short presentation of this congregation, see Part I, chapter 9.5.2.

in obedience to that which the Word of God illuminates affects our spiritual growth.[144]

It is interesting that the idea of improper baptism can be used by a Baptist with reference not only to infant baptism but also to believers' baptism.

After this discussion about "re-baptism", I want to look at the dilemma of "re-baptism" from a more unusual point of view, which is seldom discussed. It is the question of "re-baptizing" a person already baptized by believers' baptism. I want to illustrate this topic by describing several alternatives.

A person experiences a conversion, *metanoia*, to the Lord, i.e. he becomes a true and right believer and is baptized by the proper biblical believers' baptism. He has heard and received the Word and made a personal, conscious response. For some reason he abandons the Lord. He no longer believes in the Lord or in his baptism. From being a believer and an active member of a Baptist congregation, he becomes a non-believer, an "outsider".

After a few years he experiences, however, another *metanoia*. It is once again a genuine conversion and he repents. In this example we find a break in time between his first conversion (and baptism) and his second. During the time between giving up his faith in the Lord and his second conversion, he regards himself as a non-believer. In other words, there is no conscious faith; it is not either a question of continuity in faith but rather discontinuity. Does this imply that he has to be baptized once more by believers' baptism? If not, we have to ask why, in the light of the discussion about infant baptism and "re-baptism".

I will give another example. A person is going to be baptized by believers' baptism. He is convinced that he *now* believes in God. Later on, however, through a genuine conversion, he is convinced that it is first now he is a true believer. The occasion when he was first baptized by believers' baptism and gave what he thought was a conscious response in faith and said his "yes" to the Lord, after his "real" encounter with the Lord, and on the basis of his new conviction, no longer appears as genuine. The reasons for his first baptism may have been many, for instance pressure from parents, friends, relatives, the congregation. He felt perhaps that he was

---

[144] Karlsson, Birgit, "Tillbaka till dopet", *VP*, No. 46, 1987, p. 6. See also Karlsson, Birgit, "Baptistisk tro är inte till salu – men vi vill ge den vidare", *VP*, No. 43, 1991, p. 5.

more or less forced, but he was in fact without any inner conviction and personal faith in Christ.

Do not such believers' baptisms loose their sense if they are performed for the wrong reasons, for example without any *metanoia* or with inadequate faith, or even without any authentic personal conscious faith at all? And the question is, whether the first baptism is then to be regarded as invalid (as a non-baptism)? Are there reasons for "re-baptizing" such a person, baptized by believers' baptism, i.e. similar arguments to those which Baptists hold concerning infant baptism?

Baptism of a person earlier baptized by believers' baptism seems in fact a possibility. Torsten Bergsten writes in 1957:

> If it becomes evident that a man has demanded and received the Baptist baptism without faith and with false motives, the necessity of re-baptism must be seriously considered if he comes to true repentance and faith.[145]

This statement must, however, most probably be regarded as an expression of a theoretical possibility, without any practical consequences within the Baptist Union of Sweden of today. The Baptist Olof Granander (b. 1937) writes:

> We have many in our congregations who have been baptized according to early Christian custom, but who no longer live in their baptism. Despite this they are considered as full members on account of the fact that they have been baptized by immersion in water. There are many children of Baptists, once baptized perhaps on account of the parents' pressure, and who for decades have not attended any services in the congregation. Despite this they are members.[146]

We can probably take it more or less for granted that according to Baptists, believers' baptism cannot and does not need to be repeated.[147] The question is why? We find an answer from Franzén:

---

145 Bergsten, Torsten, "Baptism and the Church. Baptist Faith and Practice in a Biblical and Ecumenical Light", *The Baptist Quarterly*, Vol. 18, No. 4, 1959, p. 171. (Bergsten uses in this context the concept "Baptist baptism" *(det baptistiska dopet [1957, p. 23])* a concept to which I put a question-mark. I do not think it is appropriate to qualify baptisms with confessional epithets. I rather prefer the concept "believers' baptism".)

146 Granander, Olof, "Bör vi erkänna barndopet?", *VP*, No. 10, 1985, p. 10.

147 See for example Franzén, Bert, "Anden och det kristna livet, II. Låt er uppfyllas av ande!", *VP*, No. 35, 1987, p. 7; See also Öman, Torsten, "Frälsningens mottagande", *VP*, No. 25, 1976, p. 4.

We are always allowed to fall back on what God has done to us, for we can never destroy this so completely that it will not be sufficient as a new basis for renewal in the Spirit.[148]

Note that there is the hint here of an instrumental view. Baptism as an instrumental act will be discussed more in the next chapter.[149]

Bergsten also rejects "re-baptizing" a person who has already been baptized by believers' baptism. This is perhaps at first surprising in view of the statement above. He holds that if a person questions his relationship with God, baptism has the function of being a help and support for faith.[150] In baptism God acted on the person. If that person is faithless, God remains, however, faithful to his Word, the Word that was pronounced over the person at baptism. If the disturbing question arises of whether the person had the right faith at the moment of baptism, it is of the utmost importance that a correct teaching about faith is given, so that this is not conceived as "a human achievement necessary as a prerequisite for God's acting." Above all, the attention of the doubter ought, according to Bergsten, to be directed towards God and to the many words of promise in the Bible which are connected to baptism. "Thus the fact that I was baptized in Christ's name can be a permanent source of new power and blessing, and baptism becomes a true 'means of grace'." If a person has once received believers' baptism in faith it should never be administered again. The person in question will instead be reinstated as that child of

---

[148] "Andedop - och just i det här perspektivet spelar det faktiskt ingen roll, hur vi definierar det: så som man började göra det i 'den nya rörelsen' för 80 år sedan eller så som det sker i den här artikelserien - är alltså ingen garanti för en förblivande och djupnande Andens fullhet. Men det kan inte och behöver inte 'göras om'. Vi får alltid falla tillbaka på vad Gud har gjort med oss, ty det kan vi aldrig förstöra så fullständigt, att det inte duger som en ny utgångspunkt för en förnyelse i Anden." Franzén, Bert, "Anden och det kristna livet, II. Låt er uppfyllas av ande!", VP, No. 35, 1987, p. 7. For Franzén, there are not two baptisms, baptism in the Spirit and water-baptism, but only one, i.e. believers' baptism. This is a baptism in water and Spirit. Franzén, Bert, "Anden och det kristna livet, I. Döpta i en och samma ande", VP, No. 34, 1987, p. 7. See also Franzén, Bert, "Jesu dop – och vårt", VP, No. 1/2, 1986, p. 4.

[149] See also Part II, chapter 8.

[150] In the following I am on the whole referring to Bergsten, Torsten, "Baptism and the Church. Baptist Faith and Practice in a Biblical and Ecumenical Light", The Baptist Quarterly, Vol. 18, No. 4, 1959, p. 171.

God which he once became through faith and baptism, when he returns and repents.[151]

Bergsten's thoughts are interesting and a couple of keywords may be noticed. One is *faith*, the other *the action of God*. The question is how do they relate to one another? If there is no faith (or false motives) at the time of believers' baptism there seems, however, to be a possibility of "re-baptism" according to Bergsten - as quoted above. But if faith is present in the baptizand and the person later on in his life turns away from God, believers' baptism should, however, not be administered even in such a case. Then the question is what is true faith? Bergsten also raises this question.

Another question concerns the action of God in the rite of baptism, and its meaning for the validity to the "once-for-all" act. Ought not Bergsten's statement, "In baptism God acted on the person", to imply an exclusion of "re-baptism"? If this, however, is not the case, "re-baptism" may be administered more than once if there are many "backslidings", in view of Bergsten's statement: "If... received the Baptist baptism without faith and with false motives, the necessity of re-baptism must be seriously considered". It seems in one way as if his statements above contradict one another. Nevertheless, what is of particular interest to us is that "re-baptism" of believers' baptism is not practised. The question of why a discussion similar to that on believers' baptism is not found in the case of infant baptism must inevitably be raised, for example "... to fall back on what God has done to us" (see Franzén above).

Among Baptists with an open attitude, those believers' baptisms which by many are regarded as "re-baptism" take place primarily on account of the practice of indiscriminate baptism, i.e. that infant baptism is administered without, from their point of view, a faith-context. There are theological as well as pragmatic arguments for continuing the practice of "re-baptism".[152] Birgit Karlsson writes about the absurd consequences from an ecumenical point of view, if

---

[151] Ibid. Bergsten writes: "On this view there can be no question of rebaptizing a backslider when he comes to faith again. If he once received baptism in faith it can never be repeated. If he goes away, it will be a permanent judgement and reminder of what he lost. If he returns, he is reinstated to membership of the Family of God which he once gained by faith and baptism." Ibid.

[152] Something which should not be forgotten in this discussion is the so-called "individual" argument, i.e. the importance of the individual's own personal opinion concerning his own baptism for the validity of the baptism, which has been discussed earlier in the thesis.

every believers' baptism of a person baptized by infant baptism should be regarded as a "re-baptism". She states:

> In a country with a National Church and a tradition of infant baptism, there would not be more than a marginal place for a Baptist movement's preaching and practice.[153]

This is, of course, true. The question remains, if it despite this pragmatic fact is theologically correct?

In discussing believers' baptism it appears at first sight remarkable to mention the Church of Sweden – a church baptizing infants. I want, however, to say something more about this church - among other things since both Birgit Karlsson and Torsten Bergsten refer to it. As a matter of fact the number of believers' baptisms during recent years is greater within the Church of Sweden than within for example the Baptist Union of Sweden or within the Pentecostal Movement.[154] In the ecumenical (and also secularized)

---

[153] Karlsson, Birgit, "Dopet - en central fråga när församlingar går samman. Missionsföreståndaren kommenterar", VP, No. 40, 1987, p. 11. See also Bergsten who gives expression to a similar opinion, that if all the indiscriminate baptisms should be respected in the Baptist congregations, there would not be many people to baptize, as long as the custom of infant baptism is so general and widely spread as it still is in Sweden. "Dopet som förenar. En dialog mellan Torsten Bergsten, Svenska baptistsamfundet, och Björn Svärd, Svenska kyrkan", Till hembygden, 1988, p. 84

[154] There are no complete statistics on the number of those baptized by belivers' baptism in the Church of Sweden, except after 1980, according to Skog, see Letter to Lennart Johnsson: Skog, Margareta, 28/1/97. She there gives the following figures for those baptized during preparation for confirmation 1980-1995, and adults baptized (vuxendöpta) after 1988. In parenthesis the figures of those baptized within the Baptist Union, see Letter to Lennart Johnsson: Skog, Margareta, 17/1/97. (Abbreviations in the following table: PCB = pre-confirmation baptism, BB = believers baptism, C of S = Church of Sweden, BU = Baptist Union of Sweden.)

	PCB	BB in BU		PCB	BB in CS	BB in BU
1980	1476	(251)	1988	2215	219	(215)
1981	1725	(233)	1989	2328	336	(222)
1982	1803	(291)	1990	1989	246	(163)
1983	1932	(262)	1991	2060	291	(158)
1984	2079	(314)	1992	2501	385	(161)
1985	2297	(267)	1993	2810	326	---
1986	2618	(239)	1994	2905	463	(167)
1987	2579	(210)	1995	2994	533	(104)

Skog makes the following comment: "If we combine the figures from 1995 for both categories (2994+533), we find that 3527 persons were baptized by

Swedish context, reconsidering baptism in general, this interesting perspective has not to be forgotten that at the same time as believers' baptisms are taking place in non-Baptist contexts, the number of unbaptized in Sweden (i.e. secularized people neither baptized by infant nor by believers' baptism) seems to increase or to be at a *status quo*. One consequence of this "secularization-process" may be that the number of infant baptisms will decrease and the questions of both "indiscriminate baptism" and "re-baptism" will develop into a new, and in one way, less problematic position. On this process Harry Månsus has an interesting idea.

Månsus writes:

> Secularization has resulted in a manifest consciousness concerning baptism in the European Lutheran and Reformed traditions. An ever stronger theological opinion maintains that the church ought to baptize only such infants who will grow up in a faith-context.[155]

He says on the increasing number of unchristened infants, that the church will have to preach the Gospel to these unchristened people. The church will then invite them to faith and baptism totality. On account of the deep baptismal theology which the Lutheran tradition historically has, "an apostolic baptismal preaching will develop which will be an unexpected and unusual challenge to the traditional Baptist preaching."[156] The conclusion is evident; believers' baptisms (not in the sense of "re-baptism") will then possibly increase.

---

believers' baptism that year. This means that my colleague Jørgen Straarup is quite correct when he claims that the Church of Sweden is the denomination in the country that has most believers' baptisms. In the Pentecostal Movement, the largest Baptist denomination, 1539 were baptized that year." ("Om vi lägger samman uppgifterna från 1995 för dessa båda kategorier (2994+533) finner vi att det året 'troendedöptes' 3527 personer. Det innebär att min kollega Jørgen Straarup har helt rätt när han hävdar att Svenska kyrkan är det samfund i landet som har flest vuxendöpta. I pingströrelsen, det största av döparsamfunden, döptes under samma år 1539.") Letter to Lennart Johnsson: Skog, Margareta, 28/1/97. It must, however, be noted that expressed as a percentage of the membership, there are great differences between the number of believers' baptisms in the Baptist Union of Sweden and the Church of Sweden.

[155] Månsus, Harry, "Bibliskt dop eller surrogatdop?" *Tro och Liv*, No. 5, 1975, pp. 217f.

[156] Ibid. pp. 218. See also Bergsten, Torsten, "Dop och kyrkotillhörighet", *Nordiska röster om dop och kyrkotillhörighet*, 1988. p. 92.

The interesting question is in what context they will then be administered, for example in a Baptist congregation or in the Church of Sweden? Irrespective of believers' baptisms taking place within the Baptist Union of Sweden or in a non-Baptist church or denomination, may there not be a danger that tradition, routine and ritualism will also accompany some of these believers' baptisms or "confirmation-baptisms". These baptizands may in other words sometimes be without any inner, personal, conscious faith, without making a personal confession of faith at the time of baptism. It can thus be expected that some of these baptisms might be regarded as indiscriminate baptisms for similar reasons as with infant baptisms. The question remains of whether they are then going to be "re-baptized"? It would, of course, be of interest to study the opinions within the Baptist Union of Sweden on these tendencies to practise believers' baptism within infant baptizing churches.[157] Many of these believers' baptisms taking place in non-Baptists circles are baptisms in connection with confirmation, usually at the age of 14 or 15 within the Church of Sweden.

A question may be asked from an ecumenical perspective concerning these believers' baptisms, about whether it is of any significance for their validity if they are administered by immersion or not, when all are considered and recognized as valid by Baptists in general. Baptism is often, if not from the very beginning of Baptist history, done by immersion (i.e. "in" rather than "with" water).[158] Baptists have mostly paid attention to the exterior side of baptism - the emphasis seems to have been on the proper administration of baptism, i.e. that the baptism has taken place by

---

[157] See, however, for example Bergsten who writes: "From their perspective [those baptized by believers' baptism, i.e. Baptists, my remark] the Church of Sweden lacks Christian baptism, i.e. one rejoices over the increasing number of unbaptized confirmation candidates who are baptized in the church at a conscious age, in the hope that it then really is a question of believers' baptism." Bergsten, Torsten, "Svenska kyrkan i den aktuella debatten. Tre perspektiv", *Kyrkohistorisk årsskrift* 84, 1984 p. 35. See also Eurell, Pehr-Erik, "Med luthersk dopförrättare. Historiskt dop i Vallersvik", *VP*, No. 37, 1991, p. 7.

[158] In for example Nordström, Nils Johan, *En kulturbild från 1800-talets religiösa brytningstid*, 1926, pp. 61f., the importance of immersion is commented on. See also Part II, and especially chapter 9. concerning the discussion about "in" and "with" water.

immersion.[159] As regards the content of baptism, Baptists have often mentioned what baptism is *not*. The question about the meaning of baptism has tended to be left in the background.

One Swedish Baptist states:

> The question of *how* baptism should be administered and of *how* a person was baptized may hide the very much more important question of what it means to *be* baptized, to *live* as a baptized Christian. That risk has been close for us Baptists... Surely it would be a meagre thing if to be a Baptist should mainly consist of the memory that I once was baptized in *the right way*, a memory which fades year after year.[160]

Another Baptist complains that Baptists too often concentrated on the method of baptism:

> What has been of importance is that the person has been immersed according to all the recognized rules... it is dangerous if we let our faith depend on the method of baptism being important and that everything is all right if only the person is baptized in the right way.[161]

From a traditional Baptist baptismal point of view it is of interest to find the above utterances coming from Baptists. And in the Swedish Baptist manuals of 1924, 1940, 1955 and 1974 immersion seems more or less to be taken for granted.[162] However, the manual of 1987 also says:

---

159 See for example Anders Wiberg who writes a chapter about this: "Kyrkohistoriens vittnesbörd med afseende uppå sättet för dopets förrättande" (The witness of church history concerning the manner of baptism), pp. 262-270, in his book *Hvilken bör döpas? och Hvaruti består dopet?* 1852. See also Wiberg, Anders, *Det Christliga Dopet*, 1854, pp. 250-258; and Österberg, Edvin, "Evangelisk kristendom", *VP*, No. 48, 1978, p. 10.

160 "... Men visst vore det torftigt om detta att vara baptist skulle bestå huvudsakligen i ett minne att man en gång blev döpt på *rätt sätt*, ett minne som förbleknar för varje år som går." Persson, Larsåke W., "Vad betyder det att vara döpt?", *VP*, No. 1, 1978, p. 4.

161 "... Personligen tror jag, att det är farligt om vi bara hänger upp vår tro på att dopsättet är det viktiga och att allt är gott och väl bara man är döpt på rätt sätt." Granander, Olof, "Bör vi erkänna barndopet?", *VP*, No. 10, 1985, p. 10.

162 In the manuals of 1924, 1940 and 1955 it is said: "Then the candidate for baptism is immersed in water so that water pours over his face." *Formulär för vigsel, begravning, dop och nattvard*, 1924, p. 27; *Handbok för dop, nattvard, vigsel och begravning inom Svenska Baptistsamfundet*, 1940, p. 10; *Handbok för Svenska Baptistsamfundet*, 3rd ed., 1955, p. 14. In the manual of 1940 there is a print of a painting by G. Cederström called "Baptisterna", not to be

Baptism takes place by immersion. Immersion can be done in different ways. The most common is that the baptizand is submerged backwards in the water. The baptizand may also kneel and lean forwards in the baptismal pool and be submerged under the water or may sit on a stool in the baptismal pool and be submerged under the water.[163]

Complete immersion is, however, not absolutely necessary for all Baptists in order to regard a baptism as valid. This implies a greater possibility of recognizing other churches' baptisms. Bert Franzén means that Baptists usually recognize them, even if they have not been administered by immersion, as long as baptism takes place after a confession of personal faith.[164] That immersion is not a "must" in order to recognize baptism as valid also indicates an opening towards other churches (without immersion) and a reconsideration of baptism within traditional Baptist opinion, where the immersion almost has been a "must".

In the next chapter I will take up a discussion about baptism as an expressive or instrumental act. We may take it for granted that the view of baptism - whether it is expressive or instrumental - may have a certain significance for whether infant baptism is to be recognized as valid or not, and consequently if "re-baptism" should be practised or not.

---

found in the following manuals, which shows believers' baptism by immersion in the open air in a lake or something similar. Concerning immersion we read in the manual of 1974 in the first alternative: "Then the candidate for baptism is completely immersed in water." *Handbok för församlingens gudstjänstliv*, 1974, p. 25; in the other: "The one to be baptized is immersed in water." Ibid. p. 27.

[163] *Till församlingens tjänst*, 1987, p. 115.

[164] "Det bör betonas att troendedöpande kyrkor i regel inte tvekar att erkänna andra kyrkors dop, under förutsättning att dopet skett efter bekännelse av personlig tro. *Åtskilliga är beredda att låta detta gälla även dop som inte skett genom nedsänkning.*" Franzén, Bert, "Inledningsanförande till grupparbete: Dopet som ekumeniskt problem", 1974, p. 23, [conference documentation]. Italics mine.

293

6.   Baptism as an Expressive or an Instrumental Act

In this chapter I will study a subject which has already been touched on in this thesis, the question of baptism as an expressive or instrumental act.[165] This topic is associated with many problems.

In *BEM* there is an emphasis on the instrumental view. Baptism is mainly understood as a divine act, that is baptism *per se*, i.e. without necessarily involving the personal confession of faith, effects something.[166] The baptizand, may be a believer, but does not need to be a believer with a personal, conscious faith, in order to be baptized.[167]

Turning to the Baptist Union of Sweden, there have been different opinions and emphases concerning this issue. There is an instrumental aspect in *BUS*, which has been indicated previously. The expressive or symbolic view of baptism has, however, dominated within the Swedish Baptist tradition. Not least through influences from the beginning of Swedish Baptist history, for

---

[165] See especially Part II, chapter 8. See also chapter 8.2.2. in this part.

[166] Baptism, believers' baptism and infant baptism, gives according to *BEM* with references to the Bible a number of gifts. See for instance *B 2* mentioning participation in Christ's death and resurrection, a washing away of sin, a new birth, an exodus from bondage etc.

[167] We must not, however, forget in this context that *BEM* on the one hand emphasizes the corporate faith, that baptism is administered in a faith-context. *BEM* writes for example: "Both the baptism of believers and the baptism of infants take place in the Church as the community of faith." *B 12*, and *"The practice of infant baptism emphasizes the corporate faith and the faith which the child shares with its parents." B com 12*. Further it does on the other hand also emphasize the necessity of faith for the reception of the salvation, the importance of the personal commitment *(B 8)*, and the personal faith of the recipient of baptism for its full fruit *(B com 12)*. This personal conscious faith is, however, not an absolutely necessary presupposition, as in for example *BUS*, in order to recognize baptism as valid. Infant baptism is regarded and recognized not as a blessing but as a baptism in *BEM*.

example K.O. Broady who trained Baptist preachers and pastors, the symbolic view of baptism has been predominant.[168]

Baptism *per se* (of course in a faith-context) does not in general terms, in comparison with many other churches' view of baptism as well as that of *BEM*, seem to effect anything. Within the Baptist Union the emphasis has been primarily laid on the commitment of the baptizand. In other words, the baptizand has to be not a passive but an active, conscious and responsive person in the act of baptism – the faith-context plays in general no role at all for the validity of baptism. This attitude appears also in the Swedish Baptist manuals of 1924, 1940 and 1955. In baptism, the motif of confession of faith and baptism as an act of obedience dominates in all three manuals.[169] Such a view, which presupposes an active, conscious participation of the baptizand, excludes among other things infants and (small) children - in comparison with the view of for example *BEM* - who do not have the ability to give a conscious response.

---

[168] See Part I, chapter 6; and also Bergsten, Torsten, "Dop och kyrkotillhörighet", *Nordiska röster om dop och kyrkotillhörighet*, 1988, p. 84; Bergsten, Torsten, "Svenska Baptistsamfundet", *Svenska Trossamfund*, 8th ed., 1990, pp. 68f.

[169] The confession of faith can consist of either the baptizand telling about his conversion and his assurance of being a son of God and his request for baptism and membership, or in answering some questions asked by the principal. The questions can be as follows: Do you believe in Jesus Christ as your personal Saviour? Do you want to confess your faith in holy baptism? The formula of baptism is in all three manuals: *"On account of the command of Jesus Christ and your confession of conversion and faith in our Lord Jesus Christ, I baptize you...",* *("På grund av Jesu Kristi befallning och din egen bekännelse om sinnesändring och tro på vår Herre Jesus Kristus döper jag dig...")*, *Formulär för vigsel, begravning, dop och nattvard*, 1924, p. 27; *Handbok för dop, nattvard, vigsel och begravning inom Svenska Baptistsamfundet*, 1940. p. 10; *Handbok för Svenska Baptistsamfundet*, 3rd ed., 1955, p. 14.

Eckerdal writes that a preliminary study of the Baptist hymn book *Psalmisten* also suggests that "the contours of an act of obedience appear, to 'follow Jesus into the grave'." ("Närmast framträder konturerna av lydnadshandlingen, att 'följa Jesus efter i graven'.") Eckerdal, Lars, *Vägen in i kyrkan*, 1981, p. 372. Concerning the motif of baptism as "following Jesus into the grave" *(följa Jesus efter i graven)*, see also Persson, Larsåke W., Vad betyder det att vara döpt?", *VP*, No. 2, 1978, p. 4, ("Det är en verklig begravning."); "En framtid och ett hopp", [editorial], *VP*, No. 1/ 2, 1981, p. 2; Fahlgren, Sune, "Baptismen och baptisternas gudstjänstliv", *I enhetens tecken*, 1994, pp. 257f. See also the discussions about the manuals of 1974 and 1987 below.

An instrumental view is, nonetheless, discernible within the Baptist Union and there are Baptists who explicitly declare that God acts through the sacraments. The words of institution of baptism and the words of promise are regarded to be more than human words. These words make the baptism into a holy act and much more than just an external act.[170] Baptism is not only a symbolic act, an act of obedience. It is something more; it is a gift.[171] Baptism is not looked upon either as an isolated act, a final point of decision, but as growth, it has consequences for the whole of our lives etc.[172]

Baptism has to be put in a greater context; it is regarded as the beginning of discipleship.[173] David Lagergren discusses the problem within the Baptist tradition that from fear of the idea of "salvation in baptism", baptism has become an act of confession of faith and little more. He gives expression to a desire that Baptists present

---

[170] Engberg, Sigurd, "Det kristna dopet", VP, No. 7, 1976, p. 6. See also Engberg, Sigurd, "Det kristna dopet", VP, No. 8, 1976, p. 4; Engberg, Sigurd, "Det kristna dopet", VP, No. 9, 1976, p. 6.

[171] Wendel-Hansen, Erland, "Under Kristi lydnad", VP, No. 14, 1975, p. 4.

[172] "... the consequence of being baptized into Christ is a growth and maturity in seeing and claiming the blessings of the Lord, and in accepting responsibility for being 'the salt of the earth' and 'the light of the world'. Baptism has consequences for the whole of our lives." Persson, Larsåke W., "Vad betyder det att vara döpt?", VP, No. 1, 1978, p. 4.

[173] Lagergren gives in an article expression to the idea of conversion and baptism as a beginning with a continuation, i.e. like the wording of BEM that baptism is a beginning of a process. He writes: "Kristi liv är inte i första hand punktupplevelser och punktinsatser. Hur stor vikt Nya testamentet än lägger på begynnelser som omvändelse och dop, gör det fullt klart att allt hänger på fortsättningen." Lagergren, David, "Kontinuitet", VP, No. 41, 1976, p. 2. See also Bergsten, Torsten, "Kyrkotillhörighet - medlemskap - bekännelse", Tro och Liv, No. 1, 1980, pp. 44f.; Bergsten, Torsten, "Barnet i frikyrkan. En historisk-teologisk studie", Tro och Liv, No. 3, 1985, p. 17, he states: "Initiationen är ett kontinuerligt skeende."; Paul Beasley-Murray (the son of George Raymond Beasley-Murray) says on a visit to Sweden: "We are not only to baptize people but make them disciples! After baptism the new members must be taught and their faith deepened." Lantz, Ragni, "Paul Beasley-Murray: -Dopet bara början till lärjungaskap", VP, No. 48, 1986, p. 4. Note, teaching after baptism. See also Graninge III, for example Eckerdal, Lars, "Sektionsrapport III B", Tro och Liv, No. 1, 1980, p. 54; Dopet en livstydning. [Lars Eckerdal, Per Erik Persson], 1981.

baptism "in all its richness."[174] What this "richness" implies is, however, not made concrete by Lagergren. Valter Mattsson is of the opinion that Baptists need to consider and use what Lutherans assert, that baptismal texts in the New Testament talk about God as acting in baptism.[175] And Harry Månsus asserts that the New Testament strongly emphasizes the action of God in baptism, i.e. with our terminology an instrumental or sacramental view of baptism. The Baptists are still, however, according to Månsus, talking about "the blessing of baptism".

Whilst the New Testament emphasizes so strongly that it is God who acts with us in baptism, baptism amongst Baptists is becoming to a great extent a human act, as it is *we* who obey, confess, yes even 'fulfil all righteousness' like Jesus.[176]

The Baptist pastor Ulla Bardh maintains also that God acts in baptism. She writes:

Is father Zwingli a living prophet for Swedish Baptism of today? He is not for me. I have never seriously doubted that the bread and wine really involve a participation in Christ himself (real presence). I am also convinced that most people who have received the gift of the Supper share my belief that God really acts in baptism and Holy Communion. (She refers to John 6 and 1 Cor. 10:16f.)[177]

---

174 "Det gäller då för oss döpare att kunna presentera dopet i all dess rikedom. Där har det i vår tradition tidigare skett en allvarlig reduktion, i det att man i rädslan för 'frälsning i dopet' gjort detta till en bekännelsehandling och föga eller intet mer." Lagergren, David, "Tradition och förnyelse II", *VP*, No. 26, 1984, p. 6.

175 Mattsson, Valter, "Kristus och människan i doptexternas centrum", *VP*, No. 5, 1981, p. 4.

176 "Medan Nya testamentet så starkt betonar, att det är Gud som handlar med oss i dopet, håller dopet inom baptismen på att bli en i hög grad mänsklig handling, då det är *vi* som lyder, bekänner, ja till och med 'uppfyller all rättfärdihet' likt Jesus". Månsus, Harry, "Bibliskt dop eller surrogatdop?", *Tro och Liv*, No. 5, 1975, p. 215. And Gunnar Kjellander states that what takes place in baptism is a true reality, the promise of the Spirit and resurrection with Christ. To live a new life with Christ. Wiktell, Sven, "Gunnar Kjellander: - Det är dramatik i dopet", *VP*, No. 10, 1979, p. 5. See also Juhlin, Lars, "Behövs dopet?", *VP*, No. 40, 1989, p. 7; Sundberg, Hans, Åqvist, Berit, "Bekännelse och bärande idéer", *Liv och tjänst*, 1988, p. 99; *Gemensam väg*, 1968.

177 "Är fader Zwingli en levande profet i svensk baptism idag? Ja, inte är han det för mig. Jag har aldrig ett ögonblick seriöst tvivlat på att brödet och vinet verkligen innebär en delaktighet med Kristus själv (realpresensen). Jag är

And she asks the challenging question:

Are we, the children and grandchildren of the revival and evangelization-campaigns, afraid to be called sacramentalists?[178]

Birgit Karlsson also seems to be one of the Baptists who holds some kind of an instrumental view of baptism, and explicitly criticizes her own tradition:

Other traditions have better than ours understood and emphasized what God does and what He lets us receive in baptism.[179]

She talks about baptism as a gift, as an incorporation into the Body of Christ.[180]

---

därtill övertygad om att de flesta människor som fått tag på nattvardens gåva delar min tro att Gud verkligen handlar i dop och nattvard. Läs på nytt de oerhört laddade texterna i Joh 6: och i [1, my remark] Kor 10:16-17." Bardh, Ulla, "Har baptister behov av nattvarden?", VP, No. 16, 1978, p. 9.

178 "Är vi rädda, väckelsens och evangelisationskampanjernas barn och barnbarn, att bli kallade sakramentalister?" Ibid. Cf., however, BUS and the tendency towards a critical attitude to sacramentalism and a sacramental view of baptism. See further Larsson, Disa, "Upprörd över korstecken", (Excited about making the sign of the Cross), VP, No. 14/15, 1990, p. 16, it concerns pastor Ulla Bardh and a TV-service, where she made the sign of the Cross.

179 "Låt mig därvid få uttrycka ett mått av besvikelse gentemot den baptistiska dopsyn som kommit att fixera dopets värde och välsignelse på tidpunkten och dopsättet. Det är självfallet ett ytligt sätt att nalkas en andlig verklighet. Andra traditioner har bättre än vår förstått och betonat vad Gud gör och låter oss ta emot i dopet." Karlsson, Birgit, "Dopet - en central fråga när församlingar går samman. Missionsföreståndaren kommenterar", VP, No. 40, 1987, p. 11. Birgit Karlsson states also: "Det [troendedopet] är verkligen inte bara ett dopsätt... Det är fråga om en religiös grundsyn", Swedberg, Bo, "Birgit Karlsson: -Ett andligt genombrott är min hetaste önskan", VP, No. 50, 1983, p. 5.

180 "För mig är dopet en omistlig gåva till hjälp vid ingången till medveten tro och som stöd under hela det fortsatta livet som lärjunge och kristen." Karlsson, Birgit, "Baptistisk tro är inte till salu - men vi vill ge den vidare", VP, No. 43, 1991, p. 5; Karlsson, Birgit, "Nya människor genom Guds ord: Församlingen – Guds folk", VP, No. 38, 1978, p. 4, "Dopet var inte bara en bekännelse till lärjungaskap och väntan, det var inlemmandet i Kristus."; Karlsson, Birgit, "Nya människor genom Guds ord: Församlingen – Kristi kropp", VP, No. 40, 1978, p. 4, "Dopet uttrycker det skeende där vi införlivas med Kristi kropp." See also Sehlstedt, Berndt, "Barndop och tuggummi", VP, No. 38, 1976, p. 11, "Tack Gud för Dina sakrament.";

The Baptist theologian George Raymond Beasley-Murray must be mentioned in this context.[181] He has had significance amongst Baptists in general. He has transcended the traditional Baptist expressive view of baptism, above all because of his exegetical research. Beasley-Murray writes concerning 1 Peter 3:21:

> In the light of these statements I am compelled to conclude that the understanding of baptism as 'a beautiful and expressive symbol', *and nothing more*, is irreconcilable with the New Testament... If Baptists in earlier generations did not see this, they may thank God that at least they are now seeing it, and that they are proving again the truth of the hymn they often sing, 'The Lord hath yet more light and truth to break forth from his Word.'[182]

Another Baptist, besides the international Baptist theologians George Raymond Beasley-Murray, Johannes Schneider and Günter Wagner,[183] who without doubt can be seen, especially within the Baptist Union of Sweden, as a promotor of the process taking place during the last decades to complement an expressive view of baptism with an instrumental view, is the already frequently mentioned Torsten Bergsten. He holds, already in the 1950's, the view that baptism is an instrumental act, a sacrament:

> Baptism is a sacrament in the sense that it means an activity of God with man.[184]

Eklund, Mauritz, "Dopet är en gåva", *VP*, No. 27/28, 1992, p. 11, talking about baptism not as a demand *(krav)* but as an offer *(erbjudande)*, a gift.

[181] See also *Introduction: Some Short Remarks about my Dissertation:* "Beasley-Murray's dopuppfattning".

[182] Beasley-Murray, George Raymond, *Baptism Today and Tomorrow*, 1966, pp. 32f.

[183] All three New Testament exegetes.

[184] Bergsten, Torsten, "Baptism and the Church. Baptist Faith and Practice in a Biblical and Ecumenical Light", *The Baptist Quarterly*, Vol. 18, No. 3, 1959, pp. 125f. Bergsten writes that "the act of baptism can never be without effects." Ibid. p. 171. In Swedish "ett förrättat dop [kan] aldrig förbli utan verkningar." Bergsten, Torsten, "Dopet och församlingen. Baptistisk tro och praxis i biblisk och ekumenisk belysning", *Dopet Dåben Dåpen*, 1957, p. 23. This implies that infant baptism as well as believers' baptism either serves the building up of the Church of Christ, if the baptism is rightly administered, or its destruction and secularization, if the baptism is misused. "... On the other hand, a Baptist 'no' to infant baptism does not mean that paedo-baptist churches are denied their character as Christian churches, nor that their infant baptism is wholly denied as baptism." Bergsten, Torsten,

A couple of decades after his article in 1957, Bergsten writes a comment on among other things the quotation from Beasley-Murray above.[185] He writes:

The quotations given from G. Beasley-Murray are representative of the interpretation of baptism which has become the totally dominating one within Baptist theology during the post-war period.[186]

He states in another article that after the Second World War a powerful change of emphasis was taking place within parts of the international Baptist community from a symbolic to a sacramental interpretation of baptism.[187] And he writes:

"Baptism and the Church. Baptist Faith and Practice in a Biblical and Ecumenical Light", *The Baptist Quarterly*, Vol. 18, No. 4, 1959, p. 169f. "According to the thought presented above which regards baptism as functioning 'to damnation' if it is not administered according to the New Testament, the act of baptism can never be without effects. It serves either to the edifying of the Church of Christ if it is rightly administered, or to its destruction and secularization, if it is misused. Both these possibilities are open to Baptists as well." Ibid. p. 171. "It is thus a serious matter both to declare every infant baptism to be a 'no baptism' and to speak of Christian Churches without baptism." Ibid. p. 166.

[185] Bergsten quotes also (in Swedish) the following words by Beasley-Murray, "... it is evident that God's gift to baptism and to faith is one: it is his salvation in Christ. There is no question of his giving one part in baptism and another to faith, whether in that order or in the reverse. He gives *all* in baptism and *all* to faith." Beasley-Murray, George Raymond, *Baptism Today and Tomorrow*, 1966, p. 37; "The hearing of the Gospel in faith goes *before* baptism; faith receives the gift of God *in* baptism; and faith is the constitutive principle of the Christian life *after* baptism. There is not a line in Paul's writings that justifies a reversal of this emphasis in the relationship between faith and baptism." Ibid. pp. 40f. See Bergsten, Torsten, "Dopet igår och idag", *Tro och Liv*, No. 2, 1979, p. 6.

[186] Ibid.

[187] Bergsten, Torsten, "Anders Wiberg, dopet och de kristnas enhet", *Tro och Liv*, No. 4, 1988, p. 25. He mentions two pioneers, Johannes Schneider in German and George Raymond Beasley-Murray in English. One explanation of this development is, according to him, that these two and other Baptist theologians more actively took part in the work of Faith and Order in the WCC, and in international, exegetical research. Ibid. See Bergsten, Torsten, "Dopet igår och idag", *Tro och Liv*, No. 2, 1979, p. 6, where also Günter Wagner is mentioned together with the two mentioned above. See also Johnsson, Lennart, *Beasley-Murray's dopuppfattning*, 1987, pp. 45ff.

During the 20th century the one-sided and impoverished interpretation of baptism has been revised and enriched within large parts of the Baptist fellowship, not least on account of impulses from the international exegetical field of research and the work of Faith and Order. Baptism is nowadays, amongst Baptists, to a greater extent interpreted also as God's acting with man.[188]

This idea that baptism is not merely a symbol for something which has happened (an expressive view of baptism) – provocatively called by Bergsten, an "impoverished interpretation of baptism"[189] - but that God acts with the baptizand in baptism (an instrumental view of baptism) is evidently step by step gaining ground within the Baptist Union of Sweden.[190] The statements above indicate a reorientation of the view of baptism among Baptists.[191]

There are Baptists who react to and criticize this development within the Baptist Union. Edvin Österberg for example noticed in 1982, based on the book *När vi bryter det bröd...*, 1981, (When We

---

[188] Bergsten, Torsten, "Dop och kyrkotillhörighet", *Nordiska röster om dop och kyrkotillhörighet*, 1988, pp. 84f. He writes also: "I tolkningen av dopet kan man i SB, SMF och ÖM notera samma tendens som i nattvardsförståelsen. I dessa samfund har man mer och mer kommit att uppfatta dopet som ett nådemedel: Gud handlar med den troende människan i dopet. Detta är inte bara en människans lydnads- och bekännelsehandling." Bergsten, Torsten, *Frikyrkor i samverkan*, 1995, pp. 181f.

[189] "...denna ensidiga och utarmade doptolkning". Bergsten, Torsten, "Dop och kyrkotillhörighet", *Nordiska röster om dop och kyrkotillhörighet*, 1988, p. 84.

[190] Ibid. pp. 84f.

[191] Of course, the Swedish Baptist ecumenical commitment during the decades has had an influence in this process - all the different conferences and consultations in which Baptists have participated and the issue of baptism has been discussed (*Free Church Conferences, Ecumenical Consultations, Gemensam grund, Gemensam väg, En bok om dopet i ekumenisk belysning*, G 72, V 77, J 83, Ö 89, *Graninge I, Graninge II* (where the Baptist David Hellholm states that we do not have *one* theology of baptism in the New Testament), *Graninge III* etc., where different interpretations and views of baptism were treated and have been discussed). This has certainly contributed to and implied a more open and pluralistic understanding of baptism. See the discussion in Part I, especially chapter 9. See Part I, chapter 6. (about one of the Swedish Baptist pioneers, Anders Wiberg, and his view on baptism as a means of grace, even as a sacrament (1850)). See also Franzén, Bert, "Tro och liv i förändring", *Tro, Frihet, Gemenskap*, 1998, pp. 198f.

Break this Bread...),[192] that the sacramental view of baptism and Holy Communion is increasingly expressed within the Baptist Union of Sweden. Baptists are thereby, according to him, departing from the teaching of the New Testament and the ancient Christian church.[193]

It is, of course, natural, in discussing the topic of baptism as expressive or instrumental act, to look once more at the Baptist manuals. For some of the aspects of this development towards regarding baptism as an instrumental act are to be found in the later Baptist manuals of 1974 and 1987; in the manual of 1955 baptism is also apprehended as an action of God.[194] In the manual of 1974, there is a careful revision in comparison with the manuals of 1924 and 1940. It points towards an opening and a fuller view of baptism. Baptism should appear as a baptism *to Christ*,[195] and not as an act of obedience through which the faith in an already acquired sonship was confirmed. For example the term *överlåtelsehandling (act of commitment)* is used instead of *lydnadshandling (act of obedience)* or *bekännelsehandling (act of*

---

192 This book *När vi bryter det bröd...*, about Holy Communion, is a result of three years of study by a working party of the Baptist Union of Sweden consisting of Göte Aourell, Ulla Bardh, Else-Marie Carlsson, David Lagergren, Larsåke W Persson, Nils-Eije Svensson. This book describes a departure from an old closed Holy Communion. There is a careful recommendation that children be allowed to participate in Holy Communion (in company with their parents). Lagergren registers, however, as has already been noted, a reservation to this recommendation, see "Särskilt yttrande: Barnen och nattvarden", [David Lagergren], *När vi bryter det bröd...*, 1981, pp. 235-236.

What is said in a presentation of this book in *Veckoposten* may presumably also be said about baptism: that the fact that the relations to other denominations have influenced the view and the practice of Holy Communion in many of the Baptist congregations is not difficult to understand. Nilsson, Per-Olov, "Nattvardsboken presenteras", *VP*, No. 49, 1981, p. 9. See also Åqvist, Berit, "Får barnen vara med?", *VP*, No. 49, 1981, p. 9.

193 Österberg, Edvin, "Nattvarden", *VP*, No. 3, 1982, p. 10.

194 See also Eckerdal, Lars, *Vägen in i kyrkan*, 1981, pp. 373ff.

195 This wording "to Christ" *(till Kristus)*, is something new in comparison with earlier manuals. *Handbok för församlingens gudstjänstliv*, 1974, pp. 22, 25, 27.

confession), and baptism is regarded as reception of God's grace.[196] In one of the orders of baptism in the manual of 1974,[197] there is also an indication of a process from an expressive to a more instrumental view of baptism. This becomes apparent in a prayer:

> Lord, fulfil your promises, when we act with faith in your word. Baptize in the Holy Spirit, when we baptize in water. Let us together experience the power of being baptized in the name of Jesus and of belonging to you. Amen.[198]

We turn to the latest manual of 1987. There is a clearly expressed instrumental view. It states in the introduction to the order of baptism: "In baptism God acts through his Holy Spirit and realizes the promises associated with baptism."[199] It is explicitly said that "something" happens in baptism and this because God acts with the baptizand.

---

[196] Ibid. p. 22. This tendency towards openness and completing baptism also characterizes the suggestions for prayers and hymns in the manual. See ibid. pp. 117ff., and pp. 135ff. See also Eckerdal, Lars, *Vägen in i kyrkan*, 1981, pp. 377f.

[197] There are two orders of baptism in the manual of 1974. The formula of baptism runs in both: *"På min Mästares uppdrag och din egen bekännelse om tro på Jesus Kristus som Herre och Frälsare döper jag dig [NN, in the alternative, remark mine] till Kristus i Faderns, Sonens och den helige Andes namn."*, *Handbok för församlingens gudstjänstliv*, 1974, p. 25, resp. p. 27.

[198] "Herre, uppfyll dina löften, när vi handlar i tro på ditt ord. Döp du i helig Ande, när vi döper i vatten. Låt oss gemensamt uppleva kraften i att vara döpta i Jesu namn och tillhöra dig. Amen." Ibid. p. 27.

[199] "I dopet handlar Gud genom sin heliga Ande och förverkligar de löften som är knutna till dopet." *Till församlingens tjänst*, 1987, p. 110. It is said in the first one of the two alternative baptismal prayers: "Let your Holy Spirit fill *the one* who is now baptized with life and light and hope." ("Låt din heliga Ande fylla *den* som här döps med liv och ljus och hopp. Amen.") And in the other prayer: "When we baptize with water, give your Holy Spirit". ("När vi döper med vatten, ge du din heliga Ande".) Ibid. p. 114. Franzén makes the following comment concerning the second alternative: "Another approach would have been to pursue the parallel with the formulation 'baptize with/in the Holy Spirit'. I believe that the committee that produced the manual considered this formulation during a certain period of its work." Franzén, Bert, "Anden och det kristna livet, II. Låt er uppfyllas av ande!", *VP*, No. 35, 1987, p. 7. What can also be noted in the manual of 1987 is that the words "to Christ", found in the manual of 1974, are omitted in the order of baptism.

This view is emphasized in the *Tacksägelse och bön* (Thanksgiving and prayer) after the baptismal rite, where the words run:

We thank you for the gift of baptism and for being allowed to be baptized into Christ... We thank you for this reminder of how we committed ourselves to you in baptism and how you acted with us. We thank you for the gift of the Spirit. Help us to live in our baptism.[200]

This does not, however, imply any recognition of infant baptism.

In the manual of 1987 we find that baptism, in comparison with earlier manuals, is put in a wider context. It is said: "Holy Communion belongs according to early Christian tradition to a complete service of baptism."[201] It can be further noted that the imposition of hands is not mentioned in any of the Baptist manuals (including the manual of 1987), nor the anointing with chrism in connection with the act of baptism. It may also be mentioned that in this manual of 1987 there is an order for Confession *(bikt)*[202] and an order for Intercession and anointing with oil.[203]

This manual has been criticized by Baptists and even been regarded as unbiblical on some points.[204]

I am not quite sure how prevalent the sacramental view of baptism de facto is among Swedish Baptists. Nevertheless, a certain adjustment of the purely symbolic view and a shift of accent towards an instrumental view of baptism are discernible within the Baptist Union,[205] which is to be found in the later Baptist manuals.

---

[200] "Tack för dopets gåva och för att vi får döpas in i Kristus... Tack för denna påminnelse om hur vi i dopet fick överlåta oss åt dig och hur du handlade med oss. Tack för Andens gåva. Hjälp oss att leva i vårt dop". *Till församlingens tjänst*, 1987, p. 116.

[201] "Till fullständig dopgudstjänst hör enligt tidig kristen tradition nattvardsfirande." Ibid. p. 111.

[202] Ibid. pp. 242ff. Concerning this order see Ingvar Gustafsson: "Bikten har ju i vår tradition varit (och är) mycket litet praktiserad. Vi har i varje fall sällan kallat det bikt. Det är önskvärt att fler och fler blir medvetna om den själavårdande tillgång bikten är." Gustafsson, Ingvar, "Till församlingens tjänst", *VP*, No. 34, 1987, p. 6.

[203] *Till församlingens tjänst*, 1987, pp. 246ff.

[204] See for example Svenson, Sven, "Förhandskritik", *VP*, No. 6, 1987, p. 15.

[205] There seems to be at least a certain similarity with the view which Wiberg tried to maintain. Bergsten states: "during recent decades the interpretation which Wiberg advocated has found greater response." Bergsten, Torsten,

This ought in my opinion to imply that one of the stumbling blocks for Baptists, infant baptism and its validity, is closer to being overcome (even if not completely).

In other words, the work towards mutual recognition of baptism and thus church unity has made important progress. For the question is whether the instrumental or sacramental view of baptism ought not to result in infant baptism in general being recognized as valid. Or to put the question in another way: how can the Baptists who regard baptism as an instrumental act hold to such an ambivalent attitude towards infant baptism, as that which I have pointed out earlier in this part, i.e. that sometimes infant baptism is valid, at other times not.

The problem may be that too much emphasis is put on the baptized person who has to decide if baptism is valid or not.[206] For is it not the case that if God acts in baptism, he also gives a gift to the baptizand? Therefore, it seems remarkable if this gift could disappear so that baptism does not for ever but only for a certain period of time depend on certain conditions. Is not a gift a gift, and this gift can either be received or rejected by the person? If a person rejects it, he has nevertheless (although baptized by infant baptism) been baptized and has in and through the baptism received the gift. He can, however, rediscover this gift (baptism) whenever he wants, and figuratively speaking open his parcel and make use of its content - in a similar way to the idea we have found among Baptists concerning believers' baptism of the possibility of returning to this baptism without being "re-baptized".[207]

"Anders Wiberg - väckelseman, samfundsledare och teolog", *Kyrkohistorisk årsskrift*, 81, 1981, p. 90.

[206] See for example Lagergren, David, "Ekumenisk barnteologi", *VP*, No. 17, 1991, p. 6. He is writing in a discussion with Bergsten about this dilemma - to recognize infant baptism *sometimes* - which according to the former results in a fatal subjectivism. He concludes that "it implies taking a dubious path", ("[det] är att slå in på en oklar väg".) Ibid. Bergsten later comments on his article and agrees that such an opinion on baptism as his implies a compromise: "Jag instämmer i Lagergrens omdöme att detta är en kompromiss." Bergsten, Torsten, "Tro och tvivel på barndopet", *VP*, No. 19/20, 1991, p. 7. See also Bergsten, Torsten, "Förändring genom konfrontation och dialog. Svenskt perspektiv", *Samfund i förändring*, 1997, p. 51.

[207] See the discussion above, chapter 5, concerning the question of "re-baptism" of a person already baptized by believers' baptism, and also Bergsten,

We are obviously confronted with another dilemma in this discussion. On the one hand baptism is regarded as an instrumental act; baptism is a divine act; God acts in baptism with the baptizand.

As Swedish Baptists we no longer uphold an one-sided symbolic interpretation of baptism. We accept and recognize the common Christian teaching about the meaning of baptism which has been exceptionally well formulated in 'Baptism, Eucharist and Ministry'.208

Further infant baptism is recognized as valid by some Baptists, which from an instrumental or sacramental point of view seems obvious. On the other hand, despite holding this instrumental, sacramental view, all infant baptisms are not recognized as valid.

In comparing a Baptist instrumental, sacramental view of baptism with a Catholic or Lutheran one, we find that there must be different meanings and interpretations of what a sacramental, instrumental view of baptism means. For although baptism is increasingly looked upon as an instrumental act by Baptists and

---

Torsten, "På väg mot ett ömsesidigt doperkännande?", 1989, p. 3, [unpublished paper]; Lagergren, David, "Ekumenisk barnteologi", VP, No. 17, 1991, p. 6.

208 "Som svenska baptister driver vi inte längre en ensidig symbolisk doptolkningstradition vidare. Vi bejakar den allmänkristna förkunnelse av dopets mening som på ett så förträffligt sätt formulerats i 'Dop, nattvard, ämbete'." Bergsten, Torsten, "Anders Wiberg, dopet och de kristnas enhet", Tro och Liv, No. 4, 1988, p. 25. And in a footnote he writes that this concerns especially B 2-16 in BEM. Ibid. p. 27, footnote 57.

The statements by Bergsten are in one way correct, but in another not, see for example BUS (Part II) where we do find a more restrictive attitude. See also Bergsten, Torsten, "Kyrkotillhörighet - medlemskap - bekännelse", Tro och Liv, No. 1, 1980, p. 40, where he also refers to the document, Report of theological conversations. Sponsored by the World Alliance of Reformed Churches and the Baptist World Alliance 1973-77, where it is stated: "Baptism is a powerful sign of God's saving grace and, by virtue of the action of the Holy Spirit in it, an effective instrument of grace, actually imparting what it promises: the forgiveness of sins, union with Christ in his death and resurrection, regeneration, elevation to the status of sonship, membership in the church, the body of Christ, new life in the Spirit, the earnest of the resurrection of the body. The New Testament looks upon the operation of the Spirit in baptism as the application of the fulness of saving grace." (p. 15), quoted in Bergsten, Torsten, "Kyrkotillhörighet - medlemskap - bekännelse", Tro och Liv, No. 1, 1980, p. 40.

the term *sacrament* is used - also in a Baptist manual[209] - there are still hesitations about recognizing all infant baptisms as valid.

Baptism as an instrumental, sacramental act seems to be interpreted by Baptists more in terms of a contract under oath between two "conscious", active partners.[210] This Baptist interpretation thus presupposes two active participators. In other words, God acts with the believer in baptism (i.e. with the person who himself has the ability to make an active, conscious profession of faith) and something happens. Provocatively expressed, we ourselves seem to effect baptism, together with the action of God, otherwise it is at best a blessing. This interpretation of the sacramental or instrumental view of baptism does not correspond totally with the view in other churches of what the instrumental, sacramental view means - that God acts (and gives His grace and gifts) sovereignly, without necessarily any personal, conscious response of the baptizand at the time of the baptism.

In this chapter I have tried to point out further examples of a complementary view of baptism, in relation to the traditional, symbolic one, within the Baptist Union of Sweden, a tendency increasingly to regard baptism as an instrumental act, which indicates that there is a reconsideration of baptism. This ought to be noticeable in other ways within the Baptist Union.[211] In relation

---

[209] The term *sacraments* is mentioned for the first time in the Swedish Baptist manual of 1974. In the preface it is stated: *"By openness and receptivity to the Spirit, the Word and sacraments can be means of God's grace and an abundant spiritual life."* (*"Genom öppenhet och mottaglighet för Anden kan Ordet och sakramenten bli medel för Guds nåd och ett överflödande andligt liv."*), *Handbok för församlingens gudstjänstliv*, 1974, p. 8. See also Bergsten's two theses: firstly that baptism is a sacrament that God acts with man in baptism (the objective part); secondly that baptism is also an expression of man's surrender to God, (the subjective part). He writes: "Only that Baptism is a right Christian Baptism, which is preceded by repentance and which is received in faith in Christ." Bergsten, Torsten, "Baptism and the Church. Baptist Faith and Practice in a Biblical and Ecumenical Light", *The Baptist Quarterly*, Vol. 18, No. 3, 1959, pp. 125f.

[210] The term *sacramentum* originally meant for example a soldier's oath to his superior. See also my dissertation and discussion about this, Johnsson, Lennart, *Beasley-Murray's dopuppfattning*, 1987, pp. 105ff.

[211] For example Carl-Göran Bergman notes a change in a sacramental direction in newly built Baptist churches [formerly more frequently named chapels, my remark]: an altar-like table at the centre and the pulpit at the side. Bergman,

to the background and history of the Swedish Baptists all this must
be regarded as notable, not least in a Swedish ecumenical and
international perspective. This has, of course, also implications for
the issue of ecclesiology, the incorporation into the church and the
local congregation.

Carl-Göran, "Eucharistins plats i kyrkorummet", *Svenskt gudstjänstliv*, 62,
1987, p. 27, see also especially pp. 27-30.

7. Ecclesiology: The Question of Incorporation into the Church - by Baptism or by Faith?

The question of incorporation into the church - and in fact into Christ - is an important and difficult issue to deal with.[212] There are many different ecclesiological questions. Are for example the universal church and the local church, i.e. the congregation, one and the same, or are there any differences? What should constitute the basis and foundation of the church? When does a person become a member of the church - is it by faith, by baptism or by birth, by faith *and* baptism? Is the church equivalent to those baptized (by infant baptism or believers' baptism) - an idea held by *BEM*, or is it equivalent to those baptized exclusively by believers' baptism (or possibly as exceptions without any believers' baptism at all) - an idea which has largely prevailed within the Baptist Union. Or is the church equivalent to conscious believers? Are there even different memberships, one of the universal church and another of the local church or congregation, an idea which has been indicated previously in this study? And what about the relation between

---

[212] A discussion among Baptists about the concept "church" is found in for instance Bergsten, Torsten, *Frikyrkor i samverkan*, 1995, pp. 198f. There is a section *Vad är Kristi kyrka? Baptister svarar* (What is the Church of Christ? Baptists answer). Bergsten refers to a discussion in *Baptistpredikanternas Studieblad* 1963, between Gunnar Westin and himself, starting from the question: "Is the Baptist denomination a church?" They have different views. Westin objects to the use of the term *church* amongst Baptists and writes: "The term church with its negative overtones cannot be applied to our denomination without its entailing an interior process of change.", quoted in Bergsten, Torsten, *Frikyrkor i samverkan*, 1995, p. 198. Bergsten argues for its use: "What hinders us, on the basis of terminology in recent biblical theology, from accepting, in addition to the word congregation, the word church as a term for the New Testament ekklesia? If we were to, we would contribute to strengthening the character of the word as a biblical term and to weakening its nuances of legal institution and territorial church." In ibid. p. 199. See also Franzén, Bert, "Tro och liv i förändring", *Tro, Frihet, Gemenskap*, 1998, pp. 191f. We note that *BUS* uses the term *church*, for example, "the Swedish Baptist churches", *BUS* p. 204; "most Baptist churches in Sweden", Ibid. p. 206.

belonging and membership? What should be the basis in the work towards church unity - infant baptism, believers' baptism, both or even none of them? What is the relation for example between the church and the local congregation, the Kingdom of God, the Body of Christ etc? There are various answers to these questions. More questions could be asked. They all indicate the importance of further studies concerning ecclesiology and baptism.

To generalize there are at least four different categories of churches and denominations. They are:

1) Churches and denominations which practise infant baptism, also accepting believers' baptism (but not "re-baptism").[213]

2) Churches and denominations which exclusively practise believers' baptism (and "re-baptisms").[214]

3) Churches and denominations which practise infant baptism and believers' baptism, and sometimes "re-baptism".[215]

4) Churches and denominations which do not have any baptism at all.[216]

In *BEM* it is said:

> Through baptism, Christians are brought together into union with Christ, with each other and with the Church of every time and place. Our common baptism, which unites us to Christ in faith, is thus a basic bond of unity.[217]

In other words, baptism is regarded as the foundation of the church, and through baptism man is incorporated into Christ, i.e. the church, concretely present in the local church. Both infant baptism and believers' baptism are recognized as valid by *BEM*, and baptism is also the sign of unity, "For we were all baptized by one Spirit into one body" (1 Cor. 12:13).[218] As I pointed out in Part II this

---

[213] Most of the "great" traditional churches, as for example the Roman Catholic Church. See also *BEM* which also holds this view.

[214] Most of the Baptist denominations, see also *BUS*.

[215] For instance the Mission Covenant Church of Sweden and also some of the ecumenical congregations, where also the Baptist Union of Sweden is involved.

[216] For example the Salvation Army and the Society of Friends.

[217] *B 6*.

[218] See also *B 2*.

view results in infants through baptism being transformed from one ontological level to another, the newly born are incorporated into the church, i.e. both the universal and the local.

We touch here upon still another difficult and controversial question, already discussed, that of original sin.[219] The place of children in the church or congregation seems a difficult theological problem for Baptists.[220] For children (of Baptist parents within the Baptist Union of Sweden) have formally been placed outside the Baptist congregation (church) and also outside the Body of Christ according to a certain interpretation by some Baptists of the theology of conversion.[221] That children are considered to be outside the Body of Christ must, however, be controversial for other Baptists - not least for those who are of the opinion that infants share in the redemption of Christ.[222] But obviously a change takes place from the strict theology of conversion towards the theology of the covenant with the result that children are regarded also by Baptists as by birth within the one universal church, the Body of

---

[219] See Part II, chapter 4. discussing original sin, and also chapter 2.2. in this part.

[220] See especially Franzén who discusses children in the congregation and the question of belonging and membership, the spiritual position of children etc. Franzén, Bert, "Barnen i församlingen. Frågan om tillhörighet och medlemskap", Tro och Liv, No. 3, 1985, pp. 32ff.; Franzén, Bert, "Barnen och änglarna i vår tid", VP, No. 40, 1986, p. 4; Franzén, Bert, Guds försprång, 1991; Franzén, Bert, "Tro och liv i förändring", Tro, Frihet, Gemenskap, 1998, pp. 209f. See also BUS.

[221] "Svenska Baptistsamfundet och övriga döparsamfund har formellt placerat barnen utanför församlingen." Franzén, Bert, "Barnen i församlingen. Frågan om tillhörighet och medlemskap", Tro och Liv, No. 3, 1985, p. 32. He also refers to the meeting of The Commission on Doctrine and Inter-Church Co-operation, in connection with the congress of BWA in Toronto 1980, where the Baptist, Dr. William E. Hull, gave a speech. Hull said that the Reformed churches (kyrkorna) have built on the theology of the covenant with the result that they see the children of believers as a part of the fellowship of faith already by birth. The Baptist denominations (samfunden) in their turn have built on the theology of conversion in the New Testament and as a consequence placed children outside the Body of Christ (Kristi kropp), until they are spiritually reborn through conversion and faith. It is high time, Hull claims, to seek a synthesis between these two extremes. Franzén, Bert, "Barnen i församlingen. Frågan om tillhörighet och medlemskap", Tro och Liv, No. 3, 1985, p. 37.

[222] See for example BUS.

Christ. Some would prefer to say the Covenant or the Kingdom of God.

The cause of this ambiguity concerning the place of children can certainly partly be explained by the Baptist view of man, and partly by the traditional Baptist emphasis on repentance and conversion in order to be a member of the congregation.[223] Children cannot be members of a Baptist congregation until they have repented and been baptized by believers' baptism.[224] First then they become "full members".

Concerning the Kingdom of God (the universal church), however, there are the following possibilities from a Baptist point of view, as regards becoming a member: 1) by birth children of God, 2) by conscious response and baptism - which sometimes is a "re-baptism", 3) by conscious response alone. Points 2 and 3 presuppose a "fall" of which the person in question repents, or these alternatives can sometimes also be regarded as acts of manifestation or obedience.

It can be observed that there is a change of emphasis from regarding children as outside the local church, i.e. the congregation, to giving them a place in it.[225] Bert Franzén refers to some internationally well-known Baptist theologians (N.J. Engelsen, Bent Hylleberg, G.R. Beasley-Murray, Arthur G. Patzia and William E. Hull).[226] He concludes:

---

[223] "Even if one can with some justice say that the emphasis on conversion and decision in the Free Churches has contributed to keeping children at a distance, it has also maintained respect for personal decision and responsibility." Franzén, Bert, "Barnen i församlingen. Frågan om tillhörighet och medlemskap", Tro och Liv, No. 3, 1985, p. 39.

[224] See Part I, chapter 2. and chapter 6.; see also chapter 9.3. in Part I, the discussion in for example Gemensam grund, baptism is necessary for membership of a congregation (but also exceptions); and also Part II, chapter 4. and chapter 10., BEM's opinion that baptism (infant baptism or believers' baptism) is the incorporation into the church, i.e. Body of Christ, the New Covenant.

[225] See also BUS.

[226] Franzén, Bert, "Barnen i församlingen. Frågan om tillhörighet och medlemskap", Tro och Liv, No. 3, 1985, pp. 33-39.

that it's no longer possible not to count children as part of the fellowship of the congregation, if one wants to take clearly noticeable features of New Testament theology seriously.[227]

Franzén observes, however, that none of these theologians write about *membership* for children. Children *belong* to the Baptist congregation.[228] We touch once again on the topic of membership and belonging.

Another concept, put forward by Bergsten, is "child member" *(barnmedlem)*. This further illustrates the difficulty and complexity of incorporation and membership. He is of the opinion that an infant or a child can also be at the stage of not "only belonging to" but also of being a member of the local church, congregation, and this without baptism.[229] He argues that the common Free Church conviction is that children without faith and baptism share in the atonement of Christ, i.e. they have an individual relation to Christ. If so, the child participates at the same time in the visible congregation (the local church). It is a child member.[230] The child is

---

[227] "Samtliga anförda exempel talar för slutsatsen, att det inte längre är möjligt att inte räkna barnen till församlingens gemenskap, om man vill göra allvar av klart framträdande drag i nytestamentlig teologi." Ibid. p. 39.

[228] "Ingen av de här refererade teologerna talar emellertid om *medlemskap*, när det gäller de små barnen." Ibid. And Bergsten writes in his review of Franzén, *Guds försprång*, 1991: "The author maintains energetically and correctly that all children belong to God and are his children because of the redemption of Christ. 'Christian children', that is children who grow up under the influence of Christian parents and congregations, belong moreover to the congregation. They do this until they are ready to become by faith, confession and baptism members of the congregation." Bergsten, Torsten, "Ekumenisk barnteologi", *VP*, No. 15, 1991, p. 4.

[229] Bergsten, Torsten, "Barnet i frikyrkan. En historisk-teologisk studie", *Tro och Liv*, No. 3, 1985, pp. 12ff. Cf., however, the note just referred to above and also Bergsten, Torsten, "Den gemensamma församlingen - ett tecken om enhet", *Levande*, 1996, pp. 50-52, where he prefers and pleads for "belonging".

[230] Bergsten, Torsten, "Barnet i frikyrkan. En historisk-teologisk studie", *Tro och Liv*, No. 3, 1985, p. 16. See also "Församlingen och barnen", [editorial], *VP*, No. 16, 1985, p. 2, discussing among other things this concept "child member". I want also to quote the words of Bergsten, reviewing Franzén, *Guds försprång*, 1991, where he uses the terms *belonging* and *membership*: "There cannot be different kinds of child-relationship to God, belonging and membership." ("Inför Gud kan det inte gärna finnas olika slag av barnaskap,

in this view a member of both the universal church and also of the local Baptist congregation, and does not "only belong" to the local one.

Then, however, another problem arises, also dealt with earlier in this part: what will baptism as an act of incorporation or initiation mean to this person in such a case? Bergsten himself is conscious of this dilemma and asks, without giving any explicit answer, what is to be done with baptism as an act of initiation?[231] For if a person already is within the church, why baptize? What meaning does it in such case have? It is not a baptism into the church, the Body of Christ, nor into the congregation, the local church.

All the foregoing gives rise to questions from both ecclesiological and ecumenical perspectives: Who is "inside" and who is "outside"? What is the relation between the church and the local congregation? Are repentance/conversion and the "fall" presuppositions or not for membership of the church. There seems then to be one vital presupposition for Baptists in order to become a member of both the local Baptist congregation and the universal church. That is a "fall". It seems as if it is impossible for a person, in spite of the positive view of man, to remain within the Kingdom or church from birth onwards. For all are in one way predestined to "fall", even the best from a moral point of view. Everybody needs to repent.[232] Through awareness of the "fall" and a consciousness of the need of repentance, man may "return" to the Kingdom. A person has thus to be conscious of his position (his guilt and turning away

---

tillhörighet eller medlemskap.") Bergsten, Torsten, "Ekumenisk barnteologi", VP, No. 15, 1991, p. 4.

[231] "Men hur blir det då med dopet som initiationshandling?", Bergsten, Torsten, "Barnet i frikyrkan. En historisk-teologisk studie", Tro och Liv, No. 3, 1985, p. 16.

[232] Franzén writes that all adults have to repent in order to come into the Kingdom of God, and Jesus made it clear "that no one can earn by merit a place in this Kingdom. The only ones who have a privileged position in this case are children, Matt. 19:14; Mark. 10:14; Luk. 18:16." Franzén, Bert, "Tre evangelister om mission", Liv och tjänst, 1988, p. 48. Lagergren writes in his book about the Baptist Union of Sweden during the years 1914-1932 that the message which at that time was proclaimed was pronouncedly evangelical. It emphasized that all human beings, even the best from a moral point of view, need to repent in order to be the children of God in a conscious and qualified sense. Lagergren, David, Framgångstid med dubbla förtecken, 1989, p. 27. See, however, for example the discussion above in chapter 2.2. about Ann-Christine Lindholm, Marcus and Birgitta Brynfors.

from God), and from this he turns to God and gives a conscious response to Him. This emphasis among Baptists, that the main point is the subjective aspect, (emphasis primarily on the conscious, personal faith, man's personal acceptance of salvation - instead of the emphasis primarily on God's action), has often been at the expense of the more objective side (emphasis primarily on the action of God in a faith-context to avoid an individualization).

In other words, the objective and the subjective dimensions are often not balanced, which may possibly result in baptism sometimes tending to be "forgotten" or marginalized - with the emphasis "only" on the conscious, personal faith.

Awareness (medvetenhet) is evidently regarded as another important presupposition in order to be baptized and be a member. But what does this concept imply? When does a human being become "aware" in order to give a personal conscious response? In a way it looks as if awareness is connected with the intellect.[233] Such an opinion results for instance in the exclusion of infants and children, as well as of the so-called mentally retarded.[234] There are also problems with the interpretation of the concepts "confession", "consciousness", and "faith", and their relation to incorporation into the church.

From the discussion we find that an infant/child according to Baptists on the one hand is within the Kingdom - some say the church - by birth. It sometimes grows up in a faith-context and is thus not really "outside" the Kingdom. Baptism, as *baptism of metanoia,* is consequently in one view not needed. On the other hand, moral aspects are maintained by other Baptists: all need to repent and be baptized (even if they are "inside"). This sometimes implies, however, a baptism of people who already believe, "those who already are 'in Christ'".[235] Baptism is then more an act of

---

[233] See Fahlgren, Sune, "Baptismens spiritualitet – speglad i gudstjänstlivet. Svenskt perspektiv", Samfund i förändring, 1997, pp. 107f.

[234] The child is, according to Bergsten, an unaware human being from a psychological and spiritual point of view: "In this context theological reflection about the relationship of children to God must be analysed in an historical perspective. By child we here mean a psychologically and spiritually unaware (omedveten) person. From this point of view a mentally retarded person is and will remain a child." Bergsten, Torsten, "Barnet i frikyrkan. En historisk-teologisk studie", Tro och Liv, No. 3, 1985, p. 2.

[235] Månsus, Harry, "Bibliskt dop eller surrogatdop", Tro och Liv, No. 5, 1975, p. 218.

obedience or a manifestation of a faith which has existed for a long time, than an incorporation into the church (possibly it is an "incorporation" into the local congregation), and that discrepancy between the universal church and the local church, i.e. congregation, which Månsus writes about is continued and preserved. According to at least some Baptists "indiscriminate" believers' baptism, or according to others improper baptism, takes place.[236] And what about confession and faith? An explicit confession can be heard, but what about faith? How does one decide if it is present, and if it is sufficient or when it has been lost? And who has the qualification to judge that a proper confession of faith has been made?[237]

That incorporation into the church and the local Baptist congregation occurs through believers' baptism has been a predominant view within the Baptist Union of Sweden.[238] This view has been held among Baptists among other things on the principle of biblical authority, and also - not least during recent years - with reference to the fact that in the ancient church baptism was the

---

[236] See for example the discussion above, chapter 5.

[237] Cf. *fides infantium* and *fides ecclesiae; fides explicita,* i.e. an outspoken confession, and *fides implicita,* i.e. a possibly passive faith in an infant (or *fiducia*).

[238] See Bert Franzén, who himself was involved in the work of *BUS*. He writes: "And when we talk about being baptized into Christ, this is also clear. It means that we are baptized into his Body, which is the Christian congregation. For this reason it is of importance that we preserve the connection between baptism and the congregation. We are baptized in order to become members of the Body of Christ or members of the Christian congregation." Franzén, Bert, "Dopet in i Kristus", *VP*, No. 22, 1988, p. 26. Franzén emphasizes thus the connection between baptism and membership of the church, the congregation, which is the Body of Christ. Note the identification.

Lars Eckerdal writes that in the Baptist revival in the 19th century, it was an obvious presupposition that there was only one way to the believers' fellowship in Christ: through the only valid baptism on the basis of baptizand's personal confession of faith. Eckerdal, Lars, "Dopet", *Dop, Nattvard, Ämbete,* 2nd ed., 1983, p. 85. See also Bergsten, Torsten, "Kyrkotillhörighet - medlemskap - bekännelse", *Tro och Liv,* No. 1, 1980, p. 40.

way into the church and into the local congregation.[239] And also the Baptist pioneers in Sweden held that believers' baptism was necessary for membership of a congregation.[240]

Concerning membership and its relation to the church, a difficulty often arises, as has been stated, for Baptists. Sometimes the membership of the universal church and the local congregation coincide, at other times, however, it does not. There has been and still is an explicit desire to hold together the membership of the universal church *and* the local congregation, i.e. that one is incorporated into the Body of Christ and the congregation by *baptism of metanoia*, faith and baptism.[241] Bergsten writes:

---

[239] See for example Sundberg, Hans, Åqvist, Berit, "Bekännelse och bärande ideer", *Liv och tjänst*, 1988, p. 98; Månsus, Harry, "Bibliskt dop eller surrogatdop?", *Tro och Liv*, No. 5, 1975, p. 214.

[240] See for example the Confession of Faith (approved in 1848) from the oldest Baptist congregation in Sweden – in Borekulla, Landa parish -, which says in Article 10, already quoted in Part I: "Through baptism we are received into Christ's congregation on earth, and the Lord has ordained this to be a means of grace for us." Quoted in Nordström, Nils Johan, *En kulturbild från 1800-talets religiösa brytningstid*, 1926, p. 63. (This statement seems to come close to the opinion of *BEM*.) See also ibid. pp. 54-57; and pp. 57-74, (*Trosbekännelse*, Articles 1-15). There is, however, an important difference if infant baptism is recognized as valid or not. And Bergsten writes that Wiberg for example defended the Baptist view that believers' baptism was a necessary presupposition for membership of a congregation. See Bergsten, Torsten, "Anders Wiberg, dopet och de kristnas enhet", *Tro och Liv*, No. 4, 1988, p. 12. See also Part I, chapter 6.

[241] See for example Karlsson, Birgit, "Församling med uppdrag i världen", *Liv och tjänst*, 1988, where she declares that the congregation is the Body of Christ, (ibid. p. 18), and that the congregation in the New Testament can be interpreted in two ways, partly as a universal reality, ("Dels är den en universell storhet som sträcker sig över tidens gräns, över varje geografisk gräns och med mål att bli den skara som på Herrens dag består av människor från alla folk, stammar och tungomål."), ibid. p. 19, partly as a very concrete fellowship of people in a specific place. ("Dels är församlingen en mycket konkret gemenskap av människor i en given tid och på en bestämd ort.") Ibid. Karlsson writes also: "Församlingen måste vara lokal och konkret samtidigt som den gestaltar gemenskap över alla gränser." Karlsson, Birgit, "Liv och tjänst inför år 2000", *Liv och tjänst*, 1988, p. 225.

According to *sacramental Baptist conviction* a person is incorporated into the church - congregation - the Body of Christ through faith and baptism.[242]

At other times, however, the church and the local congregation seem to be separated - at least for some time, so even if there is a desire by Baptists to keep together the universal church and the local church, there are difficulties in maintaining this in practice. As already quoted, a fatal discrepancy has developed between the universal church and the local church.[243]

The question remains of when a person really becomes a member of the universal church and when of the local church or congregation, according to Baptist opinion? And are the church and/or the local church identical with the baptized?

Because of the dilemma in maintaining the genuine or proper believers' baptism in the Baptist sense, we can from the discussion so far expect different answers. For most Baptists children are by birth God's children and thus within the Kingdom of God but outside the local church, i.e. still not members of a local Baptist congregation. This has the following implication. Through believers' baptism, a *baptism of metanoia*, a person becomes a member of the Baptist church (for the first time) and a member of the Body of Christ, the universal church, possibly for the second time - on account of a "fall". This incorporation into the church may also sometimes occur, as has been mentioned, without any baptism, as a person often becomes a member of the universal church by faith - and often considerably later a member of the local Baptist church by baptism.[244] The separation between baptism and membership

---

[242] "Enligt *sakramental baptistisk övertygelse* inlemmas människan ju genom tro och dop i kyrkan – församlingen - Kristi kropp." Bergsten, Torsten, "Kyrkotillhörighet - medlemskap - bekännelse", *Tro och Liv*, No. 1, 1980, p. 43. See also: "... I den föregående framställningen har gång på gång framhävts att trons och dopets djupaste gemensamma väsen är att införliva människan med Kristus och hans församling, både i betydelsen den universella kyrkan och den lokala församlingen." Bergsten, Torsten, "Dopet igår och idag", *Tro och Liv*, No. 2, 1979, p. 13. See also the previous discussions in chapter 6. and also Part II, chapter 8.

[243] "... en mycket ödesdiger diskrepans [har] uppkommit mellan den universella församlingen, Kristi kropp, och lokalförsamlingen." Månsus, Harry, "Bibliskt dop eller surrogatdop?", *Tro och Liv*, No. 5, 1975, p. 215.

[244] I want to mention possible consequences in this context. A believing person, not baptized by believers' baptism but who is active in a Baptist congregation, can be a member of for instance the Church of Sweden but not necessarily of

seems to be still more obvious and frequent within the Baptist Union of Sweden in the 1970's-1990's than earlier, on account of among other things open membership and the ecumenical congregations.

It can be useful to recall that from the very beginning of the Baptist movement in Sweden, a person did not become a member of a Baptist church or congregation through believers' baptism alone. It is generally thought that Baptists have always held that a person becomes a member of a Baptist church through believers' baptism. According to the first Baptist Confession of Faith something else was needed in addition to believers' baptism. The vote of the congregation was also necessary.[245]

This points partly to a separation between baptism and membership, partly to an ambiguity in the relation between the universal church and the local Baptist church – already from the beginning of the Baptist movement - which, of course, has implications for ecclesiology and eventually ecumenism. Baptism was then connected with membership of the universal church, the

---

the local Baptist congregation to which he "just belongs", since he is not baptized by believers' baptism. As for membership of the Church of Sweden, it has been the case (until 1996 as mentioned in Part I) that children became members of the Church of Sweden by birth, if at least one of the parents (the mother) was a member of this church. This led thus to the odd consequence that a child growing up in a Baptist home could be a member of the Church of Sweden but not yet be a member of, but just belong to the Baptist Union until he is baptized in the Baptist congregation, (or, of course, a member through open membership). There are some Baptists who, in spite of the incompatibility, have been and still are members of both the Baptist Union of Sweden and of the Church of Sweden. Janarv writes that the National Church system (statskyrko- eller/och folkkyrkosystem) is incompatible with the Baptist one. All Swedish Baptists do not realize this, as they usually belong to both. Janarv, Ruben, "Församlingen de troendes gemenskap", [del 3], VP, No. 16, 1978, p. 6. Agneta Magnusson (Valsätrakyrkan) states: "Medlemmar från Svenska kyrkan har ju varenda frikyrkoförsamling", Swedberg, Bo, "25 år efter New Delhi: Nu har lokalekumeniken börjar blomma för fullt", VP, No. 7, 1986, p. 3.

[245] See Article 10, (already quoted in Part I) "an admission of a new member can occur only by a vote..." ("En ny medlems intagande kan endast efter föregående bekantskap om hans själstillstånd och efter personlig aflagd bekännelse genom röstning ske. Wid en sådan omröstning är det på det högsta önskanswärdt, att enhällighet af rösterna finner rum.") quoted in Nordström, Nils Johan, En kulturbild från 1800-talets religiösa brytningstid, 1926, p. 66. Italics mine.

vote, however, with membership of the local Baptist church. And David Lagergren writes:

> In the earlier Baptist congregations in our country, it was probably the case that a person became a member not through baptism in itself but through a decision of the congregation.[246]

Such a separation between baptism and membership of the congregation does not, however, according to Lagergren, have any support in the New Testament where the congregation was the same as those baptized.[247] There are in his opinion - referring also to *BEM* - strong reasons for maintaining baptism as the way into the congregation also in the future.[248]

There are obviously problems for Baptists in regard to ecclesiology, membership and the incorporation into the church and congregation, if the incorporation takes place by baptism and/or by faith (or, at least earlier, also by vote). Baptists have had,

---

[246] Lagergren, David, "Historia och konservatism", *VP*, No. 2, 1978, p. 2. Janarv writes, with reference to the congregation in Borekulla and Article 10: "I den *universella församlingen* blir man upptagen genom dopet, men i den *lokala* blir man intagen genom omröstning." Janarv, Ruben, "Vem fick bli - och vara - medlem i fädernas baptistförsamling?" [del 1], *VP*, No. 12, 1978, p. 3. See also Bergsten, Torsten, "Förändring genom konfrontation och dialog. Svenskt perspektiv", *Samfund i förändring*, 1997, pp. 33ff.; Franzén, Bert, "Tro och liv i förändring", *Tro, Frihet, Gemenskap*, 1998, pp. 210f.

[247] Lagergren, David, "Historia och konservatism", *VP*, No. 2, 1978, p. 2. He also writes about another example from Swedish Baptist history, from the 1920's. The notable thing is that the necessity of believers' baptism was so successfully upheld, despite it not being considered as part of salvation. A person was saved at conversion; baptism was the next step. It was the step into the congregation. Lagergren, David, *Framgångstid med dubbla förtecken*, 1989, p. 27. Westin writes about the work of the Baptist J.W. Wallin in the 19th century in Florakyrkan in Stockholm, where open Holy Communion was practised and members were incorporated into this Baptist congregation without believers' baptism. There was thus, according to Westin, some opposition in certain congregations to the policy of the denomination. Westin, Gunnar, *Svenska Baptistsamfundet 1887-1914*, 1965, pp. 45f.

[248] "Den som döps, införlivas med församlingen, med skaran av dem som tror på Jesus. Detta har fasthållits av de flesta kyrkor... och har senast bekräftats av det s k Lima-dokumentet... Det finns därför mycket starka skäl för oss att också för framtiden hävda att dopet är vägen in i församlingen, även om undantag kan göras, framför allt för dem som länge stått i en annan församlingsgemenskap." [David Lagergren], *Svenska Baptistsamfundets Årsbok* 1984, pp. 6f.

according to Lagergren, a tendency to reduce the enormous importance which the New Testament ascribes to baptism in their discussions about open membership and uniting with congregations of the Mission Covenant Church of Sweden. Particularly the function of baptism for incorporation into the Christian congregation has been questioned. The discussions within the Church of Sweden about baptism and membership/belonging, and also in BEM, ought to be a memento to the Baptists not to abandon the connection between baptism and membership preserved since the ancient church throughout church history. He states: "The congregation is not an association which a person joins - it is the Body of Christ into which a person is incorporated."[249]

He tries here as an advocate of the classic, Baptist teaching and practice to plead for believers' baptism: this baptism is an incorporation into both the universal church and the local church/congregation. On Baptist principles, membership of a Baptist church or congregation without baptism is impossible. It has been regarded as an absurdity.[250] And Franzén is of the opinion that conversion or commitment is not completed until the person is baptized and received into the congregation.[251]

As has been pointed out, also in BUS, membership in a local Baptist church without baptism has nevertheless in practice been, and still is, a possibility within the Baptist Union of Sweden. The connection between baptism and membership is not obvious. It is thus possible according to the statutes of some Baptist congregations because of for instance open membership, to be a Baptist member through confession of faith in Jesus Christ alone, i.e. without believers' baptism.[252] Associative and transferred

---

[249] "Församlingen är inte en förening som man går in i - det är Kristi kropp som man införlivas med." Lagergren, David, "Tradition och förnyelse II", VP, No. 26, 1984, p. 6.

[250] See the title "Församlingstillhörighet utan dop - en absurditet", Bergsten, Torsten, "Kyrkotillhörighet - medlemskap - bekännelse", Tro och Liv, No. 1, 1980, p. 38.

[251] Franzén, Bert, "Dopet och frälsningen. Kommentar till en artikel", VP, No. 42, 1989, p. 10.

[252] See for example Mjölby baptistförsamling and Norrmalms baptistförsamling, in Bergsten, Torsten, "Kyrkotillhörighet - medlemskap - bekännelse", Tro och Liv, No. 1, 1980, pp. 36f.

membership in addition to open membership may also be mentioned in this discussion.

The separation between baptism and membership is also found in the Baptist manual of 1955, where two different acts are mentioned. These seem to create the possibility of being a member of a Baptist church either through believers' baptism,[253] or through admission without any baptism,[254] which, however, has been questioned.[255]

Let us look at another example of alternative methods of incorporation from the latest manual of 1987. This manual shows understandably because of its ecumenical character openness towards other churches and traditions.

In the introduction, under the title *Välkomnande av nya medlemmar* (Welcoming of new members), it is said:

A word of welcome usually takes place at a Holy Communion service and is given the form of a festival, characterized by joy, kindness and warmth. Form A is for the welcome of those who are newly baptized. Form B, however, is for the welcome of those who have newly moved in with a

---

[253] *Handbok för Svenska Baptistsamfundet,* 3rd ed., 1955, pp. 11ff.

[254] Ibid. pp. 79ff. Eckerdal writes concerning the section *Medlemsintagning* (Admission as a Member) in this manual of 1955: "Baptists had been given two competing acts of admission in the manual." ("Baptismen hade i handboken fått två konkurrerande initiationshandlingar.") Eckerdal, Lars, *Vägen in i kyrkan,* 1981. p. 375. He makes the following comment: "In this act there is a connection with baptism both in the Scriptural reading (Acts 2:41) and in the concluding symbolic act (baptismal certificate). What is remarkable is rather that such an act exists at all, that is that baptism was not the act of admission *(att dopet inte utgjorde upptagningsakten).* Undoubtedly, this was an expression of the fact that baptism had become a private act of obedience, and that the connection between baptism and fellowship in the congregation was no longer self-evident. At the same time the new ritual is a sign of the dependence on and fellowship with the Swedish Free Churches." Ibid. He makes a reference to Torsten Bergsten, "Dopet och församlingen. Baptistisk tro och praxis i biblisk och ekumenisk belysning", *Dopet Dåben Dåpen,* 1957, in a footnote and writes: "The broken relation baptism - congregational fellowship is a theme in Bergsten 1957." Eckerdal, Lars, *Vägen in i kyrkan,* 1981. p. 375, footnote 77.

[255] Eckerdal's statement about the two competing acts is said by David Lagergren to be an overinterpretation *(övertolkning).* In Bergsten, Torsten, "Förändring genom konfrontation och dialog. Svenskt perspektiv", *Samfund i förändring,* 1997, p. 35.

certificate of changed domicile and of those who are received after confession of faith.[256]

We note the possibilities for becoming a member: by baptism, by certificate of changed domicile or by confession of faith. There are in this manual thus two alternatives, A and B, the latter with the heading: *Välkomnande av nyinflyttade och av dem som tas emot på bekännelse*, (Welcome of those who have newly moved in and those admitted after confession of faith).[257] In this last alternative there is not a word about baptism and membership. Some Scriptural references, John 15:4, 1 Cor. 12:27 and Jud. 20-21, are used when a person is admitted as a new member of a Baptist church.[258]

It seems possible, at least on certain occasions, to avoid the question of baptism altogether. For some statutes contain the possibility of becoming and remaining a member of a congregation without any baptism, by faith alone or by an expression of intent.[259]

---

[256] "Välkomnandet sker i regel vid nattvardsgudstjänst och formas till en högtid präglad av glädje, innerlighet och värme. Ordning A avser välkomnande av nydöpta, ordning B välkomnande av nyinflyttade med flyttningsbetyg och av dem som tas emot på bekännelse." *Till församlingens tjänst,* 1987, p. 192. We may note that the welcome, according to this manual, should preferably take place at the Holy Communion.

[257] *Till församlingens tjänst,* 1987, p. 195.

[258] Ibid.

[259] One of the many ecumenical congregations may be mentioned in this context Valsätrakyrkan in Uppsala, already dealt with in Part I. In its former statute (the constitution from 1978/1982) about membership it was said that, "the congregation in Valsätrakyrkan is an open fellowship which wants to realize the presence of Christ through being a Christian congregation. As members in the congregation we want, individually and as a group, to make the Gospel known and believed in our neighbourhood by pointing to the love of Christ through service, testimony and discipleship. Everybody who wants to live in communion with God through faith in Jesus Christ as Saviour and Lord can be a member of the congregation." Fridborg, Gunnar, "Ekumenik: Så här fungerar det i Valsätra", *VP,* No. 40, 1982, p. 8. (Note that the term *medlem (member)* is used and this regardless of baptism. The difficulty with the terminology - concerning for instance *belonging* and *membership* - has been noticed several times in the thesis.) The text of the statute is also to be found on the credal cards *(bekännelsekorten),* which are available in the church. The text is: "I have become acquainted with the text above and I want to share the fellowship, and to realize the aim expressed therein. Uppsala ... (date and name)." ("Jag har tagit del av ovanstående text och vill vara delaktig i den gemenskap och förverkliga den

This is also the case in some other ecumenical congregations in their presentations of themselves.[260]

The traditional, closed Baptist attitude, maintaining biblical believers' baptism, a *baptism of metanoia*, and a congregation consisting of members baptized by believers' baptism often by immersion, seems slowly to be weakened. Instead there is a more general Free Church attitude where faith alone may be sufficient for membership and incorporation into the (Baptist) church, and in ecumenical congregations (where Baptists also are involved). There are thus not only tendencies within the Baptist Union of Sweden but also examples at both the denominational and congregational levels of attempts to found membership and church unity not on the basis of faith and baptism (i.e. believers' baptism), but "only" on the basis of faith.[261] This is underlined in an editorial in *Veckoposten:*

Surely people attach importance to what the church believes and confesses. But how many people are not intensively longing for a spiritual home? And the chance to find such a place, where personal warmth and religious care

---

målsättning som där uttrycks. Uppsala ... (datum och namn)."), quoted in Bardh, Ulla, "Dop och medlemskap. En jämförelse mellan två ekumeniska församlingar; Storvreta frikyrkoförsamling och Valsätrakyrkan, baserad på eller speglad i 155 medlemmars svar på en enkät, hösten 1989", 1990, p. 11 note 5, [unpublished paper]. Ulla Bardh also discusses a new kind of member in the Valsätrakyrkan. See Lindberg, Erik, "1+1=mer än 2 vid samgående", *VP*, No. 40, 1991, p. 4. Cf, however, a new statute of this congregation, the constitution from 1995, where there is a tendency to give baptism a stronger position. See Bergsten, Torsten, "Den gemensamma församlingen – ett tecken om enhet", *Levande*, 1996, pp. 50-52, he discusses both this last constitution/statute and the earlier.

260 See for example Vårdkasekyrkans samkristna församling in Järfälla, Falkenbergs frikyrkoförsamling, which are both connected with the Baptist Union of Sweden and the Mission Covenant Church of Sweden, in Bergsten, Torsten, "Kyrkotillhörighet - medlemskap - bekännelse", *Tro och Liv*, No. 1, 1980, pp. 35f. See also ibid. p. 43, stating that the number of unbaptized will possibly increase in the ecumenical congregations *(ekumeniska frikyrkoförsamlingarna)*.

261 The radical suggestion by Baptist pastor, Harry Månsus, to abandon believers' baptism - although it certainly ought to be regarded as an exaggeration – cannot for that reason only be seen as a drawing-board product or curiosity. A tendency to attach less importance to baptism in regard to membership and incorporation into the church and the local congregation de facto exists. See earlier discussion in this part, chapter 2. 2.

mean more than upholding special points of dogma, will be of vital importance in the choice of church belonging *(kyrkotillhörighet).*262

If this is an expression of diversity and possibiblities for church unity may be questioned. Maybe it is an expression of another one-sided direction based on faith instead of (believers') baptism.

One of the other fundamental Baptist principles which probably has contributed to this reconsideration is the principle of freedom. The two Baptist pastors Hans Sundberg[263] and Berit Åqvist write:

> The idea of the congregation is a consequence of the biblical principle but it is also connected with the view of freedom... Only those who in faith place their lives personally and voluntarily under the lordship of Jesus can belong to the congregation.264

We find unchristened members or members baptized by infant baptism as well as "full" members, i.e. baptized by believers' baptism, not to forget the idea of "those ministered to", discussed earlier in the thesis – all in a Baptist context. Baptism is thus not at all necessary in order to be incorporated into a Baptist congregation, since faith alone is sufficient for incorporation and membership of the church. This is accepted by Baptists, but some

---

262 "Visst fäster människorna avseende vid vad kyrkan tror och bekänner. Men hur många längtar inte så intensivt efter ett andligt hem, att utsikten att finna ett sådant, där personlig värme och saklig religiös omsorg betyder mer än framhävandet av dogmatiska specialiteter, blir avgörande för valet av kyrkotillhörighet." "Ett trossamfund", [editorial], *VP*, No. 10, 1988, p. 4.

263 Sundberg became later on leader of Vineyard in Sweden.

264 Sundberg, Hans, Åqvist, Berit, "Bekännelse och bärande idéer", *Liv och tjänst*, 1988, p. 105. Note "belong" and not "member" is used. A reference is also made to the English Baptist theologian Wheeler Robinson in support of the idea that "The congregation is a spiritual fellowship made up of converted people who ackowledge the sovereign lordship of Christ." ("Församlingen är en andlig gemenskap, som utgöres av omvända människor, som erkänner Kristi suveräna herravälde.") Ibid. And Birgit Karlsson says that the congregation, which is the Body of Christ, is formed through the Word and deed of Christ and built up of those who confess Christ as Lord; "Församlingen är Kristi kropp, skapad genom Kristi ord och gärning och byggd med dem som bekänner Kristus som Herre." Karlsson, Birgit, "Församling med uppdrag i världen", *Liv och tjänst*, 1988, p. 18. She writes also: "The New Testament's picture of Christian discipleship is of a fellowship which is built up of those who believe in and confess Jesus Christ as Lord." Ibid. p. 17. Not a word is said about baptism in these examples, which may be interpreted as accidental or be regarded as something symptomatic of the Baptist Union.

form of baptism is preferable, i.e. believers' baptism or infant baptism.[265] This development in the Baptist Union of Sweden is not surprising in one way, due to the principle of freedom, open membership and the development of ecumenical congregations etc. It has, however, also been criticized.[266]

I have pointed out that there is openness within the Baptist Union of Sweden to recognize that a Baptist local church need not be identical with those baptized by believers' baptism. It may also include those baptized by infant baptism and even include unbaptized. This possibility of being a member of a church, and also, although not explicitly at least implicitly, working towards a church unity without baptism, is opposed to classic Baptist teaching and practice as well as to the view of *BEM* and to most of the other churches and denominations world-wide. It is an

---

[265] See for example the pastors Ulla Bardh and Christina Lindgren (Lindgren not a Baptist pastor but working within a Baptist context). Both discuss a generous concept of membership, with some form of baptism, see Lindberg, Erik, "1+1=mer än 2 vid samgående", *VP*, No. 40, 1991, p. 4. A distinction between *members* of and *"only friends"* of the congregation is also made, by the pastor Christina Lindgren, implying that the congregations today have at least "a double concept of membership" ("I de flesta församlingar finns 'vänner' till församlingen... en del inte har velat gå med för att de inte är säkra på sin tro...", "Uppdelningen i 'vänner' och 'medlemmar' innebär att församlingarna idag i praktiken har ett dubbelt medlemskapsbegrepp."), see Lindberg, Erik, "1+1=mer än 2 vid samgående", *VP*, No. 40, 1991, p. 4. And in for instance "Det finns en väg" it is stated: "Baptists do not deny that a person can become a member of the Body of Christ in other ways than by baptism, but maintain the practice of the early church as the normal way." ("Baptismen förnekar inte att en människa kan bli en lem i Kristi kropp på annat sätt än genom dop men håller fast vid urkristen praxis som den normala vägen.") "Det finns en väg", 1982, p. 12, [unpublished paper]. And the Baptist Lars Juhlin questions the need of baptism for membership. Juhlin, Lars, "Perspektiv på dopet", *VP*, No. 45, 1989, p. 7, see also Juhlin, Lars, "Behövs dopet?" *VP*, No. 40, 1989, p. 7; and in Nacka everyone who believes or seeks a faith and a working Christian fellowship is welcomed to membership (in the Baptist congregation). "Kyrkan i Nacka centrum byggs för alla som tror", *VP*, No. 5, 1991, p. 1; Ragni Lantz writes also about this church in Nacka, Lantz, Ragni, "Glädjedag i Nacka", *VP*, No. 5, 1991, p. 3.

[266] See for example Ruben Mild. He writes critically about this development in the Baptist Union: the conditions for membership have become lax etc. He is of the opinion that the fundamental biblical rules are abandoned; the ecumenical congregations are also a sign of the time. Mild, Ruben, "Var står vi och vart går vi?" *VP*, No. 14/15, 1990, p. 16.

intriguing finding that baptism does not (always) play as great a role for Baptists as is usually assumed.[267]

From this study we can understand that it is not an easy task to identify the ecclesiology of the Baptist Union, if incorporation into the universal church and the local church takes place by baptism and/or faith, for there is thus more than one possibility. The Baptist Union of Sweden of today may in one way be characterized as combining different "church-traditions". It has officially for decades exclusively practised believers' baptism (see category 2 above).[268] There is, however, also especially due to open membership and the development of the ecumenical congregations an openness for category 4, i.e. that baptism is not absolutely necessary for membership, and also an openness for category 3, in that there is a recognition of some infant baptisms.

Briefly, the discussion above has revealed that there are apparent problems with ecclesiology, and the issues of baptism and membership. There are different answers to the questions of ecclesiology and the incorporation (by faith and/or baptism) into the universal church and/or into the local Baptist congregation. This also concerns the meaning of the concepts "church", "congregation", "Kingdom of God", "the Body of Christ", "belonging" and "membership" etc.

BUS writes for example about a line of demarcation between belonging and membership. We have, however, in this last discussion found that there is confusion about these concepts. There is thus a difference not only between belonging and membership, but also between membership and membership etc. So far, it can be established that there is no unequivocal opinion concerning the concepts of "belonging" and "membership", nor

---

[267] A Swedish Lutheran professor, Per Erik Persson, has also pointed this out: "I have had the peculiar experience in the dialogue between Lutherans and Baptists at the global level which has now ended, that baptism obviously means more to a Lutheran than to the average Baptist." ("En egendomlig erfarenhet jag gjort vid den nu avslutade dialogen mellan lutheraner och baptister på global nivå är att dopet uppenbarligen betyder långt mer för en lutheran än för baptister i gemen.") Persson, Per Erik, " 'Ni utgör Kristi kropp och är var för sig delar av den' (1 Kor 12:27), Vad innebär det att vara församling eller kyrka i Norden i dag?", Ekumenisk Orientering, No. 2, 1990, p. 8. See also Österberg, Edvin, "Evangelisk kristendom", VP, No. 48, 1978, p. 10, "Majoriteten av världens kristna, som praktiserar spädbarnsbegjutning, lägger större vikt vid dopet än vad exempelvis baptisterna gör."

[268] This is also the view of BUS.

concerning the question of the incorporation into and membership of the church (i.e. universal church and the local Baptist congregation). The incorporation can according to Baptist opinions take place in different manners, for example by baptism and/or by faith. This is also seen concretely in many different ways, for example in congregational statutes. To generalize, the Baptist Union tries to associate on the one hand with other Baptist denominations or "groups", and on the other hand with infant baptizing churches.

The classic Baptist view of baptism and the congregation consisting of those baptized by believers' baptism (through immersion) - sometimes implying "re-baptism" - has often been, and as a matter of fact still is, a stumbling block in ecumenical, bi- and multilateral dialogues, and in the realization of church unity. In this and former chapters we have, however, seen proof that a reconsideration of baptism, with implications on ecclesiology and membership, incorporation into the church and the local Baptist congregation (or ecumenical congregation), is in progress in the Baptist Union of Sweden.

The openness, ambiguity and plurality concerning baptism and ecclesiology, which may be regarded problematic and challenging, nevertheless opens up interesting possibilities for it. Obviously the ecclesiological issue needs to be deepened and made theologically more precise, as do the issues of the "fall", the relation between *metanoia* and baptism, the relation between baptism and the Kingdom of God, the church and the local congregation etc. When, however, different confessional and denominational traditions meet and are sometimes united – in meetings, congregations, consultations, ecumenical work and in theological discussions, articles, papers etc. - a diversity appears which can result in a dogmatic and organisational vagueness, sometimes even confusion. Something of the diversity within the Baptist Union will be dealt with in the next chapter.

8. Diversity within the Baptist Union of Sweden – Opening up Possibilities of Church Unity

For many decades the Baptist Union of Sweden has taken a challenging position in its emphasis on believers' baptism in relation to many of the other churches and denominations in Sweden, with implications for ecclesiology (the congregation of believers, baptized by believers' baptism) and ecumenism. There has, however, also been openness towards ecumenical strivings.[269] This has become concrete especially in later decades when Baptists have co-operated with other congregations and also been integrated into other contexts than exclusively Baptist ones. This has certainly influenced its theology and contributed to a reconsideration of baptism.

There are, however, as has already been indicated earlier in the thesis, various opinions about this development. This will be further dealt with in this chapter in the study of some interesting articles. They point partly to compromises and displacements of accent on the question of baptism ("having it both ways"), and partly to the difficulties in handling the question of baptism in both an ecumenical and an intra-Baptist context.

Two bilateral, ecumenical discussions will be added as examples of what happens to the question of baptism in a Baptist-ecumenical context: *Baptism in Baptist - Congregationalist Discussions - Steps towards Church Unity?*, and *Baptism in Baptist - Catholic Discussions - Further Steps towards Church Unity?* These two discussions point to various emphases within the Baptist Union concerning baptism, which, of course, have consequences in ecclesiology as well as in ecumenism.

---

[269] See Part I, especially chapter 9.

8.1. Compromises Concerning the Question of Baptism

That the issue of baptism is problematic in the ecumenical context has become apparent several times. There is sometimes an emphasis on believers' baptism.[270] David Lagergren declares for example that it is *"important today in the same way as a hundred years ago to preach, practise and struggle for believers' baptism."*[271] He even gives expression to the idea that it is the mission of the Baptists to work for believers' baptism, or with his own words, "to work for a return to ancient baptismal practice and theology."[272] He does not explain what is meant with this statement.

Lagergren refers in another article to a statement from the conference *Graninge II*, that representatives from the denominations practising believers' baptism do not find it possible to regard infant baptism as a baptism in accord with the New Testament.[273] We have, however, also seen other opinions within the Baptist Union of Sweden.

The issue of baptism is still a theologically and consequently ecumenically unsolved problem which delays the process of church unity. In spite of the intricate theological issues of baptism, a

---

270 See *BUS*.

271 "Det bör också sägas att det är alltför enkelt att förklara de delar av vår tro, där vi i de olika samfunden skiljer oss åt, för oviktiga. Som jag ser det, är det *lika nödvändigt i dag som för hundra år sedan att förkunna, praktisera och kämpa för de troendes dop.* Detta dop har vunnit terräng på ett nästan otroligt sätt under vårt eget århundrade, men fortfarande har det litet eller intet utrymme i flertalet av de stora kyrkofamiljerna i världen." Lagergren, David, "Ekumenik 83", *VP*, No. 1/2, 1983, p. 2. Italics mine. See also Axelson, Einar, "Klara signaler!", *VP*, No. 7, 1986, p. 10. He writes: Have not the Baptists struggled for the biblical baptism, so can we wave it aside?... We have a responsibility towards the Bible and our fathers, who often were killed on account of their faith. Baptism [i.e. believers' baptism, my remark] and the congregation of believers are the great Baptist contributions to Christianity. ("Har inte baptisterna kämpat för det vi ser vara ett bibliskt dop, kan vi verkligen fuska bort det?... Vi har en helig förpliktelse mot bibeln och våra fäder, som ofta med sitt liv fått plikta för sin tro. Dop och troendeförsamling är baptisternas stora bidrag till kristenheten.") Axelson, Einar, "Ekumenisk besinning", *VP*, No. 27, 1987, p. 15.

272 "Sex frågor till David Lagergren, intervju: Birgit Karlsson", *Året*, 1971, p. 9.

273 Lagergren, David, "Dopsamtal", *VP*, No. 3, 1977, p. 2. See also Part I, chapter 9.3. where *Graninge II*, and also *Graninge I* and *III*, are discussed.

---

process towards church unity, in particular at the grass-root level in the establishment of new kinds of constellations such as the ecumenical congregations (or united churches), can be discerned. Of course, difficulties arise on more than one level when congregations are united to one another, among other things since there is often not only one baptismal understanding or practice but several. We understand that from a classic Baptist point of view it is difficult, for many even impossible, to recognize other churches' baptisms (in this case infant baptism) for the sake of ecumenism.

Although there on the whole is a sceptical attitude towards tradition within the Baptist Union of Sweden,[274] it is obvious that traditions of different kinds also have influence.[275] And the problem of baptism becomes concrete for the Baptist Union of Sweden in relation to the Mission Covenant Church of Sweden in particular.[276] It might seem more natural to approach other Baptist denominations or "groups", such as the Pentecostal Movement, Örebro (Baptist) Mission, Holiness Union Mission etc.,[277] where all have the same practice and partially the same view of baptism. There are, however, not only theological, ideological reasons which determine whether church unity is possible, but also pragmatic, rational and psychological causes.

---

[274] See Part I, for example chapter 2., (for example *sola Scriptura*).

[275] Valter Mattsson is of the opinion that the greatest obstacle to ecumenical co-operation is loyality towards one's own tradition (*den egna traditionen*), and that congregations with a higher average age often have more difficulty in breaking with tradition. See "Baptisterna vill samverka i ödesfrågor", *Svenska Kyrkans Tidning*, No. 31/32, 1989, p. 9.

[276] Lagergren writes concerning the establishment of an ecumenical congregation from a Baptist and a Mission Covenant Church congregation: "Naturally the question of baptism caused problems, when these congregations were going to write their statutes and congregational order." Lagergren, David, "Lokalekumeniken och dopet", *VP*, No. 37, 1978, p. 2. See also Lagergren, David, "Dopet och enheten", *VP*, No. 15, 1978, p. 2; Österberg, Edvin, "Enhet och samverkan", *VP*, No. 25/26, 1982, p. 10. See, however, what I write about ecumenical congregations in Part I, chapter 9.5. and also in this part, for example in the discussion between Birgit Karlsson and Lars Lindberg later on, chapter 8.2.1.

[277] This is also stated for example by Einar Axelson: "Låt oss därför gå samman med de andra döparsamfunden först." Axelson, Einar, "Viktigare än ekumeniken", *VP*, No. 18, 1988, p. 11.

Difficulties and ambiguities may thus also exist although the two congregations which are going to unite with each other do not have any greater problems regarding theological matters. As a matter of fact, an agreement on the issue of baptism does not necessarily imply better conditions for church unity. I will give one example which may illustrate this, i.e. Kristianstads baptistförsamling.

Before this congregation was established in 1986, an inquiry was made in 1983 in the two existing Baptist congregations on the attitude of their members towards the establishment of an ecumenical congregation. A majority of the members in Elimförsamlingen, which co-operated with the Örebro (Baptist) Mission, was against unification. This indicates that unity and unification (on the congregational level and we may suspect also on the denominational) depends on more than agreement or consensus in the question of baptism. In Betelförsamlingen or Kristianstads baptistförsamling, which belonged to the Baptist Union of Sweden, the majority was, however, positive to establishing a union. The result of the decision to unite these two congregations and establish a new congregation was that five members left Elimförsamlingen.[278] The new congregation was affiliated to both the Baptist Union of Sweden and the Örebro (Baptist) Mission.[279]

David Lagergren finds an explanation of this problem. He writes that experiences from several places in Sweden confirm an observation that has been made earlier that the result of unification depends completely on the situation.[280] He develops this:

Where two congregations approach each other seriously, look at the difficulties, and overcome them, it bears fruit for the Kingdom of God; while ecumenism for the sake of cutting costs or fatigue hardly produces any

---

[278] At the vote which preceded and led to the decision to establish a new congregation, there were two persons, one member from each congregation, who voted against the proposal. One member refrained from voting. Others who hesitated or were negative did not participate at all in the vote. Those who participated, the majority from both congregations, were positive to the proposal. Swedberg, Bo, "När ni nu enats kan man ju tro", VP, No. 11, 1986, p. 4.

[279] Ibid.

[280] The places he mentions here are Boden and Piteå in the very north of Sweden.

change at all. *What matters is renewal in the Spirit.* To try to come together may be a stage in the renewal.[281]

And Birgit Karlsson writes in a similar vein as Lagergren concerning two congregations united into one:

Practical, personnel or economic reasons should never be sufficient to unite two congregations. The power to grow in unity is of a profounder kind.[282]

It is of special interest, bearing in mind Lagergren's view on believers' baptism, to find that he as a matter of fact is positive to co-operation between the Baptist Union of Sweden, the Mission Covenant Church of Sweden and the Örebro (Baptist) Mission, where different baptismal teachings and practices obviously exist. This also appears strange in the light of the discussion above where he strongly pleaded for believers' baptism. But he writes himself:

One thinks that it should be easier for a local Baptist congregation to co-operate with a congregation of the Örebro (Baptist) Mission, since they have the same view of baptism. The psychological situation, however, due in part to a similar development, the Trilateral Denominational Consultations etc., makes it in several places just as natural to co-operate with congregations of the Mission Covenant Church of Sweden as with congregations of the Örebro (Baptist) Mission.[283]

Lagergren does, however, not only mention co-operation, but also the possibility of a new constellation of denominations between the three. He writes:

Such a constellation has hardly been imaginable previously but is today on account of the changes which have occurred, most recently exemplified by the first fusion between a congregation of the Mission Covenant Church of Sweden and a congregation of the Örebro (Baptist) Mission.[284]

---

[281] Lagergren, David, "Samgående och förnyelse", *VP*, No. 50, 1982, p. 2. Italics mine.

[282] Karlsson, Birgit, "Dopet - en central fråga när församlingar går samman. Missionsföreståndaren kommenterar", *VP*, No. 40, 1987, p. 11.

[283] "Sagt i veckan: David Lagergren i Svensk Veckotidning", *VP*, No. 10, 1977, p. 2. Lagergren states concerning the relation of the Baptist Union of Sweden to the Örebro (Baptist) Mission and the Mission Covenant Church of Sweden, in a possible new federation: "Both or nothing.", see Arvidson, Thorvald, "Baptistsamfundet. Missionsförbundet. Hur har vi det? Hur vill vi ha det? Samtalskonferens om möjligheter och problem i gemensam verksamhet", *VP*, No. 50, 1982, p. 6. Concerning the Trilateral Denominational Consultations, see Part I, for example chapter 9.2.

[284] Lagergren, David, "Ekumenik 83 (II)", *VP*, No. 3, 1983, p. 2.

He thus supports unity between the Baptist Union and the Mission Covenant Church of Sweden, in spite of at least one important theological difference, i.e. that the Mission Covenant Church of Sweden also practises infant baptism.[285]

To co-operate and even work for unity with a church that baptizes infants must have been an impossibility in the first years of the Baptist Union. Lagergren is, of course, conscious of the dilemma. It is, however, according to him, considerably lessened on account of the fact that believers' baptism has a strong position within many of the congregations of the Mission Covenant Church of Sweden. He also gives another argument for the work with the Mission Covenant Church of Sweden in this context, namely that the similarity of church structure based on congregationalist principles is, of course, an advantage.[286] There seems to be a modification here in comparison with other statements by him.[287]

That the issue of baptism must necessarily be a stumbling block in ecumenical work seems therefore not always to be the case. There is an openness to diversity. The statements by Lagergren imply a unity which may consist of denominations holding different views on such crucial issues as baptism, ecclesiology and membership. He includes the Mission Covenant Church of Sweden in the work for church unity, stating:

> We are closest to the congregations of the Örebro (Baptist) Mission and of the Mission Covenant Church of Sweden... The Mission Covenant Church of Sweden cannot and shall not be left out. A fellowship in our country which includes the Mission Covenant Church of Sweden, the Baptist Union of Sweden and the Örebro (Baptist) Mission would have a vitality and

---

[285] This act, infant baptism ought by Lagergren to be interpreted as a blessing. Lagergren writes, however, already in 1969 about faith alone without baptism, as the basis of membership of a congregation. ("... tron är så viktig i dopet att den kan fungera också utan dop.") Lagergren, David, *Enhetsförslaget och dopfrågan*, 1969, p. 10. See also *BUS*.

[286] Lagergren, David, "Ekumenik 83 (II)", *VP*, No. 3, 1983, p. 2. See also, for example, chapter 8.2.1. below, and Part I, chapter 9.4.2.

[287] Even in the same article he writes, concerning the Mission Covenant Church of Sweden, that a marked difference remains, in that infants are baptized within the Mission Covenant Church of Sweden, which is not the case in Baptist congregations. Ibid. See also for instance Lagergren, David, "Ekumenik 83", *VP*, No. 1/2, 1983, p. 2; Lagergren, David, "Inlägg är välkomna", *VP*, No. 51/52, 1983, p. 9.

importance which would benefit the Kingdom of God in Sweden and in other countries.[288]

If this vision or expectation is realistic or not, is difficult to say – at least as far as concerns the Baptist Union of Sweden.

New perspectives and possibilities in the work for church unity also with other congregations than the traditional Baptist ones, the Örebro (Baptist) Mission, the Pentecostal Movement, seem to open up. Bergsten writes:

> Despite the practice of infant baptism within the Mission Covenant Church of Sweden, in addition to believers' baptism, the Baptist Union of Sweden has more in common with this denomination in vital respects than with the Baptist Pentecostal Movement and the Örebro (Baptist) Mission. It is a question of similarity in mentality, spirituality, piety and *not of doctrinal unity.*[289]

He also points to their common root in the 19th century revival, the closeness in the life of faith and piety, several projects of co-operation etc. He gives expression to the expectation that a common Free Church will be established.[290]

That a change is taking place both on a denominational and in particular on a congregational level is confirmed by the former General Secretary, Birgit Karlsson, who states:

> It would be to flee from and falsify reality if it was not realized that the situation in the Swedish Free Church movement is much changed, also in a

---

[288] Lagergren, David, "Jag har en dröm", *VP*, No. 24, 1981, p. 2. See a comment on this in "Lokalekumeniken trycker på", [editorial], *VP*, No. 30, 1981, p.2; and also Wiktell, Sven, E., "Missionsföreståndare i samspråk: Nu är det dags att sluta sucka – det finns så mycket inspirerande", *VP*, No. 31/32, 1981, pp. 11-12. See also Swedberg, Bo, "Börje Hammarroth efter 18 år: - Jag skulle önskat få se nya samfundsmönster växa fram", *VP*, No. 20/21, 1985, p. 3, Börje Hammarroth states that *if* the three churches, the Baptist Union of Sweden, the Mission Covenant Church of Sweden and the Örebro (Baptist) Mission, were joined in a new fellowship, it would have far-reaching consequences for other denominations.

[289] "...Det handlar om överensstämmelse i mentalitet, spiritualitet, fromhetsart och *inte om läromässig enhet.*" Bergsten, Torsten, "Samfundsmedvetande och kongregationalism i svensk frikyrklighet", *Kyrkohistorisk årsskrift* 93, 1993, p. 144. Italics mine.

[290] Ibid. p. 145.

relatively short perspective. I would hold that the most decisive changes concern the situation of the local congregations.[291]

She is of the opinion that within a number of years the picture of the denominational structures will no longer be recognizable, and that no denomination will remain intact (inget samfund bevaras intakt) when the changes start seriously taking place.[292]

We find thus that there is a questioning within the Baptist Union of Sweden itself of its continued existence. Börje Hammarroth, former president of the Central Board, is himself convinced that a radical change of denominational pattern must occur.[293] It is the existence of ecumenical congregations which has basically changed the situation.[294] These ecumenical congregations, which are not even mentioned in BUS, have thus many consequences. They have had, and still have, an impact on the Baptist Union of Sweden and on other denominations as well.[295]

---

[291] Karlsson, Birgit, "Det nödvändiga samtalet om tron och praktiken", VP, No. 47, 1987, p. 4.

[292] "Min tro är att bilden av samfundsstrukturerna inom ett antal år inte längre är igenkännlig. Det finns ingenting som säger att t ex Svenska baptistsamfundet skulle försvinna i den omstöpning som säkert kommer. Mycket tydliga tecken talar för att när förändringarna på allvar tar sin början inget samfund bevaras intakt." Swedberg, Bo, "Både det tveklösa hoppet och en utväg trots allt", VP, No. 15, 1987, p. 3. This has, however, partially been confirmed, see for example Nybygget – kristen samverkan.

[293] "Jag är personligen helt övertygad om att det måste bli en radikal förändring av samfundsmönstret." Swedberg, Bo, "Börje Hammarroth efter 18 år: -Jag skulle önskat få se nya samfundsmönster växa fram", VP, No. 20/21, 1985, p. 3.

[294] See for instance "Nu!", [editorial], VP, No. 51/52, 1987, p. 4, which maintains that the situation within Free Church ecumenism has since ten years ago totally changed. The reason for this is the existence of ecumenical congregations. See also Swedberg, Bo, "25 år efter New Delhi: Nu har lokalekumeniken börjar blomma för fullt", VP, No. 7, 1986, p. 3.

[295] Besides the Baptist Union of Sweden, denominations such as for instance the Scandinavian Independent Baptist Union, the Holiness Union Mission, the United Methodist Church in Sweden, the Pentecostal Movement, the Swedish Alliance Mission, the Mission Covenant Church of Sweden and the Örebro (Baptist) Mission have been involved. Tecken om enhet, 1991, p. 17. Bergsten also mentions the Church of Sweden and the Swedish Evangelical Mission. Bergsten, Torsten, "Ekumenik, vision och verklighet", Tro och Liv, No. 1, 1986, p. 12. See also Palm, Irving, "Frikyrklig lokalekumenik – exemplet gemensamma församlingar", Tro & Tanke 1997:3, pp. 45-68; Skog,

Because of all this there is, of course, a discussion about baptism within and also beyond the Baptist Union of Sweden. It is not unimaginable that the traditional Baptist congregations will cease to exist, as a change from a closed Baptist attitude (recognizing only believers' baptism, the principle of congregationalism etc.) towards a more open Baptist/Free Church attitude (recognizing infant baptism, questioning some believers' baptism, congregation consisting also of "only" believers etc.) takes place. This so-called open attitude has sometimes had an impact on the Baptist Union through the decades. It has become concrete in different ways and may be confirmed for example by open Holy Communion, open membership, ecumenical commitment, common service manuals etc., and especially ecumenical congregations, where there is diversity and compromise, also concerning baptism.[296]

BEM writes about the *one baptism*, which may be either infant baptism or believers' baptism. Baptists have, as I have pointed out, in general problems with this wording, and consequently also when the importance of mutual recognition of baptism is underlined.[297] This is also the case in *BUS*.

We recall that the Baptist movement started as a protest against infant baptism and against the ecclesiology of the monolithic State Church practising infant baptism. There are, however, congregations with members of the Baptist Union having *both* infant baptism *and* believers' baptism, and having both a baptismal font and a baptismal pool.[298] The Baptist Union of Sweden is in a

---

Margareta, "Frikyrkosamfundens medlemstal i landets kommuner 1995", Ibid. pp. 69-147.

[296] Bergsten, Torsten, "Enheten i Kristus", *Tro, Frihet, Gemenskap*, 1998, p. 232, pp. 228ff.; Bergsten, Torsten, "Anders Wiberg, dopet och de kristnas enhet", *Tro och Liv*, No. 4, 1988, pp. 19ff.

[297] Bergsten states that Baptists have certain difficulties with the statement in *BEM* that many of the churches in Christianity are on the way towards mutual recognition of baptism. According to him these difficulties are a challenge, however, to deal with the issue of baptism. He states that the vision in the New Testament of one faith and one baptism into the one Body, which is Christ's Church on earth, puts Baptists under the obligation not to remain in positions inherited from the past. Bergsten, Torsten, "Svenska kyrkan i den aktuella debatten. Tre perspektiv", *Kyrkohistorisk årsskrift* 84, 1984, p. 36.

[298] See *Tecken om enhet*, 1991, especially pp. 91-96. Another example of compromises, an "openness" and reconsideration is that infant baptism is practised in a Baptist congregation; it is, however, administered by priests of

dynamic and challenging process - having also unbaptized (young or adult) members in its midst. This is an interesting "opening process", and I want to illustrate it.

For example in Hult (from the 1880's and onwards), men and women were gathering, as in some other places in Sweden, for pietist meetings, exclusively practising believers' baptism - sometimes as in Hult in the mill-pond.[299] Hults baptistförsamling (Hult Baptist Congregation) was, however, established (by 30 people) first in 1919. What has happened to this Baptist congregation?

In 1965 Hult Baptist Congregation was dissolved. The cause was the decreasing number of members. The remaining 23 members then became members of Eksjö Baptist Congregation.[300] In 1985 the Baptists in Hult, who then were members of Eksjö Baptist Congregation, were united with a Mission Covenant Church congregation in Hult in a new congregation, Hults frikyrkoförsamling (Hult Free Church Congregation). It was affiliated to both the Baptist Union of Sweden and the Mission Covenant Church of Sweden.[301] The leader of this congregation, Bruno Gustafsson, comments on the change which has resulted in this ecumenical congregation:

what was not feasible ten years ago is now the result of a natural development.[302]

---

the Church of Sweden, see for example Wiktell, Sven, E., "Svenska kyrkans präst döpte 'baptistiskt' i baptistkapellet", VP, No. 51/52, 1979, p. 8; Sundell, Dan-Gustaf, "Rissnekyrkan efter fyra år. Nu på god väg att bli hela samhällets kyrka", VP, No. 10, 1989, pp. 2f. Earlier in this part, I also gave examples of Swedish Baptist pastors administering infant baptism, see chapter 2.1.

[299] Wiktell, Sven E, "Hult i Småland. Frikyrkoförsamlingen som växte fram ur behovet", VP, No. 5, 1985, p. 15.

[300] Eksjö is a small town not far from Hult in the southern part of Sweden.

[301] Wiktell, Sven E, "Hult i Småland. Frikyrkoförsamlingen som växte fram ur behovet", VP, No. 5, 1985, p. 15. When the Baptists in Hult were asked about being members of this new ecumenical congregation, 11 out of 12 members answered that they intended to become members of the new congregation. Ibid.

[302] "... det som för bara 10 år sedan inte hade varit genomförbart är nu resultatet av en naturlig utveckling." Ibid.

This is only one concrete example, there are others. I have mentioned some of them earlier,[303] and there are both theological reasons and other causes for this unitive process.[304] In other words, some Baptist congregations are changed and even dissolved, or rather integrated with other congregations.[305]

---

[303] See Part I, especially about the ecumenical congregations, chapter 9.5.

[304] See Wiktell, Sven, E., "Åseda. Grunden för arbetet är bönegrupperna", VP, No. 3, 1989, p. 2, mentioning the spiritual dimension, prayer groups; "Baptist- och missionsförsamlingar går samman", VP, No. 26/27, 1990, p. 12 and Swedberg, Bo, "Mariakyrkans församling i Katrineholm: Ungdomarna visade vägen till enhet", VP, No. 50, 1990, pp. 8f., mentioning that the youth groups have been the driving force towards the uniting of the two into one ecumenical congregation; Klingsbo, Karl-Edward, "Vasakyrkan i Filipstad. Två år under Guds ledning", VP, No. 6, 1990, p. 5, mentioning financial problems and the high age of the members; Hultberg, Per-Åke, "En baptistpojkes funderingar", VP, No. 36, 1992, p. 11, also discusses the role of economics in forcing different congregations to unite. See also Tecken om enhet, 1991, pp. 19f.

[305] Some further examples of ecumenical congregations may be mentioned which are dealt with in Veckoposten (round 1990), see for example Swedberg, Bo, " -Vi vill ha en öppen kyrka i Fjugesta", VP, No. 37, 1990, pp. 8f., (between Baptist Union of Sweden and Mission Covenant Church of Sweden); Skoglund, Gunnar, "Två församlingar blev en i Sveg", VP, No. 9, 1992, p. 6, (Baptist Union of Sweden and Mission Covenant Church of Sweden); "Ny församling i Malmö", [Ref.], VP, No. 17, 1989, p. 5, (Baptist Union of Sweden and Örebro (Baptist) Mission); Lantz, Ragni, "Östermalmskyrkan öppnar sin famn", VP, No. 49, 1989, pp. 10f., (Baptist Union and Örebro (Baptist) Mission); Björkman, Bertil, "Köpings baptister återförenade", VP, No. 27/28, 1991, p. 5, (Baptist Union and Örebro (Baptist) Mission); Swedberg, Bo, "Kristianstad: Här fungerar en gemensam församling", VP, No. 11, 1992, pp. 8f., (Baptist Union and Örebro (Baptist) Mission); "Levande stenar i nytt församlingsbygge", [Ragni Lantz p. 8, Bo Swedberg p. 9], VP, No. 16, 1990, pp. 8f., (Baptist Union, Scandinavian Independent Baptist Union and Holiness Union Mission); "Gemensam församling i Katrineholm", VP, No. 50, 1990, p. 1, and Mattsson, Valter, "Högtidlig invigning med fullsatt kyrka", VP, No. 50, 1990, p. 9, about the same congregation, (Baptist Union of Sweden and Mission Covenant Church of Sweden); Lagerström, Christine, "Alla är välkomna till Vasakyrkan", VP, No. 17, 1991, p. 5, in Hedemora, (Baptist Union of Sweden, Scandinavian Independent Baptist Union and Mission Covenant Church of Sweden); "Framtid för frikyrkan?" [editorial], VP, No. 15, 1989, p. 4.

See also Bergsten, Torsten, "Enheten i Kristus", Tro, Frihet, Gemenskap, 1998, p. 232, writing about Örebro första baptistförsamling Betel, an ordinary Baptist congregation that has had significant influxes of members

We can take it more or less for granted that in some of these ecumenical congregations it is in all likelihood difficult, if not impossible, to maintain the traditional, Baptist "protest" against an ecclesiology which is based on infant baptism. Originally diametrically opposed opinions, teachings and practices are now under the same roof. This implies that former antagonists do not only today recognize each other as Christian sisters and brothers. Baptists also work together with Christians from other churches and denominations. Sometimes even within one and the same congregation, where infant baptism, an abomination to traditional, closed Baptism, and believers' baptism are practised. There are obviously, although very few, some unbaptized members within the Baptist congregations,[306] but this is evidently still more usual in the ecumenical congregations.

There is a change taking place within the Baptist Union towards a great variety of possibilities in the ecumenical process - a step which sometimes seems to be close for example to the position which the Mission Covenant Church of Sweden has defended for more than 100 years.[307]

---

from other denominations since the 1980's. In 1997, there were about 500 members, about 180 from other denominational traditions than the Baptist Union: from the Pentecostal Movement, the Mission Covenant Church of Sweden, Örebro (Baptist) Mission, Salvation Army, Scandinavian Independent Baptist Union, Holiness Union Mission, the United Methodist Church in Sweden, Swedish Alliance Mission, the Church of Sweden. Eighteen new members were received on the basis of a confession of faith without baptism. Ibid. See also Palm, Irving, "Frikyrklig lokalekumenik – exemplet gemensamma församlingar", Tro & Tanke 1997:3, especially pp. 56f.; Skog, Margareta, "Frikyrkosamfundens medlemstal i landets kommuner 1995", Tro & Tanke 1997:3, especially pp. 72ff., 78f., p. 118.

[306] Bergsten, Torsten, "Dopet i ekumeniskt perspektiv", VP, No. 9, 1988, p. 7.

[307] See Part I about the Mission Covenant Church of Sweden, chapter 9.4.2. See also for instance the constitution of the Mission Covenant Church of Sweden, adopted by the General Conference in 1964, with the emphasis on faith (not baptism). It states that the congregation wants to admit into its fellowship anyone who confesses faith in Jesus Christ as Lord and Saviour. Further, the church as the universal congregation is one, holy and catholic (en, helig och allmännelig). A making visible of the fellowship of the saints would mean that all those who believe in Christ in the same place were united and brought into a completely committed fellowship with each other by the Holy Spirit. Svenska Missionsförbundets Årsberättelse 1964, 1965, pp. 115f.

This displacement of emphasis within the Baptist Union of Sweden must be regarded as a deviation from the earlier predominant teaching and practice of believers' baptism, and also from Baptists' efforts to maintain the principle of believers' baptism on the biblical principle that baptism is regarded as the command of the risen Lord.[308] In view of classic Baptist principles and of Baptist history, the compromises concerning baptism have unavoidable implications for the Baptist Union of Sweden at both the congregational and denominational levels, and are, of course, a challenge. Therefore, it is understandable to find criticisms and protests by some Baptists against the development taking place within the Baptist Union of Sweden.[309]

This development is partially urged on by a number of Baptists - due naturally to what is taking place in theological research and in ecumenical discussions, and also in the practical field especially at the congregational level - through among other things *Veckoposten.* The Baptist pastor Ruben Mild (1918-1998) writes about concessions by leaders concerning the vital questions of baptism and membership in the Baptist congregations.[310] He accuses the Baptist organ, *Veckoposten,* since this works for church unity

---

[308] Bergsten writes in 1964 that baptism in some form, by the command of the Lord, must be regarded as unavoidable for belonging *(tillhörighet)* [Bergsten here uses the term *belonging*, i.e. not *membership*, my remark] to a Baptist congregation. Bergsten, Torsten, "Associativt och öppet medlemskap", *Baptistpredikanternas studieblad*, No. 2, 1964, p. 11. This was before the decision on open membership in 1969. See also *BEM*, refering to the command of the Lord: "St Matthew records that the risen Lord, when sending his disciples into the world, commanded them to baptize (Matt. 28:18-20)." *B 1*.

[309] The Baptist pastor Andor Gustafsson states: "It must be considered a tragedy, if we both as individuals and congregations betray our vocation in this respect [to preach and practise believers' baptism in accordance with the New Testament]." Gustafsson, Andor, "Att förverkliga Jesu bön om enhet", *VP*, No. 13, 1984, p. 15.

[310] Mild, Ruben, "Nya testamentets dopsyn bör gälla!", *VP*, No. 48, 1987, p. 6. Mild refers in his article to Franzén, 1965. Bert Franzén writes that he does not see that two qualified baptismal forms can exist side by side in the same denomination. This cannot be the milieu for a strong Baptist movement. Franzén, Bert, "Har dopet någon enande kraft?" *VP*, No. 8, 1965, p. 10. Bergsten writes: "Även om antalet odöpta frikyrkomedlemmar är ringa, är deras existens principiellt likväl tänkvärd." Bergsten, Torsten, "Dopet i ekumeniskt perspektiv", *VP*, No. 9, 1988, p. 7.

between the Baptist Union of Sweden and the Mission Covenant
Church of Sweden:

A good deal of the material in *Veckoposten*, also outside the editorial,
encourages the ecumenical trend between the Baptist Union of Sweden and
the Mission Covenant Church of Sweden. Those 'who preserve tradition and
guard older positions' are criticized.[311]

He states that individuals and congregations suffer agony
because well-founded biblical truths are being abandoned.[312]

David Lagergren also writes, (cf., however, his earlier discussions
above), about the risk of a weakening of the Baptist fellowship and
troublesome compromises particularly concerning the question of
baptism.[313] He claims regarding the question of baptism and also
regarding the relation between the Baptist Union of Sweden and the
Mission Covenant Church of Sweden that the demarcation line
between these denominations is above all about the issue of

---

[311] "Åtskilligt material i VP, även utanför ledarsidan, puffar för den ekumeniska
trenden Baptistsamfundet - Missionsförbundet... 'Traditionsbevararna och
positionsbevakarna' får en kraftig släng". Mild, Ruben, "Vart är vi på väg?",
VP, No. 9, 1988, p. 10.

[312] "Risken är stor att vi håller på att göra oss urarva vårt religiösa arv! ... Hur
ska baptisternas ledning ha det? Talar man inte med dubbla tungor om
viktiga frågor? Och under tiden våndas enskilda och församlingar över att
välgrundade bibliska sanningar håller på att överges." Ibid.

[313] "I intet annat samfund har så många lokalförsamlingar gått samman under
1970- och 1980-talen med församlingar från andra samfund. Det skall inte
fördöljas att varnande röster höjts mot denna utveckling. Risken för en
urholkning av den egna gemenskapen och för en minskning av den
ekumeniska handlingsfriheten har påpekats. Vidare har besvärliga
kompromisser i trosfrågor, särskilt dopfrågan, måst utarbetas." Lagergren,
David, "ÖM och ekumeniken", *VP*, No. 15, 1983, p. 2. Implicit criticism is
found also from Baptists coming from abroad to visit Sweden. Noel Vose,
from Australia and former chairman of *BWA*, says in an interview, on the
question of how he looks at the development towards more ecumenical
congregations in Sweden, that he is convinced from his historical studies
(especially concerning the Anabaptists and their sacrifices in the 16th
century, where some were killed on account of their conviction on the
question of baptism) that "God has given us *Baptists a special mission
concerning believers' baptism."* If Baptists fail in regard to this, God will,
according to Vose, raise up another church to preserve the Baptist line. See
Lantz, Ragni, "Noel Vose vill föra de små samfundens talan", *VP*, No. 30,
1985, p. 3. Italics mine.

baptism.[314] He wonders if Waldenström and subsequent leaders within the Mission Covenant Church of Sweden have realized how incompatible the practice of baptism in the Mission Covenant Church of Sweden is with a Baptist view of baptism.[315]

One cause of the reconsideration of baptism and ecclesiology which is given by Baptists is the open membership already mentioned, which is also criticized by some Baptists and regarded as an obstacle and as inconsistent with New Testament doctrine.[316] David Lagergren discusses open membership because of a contribution by the Baptist Professor in Systematic Theology and Ethics, Thorwald Lorenzen, (Germany/Australia, former teacher at the Baptist Theological Seminary in Rüschlikon), at a consultation in 1979. This was arranged by the WCC at the Southern Baptist Seminary in Louisville. Lorenzen questions the usual assumption in ecumenical documents that baptism is important for membership in a congregation and that baptism is necessary for salvation. He is of the opinion that common recognition of Christ as Lord is more important than common convictions about baptism. Baptists

---

314 "Skiljelinjen mellan SMF och Svenska Baptistsamfundet ligger framför allt i dopfrågan." "Så ser ledare för andra samfund på SMF", [David Lagergren], *Liv och frihet,* 1978, p. 293.

315 Ibid. Cf., however, also the discussion below in this chapter 8.2.1.

316 See for example Ericson, Bertil, "Öppet medlemskap - raka vägar?", *VP,* No. 37, 1976, p. 12; Mild, Ruben, "Nya testamentets dopsyn bör gälla!", *VP,* No. 48, 1987, p. 6. See also Bergsten, who writes that open membership causes hesitation and scruples of conscience *(samvetskonflikt)* among many Baptists. Bergsten, Torsten, "Öppet nattvardsbord, överfört medlemskap och en öppen baptism", *VP,* No. 3, 1986, p. 6.

Criticism of open membership and the developing of ecumenical congregations and the decision of 1969 has been made by Mild. He writes in 1987, about 20 years after the conference decision not to recommend open membership: "However, this was already being done and those who had the opposite opinion about this were to be silenced by the leaders of the denomination. Contrary to the wishes of the congregations and the decision of the conference this has continued. In a similar way proposals concerning the establishment of ecumenical congregations." Mild, Ruben, "Nya testamentets dopsyn bör gälla!" *VP,* No. 48, 1987, p. 6. See also Franzén who writes some years earlier that open membership does not imply an acceptance of infant baptism. Franzén, Bert, "Dopet i kyrkornas gemenskap", *VP,* No. 1/2, 1975, p .14. This is true, but indirectly it seems together with other factors to have had the consequence that the position of believers' baptism has been weakened amongst Baptists.

favouring open membership have, according to Lorenzen, gone in this direction ever since the days of Bunyan.[317]

Lagergren makes the following comment on this: "This is without doubt a more practical way to achieve unity than by trying to reach unity in the question of 'one baptism'."[318] He himself gives, however, expression to the fear that open membership will result in a playing down of baptism, which for him is inconsistent with the emphasis the New Testament puts on baptism: "It does not seem to be a sure way to the solution of the question of baptism and unity."[319]

He seems in this last statement to have a long-term perspective and realize the complexity of the problems and the consequences that open membership as a matter of fact may imply for the Baptist Union of Sweden in the future. Briefly, baptism will probably be weakened, for what primarily seems to matter to Lorenzen and other Baptists pleading for open membership is not necessarily believers' baptism - the typical, classic mark of a Baptist congregation - (nor infant baptism and later on personal faith) but faith alone, which is the *sine qua non* and also the foundation of the church.

The Baptist Union may have to pay a high price in the work towards church unity. Some Baptists also give expression to astonishment that Baptists question the view of baptism which is the basis of the Baptist faith all over the world *(den dopsyn som ligger till grund för baptismen i hela världen)*: "what are some of the pastors within our denomination doing?"[320] One Baptist argues that the Bible should be the only guiding principle: "Let us not be

---

317 See Lagergren, David, "Dop och enhet", *VP*, No. 36, 1980, p. 2. (John Bunyan 1628-88, he is well known as the author of the famous *The Pilgrim's Progress*, 1678, 1684.) Cf., however, below in this chapter, 8.2.2. concerning membership and salvation (Bergsten and Seiler).

318 "Det är ingen tvekan om att denna väg är mera framkomlig än försöken att vinna enhet kring 'ett dop'." Lagergren, David, "Dop och enhet", *VP*, No. 36, 1980, p. 2.

319 "Någon säker väg till lösningen av frågan om dop och enhet syns den inte vara." Ibid.

320 "Vad sysslar vissa pastorer med i vårt samfund?" Gerdin, Bertil, Näslund, Roland, "Skall vi erkänna barndopet?", *VP*, No. 7, 1985, p. 10. See, however, for example Lorenzen.

concerned with the Koran and Catholic heresies".[321] Baptists refer to how clear the Bible is in its description of baptism and its content, and that Jesus himself chose this way. They cannot understand for example why Baptists should recognize infant baptism for ecumenical reasons. They have never heard anyone representing the Church of Sweden say that they should recognize the Baptists' baptism in order to promote ecumenism. The Baptists should boldly preach the biblical message about the necessity of baptism, when a person has come to faith and been saved.[322]

Nevertheless, many Baptists have reconsidered baptism and have been ready also to compromise on one of its most important issues, which seems in a Swedish Baptist perspective to open up ways towards church unity – especially on the congregational level. This unity is, however, based on something else than what *BEM* and many other churches and denominations recommend, teach and practice.

In the light of this section it is urgent to continue the discussion of the issue of baptism in a Baptist ecumenical context, especially in the thought of two of the well-known Free Church leaders in Sweden, Birgit Karlsson and Lars Lindberg.

---

[321] "Låt oss inte befatta oss med koranen och katolska irrläror utan låt *bibeln* vara vårt enda rättesnöre!" Grudewall, Erik, "Bör vi erkänna barndopet?", *VP*, No. 6, 1985, p. 10. See also Hultberg, Per-Åke, "En baptistpojkes funderingar", *VP*, No. 36, 1992, p. 11; Herfert, Mischa, Axelsson, Erik, "'Jag ber att de alla skall bli ett...'", *VP*, No. 36, 1992, p. 11; cf. for instance Sjöqvist, Eric, "Ekumenik och bibelsyn", *VP*, No. 38, 1992, p. 12, stating that there are different views on the Bible in the congregation.

[322] "Har aldrig hört en Svenska kyrkans företrädare säga, 'skall vi inte erkänna baptisternas dop, så vi kan ha bättre ekumenik'... vi skall frimodigt förkunna bibelordet om nödvändigheten att gå dopets väg, när man kommit till tro och blivit frälst." Gerdin, Bertil, Näslund, Roland, "Skall vi erkänna barndopet?", *VP*, No. 7, 1985, p. 10. See also a reaction by Erik Grudewall concerning the article in *Svenska Journalen* quoted above. He writes that there is no support in the Bible for infant baptism. Grudewall, Erik, "Bör vi erkänna barndopet?", *VP*, No. 6, 1985, p. 10; see also Granander, Olof, "Bör vi erkänna barndopet?" *VP*, No. 10, 1985, p. 10 and Grudewall, Erik, "Bör vi erkänna barndopet. Svar till Olof Granander". *VP*, No. 12, 1985, p. 14. Lagergren refers on one occasion to the Danish Baptist theologian Per Nørgaard, who claims that infant baptism is not only regarded by Baptists as an improper or a doubtful baptism *(oklart dop)* but as a serious change of New Testament baptism, "en allvarlig ändring av Nya testamentets dop". Lagergren, David, "Dopet och enheten", *VP*, No. 15, 1978, p. 2.

8.2. Baptism in Two Ecumenical Dialogues

8.2.1.   Baptism in Baptist - Congregationalist Discussions - Steps towards Church Unity?

This section has a different structure compared with the others. It consists above all of a discussion primarily between two influential Free Church leaders. They are Birgit Karlsson (b. 1935), Baptist Union of Sweden, and Lars Lindberg (b. 1931), Mission Covenant Church of Sweden.[323] We will have in this section an opportunity to look at Karlsson's articles in their context.[324] Her articles have been quoted and referred to several times in the thesis, therefore reiterations are unfortunately unavoidable.

In the discussion in this chapter, we also use articles by Torsten Bergsten, Edvin Österberg and Ruben Mild. This section illustrates ecumenical approaches but also problems concerning baptism, ecclesiology and ecumenism, partly for the denominations, partly for and within Baptist congregations in particular.[325]

---

[323] Lars Lindberg is one of the most influential theologians within the Mission Covenant Church of Sweden. He has been pastor, teacher and principal at Lidingöseminariet, Stockholm.

[324] It is difficult on the whole to know if utterances by Karlsson (and also by other leaders) are to be regarded as official reflections or if they are expressions of private opinion. I suggest that because of her position they must be interpreted as official.

[325] The main texts which are treated in this chapter in chronological order are:

Lindberg, Lars, "Dop och omdop", *Svensk Veckotidning*, No. 22/23, 1987, p. 2, (in English Baptism and Re-baptism.)

Mild, Ruben, "Dopet - en central fråga när församlingar går samman", *VP*, No. 40, 1987, p. 10, (in English Baptism - a Central Question when Congregations are United.)

Karlsson, Birgit, "Dopet - en central fråga när församlingar går samman. Missionsföreståndaren kommenterar", *VP*, No. 40, 1987, pp. 10f., (in English Baptism - a Central Question when Congregations are United. The General Secretary Comments.)

I will give a short summary of Birgit Karlsson's attempt to take a *via media*. It is not easy to grasp the ambiguous attitude which I mean is to be found in Karlsson's texts.

She talks, on the one hand, about infant baptism as a valid baptism and apparently as equivalent to believers' baptism. She writes for example: "In both cases it is a question of a call to discipleship - to live in one's baptism."[326] Karlsson elucidates this and writes that God gives his grace and blessing in baptism, and makes an important addition: "but his gifts become our joy and richness when we have so much insight that we recognize them."[327] This evidently does not concern only believers' baptism but also infant baptism, and she writes de facto explicitly:

Of course these, [persons baptized by infant baptism, brought up in a Christian faith-context, remark mine], should *not been baptized once more...* I do not either want to baptize such a person once again.[328]

She makes, on the other hand, important addition to these last words: "unless it is necessary for pastoral reasons as an answer to a very clear conviction in such a person."[329] And in another article

---

Lindberg, Lars, "Lars Lindberg om dopfrågan, Upphör med omdop", *Svensk Veckotidning*, No. 42, 1987, p. 8, (in English Lars Lindberg about the Question of Baptism; Cease with Re-baptism.)

Karlsson, Birgit, "Tillbaka till dopet", *VP*, No. 46, 1987, p. 6, (in English Back to Baptism.)

Mild, Ruben, "Nya testamentets dopsyn bör gälla!", *VP*, No. 48, 1987, p. 6, (in English The Baptismal View of the New Testament ought to be Accepted.)

[326] "I båda fallen gäller efterföljelsekallelsen - att leva i sitt dop". Karlsson, Birgit, "Dopet - en central fråga när församlingar går samman. Missionsföreståndaren kommenterar", *VP*, No. 40, 1987, p. 10. She adds: "The person baptized by infant baptism can do this in the knowledge that he is baptized and thereafter has been brought up and guided into the faith which is related to baptism." ("Den barndöpte kan göra det i vetskap om att vara döpt och därefter fostrad och vägledd in i den tro som hör samman med dopet. Den troendedöpte minns sitt dop som ett avgörelse- och överlåtelseskeende han själv var beredd för och efter vilket han fortsätter sitt kristenliv i växande.") Ibid.

[327] "Gud ger nåd och välsignelse i dopet, men hans gåvor blir vår glädje och rikedom då vi anar dem så mycket att vi kan bejaka dem." Ibid.

[328] "Naturligtvis skall *inte* dessa *döpas en gång till...* Jag vill inte inte heller döpa en sådan person igen". Ibid. p. 11. Italics mine.

[329] " - om det inte av själavårdsmässiga skäl kan bli nödvändigt som svar på en mycket bestämd övertygelse hos en sådan person." Ibid.

she makes a clear statement that she cannot place infant baptism and believers' baptism on an equal footing as equivalent alternatives, since there are fundamental differences in the biblical explanation of the practice of baptism. There are differences of motive. In churches baptizing infants there are, in comparison with those practising believers' baptism, other motives which justify the practice of infant baptism. Infant baptism occurs independently of the ability of a person to receive this grace with a conscious will, and this baptism is a sign of God's prevenient grace. The Baptists baptize believers who through faith have found that baptism is a climax in the experience of conversion and leads to the congregation.[330]

We notice here among other things that conversion and incorporation into the church are connected with baptism. We may compare with the previous discussions, where I pointed to the deviations from this. The ambiguity is apparent also when Birgit Karlson writes that in the case of a person baptized by infant baptism, who recognizes his infant baptism as a baptism and does not ask for baptism again, she must refrain from baptizing him again because of his conviction. His infant baptism is, however, in this case not a baptism, but

> his faith testifies that he lives in a fellowship with Christ even with an in my opinion improper baptism *(oklart dop)* in his background.[331]

Judging by this last quotation there is for me an evident uncertainty, as to whether Karlsson regards infant baptism as a non-baptism *or* as a baptism, though improper. So although we find that Karlsson does not want to baptize a person again, there is as a matter of fact a condition both in her first and especially in her second article. This thus gives the possibility of continued practice of "re-baptism".

Lars Lindberg also discusses baptism and refers to an open ecclesiology:

> God gave our fathers in the 1870's theological wisdom which led to the open ecclesiology which unites different Christian believers, and which at the same time has great openness towards different theological points of view. An open embrace for all types of the life of faith. This is in among other things expressed in an excellent way, when both the tradition of infant

---

330 Karlsson, Birgit, "Tillbaka till dopet", *VP*, No. 46, 1987, p. 6.

331 "... hans tro betygar att han lever i Kristus-gemenskap också med ett för mig oklart dop i sin bakgrund." Ibid.

baptism and that of believers' baptism are united in one and the same denomination... Within the Mission Covenant Church of Sweden we say *yes to a double baptismal practice...* We have room for both traditions in our denomination.[332]

He comments on *BEM's* reference to *"churches which unite both infant-baptist and believer-baptist traditions"*[333]:

This is presumably the only ecumenically practicable way, namely to let both kinds of baptism be practised within the same congregation.[334]

He suggests that this could be the contribution of the Mission Covenant Church of Sweden to ecumenical thought. It is also stated in the other article that this is the *one* baptism.[335] This baptism may, according to Lindberg, occur in different ways, and above all as concerns the point in time, in two different forms as infant baptism and as believers' baptism. He is of the opinion that the Mission Covenant Church of Sweden ought to build on that basis.[336]

If there has been exclusiveness within the Baptist Union of Sweden, there is an inclusiveness and openness within the Mission Covenant Church of Sweden (which *de facto* is also partly to be found within the Baptist Union nowadays). This results obviously in difficult implications for deciding if a baptism is valid or not, proper or improper etc., and because of this, if so-called "re-baptisms" will be practised in the future.

There is, according to Lindberg, a sensitive point where *BEM* challenges the Mission Covenant Church of Sweden. It concerns the

---

[332] Lindberg, Lars, "Dop och omdop", *Svensk Veckotidning*, No. 22/23, 1987, p. 2.

[333] *B com 12.*

[334] "Detta är nog den enda ekumeniskt framkomliga vägen, att bägge dopformerna får finnas inom samma församling." Lindberg, Lars, "Dop och omdop", *Svensk Veckotidning*, No. 22/23, 1987, p. 2. Cf., for example, Franzén, Bert, "Har dopet någon enande kraft?" *VP*, No. 8, 1965, p. 10, referred to above.

[335] "Det handlar om ett dop, ett dop in i Jesus Kristus." Lindberg, Lars, "Lars Lindberg om dopfrågan, Upphör med omdop", *Svensk Veckotidning*, No. 42, 1987, p. 8.

[336] Ibid. We can also note that the Mission Covenant Church of Sweden is open to both the Baptist Union of Sweden and the Church of Sweden, and this in spite of these churches' different opinions and partly different teachings and practices of baptism. See for example *Guds kyrka och en levande församling*, 1996.

question of "re-baptism". He states that this is "the doctrine where the Mission Covenant Church of Sweden is most sectarian!"[337]

His opinion must imply that the Baptist teaching and practice of baptism also is sectarian. And in view of the fact that "re-baptism" occurs relatively frequently also within the Mission Covenant Church of Sweden, there are

> good reasons to say that this is the weakest point in ecumenical dialogue for the Mission Covenant Church of Sweden, for instance in the dialogue with the Church of Sweden.[338]

This is also noteworthy, since the Mission Covenant Church of Sweden is at the same time highly involved in and partly integrated with the Baptist Union.[339] With this co-operation and involvement (with especially the Baptist Union of Sweden), the following words are challenging:

> Within the Mission Covenant Church of Sweden we ought to say *no to 're-baptism'*. Baptism is a once for all act and it is the beginning of the Christian life. Something serious and most problematic is done if a person is 're-baptized'.[340]

He refers once again to *BEM* and quotes *B 13:* "Baptism is an unrepeatable act. Any practice which might be interpreted as 're-baptism' must be avoided."[341]

"Re-baptism" is thus problematic for Lindberg, and for biblical, theological and ecumenical reasons. He refers in his article to his

---

337 "Man kan säga, att detta är den läropunkt, där Svenska Missionsförbundet är mest sekteristiskt!" Lindberg, Lars, "Dop och omdop", *Svensk Veckotidning*, No. 22/23, 1987, p. 2.

338 "Det finns goda skäl att säga, att detta är Svenska Missionsförbundets svagaste punkt i den ekumeniska dialogen, t ex med Svenska kyrkan". Ibid.

339 See for instance Part I, chapter 9. especially 9.4.2. and 9.5.

340 "Inom SMF bör vi säga *nej till omdop*. Dopet är en engångshandling och står i början av det kristna livet. Man gör något allvarligt och ytterst problematiskt, om man döper om en människa." Lindberg, Lars, "Dop och omdop", *Svensk Veckotidning*, No. 22/23, 1987, p. 2.

341 Ibid. Lindberg also refers to the joint manual of the Swedish Alliance Mission and Mission Covenant Church of Sweden, *Handbok till den kristna församlingens tjänst*, 1983, where it is stated that baptism is a baptism into Christ and into the Christian congregation. It is an act once for all (*engångshandling*) and does not need to be repeated. In Lindberg, Lars, "Dop och omdop", *Svensk Veckotidning*, No. 22/23, 1987, p. 2.

book *Dopet in i Kristus*, 1982, (Baptism into Christ), where he gives three arguments against "re-baptism". 1) Baptism is a once-for-all act according to the New Testament. 2) It is obvious that in the ancient church there was one conversion and one incorporation into the congregation. Therefore there was, of course, only one baptism. If a person abandoned his faith and his Lord, but later on, however, wanted to return to the congregation, this did not happen through baptism, but through a new dedication in confession and penance. 3) The Baptist denominations do not include "re-baptism" in their theology. They choose instead "to declare infant baptism as a non-baptism." This cannot, however, be an option for the Mission Covenant Church of Sweden, where both infant baptism and believers' baptism are legitimate forms.[342] For it says:

> yes to baptism, it is a gift from God, it is a sacrament. Baptism does not appear as an obligation within the Mission Covenant Church of Sweden but as a gift and a possibility.[343]

Lindberg says very plainly that pastors and other spiritual leaders should carefully avoid making younger and older people doubt their infant baptism and be baptized a second time.[344]

> It cannot be an option for the Mission Covenant Church of Sweden to disapprove of infant baptism and practise 're-baptism', and this is an obstacle from an ecumenical point of view.[345]

We find a sacramental view of baptism, and recognition and practice of infant baptism. Baptism is also connected with salvation and incorporation into Christ, i.e. the church.

While the Mission Covenant Church of Sweden and the Baptist Union of Sweden work together, in among other things ecumenical congregations, we might expect that this plain statement by

---

[342] Lindberg, Lars, "Dop och omdop", *Svensk Veckotidning*, No. 22/23, 1987, p. 2. See also Lindberg, Lars, *Dopet in i Kristus*, 1982, pp. 74ff.

[343] "Inom SMF säger vi *ja till dopet*, det är en gåva från Gud, det är ett sakrament. Dopet framställs inte i Svenska Missionsförbundet som ett krav utan som en gåva och en möjlighet." Lindberg, Lars, "Dop och omdop", *Svensk Veckotidning*, No. 22/23, 1987, p. 2.

[344] "Men pastorer och andliga ledare bör akta sig noga för att söka få människor, yngre och äldre, att betvivla sitt barndop och låta döpa sig en andra gång." Ibid.

[345] "Det kan inte vara någon väg för Svenska Missionsförbundet att underkänna barndopet och förrätta omdop och det är ur ekumenisk synpunkt ett hinder." Ibid.

Lindberg would cause reactions and not pass uncontradicted. Eventually his article does indirectly result in Birgit Karlsson's article, "Dopet - en central fråga när församlingar går samman. Missionsföreståndaren kommenterar".[346] Her article seems, as has been stated above, to have been explicitly caused by another article, Ruben Mild's, "Dopet - en central fråga när församlingar går samman".[347] Mild writes among other things in this article that during recent years the Baptist movement has been influenced by a weaker Baptist view of baptism and thoughtless action. An opposite tendency also exists.[348]

There is no explicit or official reaction among the Baptists to Lindberg's article before Mild's text in *Veckoposten* No. 40, in October 1987 - more than four months after his article in May. (In the same issue there is also Birgit Karlsson's commentary on Mild's contribution.[349]) Mild writes that Lindberg can be called "chief theologian and ideologist" of the Mission Covenant Church of Sweden. His article is according to Mild an expression of the opinion at the central, denominational level of the Mission Covenant Church of Sweden on the issue of baptism.[350] Lindberg has further a distinct intention seriously to warn pastors and other leaders in the congregations against "re-baptism": "bearing in mind confirmations, camps, revival meetings and summer-weeks, when

---

346 It can be noted that in the discussion between Birgit Karlsson and Lindberg, there is an interesting circumstance. For it looks in one way as if Lindberg has caught Karlsson in a trap; she writes something in the article, "Dopet - en central fråga när församlingar går samman. Missionsföreståndaren kommenterar", which she later on in another article, "Tillbaka till dopet" seems partly to retract.

347 Mild, Ruben, "Dopet - en central fråga när församlingar går samman", *VP*, No. 40, 1987, p. 10.

348 Ibid.

349 See "Dopet - en central fråga när församlingar går samman. Missionsföreståndaren kommenterar", *VP*, No. 40, 1987, pp. 10f.

350 Mild, Ruben, "Dopet - en central fråga när församlingar går samman", *VP*, No. 40, 1987, p. 10.

the Christian faith, the congregation and baptism are brought to the fore."[351]

Mild gives expression to his astonishment at the silence about Lindberg's article, "a remarkable silence" (en märklig tystnad), not least in view of the fact that he is one of the most influential leaders within the Mission Covenant Church of Sweden, and also indicates that the question is an obstacle from an ecumenical point of view. For no reaction, whether questions or comments, is found in Veckoposten, neither from the editor, and Baptist leaders nor from Baptist pastors etc. Mild asks what their reaction is?[352] He also wonders if Baptist pastors feel free to preach their view of baptism in ecumenical congregations.[353]

An answer to Mild's article is then given in the same number of Veckoposten by the then General Secretary, Birgit Karlsson.[354] She writes, in one sense unexpectedly from a traditional Baptist point of view, on children baptized by infant baptism growing up in a Christian faith-context:

> As I understand infant baptism, the intention is that the faith should be transmitted to the baptizand by family and congregation, in order gradually to become a consciously assented faith, often expressed explicitly at the time of confirmation. Faith grows into baptism. This is often the development of children within believing families in infant-baptism contexts, for example in the Mission Covenant Church of Sweden. They are looked after and brought up for the fellowship of the congregation in which they gradually will live and serve. *Of course these should not been baptized once more. Just as Lars Lindberg asserts.*[355]

---

351 "Denna varning vill Lindberg ge med tanke på konfirmationshögtider, läger, väckelsemöten och sommarveckor då den kristna tron, församlingen och dopet aktualiseras." Ibid.

352 Ibid. He adds that there have been no comments either in Missionsbaneret [Örebro (Baptist) mission] or in Dagen [Pentecostal Movement], organs which usually discuss controversial questions. Ibid.

353 "Känner baptistpastorer frihet att i 'blandförsamlingarna' förkunna sin dopsyn? Vilket aktuellt budskap har Baptistsamfundets ledning i dag till dem som ute i landet funderar och beder med tanke på framtiden." Ibid.

354 Karlsson, Birgit, "Dopet - en central fråga när församlingar går samman. Missionsföreståndaren kommenterar", VP, No. 40, 1987, pp. 10f.

355 "Som jag förstår barndopet är avsikten att tron ska överföras till det döpta barnet av familj och församling för att så småningom bli en medveten bejakad tro, oftast klart uttryckt i konfirmationen. Tron växer in i dopet. Ofta är detta utvecklingen för barn i troende barndöparfamiljer, t ex i SMF. De

It is, of course, surprising that Lars Lindberg, a theologian and leader of a denomination practising infant baptism, believers' baptism, (and also "re-baptism"), is backed up in this way by the Baptist General Secretary in his stance against the teaching and practice of "re-baptism". We can compare with the clear rejection of infant baptism in *BUS* - a document which had also been signed by Birgit Karlsson. Her article seems to a great extent to be in agreement with *BEM*,[356] which is significant particularly from an ecumenical perspective. For her opinion gives recognition to (at least some) infant baptisms, and Bergsten writes concerning her statement:

> This *official* [italics mine] standpoint from the Baptist side is in agreement with the ecumenical document *Baptism, Eucharist, Ministry*.[357]

Mild's article, "Dopet - en central fråga när församlingar går samman", is not commented on at all by Lars Lindberg in his next article "Upphör med omdop", not even implicitly. He makes,

---

vårdas och fostras för den församlingsgemenskap de så småningom skall leva och tjäna i. *Naturligtvis skall inte dessa döpas en gång till. Precis så som Lars Lindberg hävdar."* Ibid. Italics mine.

[356] *BEM* writes: "When an infant is baptized, the personal response will be offered at a later moment in life... the baptized person will have to grow in understanding of faith." *B 12.* "Baptism is an unrepeatable act. Any practice which might be interpreted as 're-baptism' must be avoided." *B 13.* See also *B com 12* and *B com 13.* *B 16* about the importance for those who practise infant baptism to "... take more seriously their responsibility for the nurture of baptized children to mature commitment to Christ."

[357] Bergsten, Torsten, "Anders Wiberg, dopet och de kristnas enhet", 1987, p. 20, [unpublished paper].

There are two versions of this paper, in which Bergsten refers to the statement by Karlsson. We can hardly find any differences at all between the two versions. Note, however, the change of terms by Bergsten in his two versions. In the first [unpublished paper] he writes about the *official* opinion, ("Detta *officiella* [italics mine] ståndpunktstagande från baptistisk sida står i god samklang med det ekumeniska dokumentet *Dop, nattvard, ämbete.")* Bergsten, Torsten, "Anders Wiberg, dopet och de kristnas enhet", 1987, p. 20, [unpublished paper]. This version was given as a lecture in connection with a symposium about Anders Wiberg at *Betelseminariet* in Stockholm. In the other, however, he writes about the *authoritative* opinion, ("Detta *auktoritativa* [italics mine] ståndpunktstagande från baptistisk sida står i god samklang med det ekumeniska dokumentet *Dop, nattvard, ämbete.")* Bergsten, Torsten, "Anders Wiberg, dopet och de kristnas enhet", *Tro och Liv*, No. 4, 1988, p. 24.

however, some comments on the article by Karlsson just referred to: "I have now received support from an unexpected quarter, at least perhaps for some."[358] He refers to Birgit Karlsson as his authority in maintaining that "re-baptism" should cease.

Credit to such an ecumenical Baptist theology! Listen, you pastors and others within the Mission Covenant Church of Sweden helping young and older people to reject their infant baptism, even though they have lived in that baptism in security until the 'baptist propaganda' begins.[359]

Lindberg is concise:

Let us cease with the re-baptism! This *theology of rejection* which is to be found in our congregations is a bad thing, which does not help young people to rest secure in the joy of being baptized as an infant, but instead questions, rejects and redoes.[360]

These discussions and rejoinders illustrate de facto something about the issues of baptism, ecclesiology and the ecumenical context in Sweden in general, and about the process within the Baptist Union of Sweden in particular. This is an example partly pointing to the diversity and ambiguity within the Baptist Union of Sweden, partly indicating a reconsideration of baptism and ecclesiology, a change from a closed attitude, restrictiveness, towards greater openness and pluralism.

Lindberg writes:

The contribution by Birgit Karlsson is an extraordinarily good example of how Baptist theology has become more and more ecumenical and open, and that the interpretation of baptism has become more explicitly sacramental.[361]

---

358 "Nu har jag fått stöd från ett håll, som kanske är oväntat för en del." Lindberg, Lars, "Lars Lindberg om dopfrågan, Upphör med omdop", *Svensk Veckotidning*, No. 42, 1987, p. 8.

359 "Heder åt en sådan ekumenisk baptistisk teologi! Lyssna ni pastorer och andra inom Svenska Missionsförbundet, som hjälper unga och äldre att underkänna sitt barndop, fastän man levt i dopet i trygghet till dess att en 'doppropaganda' sätter in." Ibid.

360 "Låt oss upphöra med omdopet! Det är ett oskick med den *underkännandets teologi* som finns med i våra församlingar, där man hjälper unga människor inte att vila i glädjen att man är döpt som barn utan ifrågasätter, underkänner och gör om." Ibid.

361 "Birgit Karlssons inlägg är ett utomordentligt fint exempel på, hur den baptistiska teologin blivit alltmer ekumenisk och öppen och hur doptolkningen blivit allt tydligare sakramental." Ibid.

Besides Birgit Karlsson he also mentions Torsten Bergsten, as one who has paved the way for this view within the Baptist Union, i.e. an open and ecumenical one.[362]

The ideas of Birgit Karlsson in "Dopet - en central fråga när församlingar går samman. En missionsförståndare kommenterar" have obviously caused reactions - and not only in a positive sense as from Lindberg. We could expect that they would be criticized, very harshly from some quarters, which is understandable as they could be regarded as a betrayal of traditional Baptist teaching and practice. She then retracts to a certain extent in the article "Tillbaka till dopet", where she wants to clarify some formulations in her first article, which "obviously have resulted in misunderstandings."[363]

In this second article believers' baptism is strongly vindicated. She states with reference to the appeal from Lindberg to pastors within the Mission Covenant Church of Sweden to cease with the practice of "re-baptism" and to recognize every infant baptism as a baptism:

It is of course completely impossible to make the same urgent request to Baptist pastors, even if they work in ecumenical congregations.[364]

Let us examine Karlsson's argumentation for believers' baptism in this article. Her starting point is that the teaching of baptism must be based on the New Testament. This teaching must be combined with the practice of baptism into a unified whole, which is tested in honest study.[365] She asserts, partly in opposition to BUS it seems, that the dividing line between those practising believers' baptism

---

362 Ibid.

363 "Vi måste ägna möda åt att försöka förstå och att försöka göra oss förstådda. Därför vill jag återkomma med några synpunkter: främst för att försöka förtydliga vissa formuleringar i min tidigare artikel vilka uppenbarligen gett utrymme för missförstånd." Karlsson, Birgit, "Tillbaka till dopet", VP, No. 46, 1987, p. 6.

364 "Den uppfordran Lars Lindberg ger pastorer i sitt samfund (Svensk veckotidning 42/87) att inte medverka till att barndöpta medlemmar underkänner sitt barndop utan i stället stödja dem i dettas innebörd även då nya insikter kommer är naturligtvis ett bevis för svårigheten, inte minst själavårdsmässigt, att leva med dubbel dopraxis som Svenska missionsförbundet gör. Det är självfallet helt omöjligt att rikta motsvarande uppmaning till pastorer av baptistisk övertygelse även om de är verksamma i förenade församlingar." Ibid.

365 Ibid.

and those practising infant baptism does not concern only the practice of baptism but also *(nota bene)* the understanding of the New Testament.[366] *BUS* writes:

After all, different churches with various traditions can say the same things about baptism. *The difficulties* have been evident when it comes to the point of *putting the common view into practice.*367

Karlsson mentions three arguments for believers' baptism. These are not to be found in the article "Dopet - en central fråga när församlingar går samman. En missionsföreståndare kommenterar", but in her "retraction" "Tillbaka till dopet". They are: 1) Believers' baptism is based on *the words of Jesus about faith and baptism* for discipleship and salvation.[368] 2) Believers' baptism is based on the fact that *the New Testament clearly shows only believers' baptism.* This believers' baptism is a *baptism of metanoia* (conversion).[369] 3) Believers' baptism is further based on the fact, that *the teaching in the New Testament on the meaning and content of baptism cannot be understood otherwise than from a practice of baptism which implies that believers are baptized* as a part of their conversion. And she asks: "How are the illustrations of baptism, given in the New Testament, otherwise to be understood?"[370]

---

366 "I mötet mellan baptister och barndöpare är det helt uppenbart att skiljelinjen inte ligger bara i praktiserandet av dopet, utan i hur man förstått NT." Ibid. She writes also: "Alldeles fel hamnar vi om man bara ser på praxis och inte ställer frågan varför den utformats och vad man vill uttrycka med den." Ibid.

367 *BUS* p. 200. Italics mine. See also the discussion in Part II.

368 Karlsson, Birgit, "Tillbaka till dopet", *VP*, No. 46, 1987, p. 6. She refers to Mark. 16 and Matthew 28.

369 "... att *NT tydligt exemplifierar endast dop av troende.* I NT är dopet höjdpunkten i ett omvändelseskeende när människan bekänner personlig tro och i konsekvens av denna begär dop som tecken och bekräftelse till fördjupning av sin erfarenhet att lämna hela livet åt Kristi efterföljd och liv i hans församling. Troendedopet är ett omvändelsedop." Karlsson, Birgit, "Tillbaka till dopet", *VP*, No. 46, 1987, p. 6.

370 "... att *NTs undervisning om dopets mening och innebörd inte kan förstås annat än från en doppraxis som just innebär att troende döps* som ett led i sin omvändelse. Hur ska man eljest förstå bilderna av dopet som NT ger?" Ibid. Karlsson refers to Rom. 6:3f., Col. 2:12, 1 Peter 3:21, Hebrews 10:22, Titus 3:5.

In spite of this elucidation by Karlsson to avoid misunderstandings, critical remarks have also been made on her second article. One of the critics is Ruben Mild. After his contribution "Dopet - en central fråga när församlingar går samman", and the answer by Birgit Karlsson to this, he continues the debate in another article. He is of the opinion that Karlsson does not say anything new in her second article, but holds to the same opinion as in the first one. She argues thus for abandoning the biblically and evangelically motivated view of baptism.[371]

He declares:

> When Birgit Karlsson without hesitation agrees with the view of principal Lindberg regarding 're-baptism', one understands *the change which has taken place within the Baptist movement and its foundation in the Bible.*[372]

Edvin Österberg also belongs to the critics, and accuses among others Birgit Karlsson of heresy.[373] Infant baptism, which Österberg designates with the term *sprinkling (begjutning, bestänkning)*,is according to him a denial of the biblical teaching of salvation and

---

[371] "What she and others among the leadership believe is guidance to many. The enthusiastic applause from the principal Lars Lindberg was expected...also that Lindberg praises Torsten Bergsten". ("Och nu får man höra missionsföreståndaren plädera för uppgivande av den bibliskt och evangeliskt motiverade dopsynen. Vad hon och andra i ledningen anser är för många vägledande. De kraftiga applåderna från rektor Lars Lindberg (Svensk veckotidning nr 42) var väntade... Lindberg prisar också Torsten Bergsten".) Then his words are directed above all at Lindberg: "Doctors of theology have apparently not always understood what the most important thing is, documents produced by human beings or the Word of God." Mild, Ruben, "Nya testamentets dopsyn bör gälla!", *VP*, No. 48, 1987, p. 6.

[372] "När Birgit Karlsson tveklöst ansluter sig till rektor Lindbergs uppfattning i fråga om omdop förstår man *vilken förändring som ägt rum inom baptismen och dess förankring i skriften.*" Mild, Ruben, "Det finns en väg - går vi den?", *VP*, No. 42, 1987, p. 14. Italics mine. The principle for Birgit Karlsson may now read, according to Mild: "Whoever believes and has been baptized by infant baptism or believes and is baptized will be saved." He argues, however, that the wording does not read so in Mark 16:16. Ibid.

[373] "The Baptists are busy revaluing the form and meaning of baptism. Those who in the first place ought to defend the statutes of the Baptist Union as well as of the Örebro (Baptist) Mission, presupposing the baptism of the New Testament for membership, are now leading the struggle for centuries old heresies of a serious kind. I mean our General Secretaries and teachers." Österberg, Edvin, "Den aktuella dopdebatten", *VP*, No. 13/14, 1988, p. 12.

an invalidation of the biblical concept of congregation, [374] which for membership demands conversion, faith and personal confession of faith as conditions for baptism.[375]

As for Birgit Karlsson, it can be stated that it is not easy for her to take the *"via media"*. We can assume that it must have been a hard time especially for her to continue as a General Secretary of the Baptist Union of Sweden.[376] Neither is it easy to grasp her ambiguous attitude. Her approach to infant baptism and to "re-baptism" is complex. It seems on the one hand to be recognition of infant baptism and a "no" to "re-baptism", (*Naturligtvis skall inte dessa döpas en gång till*). On the other hand, as a conclusion of the

---

374 "Spädbarns neddoppning, som med tiden blev begjutning och bestänkning, är en förnekelse av Bibelns frälsningslära... ett upphävande av Nya testamentets församlingsbegrepp". Ibid.

Other terms are sometimes used instead of *infant baptism* - sometimes just to stress the fact that infant baptism is not a baptism. Österberg does not want, however, to see either infant baptism or adult baptism in *Veckoposten*. The cause, he writes earlier in *Veckoposten*, is that the age of baptism does not play any role. What matters is faith. ("Låt oss slippa se ordet 'vuxendop' och även 'barndop' i VP:s spalter, eftersom dopåldern inte spelar någon roll. Det är tron det gäller.") Österberg, Edvin, "Veckans insändare", *VP*, No. 6, 1975, p. 10. Note his choice of term, not only concerning infant baptism (as *sprinkling* etc.) but also concerning believers' baptism, designated as *vuxendop (adult baptism)*.

375 Österberg, Edvin, "Den aktuella dopdebatten", *VP*, No. 13/14, 1988, p. 12.

376 An indication of this can be detected in comparing the two versions by Bergsten: Bergsten, Torsten, "Anders Wiberg, dopet och de kristnas enhet", 1987, [unpublished paper], and Bergsten, Torsten, "Anders Wiberg, dopet och de kristnas enhet", *Tro och Liv*, No. 4, 1988, pp. 12-27.

By comparing these two versions, we can note that Bergsten has been criticized by some Baptists after he had reproduced the view of Karlsson regarding infant baptism and "re-baptism" in a lecture (his first version). In all probability he was accused after this lecture either of having misinterpreted her or having made an over-interpretation. After this lecture, i.e. version 1, he consulted Birgit Karlsson before he wrote version 2. For in version 2 he refers to an answer from Birgit Karlsson herself, where she confirms the interpretation which he had given to one of her statements in his lecture (i.e. version 1) - that infant baptism, followed by a faith-context, is not a "non-baptism" but as a matter of fact an improper (*oklart*) baptism. Bergsten, Torsten, "Anders Wiberg, dopet och de kristnas enhet", *Tro och Liv*, No. 4, 1988, p. 24. See also the discussion about *official* and *authoritative* above.

discussion above, believers' baptism is sometimes not regarded at all as a "re-baptism", while infant baptism "suddenly" due to some preconditions is no longer a baptism but just a blessing,[377] - i.e. a similar opinion to that in *BUS*.

It is possible that there are, concerning infant baptism, two issues for Karlsson. Firstly, that the faith-context (the closed one) makes the practice of infant baptism acceptable. Secondly, that the making of a confession of faith by a person in his infant baptism gives validity to that particular infant baptism.

In the discussions between Karlsson and Lindberg we must not forget that there are, in spite of some convergence, still differences concerning the issue of baptism between these two denominations, represented by these two prominent and influential Christian leaders. Lindberg cannot for example declare an infant baptism invalid, even if the practice is bad and those baptized are not given a Christian upbringing. He regards the practice of baptism, especially within the great National Churches, with hesitation; their practice may be indefensible (he mentions explicitly the Church of Sweden). In spite of this, he wants, however, with reference to Karl Barth, to recognize these baptisms as improper, but nevertheless as valid.[378] Birgit Karlsson cannot, on the other hand, recognize every infant baptism as a valid baptism, even if it (according to some) is duly performed. For some are as a matter of fact regarded as non-baptisms, at best as blessings. That there is a difference becomes more evident in Karlsson's article "Tillbaka till dopet".

Briefly, from this section and the previous chapters we can state that there are compromises and a diversity within the Baptist Union of Sweden. There are various emphases and different opinions, giving different openings concerning the issue of baptism, which, of course, have implications for ecclesiology, for the work towards church unity etc. Approaches towards mutual recognition of baptism are partly to be discerned. These involve explicitly and

---

377 "Är det inte just välsignelsemomentet som består i det barndop som inte får sin fortsättning i fostran till tro?" Karlsson, Birgit, "Dopet - en central fråga när församlingar går samman. Missionsförståndaren kommenterar", *VP*, No. 40, 1987, p. 11. See also the discussions previously in this part, especially chapter 2., chapter 4. and also in Part II, chapter 6.

378 Lindberg, Lars, "Lars Lindberg om dopfrågan, Upphör med omdop", *Svensk Veckotidning*, No. 42, 1987, p. 8; Lindberg, Lars, *Dopet in i Kristus*, 1982, pp.75f.

implicitly also steps and approaches towards church unity. At the same time, there are, however, difficulties - which sometimes even may be designated as tensions - within one and the same denomination, the Baptist Union of Sweden, with its own classic tradition and its principles of believers' baptism and the congregation of believers; even a certain tendency to abandon baptism emphasizing faith alone.

There is thus a tendency within the Baptist Union of Sweden, due to the diversity and reconsideration of baptism and the difficulties in maintaining proper biblical believers' baptism, and baptism as a basis of membership, opening up possibilities towards another kind of church unity, based not on baptism but on faith alone.

8.2.2. Baptism in Baptist - Catholic Discussions – Further Steps towards Church Unity?

I want to follow up the previous section by examining some articles illustrating another unexpected Baptist approach, in this case towards Catholics and their view of baptism.

The two churches which historically have had few contacts with each other - and when they have met, it has been in confrontation - [379] are, however, nowadays involved in a dialogue on both a national and international level.[380] And the following discussion may be a further illustration of how "old bones of contention" are dealt with.

One of the articles is by pater Herman Seiler (b. 1910) SJ,[381] representing the Roman Catholic Church. Seiler was one of the

---

[379] See for example Bergsten, Torsten, "Kyrkotillhörighet - medlemskap - bekännelse", *Tro och Liv*, No. 1, 1980, p. 38, he writes: "När baptismen kommit i närmare kontakt med Katolska kyrkan, framför allt i form av baptistisk mission i katolskt präglade områden såsom det fransktalande Afrika och Latinamerika, har ett sådant möte oftare utlöst ömsesidig misstro och agressivitet än gemenskap över samfundsgränserna."

[380] See Part I, chapter 8.; and for example Erik Lindberg commenting the report "'Summons to Witness to Christ in Today's World': A report on the Baptist-RC International Conversations, 1984-88", *One in Christ*, No. 3, 1990, pp. 238-255, in Lindberg, Erik, "Baptister och katoliker är ense om Jesus", *VP*, No. 50, 1991, p. 4.

[381] Seiler, Herman, "Dop och kyrkotillhörighet i den katolska kyrkan. Dopet som sakramentalt inlemmande i kyrkan", *Ekumenisk samsyn om dop och kyrkotillhörighet*, 1978, pp. 33-42.

Catholics in Sweden who had been involved among other things in the Swedish ecumenical dialogue. The other article is by Torsten Bergsten, representing the Baptist Union of Sweden.[382]

Herman Seiler gives in the article *Dop och kyrkotillhörighet i den katolska kyrkan*, (Baptism and Church-belonging in the Catholic Church) a contribution to the ecumenical dialogue about baptism. He sums up the Roman Catholic view of baptism in three points: 1) Baptism is fundamental for belonging to the church *(kyrkotillhörigheten)*.[383] 2) Baptism is of a sacramental character. 3) The necessity of baptism for salvation.[384] Going not so much into the article by Seiler in itself, but the discussion about it by Bergsten, we find some valuable points.

One statement by Bergsten is exceedingly interesting. He states that in essentials there is a far-reaching convergence between Catholic and Baptist conviction on baptism.[385] According to this statement one is close to reaching one presupposition for what *BEM* calls "a basic bond of unity",[386] that is not just faith alone, but also *baptism*. This may be regarded as an example of what *BEM* says: "Churches are increasingly recognizing one another's baptism as the one baptism into Christ".[387]

---

382 Bergsten, Torsten, "Kyrkotillhörighet - medlemskap - bekännelse", *Tro och Liv*, No. 1, 1980, especially pp. 39-41, see also pp. 43-45. He conducts an interesting discussion in this dialogue on pre- and postbaptismal catechumenate, and on baptism as a process rather than an isolated event.

383 We note that Seiler does not use the term *member* in relation to baptism, a term which is preferred by many Baptists. This distinction is made within the Baptist Union in order to try to make a distinction between those not baptized, who then *belong* to the Baptist church, and those baptized, who are *members* of the Baptist church. Concerning the dilemma concerning these concepts, "belonging" and "membership", see for example in this part, chapter 7. and also in Part II, chapter 10.

384 Seiler, Herman, "Dop och kyrkotillhörighet i den katolska kyrkan. Dopet som sakramentalt inlemmande i kyrkan", *Ekumenisk samsyn om dop och kyrkotillhörighet*, 1978, p. 33, "Tre fakta är och har alltid varit *av grundläggande betydelse* i den katolska trostraditionen: Dopets konstitutiva roll angående kyrkotillhörigheten, dopets sakramentala karaktär och dopets nödvändighet för människans frälsning."

385 Bergsten, Torsten, "Kyrkotillhörighet - medlemskap - bekännelse", *Tro och Liv*, No. 1, 1980, p. 40.

386 See *B 6*, and also Eph. 4:4-6.

387 *B 15*. Cf., however, with *BUS* in Part II.

I will consider Bergsten's discussion concerning the three points in Seiler. As far point 1 is concerned, he writes briefly: "To this most Baptists agree."[388] Concerning point 2, that baptism has a sacramental character, he makes an addition. He writes that this point of view is obvious to him, but it is controversial within the Baptist movement.[389] I want to analyse point 3 in greater depth: the necessity of baptism for salvation.

Bergsten writes that if this statement is interpreted in the same way by Catholics as he himself does, it implies that Baptists and Catholics are in agreement about the necessity of baptism for salvation.[390]

Bergsten's argumentation is the following. One is bound by the structures instituted by Jesus, where we among other things find baptism. God is, however, not himself bound by them. Jesus could therefore on the cross say to the repentant unchristened robber: "I tell you the truth, today you will be with me in the paradise." God is sovereign in his salvific will and in his salvific action. Man must, however, follow the way revealed to him in the Holy Scriptures for his salvation.[391] In other words, the way to man's salvation is revealed in the Bible. Baptism, as an ordained structure, belongs to the way of salvation, and is necessary for salvation.[392]

This is a different basis of church unity than the one which is built on faith alone. For it has several times above been stated that baptism is not a condition at all for incorporation into or membership of the church or into the local church, still less for

---

388 Bergsten, Torsten, "Kyrkotillhörighet - medlemskap - bekännelse", *Tro och Liv*, No. 1, 1980, p. 40.

389 Ibid. See also the previous discussions about baptism as expressive or instrumental act, in this part, chapter 6. and in Part II, chapter 8.

390 Bergsten, Torsten, "Kyrkotillhörighet - medlemskap - bekännelse", *Tro och Liv*, No. 1, 1980, p. 40.

391 Ibid.

392 Of course, the concept "faith" is involved in talking about baptism in this case. The concept "baptism" cannot stand alone in such a definition. See also the Örebro (Baptist) Mission document *Vattnet som förenar och skiljer*, 2nd ed., 1986. Juhlin refers to this document and writes that it states the point of view that there is a very solid connection between baptism and salvation. Juhlin, Lars, "Behövs dopet?", *VP*, No. 40, 1989, p. 7.

salvation.[393] We find in this "Baptist - Catholic discussion" - in opposition to some other Baptist opinions - that baptism is also regarded as a sacrament. Further, baptism is not only important but even necessary for salvation. We may assume that the statement by Bergsten, that Baptists and Catholics are in agreement about the necessity of baptism for salvation from the perspective of man, ought to be looked upon as a generalisation to which not all Baptists would subscribe.[394]

From this Baptist - Catholic discussion together with the previous discussions, we understand even more how delicate and difficult the subject of baptism is within the Baptist Union of Sweden, not least in relation to the work towards church unity. Beyond similarities and some convergence, there are after all still fundamental differences between the churches and denominations - as well as obviously also variations within one and the same denomination. For there is an ambiguity or rather pluralism within the Baptist Union of Sweden in more than one direction. Unfortunately this is not evident in *BUS*.

These Baptist - Congregationalist and Catholic discussions may indicate and open up further interesting possibilities for co-operation between these churches, as well as with other churches and denominations. All this also creates, as has been noted, a tension within the Baptist Union, especially in regard to the questions of baptism and church unity. This may in one way be something healthy and valuable despite all its difficulties, but fateful and dangerous in another way. For what will happen to baptism in the Baptist Union of Sweden in the future?

An indication of an answer is possibly found in the Baptist document *På väg mot kristen enhet.* There is a paragraph stating:

Membership in the congregation is founded on personal faith in Jesus Christ as Lord and Saviour. Membership can be gained a) through baptism after confession of faith, b) through confession of faith, c) through certificate

---

[393] See for example also Mattsson writing that baptism is not a condition for our salvation, Mattsson, Valter, "Dopet till Kristus, ett maktskifte i vårt liv", *VP*, No. 6, 1981, p. 4, "Ingenstans står det i Nya testamentet att dopet är den enda mötesplatsen mellan Kristus och människan. Dopet är inte ett villkor för vår frälsning. Men det är den plats där Jesus stämt möte med var och en som kommit till tro på honom." In the Salvation Army for example, discussed also in *BUS*, baptism is not administered at all.

[394] See for example the discussion by Lagergren about Lorenzen and open membership above.

of change of domicile from another Christian congregation, d) through associative membership.[395]

Believers' baptism is thus not something absolutely necessary for membership. Already in 1969, as already has been mentioned above, David Lagergren, the General Secretary at that time, says that faith alone is sufficient for membership. He indicates the fact that there is a tendency among Baptists to give up believers' baptism as a criterion and condition of being a member, in order to try to achieve unity.[396] He explicitly states that Swedish Free Churchmanship cannot be built on baptism.[397]

The work for church unity has possibly contributed to this tendency, which implicitly has resulted in a reconsideration of baptism, an openness for the recognition of infant baptism and also of faith alone being sufficient in order to be a member of a Baptist congregation. And conversely, the lesser emphasis on believers' baptism has possibly resulted in a growing openness with regard to ecumenism and church unity built on faith.

In comparing the two former General Secretaries, David Lagergren and Birgit Karlsson, there are several more new signs, and in part a different attitude in Karlsson than in Lagergren. There is a broader, pluralistic, ecumenical and more "open" perspective and attitude. It is not so much a question of a Baptist emphasis but more of a general Free Church approach.

We are not ready to risk the Free Churchmanship we are and have. We are a congregational movement and the idea of the free congregation is central to us. The confession of personal faith must be at the centre of the fellowship we want to live in and develop.[398]

---

395 "På väg mot kristen enhet", 1984, p. 3, [unpublished paper]. See also "På väg mot kristen enhet för församlingar som planerar att förenas", 1988, p. 4, [unpublished paper]. Torsten Bergsten comments on this, that a) is about the dominant practice in Baptist congregations, b) about open membership, c) about transferred membership. Bergsten, Torsten, "Dopsyn och församlingstillhörighet i gemensamma församlingar", 1989, p. 2, [unpublished paper].

396 Lagergren, David, Enhetsförslaget och dopfrågan, 1969, pp. 8ff.

397 "... klart att svensk frikyrklighet inte kan byggas på dopet, i varje fall inte idag." Ibid. p. 7.

398 "Vi är inte beredda att riskera den frikyrklighet vi är och har. Vi är en församlingsrörelse, och friförsamlingstanken är central för oss. Bekännelsen av personlig tro måste vara i centrum för den gemenskap vi vill leva i och utveckla." Birgit Karlsson in "Konkret förslag i enhetsfrågan: Förena SFR och

Of course believers' baptism is not to be excluded from this statement, but it is to be noticed that Birgit Karlsson does not explicitly mention confession of faith *and* believers' baptism, but only confession of faith. Such a statement must be intentional. She gives in other words a great number of clear indications which may be interpreted as meaning that believers' baptism does not need to be the basis of church unity. This openness is also indicated in the way that Karlsson de facto, in comparison with her predecessor Lagergren, regards some infant baptisms as valid - they are recognized on certain conditions.

This pluralism within the Baptist Union creates uncertainty and tension also in relation to the other churches and denominations; one wonders which direction the Baptist Union ultimately will choose in its ecumenical work. Will church unity for the Baptist Union of Sweden be based either (exclusively) on believers' baptism (i.e. the Baptist Union with other Baptist denominations - for example the Örebro (Baptist) Mission etc. (i.e. Interact), or the Pentecostal Movement) *or* mainly on the personal confession of faith, *or* possibly both believers' and infant baptism, i.e. a growing co-operation and even integration and unification with for example the Mission Covenant Church of Sweden?[399] *Or* will church unity be

---

Samråd!", *VP*, No. 9, 1988, p. 3. And she also states: "Dopet får inte bli ett teologiskt problem som man hett debatterar eller trött tiger om bland trons folk, utan måste få förbli en del av frälsningens evangelium som vi tillsammans samtalar om, gläds i och fritt förkunnar." Karlsson, Birgit, "Tillbaka till dopet", *VP*, No. 46, 1987, p. 6. See also Swedberg, Bo, "Birgit Karlsson om ekumeniken: -Också centralt stärks nu samfundens gemenskap", *VP*, No. 50, 1989, p. 3, that Karlsson dreams about a new fellowship between the denominations plainly emphasizing in their evangelization the personal confession of faith.

[399] See for example *Svenska Baptistsamfundets Årsbok* 1981, p. 81, *"Huvudsvårigheten* i de lokalekumeniska relationerna till SMF består i frågan *om såväl barndop som troendedop* skall kunna praktiseras också i de förenade församlingarna. Motsvarande *stötesten* när det gäller ÖM, är *anslutningsformen.* Eftersom det i ÖM är så att lokalförsamlingarna inte är anslutna till ÖM utan endast samarbetar med denna, är det svårt för ÖM-församlingar som går samman med SB-församlingar att tänka sig att ansluta sig till vårt samfund. Denna fråga har varit föremål för samtal upprepade gånger och är just nu en huvudfråga för SB - ÖM-delegationen. Det bör också påpekas att de båda pastorsmötena - i Örebro 1978 och i Linköping 1980 - betytt mycket för närmandet mellan de båda jämnstora baptiströrelserna i vårt land." Italics mine.

expanded, due to the openness for the recognition of infant baptism and the questioning of "re-baptism", and also to regarding baptism as an instrumental act, a sacrament, to include an even greater rapprochement (and even integration with as the time goes on) to other churches such as the Church of Sweden and/or the Catholic Church?

The Baptist Union of Sweden is without doubt in a challenging process. It is a question of identity, ultimately Baptist identity in *oecumene.* This will be dealt with in the next chapter.

9. Reconsideration of Baptism and Baptist Identity

Baptist identity has been very closely related to believers' baptism and the belief that the congregation consists of believers baptized in this way. I have several times in this thesis pointed to a reconsideration of baptism within the Baptist Union of Sweden - there is diversity concerning baptism. This is not evident in *BUS*, which maintains a traditional, closed Baptist opinion concerning infant baptism and believers' baptism, (however, not forgetting a more instrumental view on baptism in comparison with the earlier, traditional, symbolic Baptist view).

The question of church unity is, of course, an urgent, but difficult issue. It concerns many questions and many levels: congregational, denominational, theological, practical etc. There are biblical reasons for church unity - in particular Jesus' own desire for unity. And *BEM* writes of "a call to the churches to overcome their divisions and visibly manifest their fellowship" and "we are one people and are called to confess and serve one Lord in each place and in all the world".[400] There are still, however, voices expressing a more critical standpoint towards ecumenism, among other things on account of the issue of baptism. Sometimes it is claimed that the ecumenical movement has come to a standstill.

The reconsideration of baptism and ecclesiology also implies a reconsideration of the Baptist Union of Sweden itself and its identity, which will be the subject in this last chapter. In comparison with an earlier more traditional, closed Baptist attitude, the Baptist Union of Sweden of today - especially at the congregational level - has a more open, pluralistic attitude concerning baptism, with implications for ecclesiology and ecumenism.

The general changes in Swedish society and particularly the importance of the ecumenical congregations in the development of the Baptist Union cannot possibly be emphasized enough. The

---

400 *B 6.*

increasing number of ecumenical congregations has without doubt also contributed to the diversity within the Baptist Union of Sweden and the reconsideration of baptism and Baptist identity.[401] This ought to imply that the number of genuine Baptist congregations and thus the number of "strict" Baptist members will decrease. This will possibly lead to the Baptist movement being weakened in some ways.

In an editorial in *Veckoposten* it is said that the most important thing which has happened during recent years in practical work towards Christian unity in Sweden is neither the General Assembly of the World Council of Churches in Uppsala 1968, nor the National Christian Conferences such as *G 72, V 77, J 83, Ö 89.* (All these four conferences can be regarded as partly inspired by the meeting in Uppsala in 1968, and have in fact played a vital role in keeping ecumenical work alive in Sweden, in addition to *BEM.*) *"It is instead the creation of a series of united congregations."*[402]

What is then happening to baptism and Baptist identity in this ecumenical context? The ecumenical congregations are, of course, a challenge to Baptists not only at the congregational level but also and especially at the denominational level, and to its leaders.[403] Birgit Karlsson herself gives expression to this new and demanding situation in the Baptist Union:

---

[401] See also chapter 7. in this part, and also Part I, especially chapter 9.5.

[402] *"Det viktigaste som hänt när det gäller praktiskt fungerande kristen enhet i vårt land under senare år är varken Kyrkornas världsråds generalförsamling i Uppsala 1968 eller de kristna riksmötena. Det är istället tillkomsten av en rad förenade församlingar."* "Förenade", [editorial], *VP*, No. 49, 1983, p. 2. See also Freij, Torbjörn, "Uppbrott, kollaps och sedan...? Så växte det frikyrkliga samarbetet fram – del II", *VP*, No. 45, 1978, p. 10.

[403] "Lokalekumenik – betydelsefull fråga i missionsstyrelsens höstsammanträde", [NK], *VP*, No. 48, 1978, p. 16; Lagergren, David, "ÖM och ekumeniken", *VP*, No.15, 1983, p. 2: "Det är ju alldeles klart - vilket också uttryckligt framhålles i 'Det finns en väg' - att de lokala samgåendena så småningom måste få konsekvenser för samfunden. Vad är samfunden om inte en gemenskap av församlingar?" He writes also: "att samfunden ingalunda kan stå oberörda av dessa lokala skeenden."; See also Swedberg, Bo, "Samfunden ger goda råd om dop och medlemskap", *VP*, No. 49, 1983, p. 9; Bergsten, Torsten, "Ekumenik, vision och verklighet", *Tro och Liv*, No. 1, 1986, p. 12; Swedberg, Bo, "Förenade församlingarna utmaning för samfunden", *VP*, No. 21, 1987, p. 5; Karlsson, Birgit, "Budskapet, gemenskapen och de vita fälten", *VP*, No. 19/20, 1991, p. 5. See also the discussion in Part I, for example about the reactions to the ecumenical congregations, chapter 9.5.3.

It is one thing to be a Baptist among Baptists and be confirmed in one's own faith by those who have their roots in the same soil as oneself, but it is another matter to be a Baptist among people practising infant baptism who have their roots somewhere else on the spiritual map.[404]

The ecumenical congregations are understandably not Baptist congregations in the strict sense of the word.[405] Normally less specific labels are used. They are not called for example the Baptist congregation of Alunda, Knivsta or Uppsala etc., but their names are often taken from the area. Their chapels (later also called churches) are also named in the same manner - Centrumkyrkan, Norrmalmskyrkan, Valsätrakyrkan etc. -, instead of earlier more usual names as Elim, Betel etc.

The challenging situation is also apparent in the relations between the Baptist denominational and the congregational levels, which have certainly been strained more than once during recent decades and this has resulted in a dynamic state of tension.[406] As a

---

[404] "Det är en sak att vara baptist bland baptister och bekräftas i sin tro av dem som har sina rötter i samma jord som jag själv, och en något annan situation att vara baptist bland sina barndöpande vänner som har sina rötter på ett annat håll i det andliga landskapet." Karlsson, Birgit, "Det nödvändiga samtalet om tron och praktiken", *VP*, No. 47, 1987, p. 4.

[405] See for example "Ekumenik på 80-talet", [editorial], *VP*, No. 44, 1978, p. 2.

[406] A hint of this tension, between the denominational and congregational levels, can be found in a letter from Lagergren to Bergsten. He writes in connection with criticism for centralization which has been made against the denominations that such is "always a risk and no ideal for a Free Church. But a congregation which ignores advice and admonishments which it receives from the denomination to which it belongs, and which reduces or stops its support for it must make sure it does not come in conflict with the spirit and letter of the New Testament." Bergsten quotes the letter from Lagergren to him, dated 20th December 1988, Bergsten, Torsten, "Samfundsmedvetande och kongregationalism i svensk frikyrklighet", *Kyrkohistorisk årsskrift* 1993, p. 144. He makes the following comment on the words of Lagergren: "The ideas of Lagergren referred to here mirror the denominational consciousness which is alive today in this community of faith." ("Lagergrens här refererade tankegångar speglar väl det samfundsmedvetande som i dag är levande inom denna trosgemenskap.") Ibid. See also "Lokalekumeniken trycker på", [editorial], *VP*, No. 30, 1981, p. 2; Lagergren, David, "Ekumenik 83 (II)", *VP*, No. 3, 1983, p. 2, "Det har hävdats att lokalekumeniken utgör en risk för samfunden. Identiteter och lojaliteter förändras - ibland mycket snabbt."; Swedberg, Bo, "Frågor", *VP*, No. 7, 1984, p. 8; "Samgående - på sikt!", [editorial], *VP*, No. 25, 1984, p. 2; Swedberg, Bo, " -Vi saknar samfundens stöd men lokalt fungerar det fint", *VP*, No. 41, 1984, pp. 8f.; "Åsna mellan hötappar?", [editorial], *VP*, No. 19,

matter of fact this dilemma concerning baptism, ecclesiology, ecumenical congregations and Baptist identity becomes concrete in one and the same person, David Lagergren. He certainly has a true desire to work for one church, but not at any cost. How does he for instance justify, as a *Baptist* General Secretary, participating in inaugurations of the churches of ecumenical congregations where infant baptism will also be practised?

We have fortunately a statement from Lagergren himself - just before retirement.

> I would have refused to participate, if I had followed my feelings. In order not to do harm and damage *I fulfilled my ministry, but my inner protest did not become weaker.*[407]

We thus encounter a leader of the Baptist Union of Sweden who has to compromise with his conscience and interior conviction. On the one hand, there is a conviction which would refrain from participating in these ecumenical events - much on account of baptism and ecclesiology, i.e. theological reasons. On the other hand, there are other mainly external considerations - pragmatic, financial, psychological, and ecumenical - which require something else. In brief, there is an inner conflict and the result will be an act of compromise. It is when he is going to retire that he first feels "free" to express publicly his honest opinion. This phenomenon of compromise surely exists also among other Baptists (pastors and laymen) and thus also in the Baptist as well as in the ecumenical congregations.[408]

1985, p. 2; Swedberg, Bo, "Förenade församlingarna utmaning för samfunden", *VP*, No. 21, 1987, p. 5; Öhnell, Urban, "Konferens gav råg i ryggen åt ekumeniska församlingar", *VP*, No. 16/17, 1987, p. 2.

[407] "Vid två tillfällen har jag inbjudits att medverka vid invigningen av sådana kyrkor. Vid båda tillfällena skulle jag ha avstått från att medverka, om jag lytt min känsla. För att inte såra och riva sönder *fullgjorde jag min tjänst, men den inre protesten blev inte mindre för det.*" Lagergren, David, "Varför gör inte samfunden mer...", *VP*, No. 9, 1984, p. 2. Italics mine.

[408] The compromises concern both major and minor theological and organizational issues, such as the denominational affiliation of ecumenical congregations, collections (to which organization is the ecumenical congregation supposed to give?), youth camps (to which "church-camp" is the congregation to send its youngsters?) etc. See for example "Utan historia?" [editorial], *VP*, No. 17, 1985, p. 2; Swedberg, Bo, "Frågor", *VP*, No. 7, 1984, p. 8.

Evidently Baptist identity is discussed. Ingvar Paulsson, the chairman of the Central Board 1985-1995, states:

We do really have reason to consider both who we are, in what context we find ourselves and what our tasks are.[409]

And from a survey it is obvious that especially the ecumenical congregations need guidance concerning among other things the question of baptism.[410] That baptism is one of the stumbling blocks in all this is quite clear and has been discussed previously. It is not a matter of course any more that believers' baptism alone is at the centre - in order to be (incorporated and) a member of the church and of the local congregation. Nor does the low number of believers' baptisms contribute to strengthening Baptist identity but is rather, according to some Baptists, a disturbing factor in the Baptist Union.[411]

For the sake of among other things avoiding conflicts in ecumenical talks and discussions with other churches and denominations, there is on the one hand a tendency to avoid the issues of baptism. Something other than faith *and* believers' baptism seems to be the basis of the church and the local congregation and of church unity, namely faith alone, i.e. personal conscious faith.[412] This is a deviation from the classic Baptist

---

409 Swedberg, Bo, "Ingvar Paulsson: -Årskonferensen är hela samfundets angelägenhet", *VP*, No. 19/20, 1991, p. 3.

410 See Bergsten, Torsten, "Dopet i ekumeniskt perspektiv", *VP*, No. 9, 1988, p. 7. Bergsten refers in this article to a survey done in 1987, in which 31 congregations affiliated to the Baptist Union of Sweden and the Mission Covenant Church of Sweden participated. He points out that, "The survey shows that the ecumenical congregations need further guidance from the denominational leaders. More light is needed on different questions, among them baptism."

411 See for example Karlsson, Birgit, "Budskapet, gemenskapen och de vita fälten", *VP*, No. 19/20, 1991, p. 5.

412 Janarv, Ruben, "De baptistiska grundsatserna och framtiden", [del 6], *VP*, No. 31/32, 1978, p. 12. Ruben Janarv writes for instance that, "in our denomination we have examples of how one congregation merges with another, often a Mission Covenant Church. That this is possible is due to the fact that both sides emphasize *that the congregation is to be formed by believers*. That this nonetheless can be felt difficult from a Baptist point of view depends on the fact that the Mission Covenant Church of Sweden practises a congregational act - infant baptism - which in our view makes this foundation of the congregation unclear..." Ibid. Italics mine.

principles. On the other hand, (believers') baptism is emphasized by Baptists.[413]

The Baptist Göte Aourell states that on the question of baptism, the position of the Baptists seems to be "contradictory".[414] Of course, such a contradictory position on baptism also has implications for Baptist identity. This question of identity becomes even more obvious to the members of the ecumenical congregations who cannot always identify themselves with either of the denominations to which the congregation has a relation or is affiliated.[415] It is stated by Berit Åqvist that there is a risk that the members of ecumenical congregations pay such great attention to the local fellowship and to the tasks of the congregation, that solidarity with their respective denominations grows weaker.[416] And the Baptist pastor Sven Gösta Fasth maintains that in the ecumenical congregations nobody knows how many are now Baptists and how many are members of the Mission Covenant Church of Sweden.[417]

---

[413] See *BUS*, and also for example Birgit Karlsson, David Lagergren, Bert Franzén, Martin Jansson, Ruben Mild, Edvin Österberg among others mentioned earlier in this study.

[414] "I denna svåra och viktiga fråga [dopfrågan, my remark] synes mig vår hållning som baptister motsägelsefull." Aourell, Göte, "Dopet och frikyrklig enhet", *VP*, No. 42, 1992, p. 12.

[415] See for instance Swedberg, Bo, "I Höör längtar man inte tillbaka till det som var", *VP*, No. 8, 1992, p. 7.

[416] See Swedberg, Bo, "Förenade församlingar visar: -Samfunden har redan valt gemenskapens väg", *VP*, No. 9, 1988, p. 2.

[417] Swedberg, Bo, "Baptister och missionsförbundare om förenad församling i Mölndal: -Det bästa som hänt oss", *VP*, No. 10, 1985, p. 7. Ulfgöran Bergquist, pastor in an ecumenical congregation of Lindesberg, Baptist Union of Sweden and Örebro (Baptist) Mission, talks about the dilemma of the congregation gradually losing its roots in both denominations. The local congregation is the only important thing. See Lantz, Ragni, "Övervägande positiva reaktioner till samverkan", *VP*, No. 6, 1986, p. 7. (Lindesberg's present Baptist congregation was established in 1954 through a union of two different Baptist congregations, the Baptist Union of Sweden and the Örebro (Baptist) Mission.) See also Lindberg, Erik, "1+1=mer än 2 vid samgående", *VP*, No. 40, 1991, p. 4; Ringsvåg, Ingemar, "Tappar man samfundskänslan när församlingar går samman?", *VP*, No. 25/26, 1981, pp. 8f.; Swedberg, Bo, " -Vi måste lära av de lokala erfarenheterna", *VP*, No. 16, 1989, pp. 2, 12;

Editorials in Baptist journals confirm this development. It is stated in 1987:

The situation within what usually a little improperly is called Free Church ecumenism has since about ten years ago totally changed.[418]

And another editorial says:

Nor is it at all clear that the denominations which we have to take into account today and thank God for will continue to exist unchanged for much longer.[419]

What is remarkable, in both a Baptist and a common Christian tradition, is that baptism, interpreted in the Baptist context as believers' baptism and as a requirement for membership, in one way seems to play a less significant role in the ecumenical context - also where Baptists are involved.[420] There is recognition of both infant baptism and also of faith alone, i.e. membership without any baptism at all.

In the document *Vattnet som förenar och skiljer* (The Water Which Unites and Divides) from the Örebro (Baptist) Mission, it is said:

Mild, Ruben, "Varning från SMF", *VP*, No. 11, 1992, p. 11; Fristedt, Axel, "Vart är vi baptister på väg?", *VP*, No. 14, 1992, p. 4.

[418] "Situationen inom det som lite oegentligt brukar kallas frikyrkoekumeniken är sedan något tiotal år i grunden förändrad." "Nu!", [editorial], *VP*, No. 51/52, 1987, p. 4. See also *Svenska Baptistsamfundets Årsbok* 1983, p. 81; *Svenska Baptistsamfundets Årsbok* 1989, p. 62; *Svenska Baptistsamfundets Årsbok* 1992-93, pp. 3-6, [Karlsson, Birgit, "Baptistisk tro - utmanad och uttalad"], pp. 7-12 [Om baptistisk identitet]; "Några måste vara djärva nog att börja gå enhetens väg", [Nils Sköld, Kurt Naess], *VP*, No. 45, 1991, p. 12, "Den stillastående ekumenikens tid är förbi. Det finns idag en klar kristen enhet som löper över snart sagt alla samfunds gränser."

[419] "Det är inte heller något självklart att de samfund som vi idag har att räkna med och tackar Gud för kommer att leva vidare oförändrade särskilt länge till." "Ett trossamfund", [editorial], *VP*, No. 10, 1988, p. 4. See also "Framtid för frikyrkan?", [editorial], *VP*, No. 15, 1989, p. 4; "Ta ställning", [editorial], *VP*, No. 36, 1992, p. 2, and also Bergsten, Torsten, "Samfundsmedvetande och kongregationalism i svensk frikyrklighet" *Kyrkohistorisk årsskrift* 93, 1993, p. 145.

[420] *Tecken om enhet* warns in fact that baptism may be marginalized in the Swedish Free Churches on account of the ecumenical congregations, ("risk för marginalisering av dopet i svensk frikyrklighet."), *Tecken om enhet*, 1991, p. 94. See also Bergsten, Torsten, "Gemensamma församlingar", *Nordisk Ekumenisk Orientering*, No. 2, 1994, pp. 3-5, commenting on *Tecken om enhet*.

It is certainly *possible* to have a completely consistent Baptist attitude, but is it *reasonable*, when one acknowledges in many ways other Christians as genuine Christians?[421]

And Torsten Bergsten refers to this document:

Finally I want with great sympathy to agree with the rhetorical question which concludes the document *Vattnet som förenar och skiljer...* I understand this as an unreserved confession of *open baptism*.[422]

There is a Baptist reconsideration of baptism and ecclesiology, which results in a reconsideration of Baptist identity - or a mutual interchange. The question of Baptist identity is put by the Baptists themselves. In a discussion between David Lagergren and Torsten Bergsten, the former wonders if the Baptist movement is not superfluous if New Testament believers' baptism is not to be practised.[423] According to him baptism is a prerequisite for membership of the Baptist movement,[424] whilst for some other Baptists, as I have pointed out, it is certainly desirable but not absolutely necessary. The Baptists have "to get used even to infant baptism being administered in their new congregations."[425]

---

[421] "Det är visserligen *möjligt* att inta en helt konsekvent baptistisk hållning, men är det *rimligt*, när man på så många andra sätt bejakar andra kristna som fullvärdiga kristna?" *Vattnet som förenar och skiljer*, 2nd ed., 1986, p. 42.

[422] "Till sist vill jag med varm sympati instämma i den retoriska fråga som avslutar dokumentet *Vattnet som förenar och skiljer...* Detta uppfattar jag som en förbehållslös bekännelse till *öppen baptism.*" Bergsten, Torsten, "Öppet nattvardsbord, överfört medlemskap och en öppen baptism", *VP*, No. 3, 1986, p. 6.

[423] Lagergren, David, "Ekumenisk barnteologi", *VP*, No. 17, 1991, p. 6.

[424] Ibid. See, however, also other statements above by Lagergren.

[425] "Amongst Free Churches more and more ecumenical congregations are being formed, affiliated with two or more denominations. In several of them Baptists have to get used even to infant baptism being administered in their new congregations." ("Inom frikyrkligheten bildas fler och fler förenade församlingar, anslutna till två eller flera samfund. I åtskilliga av dem får baptister vänja sig vid att även barndop förekommer i deras nya församlingsgemenskap.") Bergsten, Torsten, "På väg mot ömsesidigt doperkännande?", 1989, p. 3, [unpublished paper]. He declares also: "The bitter experiences, which the Swedish Baptist movement and the Baptist denominations *(döparrörelse)* have had during the past century, have taught us that to isolate the unity of truth at the expense of that of love, as Wiberg did, is not a blessing... For a Christian movement of life cannot in the long run with continued vitality and fidelity to the Gospel live in a one-

Bergsten states on another occasion that believers' baptism is not sufficient as a basis of unity and co-operation between congregations and denominations.

Different opinions about and experiences of the spiritual gifts, evangelization, mission and social responsibility have greater importance than a common view of faith, baptism and congregation.[426]

These statements by an ideological and theological leader amongst Swedish Baptists are remarkable, not least in the light of Baptist history, where Baptists have fought for believers' baptism and have also literally been martyrs on account of this question - also in Sweden.[427]

The term *baptimister* does not exist in Swedish vocabulary; nevertheless it is said in *Veckoposten* that the phenomenon exists. It is an attempt to describe what has happened in a continually increasing number of places in Sweden, for example congregations consisting of Baptists and Mission Covenanters. This term was coined in an article to describe the uncertain identity which certain members of ecumenical congregations can experience. They are neither clear-cut Baptists nor Mission Covenanters, but a mixture "Baptimister".[428] It is said in another article (discussing a possible federation between the Baptist Union of Sweden and the Mission

---

sidedly negative and polemical relation with the rest of Christianity." Bergsten, Torsten, "Anders Wiberg, dopet och de kristnas enhet", *Tro och Liv*, No. 4, 1988, pp. 21f. He also states: "Luckily we do not have to live in a narrowly confessional situation of confrontation as Wiberg and Waldenström did in their time. It is our good fortune to pass on the essential inheritance from Wiberg without having to adopt the exaggeratedly negative attitudes to other faiths that it contains." Ibid. pp. 25f.

[426] "Erfarenheter från de gångna hundra åren av svensk frikyrkohistoria, särskilt baptisthistoria, visar att troendedopet inte räcker som bas för enhet och samverkan mellan församlingar och samfund. Olika uppfattningar och upplevelser beträffande de andliga nådegåvorna, evangelisation, mission och socialt ansvarstagande väger tyngre än gemensam syn på tro, dop och församling." Bergsten, Torsten, "Baptismen, trosfriheten och ekumeniken", *Liv och tjänst*, 1988, p. 195.

[427] Concerning this see Part I, especially chapter 5. and chapter 6.

[428] "Baptimister?", *VP*, No. 37, 1987, p. 4. See also Bergsten, Torsten, "Vad är omistligt i bekännelsen av den kristna tron?", *VP*, No. 12, 1990, p. 4, "Nog vore det en befrielse om vi kunde slippa alla våra många samfundsetiketter!"

Covenant Church of Sweden),[429] that in the long run the Baptist Union will be swallowed up by a denomination which practises infant baptism, and it is asked whether it is there they belong as Baptists?[430] – The "giant Mission Covenant Church of Sweden" is mentioned.[431]

The former president of the Swedish Baptist Youth Association (SBUF), Bengt Jansson, is of the opinion that youth in the ecumenical congregations are in a particular crisis of identity. He illustrates this by giving the following example.

A youth group from one congregation wants to go together to a conference. Because some feel at home in one context and others in another, the result is very often that the group does not participate in any conference at all, either on the district or on the national levels.[432] He writes that a "non-denominational" generation ("samfundslös" generation) is unconsciously created where different movements outside the traditional denominations and churches may acquire greater freedom to act. And according to Jansson, the questions of identity are in the long run - or maybe already now? - a problem, not only for the youth associations but also for the denominations.[433] New, previously unknown patterns are growing,

---

[429] Concerning the idea of federation see more below. See also Part I, chapter 9.1.

[430] "Jag frågar: är det där vi hör hemma som baptister?", Hultberg Walter, "Var hör vi hemma?", VP, No. 42, 1992, p. 12; Mild, Ruben, "Skriv själv, Tomas!", VP, No. 16/17, 1992, p. 16.

[431] Eriksson, Klas, Persson, Håkan, "Helhjärtad ekumenik?", VP, No. 42, 1991, p. 6, "Risk att slukas av 'jätten SMF'".

[432] Jansson, Bengt, "Svar på Berits utmaning: -Det brister i prioriteringen", VP, No. 16, 1985, p. 6. About 30% of the members in the Swedish Baptist Youth Association (SBUF) came in 1985 from ecumenical congregations, where they were affiliated with two or more Youth Associations. Ibid. See also Åqvist, Berit, "Öppen fråga", VP, No. 13, 1985, p. 2; "Utan historia?", [editorial], VP, No. 17, 1985, p. 2.

[433] Jansson, Bengt, "Svar på Berits utmaning: -Det brister i prioriteringen", VP, No. 16, 1985, p. 6. See also "Utan historia?", [editorial], VP, No. 17, 1985, p. 2. Berit Åqvist is of the opinion that above all youth are threatened by deficient relations with the national organizations. Åqvist, Berit, "Varför inte steget före?", VP, No. 22, 1985, p. 2. See also Fahlgren, Sune, "Baptismens spiritualitet – speglad i gudstjänstlivet. Svenskt perspektiv", Samfund i förändring, 1997, pp. 106f.

and sometimes a kind of new congregation, "denomination" or movement is established.

As a recent example of the latter the so-called *Trosrörelsen* (The Faith Movement) may be mentioned.[434] This movement has had a certain impact on the Free Churches, for example on the Baptist Union of Sweden and the Pentecostal Movement,[435] just as the Baptist Union of Sweden once influenced in the 19th century the monolithic National Church and Swedish society. We have also to observe other processes and movements going on throughout the congregations and denominations, indicated in the thesis.[436]

---

[434] *Trosrörelsen (The Faith Movement)*, called by its opponents *Framgångsteologin (The Theology of Success)*, is a movement which according to its own statistics (1990) includes about 100 congregations with approximately 20-30,000 members, plus "associative" members and sympathizers. This movement only practises believers' baptism. "Re-baptism" is practised. Agnarsson, Ruben, "Livets Ord", *Svenska Trossamfund*, 8th ed., 1990, pp. 101-105. The number of members is called into question: Skog mentions 84 congregations and about 7,100 members in *Trosrörelsen*, (in 1992), Skog, Margareta, "Trosrörelsen i Sverige", *Tro & Tanke* 1993:5, p. 104. See also Skog, Margareta, "Frikyrkosamfundens medlemsantal i landets kommuner 1995", *Tro & Tanke* 1997:3, pp. 92ff, mentioning about 40 congregations and about 6000 members in 1995.

See also Holmström, Krister, *Biblisk framgångsteologi*, Uppsala 1986; Gustafsson, Göran, *Tro, samfund och samhälle*, 1991, (especially pp. 109-122); Skog, Margareta, "Trosrörelsen i Sverige", *Tro & Tanke* 1993:5, especially pp. 89-124. Aronson, Torbjörn, *Guds eld över Sverige*, 1990, also gives a presentation of *Livets Ord och trosväckelsen* (pp. 191-233). *Trosrörelsen* has (whether legitimately or not) been criticized and also got quite a lot of publicity in the mass media. See also for example *Succé med Gud?* 1988; Nilsson, Fred, *Parakyrkligt*, 1988, especially pp. 205-252; Hellberg, Carl-Johan, *Gud och pengar*, 1987.

[435] See *Svenska Baptistsamfundets Årsbok* 1990/91, pp. 49f.; Karlsson, Birgit, "Det nödvändiga samtalet om tron och praktiken", *VP*, No. 47, 1987, p. 4. Besides the Faith Movement, the Vineyard Movement, and the so-called Toronto Blessing may also be mentioned. Karlsson, Birgit, "150 händelserika år", *Tro, Frihet, Gemenskap*, 1998, p. 36. Concerning another movement the Oasis Movement *(Oas-rörelsen)*, and also the Vineyard Movement *(Vineyardrörelsen)*, see Skog, Margareta, "Trosrörelsen i Sverige", *Tro & Tanke* 1993:5, pp. 125ff.

[436] As additional examples of constellations and co-operation across the denominational and congregational boundaries in Sweden, we find for example, besides the ecumenical congregations, joint open Bible studies, prayer and Bible study groups, retreat and meditation movements, charismatic gatherings, worship and intercession meetings, house churches

We find that the Baptist Union of Sweden has co-operated and still co-operates with other congregations, churches and denominations despite diversities of opinions and differences between the churches in regard to theological and practical issues. Birgit Karlsson writes:

The lines of affinity do not run any more along denominational or congregational boundaries but transcend old limits.[437]

There are on the one hand promising convergences from an ecumenical point of view. It is, however, on the other hand not clear that all this contributes to uniting churches and denominations. As Birgit Karlsson says: "It is reasonable to ask if this is a movement towards unity or towards division?"[438]

The Baptists have been challenged. Ruben Janarv asks:

how many denominations have since the days of the Trilateral Denominational Consultations been capable of reconsiderations comparable with those which the Baptist Union has sustained?

He puts the question directly to another denomination without giving any answer: "Has the Mission Covenant Church of Sweden?"[439] In another article the Baptist pastor Martin Jansson (b. 1903) also discusses the problem of Baptist identity. He asks:

how will it be possible in the long run for the General Secretary and other leaders in our [i.e. Baptist, my remark] denomination to stand the pressure and the demand on the one hand to inspire and work for an expansion of the work of the denomination, and on the other hand to give support and

---

etc. See for instance Irving Palm in Lindberg, Erik, "Gemenskapsgrupper - frikyrkans framtid", VP, No. 42, 1991, p. 5; Swedberg, Bo, "Angelägen uppgift nu: Att plantera församlingar", VP, No. 15, 1992, p. 5.

[437] "Samhörighetslinjer löper inte längre samfunds- eller ens församlingsvis utan söker sig över gamla gränser." Karlsson, Birgit, "Baptistisk tro är inte till salu - men vi vill ge den vidare", VP, No. 43, 1991, p. 5.

[438] "Det är rimligt att fråga om detta är en rörelse i enhet eller en i splittring?" Ibid. See also Eriksson, Klas, Persson, Håkan, "Helhjärtad ekumenik?", VP, No. 42, 1991, p. 6.

[439] "Jag vågar en fråga: hur många samfund har sedan tresamfundssamtalens dagar orkat med omprövningar jämförliga med dem SB gjort? Har SMF?" Janarv, Ruben, "Gemensam väg?" VP, No. 17, 1983, p. 11.

inspiration to a movement which results in the congregations of the denomination uniting with and integrating into other denominations?[440]

In view of this unitive process, he asks a really most relevant and serious question:

Can the Baptist Union of Sweden, which according to its regulations is a union of Baptist congregations, still continue to exist as a denomination?[441]

In an inquiry it is found that most of the ecumenical congregations receive new members on confession of faith independent of whether the person in question is baptized or not.[442] Of course, these ecumenical congregations stir up different reactions, both positive and negative.[443]

Baptist identity is questioned. There are voices critical to the ecumenical process which has contributed to a reconsideration of baptism and ecclesiology and consequently to a reconsideration of the Baptist Union itself. But, and this is also important to note, there are other voices who are ready to pay the price. Theological and dogmatic differences, concerning the question of baptism for

---

[440] Jansson, Martin, "Hur skall Baptistsamfundet ha det?", *VP*, No. 9, 1984, p. 14.

[441] "Kan Baptistsamfundet, som enligt stadgarna är en sammanslutning av baptistförsamlingar, ändå i verkligheten fortsätta att existera som samfund?" Jansson, Martin, "Skall vi ha Svenska Baptistsamfundet?" *VP*, No. 25/26, 1982, p. 10. Jansson asks this question because of the report "Det finns en väg", where it is stated: "Det bör vara en bestämd strävan från vårt samfunds sida att medverka till att antalet samfund i vårt land minskas. Den lokalekumeniska utvecklingen pekar mot att vi för vår del i första hand arbetar med sikte på förening både med Örebromissionen och med Svenska Missionsförbundet." "Det finns en väg", 1982, p. 19. [unpublished paper]. This is quoted by Jansson. See also "Konferensbeslut. Fred och och arbetslöshet tungt vägande frågor", *VP*, No. 22, 1982, p. 7; Arvidsson, Rune, "En dopsyn?", *VP*, No. 39, 1985, p. 12, He writes: "Många av Svenska baptistsamfundets församlingar har på senare tid lättat på 'inträdeskravet' - om jag får uttrycka mig lite vanvördigt. Allt fler medlemmar tas tydligen in enbart på bekännelse, och det gör att jag - och många med mig - frågar sig vart samfundet är på väg. Vuxendopet har ju varit grunden för vår tro och bör så vara allt framgent. Det borde helt enkelt vara självklart. Vi är ju baptister!"

[442] *Tecken om enhet,* 1991, p. 94.

[443] See Part I, chapter 9.5.3.

example, are not always regarded as important; there are no "rights" or "wrongs".[444] This position also has implications on other subjects such as ecclesiology, christology, ecumenism, and (Baptist) identity.

In the Baptist document "Det finns en väg" it is stated:

This motley picture of fusion and co-operation may appear as confused and it has sometimes been interpreted as *a threat* to the existence of our denomination. The threat is real if we count on preserving our denomination in its present form for all time. If it is instead the case that the constellations within Swedish Free Churchmanship need radically to change, our situation on the contrary is *promising*, precisely because of the great variety and the possibilities which thereby are opened up for unity on the denominational level.[445]

"Det finns en väg" regards this process and change within the Baptist Union as positive:

As far as ecumenism has an expanded co-operation in view, it hardly causes any problems for our denomination nowadays. We have realized its usefulness and experienced its joys, and we have little by little learned also to appreciate those who traditionally have been far from us as Christian sisters and brothers.[446]

It is said that the breaking up into a number of different churches is post-biblical, yes even unbiblical. The ecumenical movement is in

---

[444] See for instance Naess, Kurt, "Oacceptabelt alternativ?" *VP*, No. 19, 1992, p. 12. He writes: "Som jag förstår det kommer inte frågan om dopsyn eller hur man själv är döpt att spela någon som helst roll den dag då vi alla skall avlägga räkenskap för våra liv" and he concludes: "Låt oss därför inte fastna i dogmer och det som är historia."; see also Naess, Kurt, "Det finns inte rätt och fel i dopfrågan", *VP*, No. 36, 1992, pp. 11, 13; Lantz, Ragni, "Ebbe Sundström: -Teologin får vika om helheten gagnas", *VP*, No. 50, 1989, p. 2.

[445] "Denna brokiga bild av samgående och samarbete kan synas förvirrad och har ibland uppfattats som ett *hot* mot vårt samfunds existens. Det hotet är verkligt, om vi räknar med att bevara vårt samfund i dess nuvarande form för all framtid. Om det i stället är så att konstellationerna inom svensk frikyrklighet behöver radikalt förändras, är vår situation tvärtom *löftesrik* just genom sin mångfald och genom de möjligheter som därmed öppnas till enhet på samfundsplanet." "Det finns en väg", 1982, p. 18, [unpublished paper]. Italics mine.

[446] "Så långt ekumeniken syftar till vidgat samarbete, vållar den numera knappast några problem för vårt samfund. Vi har insett dess nytta och erfarit dess glädje, och vi har efterhand lärt oss värdesätta också dem som traditionellt stått långt ifrån oss, som kristna systrar och bröder." Ibid. p. 17.

this report looked upon as one of the most important revivals, which tries to find a remedy for this unsatisfactory state of affairs and has found a place within and to a great degree influenced the Baptist Union of Sweden. This must according to the report be judged as a positive development.[447]

Boundary lines have been modified, as I have pointed out in the thesis, within the Baptist Union of Sweden. The adjustment to ecumenical congregations is also reflected in changes in the statutes of the Baptist Union of Sweden. New challenges are waiting, also concerning baptism.

One of the movements which sometimes seems to be neglected in theological research, but which in fact has also had an important role in the ecumenical process, is the charismatic movement or renewal. It challenges the traditional congregations and denominations. Birgit Karlsson writes about this in the final number of *Veckoposten*. She states:

the spiritual experience creates a unity and fellowship which sometimes transcends the foundations of faith which we feel are indispensable such as baptism and belonging to a congregation.[448]

---

[447] Ibid. pp. 16f. David Lagergren writes a couple of years earlier that a reduction of denominations in Sweden is desirable. "Så ser ledare för andra samfund på SMF", [David Lagergren], *Liv och frihet*, 1978, p. 293; see also Lagergren, David, "Försonad mångfald", *VP*, No. 43, 1986, p. 5. Bergsten writes for example that the ecumenical congregations are a challenge and stimulation to leaders and to larger congregations to seek new ways to co-operation and fellowship at both the central and the local levels. Bergsten, Torsten, "Baptismen, trosfriheten och ekumeniken", *Liv och tjänst*, 1988, p. 200.

[448] "Karismatisk förnyelse... utmanar identiteten... Den andliga upplevelsen skapar enhet och gemenskap som stundom går förbi de trons grunder vi känner omistliga som dop och församlingstillhörighet." Karlsson, Birgit, "Baptistisk tro - utmanad och uttalad", *VP*, No. 44/45, 1992, p. 5. See also Johnny Jonsson who writes that the Holy Spirit has a decisive function in God's mission, in the rebirth of the human being and his incorporation into the Kingdom of God. Jonsson, Johnny, "Mission enligt Johannes evangelium", *Liv och tjänst*, 1988, pp. 68ff.; Lagergren, David, "Frikyrkans framtidsväg", *VP*, No. 43, 1991, p. 4, referring to Nigel Wright, teacher at Spurgeon's College, and his book *Challenge to Change. A radical agenda for Baptists*, where he recommends opening up to the charismatic movement. Lagergren writes: "En väg som Wright rekommenderar är att öppna för den karismatiska rörelsen. Den har inneburit en andlig förnyelse av den enskilda medlemmen men också en kulturell förnyelse av församlingen... Wright menar att det karismatiska inslaget bidragit till att bryta ner de speciella kyrko- och kapellkulturer som skapats bland baptister och andra frikyrkliga

A question which for explicable reasons has arisen in a specific way is, especially because of the development of the ecumenical congregations: where are the limits to be drawn[449] between the Baptist congregations, the Baptist denomination, and other *non*-Baptist congregations, churches and denominations – in short who is a Baptist? For it seems to be more and more difficult to maintain the traditional denominational boundaries, both between all the different congregations (at the local congregational level) *and* between the different Free Church denominations (at the central denominational level). As it is said in "Det finns en väg":

> When the ecumenical revival advances towards its utmost goal, a complete organic unity among all Christians, it becomes, however, more difficult.

And it continues that different views of faith, which sometimes are irreconcilable, confront each other:

> An identity which has been growing up for generations is questioned. Different activities and institutions, which all have dimensions suitable for their own denomination, *must merge* into their equivalents elsewhere. This involves a long and difficult process, which demands patient work.[450]

A fundamental question to ask in this process is: how open can the Baptist Union of Sweden be and still be a *Baptist* denomination? What criteria must then exist? For from the reconsideration of baptism within the Baptist congregations and the Baptist Union of

---

men som nu överlevt sig själva... Vad det rör sig om är öppenhet för Anden. Om Gud är i denna rörelse, bör vi också vara i den, deklarerade Wright rakt på sak." Wright also discusses introducing the title of bishop, "införandet av biskopstiteln för dem som övar tillsyn inom ett antal församlingar. Men biskopen skall då främst ha evangelisation och andlig vård som uppgift." Ibid. See also Karlsson, Birgit, "150 händelserika år", *Tro, Frihet, Gemenskap*, 1998, pp. 35-37 ("Social och karismatisk väckelse"); Lidén, Sven Gunnar, *Tema*: "Svensk baptistungdom och dess verksamhet", *Tro, Frihet, Gemenskap*, 1998, pp. 89f.

449 Limits interpreted in a wider way which includes for example theology, doctrines, ideology, practice.

450 "När den ekumeniska väckelsen går vidare mot sitt yttersta mål, en fullständig organisk enhet alla kristna emellan, blir det svårare. Här konfronteras trosåskådningar som ibland är oförenliga. Här ifrågasätts en identitet som växt fram genom generationer. Här *måste* arbetsgrenar och institutioner, som dimensionerats för arbete inom det egna samfundet, *sammansmältas* med sina motsvarigheter på andra håll. Detta innebär en lång och svår process, som kräver tålmodigt arbete." "Det finns en väg", 1982, p. 17, [unpublished paper]. Italics mine.

Sweden – and on the traditional and fundamental Baptist principles –[451] the provocative question may be put: is it possible for the Baptist Union of Sweden to continue to exist as a *Baptist* denomination?

The development especially at the congregational level may result in the Baptist Union of Sweden co-operating in one way or another to an increasing degree, but also being integrated in a new church unity, not only at the congregational level, which already to a large extent is a fact, but also at the denominational level. The question of the extent to which co-operation can go has also been explicitly put within the Baptist Union of Sweden itself.[452] It is thus possible that what is taking place within the Baptist Union, and between the churches and denominations, is a step towards the realization of church unity also on the denominational level. The idea of unification is once again expressed.[453]

The idea of a federation is put forward, an idea which in later years has been launched by among others Birgit Karlsson and was

---

451 See Part I, chapter 2.

452 See for instance Jansson, Martin, "Tveksamma och frågande baptister", *VP*, No. 13/14, 1988, p. 12, he writes: "Frågan är nu denna: kan Baptistsamfundets verksamhet fortsätta, kan verksamheten här hemma, verksamheten på missionsfälten tillsammans med de inhemska baptistsamfunden, gemenskapen och samarbetet med Baptisternas världsallians och andra verksamheter fortsätta, om församlingarna upphör att vara baptistförsamlingar och helt går upp i gemenskap med flera andra samfund?" He continues: "Mer än 30 procent av våra medlemmar är med i de förenade församlingarna. Inom Missionsförbundet är det endast 7 eller 8 procent. Pingströrelsen berörs nästan inte alls, och ändå finns inom den nära hälften av frikyrkans medlemmar i Sverige."

453 "As a continuation of this process [i.e. ecumenical Free Church congregations, remark mine] there is a possibility that a common Free Church is being created, an idea... ever since the 1910's." Bergsten, Torsten, "Samfundsmedvetande och kongregationalism i svensk frikyrklighet" *Kyrkohistorisk årsskrift* 93, 1993, p. 145. In 1994 he also writes: "That the ecumenical congregations join together to form a new Free Church denomination is excluded. One of their aims is to influence existing denominations to unite." ("Det är uteslutet att de gemensamma församlingarna sluter sig samman till ett nytt frikyrkosamfund. Ett av deras syften är ju att påverka de bestående samfunden att förenas."), Bergsten, Torsten, "Gemensamma församlingar", *Nordisk Ekumenisk Orientering*, No. 2, 1994, p. 4. See also "Framtid för frikyrkan?", [editorial], *VP*, No. 15, 1989, p. 4; "Ta ställning", [editorial], *VP*, No. 36, 1992, p. 2, "Samtidigt omprövas också själva samfundsstrukturerna." etc.

discussed a lot around 1990 within the Baptist Union of Sweden. This meant that some kind of a covenant would be made between independent Free Churches.[454] Some are, however, of the opinion that this step is not enough since the federation will probably result in the denominations being preserved. Therefore, another, more radical step must be taken. This has been proposed within the Baptist Union as well as within other denominations.[455] In order to

[454] See Swedberg, Bo, "Birgit Karlsson om ekumeniken: -Också centralt stärks nu samfundens gemenskap", VP, No. 50, 1989, p. 3; "'En federativ gemenskap'", VP, No. 50, 1989, p. 3; Mattsson, Valter, "Gemensamma församlingar: Förväntningar på federativ gemenskap", VP, No. 16, 1990, p. 5; "Nu är tiden inne för nya perspektiv i enhetssamtalen", [Sigvard Karlehagen, Gustav Sundström, Ingvar Paulsson, Birgit Karlsson], VP, No. 12, 1991, p. 3; Swedberg, Bo, "Baptistledarna: -Nu krävs vidgade perspektiv i vårt arbete för kristen enhet", VP, No. 13/14, 1991, p. 5; Swedberg, Bo, "Deklarationen", VP, No. 16, 1991, p. 2; Lindblom, Sven-Gunnar, "Hur skall frikyrkornas samhörighet utformas?" VP, No. 18, 1991, p. 4; "Öppna dörrar", [editorial], VP, No. 19/20, 1991, p. 2; Swedberg, Bo, "Ingvar Paulsson: -Årskonferensen är hela samfundets angelägenhet", VP, No. 19/20, 1991, p. 3; "Över alla gränser", [editorial], VP, No. 21/22, 1991, p. 2; "Vägen till målet", [editorial], VP, No. 39, 1991, p. 2; Karlsson, Birgit, "Baptistisk tro är inte till salu - men vi vill ge den vidare", VP, No. 43, 1991, p. 5; "Från ord till handling. Samfundsstyrelserna vill frikyrklig enhet", VP, No. 5, 1992, p. 1, where Birgit Karlsson states: "För mig framstår en federation som den bästa lösningen. Federationen pekar utöver sig själv, och jag skulle se det som naturligt att resultatet på sikt blir ett gemensamt samfund."; "Förverkliga federationen!", [editorial] VP, No. 5, 1992, p. 2; Swedberg, Bo, "Samfundsstyrelserna redo ta nya steg mot frikyrklig enhet", VP, No. 5, 1992, p. 5; Swedberg, Bo, "Birgit Karlsson: -Förord för federation!", VP, No. 5, 1992, p. 5; "Är vi på väg mot målet?", [editorial], VP, No. 8, 1992, p. 2; Bergsten, Torsten, "Att respektera varandras dop", VP, No. 9, 1992, p. 12; "Ja till samverkan", [editorial], VP, No. 41, 1992, p. 2; Svenska Baptistsamfundets Årsbok 1992-93, pp. 52f. See also Tecken om enhet, 1991.

[455] See for example "Ett stort kliv", VP, No. 13/14, 1991, p. 2; Swedberg, Bo, "Missionsförbundet vill ta ett rejält kliv", VP, No. 13/14, 1991, p. 3; "En förenad fri och öppen frikyrka", [editorial], VP, No. 27/28, 1992, p. 2. It is stated: "The General Secretary of the Baptist Union, Birgit Karlsson, has earlier proposed the idea of a federation, a sort of covenant between half a dozen independent Free Churches. However, Walter Persson and the Mission Covenant Church of Sweden want to go further: a denomination is not an aim in itself and a federation would preserve denominations. The day that a larger constellation is formed the Mission Covenant Church of Sweden should be dissolved and be absorbed by it... My dream is a denomination that does not build on any creedal documents, but only on confession of faith in Jesus Christ as Lord, and belief in the Trinity. Independent congregations can join this denomination." Italics mine, see Wallander, Cecilia, "'Det är dags

achieve this, not only the creation of a federation has been discussed, but of something completely new, i.e. the unification of some Free Churches into a new church unity at the denominational level.[456]

This idea, not necessarily of creating a new church, but of uniting already existing churches or denominations, has existed more or less consciously for a long time in the Swedish Baptist movement, and is still present. Berit Åqvist gives expression to this in her question:

> And when we can live together at the local level across denominational borderlines with our different backgrounds and diverse views on baptism, why can we not do so at the denominational level?[457]

And we also find once again that young people, for example in the youth association *SBUF* (the Swedish Baptist Youth Association), are one or two steps ahead also in this process, working towards church unity.[458]

---

att komma till klarhet' Missionsföreståndare Walter Persson om ekumeniken", *Svenska Kyrkans Tidning*, No. 25/26, 1991, p. 16.

[456] "Ett stort kliv", *VP*, No. 13/14, 1991, p. 2; "En förenad fri och öppen frikyrka", [editorial], *VP*, No. 27/28, 1992, p. 2; Svensson, Alvar, "Låt inte mörkermännen ta över!", *VP*, No. 45, 1991, p. 12. (Cf., however, Bergsten, Torsten, "Gemensamma församlingar", *Nordisk Ekumenisk Orientering*, No. 2, 1994, p. 4, just quoted above.)

[457] "Och kan vi leva tillsammans lokalt, över samfundsgränserna, med våra olika bakgrunder och våra skilda dopsyner, varför skulle vi då inte kunna göra det på samfundsplanet?", in Swedberg, Bo, "Förenade församlingar visar: - Samfunden har redan valt gemenskapens väg", *VP*, No. 9, 1988, pp. 2f.

[458] See for example "SBUF och SMU visar vägen", *VP*, No. 17, 1991, p. 1; "Ungdomen visar vägen", [editorial], *VP*, No. 17, 1991, p. 2; Swedberg, Bo, "SBUF och SMU överens: -Nu ska vi gå samman i ett gemensamt förbund", *VP*, No. 17, 1991, p. 3; "Framåt!", *VP*, No. 24, 1991, p. 2. Nils Sköld, then chairman of *SBUF*, states: "We wanted to make sure that the mother denominations [i.e. the Baptist Union of Sweden and the Mission Covenant Church of Sweden, my remark] have the same aim as the youth associations, that is, that they are on the way towards a federative unification, and I feel that we received such support." ("Vi ville försäkra oss om att modersamfunden har samma inriktning som ungdomsförbunden, dvs är på väg mot ett federativt samgående, och det stödet tycker jag att vi fick."), "Samgående får helhjärtat stöd", *VP*, No. 39, 1991, p. 1. See also "Några måste vara djärva nog att börja gå enhetens väg", [Nils Sköld, Kurt Naess], *VP*, No. 45, 1991, p. 12, [Sköld Chairman of *SBUF*, Naess National Chairman (förbundssekreterare) of *SBUF*]; Swedberg, Bo, "I Höör längtar man inte

There is even explicit talk about not integration, but dissolution of the Swedish Baptist Youth Association (SBUF):

> SBUF is, as little as any denominational body, an end in itself. If we can see that Christian unity is advanced by our dissolution, we will take such a step.[459]

Congregations and (some) denominations work for the ecumenical strivings towards some kind of church unity and they often discover that they have much more in common than they probably - because of prejudices and negative statements about each other - had expected. The Baptist Union of Sweden as a whole has been forced in different ways by above all this ecumenical process into a less categorical position concerning believers' baptism (not least at the local level in the congregations) than the one which is found in for example BUS (at the official level). Classic Baptist principles seem to be less certain.

The ecumenical development which is taking place within the Baptist Union may possibly be regarded as one step towards a realization of what is said in BEM "to realize the goal of visible Church unity",[460] and also of the declaration made already in New Delhi in 1961 about the unity of "all in each place".[461] The process

---

tillbaka till det som var", VP, No. 8, 1992, p. 7 ("Ungdomarna drev på"); Lantz, Ragni, "Vasakyrkan i Filipstad: Tre frikyrkosamfund i stimulerande gemenskap", VP, No. 9, 1992, p. 8 ("Ungdomarna visade vägen"); "SBUF sade ja till gemensamt ungdomsförbund", VP, No. 25/26, 1992, p. 1; Lagerström, Christine, "Historisk årskonferens i ekumenikens tecken", VP, No. 25/26, 1992, pp. 8f. See also Part I, chapter 9.2. etc., on the role of the youth in the ecumenical process.

[459] "SBUF är, lika lite som någon samfundskropp, ett självändamål. Kan vi se att den kristna enheten främjas av vår upplösning, ska vi gå däråt." "Några måste vara djärva nog att börja gå enhetens väg", [Nils Sköld, Kurt Naess], VP, No. 45, 1991, p. 12; see also Lidén, Sven Gunnar, Tema: "Svensk baptistungdom och dess verksamhet", Tro, Frihet, Gemenskap, 1998, pp. 93f., about a joint declaration of intent in 1992, to form a common youth association, and mentioning that the three youth associations of the Baptist Union of Sweden, the Mission Covenant Church of Sweden and the United Methodist Church in Sweden (SBUF, SMU, MKU) moved into joint headquarters in 1993.

[460] BEM p. vii.

[461] The New Delhi Report, 1962, p. 116. See also for example "Alla på samma ort", [editorial], VP, No. 7, 1986, p. 2.

towards church unity is also expressed in among other things the common hymn books, the common service manuals, shared witnesses, common services etc., which I have also dealt with in this study. We find at least partially how the ecumenical vision of church unity begins to be realized.

The united Free Church has not until now, however, been realized as far as the Baptist Union of Sweden is concerned on the denominational level, but as a matter of fact some other denominations in Sweden have gone further.[462] The denominational level is, in comparison with the congregational level, as it has been almost from the very beginning, "involved in ecumenical matters but without being involved". In other words, it holds the door open for different future possibilities and combinations - with other churches and denominations such as the Örebro (Baptist) Mission [i.e. after 1996/97 Interact], the Mission Covenant Church of Sweden, the Church of Sweden etc. - without coming to a definite decision to unite totally with another church or denomination.[463]

Sometimes disappointment is expressed among Baptists at the congregational level towards the denominational level, or as I have already pointed out in this chapter a state of tension between the

---

[462] In 1994 two denominations were united: the Holiness Union Mission and the Scandinavian Independent Baptist Union, HF/FB (HF/FB Mission). In New Year 1997 a union NYBYGGET - kristen samverkan, with the international name Interact, was formed. Behind this phenomenon we find the Örebro (Baptist) Mission and HF/FB Mission. Skog, Margareta, "Antal medlemmar i valda samfund 1975-1996", 1996:6, p. 48. In Interact there are about 29,000 members in 370 congregations. See for example "Landet runt", Trons Värld, No. 2, 1997, p. 11.

[463] As a matter of fact there is still almost the same number of churches and denominations in Sweden as 20 or 40 years ago - or in fact even more. One reason for this is, of course, the so-called immigrant churches, such as for instance the Roman Catholic Church and all the different Orthodox Churches (which have increased in number), as well as other movements, churches etc. See for example Skog, Margareta, "Antal medlemmar i valda samfund 1975-1996", Tro & Tanke, 1996:6, pp. 45-55, especially pp. 53-55, and also "Sommarstiltje", [editorial] VP, No. 26, 1986, p. 2.

"It can be noted at the end of this book that little has happened in the Free Church ecumenical development here described in regard to the denominational level. *Optimistic visionaries have fought an unequal battle against the cautiousness of the leaders of the denomination.* The Swedish Free Church ecumenism of the 20th century may from one point of view be briefly summarized so." Bergsten, Torsten, Frikyrkor i samverkan, 1995, p. 297.

Baptist denominational and congregational levels exists,[464] and also in the Baptist organ *Veckoposten* itself (in for example editorials), it is claimed that nothing has been done for decades, in fact since the 1950's, at the central, denominational level, concerning unity work.[465]

At the same time there are voices at the denominational level which deny this. It is claimed that one also desires and works for church unity at the central, denominational level.[466]

---

[464] See for example Swedberg, Bo, "Frågor", *VP*, No. 7, 1984, p. 8; Swedberg, Bo, " -Vi saknar samfundens stöd men lokalt fungerar det fint", *VP*, No. 41, 1984, pp. 8f; Swedberg, Bo, "Förenade församlingarna utmaning för samfunden", *VP*, No. 21, 1987, p. 5; Öhnell, Urban, "Konferens gav råg i ryggen åt ekumeniska församlingar", *VP*, No. 16/17, 1987, p. 2; "Efter 126 års parallelldrift. Två förenade församlingar har bildats i södra Närke", *VP*, No. 8, 1988, p. 3; Swedberg, Bo, "Lokalekumener: -Vi har ett budskap till våra samfund", *VP*, No. 35, 1989, p. 8; Swedberg, Bo, "Pastor i förenad församling: -Samfunden bör ta större hänsyn till utvecklingen i församlingarna", *VP*, No. 51/52, 1989, p. 9.

[465] "Handling för enhet", [editorial], *VP*, No. 16, 1989, p. 4. See also "Samgående - på sikt!", [editorial], *VP*, No. 25, 1984, p. 2; "Åsna mellan hötappar?", [editorial], *VP*, No. 19, 1985, p. 2; "En årskonferens", [editorial], *VP*, No. 24, 1987, p. 4; "Framtid för frikyrkan?", [editorial], *VP*, No. 15, 1989, p. 4, (it states: "Samfunden centralt har kommit på efterkälken."); "När vi samlas...", [editorial], *VP*, No. 18/19, 1989, p. 6; "Ord om enhet", [editorial], *VP*, No. 1/2, 1991, p. 2; "Ledaransvar", [editorial], *VP*, No. 49, 1989, p. 4; "Traditioner och reaktioner", [editorial], *VP*, No. 16, 1990, p. 2; "Om politikerna kan...", [editorial], *VP*, No. 40, 1992, p. 2.

[466] See for example Swedberg, Bo, "Samfunden ger goda råd om dop och medlemskap", *VP*, No. 49, 1983, p. 9; "Samfunden svarar Lysekil: -Visst får de förenade församlingarna vårt stöd", *VP*, No. 42, 1984, p. 15; "Enheten kan inte vänta", *VP*, No. 16, 1989, p. 1; Elmquist, Karl-Axel, "Viktig arbetsgrupp tillsatt: Sex samfund börjar nu samråda om de förenade församlingarna", *VP*, No. 16, 1989, p. 2, writing about a working party consisting of representatives from six denominations discussing and consulting about the ecumenical congregations. They were the Baptist Union of Sweden, the Mission Covenant Church of Sweden, the Örebro (Baptist) Mission, the Holiness Union Mission, the United Methodist Church in Sweden and the Swedish Alliance Mission. This group produced *Tecken om enhet*, 1991, referred to several times; Swedberg, Bo, "Vi måste lära av de lokala erfarenheterna", *VP*, No. 16, 1989, pp. 2, 12; Swedberg, Bo, "Birgit Karlsson om ekumeniken: -Också centralt stärks nu samfundens gemenskap", *VP*, No. 50, 1989, p. 3; "Från ord till handling. Samfundsstyrelserna vill frikyrklig enhet", *VP*, No. 5, 1992, p. 1; Swedberg, Bo, "Samfundsstyrelserna redo ta nya steg mot frikyrklig enhet", *VP*, No. 5, 1992, p. 5; Swedberg, Bo, "Birgit

In short, it can be said that the relations between the congregational and denominational levels, between the Baptist Union of Sweden and other churches and denominations, as well as central issues such as baptism, ecclesiology and church unity, and the question of the Baptist identity, are more complex and difficult to handle than they may first appear. There are no simple, unambiguous answers. Even if the Baptist Union of Sweden should not necessarily cease to exist, should one of the basic and characteristic Baptist principles – believers' baptism - disappear, the Baptist movement as a theological current would be modified in comparison with its classic identity.

The question is, of course, how open the Baptist Union of Sweden can be and still be, partly in its own opinion, and partly also that of others, regarded as a *Baptist* Union – if infant baptism is recognized, if baptism is not a condition for membership of and incorporation into the church etc?[467] A modification towards a less strict position has in fact taken place within the Baptist Union of Sweden in more than one area.

Berit Åqvist is of the opinion that the Baptist Union of Sweden has already chosen its direction.[468] How does one know this? The

---

Karlsson: -Förord för federation!", *VP*, No.5, 1992, p. 5. See also the discussion about the federation above and also in Part I, especially chapter 9.1.

[467] It can be pointed out that the Baptist movement in England has not ceased to exist, where for instance open Holy Communion has been practised since the 17th century. See also Lagergren, David, "Lokalekumeniken och dopet", *VP*, No. 37, 1978, p. 2; in this part, chapter 2.1. Cf., however, Janarv's statement (already quoted) that the Baptist Union of Sweden cannot recognize infant baptism as a baptism, for *"then we would no longer be Baptist congregations."* "Baptistpastor om dopdokument: -Baptister bör erkänna barndopet", *Svenska Journalen*, No. 1, 1985, p. 12. Italics mine. And Lagergren states: "Det är inga riktiga baptister längre som tvingas att acceptera barndopet", in Naess, Kurt, "Krossa församlingen och gå ut i 'världen'", *VP*, No. 50, 1978, p. 10.

[468] She states: "Vi *har* redan valt väg." Swedberg, Bo, "Förenade församlingar visar: -Samfunden har redan valt gemenskapens väg", *VP*, No. 9, 1988, p. 2. See also "Förenade församlingar visar vägen till enhet", *VP*, No. 9, 1988 p. 1. Berit Åqvist is a Baptist pastor, in 1988 teacher at Betelseminariet and chairman of Vårdkasekyrkans församling in Järfälla, an ecumenical congregation affiliated with the Baptist Union of Sweden and the Mission Covenant Church of Sweden.

sign is in her opinion the ecumenical congregations, which are affiliated with more than one denomination.[469] She states that members of the ecumenical congregations, of one of which she herself is a member, step by step have discovered that they are no longer just Baptists or members of the Mission Covenant Church of Sweden which they once had been.

We have got a new identity, and we must be prepared to take decisive consequences of this.[470]

Her aim is one united Free Church.[471] Another Baptist pastor Ulla Bardh is referred to as saying: "... one loses one's old denominational identity" (i.e. in the ecumenical congregations),[472] and she is of the opinion that even a new theology is born in the ecumenical congregations, due to the fact that different theologies and traditions have met.[473] What this new theology would consist of is, however, not stated.

In spite of all this taking place in the local Baptist congregations, especially in the ecumenical congregations, in youth organizations etc. which I have tried to exemplify (especially in this part),[474] there are other Baptist voices which defend the traditional, Baptist

---

[469] Swedberg, Bo, "Förenade församlingar visar: -Samfunden har redan valt gemenskapens väg", *VP*, No. 9, 1988, pp. 2f.

[470] "Vi har i den församlingen aldrig känt att vi skulle vara särskilt olika. Däremot har vi undan för undan upptäckt att vi inte längre är bara de baptister och de missionsförbundare vi en gång var. *Vi har fått en ny identitet,* och det måste vi vara beredda att ta bestämda konsekvenser av." Ibid. p. 2. Italics mine. See also "Handling för enhet", [editorial], *VP*, No 16, 1989, p. 4.

[471] Swedberg, Bo, "Förenade församlingar visar: -Samfunden har redan valt gemenskapens väg", *VP*, No. 9, 1988, pp. 2f. And a pastor with roots in the United Methodist Church in Sweden, Tomas Lindell, working in an ecumenical congregation where three denominations are involved (the United Methodist Church in Sweden, the Mission Covenant Church of Sweden and the Baptist Union of Sweden), states that within 10 years these denominations will have been united into one. ("Inom högst tio år har även våra respektive samfund gått samman, tror Tomas Lindell, församlingens pastor med rötter i Metodistkyrkan.") "Framtidshopp i Filipstad. Vasakyrkan har band till tre frikyrkosamfund", *VP*, No. 9, 1992, p. 1.

[472] "... man förlorar sin gamla samfundsidentitet." Lindberg, Erik, "1+1=mer än 2 vid samgående", *VP*, No. 40, 1991, p. 4.

[473] Ibid. See also Bardh in Swedberg, Bo, " -Vi måste lära av de lokala erfarenheterna", *VP*, No. 16, 1989, p. 12.

[474] See also Part I.

principles, strongly advocating among other things believers' baptism. This seems to be emphasized at the central, denominational level with a few exceptions, as is evident in Franzéns book *Guds försprång*, 1991, as well as in *BUS*. And Lagergren writes concerning *BUS*: "It can thus rightly be said to be the opinion of our denomination."[475] This is a statement which I, however, would question because of what was found in this study at the Baptist congregational level, and in particular in the ecumenical congregational context, where Baptists are involved.

Such an opinion as that which Lagergren holds can be discerned not only in a Swedish context but also, if we widen the perspective, in a European one (and returning to the starting point of this study, the international, ecumenical perspective with *BEM)*, to which for example *Svenska Baptistsamfundets Årsbok* 1992-93, refers. It quotes a document issued by the European Baptist Federation *(EBF)* in 1992.[476] This document in 13 clauses was to be distributed to the denominations in Europe as a basis for continued talks about Baptist identity. It states: *"We practise baptism, for believers only, into the Body of Christ."*[477] It continues:

> Baptists find that baptism in the New Testament and the earliest church was normally immersion into water, in the triune name of God, of those who could confess their personal allegiance to Jesus Christ as Lord. In baptism there is a sharing in the death and resurrection of Christ, so that there is a coming together of the grace of God with the faith of the believer.[478]

---

[475] "Det kan alltså med viss rätt sägas vara vårt samfunds uppfattning." Lagergren, David, "Ekumenisk barnteologi", *VP*, No. 17, 1991, p. 6.

[476] See *Svenska Baptistsamfundets Årsbok* 1992-93, pp. 7-12.

[477] "Document for Comment by the Baptist Unions of Europe. What are Baptists? A Statement of Identity by Baptist Christians in Europe.", 1992, p. 2, clause 5, [unpublished document]. (In Swedish (translated by Ragni Lantz) *"Vi praktiserar dop enbart av troende in i Kristi kropp." Svenska Baptistsamfundets Årsbok* 1992-93, p. 9, point 6.) The principles of congregationalism and freedom are also evident in this document, as well as, of course, the principle of the authority of the Bible. See also Part I, chapter 2. in this thesis.

[478] "Document for Comment by the Baptist Unions of Europe. What are Baptists? A Statement of Identity by Baptist Christians in Europe.", 1992, p. 2, clause 5, [unpublished document]. (In the Swedish translation, "Baptister anser att dopet i Nya Testamentet och i den tidigaste kyrkan normalt innebar nedsänkning i vatten, i den treenige Gudens namn, av dem som bekänner en personlig tro på Jesus Kristus som Herre. En människa

It says clearly: "... this makes the act inappropriate for infants or young children."[479] Further

Baptism is inseparable from entrance into membership of the church as the Body of Christ, though Baptists allow freedom of conscience among themselves about the way this is to be worked out. Many churches insist that members must be baptised as believers.[480]

The conclusion and aim is quite clear:

Notwithstanding these differences, *all Baptists believe that a return to the New Testament practice of baptism is essential* for true understanding of the nature of faith, the church and discipleship.[481]

---

måste därför ha tro innan hon kan döpas. I dopet förenas denna mänskliga tro med Guds nåd, då den troende delar Kristi död och uppståndelse och därmed också bär vittnesbörd om frälsningen." *Svenska Baptistsamfundets Årsbok* 1992-93, p. 9, point 6.)

[479] "Document for Comment by the Baptist Unions of Europe. What are Baptists? A Statement of Identity by Baptist Christians in Europe.", 1992, p. 2, clause 5, [unpublished document]. (In the Swedish translation, "Allt detta gör att akten är olämplig för spädbarn." *Svenska Baptistsamfundets Årsbok* 1992-93, p. 9, point 6.)

[480] "Document for Comment by the Baptist Unions of Europe. What are Baptists? A Statement of Identity by Baptist Christians in Europe.", 1992, p. 2, clause 5, [unpublished document]. It states also: "... others, recognising with sadness the broken nature of the Church Universal, will accept those who have been baptised as infants and confirmed in other Christian churches; still others, in special circumstances, will permit membership simply on confession of personal faith in Christ." Ibid. (In the Swedish translation, "Dopet är oskiljaktigt från medlemskapet i församlingen som Kristi kropp, fastän baptister tillåter samvetsfrihet bland sig själva om hur detta skall skötas i praktiken. Många samfund insisterar på att de som sluter sig till en församling först måste döpas som troende; andra, som med sorg inser den universella kyrkans splittrade natur, accepterar dem som har döpts som barn och konfirmerats i andra kristna samfund; ytterligare några tillåter medlemskap enbart efter bekännelse om personlig tro på Kristus, under särskilda omständigheter." *Svenska Baptistsamfundets Årsbok* 1992-93, p. 9, point 6.)

[481] "Document for Comment by the Baptist Unions of Europe. What are Baptists? A Statement of Identity by Baptist Christians in Europe.", 1992, p. 2, clause 5, [unpublished document]. Italics mine. (The Swedish translation, "Oavsett sådana skillnader *tror alla baptister att en återgång till det nytestamentliga troendedopet är väsentligt* för att man verkligen ska förstå trons, församlingens och lärjungaskapets innebörd." *Svenska Baptistsamfundets Årsbok* 1992-93, p. 9, point 6. Italics mine.)

Birgit Karlsson refers among other things, after the talks among Baptist leaders from 23 European Baptist Unions in Dorfweil, Germany, (besides Birgit Karlsson, Berit Åqvist also participated from the Baptist Union of Sweden), to the following traditional characteristics of Baptist identity: believers' baptism into the Body of Christ and the fellowship of the congregation, and the congregation as a fellowship of believers who meet at Holy Communion.[482]

Infant baptism (and thus also so-called "re-baptism") seems thus still to be a stumbling block in ecumenical work, at least at the official, international and denominational Baptist levels, which also *BUS* confirms and of which it is one example, *but* obviously less at the congregational level – bearing in mind in particular the ecumenical congregations. The question is how well integrated this traditional, Baptist fundamental principle and characteristic of Baptist identity as a matter of fact is "in reality", i.e. at the grass-root level, which, of course, is in interaction with the other levels.

I have pointed out that there is a reconsideration of baptism, ecclesiology and Baptist identity within the Baptist Union of Sweden, especially at the local, congregational level, which becomes even more evident in comparison with Part II, and also from the presentation of the Baptist movement and the Baptist Union of Sweden and its early history in Part I. This more open and pluralistic position among Swedish Baptists, especially seen in this part, has implications for ecclesiology, ecumenism and Baptist identity - for the Swedish denominational level as well as for the congregational level (and also the individual one) - as I have tried to demonstrate. There is a Baptist diversity. For there are obviously different opinions within the Baptist Union of Sweden concerning baptism with implications in the future.

There are at least two baptismal theologies and practices in the Baptist Union of Sweden, each of them with different presuppositions. To generalize they imply on the one hand an approach close to that of *BEM* (recognition of infant baptism etc.), on the other hand an approach in line with *BUS* (recognition of believers' baptism alone etc.), - not to forget the tendency to abandon baptism (both infant baptism and believers' baptism) on account of faith alone.

---

[482] Karlsson, Birgit, "Baptismens röst i det nya Europa - samtal om identitet och insats", *VP*, No. 7, 1992, p. 4. See also "Europas baptistledare: -Vi vill samarbeta!", *VP*, No. 7, 1992, p. 4.

We can once again point out that there is a fascinating, but difficult, process taking place within the Baptist Union of Sweden in the *oecumene*. The Baptist Union of Sweden has in different ways dealt with one of its most central and important principles, which for most Baptists also is a very sensitive question personally as well as collectively. It involves the difficult task of letting different, sometimes painful and disagreeable, opinions appear. This is worthy of imitation in other churches and denominations. The diversity is, however, not easy to cope with, but the Baptist Union of Sweden as a matter of fact has managed to do this at the different levels, letting not only the official level, for example *BUS*, the General Secretaries etc., express itself, but also other different, individual voices who give expression to both traditional, "closed" Baptist opinions and pluralistic, "open" ones. The Baptist Union of Sweden has been regarded as one of the most ecumenical denominations in Sweden, as a bridge builder,[483] between different churches and denominations.[484]

Possibly one of the Baptist principles which is treated least in this study - at least explicitly - the principle of freedom, implying among other things respect for the individual,[485] is the most significant one for the Baptist movement and the Baptist Union, and which has also been the decisive cause of the reconsideration of baptism, of the congregation of believers and of the Baptist Union in the *oecumene*. This principle has consequences for the individual person, the fellowship, the congregation, the denomination, and

---

[483] Bergsten, Torsten, "Enheten i Kristus", *Tro, Frihet, Gemenskap*, 1998, p. 227.

[484] See for example Palm, Irving, "Frikyrklig lokalekumenik – exemplet gemensamma församlingar", *Tro & Tanke* 1997:3, pp. 56f.; Skog, Margareta, "Frikyrkosamfundens medlemstal i landets kommuner 1995", ibid. pp. 72ff., pp. 78f., and also the appendices. She states: "The Baptist Union of Sweden is on the whole that denomination which shows the greatest openness towards co-operation across the denominational boundaries." Ibid. p. 74.

[485] See for example Bergsten, Torsten, "På väg mot ett ömsesidigt doperkännande?", 1989, p. 3, [unpublished paper]. Bergsten writes: "A fundamental position in Baptist tradition is respect for a person's seriously held views and convictions." Ibid.

also theology and contributes also, in my opinion, to the diversity within the Baptist Union of Sweden.

Because of the diversity which undeniably exists in the Baptist Union of Sweden and also because of the principle of congregationalism (no central authority, nor normally any official documents etc.), it is not easy to identify what the Baptist baptismal theology and practice as a matter of fact is today - especially in Sweden – and thus find out what is happening to and within the Baptist Union of Sweden. This dilemma has obviously contributed to the difficulties I have had in my work with this thesis. I have, however, managed to show that there is a Baptist reconsideration of baptism and ecclesiology. This has been proved by studying the Swedish Baptist history (Part I), and comparing *BUS* with *BEM* (Part II), and also with these parts in mind by studying the public discussions, comparing the latter with the former (Part III).

Conclusion:

Baptist Reconsideration of Baptism and Ecclesiology - From Traditionalism to Pluralism

I want to make some concluding remarks on this thesis.

The Baptist Union of Sweden is involved in the ecumenical process at local, congregational, central, denominational and also global levels. A further expression of the present ecumenical process is that the Baptist Union of Sweden responded to *BEM* (also called the Lima-document, 1982). In this thesis I have made an analysis of *BUS*, the official response of the Baptist Union of Sweden to *BEM*, concerning baptism, and an examination and comparison of *BUS* with what I call the public discussions in the Baptist Union of Sweden. The thesis can been seen as a case study on the representativeness of an official document written for an international forum. It can hopefully also be of value to other future examinations of this type.

From the presentation of the Baptist Union of Sweden in an historical and ecumenical context (in Part I), and this in relation to *BUS* and *BEM* (in Part II) and the public discussions (in Part III), it is obvious that there is a change of emphasis in Baptist fundamental principles. There is a Baptist reconsideration of baptism and ecclesiology. This has taken place, in my opinion, as a result of among other things one of the Baptist principles, the principle of freedom. There is today a diversity within the Baptist Union of Sweden concerning baptismal understanding and baptismal practice. This results in a reconsideration also of the other Baptist principles (the principle of biblical authority as the sole authority for the theology and practice of baptism, the principle of congregationalism). Of course, there is an interchange between these principles.

One of the most fundamental ecumenical issues is baptism. In churches all around the world there are, however, diverse theologies and practices of baptism. These concern among other things the difficult questions of infant baptism, believers' baptism and "re-baptism", indiscriminate baptism; the institution of baptism, the meaning of baptism, the relation between baptism and faith; the relation of baptism, catechism, confirmation and Holy Communion; the celebration of baptism; baptism in relation to the concepts "belonging" (tillhörighet) and "membership" (medlemskap), church unity etc.

We can see that the problem of baptism has generally speaking resulted in two different kinds of churches. On the one hand, there are the so-called infant baptizing churches and, on the other hand, there are the churches exclusively teaching and practising believers' baptism, which is considered the only valid one – this, however, according to the infant baptizing churches involves the practice of "re-baptism". Baptism, i.e. on the one hand infant baptism which is not recognized by Baptists as a baptism and on the other hand "re-baptism" regarded by the opponents as null and void, is regarded as one of the stumbling blocks in the relations between for example the Baptist Unions and other churches, and an obstacle to the one visible church. The Baptist congregations and denominations may be regarded as a movement of protest against an ecclesiology built on infant baptism.

One of the Baptist principles, believers' baptism (baptism of metanoia, by immersion - which I call a proper baptism) has been regarded the gateway to membership of the church, i.e. incorporation into the Body of Christ (the universal church) and to the local Baptist congregation. This is motivated by another Baptist principle, the principle of biblical authority as the sole authority for the theology and practice of baptism among Baptists. The task of this thesis has been to study baptism (baptismal theology and practice) within the Baptist Union of Sweden – in an ecumenical context. I thus relate baptism also to some other issues, which I found are of importance to include in a study like this. They are among other things ecclesiology, church unity and the ecumenical context.

Such a study is problematic in more than one way, especially since the Baptist Union of Sweden does not have any official doctrinal documents or creeds, like for example the Lutheran, Anglican or Roman Catholic Churches. Baptists do not in principle have any central authority – except the Bible.

The Baptist principle of congregationalism must also be mentioned in this context. It implies that every congregation, also on the principle of freedom, is free to decide about itself without any central authority (for instance council, synod, or Pope) but the Bible.

In *BUS* (approved 1985, published 1987), an explicit theology of baptism is formulated. The question is, however, how representative *BUS* is. Through a comparison with the public discussions – dealing mainly with the period 1970's and onwards - I have found nuances, similarities, complementary ideas, but also other opinions which are not found in the official document *BUS*.

In order to understand the views of baptism within the Baptist Union of Sweden during that time, I have had to create a forum out of mainly Swedish Baptist periodicals (primarily *Veckoposten*), which I call public discussions. There we find various Swedish Baptists, mainly pastors and theologians, each one representing certainly their own version of the Baptist Union of Sweden. I try in this way to get a broader picture of the Baptist Union of Sweden in regard to baptism and ecclesiology. And one result of this study is that there is a *Baptist reconsideration of baptism and ecclesiology*.

The choice of the period from the 1970's and onwards is motivated by the two documents *BEM* (1982) and *BUS* (1985). It was also a very intensive period for the Baptist Union of Sweden in an ecumenical perspective, with for example the growing development of the ecumenical congregations.

This study about *Baptist reconsideration of baptism and ecclesiology* also gives a presentation of the Baptist Union of Sweden and its history (from the 1840's and onwards) - in an ecumenical context – and also of its fundamental principles. This is done in Part I where different issues are treated which directly or indirectly are connected with Parts II and III. I have found it useful to present the Baptist Union of Sweden in this way especially with non-Swedish readers in mind, as *BUS* as well as *BEM* are international documents.

The Baptist Union ought to be understood in the Swedish context, where it has grown and developed together with other movements – as for example other revivalist movements, and the labour and temperance movements. Another context which must not be forgotten is the State Church system. The Baptist movement which may be characterized as a popular movement - "a power to the people movement" - adopted a different understanding, teaching and practice of baptism through their interpretation of the Bible, than that prevailing in the State Church with infant baptism.

In Part I, I have discussed the beginnings of the Baptist movement, its fight against the State Church for freedom and independence, strongly vindicating freedom of conscience and freedom of religion. This became concrete particularly through the rite of believers' baptism. This rite implied a person's own individual, voluntary, free, conscious choice of baptism (not "forced baptisms"), and incorporation into membership of a voluntary church. The other Baptist principle, congregationalism, implied that the congregation consisted only of believers who had repented, been converted, experienced salvation, and made a public confession of their faith, and thereafter been baptized by believers' baptism.

The Baptist movement, and when consolidated the Baptist Union of Sweden, was, however, itself to experience anxiety, tensions and also divisions within itself. Some of these resulted in new "denominations": the Scandinavian Independent Baptist Union *(Fribaptistsamfundet)* 1872, the Pentecostal Movement *(Pingströrelsen)* (1913) and the Örebro (Baptist) Mission *(Örebro Missionsförening)* 1936/37.

It has also been involved in an ecumenical process, (even if the term *ecumenical* was unknown at the end of 19th century). This process has continued and become increasingly more concrete and obvious, particularly from the 1970's onwards, especially in the continued development of the so-called ecumenical congregations.

There are different kinds of ecumenical congregations, dealt with in both Part I and III, where for example one Baptist congregation may unite with another Baptist congregation, for example affiliated with the Örebro (Baptist) Mission [Interact], or even with a non-Baptist congregation, for example affiliated with the Mission Covenant Church of Sweden or the United Methodist Church in Sweden (infant baptizing churches). These congregations not only co-operate with each other (which as a matter of fact has occurred between Baptist congregations from the Baptist Union and the Örebro (Baptist) Mission ever since the division in the 1930's), but have also been united into one congregation.

Such a unification occurs sometimes despite different theologies and practices of for example baptism, so that one can find both a baptismal font and a baptismal pool in one and the same building. Different doctrines and practices are brought together under the same roof. The ecumenical congregations are thus examples of a unitive process across traditional, confessional divisions moving towards "unity in a reconciled diversity", and towards church unity. The ecumenical congregations are, however, not Baptist congregations in the strict sense. They are not mentioned in *BUS*.

In Part I, I have indicated that the Baptist Union of Sweden from the beginning may be characterized as a closed Baptist fellowship with for example strict membership requirements. But with time and especially during recent decades, the Baptist Union of Sweden has become more open and pluralistic. At present it may be regarded as one of the most ecumenical denominations in Sweden, in particular on account of the ecumenical congregations. This change has, however, implied an ambiguity within the Baptist Union of Sweden, which is also found in regard to the issue of baptism where the boundaries have not always been evident or absolute. The Baptist reactions to the ecumenical congregations vary.

In Part II baptism is studied and analysed in *BUS* and in comparison with *BEM*. A natural starting point is thus taken in *BEM's* texts about "our one baptism", "our common baptism", and also its writing about *"The need to recover baptismal unity"*. I also analyse the work by the working party within the Baptist Union of Sweden which preceded the final product, *BUS*.

In *BEM* baptism is regarded as the basis of the church. It is in other words fundamental for church unity, and through baptism a person is "christened", incorporated into the church, the Body of Christ. *BEM* recognizes both infant baptism and believers' baptism, but not "re-baptism". It discusses believers' baptism and states that this was the most clearly attested pattern in the New Testament documents in the apostolic age. It shows a cautious attitude to the question of whether infant baptism was administered at that time. Because of this, it might have been expected that *BEM* would plead more strongly for believers' baptism than is now the case. Instead it argues for infant baptism and against "re-baptism". This may be interpreted as *BEM*, in comparison with the Baptists, considering more the importance of the tradition of the church than that of the New Testament alone.

In *BUS* we do nevertheless find agreements with and a positive attitude to *BEM*. The former writes for example that the work within the frame of Faith and Order has led to a common understanding of baptism in many respects, especially regarding the meaning and importance of baptism. And it comes to a point of agreement with *BEM* as concerns, for example, the importance of baptism and the description of the meaning of baptism. *BUS* also states that after all different churches with various traditions can say the same things about baptism. It is also of the opinion that there is only *one* baptism, but asks the most relevant question from its position: "Can we in earnest talk about 'our one baptism' as long as baptismal practice in a decisive way divides us?"

In the analysis I have found that *BUS* holds to a traditional, closed Baptist view. This means that believers' baptism is for it the only valid baptism. It cannot recognize infant baptism as valid and denies thus that "re-baptism" is practised.

A delicate question arises, however, concerning infant baptism: why does *BUS* not recognize infant baptism as valid but "only" as a blessing, if there is, which it states, a common understanding of baptism - regarding its meaning and importance – between it and *BEM*? Something more must obviously be included by *BUS* than that baptism is practised in water, in the name of the Trinity etc. There is an explicit answer: "For Baptists the baptism belongs together with a personal conversion". This conversion, *metanoia*, is thus the *sine qua non*, a fundamental condition for proper, biblical baptism, believers' baptism.

This condition does not, however, only concern, in my opinion, the form, the baptismal practice, but the baptismal theology, depending also on anthropology, ecclesiology etc. It seems, however, as if *BUS* is of the opinion that it is "only" baptismal practices which divide the churches.[1] I have, however, indicated in the thesis that baptismal practice also includes baptismal theology, and vice versa. The practice and theological understanding relate to one another. It is both baptismal practices *and* baptismal understandings which divide the churches and denominations (or unite them), not only the baptismal practices.

---

[1] *BUS* states: "various *baptismal practices* indicate different consequences of this common understanding." (*BUS* p. 201, italics mine), and "With the present varied *practices* in different churches it is hardly possible to come to a united standpoint." (*BUS* p. 200, italics mine).

There is in the light of my analysis of *BUS* and *BEM* not one but sometimes two baptisms: infant baptism, not recognized at all by *BUS* but by *BEM*, and exclusively believers' baptism (i.e. sometimes meaning "re-baptism") which is regarded as the proper, genuine biblical one by *BUS*. In other words, there are at least two baptismal theologies and practices, each of which has different presuppositions and implications for ecclesiology. For *BEM* baptism may be a "starting-point" of a process in a Christian's life, while it tends to be rather the climax of a process in *BUS*.

The issue of baptism is also, as already has been indicated, connected with many other questions, concerning for example the question of anthropology. In *BUS* there is, in comparison with *BEM*, a more positive view of man. As infants are within the Kingdom of God by birth, there is no need of any "special performance" (i.e. infant baptism) in order to transform a person from one ontological level to another (an exodus from bondage for example). Children are already, according to *BUS*, under the atonement of Christ. On the other hand, it writes about an obligation to express the fact that children are under the protection of God's grace. It discusses the blessing of children. One reason for *BUS* to discuss this, besides the "baptism-dilemma", is of course the problematic situation which has existed within the Baptist Union itself, that infants have formally been regarded to be "outside" the Baptist congregations.

A concept which also turns up in discussing anthropology is the "fall". According to *BUS* infants are not "fallen". I have discussed what this "fall" may consist of, and what significance believers' baptism may have, if a person grows up, for example, in a close faith-context (i.e. in a Christian family or environment), and never has "fallen", i.e. been outside the Kingdom of God. A baptism in such a case may hardly be regarded as a *baptism of metanoia* or an incorporation into the Body of Christ, a new birth, an exodus from bondage etc. It could be questioned if this is a proper, genuine believers' baptism in the sense of traditional Baptist understanding of *baptism of metanoia.*

I have also treated the concept "faith", with its various meanings (*fides qua, fides quae etc.*), and "faith-context". There is, according to *BUS*, a difference between children growing up in Christian faith-context, having an advantage (living under the protection of God's grace, of the faith of their parents and of the church fellowship), in relation to those growing up without any closer faith-context.

In the question of anthropology (if for example original sin is to be taken into consideration or not) there is another subject: the two rites of the blessing of children and infant baptism. How are these two acts related to one another? For *BUS* it is simple, because it equates infant baptism with the blessing of children. This implies among other things that for *BUS* both those who are baptized by infant baptism or those blessed by the blessing of children are regarded as catechumens - preparing for baptism, which in some churches actually means (for those baptized by infant baptism) a "re-baptism". I have, however, put a question mark to this identification of the blessing of children with infant baptism. There are differences between these rites: for example the intention, the use of water, and of course the rite (if blessing or baptism), and also the theology behind the rites.

I want, however, also to note that there is in *BUS*, in comparison with traditional Baptist theology, a shift in the view of infant baptism, from regarding it as a non-baptism towards a blessing.

I discuss the role of the baptizand as an active subject in baptism, and also the role of God. The issue concerns in other words the expressive/symbolic *and* instrumental/sacramental views on baptism. The question is if baptism has any effect *per se*, i.e. if it is valid without any personal faith of the baptizand? I have found that *BEM* holds an instrumental/sacramental view, i.e. baptism *per se* is valid (of course in a faith-context, or as *BEM* puts it "in the Church as the community of faith"). For *BUS*, however, baptism does not have any effect without this personal conscious response of the baptizand.

There is also to be found in *BUS* a reaction against "sacramentalism" in *BEM:* in other words, that baptism could be an external, effective act on an unaware person who does not have any freedom to decide for himself, and that this act (and the theology associated with it) may also undermine the necessity of personal faith.

In spite of this reaction *BUS*, as well as the latest manual *Till församlingens tjänst* (1987), do not deny that God acts and even effects "something" in (believers') baptism. This cannot, however, be applied to infant baptism. The fact is, that in spite of having an instrumental view of baptism, infant baptism is not recognized as a baptism - even if it is administered in a (close) faith-context, i.e. with believing parents in the church-fellowship. For the baptizand himself must also act, i.e. give his conscious response in faith, in order to have, in the view of *BUS*, not a blessing but a baptism. This baptism, i.e. believers' baptism, is of course also possible according to *BEM*, but the response of the baptizand himself is not absolutely necessary.

Concerning the validity of baptism, baptism by immersion is generally regarded by Baptists as necessary. Without doubt immersion is recommended by *BUS*, as this expresses "in a better way" participation in Christ's death, burial and resurrection. Baptism takes place preferably *in* (i.e. immersion, not *with*) water and in the name of the Trinity. There is, however, in any case a possibility of interpreting *BUS* as recognizing baptism without immersion as valid – if there is a confession of faith by the baptizand.

BEM and *BUS* seem to be in agreement concerning the celebration of baptism. The latter acknowledges the list of elements which should be included in the order of baptism according to the former. A hesitation is, however, expressed by *BUS* in regard to "over-explicit explanations". Going not to *BUS*, where this is not explained, but to the working party which wrote the document (in Swedish, before the definitive English edition *BUS*) an indication of what this means is given. It concerns "the renunciation of evil".

It is also evident that *BUS* has some difficulties with the *BEM* texts about the Spirit and the gifts of the Spirit. This has been a delicate issue and still is in the Baptist Union.

BEM also discusses another issue, indiscriminate baptism. The indiscriminate baptisms have without doubt obstructed the work towards recognition of baptism by Baptists. This topic is discussed in many churches. It is, however, not discussed in *BUS*. The latter, however, underlines *BEM's* statement that baptism is connected with the corporate life and worship of the church. In spite of this the working party behind *BUS* states: "The crucial point on the question of infant baptism is not after all the fact that it is practised indiscriminately."[2] We understand why: neither the act *per se*, nor the faith-context plays any role for the validity of infant baptism. According to *BUS* infant baptism is not recognized as a baptism and therefore "re-baptism" is not administered.

BEM's thesis that "the one baptism" could be regarded as the basis of the church and of church unity, is after an analysis of *BUS* to be questioned. Recognizing both baptisms, i.e. infant and believers' baptism (not, however, "re-baptism"), as valid as *BEM* does, seems to end up in a blind alley with *BUS*. It states explicitly: "With the present varied practices in different churches it is hardly

---

[2] "Den springande punkten i fråga om barndopet är trots allt inte att det praktiseras urskillningslöst." Supplement to Minutes 2/11/83.

possible to come to a united standpoint. The question is if the Lima text initiates a new start."

And in spite of *BUS'* words: "we want to emphasize that a terminology should be used that is not depreciating or insulting", it certainly uses itself the term *infant baptism* but gives it, however, a quite different content (it is a blessing). *BUS* holds partly that infant *baptism* is a non-baptism, and talks partly, however, about different kinds of *baptismal* practices, which obviously includes the practice of both believers' baptism and also infant baptism, not called a blessing in this case. There is an ambiguous vocabulary here. There is obviously a problem with "the mutual recognition of baptism."

In both the early Swedish Baptist movement and later on in the Baptist Union of Sweden it has been maintained that *baptism of metanoia* means incorporation into the church, the Body of Christ, and the local congregation. Therefore baptism has been administered as close as possible in time to conversion. In *BUS*, however, there is a reconsideration of this. We find there that a Baptist congregation can also include unbaptized members. What ultimately matters for membership of the church is the personal faith (compare with the traditional Baptist principles and its history, see Part I). Baptism is thus not a necessary condition for becoming or remaining a member of a Swedish Baptist congregation any more.

This has had as a consequence that Baptist congregations also invite believers (i.e. not necessarily baptized at all) to the Lord's table, open Holy Communion. We may compare this for example with the earlier conflict in Baptist history when most Baptists urged for closed Holy Communion, closed membership with believers' baptism as a presupposition for membership, and how then open Holy Communion contributed to divisions.

The question is from both a theological and ecumenical point of view what ought to be regarded as necessary or sufficient in order to be a member of the church, i.e. both in the sense of the universal church and the local congregation. The fundamental difference in answer to that question is if baptism should be regarded as the basis of membership of the church and of church unity (as *BEM* states) – with an emphasis on God. Or if faith alone, i.e. the personal, conscious response, should be regarded as the basis - with more emphasis on the human being.

Studies of official documents at central, denominational levels can be compared with studies of *public discussions* (Part III). "Reality" is sometimes more complex and therefore more difficult to grasp than is possible "only" in an official response. Official documents often give the expected opinions and answers, holding to the tradition of a church or denomination. This is obviously also the case in *BUS*. It has therefore been of value also to study the public discussions (Part III) in order to see how representative *BUS* is of the Baptist Union of Sweden, fully conscious of the methodological difficulties in comparing different types of material. In other words, does *BUS* reflect the contemporary situation of the Baptist Union of Sweden *or* are there possibly other, complementary or contradicting aspects?

BEM's own words are another motive for my approach. It states: "Perhaps even more influential than the official studies are the changes which are taking place within the life of the churches themselves." In analysing an official document and the public discussions in the Baptist Union of Sweden, I hope to meet this expectation in *BEM.*

Part III contains the same topics as were dealt with in Part II, but also some complementary subjects not dealt with at all in *BUS*. It is the question of the ecumenical congregations and the impact of these congregations on the Baptist Union, Baptist baptismal theology and practice, and Baptist identity.

There seems in general to be a more relaxed view of infant baptism among many Swedish Baptists in comparison with *BUS*. I have proved that there is some recognition within the Baptist Union of Sweden of infant baptism as valid baptism. There are even examples of some Baptist pastors administering infant baptisms. This finding might be regarded as a step towards increasing mutual recognition of baptism and towards "the one baptism" and church unity which *BEM* writes about. This development and "opening" is not even indicated in *BUS.*

In other words there is not only the opinion of *BUS* within the Baptist Union but also a growing opening towards mutual recognition of baptism. It is also of interest to observe, not least in light of Baptist history (Part I), that in the Baptist manual of 1987 (then common to five Baptist denominations), there is a rite, *Förnyelse av dopförbundet* (Renewal of the Baptismal Covenant), in which there is the possibility for Christians from different baptismal traditions to confess and preach together the meaning of baptism. In ecumenical services there may thus be a renewal of the baptismal covenant.

I want to add in this context another problem for some Baptists, namely that sometimes some of the "believers' baptisms" tend to be infant baptisms on account of the low age of these involved.

From the reconsideration of infant baptism within the Baptist Union of Sweden, it is more or less to be expected that one of the most characteristic principles in Baptist history is also reconsidered, namely that of believers' baptism. I have indicated this in my work. It has been increasingly evident for the Baptists that to maintain their traditional biblical believers' baptism (especially in practice), a *baptism of metanoia*, i.e. conversion/repentance, personal confession of faith and baptism as one act closely connected in time, which I call a proper baptism, is often difficult. For based on traditional Baptist interpretation of the New Testament, baptism and faith are expressions of the same reality. To be a believer is to be baptized, and baptism and conversion coincide in time. There also exist, in my terminology, improper believers' baptisms. This means that often because of what I characterize as a "time-problem", the believers' baptism is administered not to the newly converted but to people who have been believers already for a long time (i.e. they are already within the church), or have had a faith "as long as they can remember". There are sometimes temporal disjunctions between conversion, faith, and baptism.

This has ecclesiological implications. A consequent question arises: why baptize those who already are in the church, if baptism should be an incorporation into that church? Instead of being one act – *a baptism of metanoia* - they become two different experiences and stages.

Another cause which may not be forgotten as an explanation of the reconsideration of baptism and its relation to the church, but which is too often neglected, originates in early Swedish Baptist history, namely the vote. The vote implied that believers' baptism was not enough in order to be a member of a Baptist congregation. The vote of the congregation was also necessary. It was said that an admission of a new member could occur only by a vote after prior acquaintance with a person's spiritual state and after personal confession of faith. At such a vote it was most desirable that unanimity among the voters was reached.

It is not improbable that this system (from the 1850's) has more or less consciously haunted the Baptists and their ecclesiology, and teaching and practice of baptism, and also indirectly resulted in the tendency, which can be discerned within the Baptist Union during the 1970's and onwards, that the personal faith, not baptism, is the *sine qua non* of membership of the church, despite the explicit commandment in the Bible to baptize. It may also be added that the personal, conscious faith depends in the Baptist context to a large extent on the person's intellectual, spiritual abilities to understand and profess the faith – in other words there is an emphasis on the intellect, faith as *cognitio.*

This points partly to a separation between baptism and membership, partly to an ambiguity in the relation between the universal church and the local Baptist congregation. Baptism was connected with membership of the universal church, the vote, however, with membership of the local Baptist congregation. Such a separation between baptism and membership of the congregation does not have any support in the New Testament, according to the former General Secretary David Lagergren, where the congregation was equivalent to those baptized.

One Baptist pastor, Harry Månsus, states that a fatal discrepancy has developed within the Baptist Union of Sweden between the universal church and the local church. This has also had the consequence that we find unbaptized Baptist members, and also both members baptized by infant baptism and members baptized by believers' baptism within a Baptist congregation. Open membership ought also to be mentioned here.

Speaking once more about "the fall" and the view of man, it can be noted that Baptists reject the doctrine of original sin, which has often motivated infant baptism. Instead a "fall", caused by some kind of sin, has been a presupposition of believers' baptism and the membership of the church. Man is born into a broken world, and as time goes on, he later "falls" through a sinful act. The person does something sinful and this breaks the spontaneous relation to God, and he is then "outside" the Kingdom of God. The person has to be conscious of his fallen state and then, through *metanoia* and baptism, he (re-) turns to God (the Kingdom), and is incorporated into the church, the Body of Christ.

There are a couple of problems in this that I want to discuss. How does one know, for example, when the ontological status of the child is changed? In other words, when is it no longer within the Kingdom but instead in need of *metanoia* (repentance/conversion) and of being baptized and incorporated into the church? Further, how does one know if and when the "proper conditions" ("real" conversion, sufficient faith etc.) are present?

It seems to me that there is often a great emphasis in a Baptist context on the individual's ability to decide this (possibly together with his or her pastor). I have found in my study that on the principle of freedom and out of respect for the individual it is also very much in the hands of the baptized individual to decide if his or her infant baptism is valid or not.

The concept *"metanoia"* is ambiguous, like "faith" and "faith-context" etc. *Metanoia* may mean, as I have indicated in the thesis, a conversion in a continuing process of maturing. *Metanoia* has, however, often in Baptist tradition not been associated with this interpretation but more with that of a sudden, radical conversion. There is then sometimes a problem for Baptists concerning "the timing". In short, some believers' baptisms take place too early in time in relation to the awareness and the *metanoia;* others, however, too late. Some of the believers' baptisms imply thus baptizing those who have already been Christian believers for a long time.

The "traditional" believers' baptism with radical conversion and baptism close to this event, often earlier in Swedish Baptist history in connection with tent meetings and revival meetings, no longer occurs so frequently. A proper believers' baptism implied a farewell to sin and the world, a conversion from the world to Christ and then the person in question was incorporated into and became a member of both the church and the congregation – through baptism of *metanoia* (and vote). The concept *"metanoia"* has also, however, been widened among Baptists to mean not only a radical conversion/repentance.

Another problem in this context is the place of children. In the Baptist theology of conversion, children have been regarded as inside the Kingdom of God by birth but outside the Baptist congregation, until they have repented, made a personal confession of faith, and been baptized by believers' baptism (by immersion). Then the person in question has been regarded as "inside", i.e. within the church.

One question is, however, if they never have been "outside" the Kingdom, (also according to Baptists themselves), what will baptism as an act of incorporation mean in such cases – an act of recruitment? I have dealt with these problematic and disputed questions in the thesis. I have also discussed the catechetical teaching in relation to baptism. Some Baptists argue that such teaching ought to take place first after the conversion and the believers' baptism; others, however, that the teaching should take place first and thereafter baptism. There are different interpretations and answers among Baptists themselves to these questions.

This diversity within the Baptist Union of Sweden does not make it easier to analyse Baptist baptismal theology and practice. In short, there is among the Baptists a reconsideration of infant baptism, believers' baptism and "re-baptism". It seems as if both the teaching *and* the practice of believers' baptism have decreased. At the same time, we observe that some infant baptisms have been administered among the Baptists, and also (even if these, of course, are exceptions) some have been administered by Baptist pastors. This results, of course, in a dynamic and sometimes difficult challenge to the Baptist Union, and one Swedish Baptist pastor has given the radical suggestion that it might be best to abandon baptism altogether because of the difficulties in maintaining the proper, biblical *baptism of metanoia.*

A reconsideration of the view of infants is to be discerned in for example Baptists practising the blessing of children (there is also an act for the blessing of children in the Baptist manual). They have thus tried to solve this dilemma (about children being outside the Baptist congregation) by practising the blessing of children. This gives children a place in the congregation - the term *child-member* has even been suggested. There is also an alternative opinion within the Baptist Union holding that children are within both the Kingdom of God and the Baptist congregation from birth.

I have dealt with indiscriminate baptism in Part III. This is not discussed at all in *BUS,* but in *BEM* and also in the public discussions.

For Baptists who are ready to recognize infant baptism as valid the indiscriminate baptisms in the Church of Sweden are an obstacle, and contribute to problems in the work towards mutual recognition of baptism. Baptists have objected that in the Church of Sweden to be baptized is part of "the birth phase", which has not always involved an initiation into a continuous Christian life in the congregation. Those Baptists who are ready to recognize infant baptism cannot recognize all infant baptisms as valid particularly due to these baptisms.

There is obviously a risk of subjectivity in such an argumentation, i.e. in recognizing some but not all infant baptism (for example Torsten Bergsten, one of the leading Swedish Baptist theologians, associate professor and layman, and the former General Secretary Birgit Karlsson), which has also been stated by David Lagergren. The ambiguous attitude towards infant baptism has among other things the implication that one of the most sensitive and problematic issues in the discussion about baptism, the issue of "re-baptism", is still not solved. It has also, strangely enough in the light of its history, been a dilemma even within the Baptist Union of Sweden.

There may, however, be a danger that tradition, ritualism and routine accompany not only infant baptisms but also some believers' baptisms as well. Besides the "traditional" problems of "re-baptism", I have found that "indiscriminate" believers' baptisms occur in the Baptist Union of Sweden and we are confronted with a more unusual problem of "re-baptism". This resulted in my thesis in a discussion about the possibility of "re-baptizing" a person earlier baptized by believers' baptism. For this ought to be possible (in comparison with the problem of infant baptism) for example if the (first) believers' baptism was administered without a true change of heart; if insufficient personal faith existed at the time of baptism; or if it was performed for the wrong reasons; or if we find a break in time between the first conversion and baptism and the second, the person having become a non-believer (an apostate) in the meantime; or if a person has been baptized by "pressurized baptism" (more or less forced by parents, friends, the youth-group etc.). In other words baptism may many times be administered without a true, honest, conscious faith.

Even if I have found one Baptist who discusses this possibility of "re-baptizing", this must, however, be regarded as an exception. For it is also stated that believers' baptism should not be administered twice, even if some believers' baptisms obviously, also according to some Baptists, are regarded, with my terminology, as improper because of wrong presuppositions, motives etc. One argument for this opinion - not to "re-baptize" a person earlier baptized by believers' baptism - is that "we are always allowed to fall back on what God has done to us".

In other words the fact that God acted in baptism with the baptizand utterly excludes "re-baptism". Following on from this I discussed why a similar discussion is not found in the case of infant baptism. This resulted in a discussion about baptism as an expressive or instrumental act.

The expressive or symbolic view of baptism has dominated within the Baptist Union of Sweden. A change is, however, to be discerned and there is a certain self-criticism of the previous predominant view of baptism, which regards baptism as only a symbol for something which has happened in conversion, and not more. This is considered an impoverished interpretation of baptism.

The discussion about the proper administration of baptism, for example by immersion, has often dominated among Baptists. This emphasis has sometimes, according to them, been at the expense of the meaning and possible consequences the baptism may have. And the task of the church is not "only" to baptize (in the right manner with the right method) but also to make disciples. Complete immersion – even if it is wanted - is not absolutely necessary for all Baptists in order to recognize a baptism as valid. This implies also a greater possibility of recognizing other churches' baptisms - if there is a confession of faith by the baptizand.

An instrumental or sacramental view of baptism seems to be gaining ground in the public discussions: God acts in and through baptism. A view which seems to come close to that of *BEM*. This development is also found in the later Baptist manuals of 1974 and 1987. In the manual of 1987 it is explicitly stated: "In baptism God acts."

There is, however, also criticism among some Baptists towards this development, which they regard as unbiblical, as a departure from the teaching of the New Testament.

The interpretations of the concepts "instrumental" and "sacramental" lead to hesitations among Baptists about recognizing infant baptisms, despite regarding baptism as an instrumental act. A sacrament seems to be interpreted by Baptists more like a contract under oath between two consciously active partners. The emphasis is thus laid not only on one but on two acting subjects (God and the baptizand). This excludes infant baptism. This view has thus the action of the baptizand as one presupposition. It is not baptism *per se* that counts. Something else must be added. It is the personal faith which is the *sine qua non*, then God can act with the baptizand. Here is an important difference between Baptist sacramental theology and practice and many other churches (inclusive *BEM*), who see God acting sovereignly with the baptizand.

All that is dealt with in Part III has, as has already been stated, implications for the issue of ecclesiology. For example, we find that the definition of the church is ambiguous. The church may mean the universal church or the local congregation. Sometimes these entities are equivalent; for the most part they are not. Sometimes baptism is an incorporation into the church in both senses; at other times, however, "the church" seems to be separated partly into the universal church, partly the local church – through baptism taking place considerably later, if it is administered at all.

The incorporation into the church can thus be understood to take place in different manners depending on different anthropologies, ecclesiologies and different baptismal theologies and practices.

There is a reconsideration of ecclesiology due to the reconsideration of baptism and vice versa.

Without doubt the ecumenical congregations have contributed to this process. There are compromises concerning baptism. The Baptist Union of Sweden has, especially during the period I have studied, been in a dynamic and challenging period. The ecumenical process may even sometimes be regarded as a "costly unity" for the Baptist Union. The principle of freedom (including also respect and tolerance for others) has contributed to this dynamic ecumenical development. Some Baptists would probably say ecumenical confusion with a diversity of baptismal theology and baptismal practices within the Baptist Union. And the former General Secretary Birgit Karlsson states "that the most decisive changes concern the situation of the local congregations".

We find a dialectical process between a theology understood to be found in the New Testament (a commandment to baptize) and a theology which people formulate and practise in the congregations - where the fellowship is of great importance and sometimes almost tends to have sacramental features.

Some Baptists maintain that the Baptists have developed a new identity, and one Baptist pastor, Berit Åqvist, is of the opinion that the Baptist Union of Sweden has already chosen its direction. The sign of this is the ecumenical congregations. This also implies, according to another Baptist pastor Ulla Bardh, that a new theology has been born. The Baptist Union of Sweden at the central, denominational level has, however, not yet been united with any other church.

The Baptist position seems to be "contradictory" on more than one point. This is not apparent in *BUS*. The Baptist Union of Sweden has, however, kept this "both-and attitude" towards baptism: some Baptists advocate traditional Baptist principles (a closed Baptist attitude); others are more open and pluralistic, recognizing some infant baptisms, questioning some believers' baptisms (and also more or less explicit "re-baptism"), also allowing the possibility of being a member of the church without any baptism; also in relation to other churches some Baptists are open, working for church unity with other non-Baptist denominations or churches in spite of different baptismal theologies and practices - for example the Mission Covenant Church of Sweden - maintaining an open, pluralistic Baptist attitude; other Baptists, however, work for church unity with other Baptist denominations ("groups") - for example the Örebro (Baptist) Mission (later on Interact) - maintaining a closed, traditional Baptist attitude.

I have also found that maintaining the same understanding, teaching and practice of baptism, i.e. doctrinal unity on baptism, does not necessarily mean continued church fellowship nor necessarily an unification of churches with similar opinions into one church. Painful divisions have occurred also within the Baptist Union.

There is a mixture of cause and effect, which sometimes may result in unification, at others in divisions. This gives one cause to study doctrinal questions, but it is also necessary to take practical factors into account, such as personal relationships, leadership, finances, the press, etc. All these factors may result in a reconsideration of theology and even in a partial change of identity of a church.

A result of my work is that baptism seems to continue to be a stumbling-block, not only between believers' baptizing denominations/churches and infant baptizing churches, but, as far as concerns Swedish Baptist conditions, within the Baptist Union of Sweden itself. For in the latter, in its ecumenical context, the traditional Baptist characteristics and principles have been reconsidered – and not only that but also partly changed.

The question is if the Baptist Union of Sweden will become superfluous. It has, particularly from the 1970's onwards, become more fluid and pluralist concerning its view on baptism with implications on other issues (both in theory and practice), as for example ecclesiology and ecumenism. This has been a challenge – also to its Baptist identity. From this study of baptism in the Baptist Union of Sweden, I have proved that there is a more complex, wide and pluralistic situation than is reflected in BUS, a document which thus in one way may be questioned in regard to its representativeness for the Baptist Union of Sweden.

What will happen to the Baptist Union of Sweden in the future because of all this? For it may, of course, be questioned if two baptismal forms existing side by side are the best presupposition for a strong Baptist movement. Can a Baptist be and remain a Baptist without baptism, and is it still a Baptist church if baptism is not indispensable for membership? The Baptist pastor Ruben Janarv is explicit. He maintains that the Baptist Union of Sweden cannot recognize infant baptism as baptism "then we would no longer be Baptist congregations." This is one opinion, there are others, as for example by Torsten Bergsten. In other words the answers are not unambiguous, for we get different answers from the Swedish Baptists, which once again shows the diversity within that denomination.

After beginning my thesis with international ecumenical documents, *BEM* and *BUS*, I finished my thesis by relating to an international document, issued by the European Baptist Federation *(EBF)* in 1992 – referred to for example in *Svenska Baptistsamfundets Årsbok* 1992-93 (The Annual of the Baptist Union of Sweden). This document in 13 clauses, distributed to Baptist denominations in Europe, says: *"We practise baptism, for believers only, into the Body of Christ... this makes the act inappropriate for infants or young children."* And it states that baptism is inseparable from entrance into membership of the church as the Body of Christ. It maintains the importance of returning to the New Testament practice of baptism, i.e. believers' baptism, for a true understanding of the nature of faith, the church and discipleship. In other words, a similar opinion to that in *BUS*.

I wonder, however, if the clauses just referred to are in fact representative of the Baptists in Europe – they are obviously not completely in agreement with or representative of the Baptist Union of Sweden. For on the basis of this thesis, it may be questioned if official documents and statements in fact describe "reality". Possibly they describe a part of reality, for what has been found in *BUS* concerning Baptist baptismal theology and practice is not wholly congruent with what is found within the public discussions. This ought to be a memento for the work towards church unity in the future at all levels within all churches.

There is, starting from the Swedish Baptist background and history (Part I), partially in *BUS* (Part II) but even more in the public discussions (Part III), a complementary, revised view of baptism with implications for ecclesiology. The traditional Baptist dogmatic and categorical rejection of infant baptism and acceptance of "re-baptism" has been weakened in favour of a differentiated judgement on both. This is what I have called an open and pluralistic Baptist attitude, more evident at the local, congregational level than at the official one, where we find a "dogmatic delayed reaction".

The diversity within the Baptist Union concerning baptism has implications on other issues. Such a finding, and the process taking place especially among "the grass-roots", does not always become apparent in international documents like *BUS*. We cannot talk about "our one baptism" or "our common baptism", and thus neither about baptism as the basis of membership of the church nor baptism as a basic bond of church unity. This is evident not least in the official response to *BEM*. At the same time baptism, i.e. believers' baptism, has in one way been weakened within the Baptist Union of Sweden which is remarkable in view of its history.

A possibility of church unity founded not on faith and baptism but on faith alone seems to be developing, especially in the ecumenical congregations, which is opposed to the view of *BEM* and also to classic Baptist teaching and practice. To have unbaptized members is surely a dogmatic anomaly for Baptists.

In short, there is a Baptist reconsideration of baptism and thus of ecclesiology.

Appendix.

This appendix is copied with kind permission from WCC Publications, Geneva, *Churches respond to BEM*. Official Responses to the "Baptism, Eucharist and Ministry" text, Vol. IV, ed. Max Thurian, Faith and Order Paper No. 137, World Council of Churches, Geneva 1987, pp. 200-205.

BAPTIST UNION OF SWEDEN

Foreword

The Baptist Union of Sweden, although not a member of the World Council of Churches, has always followed with great interest the work of the Faith and Order Commission of the WCC. When the Lima document on "Baptism, Eucharist, Ministry" appeared, it seemed therefore natural that the Baptist Union of Sweden should formulate a response to this document. This response has been worked out by a committee of five persons and has been approved by the executive board of the Union.

Baptism

INTRODUCTORY NOTES

A study of many years within the frame of the Faith and Order work has led to a common understanding of baptism in many respects, especially regarding the meaning and importance of baptism. After all, different churches with various traditions can say the same things about baptism. The difficulties have been evident when it comes to the point of putting the common view into practice. As no church wants to practise "re-baptism" or have its baptismal practice looked upon as such, there will be problems in connection with the mutual recognition of baptism. New points of view must be considered in order to avoid the question ending up in a blind alley. With the present varied practices in different churches it is hardly possible to come to a united standpoint. The question is if the Lima text initiates a new start.

THE INSTITUTION AND MEANING OF BAPTISM, §§1–7

In accordance with the above we can agree with what is said here. Yet the indicated difficulty emerges in the last sentence in §6: "Therefore, our one

---

● 20,924 members, 370 churches.

baptism into Christ constitutes a call to the churches to overcome their divisions and visibly manifest their fellowship." Can we in earnest talk about "our one baptism" as long as baptismal practice in a decisive way divides us? In the subsequent commentary the importance of the practice is clear. But sure enough it is also emphasized that baptism is not the only dividing factor.

BAPTISM AND FAITH, §§8–10

Here baptism is said to be both God's gift and our human response. Likewise the necessity of faith for the reception of the salvation embodied and set forth in baptism is accentuated. It is further pointed out that personal commitment is necessary for responsible membership in the body of Christ. But various baptismal practices indicate different consequences of this common understanding.

BAPTISMAL PRACTICE, §§11–16

A. Baptism of believers and infants

The list that is presented here is not complete, at any rate not for Swedish conditions. There are churches in which the individual is at liberty to decide not only the form of baptism but also if he should be baptized at all. The Society of Friends and the Salvation Army, for example, do not practise any baptism. In these cases there is a deliberate repudiation of sacramental administration. There are, however, cases when the importance of baptism is strongly asserted but baptism is not considered to be necessary for membership in the church in question.

This raises the question: should a church be looked upon as a church if not all or even any of its members are baptized or if the sacraments are neither taken into account nor administered? Anyway, churches which are reluctant to recognize infant baptism have been prepared to answer this question in the affirmative. An answer like this can be regarded as deviation from what is said in for instance §6: "Through baptism, Christians are brought into union with Christ, with each other and with the Church of every time and place." We are, however, obliged to observe that there is an inconsistency between doctrine and practice when the necessity of baptism is strongly stressed at the same time as membership without baptism is accepted and justified. Nor is a personal response later on necessary for membership. This is best exemplified in our country by the Church of Sweden with its state church idea and increasing number of unchristened members. This naturally creates difficulties in ecumenical relations and discussions when the church and the importance of sacraments for the church are to be defined. In such circumstances it is difficult to take seriously the accusation that we Baptists deny sacramental integrity when baptizing someone who is a member of another church.

In §12 it is said that baptism always takes place in a community of faith. When someone who is a believer is baptized he confesses his faith in connection with the baptism. When an infant is baptized, it is taken for granted that a personal response will be given at a later moment in life.

One question remains unanswered. Does baptism have any effect without this response? The very stress of the fact that no baptism can be repeated or made undone possibly implies an answer in the affirmative. A supplementary question ought to be asked: Can such a kind of baptism—as long as this personal response is not given — be said to have another meaning than the blessing of children has in churches where baptism of believers is practised?

When it is said in the commentary to §12 that "both forms of baptism require a similar and responsible attitude towards Christian nurture", it should be pointed out that anyone who has been blessed as a child and consequently is not baptized, is to be regarded as a catechumen, in the proper sense of the word, whose instruction is a preparation for baptism and life as baptized. We hesitate to put someone in the situation to have a claim "laid upon" him as long as there is no possibility of response. On the other hand there is the possibility as well as the obligation to express "that children are placed under the protection of God's grace" (§16) in an act that goes back to Jesus' action. Here we want to comply with the request "to express more visibly that fact". The place and theological foundation of the blessing of children has probably not been given enough attention in this connection but should be the subject of a close study, which hopefully could give a new basis of the question of mutual acceptance of baptismal practices. Further aspects on blessing of children and its meaning are dealt with in the supplement.

In §13 with commentary it is said that any practice which might be interpreted as "re-baptism" must be avoided. We can agree with this wording. But it makes the question whether re-baptism is practised dependent on who interprets. It is doubtful whether baptism of believers with its consequences should be looked upon as a denial of the sacramental integrity of other churches. The churches that baptize believers only do not seem to find it most difficult to recognize the ministries of other churches. Moreover, it is the recognition of other churches and their members as members of the body of Christ that is the reason why open communion and sometimes even open membership are practised in our churches. We mean that unity in Christ can be manifested in spite of different baptismal practices.

B. Baptism–chrismation–confirmation

We agree that "Christian baptism is in water and the Holy Spirit", §14. We cannot see that baptism has to be completed by another act of sacramental character in order to receive the Holy Spirit or share in the eucharist. That would imply to diminish the meaning of baptism and not take its consequences seriously.

We maintain that the imposition of hands, in the baptismal rite itself or in a special ceremony afterwards is not associated with the giving of the Holy Spirit but an act of blessing with intercession for the baptized person, a consecration to membership and personal commitment in the Christian church.

C. Towards mutual recognition of baptism

Questions in connection with these items have already been touched upon and will be discussed in the supplement concerning blessing of children. However, we want to emphasize that a terminology should be used that is not depreciating or insulting. This would to a great extent contribute to an increasing mutual understanding of our convictions. We Baptists must admit that we have often used the expression "sprinkling" to demonstrate repudiation of the practice of churches baptizing infants. This is naturally perceived as offensive and we should show respect for the conviction of these churches by using the word "infant baptism" when baptism of infants is referred to. In the same way we Baptists find it insulting when our baptismal practice is described as "re-baptism" and we want others to show respect for our conviction by avoiding referring to our baptism in this way. When we want to accentuate our practice as a contrast to infant baptism we speak about believers' baptism. The matter in concern — to handle the question of how to look upon one another's baptism — will benefit from a mutual respect which also manifests itself in our choice of words.

THE CELEBRATION OF BAPTISM, §§17–23

Paragraph 17 describes what is necessary about the celebration of baptism.

For a person who practises immersion it is natural to say "baptize in water" especially since that is what was said in §14: "The Christian baptism is in water and the Holy Spirit."

Naturally enough the rich contents of baptism benefits from a form that fully does justice to it, §18. That is e.g. the reason why we baptize by immersion. We find that immersion does not only express participation in Christ's death, burial and resurrection but also other factors as e.g. when the purification that baptism aims at is described by "washing", Acts 22:16, "a body washed in pure water", Hebrews 10:22, or as "the washing of regeneration and renewal in the Holy Spirit", Titus 3:5, or when it is said: "Baptized into union with him you all put on Christ as a garment", Galatians 3:27 (quotations from *New English Bible*.) Other instances are given in the commentary to this item of the text.

Regarding what is said in §19 we refer to what we have commented on §§13 and 14 above.

One baptismal rite may differ from the other by being more or less comprehensive, §20. Such differences should not impede Christian unity.

Several elements of the baptismal ritual here enumerated are, in accordance with what was said in item 18 above, included in the very baptismal rite. Moreover, we believe that over-explicit explanations can "rationalize away" the inherent symbolic force of the rite. But we do recognize elements here enumerated which should be included, e.g. the proclamation of the scriptures referring to baptism, the creed and the *epiklesis*. See further §14 above.

Paragraph 21 accords with what was said about the proclamation of the scriptures referring to baptism in the preceding paragraph.

What is said in §22 applies to us as well.

We would like to emphasize that baptism is intimately connected with the corporate life and worship of the church, §23.

SUPPLEMENT ON BLESSING OF CHILDREN

Excursus about the blessing of children

Since the middle of the 1930s the blessing of children has been increasingly practised in the Swedish Baptist churches. There are some examples already from the 1860s as well as from the beginning of the twentieth century. The impulses seem to have come from abroad, mainly from the United States and England. Nowadays most newborn children are involved in such a practice. From the handbook of 1954 and onwards there is an agenda for the performance of the act which is followed by most pastors.

The blessing of children has a threefold content: a thanksgiving to the Lord of Life for the newborn child, an act of prayer for parents and child in which the parents also are given the opportunity to accept their Christian calling as parents and eventually an opportunity for the church to accept its responsibility for the newborn child. The act as a whole is a marking of the place of the child in the church family and points towards the day when the young man/woman presumably accepts the Christian faith and the fellowship of the church where he/she has grown up.

So performed and understood the blessing of children is an expression of the Baptist understanding of the children growing up in the church. The Baptists do not adhere to the teaching of inherited sin in the sense that the children already from birth should live under the judgment of sin. They live under the atonement of Christ and also in the protection of the faith of their parents and the church fellowship. For this no special performance is required but the blessing of children is an expression and a reminder of this situation of life. For Baptists the baptism belongs together with a personal conversion and the acceptance of faith which occur later in life.

The tendency is that the blessing of children is increasingly practised also in denominations which so far mainly have been practising infant baptism. Internationally the blessing of children is also used as a complement to baptism in situations where one wants an act of blessing in another geographic environment than parents' church or for instance with adoption.

We recommend churches that baptize children, and especially those in which uncertainty about infant baptism has arisen, to seriously consider the question of blessing of children.

Of course there are important possibilities to understand infant baptism and blessing of children as related expressions for several momentous parts of the Christian understanding of the children. Even the blessing of children "stresses the corporate faith" (see note to §12) and the participation of the child in the fruits of the parents' faith. The blessing of children underlines the being of man as a continuation of a divine act of creation. Many important biblical thoughts and sayings which often are related to the baptism of children can very well be used also for the blessing of children. For Baptists it is possible to look at infant baptism as a form of blessing of children and there are examples that priests and pastors who practise infant baptism look upon it in the same way. In the new order of baptism of the Swedish Lutheran Church there is also a special moment of blessing:

1. Against this background it is possible for a Baptist to acknowledge that infant baptism "embodies God's own initiative in Christ and expresses a response of faith made within the believing community" (B12, commentary).

2. The line of difference between "belonging" and "membership" can possibly prepare for a new understanding. Both opinions of baptism therefore count a form of relation between the church and the child.

3. So understood infant baptism can be looked upon as an alternative to the blessing of children, but the consequence is not that Baptists feel themselves prevented from baptizing people who in this manner have been blessed in the form of infant baptism.

Churches where infant baptism, and especially those where hesitation about the rise of infant baptism is at stake, should consider the possibility of offering parents blessing of children as an alternative to infant baptism. The more the blessing of children gains ground the more the need for a common study of the relation of the two acts to each other increases.

Abbreviations

ABFMS	American Baptist Foreign Mission Society.
AGF	Arbetsgruppen för gemensamma församlingar (the Working Party on Ecumenical Congregations).
B 1, B 2	etc. means paragraph 1, 2 etc. in *BEM* (the Lima document, see below).
B com 6,	
B com 12	etc. means commentary to *B 6* etc. in *BEM*.
BEM	*Baptism, Eucharist and Ministry*, Faith and Order Paper No. 111, World Council of Churches, Geneva 1982.
BUS	The official response of the Baptist Union of Sweden to *BEM*, in *Churches respond to BEM*. Vol. IV, Faith and Order Paper No. 137, World Council of Churches, Geneva 1987, pp. 200-213.
BWA	Baptist World Alliance.
Dop	"Dop Nattvard Ämbete. Svenska Baptistsamfundets svar på Faith and Order Paper No. 111", 1985, [unpublished paper], before the English translation, i.e. *BUS*.
EBF	European Baptist Federation.
G 72	The National Christian Conference in Gothenburg, Sweden.
V 77	The National Christian Conference in Västerås, Sweden.
J 83	The National Christian Conference in Jönköping, Sweden.
Ö 89	The National Christian Conference in Örebro, Sweden.
SBUF	Svenska Baptisternas Ungdomsförbund (The Swedish Baptist Youth Association).
VP	Veckoposten (The official weekly magazine of the Baptist Union of Sweden until 1992).
WARC	World Alliance of Reformed Churches.
WCC	World Council of Churches.

Bibliography

1. Unpublished Papers, Documents, Letters and Minutes

The Germanic vowels å, ä, ö and ø are ranged under a and o.

HAMBURG

THE OFFICE OF THE EUROPEAN BAPTIST FEDERATION

"Document for Comment by the Baptist Unions of Europe. What are Baptists? A Statement of Identity by Baptist Christians in Europe." Issued by the European Baptist Federation, 1992. (Dorfweil, Germany, 26-29 January 1992), [unpublished document].

ÖREBRO

THE LIBRARAY OF THE ÖREBRO (BAPTIST) MISSION SCHOOL

Cedersjö, Björn, Fahlgren, Sune, "Från separation till växande gemenskap. Relationen Svenska Baptistsamfundet - Örebromissionen som den speglas i protokollen från samtalsdelegationen 1965-1986", Uppsats vid Örebro Missionsskola, Örebro 1987, [unpublished paper].

Cedersjö, Björn, "På väg till enhet i tron!? Ef. 4:13. En kartläggning och analys av ett antal lärosamtal (åren 1963-1988) där frikyrkorna i Sverige deltagit", Tro och Liv - symposiet 1989 "Finns det en ekumenisk teologi?", Lidingö 26-27 januari 1989, [unpublished paper].

STOCKHOLM

THE ARCHIVES OF THE BAPTIST UNION OF SWEDEN, BETELSEMINARIET

"Det finns en väg". Rapport från en arbetsgrupp inom Svenska Baptistsamfundet, Stockholm 1982, [unpublished paper].

"Dop Nattvard Ämbete. Svenska Baptistsamfundets svar på Faith and Order Paper No. 111", [1985], pp. 1-19, [unpublished paper]. [Abbreviated to *Dop* in the thesis].

"På väg mot kristen enhet", 1984, [unpublished paper].

"På väg mot kristen enhet för församlingar som planerar att förenas", 1988, [unpublished paper].

"Svenska Baptistsamfundet och Kyrkornas Världsråd. En studierapport", Svenska Baptistsamfundets ekumeniska kommitté, på uppdrag av Svenska Baptistsamfundets missionsstyrelse, 1965, [unpublished paper].

Minutes from the Baptist Union of Sweden

5/10/83, §§ 1-6, Protokoll vid sammanträde med arbetsgruppen för uttalande om "Dop-Nattvard-Ämbete" Baptistsamfundets expedition, onsdagen den 5 oktober 1983 kl 17.00.

2/11/83, §§ 7-10, Protokoll fört vid sammanträde med BEM-gruppen (arbetsgruppen för uttalande om "Dop-Nattvard-Ämbete"), Baptistsamfundets expedition, onsdagen den 2 november 1983 kl.13.00.

Bilaga: Ruben Janarv: Synpunkter på översättningen av avsnittet om dopet och kommentar till vissa delar av innehållet. (Referat av gruppens kommentarer och samtal bryts in i bilagan), [Supplement to the Minutes 2/11/83].

17/1/84, §§ 11-16, Protokoll fört vid sammanträde med BEM-gruppen på Baptistsamfundets expedition tisdagen den 17 januari 1984 kl.13.00.

23/2/84, §§ 17-24, Protokoll fört vid sammanträde med BEM-gruppen på Baptistsamfundets expedition torsdagen den 23 februari 1984 kl 17.00

Bilaga 1. 84-02-23, Ruben Janarv: LIMA-dokumentet: Dopet, [Supplement to the Minutes 23/2/84].

20/3/84, §§ 25-30, Protokoll fört vid sammanträde med BEM-gruppen på Baptistsamfundets expedition tisdagen den 20 mars 1984 kl.16.00.

11/5/84, §§ 31-36, Protokoll fört vid sammanträde med BEM-gruppen på Baptistsamfundets expedition fredagen den 11 maj 1984 kl.13.30.

23/8/84, §§ 37-47, Protokoll fört vid sammanträde med BEM-gruppen på Baptistsamfundets expedition torsdagen den 23 augusti 1984.

20/9/84, §§ 48-55, Protokoll fört vid sammanträde med BEM-gruppen på Baptistsamfundets expedition torsdagen den 20 september 1984.

18/10/84, §§ 55-65, Protokoll fört vid sammanträde med BEM-gruppen i Norrmalmskyrkan torsdagen den 18 oktober 1984.

20/11/84, §§ 66-72, Protokoll fört vid sammanträde med BEM-gruppen i Norrmalmskyrkan tisdagen den 20 november 1984.

8/3/85, §§ 13, Svenska Baptistsamfundet, Protokoll 1985-03-08, Missionsstyrelsen, Kungsholms Baptistkyrka, Stockholm, Fredag kl 09.00-18.00, [Meeting of the Central Board of the Swedish Baptist Union of Sweden].

STOCKHOLM

NATIONAL ARCHIVES OF SWEDEN

Bergsten, Torsten, "Dopet i internationell belysning", in "Dopet i kyrkornas gemenskap. Material från Svenska ekumeniska nämndens konferens på Graninge Stiftsgård den 10-12 december 1974", Svenska Ekumeniska Nämnden, pp. 33-34, [conference documentation].

"Dopet i kyrkornas gemenskap. Material från Svenska ekumeniska nämndens konferens på Graninge Stiftsgård den 10-12 december 1974", Svenska Ekumeniska Nämnden, [conference documentation].

Franzén, Bert, "Inledningsanförande till grupparbete: Dopet som ekumeniskt problem", in "Dopet i kyrkornas gemenskap. Material från Svenska ekumeniska nämndens konferens på Graninge Stiftsgård den 10-12 december 1974", Svenska Ekumeniska Nämnden, p. 23, [conference documentation].

Hellholm, David, "Pistis - baptisma. Ett försök att analysera trons förhållande till dopet utifrån Rom 6", Föredrag vid dopkonferens på Graninge stiftsgård 15-17 december 1976, Graninge II, tema: "Tron och dopet", Svenska Ekumeniska Nämnden, pp. 1-22, [conference documentation].

"Konferens kring temat 'Dopet i kyrkornas gemenskap'", in "Dopet i kyrkornas gemenskap. Material från Svenska ekumeniska nämndens konferens på Graninge Stiftsgård den 10-12 december 1974", Svenska Ekumeniska Nämnden, p. 1, [conference documentation].

Lagergren, David, "Är en gemensam dopsyn en förutsättning för gemensamt nattvardsfirande?", Inledning till grupparbete vid dopkonferens på Graninge stiftsgård 15-17 december 1976, Graninge II, tema: "Tron och dopet", Svenska Ekumeniska Nämnden, pp. 1-2, [conference documentation].

"Utkast till rapport till V-77. Dopet och de kristnas enhet", Utkast vid dopkonferens på Graninge stiftsgård 15-17 december 1976, Graninge II, tema: "Tron och dopet", Svenska Ekumeniska Nämnden, [conference documentation], pp. 1-4.

"Uttalande från konferensen (1974-12-13)", in "Dopet i kyrkornas gemenskap. Material från Svenska ekumeniska nämndens konferens på Graninge Stiftsgård den 10-12 december 1974", Svenska Ekumeniska Nämnden, p. 57, [conference documentation].

UPPSALA

FACULTY OF THEOLOGY, UPPSALA UNIVERSITY

Bardh, Ulla, "Dop och medlemskap. En jämförelse mellan två ekumeniska församlingar; Storvreta frikyrkoförsamling och Valsätrakyrkan, baserad på eller speglad i 155 medlemmars svar på en enkät, hösten 1989." Delrapport av uppsats 1990, Uppsala 1990, [unpublished paper].

Bardh, Ulla, "Limadokumentet och Sv. Baptistsamfundet. En redogörelse för och kommentar kring Sv. Baptistsamfundets remissvar", Uppsala 1986, [unpublished paper].

Bardh, Ulla, "Preliminär skrivning av idépapper om SMF och ekumeniken med anledning av det s.k. folkrörelseprojektet 'Ju mer vi är tillsammans...', där SMF representerar väckelserörelserna", [s.a], [unpublished paper].

Mattsson, Valter, "Behov och problem som den ekumeniska församlingen brottas med. Praktiska, samhälleliga, psykologiska och teologiska aspekter på framväxten av Församlingen i Valsätrakyrkan", Uppsala 1981, [unpublished paper].

VÄXJÖ

AUTHOR'S COLLECTION

Bergsten, Torsten, "Anders Wiberg, dopet och de kristnas enhet", Wibergssymposium, Betelseminariet 4-5 november 1987, [unpublished paper].

Bergsten, Torsten, "Baptismens dubbla dilemma", Bidrag av Torsten Bergsten till den frikyrkoekumeniska debatten i Svensk Veckotidning och Veckoposten, Uppsala den 10 november 1991, [unpublished paper].

Bergsten, Torsten, "Dopet i ett ekumeniskt perspektiv", Föredrag på Örebro missionsskola den 4 februari 1988, [unpublished paper].

Bergsten, Torsten, "Dopsyn och församlingstillhörighet i gemensamma församlingar", Inledningsföredrag den 30 november 1989 i Norrmalmskyrkan, [unpublished paper].

Bergsten, Torsten, "Kyrka, samfund och den radikala kongregationalismen. Tro och Liv - symposium 26-27 jan 1989", [unpublished paper].

Bergsten, Torsten, "På väg mot ett ömsesidigt doperkännande?" Kyrka 89, Göteborg 27 maj 1989. Fädernas kyrka: statskyrka, folkkyrka, frikyrka, [unpublished paper].

Letters to Lennart Johnsson

Skog, Margareta, Church of Sweden, Research Department, Uppsala. Letter to Lennart Johnsson 17/1/97.

Skog, Margareta, Church of Sweden, Research Department, Uppsala. Letter to Lennart Johnsson 28/1/97.

Skog, Margareta, Church of Sweden, Research Department, Uppsala. Letter to Lennart Johnsson 24/9/99.

Wagner, Günter. Letter to Lennart Johnsson 19/2/88.

2. Published Material

A *Bibliography of Baptist writings on baptism, 1900-1968,* Bibliographical Aids, No. 1, compiled by Athol Gill, Rüschlikon - Zürich 1969.

A *Documentary History of Faith and Order Movement 1927-1963,* ed. Lukas Vischer, St. Louis, Missouri, 1963.

Agnarsson, Ruben, "Livets Ord", *Svenska Trossamfund.* Historia, tro och bekännelse, organisation, gudstjänst- och fromhetsliv, ed. Allan Hofgren, 8th ed., Uppsala 1990, pp. 101-105.

Ahlefelt, Annika, "'Nya Teologiska högskolan ska motverka kyrkosplittring'", *Svenska Kyrkans Tidning,* No. 40, 1993, p. 19.

"Alla på samma ort", [editorial], *Veckoposten,* No. 7, 1986, p. 2.

Andersson, Axel, *Svenska Missionsförbundet.* Dess uppkomst och femtioåriga verksamhet. Inre missionen, del I, Stockholm 1928.

Andersson, Krister, "Levande samtal om förenade församlingar", *Svensk Veckotidning,* No. 42, 1990, p. 2.

Aourell, Göte, "Dopet och frikyrklig enhet", *Veckoposten,* No. 42, 1992, p. 12.

Åqvist, Berit, "Baptistisk konfirmation", *Veckoposten,* No. 33, 1985, p. 2.

Åqvist, Berit, "Berit Åqvist om samverkan med Lidingö: -Inte ekumenik i uppgivenhetens tecken", *Veckoposten,* No. 40, 1992, pp. 8-9.

Åqvist, Berit, "Får barnen vara med?", *Veckoposten,* No. 49, 1981, p. 9.

Åqvist, Berit, "Förord", *Tro, Frihet, Gemenskap.* Svensk baptism genom 150 år, Örebro 1998, p. 7.

Åqvist, Berit, "Öppen fråga", *Veckoposten,* No. 13, 1985, p. 2.

Åqvist, Berit, *Porträtt:* "Baptistisk hövding", *Tro, Frihet, Gemenskap.* Svensk baptism genom 150 år, Örebro 1998, pp. 237-239.

Åqvist, Berit, "Varför inte steget före?", *Veckoposten,* No. 22, 1985, p. 2.

"Är vi på väg mot målet?", [editorial], *Veckoposten,* No. 8, 1992, p. 2.

Året, Baptistsamfundets kalender Betlehem, Stockholm 1971.

Året, Baptistsamfundets kalender Betlehem, Stockholm 1972.

Aronson, Torbjörn, *Guds eld över Sverige.* Svensk väckelsehistoria efter 1945, Uppsala 1990.

"Årskonferensens förhandlingar: Evangelisationens vägar den mest samlande frågan", *Veckoposten,* No. 21, 1986, p. 3.

Arvidson, Thorvald, "Dopet - gemenskap eller söndring", *Veckoposten,* No. 1/2, 1975, p. 3.

Arvidson, Thorvald, "Baptistsamfundet. Missionsförbundet. Hur har vi det? Hur vill vi ha det? Samtalskonferens om möjligheter och problem i gemensam verksamhet", *Veckoposten,* No. 50, 1982, pp. 6-7.

Arvidsson, Rune, "En dopsyn?", *Veckoposten,* No. 39, 1985, p. 12.

"Åsna mellan hötappar?", [editorial], *Veckoposten,* No. 19, 1985, p. 2.

Asp, Samuel, "Den svenska pingstväckelsen", *Svenska Trossamfund.* Historia, tro och bekännelse, organisation, gudstjänst- och fromhetsliv, ed. Allan Hofgren, 8th ed., Uppsala 1990, pp. 91-100.

"Att missa målet", [Wilhelm Salomonson, Jan Lundahl, Ingrid Samuelsson], *Veckoposten,* No. 21/22, 1991, p. 16.

"Att räkna medlemmar", [editorial], *Veckoposten,* No. 5, 1990, p. 2.

Axelson, Einar, "Ekumenisk besinning", *Veckoposten,* No. 27, 1987, p. 15.

Axelson, Einar, "Klara signaler!", *Veckoposten,* No. 7, 1986, p. 10.

Axelson, Einar, "Viktigare än ekumeniken", *Veckoposten,* No. 18, 1988, p. 11.

Bangalore 1978. Minutes and Supplementary Documents from the Meeting of The Commission on Faith and Order, held at The Ecumenical Christian Centre Whitefield, Bangalore, India, 16-30 August, 1978, Faith and Order Paper No. 93, World Council of Churches, Geneva, Commission on Faith and Order, 1979.

"Baptimister?", *Veckoposten,* No. 37, 1987, p. 4.

Baptism, Eucharist and Ministry, Faith and Order Paper No. 111, World Council of Churches, Geneva 1982.

Baptism, Eucharist & Ministry 1982-1990. Report on the Process and Responses, Faith and Order Paper No. 149, World Council of Churches, Geneva 1990.

"Baptist - biskop besökte Sverige", *Veckoposten,* No. 2, 1988, p. 3.

"Baptist- och missionsförsamlingar går samman", *Veckoposten,* No. 26/27, 1990, p. 12.

"Baptisterna och Anden", [editorial], *Veckoposten,* No. 6, 1979, p. 2.

"Baptisterna vill samverka i ödesfrågor", *Svenska Kyrkans Tidning,* No. 31/32, 1989, p. 9.

"Baptistpastor om dopdokument: -Baptister bör erkänna barndopet", *Svenska Journalen,* No. 1, 1985, p. 12.

Baptists and Lutherans in Conversation. A Message to our Churches. Report of the Joint Commission of the Baptist World Alliance and the Lutheran World Federation, Geneva 1990.

Bardh, Ulla, "Har baptister behov av nattvarden?", *Veckoposten,* No. 16, 1978, p. 9.

Barth, Karl, *Det kristna dopet,* Stockholm 1949.

Barth, Karl, *Die kirchliche Dogmatik,* Band 4: Die Lehre von der Versöhnung. Teil 4: Das christliche Leben: (Fragment): die Taufe als Begründung des christlichen Lebens, München 1967.

Barth, Karl, "Die kirchliche Lehre von der Taufe", *Theologische Studien* 14, Zürich 1947.

Beasley-Murray, George Raymond, *Baptism in the New Testament,* Exeter 1962.

Beasley-Murray, George Raymond, *Baptism Today and Tomorrow,* London/New York 1966.

Beasley-Murray, George Raymond, *Dopet idag och i morgon,* Stockholm 1967.

Beasley-Murray, George Raymond, "The Problem of Infant Baptism. An Exercise in Possibilities", *Festschrift Günther Wagner,* International

Theological Studies. Contribution of Baptist Scholars, Vol. 1, Rüschlikon 1994, pp. 1-14.

Benander, Carl Eric, "Tillbakablickar och framtidssyner. Minnen och intryck V", Tro och Liv, No. 4, 1943, pp. 181-183.

Bergman, Carl-Göran, "Eucharistins plats i kyrkorummet", Svenskt gudstjänstliv 62, Lund 1987, pp. 19-34.

Bergsten, Torsten, "Anders Wiberg, dopet och de kristnas enhet", Tro och Liv, No. 4, 1988, pp. 12-27.

Bergsten, Torsten, "Anders Wiberg - väckelseman, samfundsledare och teolog", Kyrkohistorisk årsskrift 81, 1981, Uppsala, pp. 84-93.

Bergsten, Torsten, "Associativt och öppet medlemskap", Baptistpredikanternas studieblad, No. 2, 1964, pp. 9-12.

Bergsten, Torsten, "Att respektera varandras dop", Veckoposten, No. 9, 1992, p. 12.

Bergsten, Torsten, Balthasar Hubmaier. Seine Stellung zu Reformation und Täufertum: 1521-1528, Diss., Kassel 1961.

Bergsten, Torsten, "Baptism and the Church. Baptist Faith and Practice in a Biblical and Ecumonical Light", The Baptist Quarterly, Vol. 18, No. 3, 1959, pp. 125-131, and No. 4, 1959, pp. 159-171, [Orig; "Dopet och församlingen. Baptistisk tro och praxis i biblisk och ekumenisk belysning", Dopet Dåben Dåpen. Tre nordiska teologiska uppsatser, Stockholm 1957, pp. 5-23.]

Bergsten, Torsten, "Baptismen, trosfriheten och ekumeniken", Liv och tjänst. Guds mission församlingens uppdrag, eds. Birgit Karlsson, Berit Åqvist, Örebro 1988, pp. 187-205.

Bergsten, Torsten, "Baptismens dubbla dilemma", Veckoposten, No. 47, 1991, p. 4.

Bergsten, Torsten, "Barnet i frikyrkan. En historisk - teologisk studie", Tro och Liv, No. 3, 1985, pp. 2-22.

Bergsten, Torsten, "Den gemensamma församlingen - ett tecken om enhet", Levande. Om församling, teologi och samhälle, 1996, pp. 37-53.

Bergsten Torsten, "Dop, barndop och församlingstillhörighet", Trons Segrar, No. 21, 1989, p. 11.

Bergsten, Torsten, "Dop och kyrkotillhörighet", Nordiska röster om dop och kyrkotillhörighet. Synpunkter och föredrag från en nordisk ekumenisk konsultation om teologi och kyrkorätt med anledning av Vägen till kyrkan - diskussionsbetänkande nr 2 från en arbetsgrupp inom Svenska kyrkan, Svenska Kyrkans Utredningar (SKU) 1988:1, KISA - rapport 1988:4, ed. Tord Harlin, Uppsala 1988, pp. 83-94.

Bergsten, Torsten, "Dop och nattvard i de gemensamma församlingarna", Tro och Liv, No. 6, 1990, pp. 2-7.

Bergsten, Torsten, "Döparrörelsen 450 år", Veckoposten, No. 33/34, 1975, p. 3.

Bergsten, Torsten, "Dopet i ekumeniskt perspektiv", Veckoposten, No. 7, 1988, p. 7.

Bergsten, Torsten, "Dopet i ekumeniskt perspektiv", Veckoposten, No. 8, 1988, p. 7.

Bergsten, Torsten, "Dopet i ekumeniskt perspektiv", *Veckoposten*, No. 9, 1988, p. 7.

Bergsten, Torsten, "Dopet igår och idag", *Tro och Liv*, No. 2, 1979, pp. 2-13.

Bergsten, Torsten, "Dopet och församlingen. Baptistisk tro och praxis i biblisk och ekumenisk belysning", *Dopet Dåben Dåpen.* Tre nordiska teologiska uppsatser, Stockholm 1957, pp. 5-23.

Bergsten, Torsten, "Ekumenik, vision och verklighet", *Tro och Liv*, No. 1, 1986, pp. 4-12.

Bergsten, Torsten, "Ekumenisk barnteologi", *Veckoposten*, No. 13/14, 1991, p. 12.

Bergsten, Torsten, "Ekumenisk barnteologi", *Veckoposten*, No. 15, 1991, p. 4.

Bergsten Torsten, "Enheten i Kristus", *Tro, Frihet, Gemenskap.* Svensk baptism genom 150 år, Örebro 1998, pp. 213-234.

Bergsten, Torsten, "Förändring genom konfrontation och dialog. Svenskt perspektiv", *Samfund i förändring.* Baptistisk identitet i norden under ett och ett halvt sekel, Tro & Liv skriftserie No. 2, ed. David Lagergren, Stockholm 1997, pp. 30-65.

Bergsten, Torsten, *Frikyrkor i samverkan.* Den svenska frikyrkoekumenikens historia 1905-1993, Örebro/Stockholm 1995.

Bergsten, Torsten, "Gemensamma församlingar", *Nordisk Ekumenisk Orientering*, No. 2, 1994, pp. 3-5.

Bergsten, Torsten, "Kontroversiella rekommendationer", *Dop, Nattvard, Ämbete.* Den officiella texten från Faith and Order - den s k Lima texten 1982 - jämte introduktion och inofficiella ekumeniska kommentarer, Nordisk Ekumenisk skriftserie 11, ed. Kjell Ove Nilsson, 2nd ed., Sigtuna 1983, pp. 134-139.

Bergsten, Torsten, "Kyrkotillhörighet - medlemskap - bekännelse", *Tro och Liv*, No. 1, 1980, pp. 33-45.

Bergsten, Torsten, "Öppet nattvardsbord, överfört medlemskap och en öppen baptism", *Veckoposten*, No. 3, 1986, p. 6.

Bergsten, Torsten, "På väg mot fördjupad gemenskap", *Dokument från Örebro*, utgivna på uppdrag av Sveriges frikyrkoråd under redaktion av Stig Svärd, Stockholm 1969, pp. 61-78.

Bergsten, Torsten, "Samfundsmedvetande och kongregationalism i svensk frikyrklighet", *Kyrkohistorisk årsskrift* 93, 1993, Uppsala, pp. 131-150.

Bergsten, Torsten, "Svenska Baptistsamfundet", *Svenska Trossamfund.* Historia, tro och bekännelse, organisation, gudstjänst- och fromhetsliv, ed. Allan Hofgren, 8th ed., Uppsala 1990, pp. 64-72.

Bergsten, Torsten, "Svenska kyrkan i den aktuella debatten. Tre perspektiv", *Kyrkohistorisk årsskrift* 84, 1984, Uppsala, pp. 30-37.

Bergsten, Torsten, "Tro och tvivel på barndopet", *Veckoposten*, No. 19/20, 1991, p. 7.

Bergsten, Torsten, "Vad är omistligt i bekännelsen av den kristna tron?", *Veckoposten*, No. 12, 1990, p. 4.

Bergström, Erik, "Stockholms Evangeliska Predikantförbunds tillkomst och utveckling", *I endräktens tecken*. Minnesskrift vid Stockholms Evangeliska Predikantförbunds 25 års högtid, Stockholm 1922, pp. 5-13.

"Beslutskonferens", [editorial], *Veckoposten*, No. 16, 1991, p. 2.

Betelseminariet 100 år, ed. Bertil Petterson, Stockholm 1966.

Bexell, Oloph, "Kyrkor i Sverige", *Kyrkans liv*. Introduktion till kyrkovetenskapen, ed. Stephan Borgehammar, 2nd ed., Stockholm 1993, pp. 66-96.

"Birgit Karlsson svarar:", *Veckoposten*, No. 50, 1990, p. 7.

Björkman, Bertil, "Köpings baptister återförenade", *Veckoposten*, No. 27/28, 1991, p. 5.

Bredberg, William, *P. P. Waldenströms verksamhet till 1878*. Till frågan om Svenska Missionsförbundets uppkomst, Diss., Uppsala/Stockholm 1948.

Bredberg, William, *Sällskap - samfund - kyrka?* Vad syftade Missionsförbundets fäder till? Stockholm 1962.

Bring, Ragnar, *Dop och medlemskap i kyrkan*, Stockholm 1979.

Brodd, Sven-Erik, *Dop - Kyrka - Struktur*. Uppsatser, föreläsningar och diskussioner, Uppsala 1980.

Brodd, Sven-Erik, *Dop och kyrkotillhörighet enligt Svenska kyrkans ordning*. Utkast och skisser, Stockholm/Lund 1978.

Brodd, Sven-Erik, "Dop och kyrkotillhörighet i Svenska kyrkan", *Ekumenisk samsyn om dop och kyrkotillhörighet*. Rapport från den officiella lutherskkatolska samtalsgruppen i Sverige med anledning av Stat - kyrka. Ändrade relationer mellan staten och Svenska kyrkan, Statens Offentliga Utredningar (SOU) 1978:1, Stockholm/Lund 1978, pp. 25-32.

Brodd, Sven-Erik, *Ekumeniska perspektiv*. Föreläsningar, KISA - rapport 1990: 4-5, Svenska kyrkans forskningsråd, Uppsala 1990.

Brodd, Sven-Erik, "Ekumeniska perspektiv. Om kristna enhetssträvanden i Sverige", *Svenska Trossamfund*. Historia, tro och bekännelse, organisation, gudstjänst- och fromhetsliv, ed. Allan Hofgren, 8th ed., Uppsala 1990, pp. 183-195.

Brodd, Sven-Erik, "Skärningspunkt mellan idé och verklighet", *Kyrkans liv*. Introduktion till kyrkovetenskapen, ed. Stephan Borgehammar, 2nd ed., Stockholm 1993, pp. 284-318.

Brunner, Emil, *Wahrheit als Begegnung*. Sechs Vorlesungen über das christliche Wahrheitsverständnis, Berlin/Zürich 1938.

Carlsson, Bertil, *Organisationer och beslutsprocesser inom Pingströrelsen*, Järna 1974.

Carlsson, Else-Marie, "Nattvarden i Svenska Baptistsamfundet 1910-1970", *När vi bryter det bröd...*, Stockholm 1981, pp. 101-119.

Churches respond to BEM. Official responses to the "Baptism, Eucharist and Ministry" text, Vol. I, ed. Max Thurian, Faith and Order Paper No. 129, World Council of Churches, Geneva 1986.

Churches respond to BEM. Official responses to the "Baptism, Eucharist and Ministry" text, Vol. II, ed. Max Thurian, Faith and Order Paper No. 132, World Council of Churches, Geneva 1986.

Churches respond to BEM. Official responses to the "Baptism, Eucharist and Ministry" text, Vol. III, ed. Max Thurian, Faith and Order Paper No. 135, World Council of Churches, Geneva 1987.

Churches respond to BEM. Official responses to the "Baptism, Eucharist and Ministry" text, Vol. IV, ed. Max Thurian, Faith and Order Paper No. 137, World Council of Churches, Geneva 1987.

Churches respond to BEM. Official responses to the "Baptism, Eucharist and Ministry" text, Vol. V, ed. Max Thurian, Faith and Order Paper No. 143, World Council of Churches, Geneva 1988.

Churches respond to BEM. Official responses to the "Baptism, Eucharist and Ministry" text, Vol. VI, ed. Max Thurian, Faith and Order Paper No. 144, World Council of Churches, Geneva 1988.

Cronsioe, Håkan, "Tack, Veckoposten!", *Veckoposten,* No. 43, 1992, p. 15.

Dahlbäck, Eva, "Trosprov vara baptist - miste lärartjänst", *Veckoposten,* No. 1/2, 1975, p. 11.

Dahlgren, Curt, "Gudstjänstbesök och livsriter i Svenska kyrkan under 1980-talet", *Tro & Tanke* 1991:10, Svenska kyrkans forskningsråd, Uppsala 1991, pp. 51-67.

Dahlgren, Curt, "Gudstjänstbesök och livsriter under 1970-talet", *Smärre meddelanden* 1980:7, Religionssociologiska institutet, Stockholm.

Danielson, Hjalmar, "Tillbakablickar och framtidssyner. Minnen och intryck VI", *Tro och Liv,* No. 4, 1943, pp. 183-184.

Davidson, Birger, "Helgelseförbundet", *Svenska Trossamfund.* Historia, tro och bekännelse, organisation, gudstjänst- och fromhetsliv, ed. Allan Hofgren, 8th ed., Uppsala 1990, pp. 79-84.

"De har funnit varandra! Men hur går det för SB och ÖM?", *Veckoposten,* No. 21, 1983, p. 1.

"Det uppgivna målet om enhet. Förenade församlingar beklagar deklaration", [Kent Malmqvist], *Veckoposten,* No. 21/22, 1991, p. 16.

"Detta lovar en god fortsättning", *Veckoposten,* No. 5, 1986, p. 6.

Documentary History of Faith and Order 1963-1993, ed. Günther Gassmann, Faith and Order Paper No. 159, World Council of Churches, Geneva 1993.

Dokument från Örebro, utgivna på uppdrag av Sveriges frikyrkoråd under redaktion av Stig Svärd, Stockholm 1969.

Dokumente wachsender Übereinstimmung. Sämtliche Berichte und Konsenstexte interkonfessioneller Gespräche auf Weltebene, Band I, 1931-1982, eds. Harding Meyer, Damaskinos Papandreou, Hans Jörg Urban, Lukas Vischer, 2., neubearb Aufl, Paderborn/Frankfurt am Main 1991.

Dokumente wachsender Übereinstimmung. Sämtliche Berichte und Konsenstexte interkonfessioneller Gespräche auf Weltebene, Band II, 1982-1990, eds. Harding Meyer, Damaskinos Papandreou, Hans Jörg Urban, Lukas Vischer, Paderborn/Frankfurt am Main 1992.

Dop, Nattvard, Ämbete. Den officiella texten från Faith and Order - den s k Lima texten 1982 - jämte introduktion och inofficiella ekumeniska kommentarer, Nordisk Ekumenisk skriftserie 11, 1983, 2nd ed., ed. Kjell Ove Nilsson, Sigtuna 1983. [Orig: *Baptism, Eucharist and Ministry,* Faith and Order Paper No. 111, World Council of Churches, Geneva 1982.]

Dop och kyrkotillhörighet. Diskussionsbetänkande från en arbetsgrupp inom Svenska Kyrkan, Svenska Kyrkans Utredningar (SKU) 1985:1, Stockholm 1985.

Dopet Dåben Dåpen. Tre nordiska teologiska uppsatser, Stockholm 1957.

Dopet - en Guds gåva, utarbetat av Evangeliska Fosterlandsstiftelsens teologiska studiegrupp: Valentin Bergqvist, Ivar Lundgren, Torsten Nilsson, Agne Nordlander, Birger Olsson, 2nd ed., Stockholm 1975.

Dopet - en livstydning. Om dopets innebörd och liturgi, [Lars Eckerdal, Per Erik Persson], Älvsjö/Stockholm 1981.

Dopet i fokus, [Björn Svärd, Birgitte Thaning, Ingegerd Sjölin]. Stockholm 1992.

"Dopet som förenar. En dialog mellan Torsten Bergsten, Svenska baptistsamfundet, och Björn Svärd, Svenska kyrkan", *Till hembygden.* Strängnäs stiftsbok. En hälsning till församlingarna i Strängnäs stift, Strängnäs 1988, pp. 73-86.

Dopet - teologiskt, kyrkorättsligt, pastoralt. Rapport från Biskopsmötets teologiska kommission 1983 om dop och kyrkotillhörighet. Utgivare: Svenska kyrkan, Biskopsmötet, Teologiska kommissionen, Älvsjö 1984.

Doyle, Kerstin, "Samling kring barnen och församlingen: Bort med åldersgränser, fram för tant Maja och Erik Fläckman", *Veckoposten,* No. 21, 1986, p. 10.

Drake, Adolf, Borgström, Johan Alfred, *Svenska baptisternas historia under de första 50 åren 1848-1898,* Stockholm 1898.

Eckerdal, Lars, "Dopet", *Dop, Nattvard, Ämbete.* Den officiella texten från Faith and Order - den s k Lima texten 1982 - jämte introduktion och inofficiella ekumeniska kommentarer, Nordisk Ekumenisk skriftserie 11, ed. Kjell Ove Nilsson, 2nd ed., Sigtuna 1983, pp. 85-90.

Eckerdal, Lars, "Sektionsrapport III B", *Tro och Liv,* No. 1, 1980, pp. 54-55.

Eckerdal, Lars, *Vägen in i kyrkan.* Dop, konfirmation, kommunion - aktuella liturgiska utvecklingslinjer. Svenska kyrkans gudstjänst. Kyrkliga handlingar. Bilaga 3. Statens Offentliga Utredningar (SOU) 1981:66, Stockholm 1981.

Ecumenical Perspectives on Baptism, Eucharist and Ministry, ed. Max Thurian, Faith and Order Paper No. 116, World Council of Churches, Geneva 1983.

"Efter 126 års parallelldrift. Två förenade församlingar har bildats i södra Närke", *Veckoposten,* No. 8, 1988, p. 3.

Ekblad, Lars, *Och hindra dem inte.* Barndopet ur pastoralt perspektiv. Prästmötesavhandling för Strängnäs stift, Stockholm 1992.

Eklund, Mauritz, "Dopet är en gåva", *Veckoposten,* No. 27/28, 1992, p. 11.

"Ekumenik på 80-talet", [editorial], *Veckoposten,* No. 44, 1978, p. 2.

Ekumeniken och forskningen. Föreläsningar vid den nordiska forskarkursen "Teorier och metoder inom forskning om ekumenik" i Lund 1991, Nordisk ekumenisk skriftserie 20, 1992, eds. Sigurd Bergmann et al., Uppsala 1992.

Ekumenisk samsyn om dop och kyrkotillhörighet. Rapport från den officiella luthersk - katolska samtalsgruppen i Sverige med anledning av Stat - kyrka. Ändrade relationer mellan staten och Svenska kyrkan, Statens offentliga utredningar (SOU) 1978:1, Stockholm/Lund 1978.

Eldebo, Runar, "Svenska Missionsförbundet", *Svenska Trossamfund.* Historia, tro och bekännelse, organisation, gudstjänst- och fromhetsliv, ed. Allan Hofgren, 8th ed., Uppsala 1990, pp. 57-63.

Elmquist, Karl-Axel, "Viktig arbetsgrupp tillsatt: Sex samfund börjar nu samråda om de förenade församlingarna", *Veckoposten,* No. 16, 1989, p. 2.

"En årskonferens", [editorial], *Veckoposten,* No. 24, 1987, p. 4.

En bok om dopet i ekumenisk belysning. Utg. av Svenska Faith and Order-kommittéen, ed. Torsten Bergsten, Stockholm 1965.

"'En federativ gemenskap'", *Veckoposten,* No. 50, 1989, p. 3.

"En förenad fri och öppen frikyrka", [editorial], *Veckoposten,* No. 27/28, 1992, p. 2.

"En framtid och ett hopp", [editorial], *Veckoposten,* No. 1/2, 1981, p. 2.

"En historisk konferens?", [editorial], *Veckoposten,* No. 19/20, 1983, p. 2.

"En tidning", [editorial], *Veckoposten,* No. 21/22, 1991, p. 2.

Enade och åtskilda. Vattnet som förenar och skiljer. Kristen enhet - Guds gåva och vår kallelse, eds. Björn Cedersjö, Lennart Thörn, Örebro 1989.

Engberg, Sigurd, "Det kristna dopet", *Veckoposten,* No. 7, 1976, p. 6.

Engberg, Sigurd, "Det kristna dopet", *Veckoposten,* No. 8, 1976, p. 4;

Engberg, Sigurd, "Det kristna dopet", *Veckoposten,* No. 9, 1976, p. 6.

"Enheten kan inte vänta", *Veckoposten,* No. 16, 1989, p. 1.

Enhetskonferensen i Örebro. Föredrag och samtal, Örebro 1946.

Ericson, Bertil, "Öppet medlemskap - raka vägar?", *Veckoposten,* No. 37, 1976, p. 12.

Eriksson, Klas, Persson, Håkan, "Helhjärtad ekumenik?", *Veckoposten,* No. 42, 1991, p. 6.

"Ett stort kliv", *Veckoposten,* No. 13/14, 1991, p. 2.

"Ett trossamfund", [editorial], *Veckoposten,* No. 10, 1988, p. 4.

Eurell, Pehr-Erik, "Med luthersk dopförrättare. Historiskt dop i Vallersvik", *Veckoposten,* No. 37, 1991, p. 7.

"Europas baptistledare: -Vi vill samarbeta!", *Veckoposten,* No. 7, 1992, p. 4.

Fagerberg, Holsten, *Svenska kyrkan i ekumeniska samtal.* Evangeliet som förenar, Svenska Kyrkans Utredningar (SKU) 1987:1, Stockholm.

Fahlgren, Sune, "Baptismen och baptisternas gudstjänstliv", *I enhetens tecken.* Gudstjänsttraditioner och gudstjänstens förnyelse i svenska kyrkan och samfund, eds. Sune Fahlgren, Rune Klingert, Örebro 1994, pp. 249-287.

Fahlgren, Sune, "Baptismens spiritualitet – speglad i gudstjänstlivet. Svenskt perspektiv", *Samfund i förändring.* Baptistisk identitet i norden under ett och ett halvt sekel, Tro & Liv skriftserie No. 2, ed. David Lagergren, Stockholm 1997, pp. 104-114.

Fahlgren, Sune, "Sju samfund - tre handböcker - en gemensam nattvardsliturgi", *Svenskt gudstjänstliv* 62, Lund 1987, pp. 35-55.

"'Folk uppskattar vår enhet'", *Veckoposten*, No. 37, 1990, p. 1.

"Förenade", [editorial], *Veckoposten*, No. 49, 1983, p. 2.

"Förenade församlingar: Gemensam tidning för samfunden - nu!", *Veckoposten*, No. 8, 1991, p. 3.

"Förenade församlingar visar vägen till enhet", *Veckoposten*, No. 9, 1988, p. 1.

Formulär för vigsel, begravning, dop och nattvard, Stockholm 1924.

"Församlingen och barnen", [editorial], *Veckoposten*, No. 16, 1985, p. 2.

"Förverkliga federationen!", [editorial], *Veckoposten*, No. 5, 1992, p. 2.

"Framåt!", *Veckoposten*, No. 24, 1991, p. 2.

"Framtid för frikyrkan?", [editorial], *Veckoposten*, No. 15, 1989, p. 4.

"Framtidshopp i Filipstad. Vasakyrkan har band till tre frikyrkosamfund", *Veckoposten*, No. 9, 1992, p. 1.

"Från ord till handling. Samfundsstyrelserna vill frikyrklig enhet", *Veckoposten*, No. 5, 1992, p. 1.

Franzén, Bert, "Adolf Drake - han skapade Veckoposten", *Veckoposten*, No. 38, 1992, pp. 8-9.

Franzén, Bert, "Anden och det kristna livet, I. Döpta i en och samma ande", *Veckoposten*, No. 34, 1987, p. 7.

Franzén, Bert, "Anden och det kristna livet, II. Låt er uppfyllas av ande!", *Veckoposten*, No. 35, 1987, p. 7.

Franzén, Bert, "Barnen i församlingen. Frågan om tillhörighet och medlemskap", *Tro och Liv*, No. 3, 1985, pp. 32-39.

Franzén, Bert, "Barnen och församlingen. Guds försprång kan behållas", *Veckoposten*, No. 24/25, 1986, p. 5.

Franzén, Bert, "Barnen och församlingen, II. Texterna om Jesus och barnen", *Veckoposten*, No. 26, 1986, p. 6.

Franzén, Bert, "Barnen och församlingen, III. Barn med andlig hemortsrätt", *Veckoposten*, No. 27/28, 1986, p. 7.

Franzén, Bert, "Barnen och församlingen, IV. En modell för mognad", *Veckoposten*, No. 29/30, 1986, p. 7.

Franzén, Bert, "Barnen och änglarna i vår tid", *Veckoposten*, No. 40, 1986, p. 4.

Franzén, Bert, "Den enhet vi söker", [editorial], *Veckoposten*, No. 38, 1975, p. 2.

Franzén, Bert, "Dopet i kyrkornas gemenskap", [editorial], *Veckoposten*, No. 1/2, 1975, pp. 2, 14.

Franzén, Bert, "Dopet i vatten och ande", *Veckoposten*, No. 1/2, 1987, p. 5.

Franzén, Bert, "Dopet in i Kristus", *Veckoposten*, No. 22, 1988, p. 26.

Franzén, Bert, "Dopet och frälsningen. Kommentar till en artikel", *Veckoposten*, No. 42, 1989, p. 10.

Franzén, Bert, "Dopet som gemenskapsfaktor", *Tro och Liv*, No. 5, 1975, pp. 194-197.

Franzén, Bert, "Dopet som kallelse och gåva", *En bok om dopet i ekumenisk belysning*. Utg. av Svenska Faith and Order - kommittéen, ed. Torsten Bergsten, Stockholm 1965, pp. 63-70.

Franzén, Bert, *Guds försprång*. Om barnen och Guds rike, Örebro 1991.

Franzén, Bert, "Har dopet någon enande kraft?", *Veckoposten*, No. 8, 1965, p. 10.

Franzén, Bert, "Individ och familj i den kristna församlingen", *Familj och församling*, Stockholm 1960, pp. 7-23.

Franzén, Bert, "Jesu dop - och vårt", *Veckoposten*, No. 1/2, 1986, p. 4.

Franzén, Bert, "Tre evangelister om mission", *Liv och tjänst*. Guds mission församlingens uppdrag, eds. Birgit Karlsson, Berit Åqvist, Örebro 1988, pp. 37-50.

Franzén, Bert, "Tro och liv i förändring", *Tro, Frihet, Gemenskap*. Svensk baptism genom 150 år, Örebro 1998, pp. 187-212.

Freij, Torbjörn, "Tre baptistprofiler kommenterar 'baptistfederationen'", *Veckoposten*, No. 4, 1979, p. 10.

Freij, Torbjörn, "TV - kyrkan i söndags: 'Det andliga spirandet fortsätter'", *Veckoposten*, No. 20/21, 1977, p. 3.

Freij, Torbjörn, "Uppbrott, kollaps och sedan...? Så växte det frikyrkliga samarbetet fram - del II", *Veckoposten*, No. 45, 1978, p. 10.

Fridborg, Gunnar, "Ekumenik: Så här fungerar det i Valsätra", *Veckoposten*, No. 40, 1982, p. 8.

Fridborg, Gunnar, "Nu kommer ditt festtåg, o Gud", *Tro, Frihet, Gemenskap*. Svensk baptism genom 150 år, Örebro 1998, pp. 137-159.

Fridborg, Gunnar, "Valsätrakyrkan i Uppsala. En ny typ av ekumenisk församling", *Årsbok*. Sveriges Frikyrkoråd, Älvsjö 1981-82, pp. 12-17.

Fridén, George, "Jag tror på vår framtid", *Mot nya tider*. Tankar om Baptistsamfundets läge och framtidsutsikter, Personliga ord, utg. av George Fridén, Seth Jacobson, Stockholm 1938, pp. 23-32.

"Frikyrklig samordning och Kyrkornas världsråd tas upp i massmotioner", *Veckoposten*, No. 12, 1986, p. 3.

"Frikyrkorna ense: Barnen tillhör Guds rike", [BF.], *Veckoposten*, No. 17, 1985, pp. 3, 12.

Frikyrkosverige. En livsstilsstudie, Älvsjö 1979.

Fristedt, Axel, "Vart är vi baptister på väg?", *Veckoposten*, No. 14, 1992, p. 4.

Fristedt, Werner, "Barn - Dop - Nattvard", *Veckoposten*, No. 6, 1976, p. 12.

Garstein, Oskar, *Rome and the Counter - Reformation in Scandinavia*. Until the establishment of the S. Congregatio de Propaganda Fide in 1622, based on source material in the Kolsrud collection, Vol. 1 (1539-1583), Oslo 1963.

Garstein, Oskar, *Rome and the Counter - Reformation in Scandinavia*. Until the establishment of the S. Congregatio de Propaganda Fide in 1622, based on source material in the Kolsrud collection, Vol. 2 (1583-1622), Oslo 1980.

Garstein, Oskar, *Rome and the Counter - Reformation in Scandinavia*. Jesuit educational strategy 1553-1622, Studies in the history of Christian thought 46, 1992, Leiden 1992.

Garstein, Oskar, *Rome and the Counter - Reformation in Scandinavia*. The age of Gustavus Adolphus and Queen Christina of Sweden 1622-1656, Studies in the history of Christian thought 47, 1992, Leiden 1992.

"Gemensam församling i Katrineholm", *Veckoposten*, No. 50, 1990, p. 1.

Gemensam grund. En skrift om frikyrklig trosåskådning. Utgiven på uppdrag av Sveriges Frikyrkoråd, Stockholm 1963.

"Gemensam tidning", [editorial], *Veckoposten*, No. 15, 1992, p. 2.

"Gemensam tidning - nu!", [editorial], *Veckoposten*, No. 8, 1991, p. 2.

Gemensam tro. Ett samtalsdokument från Metodistkyrkan, Svenska Baptistsamfundet, Svenska Missionsförbundet i samarbete med Frikyrkliga studieförbundet, Stockholm 1995.

Gemensam väg. Utgiven på uppdrag av Sveriges Frikyrkoråd, Stockholm 1968.

Gemensamt nattvardsfirande. Betänkande av Kommittén för utredning om viss gudstjänstgemenskap mellan Svenska kyrkan och andra inom riket verksamma kristna samfund, Uppsala 1975.

Gerdin, Bertil, Näslund, Roland, "Skall vi erkänna barndopet?", *Veckoposten*, No. 7, 1985, p. 10.

Granander, Olof, "Bör vi erkänna barndopet?", *Veckoposten*, No. 10, 1985, p. 10.

Growing Together in Baptism, Eucharist and Ministry. A study by William H. Lazareth, Faith and Order Paper No. 114, World Council of Churches, Geneva 1982.

Growth in Agreement. Reports and Agreed Statements of Ecumenical Conversations on a World Level, eds. Harding Meyer, Lukas Vischer, Faith and Order Paper No. 108, World Council of Churches, Geneva/New York 1984.

Grudewall, Erik, "Bör vi erkänna barndopet?", *Veckoposten*, No. 6, 1985, p. 10.

Grudewall, Erik, "Bör vi erkänna barndopet? Svar till Olof Granander", *Veckoposten*, No. 12, 1985, p. 14.

"Guds försprång i barnens liv", [SEW.], *Veckoposten*, No. 20, 1989, p. 11.

Guds kyrka och en levande församling. Rapport från den officiella samtalsgruppen mellan Svenska kyrkan och Svenska Missionsförbundet, Stockholm 1996.

Gustafsson, Andor, "Att förverkliga Jesu bön om enhet", *Veckoposten*, No. 13, 1984, p. 15.

Gustafsson, Berndt, *Svensk Kyrkogeografi*. Med samfundsbeskrivning, Lund 1971.

Gustafsson, Göran, *Tro, samfund och samhälle*. Sociologiska perspektiv, Örebro 1991.

Gustafsson, Ingvar, "En väg till salighet", *Veckoposten*, No. 25, 1984, p. 4.

Gustafsson, Ingvar, "Till församlingens tjänst", *Veckoposten*, No. 34, 1987, p. 6.

Hallberg, Edvin, *Samfundstanken i Apostlagärningarna*, 2nd ed., Stockholm 1939.

Hallqvist, Anders, Westblom, Per, *Tema:* "Viktiga händelser i Baptistsamfundets historia", *Tro, Frihet, Gemenskap.* Svensk baptism genom 150 år, Örebro 1998, pp. 241-256.

Handbok för dop, nattvard, vigsel och begravning inom Svenska Baptistsamfundet, Stockholm 1940.

Handbok för församlingens gudstjänstliv, Stockholm/Örebro 1974.

Handbok för Svenska Baptistsamfundet, 3rd ed., Stockholm 1955.

Handbok till den kristna församlingens tjänst. Svenska Alliansmissionen, Svenska Missionsförbundet, Älvsjö 1983.

"Handling för enhet", [editorial], *Veckoposten,* No. 16, 1989, p. 4.

Hellberg, Carl-Johan, *Gud och pengar.* Om framgångsteologi i USA och i Sverige, Stockholm 1987.

Hellström, Jan Arvid, *Samfund och radio.* Återspegling kontra medieanpassning ifråga om den kristna programverksamheten i Sverige fram t o m omorganisationen 1951/52, Stockholm 1979.

Henningsson, Karl-Åke, *Striden om lekmannadopet.* En studie i motsättningen mellan Svenska Kyrkan och Svenska Missionsförbundet 1878-1898, Diss., Lund 1956.

Herfert, Mischa, Axelsson, Erik, "'Jag ber att de alla skall bli ett...'", *Veckoposten,* No. 36, 1992, p. 11.

Hermansson, Werner, *Enhetskyrka, folkväckelse, församlingsgemenskap.* En utvecklingslinje till Svenska Missionsförbundet, Stockholm 1968.

"Hjortensbergskyrkan, Nyköping: Tre församlingar växte under tio år samman till en enda", *Veckoposten,* No. 49, 1983, pp. 8f.

Holmström, Krister, *Biblisk framgångsteologi.* Aktuell teologi, Uppsala 1986.

Holte, Ragnar, "Svenska kyrkan och lekmannadopet. En studie till det utgående 1800-talets kyrkohistoria", *Kyrkohistorisk Årsskrift* 50, 1950, Uppsala/Stockholm, pp. 165-215.

Hopko, Thomas, "Tasks Facing the Orthodox in the 'Reception' Process of BEM", *Orthodox Perspectives on Baptism, Eucharist, and Ministry,* eds. Gennadios Limouris and Nomikos Michael Vaporis, Faith and Order Paper No. 128, Brookline, Massachusetts 1985, pp. 135-147.

Hultberg, Per-Åke, "En baptistpojkes funderingar", *Veckoposten,* No. 36, 1992, p. 11.

Hultberg, Walter, "Var hör vi hemma?", *Veckoposten,* No. 42, 1992, p. 12.

I endräktens tecken. Minnesskrift vid Stockholms Evangeliska Predikantförbunds 25 års högtid, Stockholm 1922.

"I Kil, Knivsta och Järnboås: Allt vanligare att två blir ett", *Veckoposten,* No. 7, 1984, pp. 8-9.

"Ingen i Höör ångrar samgående", *Veckoposten,* No. 8, 1992, p. 1.

Isacsson, Seth, "Fribaptistsamfundet", *Svenska Trossamfund.* Historia, tro och bekännelse, organisation, gudstjänst- och fromhetsliv, ed. Allan Hofgren, 8th ed., Uppsala 1990, pp. 73-78.

"Ja till samverkan", [editorial], *Veckoposten,* No. 41, 1992, p. 2.

Janarv, Ruben, "Baptisterna och friheten", [De baptistiska grundprinciperna, del 4], *Veckoposten*, No. 17, 1978, p. 10.

Janarv, Ruben, "Baptisternas grundsatser och dopet", [De baptistiska grundprinciperna, del 5], *Veckoposten*, No. 27, 1978, p. 8.

Janarv, Ruben, "De baptistiska grundsatserna och framtiden", [De baptistiska grundprinciperna, del 6], *Veckoposten*, No. 31/32, 1978, pp. 12-13.

Janarv, Ruben, "Församlingen de troendes gemenskap", [De baptistiska grundprinciperna, del 3], *Veckoposten*, No. 16, 1978, pp. 6-7.

Janarv, Ruben, "Gemensam väg?", *Veckoposten*, No. 17, 1983, p. 11.

Janarv, Ruben, "Vem är baptist?", [De baptistiska grundprinciperna, del 2], *Veckoposten*, No. 14, 1978, p. 11.

Janarv, Ruben, "Vem fick bli - och vara - medlem i fädernas baptistförsamling?", [De baptistiska grundprinciperna, del 1], *Veckoposten*, No. 12, 1978, pp. 3, 12.

Jansson, Bengt, "Svar på Berits utmaning: -Det brister i prioriteringen", *Veckoposten*, No. 16, 1985, p. 6.

Jansson, Martin, "Hur skall Baptistsamfundet ha det?", *Veckoposten*, No. 9, 1984, p. 14.

Jansson, Martin, "Hur skall det bli med Baptistsamfundet?", *Veckoposten*, No. 15, 1992, p. 12.

Jansson, Martin, "'Skall vi ha Svenska Baptistsamfundet?'", *Veckoposten*, No. 25/26, 1982, p. 10.

Jansson, Martin, "Tveksamma och frågande baptister", *Veckoposten*, No. 13/14, 1988, p. 12.

Johnsson, Lennart, *Beasley-Murray's dopuppfattning*, Faculty of Theology, Uppsala University, Uppsala 1987.

Jonsson, Gunnar, O, *Ett hundra år med baptistförsamlingen Ebeneser, Stockholm.* Historisk krönika. 1883 19 aug 1983, Stockholm 1983.

Jonsson, Johnny, "Mission enligt Johannes evangelium", *Liv och tjänst.* Guds mission församlingens uppdrag, eds. Birgit Karlsson, Berit Åqvist, Örebro 1988, pp. 64-74.

Juhlin, Lars, "Behövs dopet?", *Veckoposten*, No. 40, 1989, p. 7.

Juhlin, Lars, "Perspektiv på dopet", *Veckoposten*, No. 45, 1989, p. 7.

Julén, J., "Frikyrkligt samarbete", *Tro och Liv*, No. 4, 1943, pp. 150-165.

Källstad, Thorvald, "Frikyrkofolkets ekumeniska vilja", *Frikyrkosverige.* En livsstilsstudie, Älvsjö 1979, pp. 55-71.

Källstad, Thorvald, "Metodistkyrkan och tresamfundssamtalen", *Tro och Liv*, No. 5, 1979, pp. 38-42.

Karlsson, Birgit, "150 händelserika år", *Tro, Frihet, Gemenskap.* Svensk baptism genom 150 år, Örebro 1998, pp. 9-44.

Karlsson, Birgit, "Baptismens röst i det nya Europa - samtal om identitet och insats", *Veckoposten*, No. 7, 1992, p. 4.

Karlsson, Birgit, "Baptistisk tro är inte till salu - men vi vill ge den vidare", *Veckoposten*, No. 43, 1991, p. 5.

Karlsson, Birgit, "Baptistisk tro - utmanad och uttalad", *Veckoposten,* No. 44/45, 1992, p. 5.

Karlsson, Birgit, "Budskapet, gemenskapen och de vita fälten", *Veckoposten,* No. 19/20, 1991, p. 5.

Karlsson, Birgit, "Det nödvändiga samtalet om tron och praktiken", *Veckoposten,* No. 47, 1987, p. 4.

Karlsson, Birgit, "Dopet - en central fråga när församlingar går samman. Missionsföreståndaren kommenterar", *Veckoposten,* No. 40, 1987, pp. 10-11.

Karlsson, Birgit, "Församling med uppdrag i världen", *Liv och tjänst.* Guds mission församlingens uppdrag, eds. Birgit Karlsson, Berit Åqvist, Örebro 1988, pp. 17-34.

Karlsson, Birgit, "Från min horisont", *Veckoposten,* No. 21, 1987, pp. 4, 12.

Karlsson, Birgit, "G 72 - en manifestation av enhet", *Året,* Baptistsamfundets kalender Betlehem, utges av Svenska Baptistsamfundet, Stockholm 1972, pp. 17-23.

Karlsson, Birgit, "Liv och tjänst inför år 2000", *Liv och tjänst.* Guds mission församlingens uppdrag, eds. Birgit Karlsson, Berit Åqvist, Örebro 1988, pp. 215-244.

Karlsson, Birgit, "Nya människor genom Guds ord: Församlingen – Guds folk", *Veckoposten,* No. 38, 1978, pp. 4-5

Karlsson, Birgit, "Nya människor genom Guds ord: Församlingen – Kristi kropp", *Veckoposten,* No. 40, 1978, p. 4.

Karlsson, Birgit, "Tillbaka till dopet", *Veckoposten,* No. 46, 1987, p. 6.

Kennerberg, Owe, *Innanför eller utanför.* En studie av församlingstukten i nio svenska frikyrkoförsamlingar, Diss., Örebro 1996.

Klingsbo, Karl-Edward, "Vasakyrkan i Filipstad. Två år under Guds ledning", *Veckoposten,* No. 6, 1990, p. 5.

"Konferensbeslut. Fred och arbetslöshet tungt vägande frågor", *Veckoposten,* No. 22, 1982, pp. 7-8.

"Konkret förslag i enhetsfrågan: Förena SFR och Samråd!", *Veckoposten,* No. 9, 1988, p. 3.

" -Kristen har jag väl alltid varit men nu förstår jag bibeln bättre", *Veckoposten,* No. 25/26, 1985, p. 7.

Kvist, Edvin, "Mot nya tider", *Mot nya tider.* Tankar om Baptistsamfundets läge och framtidsutsikter, Personliga ord, utg. av George Fridén and Seth Jacobson, Stockholm 1938, pp. 49-56.

"Kyrkan i Nacka centrum byggs för alla som tror", *Veckoposten,* No. 5, 1991, p. 1.

Kyrkan och dopet. En debattbok om dopet idag och i framtiden, utgiven på uppdrag av 1972 års prästmöte i Växjö stift, Lund 1974.

Kyrkans liv. Introduktion till kyrkovetenskapen, Kyrkovetenskapliga institutets skriftserie 1, ed. Stephan Borgehammar, 2nd ed., Stockholm 1993.

Lagergren, David, "Barnen och nattvarden", *Veckoposten,* No. 49, 1981, p. 2.

Lagergren, David, "Borgström och Byström - ett radarpar!", *Veckoposten,* No. 39, 1992, pp. 8-9.

Lagergren, David, "Dop och enhet", *Veckoposten,* No. 36, 1980, p. 2.

Lagergren, David, "Dopet och enheten", *Veckoposten,* No. 15, 1978, p. 2.

Lagergren, David, "Dopsamtal", *Veckoposten,* No. 3, 1977, p. 2.

Lagergren, David, "Efter etthundrafem år", *Veckoposten,* No. 50, 1983, p. 2.

Lagergren, David, "Ekumenik 83", *Veckoposten,* No. 1/2, 1983, p. 2.

Lagergren, David, "Ekumenik 83 (II)", *Veckoposten,* No. 3, 1983, p. 2.

Lagergren, David, "Ekumenisk barnteologi", *Veckoposten,* No. 17, 1991, p. 6.

Lagergren, David, *Enhetsförslaget och dopfrågan.* Inledningsanförande vid samfundsdelegationernas överläggningar i Stockholm den 11 januari 1969, Stockholm 1969.

Lagergren, David, *Förändringstid.* Kris och förnyelse. Svenska Baptistsamfundet åren 1933-1948, Örebro 1994.

Lagergren, David, "Försonad mångfald", *Veckoposten,* No. 43, 1986, p. 5.

Lagergren, David, *Framgångstid med dubbla förtecken.* Svenska Baptistsamfundet åren 1914-1932, Örebro 1989.

Lagergren, David, "Från Wiberg till Pethrus", *Veckoposten,* No. 45, 1985, p. 6.

Lagergren, David, "Frikyrkans framtidsväg", *Veckoposten,* No. 43, 1991, p. 4.

Lagergren, David, "Fyrsamfundssamtal?", *Veckoposten,* No. 11, 1979, p. 2.

Lagergren, David, "Historia och konservatism", *Veckoposten,* No. 2, 1978, p. 2.

Lagergren, David, "Inlägg är välkomna", *Veckoposten,* No. 51/52, 1983, p. 9.

Lagergren, David, "Jag har en dröm", *Veckoposten,* No. 24, 1981, p. 2.

Lagergren, David, "Kontinuitet", *Veckoposten,* No. 41, 1976, p. 2.

Lagergren, David, "Lokalekumeniken och dopet", *Veckoposten,* No. 37, 1978, p. 2.

Lagergren, David, "När föddes baptismen i Sverige?", *Veckoposten,* No. 42, 1980, p. 2.

Lagergren, David, "Nattvard och syndabekännelse", *Veckoposten,* No. 8, 1983, p. 2.

Lagergren, David, "Nattvarden i Svenska Baptistsamfundet 1848-1910", *När vi bryter det bröd...,* Stockholm 1981, pp. 89-100.

Lagergren, David, "ÖM och ekumeniken", *Veckoposten,* No. 15, 1983, p. 2.

Lagergren, David, "ÖM och SB", *Veckoposten,* No. 4, 1981, p. 2.

Lagergren, David, "Samgående och förnyelse", *Veckoposten,* No. 50, 1982, p. 2.

Lagergren, David, "Svar:", *Veckoposten,* No. 27, 1978, p. 10.

Lagergren, David, "Svenska baptistsamfundet och Örebromissionen - En tillbakablick", *Veckoposten,* No. 7, 1985, pp. 7, 12.

Lagergren, David, "Tradition och förnyelse II", *Veckoposten,* No. 26, 1984, p. 6.

Lagergren, David, "Tro och dop", *Veckoposten,* No. 3, 1975, p. 2.

Lagergren, David, "Vallfartsort och väckelsehärd", *Veckoposten,* No. 34/35, 1980, p. 2.

Lagergren, David, "Varför gör inte samfunden mer...", *Veckoposten,* No. 9, 1984, pp. 2, 12.

Lagerström, Christine, "Alla är välkomna till Vasakyrkan", *Veckoposten*, No. 17, 1991, p. 5.

Lagerström, Christine, "Historisk årskonferens i ekumenikens tecken", *Veckoposten*, No. 25/26, 1992, pp. 8-9.

"Landet runt", *Trons Värld*, No. 20, 1989, p. 3.

"Landet runt", *Trons Värld*, No. 2, 1997, p. 11.

Lantz, Ragni, "Ann-Christine Lindholm: Från frälsningssoldat till baptistpastor", *Veckoposten*, No. 8, 1988, p. 16.

Lantz, Ragni, "Birgit Karlsson: -Det ljusnar för kristna i öst", *Veckoposten*, No. 43, 1989, p. 2.

Lantz, Ragni, "Ebbe Sundström: -Teologin får vika om helheten gagnas", *Veckoposten*, No. 50, 1989, p. 2.

Lantz, Ragni, "Glädjedag i Nacka", *Veckoposten*, No. 5, 1991, p. 3.

Lantz, Ragni, "Kvinnor träder fram", *Tro, Frihet, Gemenskap*. Svensk baptism genom 150 år, Örebro 1998, pp. 117-135.

Lantz, Ragni, "Noel Vose vill föra de små samfundens talan", *Veckoposten*, No. 30, 1985, p. 3.

Lantz, Ragni, "Östermalmskyrkan öppnar sin famn", *Veckoposten*, No. 49, 1989, pp. 10-11.

Lantz, Ragni, "Övervägande positiva reaktioner till samverkan", *Veckoposten*, No. 6, 1986, p. 7.

Lantz, Ragni, "Paul Beasley-Murray: -Dopet bara början till lärjungaskap", *Veckoposten*, No. 48, 1986, pp. 4, 13.

Lantz, Ragni, "Sannerudskyrkan i Kil. Högt i tak och trångt i bänkarna", *Veckoposten*, No. 50, 1989, pp. 8-9, 11.

Lantz, Ragni, "Ulla Bardh: -Vi har mycket att lära av de gemensamma församlingarna", *Veckoposten*, No. 33/34, 1992, p. 16.

Lantz, Ragni, "Vasakyrkan i Filipstad: Tre frikyrkosamfund i stimulerande gemenskap", *Veckoposten*, No. 9, 1992, p. 8.

Larsson, Disa, "Upprörd över korstecken", *Veckoposten*, No. 14/15, 1990, p. 16.

Larsson, Rich, "Tillbakablickar och framtidssyner. Framtidsuppgifter", *Tro och Liv*, No. 4, 1943, pp. 184-187.

Larsson, Rune, *Religion i radio och TV under sextio år*, Kyrkovetenskapliga studier 43, 1988, Stockholm 1988.

"Ledaransvar", [editorial], *Veckoposten*, No. 49, 1989, p. 4.

Levande. Om församling, teologi och samhälle, ed. Lennart Molin, Stockholm 1996.

"Levande stenar i nytt församlingsbygge", [Ragni Lantz, Bo Swedberg], *Veckoposten*, No. 16, 1990, pp. 8-9.

Lidén, Sven Gunnar, *Tema:* "Svensk baptistungdom och dess verksamhet", *Tro, Frihet, Gemenskap*. Svensk baptism genom 150 år, Örebro 1998, pp. 75-94.

Lindberg, Alf, *Väckelse, frikyrklighet, pingströrelse*. Väckelse och frikyrka från 1800-talets mitt till nutid, Pingstskolornas skriftserie, Ekerö 1985.

Lindberg, Erik, "1+1=mer än 2 vid samgående", *Veckoposten*, No. 40, 1991, p. 4.

Lindberg, Erik, "Baptister och katoliker är ense om Jesus", *Veckoposten*, No. 50, 1991, p. 4.

Lindberg, Erik, "Erik Lindberg om frikyrkans framtid 'Börja förnya eller dö ut'", *Broderskap*, No. 50/52, 1993, pp. 6-7.

Lindberg, Erik, "Gemenskapsgrupper - frikyrkans framtid?", *Veckoposten*, No. 42, 1991, pp. 5-6.

Lindberg, Erik, "John Ongman - en förkämpe för kvinnans rätt", *Veckoposten*, No. 31/32, 1992, pp. 8-9.

Lindberg, Erik, "Lutheraner och baptister: Vi är ense i allt utom dopet", *Veckoposten*, No. 4, 1992, p. 5.

Lindberg, Lars, "Dop och omdop", *Svensk Veckotidning*, No. 22/23, 1987, p. 2.

Lindberg, Lars, *Dopet in i Kristus*, Nya motiv, Stockholm 1982.

Lindberg, Lars, "Folkkyrka - folkrörelse", *Tro och Liv*, No. 1, 1980, pp. 20-26.

Lindberg, Lars, "Lars Lindberg om dopfrågan. Upphör med omdop", *Svensk Veckotidning*, No. 42, 1987, p. 8.

Lindblom, Sven-Gunnar, "Hur skall frikyrkornas samhörighet utformas?", *Veckoposten*, No. 18, 1991, p. 4.

Lindström, Sven, "Jesusglöd i levande församlingar", *Veckoposten*, No. 5, 1986, p. 7.

Lindvall, Karin, *Porträtt*: "Jag älskar söndagsskolan...", *Tro, Frihet, Gemenskap*. Svensk baptism genom 100 år, Örebro 1998, pp. 73-74.

Lindvall, Magnus, "Baptismen - en rörelse i tiden", *Samfund i förändring*. Baptistisk identitet i norden under ett och ett halvt sekel, Tro & Liv skriftserie No. 2, ed. David Lagergren, Stockholm 1997, pp. 9-27.

Lindvall, Magnus, Åqvist, Berit, *Tema*: "Utbildning och det tryckta ordet", *Tro, Frihet, Gemenskap*. Svensk baptism genom 100 år, Örebro 1998, pp. 167-185.

Liv och frihet. En bok om Svenska Missionsförbundet, ed. Olof Wennås, Stockholm 1978.

Liv och tjänst. Guds mission församlingens uppdrag, eds. Birgit Karlsson, Berit Åqvist, Örebro 1988.

"Lokalekumenik - betydelsefull fråga i missionsstyrelsens höstsammanträde", [NK], *Veckoposten*, No. 48, 1978, p. 16.

"Lokalekumeniken trycker på", [editorial], *Veckoposten*, No. 30, 1981, p. 2.

Louvain 1971. Faith and Order, Louvain 1971, Study Reports and Documents, Faith and Order Paper No. 59, World Council of Churches, Geneva 1971.

Lumpkin, William L., *Baptist Confessions of Faith*, rev. ed., The Judson Press, Valley Forge, 1969.

Lundahl, J. E., "Tillbakablickar och framtidssyner. Minnen och intryck IV", *Tro och Liv*, No. 4, 1943, pp. 178-181.

Lundkvist, Sven, "Demografiska och socio - ekonomiska data", *Frikyrkosverige*. En livsstilsstudie, Älvsjö 1979, pp. 73-88.

Lundkvist, Sven, "Medlemsrekrytering och motiv för medlemskap", *Frikyrkosverige*. En livsstilsstudie, Älvsjö 1979, pp. 21-34.

Månsus, Harry, "Baptistsamfundet och 80-talets folkväckelse", *Veckoposten*, No. 27, 1979, p. 4.

Månsus, Harry, "Bibliskt dop eller surrogatdop?", *Tro och Liv*, No. 5, 1975, pp. 213-218.

Martling, Carl Henrik, "De inomkyrkliga väckelserörelserna under förra hälften av 1800-talet", *Väckelse och kyrka i nordiskt perspektiv*. Nordiska studier över brytningarna mellan kyrklig ordning och religiös folkrörelse under 1800-talet. Skrifter utgitt av Nordiskt institut för kyrkohistorisk forskning 1, 1969, ed. A. Pontoppidan Thyssen, Köpenhamn /Lund /Helsingfors /Oslo 1969, pp. 155-183.

Mattsson, Valter, "Dopet till Kristus, ett maktskifte i vårt liv", *Veckoposten*, No. 6, 1981, pp. 4-5.

Mattsson, Valter, "Gemensamma församlingar: Förväntningar på federativ gemenskap", *Veckoposten*, No. 16, 1990, p. 5.

Mattsson, Valter, "Högtidlig invigning med fullsatt kyrka", *Veckoposten*, No. 50, 1990, p. 9.

Mattsson, Valter, "Kristus och människan i doptexternas centrum", *Veckoposten*, No. 5, 1981, p. 4.

"Medlemstal", [editorial], *Veckoposten*, No. 44, 1986, p. 2.

Meyer, Harding, "'Unity in diversity' - A Concept in Crisis", *Ekumeniken och forskningen*. Föreläsningar vid den nordiska forskarkursen "Teorier och metoder inom forskning om ekumenik" i Lund 1991, Nordisk ekumenisk skriftserie 20, 1992, eds. Sigurd Bergmann et al., Uppsala 1992, pp. 43-55.

Mild, Ruben, "Åter aktuell dopdebatt", *Veckoposten*, No. 43, 1991, p. 12.

Mild, Ruben, "Det finns en väg - går vi den?", *Veckoposten*, No. 42, 1987, p. 14.

Mild, Ruben, "Dopet - en central fråga när församlingar går samman", *Veckoposten*, No. 40, 1987, p. 10.

Mild, Ruben, "Nya testamentets dopsyn bör gälla!", *Veckoposten*, No. 48, 1987, p. 6.

Mild, Ruben, "Skriv själv, Tomas!", *Veckoposten*, No. 16/17, 1992, p. 16.

Mild, Ruben, "Var det nödvändigt?", *Veckoposten*, No. 18, 1991, p. 4.

Mild, Ruben, "Var står vi och vart går vi?", *Veckoposten*, No. 14/15, 1990, p. 16.

Mild, Ruben, "Varning från SMF", *Veckoposten*, No. 11, 1992, p. 11.

Mild, Ruben, "Vart är vi på väg?", *Veckoposten*, No. 9, 1988, p. 10.

"Mission i Sverige", [editorial], *Veckoposten*, No. 11, 1991, p. 2.

Modén, Karl August, "Tillbakablickar och framtidssyner. Minnen och intryck I", *Tro och Liv*, No. 4, 1943, pp. 173-175.

"Mot nya horisonter?", [editorial], *Veckoposten*, No. 12, 1991, p. 2.

Mot nya tider. Tankar om Baptistsamfundets läge och framtidsutsikter, ed. George Fridén, Seth Jacobson, Stockholm 1938.

"Möte med konsekvenser", [editorial], *Veckoposten*, No. 38, 1992, p. 2.

"Motioner", [editorial], *Veckoposten*, No. 12, 1986, p. 2.

Naess, Kurt, "Det finns inte rätt och fel i dopfrågan", *Veckoposten*, No. 36, 1992, pp. 11, 13.

Naess, Kurt, "Glädjande klarsyn", *Veckoposten*, No. 24, 1991, p. 8.

Naess, Kurt, "Krossa församlingen och gå ut i 'världen'", *Veckoposten*, No. 50, 1978, p. 10.

Naess, Kurs, "Oacceptabelt alternativ?", *Veckoposten*, No. 19, 1992, p. 12.

Naess, Kurt, "Vad hände med motioner om Kyrkornas världsråd?", *Veckoposten*, No. 50, 1990, p. 7.

"Några måste vara djärva nog att börja gå enhetens väg", [Nils Sköld, Kurt Naess], *Veckoposten*, No. 45, 1991, p. 12.

Nairobi 1975. Breaking Barriers, Nairobi 1975. The Official Report of the Fifth Assembly of the World Council of Churches, 23 November - 10 December, 1975, ed. David M. Paton, London/Grand Rapids 1976.

"När samfundsstyrelserna möttes: - Vi är på väg mot enheten", *Veckoposten*, No. 50, 1983, p. 7.

När vi bryter det bröd..., Författad av en arbetsgrupp inom Svenska Baptistsamfundet, utgiven av Svenska baptistsamfundet, Stockholm 1981.

"När vi samlas...", [editorial], *Veckoposten*, No. 18/19, 1989, p. 6.

Nicklasson, Gösta, *Missionsförbundet och ekumeniken*, Stockholm 1971.

Nilsson, Fred, *Parakyrkligt*. Om business och bön i Sverige, Stockholm 1988.

Nilsson, Per-Olov, "Nattvardsboken presenteras", *Veckoposten*, No. 49, 1981, p. 9.

Nordin, Nils, G., "Öppet brev om samverkan mellan samfunden", *Veckoposten*, No. 24, 1991, p. 8.

Nordiska röster om dop och kyrkotillhörighet. Synpunkter och föredrag från en nordisk ekumenisk konsultation om teologi och kyrkorätt med anledning av Vägen till kyrkan - diskussionsbetänkande nr 2 från en arbetsgrupp inom Svenska kyrkan, Svenska Kyrkans Utredningar (SKU) 1988:1, KISA - rapport 1988:4, ed. Tord Harlin, Uppsala 1988.

Nordström, Nils Johan, *De frikyrkliga och statskyrkoproblemet*. Utgiven på uppdrag av tredje svenska frikyrkomötets utredningskommitté, Stockholm 1922.

Nordström, Nils Johan, *En kulturbild från 1800-talets religiösa brytningstid*. Den första svenska baptistförsamlingens uppkomst och kamp för samvetsfriheten, Stockholm 1926.

Nordström, Nils Johan, *Svenska Baptistsamfundets historia*. Första delen, Stockholm 1923.

Nordström, Nils Johan, *Svenska Baptistsamfundets historia*. Andra delen, Stockholm 1928.

Norman, Aug. V., "Tillbakablickar och framtidssyner. Minnen och intryck II", *Tro och Liv*, No. 4, 1943, pp. 175-176.

"Nu!", [editorial], *Veckoposten*, No. 51/52, 1987, p. 4.

"Nu är tiden inne för nya perspektiv i enhetssamtalen", [Sigvard Karlehagen, Gustav Sundström, Ingvar Paulsson, Birgit Karlsson], *Veckoposten,* No. 12, 1991, p. 3.

"Ny församling i Malmö", [Ref.], *Veckoposten,* No. 17, 1989, p. 5.

"Ny tidning", *Veckoposten,* No. 27/28, 1992, p. 2.

"Nya tidningen kommer i höst", *Veckoposten,* No. 27/28 (1992), p. 1.

Nyrén, J., "Tillbakablickar och framtidssyner. Minnen och intryck III", *Tro och Liv,* No. 4, 1943, pp. 177-178.

Ohm, Sven, "Rüschlikon - seminariet vårt!", *Veckoposten,* No. 25, 1989, pp. 2-3.

Öhnell, Urban, "Konferens gav råg i ryggen åt ekumeniska församlingar", *Veckoposten,* No. 16/17, 1987, p. 2.

"Om politikerna kan...", [editorial], *Veckoposten,* No. 40, 1992, p. 2.

Öman, Torsten, "Frälsningens mottagande", *Veckoposten,* No. 25, 1976, p. 4.

One Baptism, One Eucharist and a mutually recognized Ministry, Faith and Order Paper No. 73, World Council of Churches, Geneva 1975.

One Lord, One Baptism. Report on The Divine Trinity and the Unity of the Church and Report on The Meaning of Baptism by the Theological Commission on Christ and the Church. Studies in Ministry and Worship, Faith and Order Commission Paper No. 29, eds. G.W.H. Lampe and David M. Paton, World Council of Churches, Geneva/London 1960.

"Öppna dörrar", [editorial], *Veckoposten,* No. 19/20, 1991, p. 2.

"Öppning om dopet", *Veckoposten,* No. 24/25, 1986, p. 2.

"Ord om enhet", [editorial], *Veckoposten,* No. 1/2, 1991, p. 2.

Österberg, Edvin, "Den aktuella dopdebatten", *Veckoposten,* No. 13/14, 1988, p. 12.

Österberg, Edvin, "Dop och församling", *Veckoposten,* No. 42, 1984, p. 4.

Österberg, Edvin, "Enhet och samverkan", *Veckoposten,* No. 25/26, 1982, p. 10.

Österberg, Edvin, "Evangelisk kristendom", *Veckoposten,* No. 48, 1978, p. 10.

Österberg, Edvin, "Nattvarden", *Veckoposten,* No. 3, 1982, p. 10.

Österberg, Edvin, "Veckans insändare", *Veckoposten,* No. 6, 1975, p. 10.

"Över alla gränser", [editorial], *Veckoposten,* No. 21/22, 1991, p. 2.

På stugmötenas tid. Till 100-årsminnet av konventikelplakatets upphävande 1858, [Hilding Pleijel, Erland Sundström, Oscar Lövgren, Olof Thulin, Martin Gidlund, Lars Österlin], Stockholm 1958.

På väg mot frikyrklig enhet. Föredrag och handlingar från åttonde allmänna frikyrkomötet 1953, [Utgiven av] Frikyrkliga samarbetskommittén, Stockholm 1953.

Palm, Irving, "Frikyrklig lokalekumenik – exemplet gemensamma församlingar", *Tro & Tanke* 1997:3, Svenska kyrkans forskningsråd, Uppsala, pp. 45-68.

Palm, Irving, "Frikyrkofolket och ekumeniken", *Tro & Tanke* 1993:5, Svenska kyrkans forskningsråd, Uppsala, pp. 37-88.

Palm, Irving, "Gemensamma församlingar - en ny fas i den ekumeniska utvecklingen", *Tro & Tanke* 1992:4, Svenska kyrkans forskningsråd, Uppsala, pp. 29-92.

Parker, G. Keith, *Baptists in Europe. History and Confessions of Faith*, Nashville 1982.

"Pastorsutbildning med nya perspektiv", [editorial], *Veckoposten*, No. 13/14, 1991, p. 2.

Persson, Larsåke W., "Nattvarden i Svenska Baptistsamfundet på 1970-talet", *När vi bryter det bröd...*, Stockholm 1981, pp. 120-154.

Persson, Larsåke W., "Vad betyder det att vara döpt?", *Veckoposten*, No. 1, 1978, p. 4.

Persson, Larsåke W., "Vad betyder det att vara döpt?", *Veckoposten*, No. 2, 1978, p. 4.

Persson, Per Erik, "Att tillhöra Guds folk", *Tro och Liv*, No. 1, 1980, pp. 4-11.

Persson, Per Erik, "Forskning om ekumenik - en inledning", *Ekumeniken och forskningen.* Föreläsningar vid den nordiska forskarkursen "Teorier och metoder inom forskning om ekumenik" i Lund 1991, Nordisk ekumenisk skriftserie 20, 1992, eds. Sigurd Bergmann et al., Uppsala 1992, pp. 9-12.

Persson, Per Erik, "'Ni utgör Kristi kropp och är var för sig delar av den' (1 Kor 12:27), Vad innebär det att vara församling eller kyrka i Norden i dag?", *Ekumenisk Orientering*, No. 2, 1990, Eds. Virpi Pakkanen-Wiberg, Gudrun Söderman, Nordiska ekumeniska institutet, Uppsala 1990, pp. 5-11.

Petersson, Kjell, *Kyrkan, folket och dopet. En studie av barndopet i Svenska kyrkan*, Diss., Lund 1977.

Pethrus, Lewi, "De frikyrkligas alliakssträvanden och pingstväckelsen", *Evangelii Härold* 15 Dec. 1927, pp. 641-643.

Pethrus, Lewi, "De kristnas enhet. Kan detta mål nås genom de moderna samfundsorganisationerna?", *Pethrus, Lewi, Samlade skrifter*, Band 4, Stockholm 1958, pp. 129-179.

Pethrus, Lewi, "Ett brännande spörsmål", *Evangelii Härold*, 7 Nov. 1918, p. 177.

Pethrus, Lewi, Samlade skrifter, Band 4, Stockholm 1958.

Pethrus, Lewi, Samlade skrifter, Band 6, Stockholm 1958.

Pethrus, Lewi, "Vår ställning till andra kristna", *Pethrus, Lewi, Samlade skrifter*, Band 6, Stockholm 1958, pp. 157-190.

Petrén, Erik, *Kyrka och makt. Bilder ur svensk kyrkohistoria*, Lund 1990.

Ratschow, Carl Heinz, *Die eine christliche Taufe*, Gütersloh 1972.

Reimers, Eva, *Dopet som kult och kultur. Bilder av dopet i dopsamtal och föräldraintervjuer*, Diss., Stockholm 1995.

Ringsvåg, Ingemar, "ÖM och Baptistsamfundet i gemensamt styrelsemöte: Vad kan de båda göra tillsammans?", *Missionsbaneret*, No. 4, 1986, p. 3.

Ringsvåg, Ingemar, "Tappar man samfundskänslan när församlingar går samman?", *Veckoposten*, No. 25/26, 1981, pp. 8-9.

Roman, Bertil, "Tre bilder", *Veckoposten*, No. 9, 1992, p. 12.

Rothermundt, Gottfried, Ein Dialog beginnt. Die baptistisch - lutherischen Gespräche seit 1979, *Ökumenische Rundschau* 36, 1987, Frankfurt am Main, pp. 321-331.

Rudén, Erik, "Samarbete mellan de frikyrkliga", *Tro och Liv*, No. 7/8, 1948, pp. 305-312.

Rudén, Erik, "'Union Churches'", *Veckoposten*, No. 6, 1965, p. 14.

Ruuth, Anders, *Dopets rikedom enligt Bibeln och bekännelseskrifterna*, Stockholm 1975.

Rydlander, Håkan, "SBUF och ÖMU: Återförena baptismen!", *Veckoposten*, No. 50, 1983, p. 10.

" -Så mycket gemensamt!", *Veckoposten*, No. 23, 1990, p. 1.

"Så ser ledare för andra samfund på SMF", [David Lagergren], *Liv och frihet*. En bok om Svenska Missionsförbundet, ed. Olof Wennås, Stockholm 1978, p. 293.

"Sagt i veckan: David Lagergren i Svensk Veckotidning", *Veckoposten*, No. 10, 1977, p. 2.

Sahlberg, Joel, "Svensk baptism i framtiden", *Veckoposten*, No. 1, 1979, p. 12.

"Samfunden svarar Lysekil: -Visst får de förenade församlingarna vårt stöd", *Veckoposten*, No. 42, 1984, p. 15.

"Samgående får helhjärtat stöd", *Veckoposten*, No. 39, 1991, p. 1.

"Samgående - på sikt!", [editorial], *Veckoposten*, No. 25, 1984, p. 2.

Samtal om samverkan. Svenska Kyrkan, Svenska Missionsförbundet, ed. Gösta Hedberg, Stockholm 1971.

"Samtala!", [editorial], *Veckoposten*, No. 14, 1987, p. 4.

Samuelsson, Owe, *Sydsvenska baptister inför myndigheter*. Tillämpning av religionsbestämmelser i Lunds och Växjö stift 1857-1862, Diss., Lund 1998.

"Samverkan stärker banden - Bådar gott för framtiden", *Veckoposten*, No. 5, 1986, p. 1.

Sandewall, Allan, *Konventikel- och sakramentsbestämmelsernas tillämpning i Sverige 1809-1900*, Stockholm/ Göteborg/ Uppsala 1961.

Sandewall, Allan, "Konventikelplakatets upphävande - ett gränsår i svensk religionsfrihetslagstiftning?", *Kyrkohistorisk Årsskrift* 57, Uppsala/Stockholm 1957, pp. 136-152.

"Särskilt yttrande: Barnen och nattvarden", [David Lagergren], *När vi bryter det bröd...*, Stockholm 1981, pp. 235-236.

"SBUF och SMU visar vägen", *Veckoposten*, No. 17, 1991, p. 1.

"SBUF sade ja till gemensamt ungdomsförbund", *Veckoposten*, No. 25/26, 1992, p. 1.

Sehlstedt, Berndt, "Barndop och tuggummi", *Veckoposten*, No. 38, 1976, p. 11.

Sehlstedt, Berndt, "Dopfrågan", *Veckoposten*, No. 25/26, 1983, p. 10.

Seiler, Herman, "Dop och kyrkotillhörighet i den katolska kyrkan. Dopet som sakramentalt inlemmande i kyrkan", *Ekumenisk samsyn om dop och kyrkotillhörighet*. Rapport från den officiella luthersk - katolska samtalsgruppen i Sverige med anledning av Stat - kyrka. Ändrade relationer mellan staten och Svenska kyrkan, Statens offentliga utredningar (SOU) 1978:1, Stockholm/Lund 1978, pp. 33-42.

Selinder, Per-Magnus, "Öppning i dopfrågan", *Svensk Veckotidning*, No. 22, 1986, p. 2.

"Sex frågor till David Lagergren, intervju: Birgit Karlsson", *Året*, Baptistsamfundets kalender Betlehem, ed. Birgit Karlsson, Stockholm 1971, pp. 8-13.

"Siffror till eftertanke", [editorial], *Veckoposten*, No. 18, 1987, p. 4.

Sjölén, Berit, "Marcus 11 år 'kan' konferens", *Veckoposten*, No. 22, 1985, p. 9.

Sjöqvist, Eric, "Ekumenik och bibelsyn", *Veckoposten*, No. 38, 1992, p. 12.

Skog, Margareta, "Antal medlemmar i valda samfund 1975-1996", *Tro & Tanke* 1996:6, Svenska kyrkans forskningsråd, Uppsala, pp. 45-55.

Skog, Margareta, "Antalet medlemmar i valda samfund 1960-1983", *Smärre meddelanden* 1984:2, Religionssociologiska institutet, Stockholm.

Skog, Margareta, "Antalet medlemmar i valda samfund 1975-1989", *Religion och Samhälle* 1989:9, Religionssociologiska institutet, Stockholm.

Skog, Margareta, "Antalet medlemmar i valda samfund 1975-1992", *Tro & Tanke* 1992:11, Svenska kyrkans forskningsråd, Uppsala, pp. 45-61.

Skog, Margareta, "Frikyrkornas medlemstal i landets kommuner 1985", *Religion och Samhälle* 1986:13, Religionssociologiska institutet, Stockholm.

Skog, Margareta, "Frikyrkornas medlemstal i landets kommuner 1990", *Tro & Tanke* 1992:4, Svenska kyrkans forskningsråd, Uppsala, pp. 93-172.

Skog, Margareta, "Frikyrkosamfundens medlemstal i landets kommuner 1995", *Tro & Tanke* 1997:3, Svenska kyrkans forskningsråd, Uppsala, pp. 69-147.

Skog, Margareta, "Trosrörelsen i Sverige", *Tro & Tanke* 1993:5, Svenska kyrkans forskningsråd, Uppsala, pp. 89-138.

Skoglund, Gunnar, "Två församlingar blev en i Sveg", *Veckoposten*, No. 9, 1992, p. 6.

Sollerman, Erik, "Rent religiöst har ÖM och BM förts närmare varandra", *Veckoposten*, No. 28/29, 1979, p. 7.

"Sommarstiltje", [editorial], *Veckoposten*, No. 26, 1986, p. 2.

Stenström, Tomas, "Till rätt adressat?", *Veckoposten*, No. 14, 1992, p. 4.

Stockholms första baptistförsamling 1854-1954. Minnesskrift över Stockholms Första Baptistförsamlings verksamhet genom 100 år, utg. av Ernhard Gehlin till jubileumshögtiden i oktober 1954, Stockholm 1954.

"Stor utmaning att få arbeta för samgående", *Veckoposten*, No. 7, 1984, p. 8.

Straarup, Jørgen, "Den kyrkliga aktivitetens utveckling under 1990-talet", *Tro & Tanke* 1996:6, Svenska kyrkans forskningsråd, Uppsala, pp. 13-43.

Struble, Rhode, *Den samfundsfria församlingen och de karismatiska gåvorna och tjänsterna. Den svenska pingströrelsens församlingssyn 1907-1947*, Diss., Lund, Stockholm 1982.

Succé med Gud? Kritisk granskning av framgångsteologin i Sverige, [Sigbert Axelson, Rune W Dahlén, Lars Lindberg, Fred Nilsson], Stockholm 1988.

"'Summons to Witness to Christ in Today's World': A report on the Baptist - RC International Conversations, 1984-88", *One in Christ*, No. 3, 1990, pp. 238-255.

Sundberg, Hans, Åqvist, Berit, "Bekännelse och bärande idéer", *Liv och tjänst*. Guds mission församlingens uppdrag, eds. Birgit Karlsson, Berit Åqvist, Örebro 1988, pp. 95-110.

Sundberg, Kerstin, "Örebromissionen", *Svenska Trossamfund*. Historia, tro och bekännelse, organisation, gudstjänst- och fromhetsliv, ed. Allan Hofgren, 8th ed., Uppsala 1990, pp. 85-90.

Sundell, Dan-Gustaf, "Rissnekyrkan efter fyra år. Nu på god väg att bli hela samhällets kyrka", *Veckoposten*, No. 10, 1989, pp. 2-3.

Sundström, Erland, "Babylonisk sköka - konungens brud", *Veckoposten*, No. 23, 1975, pp. 8f.

Svärd, Arvid, Wange, Per, *Det hundrade året*. En krönika i ord och bild om Svenska Baptistsamfundets jubileumsår 1947-1948, Stockholm 1948.

Svärd, Björn, "Dopet i fokus", *Dopet i fokus,* eds. Björn Svärd et al., Stockholm 1992, pp. 5-6.

Svärd, Stig, "Den halvfärdiga bron - och hammaren som väntar på oss", *Veckoposten*, No. 17, 1982, p. 3.

Svensk baptism genom 100 år. En krönika i ord och bild, ed. George Fridén, Stockholm 1948.

Svensk författningssamling (SFS) 1995:1211. Lag om ändring i kyrkolagen, Stockholm 1996.

Svenska Baptistsamfundet. Statistik och adressförteckning 1969-1970, Stockholm 1969.

Svenska Baptistsamfundet. Statistik och adressförteckning 1970-1971, Stockholm 1970.

Svenska Baptistsamfundet. Statistik och adressförteckning 1971-1972, Stockholm 1971.

Svenska Baptistsamfundet. Statistik och adressförteckning 1972-1973, Stockholm 1972.

Svenska Baptistsamfundet. Statistik och adressförteckning 1973-1974, Stockholm 1973.

Svenska Baptistsamfundets Allmänna konferenser Stockholm 1963 Linköping 1964. Svenska Baptistsamfundets Ungdomsförbunds (SBUF) årskonferenser Västerås 1963 Sjövik 1964. Årsberättelser, rapporter och protokoll, Stockholm 1964.

Svenska Baptistsamfundets Årsbok 1961-1962, Stockholm 1961.

Svenska Baptistsamfundets Årsbok 1962-1963, Stockholm 1962.

Svenska Baptistsamfundets Årsbok 1963-1964, Stockholm 1963.

Svenska Baptistsamfundets Årsbok 1979, Stockholm 1979.

Svenska Baptistsamfundets Årsbok 1981, Stockholm 1981.

Svenska Baptistsamfundets Årsbok 1983, Stockholm 1983.

Svenska Baptistsamfundets Årsbok 1984, Stockholm 1984.

Svenska Baptistsamfundets Årsbok 1985, Stockholm 1985.

Svenska Baptistsamfundets Årsbok 1986, Stockholm 1986.

Svenska Baptistsamfundets Årsbok 1988, Stockholm 1988.

Svenska Baptistsamfundets Årsbok 1989, Stockholm 1989.

Svenska Baptistsamfundets Årsbok 1990/91, Stockholm 1991.

Svenska Baptistsamfundets Årsbok 1992-93, Stockholm 1992.

Svenska Missionsförbundets Årsberättelse 1964, Stockholm 1965.

Svenska Trossamfund. Historia, tro och bekännelse, organisation, gudstjänst- och fromhetsliv, ed. Allan Hofgren, 8th ed., Uppsala 1990.

Svenson, Sven, "Förhandskritik", *Veckoposten,* No. 6, 1987, p. 15.

Svenson, Sven, "Missvisande rubrik", *Veckoposten,* No. 5, 1985, p. 3.

Svensson, Alvar, "Låt inte mörkermännen ta över!", *Veckoposten,* No. 45, 1991, p. 12.

Svensson, Nils-Eije, "'Att tillhöra Guds folk' - Graninge III handlade om tro och kyrkotillhörighet", *Tro och Liv,* No. 1, 1980, pp. 2-3.

Swedberg, Bo, "25 år efter New Delhi: Nu har lokalekumeniken börjar blomma för fullt", *Veckoposten,* No. 7, 1986, p. 3.

Swedberg, Bo, "600 personer deltog i invigningshögtiden", *Veckoposten,* No. 37, 1990, p. 9.

Swedberg, Bo, "Angelägen uppgift nu: Att plantera församlingar", *Veckoposten,* No. 15, 1992, p. 5.

Swedberg, Bo, " -Att döpas var som att komma hem", *Veckoposten,* No. 45, 1989, p. 10.

Swedberg, Bo, "Både det tveklösa hoppet och en utväg trots allt", *Veckoposten,* No. 15, 1987, pp. 2-3.

Swedberg, Bo, "Baptister och missionsförbundare om förenad församling i Mölndal: -Det bästa som hänt oss", *Veckoposten,* No. 10, 1985, pp. 6-7.

Swedberg, Bo, "Baptistledarna: -Nu krävs vidgade perspektiv i vårt arbete för kristen enhet", *Veckoposten,* No. 13/14, 1991, p. 5.

Swedberg, Bo, "Birgit Karlsson: -Ett andligt genombrott är min hetaste önskan", *Veckoposten,* No. 50, 1983, p. 5.

Swedberg, Bo, "Birgit Karlsson: -Förord för federation!", *Veckoposten,* No. 5, 1992, p. 5.

Swedberg, Bo, "Birgit Karlsson om ekumeniken: -Också centralt stärks nu samfundens gemenskap", *Veckoposten,* No. 50, 1989, p. 3.

Swedberg, Bo, "Börje Hammarroth efter 18 år: -Jag skulle önskat få se nya samfundsmönster växa fram", *Veckoposten,* No. 20/21, 1985, p. 3.

Swedberg, Bo, "Deklarationen", *Veckoposten,* No. 16, 1991, p. 2.

Swedberg, Bo, " -Den lär oss förstå bibelns anknytning till vår vardagsvärld", *Veckoposten,* No. 8, 1989, pp. 3, 12.

Swedberg, Bo, " -Det här är en enhet som vi längtat efter", *Veckoposten,* No. 7, 1986, pp. 6-7.

Swedberg, Bo, "Det var missionsstyrelserna ense om: Praktisk samverkan förenar", *Veckoposten,* No. 5, 1986, p. 6.

Swedberg, Bo, "En historisk händelse - och sedan?", *Veckoposten,* No. 5, 1986, p. 2.

Swedberg, Bo, "Enkät ger klart besked: 'Bättre' eller 'mycket bättre' i de förenade församlingarna", *Veckoposten,* No. 51/52, 1987, p. 3.

Swedberg, Bo, "Förenade församlingar visar: -Samfunden har redan valt gemenskapens väg", *Veckoposten,* No. 9, 1988, pp. 2-3.

Swedberg, Bo, "Förenade församlingarna utmaning för samfunden", *Veckoposten,* No. 21, 1987, p. 5.

Swedberg, Bo, "Frågor", *Veckoposten,* No. 7, 1984, p. 8.

Swedberg, Bo, " -Fri teologihögskola bra för ekumeniken", *Veckoposten,* No. 40, 1992, p. 6.

Swedberg, Bo, *Frikyrka på väg,* Stockholm 1961.

Swedberg, Bo, "I Höör längtar man inte tillbaka till det som var", *Veckoposten,* No. 8, 1992, p. 7.

Swedberg, Bo, "Ingvar Paulsson: -Årskonferensen är hela samfundets angelägenhet", *Veckoposten,* No. 19/20, 1991, p. 3.

Swedberg, Bo, "Knud Wümpelmann, ledare för 35 miljoner baptister: -Det viktigaste är alltid lokalförsamlingens insats", *Veckoposten,* No. 21/22, 1991, p. 20.

Swedberg, Bo, "Kristianstad: Här fungerar en gemensam församling", *Veckoposten,* No. 11, 1992, pp. 8-9.

Swedberg, Bo, "Lokalekumener: -Vi har ett budskap till våra samfund", *Veckoposten,* No. 35, 1989, p. 8.

Swedberg, Bo, "Mariakyrkans församling i Katrineholm: Ungdomarna visade vägen till enhet", *Veckoposten,* No. 50, 1990, pp. 8-9.

Swedberg, Bo, "Missionsförbundet vill ta ett rejält kliv", *Veckoposten,* No. 13/14, 1991, p. 3.

Swedberg, Bo, "'När ni nu enats kan man ju tro'", *Veckoposten,* No. 11, 1986, p. 4.

Swedberg, Bo, "Nu är det klart: Den gemensamma tidningen börjar utkomma den 1 november", *Veckoposten,* No. 27/28, 1992, p. 5.

Swedberg, Bo, "Pastor i förenad församling: -Samfunden bör ta större hänsyn till utvecklingen i församlingarna", *Veckoposten,* No. 51/52, 1989, p. 9.

Swedberg, Bo, "'Psalmer och Sånger' bidrar till en rikare gudstjänst", *Veckoposten,* No. 8, 1989, pp. 2-3.

Swedberg, Bo, "Samfunden ger goda råd om dop och medlemskap", *Veckoposten,* No. 49, 1983, p. 9.

Swedberg, Bo, "Samfundsstyrelserna redo ta nya steg mot frikyrklig enhet", *Veckoposten,* No. 5, 1992, p. 5.

Swedberg, Bo, "SBUF och SMU överens: -Nu ska vi gå samman i ett gemensamt förbund", *Veckoposten,* No. 17, 1991, p. 3.

Swedberg, Bo, "Vi måste lära av de lokala erfarenheterna", *Veckoposten,* No. 16, 1989, pp. 2, 12.

Swedberg, Bo, " -Vi saknar samfundens stöd men lokalt fungerar det fint", *Veckoposten,* No. 41, 1984, pp. 8-9.

Swedberg, Bo, " -Vi vill ha en öppen kyrka i Fjugesta", *Veckoposten*, No. 37, 1990, pp. 8-9.

"Ta ställning!", [editorial], *Veckoposten*, No. 36, 1992, p. 2.

Tecken om enhet. Gemensamma församlingar. Rapport från en arbetsgrupp inom Sveriges Frikyrkoråd, 1991.

The New Delhi Report. The Third Assembly of the World Council of Churches 1961, ed. Willem Adolph Visser't Hooft, London 1962.

Theologischer Konsens und Kirchenspaltung, eds. Peter Lengsfeld, Heinz-Günther Stobbe, Stuttgart 1981.

Thunberg, Lars, "Om receptionen av ekumeniska texter", *Ekumeniken och forskningen.* Föreläsningar vid den nordiska forskarkursen "Teorier och metoder inom forskning om ekumenik" i Lund 1991, Nordisk ekumenisk skriftserie 20, 1992, eds. Sigurd Bergmann et al., Uppsala 1992, pp. 201-215.

Thurian, Max, "Introduction: The Lima document on 'Baptism, Eucharist and Ministry' the event and its consequences", *Churches respond to BEM.* Official responses to the "Baptism, Eucharist and Ministry" text, Vol. I, ed. Max Thurian, Faith and Order Paper No. 129, World Council of Churches, Geneva 1986 pp. 1-27.

"Tidigare redaktörer. Det räcker med en bra tidning", *Veckoposten*, No. 9, 1989, p. 5.

Till församlingens tjänst. Handbok för Fribaptistsamfundet, Helgelseförbundet, Svenska Baptistsamfundet, Örebromissionen, Finlands Svenska Baptistsamfund, Örebro 1987.

"Tomma ord - eller?", [editorial], *Veckoposten*, No. 30, 1985, p. 2.

Towards Koinonia in Faith, Life and Witness. A discussion paper, Faith and Order Paper No. 161, World Council of Churches, Geneva 1993.

"Traditioner och reaktioner", [editorial], *Veckoposten*, No. 16, 1990, p. 2.

Tro, Frihet, Gemenskap. Svensk baptism genom 150 år, ed. Berit Åqvist, Örebro 1998.

"Två samfund", [editorial], *Veckoposten*, No. 23, 1990, p. 2.

"Ungdomen visar vägen", [editorial], *Veckoposten*, No. 17, 1991, p. 2.

"Unikt: baptister utarbetar trosbekännelse", *Veckoposten*, No. 9, 1977, p. 1.

Uniting in Hope. Reports and Documents from the Meeting of the Faith and Order Commission, 23 July - 5 August, 1974, University of Ghana, Legon, Faith and Order Paper No. 72, World Council of Churches, Geneva 1975.

"Uppbyggelse och nytta", [editorial], *Veckoposten*, No. 21, 1986, p. 2.

"Utan historia?", [editorial], *Veckoposten*, No. 17, 1985, p. 2.

"Utbildning för tjänst", sektion 2, *Sändaren*, No. 38, 1993, pp. 1-20.

"Utökat samarbete mellan Betelseminariet och Örebro Missionsskola leder till alternativ akademisk examen", *Veckoposten*, No. 2, 1977, p. 16.

Väckelse och kyrka i nordiskt perspektiv. Nordiska studier över brytningarna mellan kyrklig ordning och religiös folkrörelse under 1800-talet. Skrifter utgitt av Nordiskt institut för kyrkohistorisk forskning 1, 1969, ed. A. Pontoppidan Thyssen. Köpenhamn /Lund /Helsingfors /Oslo 1969.

Vägen till kyrkan. Om dopet och kyrkotillhörigheten. Ett diskussionsbetänkande nr 2 från en arbetsgrupp inom Svenska kyrkan, Svenska Kyrkans Utredningar (SKU) 1988:1, Stockholm 1988.

"Vägen till målet", [editorial], *Veckoposten*, No. 39, 1991, p. 2.

"Varför inte tillsammans?", [editorial], *Veckoposten*, No. 7, 1984, p. 2.

Vattnet som förenar och skiljer. Rapport från en arbetsgrupp, tillsatt av Örebromissionens styrelse, om doptolkning och doppraxis i ett ekumeniskt perspektiv, [Sune Fahlgren, Hans Lundin, Joel Sahlberg, Tord Ström, Lennart Thörn, Bo Wettéus], 2nd ed., Örebro 1986.

Visser't Hooft, Willem Adolph, *The Genesis and Formation of the World Council of Churches*, Geneva 1982.

Wagner, Günter, *A Survey of Baptist Responses to "Baptism, Eucharist and Minsitry"*, Rüschlikon 1986.

Walan, Bror, *Året 1878*, Waldenströmföreläsningar 1977, Stockholm 1978.

Walan, Bror, "De utomkyrkliga väckelserörelserna under senare hälften av 1800-talet", *Väckelse och kyrka i nordiskt perspektiv*. Nordiska studier över brytningarna mellan kyrklig ordning och religiös folkrörelse under 1800-talet. Skrifter utgitt av Nordiskt institut för kyrkohistorisk forskning 1, 1969, ed. A. Pontoppidan Thyssen, Köpenhamn /Lund /Helsingfors /Oslo 1969, pp. 184-214.

Walan, Bror, *Fernholm och frikyrkan.* En studie i Svenska Missionsförbundets förhistoria, Stockholm 1962.

Walan, Bror, *Församlingstanken i Svenska Missionsförbundet.* En studie i den nyevangeliska rörelsens sprängning och Svenska Missionsförbundets utveckling till o. 1890, Diss., Stockholm 1964.

Wallander, Cecilia, "'Det är dags att komma till klarhet' Missionsföreståndare Walter Persson om ekumeniken", *Svenska Kyrkans Tidning*, No. 25/26, 1991, p. 16.

Wendel-Hansen, Erland, "Under Kristi lydnad", *Veckoposten*, No. 14, 1975, p. 4.

Westblom, Anne, *Porträtt*: "Pedagog i Dalabygd", *Tro, Frihet, Gemenskap.* Svensk baptism genom 100 år, Örebro 1998, pp. 163-166.

Westin, Gunnar, *Den kristna friförsamlingen genom tiderna.* Martyrer och frihetskämpar, 3rd ed., Stockholm 1955.

Westin, Gunnar, *Den kristna friförsamlingen i Norden.* Frikyrklighetens uppkomst och utveckling, Stockholm 1956.

Westin, Gunnar, *George Scott och hans verksamhet i Sverige* I, Stockholm 1929.

Westin, Gunnar, *I den svenska frikyrklighetens genombrottstid.* Svensk baptism till 1880-talets slut. Kyrkohistoriska uppsatser, Stockholm 1963.

Westin, Gunnar, *Kyrkor, sekter och kristen gemenskap*, Stockholm 1941.

Westin, Gunnar, *Samfund och enhet.* En granskning av pastor Lewi Pethrus' uppfattning om kristna missionsorganisationer, 3rd ed., Stockholm 1920.

Westin, Gunnar, *Svenska Baptistsamfundet 1887-1914.* Den baptistiska organisationsdualismens uppkomst, Stockholm 1965.

Wiberg, Anders, *Det Christliga Dopet.* Framstäldt uti Biblens Egna Ord och Beledsagadt med förklarande Anmärkningar samt Wittnesbörd af Utmärkta Theologer, Philadelphia 1854.

Wiberg, Anders, *Hvilken bör döpas? och Hvaruti består dopet?* Undersökning grundad uppå den heliga Skrifts vittnesbörd och den christna kyrkans historia, Upsala 1852.

Wiktell, Sven, "Gunnar Kjellander: -Det är dramatik i dopet", *Veckoposten*, No. 10, 1979, p. 5.

Wiktell, Sven, E., "Åseda. Grunden för arbetet är bönegrupperna", *Veckoposten*, No. 3, 1989, p. 2.

Wiktell, Sven, E., "Försoningens gemenskap vid Herrens bord", *Veckoposten*, No. 21, 1983, pp. 3, 13.

Wiktell, Sven E, "Hult i Småland. Frikyrkoförsamlingen som växte fram ur behovet", *Veckoposten*, No. 5, 1985, p. 15.

Wiktell, Sven, E., "Missionsföreståndare i samspråk: Nu är det dags att sluta sucka – det finns så mycket inspirerande", *Veckoposten*, No. 31/32, 1981, pp. 11-12.

Wiktell, Sven, E., "Öppenhjärtig intervju. Hur ser missionsföreståndarna på de många arbetsuppgifterna?", *Veckoposten*, No. 21, 1983, pp. 10-11.

Wiktell, Sven, E., "Svenska kyrkans präst döpte 'baptistiskt' i baptistkapellet", *Veckoposten*, No. 51/52, 1979, p. 8.

Wingård, Bengt-Gunnar, "Sannerudskyrkan - gemensam kyrka för missions- och baptistförsamlingarna i Kil invigd", *Veckoposten*, No. 45, 1979, p. 3.

Zettergren, Sten-Sture, "En ny psalmbok blir till", *Tro och Liv*, No. 1, 1987, pp. 5-9.

The Germanic vowels å, ä, ö and ø are ranged under a and o.

Index

The Germanic letters å, ä, ö and ø are ranged under a and o.

The Germanic letters å, ä, ö and ø are ranged under a and o.

Peter Lang · Europäischer Verlag der Wissenschaften

Daniël J. Louw

Meaning in Suffering

A theological reflection on the cross and the resurrection for pastoral care and counselling

Frankfurt/M., Berlin, Bern, Bruxelles, New York, Wien, 2000. VIII, 210 pp.
International Theology. Edited by Jürgen Moltmann, William Schweiker and Michael Welker. Vol. 5
ISBN 3-631-36173-4 · US-ISBN 0-8204-4744-7· pb. DM 65.–*

The basic assumption is that suffering, as well as its association with evil, causes an existential problem as expressed in the now classic question: Why? For what purpose? Hence the attempt to take up the challenge put forth by theodicy, and to develop a theological argument along the lines of a theology of the cross and a theology of the resurrection.

The book focuses on the following question in order to develop a theological model for pastoral care and counselling: If it is true that God-images are influenced by culture and do play a decisive role in people's reaction to severe suffering and pain, how should God be interpreted and portrayed if Christian spirituality still is an influential factor in postmodernity's quest for meaning? What God-image is appropriate for a new millennium? These questions are linked to the problem of a pastoral diagnosis.

A reinterpretation of the power of God (God's omnipotence) is proposed in terms of the following pastoral concepts: compassion/vulnerability, and transformation/empowerment.

The book has been compiled along the lines of the following basic pastoral questions posed by people who suffer due to events which befall us as a "tragedy," afflicting the innocent and the harmless: Why God? (Cause and explanation); How God? (Mode and identification); Where God and what? (Polarization and the will of God); When God? (Transformation and overcoming); For what purpose? (Our human quest for meaning).

Contents: Theodicy · God-images · The omnipotence of God (power) · Providence · Metaphorical theology · Quest for meaning · Suffering · Pastoral care and counselling · Theology of the cross · Theology of the resurrection

Frankfurt/M · Berlin · Bern · Bruxelles · New York · Oxford · Wien
Auslieferung: Verlag Peter Lang AG
Jupiterstr. 15, CH-3000 Bern 15
Telefax (004131) 9402131
*inklusive Mehrwertsteuer
Preisänderungen vorbehalten